Lawrence James studied History and ~~Engli~~ subsequently undertook a research degree at Merton College, Oxford. Following a career as a teacher, he became a full-time writer in 1985, and is the author of the acclaimed *The Golden Warrior: The Life and Legend of Lawrence of Arabia; Imperial Warrior: The Life and Times of Field Marshal Viscount Allenby; The Rise and Fall of the British Empire; and Raj: The Making and Unmaking of British India.*

'James' well-researched book . . . humanizes this history through vivid and telling vignettes' *Time*

'Authoritative and exhaustive . . . This is popular history at its very best: always accessible, always informative' *Publishing News*

'An absorbing new history of Britain . . . This is a book that will be read and reread many times and is surely destined to become a classic' *Waterstones Books Quarterly*

WARRIOR RACE

A HISTORY OF THE BRITISH AT WAR FROM ROMAN TIMES TO THE PRESENT

Lawrence James

An *Abacus* Book

First published in Great Britain in 2001 by Little, Brown
This edition published by Abacus in 2002

A CIP catalogue record for this book
is available from the British Library.

ISBN: 0 349 11486 2

Typeset in Goudy by M Rules
Printed and bound in Great Britain
by Clays Ltd, St Ives plc

Abacus
An imprint of
Time Warner Books UK
Brettenham House
Lancaster Place
London WC2E 7EN

www.TimeWarnerBooks.co.uk

Contents

• Contents •

Acknowledgements

In preparing and writing this book I have accumulated many debts. The greatest are to my wife, Mary, and my sons, Edward and Henry, who have offered assistance of all kinds and shown considerable forbearance. Thanks for help, suggestions and explanations are also due to Professor Michael Alexander, the Marquess of Anglesey, Dr Ian Bradley, Geordie Burnett-Stuart, Cyril Dawson, Richard Demarco, Mark Dunkerley, Professor Martin Edmonds, Nick Fogg, Professor Ray Furness, Dr Christine Gascoigne, Mark Hunter, Lynda Innocent, Lynda Kinloch, Andrew Lang, Professor Bruce Lenman, Colin Lindsey-MacDougall, Andrew Lownie, Joe Mahady, Dr Roddy MacDowell, Professor Tony McGelligot, Andrew MacGregor, Katie Nicholson, Professor Alan Patterson, Dr Anna Patterson, Liz Pert-Davies, Captain Cahal O'Reilly, Professor Jeffrey Richards, Bob Roberts, Professor Nick Roe, Dr Jane Roe, Trevor Royle, Alan Samson, Linda Silverman, Andrew and the late Cherry Williams, Philip Williams, A.N.Wilson, Percy Wood, Dr Martin Stephen and the Reverend Andrew Wylie.

I am also deeply grateful for the many kindnesses shown and invaluable assistance given by the staffs of the British Library and its newspaper collections at Colindale, the Buckinghamshire Record Office, the Imperial War Museum, St Andrews University Library, the Liddell Hart Centre, the National Army Museum, the National Library of Scotland, the Public Record Office and the Scottish Record Office.

Quotations from Crown Copyright collections appear by permission of the Comptroller of Her Majesty's Stationery Office.

Introduction

"Tis one thing, brother *Shandy*, for a soldier to hazard his own life – to leap first down into the trench, where he is sure to be cut to pieces: – 'Tis one thing, from public spirit and a thirst for glory, to enter the breach the first man, – To stand in the foremost rank, and march bravely on with drums and trumpets, and colours flying about his ears: – 'Tis one thing, I say brother *Shandy*, to do this, – and 'tis another thing to reflect on the miseries of war, – to view the desolations of whole countries, and consider the intolerable fatigues and hardships which the soldier himself, the instrument who works them, is forced . . . to undergo.

Laurence Sterne, *Tristram Shandy*, Book VI

Toby Shandy was right. War has always generated ambivalent and sometimes contradictory passions. There is horror at its capacity for destructiveness, but there is admiration for courage in the face of death. We are still mesmerised by the spectacle of war and want to discover what it was like, a curiosity that is now satisfied by films whose reconstructions of battle brim with grisly details. Virtual reality is complemented by actual reality, for the wonders of the high tech and high explosive battlefield are instantly transmitted by satellite TV. This also provides images of shattered buildings, uprooted and frightened people and bodies of the dead, both civilian and military. Similar scenes would have been witnessed by Toby Shandy when he campaigned in Flanders at the end of the seventeenth century.

This book examines some of the myriad individual stories of those who were swept up in the hurly burly of war. For some it was an opportunity for adventure and escape from a boring, uncongenial or threatening world. When he was drafted into Charles I's army in 1640, Richard Wright of Nursling in Hampshire evaded a maintenance order and possible whipping for fathering an illegitimate child. Of course, he exchanged the peril of appearing before the local bench for another, death in battle or from camp fever. Fate could also be generous: if Wright survived, he could enrich himself by looting and find more willing girls. Anne Leggatt, the mother of his child, like many others in her position, might too find the war a source of opportunity and become a camp follower; soldiers were notorious for spending their money freely on women and drink.

Public catastrophes, like that which overtook England in 1640, affected lives at every level. War provided an impetus that compelled many people along unlooked-for paths, not all of which led to suffering. Some years ago, a member of a Scottish landowning family told me how her ancestor, one of several sons of a crofter, had been taken by his father to enlist in a Highland regiment at Inverness. There was no alternative, for the family land could only support his eldest brother. The young man in question was literate and was promoted quickly, for he could attend to the orderly book, and the high wastage of officers in the Crimea secured him a commission. He served in the army that relieved Lucknow in 1857 and ruthless looting gained him sufficient cash to return home and purchase an estate. A similar twist of fate advanced the villains in Conan Doyle's *The Sign of Four*. Not all the Highland lads who helped suppress the Indian Mutiny were so lucky. Robert Louis Stevenson met one, a veteran of the siege and presumably the looting of Delhi, who was an impoverished road mender. An eye-witness to dramatic events that had changed history, the road man could remember little of what he had seen and was apparently unaware of its significance.

War has always provided ordinary people with an opportunity to engage in history on a grand scale, particularly in the twentieth century when it has required the mobilisation of the entire population. There can hardly be a family in Britain that has not had at least one member who served with the forces in the First and Second World Wars or undertook war work in factories or on farms. This participation still matters, which is why so many families cherish photographs, letters and medals connecting them with great events. Such tokens are also a source of pride in duty fulfilled.

This book is also about the part played by war in the evolution of the states within the British archipelago that, in 1801, became the United Kingdom. It also examines the wars fought by the British overseas to create a commercial and territorial empire. Ireland has been included in this survey because from the twelfth century until 1922 it was successively, if reluctantly, attached to English and British polities.

Britain's domestic conflicts have been of immense historical importance. Internal wars have marked the pivotal points in the nation's history and their outcome has dictated its future direction. Speculative history can be something more than an entertaining diversion just because it reminds us that much of what we take for granted has depended on a single event. What sort of country would have evolved if the Normans had been repelled at Hastings? Would a defeat at Bannockburn have marked the end of Scottish independence? If Richard III had won at Bosworth, there would have been no Tudor dynasty and, if they had occurred at all, the English and Scottish reformations might have followed different courses. The nation's political structures and the principles that upheld and defined them would have been different if Charles I's armies had prevailed at Edgehill, Marston Moor or Naseby, or if the Jacobite adventure of 1745 had succeeded.

On three occasions, the existence of Britain as an independent nation was in jeopardy. Geography dictated that its survival depended on command of the seas; if this had been lost during the French and Napoleonic wars, an invasion and possible occupation might have followed. Without naval paramountcy Britain would have been unable to fight, let alone win the First and Second World Wars. Trafalgar, Jutland and the defeat of the U-boats in 1943 were three of the most decisive battles in British history.

Wars did not always deliver irrevocable political decisions: the intermittent contests for control of Ireland have yet to reach a conclusion. Their significance has been considerable for those who have perpetuated the struggle – witness the annual Orange Order parades to celebrate battles won three hundred years ago and the nationalist invocation of martyr heroes of 1798 and 1916. In Ireland, as in the rest of the British Isles, death in battle remains one of the most elevated expressions of patriotism.

War has placed its stamp on the development of British society in ways that have either been taken for granted or overlooked. The warrior élite which secured political paramountcy in England, Scotland and Ireland between the Roman evacuation and the Middle Ages evolved into a ruling class that derived political and territorial power from its skill at arms. Its carefully cultivated concepts of personal courage, honour and self-respect based on an indifference to danger lay at the heart of chivalry. It survived, blended Christian ideals of social responsibility and Renaissance notions of virtue, and was bequeathed to subsequent generations. The result was a persistent faith in the peculiar moral qualities of gentlemen which qualified them to command in war. Their outlook and values made them the natural leaders, which was why victory at Waterloo was allegedly won on the playing fields of Eton and why the RAF was desperate to recruit former public schoolboys with an aptitude for sport and experience as prefects to fly Spitfires in 1940. What mattered, as the system's defendants always claimed, was that it worked.

Until modern times, Britain's fleet and armies were commanded by gentlemen who led by example and were filled with men who were either drafted in an emergency or driven to enlist by moral or economic disabilities. These arrangements disappeared in the twentieth century when the total wars waged by industrial nations demanded universal participation. Both the First and Second World Wars were struggles on an unprecedented scale which turned into extended and gruelling assays of the nation's capacity to endure hardship, produce food, manufacture weaponry and sustain the collective will for victory. Men and women were mobilised, surrendering themselves to a state that demanded the suspension of customary legal and political rights.

The last part of this book is concerned with these contests and their economic, political, social and psychological repercussions. Britain emerged victorious from both wars, although impoverished and shaken in spirit. Nonetheless, the experience of two world wars has done much to define national character in that the people revealed an astonishing tenacity and intensity of purpose. This matters and sets Britain apart from the nations of the rest of Europe that have suffered defeat, occupation and calculated humiliation or, in the case of Spain, a wounding civil war. Success in war generates self-admiration, understandably, and is a vindication of a nation's collective will and institutions. It also encourages hubris, which may be why the British find it hard to come to terms with their present position in the world or fail to respond to crises in a cool, competent and determined manner. Recriminations over present difficulties are tinged with a belief that such things were better managed in the past.

Perhaps this is because war is the potent father of myths and legends. Perceptions of what happened, or what ought to have happened, supplant reality and, in the twentieth century, have been given permanency by the cinema. Because a people's performance in war is so closely linked to national self-esteem, I have discussed its penetration of the public imagination. I have also, and I make no apologies for this, pursued the quirky and been wary about imposing neat patterns. These have and do exist, but the essence of history concerns individuals who are so often irrational, untidy and unpredictable in their thoughts and behaviour.

April 2001

PART ONE

—◆—

CONQUESTS
AD 43–1100

1

A warlike province: Britain, AD 43–410

Inchtuthil was once a monument to the military power and energy of imperial Rome. Today, it is an area of flattish meadowland close to the Tay, a lonely place of curlews, wild geese and the occasional buzzard. It is also home to a colony of engineers, as persistent as the Romans and of greater endurance – rabbits. Their warren has undermined one of the grass- and moss-covered banks which give a clue as to what Inchtuthil once was: an outpost on the northernmost frontier of the Roman Empire. It was a formidable fortress whose ditches and ramparts enclosed fifty-three acres and encompassed all the essentials of a military base: heated quarters for officers, barracks, granaries, storehouses and a hospital. Of lesser priority was the legionaries' bathhouse, which had been planned but was never built. A change of frontier policy in Rome led to Inchtuthil's abandonment in about 87, after just four years of intensive labour. Even incomplete, the fortress represented a triumph of will, organisation and hard grind by the soldiers who shovelled earth, felled and trimmed oaks, and quarried, carted and cut stone. Modern archaeology, in conjunction with ergonomics, tells us that this enterprise consumed at least 2.7 million man-hours, allowing for a labour force of 5000 soldiers and an eight-hour day.[1]

The scale of Inchtuthil indicates that it was intended to house a full legion, in all likelihood the 5000 or so men of the XXth Valeria Victrix.[2] A glance at the surrounding landscape reveals the fort's strategic function. To the west and north are the foothills of the Grampians, the home of the Caledones whose forces had been defeated by Gnaeus Julius Agricola at the battle of Mons Graupius in September 83. As so often, victory in a pitched battle had demonstrated beyond doubt the capacity of a Roman army to overcome a tribal one, but submission and pacification did not follow automatically. The Caledones retired into the Highlands, which were beyond Rome's reach for the moment. Penetration in sufficient force to overawe and subdue them required an immense base, and this was Inchtuthil. It was an earnest of permanent occupation and its position astride the Tay valley blocked any tribal counteroffensive. Advance warning of this or any other hostile activity was provided by a string of smaller forts and signal stations which stretched back down the valley to Bertha (Perth) and beyond along the vale of the Earn and over the Ochil hills. A further line of small fortified outposts extended north-westwards from Inchtuthil into the foothills of the eastern Grampians. The fortress was the focus of a network that provided both intelligence of enemy movements and the wherewithal to intercept any small-scale raids, for the outlying forts were garrisoned by auxiliary cavalry and light troops. In an emergency, these and the legionaries from Inchtuthil could be shifted along stone-surfaced roads which linked the outposts and, importantly, expedited the mule trains and ox-carts that carried their supplies.

This network of roads, strongholds and signal stations was an expression of the military genius of Rome. It knew no obstacles, human or physical, and its principal elements were practical experience, superior technology and the self-confidence these generated. In Scotland all were ultimately wasted, although lessons learned there were added to the already huge corpus of martial knowledge. No invasion of the Highlands materialised, Inchtuthil was methodically demolished and a million unused nails were buried; the local commander was not going to make a gift of iron to the Empire's foes. The decision to withdraw suggests that at the highest levels there were fears that the Empire had overstretched itself and could not sustain a permanent occupation of the Tay valley, let alone contemplate large-scale operations in the Highlands. Whether or not the retreat southwards from the Tay encouraged tribal restlessness is not known. What is certain is that soon after the accession of Hadrian in 117 the northern frontier region was convulsed by disorder, which prompted the emperor to visit Britain and order the construction of a frontier of stone, the wall that took his name.

II

The ebb and flow of imperial frontier in Britain has made the Roman way of war familiar. We can reconstruct Roman forts using exact archaeological evidence and, through aerial photographs, we can trace the roads along which the legions marched, pinpoint their signal stations and marching camps. We know what the Roman soldier ate, drank and wore, and how he was armed. The strategies adopted by his generals are set down in memoirs and contemporary annals, and detailed military handbooks have survived which reveal how he was trained and deployed.

We can glimpse the grisly reality of battle. Trajan's column shows the wedges of disciplined, armoured infantrymen hacking their way through a confused press of barbarians. This was how Boudicca's army was overcome in 60. 'Just keep in close order,' Gaius Suetonius Paulinus had told his legionaries, 'Throw your javelins and then carry on: use shield-bosses to fell them, swords to kill them.' It worked as it had done elsewhere, and afterwards the auxiliary cavalry swept in to cut down the fugitives. One such horseman appears on a spirited if rudely carved distance-stone found at Bridgeness on the Antonine wall, the Empire's second Scottish frontier. The rider's lance is raised to strike at the naked barbarians sprawled under his horse; one is headless. Variations of this image were popular for military tombstones. Longinus, born in what is now Bulgaria and an officer of a Thracian cavalry unit that took part in the first phase of the conquest of Britain, appears mounted on his monument at Camulodunum (Colchester). He wears armour and brandishes a spear, the symbol of authority throughout the Empire, and another bearded barbarian cowers beneath his charger. Revealingly, Mars is portrayed in this fashion on a relief discovered at Stragglethorpe in Lincolnshire, although his lance is aimed at a serpent, which makes the god resemble later representations of St George.[3]

Alongside these vivid triumphal images there is the evidence of the human remains uncovered among the earthworks at Maiden Castle in Dorset, which fell in 43 to forces under the overall command of Vespasian, a future emperor. The siege had opened with a bombardment by ballistas and one skeleton has the iron head of a bolt wedged in its backbone. Then followed an assault against the eastern defences, breakthrough and a hand-to-hand struggle along the wooden ramparts. Here the legionaries slashed with their short iron swords at the unguarded heads of their adversaries. Some wounds were possibly inflicted after death by soldiers exasperated by the stubbornness of resistance. One young Briton, aged between twenty and thirty, received at least nine, each of which had penetrated his skull. He may well have been a warrior, trained in combat, for he was the tallest casualty (just over five feet seven inches) and strongly built. Those who buried him thought him worthy of a leg of lamb for the afterlife. Lying nearby was another corpse which had taken several sword blows on the face, delivered with what a modern pathologist described as 'the utmost force of a man's arm'. The legionary sword was also a stabbing weapon, which may explain why the bones of other victims of the massacre, including eleven women, show no signs of injury to their bones. They may have been killed when the soldiers fanned out into the settlement, setting fire to some huts.[4]

The infliction of exemplary terror was as vital to a Roman campaign of conquest as defeating armies or storming hill forts. Sometimes it was all that was necessary. At another Dorset hill fort, Hod Hill, Vespasian's legionaries took its defenders by surprise, arriving in the middle of their frantic efforts to reinforce the ramparts. The Romans erected a fifty-foot-high tower upon which they set a ballista and then trained it on the chieftain's hut. To judge from the positions of the bolts, the fire was unnervingly accurate. Demoralised by this demonstration of technical expertise, the defenders must have surrendered, for archaeologists found no evidence of a fight like that at Maiden Castle.[5]

This combination of professional efficiency and alacrity of movement gave the Romans the edge in any pitched battle or siege. The native British had had their first taste of Roman methods of waging war in 55 and 54 BC, when Julius Caesar had undertaken two reconnaissance campaigns in south-eastern England. In his record of operations there, he remarked on the outlandishness of the Britons, who wore animal skins and whose aristocracy shared wives. He paid tribute to the ferocity of British warriors which made them worthy opponents for the Romans, who prided themselves on their own toughness and pugnacity. Defeating brave men enhanced the prestige of the army and the honour of its commander.[6] Cornelius Tacitus, the chronicler of the Scottish campaigns of his father-in-law, Agricola, contrasted the belligerence and tenacity of the British with the effeteness of the Gauls, who had been softened by long exposure to Roman vices. The martial spirit of the British was resilient, even after sixty years of slow subjugation. As Tacitus remarked: 'They have been framed to obedience but not yet to servitude.'

The process of piecemeal conquest had begun in 43 at the command of the new emperor, Claudius. It was undertaken for complex psychological, political and economic reasons. Britain was a mysterious land on the fringes of the world, about which little was known, although there were exaggerated rumours of mineral wealth. Claudius's invasion not only extended the frontier of the Empire, it was a step into the unknown. To undertake it added immensely to the stature of an emperor who had, in the words of a fawning poet, proved that, 'The boundary of the earth was not the boundary of the Empire.'[7] Such a bold enterprise challenged the supernatural world. The sea that separated Britain from Gaul represented the god Oceanus, the father of all rivers, themselves lesser deities. An altar to this god, symbolised by an anchor, was set up by soldiers the VIth Victrix legion at Newcastle-upon-Tyne, and his features may have decorated the pediment of the temple of Sulis Minerva at Bath. If they were those of Oceanus, then those who gazed on them would have been reminded of how Claudius's seaborne army had, as it were, overcome the god in his own element. It was a triumph that surpassed the crossings of the Rhine, Danube and Euphrates, great rivers but petty gods in comparison with Oceanus.[8]

Imperial prestige soared once it was clear that the invasion would succeed. Claudius, accompanied by elephants from the far southern fringes of his Empire, came ashore and remained with his army for sixteen days. He then returned to Rome to reap the rich propaganda rewards of the campaign. His son was named Britannicus and he ordered the building of triumphal arches at his point of embarkation,

Boulogne, and in Rome. Neither survive, but at Aphrodisias in south-west Turkey a carved panel shows Claudius, dressed only in a cloak and helmet, subduing a prostrate, distraught and déshabillé Britannia. As far away as Caesarea, coins were minted to celebrate the addition of a new province to the Empire. On the Campus Martius in Rome, the emperor's exploits were performed for the masses with a spectacular re-enactment of the capture of Camulodunum in which Claudius played himself, receiving the surrender of its actor king.[9]

If Trajan's arch in Rome or that at Orange in southern France are anything to go by, Claudius's would have been embellished by sculptures that showed every feature of the Roman war machine in action. The scenes of soldiers marching across pontoon bridges, digging ditches and setting up wooden palisades for their camps, and receiving first aid at field hospitals proclaimed Rome's supremacy in the science of war. Technical capacity was complemented by the stamina and courage of the individual fighting man. On his fingers he often wore rings with representations of the great heroes of antiquity: Theseus (one was excavated at Corbridge on Hadrian's Wall); Ajax bearing the corpse of Achilles (this was found at the Woddon Hill camp in Dorset); and Hercules wrestling the Nemean lion.[10] These were both talismans and reminders of how a brave man ought to behave. But, unlike these legendary figures, the Roman soldier fought as part of a well-drilled and tightly disciplined unit which moved with the precision of clockwork and could change formation in response to its commander's wishes, conveyed by trumpet calls and signals. By changing front and formation to suit circumstances, a Roman army was able to seize and exploit any tactical advantage the moment it appeared.

Personal honour, pride in his unit and reverence for his commanders and the state they served motivated the Roman soldier. His everyday concerns are nicely reproduced by the four devices cut on a glass intaglio once set in the ring of a soldier at the garrison of Woddon Hill. Martial virtues and their rewards are represented by the club of Hercules and the palm of victory. The rudder of Fortune reminded the ring's wearer that his calling made him a perpetual hostage to fate, and the corn-ear of Ceres indicated the soldier's eternal anxiety about regular rations.[11] When he died, the fighting man's tombstone was usually a terse record of place of birth, unit and service. One, found at

Wroxeter on the upper reaches of the Severn and on the edge of the turbulent Welsh border, may speak for many others: 'Marcus Petronius, son of Lucius of the Manenian voting tribe, aged thirty-eight with eighteen years service, a soldier of XIVth Gemina legion, he was a standard-bearer and lies here.' He came from northern Italy and had died some time before 61, when his legion was awarded the title 'Martia Victrix' for its part in the defeat of Boadicea.

In each of his eighteen years in arms, Marcus Petronius would have joined his officers and fellow legionaries on 3 January in an annual reaffirmation of their oaths to Jupiter and, through him, the emperor and Empire. These rites of rededication were performed in every garrison throughout the Empire, like those that marked the anniversaries of imperial accessions and the festivals of the greater gods under whose benevolence Rome flourished. A soldier whose fort overlooked the Severn knew that on these occasions the same rituals were being witnessed by distant brothers-in-arms on the Rhine, the Danube and, of course, the Tiber. He was participating in ceremonies that demonstrated the unity of the Empire and the common ties of loyalty that bound its guardians. Altars to Jupiter were erected as a permanent reminder of vows renewed and the nature of the soldier's duty to this god and the state he protected. Several, set up by the Ist Hispanic Cohort, have been discovered at Maryport on the Cumbrian coast.

Another such altar, dedicated by the prefect of the Vth Gallic Cohort during the second quarter of the second century, was found at Cramond above the Firth of Forth. Men from this garrison may have cut the imperial eagle that can still be seen on one of the rocks of the foreshore. It possibly represents a defiant symbol of Rome's presence, for it looks northwards across the estuary towards the lands of the Caledones; or the eagle could have been an impromptu memorial to duty undertaken in a desolate and unfriendly country, just like the regimental badges cut on rocks by British troops who served on India's North-West Frontier in the twentieth century. Like his Roman counterpart, and for the same reasons, the British soldier also took part in regular, public religious observances (church parades) and yearly imperial celebrations on the monarch's birthday.

When the Roman soldier honoured a god with the correct sacrifices and prayers he was striking a bargain. Protection was the reward for veneration, so long as it was offered in the appropriate form and with the right words. Sometimes, a fighting man would carry some token that reminded him of his guardian deity. A roundel once attached to a soldier's belt had the inscription: 'Jupiter Optime Maxime, conserva numerum omnium militantium' (O Jupiter, Greatest and Best, succour this band of fighting men).[12] When formal parades were held, cavalrymen appeared in close-fitting metal helmets embellished with masks of Jupiter, Mars and Minerva, gods from the officially approved pantheon. Individuals and units also cultivated relationships with 'unofficial' deities. The centurion M. Cossius Firmus, stationed at Auchendavy in Dumbartonshire, set up altars in honour of Jupiter, Mars and Minerva and a local lesser god, 'Genius Terrae Britannicae'. Auxiliaries, recruited in the provinces, imported their own deities, like the Rhenish campestres, mother-goddesses who were worshipped only by Gallic cavalrymen.[13] So long as religions and cults did not challenge or hold the state in contempt, as did Druidism and Christianity, they were tolerated by the Empire. Gods were equally forbearing towards each other and so it was possible to worship several at once, which must have been reassuring for a soldier, who always needed as much supernatural assistance as he could get.

The cult of Mithras not only offered the soldier supernatural security, it provided spiritual and human comforts that were ideally suited to the profession of arms. The Mithraic religion was of Indo-Persian origin and made considerable headway during the second and third centuries when it gained converts among the British garrison. One Mithraic temple, which must have been used by troops stationed on Hadrian's Wall, is at Carrawburgh in Northumberland, and there is a carving of him in his role as the god of light (the sun), which was found at Housesteads camp and is now in the Newcastle-upon-Tyne Museum of Antiquities. Worship of Mithras drew devotees into a secret world which was a blend of modern freemasonry and an old-style gentleman's club. Women were totally excluded from the cult and the seven stages of the prescribed passage from ignorance to enlightenment were marked by dramatic initiation rites. One involved a temporary burial and resurrection; the pit used for this rite of regeneration can be seen at Carrawburgh. There was much here to attract the Roman soldier. Mithraism strengthened the bonds of comradeship, for its cells were exclusive, tightly knit masculine fellowships where those who shared the divine mysteries regularly took food and wine together.[14]

Military shrines were commonly placed close to their parade grounds. Divine goodwill needed to be supplemented by skill in arms, and so men had to follow an unending and rigorous programme of training designed to foster efficiency and fitness. The compilers of military handbooks rightly suspected that the bane of garrison life, inactivity, was debilitating and idleness was the mother of mutiny.[15] Flavius Vegetius Renatus, writing in the fourth century, outlined an ideal training régime: 'The troops, both legionaries and auxiliaries, should very frequently be exercised in cutting down trees, carrying burdens, jumping over ditches, swimming in sea or river water, having route marches at full pace or even running fully armed and with packs, so that experience gained by daily practice in peacetime will not seem difficult in war.' Cavalrymen practised their horsemanship, threw lances at targets, and slashed at wooden posts with their swords. The strongest mastered the art of vaulting on to their horses' backs in full armour. In Britain, these equestrian exercises were often undertaken on the flat, open ground inside abandoned native hill forts. Wherever they trained, soldiers were under the eyes of their officers who watched from the wooden platforms that overlooked the parade grounds.

Constant training promoted confidence, as did the superiority of Roman equipment. At the end of the first century, the legionary wore a close-fitting iron helmet with cheekpieces and protection for the neck. His trunk and shoulders were protected by flexible plate armour and he carried a wooden shield with a large iron boss. He was armed with two weighted pila, which were thrown at close range, and a short sword. Auxiliary infantrymen and archers had similar helmets and body armour of mail or, in the case of some cavalrymen, small metal plates. Whatever its form, armour gave the Roman fighting man a considerable advantage over the bulk of his British opponents who lacked it.

The backbone of the armies that resisted the Roman invasion was the bands of professional warriors attached to tribal rulers. Their fighting methods were Homeric, with each man deliberately seeking to prove his audacity and prowess in the manner of a champion. Some tribes favoured light, wooden chariots that moved nimbly across the battlefield and provided mobile platforms from which warriors leapt to engage their enemies. It must have been a very spectacular display, not least because some Britons went into battle naked, their bodies tattooed or painted with greenish-blue woad. The ballast of the British army was the tribal levy whose members were untrained, unarmoured and equipped with a spear and shield.

III

The inequalities of skill and equipment tipped the balance in every pitched battle. This was proved within days of Claudius's landing in Kent, where a tribal army was decisively beaten in a two-day engagement on the Medway. Here, the long hours of exercise proved their value, for the river was crossed by Batavian auxiliaries who had been trained to swim in their armour. This victory was followed by an advance on Camulodunum and lightning strikes by Vespasian against the tribal hill forts of the south-west. Within little more than a year, the invaders had established a vast bridgehead with a front that followed the line of the Fosse Way between the lower reaches of the Severn and the Humber estuary.

The success of the campaign owed much to mobility and the army's logistical machinery which was dependent on control of the English Channel. Supply depots were established at Richborough on the Kentish coast and, once it had been taken, at Camulodunum on the River Colne. Another supply base, at Bosham, was probably used for amphibious operations along the Dorset and Devon coast.[16] This facility was provided by a collaborator, Cogidubnus, ruler of the Atrebates of the Sussex hinterland. Claudius repaid his friendship by installing him as a client king. His magnificent palace at Fishbourne was Roman in style with imported mosaic floors; it stood, appropriately, on the site of a former legionary storehouse. Accommodation was preferable to hopeless resistance, and the shrewd magnate who came to terms with the invaders could expect to retain his status and some of his powers. For this reason, Prasutagus of the Iceni, of Norfolk and Suffolk, followed Cogidubnus's example, and was rewarded with similar favours. Integration of such men into the Roman system was part of an official programme by which native aristocracies throughout the Empire were gradually Romanised. The northern flank of the frontier was secured by an agreement with Cartimandua, queen of the Brigante tribal confederacy of the Pennines, who was bribed into benevolent neutrality. Two hundred years of empire building had taught the Romans that gold could conquer as effectively as iron.

The Brigante queen's co-operation proved vital during the second phase of the conquest. The objective was the subjection of the Welsh tribes who had rallied around Caractacus during 47 and 48. He was the son of King Cunobelinus (Shakespeare's Cymbeline) of the Trinovantes and Catuvellauni of East Anglia, a resourceful leader and tactical innovator. After another, suicidal, head-on collision between tribal and Roman forces in central Wales, Caractacus turned to guerrilla warfare against lines of communication and isolated parties of foragers or detachments building forts.[17] The result was a messy war of attrition of a kind all too familiar to nineteenth- and twentieth-century colonial powers. Counterinsurgency measures included large-scale operations to uncover hidden weapons and intensive patrolling of the marshy valleys and wooded uplands of the Welsh borders. The struggle dragged on until 51, when Caractacus was captured by Cartimandua who delivered him to his enemies.

They conducted him to Rome where his noble bearing convinced many that he was a gallant adversary. According to Tacitus, he looked at the city's magnificent buildings and asked why, when they had so much, did the Romans wish to take the wretched huts of his people. He may well have expressed such sentiments, but on this and other occasions when he has British leaders delivering stirring speeches in defence of liberty, Tacitus is voicing his own misgivings about the capriciousness of imperial power. He has Caractacus, Boadicea and the Caledonian king, Calgacus, appeal to the Roman conscience in the language of the former republic, whose principles had been extinguished by Julius Caesar and his successors.

It was Druidism, rather than attachment to concepts of liberty, that animated and united tribal resistance to Rome. The Druids were a caste of priest-magicians who possessed psychic powers that put them in contact with all that was unseen and inexplicable. Through their prophecies and interpretation of natural phenomena, they exercised a tight grip on the minds of the Britons. They were also the implacable

enemies of Rome, which was why Caius Suetonius Paulinus was determined to extirpate them and their religion. He arrived as governor in
the winter of 58 to 59 and immediately began preparations for an expedition against the island of Mona (Anglesey) which was the spiritual
powerhouse of Druidism. It fell after a combined assault from sea and
land, the Druids were slaughtered and their sacred oak groves uprooted.
At the close of this campaign, Suetonius heard news of a general uprising in eastern England led by Boadicea, the widow of Prasutagus, the
puppet king of the Iceni.

IV

Boadicea, as she is mistakenly but popularly called, has made a powerful impact on the national consciousness. She has been fixed in our
imagination by the immense statue raised to her in 1902 and placed at
the end of Westminster Bridge. There she stands with her daughters in
a brazen chariot with its unhistorical scythes and rearing horses, defending, as it seems, the ancient liberties of the British people as represented
by the parliament buildings opposite. There are several ironies here.
First, her correct name, Boudicca, can be rendered as 'victorious', which
made her a fitting heroine for the age of another queen, Victoria, and
explains why Prince Albert was one of the first to support proposals for
the statue. It was finally erected at the end of a period of the British
Empire's expansion, and yet Boadicea's principal achievement was to
lead a rebellion against another imperial power. In doing so, she abandoned the passive qualities of femininity that the Victorians cherished.
Moreover, she looks towards the city that she and her followers did all
in their power to raze to the ground.

   The promotion of Boadicea as a national heroine owes everything to
Tacitus's account of her deeds and words. Her husband had made Nero
his co-heir and a dispute over his will led to a clash with the Roman
authorities, the looting of the royal palace, the rape of the queen's two
daughters and her own flogging by soldiers. For Tacitus, such outrages
against women of high birth were typical expressions of the tyranny
that Rome had become under the Caesars and a reminder that their
Empire rested on greed and injustice. Listen to her speech on the eve of

battle: 'I am descended from mighty men! But now I am not fighting for my kingdom and wealth. I am fighting as an ordinary person for my lost freedom, my bruised body and my outraged daughters. Nowadays Roman rapacity does not even spare our bodies. Old people are killed, virgins raped. But the gods will grant us the vengeance we deserve!'

Her oratory and insurrection became known in England during the sixteenth century when the hitherto unknown works of Tacitus were first published. As Bonduca, she is a central figure in Beaumont and Fletcher's play of the same name, which was first performed early in the reign of Charles I. She is portrayed as a headstrong, meddlesome woman whose attempts to play the man's game of war end in disaster. The British defeat is the direct result of her tactical misjudgement; had she heeded the advice of the professional soldier, Caractacus, things would have turned out differently. Nevertheless, she has a patriotic vision of the land she is defending which closely resembles the seventeenth-century ideal of a godly, protestant England.

> *Therefore 'tis fitter I should reverence*
> *The thatched houses where the Britains dwell*
> *In careless mirth, where blest houschold gods*
> *See nought but chaste and simple puritie.*
> *'Tis not high power that makes a place divine*
> *Nor that men from gods device their line.*
> *But sacred thoughts in holy bosoms stor'd,*
> *Make people noble and the place ador'd.*

Revealingly, at a time when England was beginning to embark on overseas expansion, Bonduca warns her enemies:

> *If you will keep your Laws and Empire whole,*
> *Place in your Romane flesh a Britain soul.*

The notion that the moral virtues of the British made them superior empire builders to the Romans is developed by William Cowper in his 'Boadicea: An Ode' of 1782. Before going into battle, she hears the prophecy of a Druid who predicts the downfall of Rome. But,

> Other Romans shall arise,
> Heedless of a soldier's name;
> Sounds, not arms shall win the prize –
> Harmony the path to fame.
>
> Then the progeny that springs
> From the forests of our land,
> Arm'd with thunder, clad with wings,
> Shall a wider world command.
>
> Regions Caesar never knew
> Thy posterity shall sway,
> Where his eagles never flew,
> None invincible as they.

Uplifted by this vision, Boadicea defies her enemies:

> Ruffians, pitiless as proud,
> Heav'n awards the vengeance due;
> Empire is on us bestow'd
> Shame and ruin wait for you.

The lines

> Regions Caesar never knew
> Thy posterity shall sway

are cut in the plinth below her statue, and so the woman who challenged an empire in the name of justice and freedom is transformed into the heroine of its humane successor. Boadicea is more than just a leader in war who sacrificed her life in defence of her country, her battle cries are those of a free people in arms against alien oppression and they would have resonances in later centuries. Like her fanciful chariot, the Westminster Bridge Boadicea is an invention, a creature of legend, but she is also a part of Britain's historical self-image. This being so, it is more than ironic that today the base of her statue is nearly obscured by a kiosk selling the tawdry knick-knacks that tourists buy as souvenirs of London.

What of the real Boadicea? There is a tantalising picture of her drawn by the historian Cassius Dio who depicts her as a tall, grim-faced woman with thick tawny hair that reached to her hips, who spoke with a deep voice, wore a golden torque and carried a spear. This sounds like an authentic description of a Celtic queen, but Dio was writing over a hundred and fifty years after Boadicea's death. Her followers were Iceni, supported by neighbouring tribes who shared her indignation against Rome. In what was a more or less spontaneous upsurge of rage they set about the eradication of everything Roman they could find. Nothing better illustrates their temper than the bronze head of Claudius, violently wrenched from a statue in Camulodunum and later thrown into the River Alde.[18] And then there is the smashed face of the cavalryman Longinus whose arrogant tombstone was overturned during the city's destruction. Here, as in London and Verulamium (St Albans), buildings were burned and Romans massacred; according to Tacitus there was a marked animus towards ex-legionary settlers and their families.

Reports of these outrages reached Suetonius on Anglesey. They revealed a political and strategic situation that was extremely dangerous; large parts of south eastern England had been wrenched from Roman control and a detachment of troops had been badly mauled near Camulodunum. Above all, Roman prestige had been gravely bruised. This had to be restored at all costs. An energetic and resolute proconsul, Suetonius gathered a scratch force of between eleven and thirteen thousand men drawn from the available legions and headed towards the disturbed region. Boadicea moved to meet him and battle was joined somewhere in the south midlands, possibly near Mancetter. It followed the familiar pattern with Roman discipline more than compensating for their opponents' superiority in numbers. Boadicea took poison, escaping the general massacre of her followers. Their casualties were heavy; one estimate, quoted by Tacitus, suggests that eighty thousand died during and after the battle, and there were no doubt many others killed in punitive operations undertaken in the winter of 60 to 61.

Such large and conveniently rounded casualty figures given by Roman and medieval annalists are often considered by modern historians as rhetorical devices employed to highlight the decisiveness of a victory. Perhaps so, but they should not all be dismissed out of hand. Recent calculations of the population of Roman Britain at the end of the fourth century suggest a total of between three and four million, so it is possible that Boadicea's forces, together with their wives and children, could have numbered as many as a hundred thousand.[19]

V

The extinction of Druidism and the crushing of Boadicea's revolt marked the consolidation of Roman rule over Wales, the midlands, East Anglia and southern England. An internal struggle between pro- and anti-Roman factions at the court of Queen Cartimandua provided the excuse for direct military intervention in Brigante territory in 69. As ever, progress was gradual and methodical with Roman forces taking ten years to advance as far as what is now the border with Scotland. The impetus for what turned out to be the final and most extended phase of the Roman conquest came from Rome, where the newly established Flavian dynasty was hungry for prestige.

The thrust northwards raised the question of where the final frontier would be fixed. If the matter was to be settled by geography alone, the Clyde and Forth valleys or the northerly coast of Scotland were obvious boundaries. Large-scale operations against the tribes of southern and central Scotland were undertaken by the capable and efficient Agricola, governor of Britain from 77 to 84. This ambitious enterprise included the occupation of the Tay valley which brought the frontier to the edge of the Highland line. At Mons Graupius, Agricola's army defeated that of a tribal alliance commanded by Calgacus who, according Tacitus, was a leader of 'courage and high birth'. These virtues were reflected in the words that the historian placed in his mouth on the eve of the battle. He described the forthcoming engagement as a last stand against a rapacious Empire bent on engrossing the whole world. Referring to the Roman army's methods of pacification and punishment, he remarked pungently: 'When they make a wilderness they call it Peace.'

Once again, Tacitus was using the speech of an enemy of Rome to express republican sentiments, a device that was particularly apposite at a time when the ruling emperor, Domitian, was eradicating the last traces of the old republican traditions. Agricola, who was Tacitus's father-in-law, told his soldiers that they were about to fight the final battle in the conquest of Britain. Mons Graupius was a victory, but not the decisive one that the proconsul had predicted. Within four years he had been recalled by Domitian and the occupation forces had withdrawn into northern England, leaving behind a few outposts.

In his appeal to his men Agricola had told them that Britain was 'held by force of arms', and Tacitus observed that despite over forty years of Roman penetration and occupation it was still 'a warlike province'. Literary evidence as to the nature or extent of British belligerence is fragmentary. There was a serious Brigante uprising between 117 and 119 and further spasmodic outbreaks of restlessness during the next sixty or so years, and the Scottish tribes intermittently raided Roman territory. A combination of Brigante sullenness and tribal hostility made northern England a region of chronic instability, which compelled the authorities to take expensive and extensive measures to impose order. Hadrian took personal charge of policy when he visited the area in 122, and the scale of his wall, completed within sixteen years, reflects the seriousness of the problem it was designed to eliminate. Vast resources of manpower and material were tapped for the construction, including 3.7 million tonnes of stone and 86,250 tonnes of timber.[20]

Hadrian's wall was an attempt to create a defensible obstacle that marked the limits of Rome's power, serving, as it were, the same function as the Rhine, Danube and Euphrates. No such natural frontier existed in Britain and so the next best thing was to create one: a barrier of earth ditches and a stone curtain wall extending across the narrowest section of northern England, between the estuaries of the Solway and the Tyne. The defences snaked south for thirty-two miles along the Cumbrian coastline as far as Bowness. This strongly suggests that containment of the Brigantes was one of Hadrian's main objectives, for they were isolated by land and sea from their natural partners in mischief-making, the Scottish tribes. One, the Votadini, had their lands sliced in two by the wall. By placing a barrier between Rome's enemies, the wall prevented them from forming an alliance, as the Scottish tribes had done during Agricola's campaigns. If this was so, then it was a classic expression of the universal maxim of empire builders: divide and rule.

The main, eighty-mile-long stretch of the wall served as a bulwark against cross-border raids, as well as a springboard for launching counterattacks and punitive expeditions. It was also an early warning system: there were strategically sited, fortified outposts beyond the wall at Birrens in Annandale, Bewcastle on the western edge of the Cheviots, High Rochester in Redesdale and Learmouth, overlooking the Northumberland coastal plain and not far from a later stronghold, Alnwick castle. Along the wall were regularly placed lookout points and mile-castles, each with a north-facing gateway. These entrances imposed tight control over those who wished to pass to or from Roman Britain and may well have been used to collect customs and restrict the import of arms. The mile-castles also made it easy to respond quickly and in force whenever and wherever an emergency occurred. Each had barrack accommodation for between eight and thirty-two soldiers who, like the bulk of the frontier garrison, were infantrymen.

Was this elaborate defence system a success? The Brigantes were not noticeably deterred, for unrest continued with a major revolt in 139 which took three years to suppress. The insurgents may have had assistance from beyond the wall, which would explain why a decision was taken to advance the frontier seventy-five miles north and bring the Scottish Lowlands under direct Roman control. Three legions commanded by Britain's governor, Quintus Urbicus, entered Scotland and began construction of the Antonine wall. It utilised another suitable neck of land, this time the forty miles between the Clyde and the Firth of Forth, and its layout and features suggest that lessons had been learned during the building of Hadrians wall, some of them hard ones. The absence of mile-castles and observation points indicates that they had probably been of limited value, and the use of turf and clay bricks (on the eastern section) for the rampart either hints at economic constraints or the possibility that the new wall was designed as a stumbling-block rather than a barrier. The defensive strength of the Antonine wall lay in its forts, placed at two-mile intervals immediately behind the wall.[21] A road connected these strongpoints and the presence of beacon towers along the wall gives the impression of a system that relied entirely on the army's capacity for what is today called a 'rapid response' to enemy activity.

The second Roman occupation of Scotland ended abruptly just after

160 when the Antonine wall was abandoned. This sudden change of policy was in all likelihood a reaction to an unexpected manpower crisis, brought about by an over-ambitious frontier policy on the Danube. A third, inconclusive invasion of the Scottish Lowlands was undertaken between 208 and 211. Thereafter, the Roman presence in Scotland was confined to fortified outposts, known as *castra exploratores*, at Netherby in lower Annandale and Risingham and High Rochester in the Cheviots. As their name indicates, they were bases for regular units whose task was to spy on the activities of the local tribes.[22] As well as keeping a close eye on these people, the military authorities may have bribed their chiefs to keep the peace, which would explain the origin of some of the hoards of Roman coins that have been discovered in Scotland.

VI

A province with a precarious border required a permanent, substantial garrison. Its average strength during the first, second and third centuries was fifty thousand, and in the fourth it fluctuated between twenty-one and thirty-three thousand. There was also the *Classis Britannica*, the Roman fleet stationed in British waters, which grew during the fourth century after an increase in seaborne raids from across the North Sea. This military and naval establishment was largely sustained from local resources and, therefore, had a formidable impact on the British economy. Its exact nature is hard to quantify simply because of a lack of precise evidence as to the relationship between military consumption and agricultural production. Nevertheless, enough is known or can be deduced to indicate that the Roman occupation was a considerable burden for those who enjoyed the security it provided.

Most of Rome's three to four million British subjects made their living by farming. The poorest paid their taxes in produce – one-tenth of a holding's gross yield. Moreover, until the beginning of the fourth century, the military authorities possessed the right to requisition food, and their demands overrode all others. Exact calculations of how much the armed forces did secure vary enormously, but one fact is beyond question: the amounts were large in proportion to what was available.

Grain formed the staple of the soldier's diet, and excavations of barrack latrines have revealed wheat, barley and oats. Each man's daily ration was between two and three pounds of grain and it has been reckoned that in a year the entire army was eating its way through the produce of between fifty-three and sixty-one thousand acres. One estimate puts the total at over two hundred thousand acres. Arithmetical exactitude is unobtainable because of variations in yields. These ranged between four and a half and six hundredweight per acre, and with exceptionally fertile soil could reach twelve hundredweight per acre, figures that represent about one-third or less of present-day production levels.[23]

By and large, the army preferred local suppliers, which saved transport costs and inevitable losses in transit caused by decay, theft and graft by venal officials. It is tempting to imagine that the fragments of quartermaster's receipts for Celtic beer, barley and venison delivered to the garrison of Vindolanda or Hadrian's wall were for deliveries from local producers.[24] Although civilians were officially excluded from the frontier zone, it seems highly likely that the cattle, sheep, pig and deer bones found at the fort were from beasts obtained nearby. Analysis of the woollen cloth discovered at Vindolanda shows that it came from indigenous sheep.[25] Evidence of a similar kind from other sites strongly suggests that the army was a major consumer not only of provender and forage but of locally manufactured pottery, metalware and leather. Regions adjacent to concentrations of Roman forces underwent a form of agrarian revolution during the occupation. Forest clearing, already well underway in southern England before the invasion, was extended during the third century to the upland regions of Wales, the Yorkshire Dales, the Lake District and southern Scotland. In each area the new land was used for arable farming.

Ploughing up the hillsides and valleys of northern England was one feature of the general economic expansion between the mid third and mid fourth centuries. It was a period of climatic stability with predominantly warmer and drier weather. Food production rose, along with the population, which was just as well considering the inroads made into the surplus by military consumption. How far these favourable economic conditions depended upon the security provided by the Roman army is hard to judge. The slow, piecemeal withdrawal of Roman forces towards the end of the fourth century and the armed migrations of the

Saxons during the early years of the fifth coincided with the onset of a period of climatic change which was marked by chillier, wetter weather. The freezing of the Rhine in 406, which enabled Germanic invaders to cross with ease, was one dramatic example of the new conditions. Another was lowland flooding in Britain and the reduction of upland arable farming.[26] Had the Roman army remained, it might well have faced severe problems in supporting itself in circumstances in which famine was a very real possibility.

VII

Nearly five hundred miles and two hundred years separate Inchtuthil from Portchester. Each is a monument to Roman energy and engineering, the fort at Portchester the more so, for it is built of stone and still largely intact. There is, however, one significant difference: Inchtuthil's earthworks were dug when Roman power in Britain was virile and aggressive, while Portchester was constructed at a time when it was defensive and less bullish. Nonetheless, those who watched its walls that might easily have believed that Rome still had the inner resolve to keep what it had conquered.

Portchester is still impressive. It stands on a flat tongue of land on the inner edge of Portsmouth harbour. Standing beneath its seaward walls one can see across the water to the modern naval dockyard and the masts and spars of the *Victory* and *Warrior*. Turn around and the view is unappealing: a bleak hinterland of suburban sprawl and dual carriageways which stretches up to chalk downland, disfigured by quarrying. Pleasure yachts moored in roads opposite the fort are a reminder of Portchester's original function: the protection of an anchorage for the Roman Channel fleet.

Work on the fort began in about 285 and was probably completed within five years. Mottled grey and white local flints bonded with reddish-brown tiles and bricks were used for the walls, which were ten feet thick and over twenty feet tall. The original parapets have disappeared, but their medieval replacements give a good impression of how they appeared. Four stout, D-shaped bastions stand at the corners of the fort and a further sixteen project from the walls. These may have mounted ballistas which, if common military practice was followed, would have been sited to fire at the right-hand, that is shieldless, side of anyone storming the walls. A single ballista bolt was among the handful of discarded military objects uncovered when the fort was excavated.

The scale of Portchester – it encompasses eight and a quarter acres – and the speed with which it was erected suggest a response to a sudden and serious crisis. During the last quarter of the third century, seaborne Saxon and Angle raiders from the Frisian and south Jutland coasts had increased their attacks on the British and northern French coasts. They breached the maritime 'frontier' between Dover and Boulogne and began operating in Breton waters. Their elimination was the task of an able and highly ambitious naval commander, M. Aurelius Carausius, who set about creating a new defensive line, a hundred miles long, between fortified bases at Portchester and Le Havre. Each provided an anchorage for galleys which patrolled the Channel and intercepted the marauders. And they did so successfully, for Portchester was decommissioned by 300.

Thereafter, the fort was intermittently occupied and the detritus left behind by its inhabitants in many ways reflects the flagging fortunes of late Roman Britain.[27] Broken swords, an arrowhead and spearheads hint at the existence of a permanent garrison during the middle years of the fourth century, but give no indication as to who they were. The Roman military system had undergone many changes over the preceding three hundred years, most importantly the recruitment of non-citizens into the legions. Barbarian units were widely deployed after 300 and a woman's or child's leather shoe of Germanic fashion raises the question whether Portchester was home to Saxon mercenaries. All that can be said is that this footwear is a fragment of evidence in a wider, often testy and yet unresolved debate among archaeologists over the presence of Saxon detachments, complete with wives and offspring, among the garrisons of Britain's coastal strongholds. Women and children were certainly present inside Portchester. The unearthing of infant skeletons, buried at random, suggests camp followers, although some of the remains are accompanied by the bones of animals whose meat was to provide sustenance for the afterlife. Another possibility is that the fort was guarded by the novel peasant militia, a body created to replace professional soldiers who were needed elsewhere or had been drawn into the power struggles waged by their superiors. If such men did defend Portchester, then they brought their families with them.

After 364 there are signs that civilian squalor, characterised by way-ward drainage channels and sprawling rubbish dumps, superseded martial orderliness. The date, attested to by coins, is in the middle of a period of chronic disorder when Britain's land and sea frontiers were under sustained attack by Scottish, Irish and Saxon (as used by the Romans this word also encompassed Angles) barbarians. Henceforward, and well into the next century, Portchester may have served as a refuge for men and women living in uncertain and violent times in which the boundary line between civilian and soldier was becoming blurred. Then and earlier, the fort was overrun by cats.

Among the coins excavated at Portchester were fifty that bore the head of its creator, Carausius, and advertised his grandiose pretensions. He was one a new breed of Roman commanders, thrusting filibusterers who exploited their reputations and the loyalty of their troops in attempts to seize control of provinces and make themselves 'little emperors'. Carausius's bid to detach Britain and northern Gaul from the Empire failed (he was assassinated in 293), but his fate did not deter others with similar dreams. In 350 the British governor, Magnentius, vainly tried to make himself emperor, and in 383 one of his successors, Magnus Maximus, followed suit. Both extracted substantial forces from the British garrison.

Reverberations of these imperial power struggles were felt beyond the northern frontier and encouraged invasions by the now increasingly unified central and northern Scottish tribes who, then and after, were called Picts – the painted people. The major outbreaks, at the end of the third century and during the middle of the fourth, were eventually contained and order restored, but only temporarily and with troops imported from the continent. The longest and most harmful incur-sions occurred during the 360s when there were simultaneous attacks on northern England by Picts and the Attacotti (a tribe from the north-ern Highlands) and amphibious raids on the western coast by the Scotti, Deisi and Ui Liathain from Ireland, and on the eastern coast by Saxons. In 367, Hadrian's wall was overwhelmed after a conspiracy that involved Picts and civilian Britons who had been permitted to settle close to the military installations.[28] The collapse of civil order offered opportunities for those with little to lose and much to gain; runaway slaves and deserters joined the barbarian raiding parties, as they did elsewhere in western Europe.[29]

The fourth-century invasions were plundering raids, probably undertaken by small, mobile bands who lived off the country. They may also have levied protection money, which is one explanation for the hoard of silverware unearthed at Trapain Law, a hog's-back hill in Lothian and once the capital of the Votadini. Whether loot or bribe, the ornaments (one with a Christian symbol) had been broken up for melting down, and coins date the treasure to about 400.[30] Other collections of Roman coins and valuables from British sources have been uncovered in Ireland.[31]

Barbarian raids were sudden and brutal. In the last decade of the fourth century a party surprised and overwhelmed the small fortified signal station on the Yorkshire coast at Goldsborough. The remains of the south-east tower contained the skeleton of a man who had fallen across a hearth and another who died nearby, defended or mourned by a large dog whose paws were stretched across his shoulder. Other human remains were found in a well, including those of a woman, an old man and a younger one who had been struck on the head with a sword. Charred timbers reveal that the fort was afterwards burned. Another signal station, a few miles north at Huntcliff, fell a few years later. The well was again a cemetery for the slaughtered; there were fourteen in all, including children, and some may have been beheaded.[32] Whether these victims were soldiers and their families or civilians who had taken refuge in a place that offered security is not known.

Nor is the identity of their assailants, although the two forts' proximity to the sea and the swiftness and ferocity of the attacks strongly suggest Saxons. Their vessels had first appeared in British waters during the second quarter of the third century. Paradoxically, given their hostile intentions, their ability to cross the North Sea may have been the result of the adoption of Roman shipbuilding technology and the replacement of paddling by rowing.[33] What emerged from the third- and fourth-century Saxon shipyards were wooden boats like that found at Nydam in southern Jutland. It was fifty feet long, clinker-built of oaken planks, with a flat bottom and high bow and stern. The early seventh-century royal ship discovered at Sutton Hoo in Suffolk was of similar appearance save for a keel, eighty six feet long and with the capacity to carry forty men, which would have allowed for a relief crew of rowers. As this ship was used for a burial, there were no signs of a mast. A recent, half-sized reconstruction of the Sutton Hoo vessel has been used to assess the seaworthiness of Saxon ships. Equipped with a sail, the model proved that with favourable winds and tides the Sutton Hoo ship could have reached speeds of up to ten knots. Similar experiments were made with a half-sized copy of the forty-foot-long, tenth-century Saxon boat found at Graveney in Kent, which had been used for coastal and estuarine voyages. Under the right conditions, and with a sail, it handled well and attained four knots.[34]

Third- and fourth-century Saxon mariners had to do without sails; these first appeared on illustrations of ships after 500. The muscle-power of oarsmen propelled the early raiders across the sea in what were perilous as well as exhausting enterprises. The low hulls of their ships forced Saxon seamen to avoid rough seas wherever possible, and contrary winds impeded progress. 'Weary shall he be who rows against the wind,' wrote a later Saxon poet.[35] The early raiders had, therefore, to move cautiously along the north German and Dutch coastline towards the Hook of Holland, from where they could head for East Anglia or the Thames estuary, a distance of a hundred or so miles. It was not just convenience of access that drew the Saxons to these shores. The abundance of creeks and rivers made it easy for the shallow-draught Saxon craft to penetrate inland.

This tactic was acknowledged by the first countermeasures against the Saxons. The coastal forts at Reculver in Kent and Brancaster in north Norfolk respectively command the waters of the Thames estuary and the approaches to the Wash. Into the latter flowed the Great Ouse and Nene and the Welland and Glen rivers which offered the Saxons routes into large tracts of eastern England. Reculver and Brancaster were built in about 230, the first defensive points in what turned out to be a chain of forts, naval bases and signal stations that extended south-wards to Portchester and northwards to the Yorkshire coast. These served as an early warning system and as bases for naval and land forces. A cavalry unit was posted at Brancaster during the second half of the third century, presumably to intercept raiding parties that had come ashore.[36] Another, complementary string of similar strongpoints was deployed across the Channel to protect what are today the Belgian and northern French coasts. Co-ordination of these defences was placed in the hands of a new official, the count (*comes*) of the Saxon Shore, while the northern, land frontier was under the overall command of a duke (*dux*) based at York.

The extension and continual refurbishment of the seaward defences during the fourth century are clear evidence of the persistence of the Saxon raids. So, too, are the caches of coins and valuables that have been uncovered in south-eastern and eastern England and northern France. These were buried either as a precaution against a raid or else, and this is more likely, as a nervous response to the news that marauders were in the vicinity. The owners did not recover their treasure. They were either killed or kidnapped as slaves, as was the future evangelist Patrick, the son of a Romano-British official whose villa near the south-west coast was plundered by Irish pirates.

Country-dwellers invariably suffered the brunt of such irruptions, whether by Saxons (who had an irrational fear of towns), Irish or Picts. The plight of the victims and the precarious state in which they lived were touched upon in a poem praising the exploits of the Vandal general, Stilicho, who had inflicted defeats on the barbarians in Britain during 398 and 399.

> Next spoke Britain clothed in the skin of some Caledonian beast, her cheeks tattooed, and an azure cloak, rivalling the swell of the ocean, sweeping to her feet: 'Stilicho gave aid to me also when at the mercy of neighbouring tribes, that time the Scots roused all Hibernia against me and the sea foamed to the beat of hostile oars. Thanks to his care I had no need to fear the Scottish arms or tremble at the Pict, or keep watch along all coasts for the Saxon . . .'[37]

Stilicho had indeed driven off the intruders, but, as with the similar campaign of thirty years before, his forces had given the Romano-British a breathing space rather than permanent peace. The inescapable truth was that the garrison had dwindled, the Roman fleet and army lacked the capacity to take reprisals against the raiders in their homelands, and there was no guarantee that troops could be brought across from the continent in the event of another emergency. These cold facts confronted Britain between 406 and 410 when it became obvious that attachment to Rome was, in military terms, valueless. Events followed a familiar and baleful sequence: in 406 the garrison elected an imperial candidate, Marcus, discarded him and chose a civilian, Gratian, who was quickly replaced by a soldier, Constantine III. He left Britain with the bulk of its forces to pursue his ambitions in Gaul, then suffering from a large-scale Germanic invasion. As usual, a military withdrawal triggered an upsurge in raids and the Romano-British were thrown on to their own resources. Only the bare outlines of their countermeasures are known, but they appear to have had some limited success.

Constantine's departure was also the signal for political disorder. Literary sources say little about its nature, but its outcome was clear: whoever assumed authority was determined to sever links with Rome. Hitherto, and at a heavy cost in taxation and sequestration of foodstuffs, Rome had enjoyed a monopoly of military power within Britain. The state alone had raised, trained, equipped and paid the armed forces, whose sole purpose was the safety of the civilian population. For the past fifty years, a diminished Roman garrison had provided security that, at best, had been fitful. This pattern of events seemed destined to perpetuate itself; the antics of the latest batch of imperial pretenders proved that. Moreover, the scale of the recent Germanic invasion of Gaul made it unlikely that reinforcements would be found for Britain in a crisis, even if the will to help was there. In 410 the Romano-British declared a form of independence; the apparatus of the Roman state was dismantled, its bureaucracy was disbanded and political links with the debilitated Empire were cut.

2

Stern in contest: Arthur and after, 410–800

Tidal metaphors come easily to mind when thinking of the barbarian penetration of the western Roman Empire: the intruders came as a 'flood' or in 'waves' which 'swamped' whole provinces. As for England, it too was 'submerged' by an Anglo-Saxon current which swept away the Romano-British who were driven back into what would become the Celtic fringe, Cornwall and Wales. Here, the fugitives mingled with Irish immigrants, and in Scotland the Scotti, from what is now Ulster, established the kingdom of Dalriada in western Argyll. Celtic fugitives could take comfort, as defeated people do, in the exploits of a dead hero, Arthur, who temporarily stemmed the flow of the Anglo-Saxons by winning twelve battles. A hundred or so years after his fruitless victories his reputation was already glowing. In *The Gododdin*, an early seventh-century elegy for Celtic warriors slain in battle, one is measured by an Arthurian yardstick: 'He glutted black ravens on the ramparts of the stronghold though he was no Arthur.'[1]

The image of carrion is another that seems fitting for an age of almost continual bloodshed. Between 600 and 850 contemporary chroniclers listed eighty-two campaigns waged within England alone, a total that excludes those fought against external enemies such as the Vikings.[2] Having expelled or neutralised the native British, the new Anglo-Saxon polities struggled among themselves for land, a pecking order and, in time, paramountcy. None of this can be denied, but the dramatic language of annalists and versifiers which makes for powerful stories also conceals much of the truth, not least about the scale of the events they were describing.

The parties of Germanic tribesmen who shifted across western Europe during the late fourth and the fifth centuries were for the greater part farmers in search of land. Their social and psychological ties were to immediate kin or clan, and the tribal differences noted by outsiders were commonly blurred, certainly among the warrior élites. The fighting man, trained to use arms, stood apart from those who toiled, and he owed his allegiance to a leader rather than a race or nation, concepts that meant nothing at this time. The barbarian warrior might gladly serve in the Roman army, and many did, showing impressive loyalty.[3] Or, he might offer his professional skills to a ruler who would reward him generously and add to his honour.

The quest for such an open-handed patron brought the fictional Beowulf to Hrothgar's great feasting hall at Heorot, for he knew that within it gallant men were favoured by gifts and well fed and wined.[4] Pride in courage and loyalty to a noble lord who rewarded it gave a warrior band cohesion to the point where, if its leader was slain, his followers would fight on to the death. For the Romans, such behaviour was another example of barbarian madness, but within the Germanic and Celtic traditions it was a mark of the highest distinction. And it long remained so. A fifth-century Roman was puzzled by the fact than among the Alani 'a man is judged happy who sacrificed his life in battle'.[5] Six hundred years later, the gravestone of a Scandinavian warrior proclaimed: 'He did not run at Uppsala, but fought while he could hold weapons.'[6]

Dedicated and skilled warriors were rare creatures among the bodies of men, women and children who wandered through the provinces of the western Roman Empire, beyond the power of the authorities either to expel or control. Accommodations were made, sometimes at the point of a sword. In 409 and 410 Alaric's attacks on Ravenna and Rome were used to extract treasure and land from the Emperor Honorius, and in 418 the authorities in Aquitaine agreed to allow Visigoth immigrants to settle. The alternative, here and elsewhere, was widespread disruption and the destruction of property. Those forced to do business with the barbarians detected a simple form of polity among them, based upon families and groups of settlements which were dominated by strong men, whom the Romans called optimates and who were attended by small bands of warriors. From these leaders descended the rulers of the states that emerged during the next hundred or so years.

The barbarians who entered Britain were organised along similar lines. The British experience of infiltration and settlement was, however, different from that of, say, Gaul. The necessity of a passage across either the North or the Irish Sea, and the capacity of the boats available to undertake it, dictated that the numbers of immigrants would be smaller and their arrival spread over a longer period. The early history of their first settlements is hard to trace, nor is it possible to assess how many colonists they contained. What is beyond question is that by the middle years of the seventh century the Anglo-Saxons had acquired dominance over large swathes of southern, eastern and midland England and were in the process of developing independent monarchies. In Scotland, the Scotti had laid the foundations of a strong state, Dalriada, which was already feared by its Pictish neighbours.

The repercussions of these shifts in power are difficult to pin down. There was a slow withdrawal of Celts into Wales, the far south-west and even Brittany. And yet there is no archaeological evidence to suggest bloody expulsions and massacres, or that the Celtic exodus was wholesale. There was no racial death struggle nor any equivalent of late twentieth-century ethnic cleansing. The proliferation of Anglo-Saxon placenames is not necessarily an epitaph for dead or vanished Romano-Britons. They merely proclaim who was politically or legally dominant in an area. In the same way, the late nineteenth-century colonial names Rhodesia and Salisbury announced that the British and not the Ndebele now controlled a large chunk of southern Africa. Irish placenames replaced Pictish in Dalriada for the same reason, but this did not mean that Picts had disappeared. Some stayed and they may well have outnumbered their new rulers.[7] Revealingly, older names for natural features such as hills and rivers were adopted by the newcomers, as also happened in colonial Africa.

While there were those who fled from the invaders, there must have been many, perhaps the majority, who chose to stay behind. Those at the bottom of the pile, slaves, obviously had nothing to lose from a change of masters. In south-western Scotland, Anglo-Saxon conquest was followed by coexistence between incomers and natives, and elsewhere assimilation occurred. Fifth-century Portchester housed people of Celtic and Germanic origins, who appear to have integrated.[8] Further east, unopposed Anglo-Saxon settlers took over vacant land between the rivers Ouse and Cuckmere.[9]

Resistance to Anglo-Saxon colonisation was led from the top. Little is known about the polities that emerged after the Roman administration had been dismantled. Strong men of some kind certainly appeared and, given the hierarchical nature of Romano-British society, they were men of property who already enjoyed the local status that went with it. One took the title Vortigern ('over king') and appears to have enjoyed a form of superiority over lesser magnates, although the limits of his authority remain unknown. Most of what is known about Vortigern comes from the polemic of Gildas, whose *De Excidio Britanniae* ('On the Ruin of Britain') was compiled between 490 and 540, using among other sources handed-down memories. His theme is the overthrow of Christian Britain by the pagan Saxons who, revealingly, are likened to the Assyrian persecutors of the Israelites. Gildas's lamentations, consciously echoing those of Jeremiah, reflected the natural bitterness of the old Romano-British élite, dispossessed of their lands and driven into exile by barbarians.

Vortigern had assumed power in England by 425. His emergence coincided with renewed Pictish, possibly Anglo-Saxon, attacks which were beyond the capacity of local forces to handle. Vortigern reacted in a typical Roman manner and hired the services of three boatloads of mercenaries commanded by two Jutes, Hengist ('stallion') and his brother Horsa ('horse'). They were warlords whose names or nicknames suggested the strength and wealth symbolised by the horse in Germanic mythology.[10] Contracts between such leaders and the Roman army and barbarian war bands had been a common feature of late imperial defence policy, a stopgap measure that usually worked well, not least because these mercenaries were perfectly happy to fight their fellow tribesmen. There is every likelihood that small bodies of these troops, known as *foederati*, were present in Britain when the connections with Rome were severed. As was usual with such detachments, the men would be accompanied by their wives and families.

This seems to have been the case with Hengist and Horsa who, in return for driving off marauders, were allow to settle on Thanet in Kent. Over the next twenty or so years, at least four further contingents arrived. Their services were invaluable, for they had the capacity to take the war into the Pictish heartland; a flotilla of forty ships commanded by Hengist's son, Octha, undertook a large seaborne operation against the Orkneys.[11] There were other influxes of Anglo-Saxons who may or may not have had any connection with the mercenary companies and who settled extensively in East Anglia. These were probably economic refugees, driven overseas by the climatic changes that led to the flooding of the Frisian coastline. The party that crossed from Federsen Wierde in Lower Saxony to Mucking on the Essex shore of the Thames intended to stay there, for they brought their own pottery.[12]

Early in the 440s relations between Vortigern and his hitherto useful army broke down. The immediate cause seems to have been a squabble about the terms of the contract, but the chronicler Nennius blamed the trouble on Vortigern's lechery: he seduced Hengist's daughter, Rowena, at a feast and soothed her outraged father with an offer of the whole of Kent, then ruled by an under-king. The offspring of Vortigern's lapse was the future theologian and saint, Faustus. Be that as it may, the disagreements between Hengist and Vortigern led to an intermittent conflict between the Romano-British and the Anglo-Saxons which extended into the next century and formed the background for the exploits of Ambrosius Aurelianus or, as he was afterwards called, Arthur.

II

Archaeology and fragmented chronicles in which fact and Celtic legend blend give a veiled impression of the course of the war. Its most impressive and tantalising monument is the hill fort at South Cadbury in south Somerset. Together with Congresbury in the north of the same county and Tintagel on a Cornish promontory, it represents part of the defensive response to Anglo-Saxon advances during the fifth and sixth centuries. Originally an Iron Age fort, South Cadbury was refurbished on a scale and in a manner that strongly suggest a ruler with extensive resources at his command. The perimeter ramparts alone needed a hundred thousand feet of dressed timber and, obviously, a large labour force, which may have worked under compulsion. A tenth-century Celtic text states that rulers could exercise the right to press their subjects to undertake work on hill forts as a form of military service.[13] Presumably the local rural population was mobilised to do the hard grind although, interestingly, what has been excavated of their efforts shows that by 500 Roman techniques of mixing mortar had been forgotten. Whoever he was, the lord of South Cadbury held his state in a great wooden rectangular hall where, if he upheld custom, he would have entertained his band of warriors.

It is tempting, especially given South Cadbury's name, to link it with the Camelot of subsequent legend, and to identify its lord as Ambrosius Aurelianus, or Arthur, who directed the defence of western England during the third quarter of the fifth century. Furthermore, there is the substantial body of folklore, largely fabricated six hundred years later by the monks of Glastonbury, that pinpoints legendary Avalon among the Somerset levels and Arthur's grave within their church. Unfortunately, or perhaps fortunately, for subsequent legend spinners and speculators, the written evidence about where Arthur actually lived and fought his battles is vague. He never held the rank of king and there is no evidence beyond conjecture that his forces were predominantly cavalry. Rather, he was the commander of a war band of indeterminate size but considerable effectiveness. It won a dozen battles, on six occasions at river crossings where, presumably, Arthur intercepted advance parties of Anglo-Saxons.[14] At his final victory, in about 495, his forces were encircled within a hill fort at Mons Badonicus, somewhere in south-western England. They broke the siege, charged downhill and scattered their enemies, who suffered heavy losses. This engagement may well have severely depleted the ranks of Anglo-Saxon warriors, which explains why there was a twenty-year lull in hostilities. According to Welsh tradition Arthur died in 515 on an unidentifiable battlefield, fighting against 'Medraut', who was possibly a rival warlord or a former follower.

The earlier battle scenarios are all convincing. Arthur waged war in a region criss-crossed by rivers, and so the invaders were compelled to travel by way of fords, which reduced their scope for strategic manoeuvre and made it possible for an adversary to prepare ambushes. Roman roads may well have been used, as one was by King Rædwald of East Anglia in 617. His army followed the Roman road that ran from Lincoln to Castleford, when it advanced to engage the forces of King Æthelfrith of Northumbria. He must have been forewarned of his enemy's route, for the two forces joined battle where the road crossed the River Idle.[15] Arthur's use of an old hill fort also fits what is known about contemporary patterns of warfare. In 1006 the Danish army took up a position in one on Ashdown hill, high on the Lambourn downs, and waited there for their Saxon opponents whom they had challenged to battle at this site.

Arthur's successes assured him a place in the annals of those he had attempted to defend. The sparse facts of his existence were eventually supplemented by all manner of fables which entertained, comforted and inspired. The feasting hall of the warlord Arthur, if it ever existed, was soon on the way to becoming the Camelot of legend, and his warriors the paladins of the Round Table. In the process, the Celtic imagination provided the Welsh with a potent self-image: they were a people capable of a greatness that would be revived when Arthur was resurrected. The fifth-century warlord was reinvented as someone he had never been: a just, Christian prince whose reign had marked a golden age. Within six hundred years of his lifetime and on the eve of his transformation into the model of western European knighthood, there were believers convinced that he and his times would return. In 1113, French visitors to Bodmin were shown Arthur's throne and a Cornishman assured them that he was still alive.[16]

In the twentieth century there would be people who imagined that Field-Marshal Kitchener and Colonel T. E. Lawrence had never died, but waited somewhere for a time when they would be needed to save their people. The developed Arthurian legend, the roots of which lay in his own age and flowered in that of chivalry, has taken an extraordinarily powerful grip on our national consciousness. Perhaps one should say subconsciousness, for many who watched the funeral of Diana, Princess of Wales, may have noted that, like Arthur, her last resting place was in a lake.

Wherever he was buried, Arthur, the champion of all that was left of Roman Britain, had fought his enemies to a stalemate. The Anglo-

Saxon thrust into the Thames valley and adjacent districts was halted, but it regained what turned out to be an unstoppable momentum in the next century. The forensic evidence for the struggle is scattered and inconclusive. Remains uncovered from a settlement at Caistor-by-Norwich overrun in the middle of the fifth century reveal that destructive raiding was still prevalent. A largish house built of wattle and daub, but including baths in the Roman manner, was burned down, and within its remains were found thirty-six skulls and other bones of what must have been the victims of a massacre. Death may have come suddenly, for a kiln excavated nearby still contained pots ready for firing.[17]

Such incidents must have been the experience of war for many during the fourth and fifth centuries. There is, of course, no reason to assume automatically that those slaughtered at Caistor-by-Norwich fell to an Anglo-Saxon war band intent on clearing the land for future occupation. The collapse of Vortigern's authority in the 440s may well have encouraged the emergence of petty warlords perpetually at loggerheads with their neighbours in a contest for power and resources. Such creatures proliferated in contemporary Ireland, where they measured their political power by their ability to make life unbearable for their rivals.[18] Their activities are grimly described in an early seventh-century verse:

> *Fire has seized Ráith Guala*
> *Save ye little from it!*
> *Swiftly do evil men kindle*
> *A fire in the fort of Áed of the [Fir] Bog.*[19]

There were also bands of young warriors who roamed the countryside, preying on those who could not defend themselves or their goods.[20] Their temper and that of their 'official' counterparts is conveyed by another verse from the same period:

> *I am thankful for what has been gained*
> *Tonight for my feast, a single morsel;*
> *I have had [many] another night*
> *[When] Mary's son gave me seven cows.*[21]

The gratitude to Jesus Christ for past plunder suggests that conversion to Christianity was not always accompanied by a softening of the old values of the warrior class.

It was men from this élite who, quite literally, provided the cutting edge for the parties of Anglo-Saxon immigrants who were moving across England during the second half of the fifth century and much of the sixth. The impulse that drove them was the need for more fertile land and, with it, a better chance of survival. Some were the surplus population from those coastal areas, such as Sussex and East Anglia, that had already been settled for two or three generations. Others were newcomers who had staked their fortunes on a perilous voyage. The dangers they faced were described two centuries later by the poet Cynewulf, who likened the hazards of a man's passage through life to those encountered by a seafarer:

> Across cold water we sail in our keels,
> Over the wide sea in our ocean steeds,
> Faring on in our flood-wood. Fearful the stream,
> The tumult of waters whereon we toss
> In this feeble world, fierce are the surges
> On the ocean lanes. Hard was our life
> Before we made harbour o'er the foaming seas.[22]

How many ventured to cross to England is not known. One plausible estimate, based upon recorded landfalls and the numbers and capacity of ships available, puts the total of immigrants at thirty-five thousand, of whom four to five thousand were fighting men.[23] Not all arrivals were mentioned in the chronicles, but those that were give an impression of one or more extended families or septs travelling independently in a handful of ships. One example, set down in the *Anglo-Saxon Chronicle*, may stand for many others: 'In this year [501] Port and his two sons Bieda and Mægla came to Britain with two ships at the place which is called Portsmouth; and there they killed a [young] man of very high rank.' Even if they had travelled in larger vessels like that found at Sutton Hoo, this party could hardly have totalled more than a hundred.

The Anglo-Saxons brought with them a pyramidal society whose gradations were revealed in the laws adopted in their embryonic kingdoms. Those of King Ine of Wessex, dating from 688 to 694, reveal that at the apex of the hierarchy was the landed nobleman, then came the landless nobleman and the ceorl (a freeman farmer) and so on, down to slaves. Divisions in life were perpetuated in death; the lord was buried with the accessories of the warrior (sword and shield) and the ceorl with a spear. Weapons signified a man's place in society rather than his ability to use them; one skeleton found alongside a spear showed the marks of spina bifida which would have rendered the owner unfit to fight.[24] As might be expected in what was a colonial, frontier society, the proportion of sword burials in English cemeteries (roughly one in five) is higher than in the more settled Anglo-Saxon homelands of north Germany.[25] Warriors were essential for the conquest and security of new lands, so their status was correspondingly high. So, too, were their chances of being well rewarded; the careers of Hengist and Horsa must have encouraged many other opportunists to try their luck in England.

III

The most significant outcome of the extended competition for land and power throughout Britain and Ireland during the Dark Ages was the physical and social ascendancy of the warrior. The survival of communities and fledgling states depended upon his strength and skill at arms. For the professional fighting man, affinities of race or tribe meant little. Celtic, Anglo-Saxon, Scandinavian, Pictish and Irish warriors held similar values, followed similar codes of conduct, admired the same qualities, and shared a common pride in their calling.

Consider Gorthryn, son of Ufai, a warrior of the sixth-century Romano-British kingdom of Gododdin: 'He was stern in contest, he slew with a spear, a hundred men bore away his harsh warning from battle.'[26] Five centuries later, the Danish king, Swein Forkbeard, was praised as a 'brave warrior who often gave the raven bloated flesh, left the imprint of sword-edge on a warrior's limbs'.[27] The measure of the fighting man was how many others he killed. When the Irish warriors of Ulaidh gathered for an annual festival, each would boast of his exploits and produce from his pouch the tongues of those he had slain that year.

Some 'threw in cattle tongues' to swell their total but, if detected, deceit could prove fatal, for the warriors 'spoke with their swords on their thighs, swords that turned against anyone who swore falsely'.[28] If he lacked personal honour, the warrior's death tally meant little.

Reputation was prized above all things. It gave the warrior status in his lifetime and renown after death, for his exploits would be relived by the versifiers and minstrels who entertained fighting men as they ate and drank in their lord's hall. At the battle of Catraeth (probably Catterick) in about 588, Nai, son of Nwython, of Gododdin 'slew a hundred princes wearing gold torques so that he might be celebrated'. After the fight, 'for many a year a minstrel was glad'.[29] The deeds of that day would be transformed into epics of courage which were recited or sung to aristocratic audiences. When Beowulf entered Hrothgar's hall at Heorot, he was greeted with the words:

> Yet sit now to banquet, where you may soon attend
> Should the mood take you, some tale of victory.

Magical and supernatural events were woven into such stories and their heroes assumed legendary, superhuman qualities. By the age of six, the Irish warrior Cú Chulaind had singlehandedly overcome 150 boys at wrestling and torn apart a great hound.

Entry into the world of warriors followed soon after, when Cú Chulaind began 'to study weaponry'. The curriculum was tough:

> The Jarl [earl] grew up in the halls;
> he swung the shield and fitted the bowstring,
> bent the bow and shafted the arrow,
> let fly the dart and wielded the spear,
> rode horses and loosed hounds,
> drew swords and swam the stream . . .[30]

The aspirant would have to become familiar with shield, sword and spear, and acquire the strength and quick reflexes to handle them in battle. All were heavy and, by the seventh and eighth centuries, he would have to accustom himself to the weight of the mail byrnie (shirt) and the iron helmet which were being worn by more and more warriors.

The apprentice fighting man developed stamina and steadiness of eye and hand through hunting which, incidentally, provided welcome additional food for himself and the community that supported him and his lord. He also needed dexterity and suppleness of limb; the tenth-century Norwegian king Olaf Tryggvasson was famed for his skill at juggling with sharp daggers and the feat of walking along a row of the outstretched oars of a longship.[31]

Physical training for warriorhood was complemented by an equally vital psychological preparation. As the time of battle approached, the fighting man had deliberately to lay aside his humanity and undergo a metamorphosis in which his body and mind became those of a predatory beast. The Irish called this process *riastarthe*, which may be rendered as 'battle fury', and in Cú Chulaind its onset was accompanied by a terrifying physical transformation. 'You would have thought that every hair was being driven into his head. You would have thought that a spark of fire was on every hair. He closed one eye until it was no wider than the eye of a needle; he opened the other until it was as big as a wooden bowl. He bared his teeth from jaw to ear, and he opened his mouth until the gullet was visible.'[32]

When this mutation was accomplished, the warrior had absorbed the strength and ferocity of an animal. One from Gododdin was described as a 'bull of battle', another as 'the serpent with a terrible sting'.[33] Germanic fighting men, who raised themselves to this pitch of fury, became 'berserk' (bear-like) or as 'mad as dogs or wolves; they bit their shields and were as strong as bears'.[34] Vulpine characteristics were particularly cherished, for wolves hunted in packs and their savagery was proverbial. Warriors clad in wolves' skins absorbed that beast's ferocity. They are described in the ninth-century Norse poem *Raven Song*: 'Wolfcoats they are called, those who bear blood-stained swords to battle; they redden spears when they come to the slaughter, acting together.'[35] Just before they joined battle at Magh Rath (Moira, County Down) in 637, the armies of Ulaidh and Dalriada 'roared in the manner of a herd of stags'.[36] Gildas's comparison of the Anglo-Saxons with lions, dogs and wolves was probably more than a rhetorical device.

A whole army might take courage from the dragon, a malevolent creature of the Devil which symbolised the havoc of war. A fabricated golden dragon was carried as a banner by the West Saxon army of King

Cuthred when it defeated the Mercians at Burford in 752.[37] A dragon standard flew over the English army at the battle of Assandun in 1016 and another appeared fifty years later at Hastings. To judge from its portrayal on the Bayeux Tapestry, this banner resembled a long, voluminous windsock, with wings, a tail and gaping jaws. The presence of such a fearsome symbol of destruction above a battlefield must have inspired terror among the credulous, who probably made up an overwhelming majority. Dragons were not mythical creatures: one, fiery-headed and breathing sulphur, was seen in 1113 at Christchurch in Hampshire by the same French visitors who had heard of the living Arthur in Cornwall.[38]

The battle of Burford in which the dragon banner made its début is tersely described in the *Anglo-Saxon Chronicle*, no doubt for lack of evidence as to what form the fighting had taken. No such inhibitions troubled Henry of Huntingdon, who wrote in the first half of the twelfth century and offered a vivid account of the engagement in terms that might easily have been applied to any battle of the eighth century or of his own. The armies drew up and then threw themselves at each other in a headlong rush. 'The thunder of war, the clash of arms, the clang of blows, and the cries of the wounded' are perhaps stock phrases, but they sound authentic, as in the description of the fighting men 'stained with blood, bespattered with brains, their spears shattered'.[39] This is combat in the Homeric fashion: a collision between warriors who fight as individuals, as anxious to add lustre to their own reputations as to overcome their lord's enemies.

Blood flowed everywhere and the wounds inflicted by heavy, bladed weapons were hideous. Only someone who has witnessed the immediate aftermath of a fatal road accident, a knife-fight or a terrorist bombing can come close to imagining how a Dark Age battlefield must have appeared. Six skeletons, all of men of between twenty and thirty-five who had died in combat, were excavated at Eccles in Kent and their injuries give a sombre reality to the annalists' battle rhetoric. One suffered sword cuts to his left elbow, which severed the tendons and rendered him unable to use his shield, and was then slain by a blow to the head. Another's skull was penetrated by a single stroke, and others died from several downward cuts to the head. Such deaths were grimly celebrated by the twelfth-century Icelandic poet Gunnlangr: 'the flame of battle [sword] destroys the dwellings of brains [heads].'[40] All those found at Eccles had died from trauma and massive loss of blood, and two had been wounded beforehand by missiles, possibly arrows or darts.[41] An unusually tall (just over six feet) skeleton of a young man exhumed at Portchester showed signs of a fatal sword cut to his lower face which would have opened the jugular vein. There are also traces of disabling cuts to his lower legs.[42] The pattern for all these casualties is similar: those who inflicted them had used their swords to cripple their adversaries before delivering the final and fatal blows to the head.

The forensic evidence points to all these injuries having been made by sword strokes. The Anglo-Saxon sword was both a weapon and a symbol of the warrior's social standing. It was between thirty and thirty-two inches long with a blade of between twenty-seven and thirty inches. It was expensive, for it took time to produce. The strength and suppleness that were the qualities prized in a sword were the result of forging together strips of iron on top of each other, a process that could require up to two hundred hours of labour and between two and three hundredweight of charcoal.[43] On completion, a blade might be inlaid or engraved with the name of its owner or maker. Hilts and scabbards were sometimes embellished with gold and silverwork, finely patterned, like the 'treasure sword' delivered to Beowulf by Hrothgar.[44]

The heavy, wooden, iron-bossed round shield was the warrior's principal defence. It served to parry bows, particularly to the legs and arms, and could be used as a bludgeon. Armour appears to have been an innovation that spread during the seventh and eighth centuries. The early seventh-century royal burial at Sutton Hoo (possibly King Rædwald, who died in about 625) included a knee-length mail byrnie, a rare and highly expensive item with rows of links alternately welded and riveted. The near-contemporary warriors of Gododdin may have possessed such garments, for the recital of their deeds mentions their 'dark blue' armour but gives no hint as to how it was made.[45] Beowulf's was 'the best of battle-dress, that protects my breast, the finest of gear; it is Hreoel's heirloom, the work of Weland'.

Three helmets survive from this period: one from Sutton Hoo; another of the mid seventh century from Benty Grange in Derbyshire; and a third, from the second half of the eighth century, from Coppergate in York.[46] Each is a practical response to the nature of contemporary combat with reinforced iron defences for the skull and, in the Sutton Hoo and Coppergate examples, cheekpieces to deflect blows away from the jaw.

These helmets and similar, contemporary pieces from Sweden were not just defensive headpieces. Their rich and elaborate decoration proclaimed the wearer's status, and its iconography celebrated the cult of the warrior and invoked supernatural forces to aid him in battle. The Benty Grange helmet is surmounted by the figure of a wild boar, a pungnacious-looking creature studded with silver, with garnets inset as eyes and gilded tusks. The boar motif appeared on the helmets of Beowulf's war band: 'over the cheekpieces, boar shapes shone out with gold, blazing and fire hard, fierce guards of their bearer's lives.' Divine protection is summoned on the Coppergate helmet which has a strip engraved 'IN NOMINE DNI NOSTRI IHV SCS D ET OMNIBUS DECEMUS AMEN. OSHERE XPI', which can be rendered, 'In the Name of Our Lord Jesus, the Holy Ghost, God and with all we pray. Amen. Oshere. Christ'. Pagan magical forces were summoned by one of the images on the Sutton Hoo helmet. Among the small silver plaques around its rim is one on which a spear-armed horseman rides over a fallen warrior. This represents Fate in the form of a Valkyrie, one of the mounted messengers of the god of war, Woden, whose task it was to choose those warriors who were to die in battle. The stricken man on the Sutton Hoo helmet attempts to reverse his destiny by thrusting at the horse with his sword, and he is helped by a smaller figure behind the rider who is trying to deflect the lance.[47] Was this some charm, contrived to raise the confidence of the helmet's owner by warding off the Valkyries?

This Anglo-Saxon warrior followed the Germanic cult of Woden. His helmet is decorated with a relief that shows two dancing men wearing horned helmets and carrying spears and a sword. These figures represent some rite of Woden, perhaps one of initiation, in which a young warrior's agility and courage were tested by his having to avoid spears and swords hurled by his elders.[48] Casts for such helmet decorations found at Torslunda in Sweden show one scene in which a warrior is fighting two bears and another in which he engages a monster. This imagery of savage beasts that the warrior must both imitate and overcome made him a formidable figure in battle. If the Sutton Hoo equipment did belong to King Rædwald, then he and others like him must have been awesome figures with their long mail shirts, richly inlaid belts and scabbards, and helmets with what the *Beowulf* poet called the 'war' or 'battle' mask. His humanity was obscured and about his head were vivid images of those predators whose fierceness he deliberately emulated.

The richness of the warrior's harness was a mark of his distinction in battle. For this his lord gave him arm rings and other gifts, as well as food and drink. King Mynyddog of Gododdin knew how to reward those who fought for him; Gorthryn, son of Urfai, 'deserved his wine' and Gwefrfraw proved invaluable 'in return for wine from the drinking horn', which may well have increased his fighting powers, for a brother-in-arms was described as 'reared and nourished on wine'.[49] To judge from other passages in the poem, alcohol helped stir the warriors of Gododdin to that battle frenzy that made them careless of their lives.

Generosity in a prince was inseparable from bravery; the legendary and therefore model ruler of the ancient Angles, Offa, 'was widely honoured in gift-giving and warfare'. This was not surprising, given his illustrious pedigree. His ancestors were all heroes, a guarantee of nobility and courage, which was why the dynasties that emerged in sixth- and seventh-century Britain and Ireland expended so much energy in compiling genealogies to prove their descent from mighty men, even gods. All the Anglo-Saxon royal families claimed a common descent from Woden and continued to do so even after their conversion to Christianity.

IV

The Germanic god of war was a fitting ancestor for the war-band leaders turned kings who were struggling for land and power during the sixth and seventh centuries. What was gained by the sword had to be defended by the sword; of the eight kings who ruled Northumbria between 600 and 700, six died in battle. A three-cornered contest for the overlordship of the Picts between 726 and 729 was marked by nine battles, and in the last one competitor was killed.[50] Seven petty kings of the Cruithi of northern Ireland perished in the battle of Móin Dairi Lothair in about 562.[51] Ruthlessness was as vital for the ambitious as personal bravery. King Penda of Mercia died on the battlefield in 655 after a career in which he had served as client commander for Cadwallon of Gwynedd, murdered a fugitive Northumbrian ætheling (prince), ravaged Northumbria and killed in battle Ecgric and Sigberht, two East Anglian kings. 'I know that the king will not live; for I never before saw so humble a king,' a cleric observed of Oswine of Deira who was noted for his exceptional piety. Unable to raise sufficient fighting men to defend his kingdom in an emergency, he was slain by his rival, Oswiu, in 642.[52]

The political moral here was that the king who attracted warriors would flourish and they, in turn, would benefit from his success. Royal presents of rings and abundant food and wine placed warriors under an obligation which was fulfilled on the battlefield. The fighting man could also expect a share in the lands conquered by his patron. 'If a nobleman who holds land neglects military service, he shall pay 120 shillings and forfeit his land,' ran one of the laws of Ine of Wessex. The landless warrior was liable for half that amount if he failed to perform his duty.[53]

The nature of this relationship between a king and his warriors was understood by the ætheling Cyneard. After he and his followers had murdered Cynewulf of Wessex in 755, he offered land and money to the dead king's adherents. They refused, invoking ancient but still vibrant warrior traditions, claiming that even though their kinsfolk had defected to Cyneard, they would stay loyal to their former master. They kept their word and overcame the usurper, killing him and all but two of his fighting men.[54]

This engagement was between two, relatively small, groups of professional fighters. The same kind of men dominated royal field armies and did the brunt of the fighting. The numbers involved were tiny by modern standards; King Ine's laws defined an army as thirty-five or more men, which fits with what is known about the size of those war bands that had first conquered large parts of England. Battles were, therefore, small-scale affairs which seldom involved more than a hundred warriors on either side. Even allowing for poetic hyperbole, contests were hard-fought, with men fighting with an eye to their standing among their fellows. Casualties cannot be easily assessed and, with the exception of kings or noblemen, were rarely mentioned by chroniclers. The figure of eighty-four dead given in the *Anglo-Saxon Chronicle* for an encounter between two Anglo-Saxon royal armies in 784 seems about right.

Military obligation extended to those beyond the royal circle of warriors. Its avoidance would cost a ceorl thirty shillings according to Ine's laws, which do not say what was expected from this soldier. An insight into one form of ceorl's duty is given by Bede. A young warrior serving King Ecgfrith of Northumbria was left for dead after a battle with Æthelred of Mercia in 679. Recovering somewhat, he tried to get away, but was captured by a Mercian nobleman who asked who he was. 'Fearing to own himself a soldier', he answered that, 'he was a peasant, poor and married, and that he came to the army with others to bring provisions to the soldiers'. When the nobleman finally discovered the young man's rank, he remarked: 'I perceived by your answers that you were no peasant.' Nonetheless, he was sold as a slave to a Frisian, but eventually ransomed. Three features of contemporary warfare emerge from this tale. The bearing and speech of a warrior were distinctive; the peasantry were corralled into providing logistical support for an army; and prisoners were treated as plunder and sold into slavery by their captors. This practice must have added to the stock of slaves who made up a tenth of the population according to the Domesday survey of 1086. In Cornwall, which had been a refuge for Romano-British refugees, the proportion was 21 per cent.[55] Revealingly, the Anglo-Saxon word for a Welshman was 'wealh', which meant slave.

Like the nobleman, the free ceorl was legally bound to serve a king in war. As Ine's laws suggest, the relationship was contractual: the crown bestowed protection in return for service. In early seventh-century Kent the laws of King Æthelberht stipulated that if one of his frigmen (free men) was murdered, his assailant would have to pay a fifty shilling fine to the crown.[56] Compensation was even due to the king for the death or injury of slaves. But personal safety had a price; kings, both great and petty, regularly traversed their kingdoms and during their journeys they and their dependants received rent or taxation in the form of livestock, grain and drink. The new states, and, for that matter, their warrior caste, rested upon the agricultural surplus of small rural communities which, in theory, enjoyed a degree of safety from depredation.

This security was brittle, to say the least, given the chronic disorder created by intermittent dynastic power struggles within states and rivalries between them. Whenever a ruler gained the upper hand over a rival he demonstrated his position by imposing tribute on the defeated prince's lands. A seventh-century Welsh poet complained of his people's cattle bellowing as they were pricked by the spears of Northumbrians collecting what was tantamount to extortion in kind.[57]

Another form of exaction, practised by Irish kings, was the systematic plunder of their enemies' territory, a process that would later be known as 'harrying'. By reiving livestock and carrying off crops, a ruler proved himself the stronger man and exposed his rival's incapacity to defend his own people and their property. Raids and counter-raids were a form of warfare by attrition, for the end result was the erosion of resources and the weakening of a state. There were also in Ireland fianna (independent war bands) which were filled with unattached warriors aged between fourteen and twenty and older men who had been expelled from their kingdoms as a result of dynastic intrigue. These freebooters preyed on communities unlucky enough to be in their path and were a considerable nuisance. And yet the fianna were tolerated by kings who were unwilling to reduce the stock of fighting men available to them; in time, the young bloods would join royal war bands, settle down, marry and become landowners. Interestingly, one exasperated Irish ruler solved the problem of a particularly disruptive example of the fianna by persuading its members to cross the Irish Sea and pester the English.[58]

V

The hill fortress of Dunadd, close to the shores of the Sound of Jura, is a striking monument to another Irish overseas enterprise, the kingdom of Dalriada. Stark and somewhat forbidding above the lush meadowlands of the Kilmartin valley, Dunadd tells us much, not only about the precarious times in which it served as a stronghold, but about the nature of early medieval kingship and war. From whichever way one approaches this isolated glacial outcrop, one looks upwards, which is fitting for a place that was the resort of kings. Among the rocks at the

summit is one on which is incised the image of a boar, a creature associated with warriors. Nearby, another stone bears an impression that
resembles the outline of a human foot, which has encouraged speculation that it played some part in the ceremonies by which a king was
installed. Tradition has it that Dunadd was a major centre of the kingdom of Dalriada as well as a formidable fort. After scrambling up the
two hundred or so feet of steep, slippery and rocky hillside, one is faced
by a narrow passage, a place of ambush where, like Horatius and his
companions, a handful of warriors could stem an army. A few iron
spearheads, knives and a broken sword were among the artefacts found
when the site was excavated, and the archaeologists calculated that 250
men could man the defences.[59] Perhaps so, but only in a dire emergency, for walking around the position one feels that they would have
been cramped and there would have been little room for provisions.

Dunadd's greatest strategic value was as an observation post. From its
highest point a watcher could see ten, perhaps fifteen, miles in the
right conditions, which would enable him to detect the approach of
seaborne forces as they sailed up the Sound of Jura. Turning inland, he
had panoramic views over the Kilmartin valley and the hills beyond,
over which invading war bands from Pictland and Strathclyde would
have to travel.

Vigilance was vital for Dark Age strategy. The earlier he was forewarned of invaders, the better a ruler could muster men to repel them.
The kings of Dalriada, like their Anglo-Saxon counterparts, had the
right to demand military service from their scattered subjects, who were
obliged to attend whenever summoned to slogad, or hosting. This could
be called if the kingdom was under attack, or when the king needed to
chastise rebels. At the beginning of the eighth century, a Dalriadan
king could call on 1500 fighting men, organised in groups of twenty
households, for service on land or sea.[60] A unit, therefore, comprised
the head of a household, or sept, his kinsmen, servants and slaves. Sea
service involved the manning of currachs, wicker-framed leather boats
propelled by oars (seven on each side) and sails, which were used for
expeditions to the isles or against the mainland of Ireland. A carefully
reconstructed facsimile of one of these vessels, based on one that would
have conveyed St Columba on his maritime missions, is displayed in
the museum at nearby Kilmartin.

The fragments of Dalriada's recorded history strongly suggests that hostings were a commonplace occurrence. Its Scotti overlords arrived in about 500 to found what was in effect a colony of the kingdom of Ulaidh which occupied the coastal area of modern Antrim. From the start, Dalriada was a pawn in a convoluted and turbulent game of Irish power politics in which dozens of kings (great, middling, small and miniature) struggled to consolidate or enlarge their polities and establish a pecking order. Dalriada faced conflict on two fronts: there was friction with Ulaidh, and a strong urge to expand southwards towards the Clyde.

As elsewhere, the fortunes of the state depended heavily on the personality of its king. Aedan mac Gabrain, who died in 608, possessed in full those qualities of pugnacity and cunning that were essential for political and military survival. He waged wars against the Picts, may have launched an expedition against the Orkneys, and detached his fledgling state from Ulaidh. At the beginning of his reign, he secured the assistance and advice of the missionary St Columba. It was an astute move, for as other contemporary monarchs were discovering, the sanction of the church added to their stature. When Aedan visited the holy man at his monastery at Iona in 574, he underwent a ritual of ordination which invested him with a spiritual authority and transformed him into a ruler consecrated by God. Columba's prayers supported Aedan's warriors in a campaign against pagans (presumably still-to-be-converted Picts) and the saint, relying on a vision, chose and blessed his heir, Eochaidh Buidhe. Moreover, Columba may have swayed his kinsman, the Irish high king Aed mac Ainmuirech, into making an alliance with Aedan against his nominal overlord.[61] The saint enjoined Aedan and his descendants to keep this treaty and warned that backsliding would have grim consequences for Dalriada, which it did. Hostilities between Dalriada and Ulaidh soon reopened; there were three battles between 626 and 629, in which one Irish and one Dalriadan king were killed.

These contests are entries in contemporary and later annals which were little more than terse lists of battles intertwined with pedigrees of illustrious but otherwise unremembered kings. Visit Dunadd today and one finds little reference to its blood-spattered past. Rather, in the excellent Kilmartin museum the emphasis is on the humblest subjects of the kings of Dalriada: the peasantry who lived thereabouts and fished, grew crops and hunted. And then there are reminders of the local presence of St Columba, the princely evangelist who brought the gospel message out of Ireland into Scotland and established the monastery of Iona as the powerhouse of Celtic Christianity.

The sixth and seventh centuries, which witnessed ceaseless wars throughout Britain and Ireland, were also a period in which pagan kings and their warriors were converted to a faith that demanded meekness and humility from its adherents. Nevertheless, there was much within the Christian faith with immediate appeal to those who occupied the upper reaches of early medieval British society, not least the concept of a single, omnipotent God who demanded absolute loyalty from his followers. Addressed as 'ruler', 'mighty' and 'lord' ('herro'), such a God was comprehensible to those already conditioned to accept pagan deities who were figures of awe and power. Moreover, those accustomed to the authority of fate could understand how the will of God worked in human affairs.

Superficially at least, the Christian faith condemned all violence, but there were significant exceptions which together added up to the canonical concept of the just war. St Augustine of Hippo argued that force could be used in defence of the weak, to chastise rebels and oath breakers and, of course, against heretics and pagans, which was why St Columba prayed for King Aedan's victory. There was little here that would have disturbed the conscience of an early medieval king who, ostensibly, only went to war to protect his otherwise defenceless subjects from aggression or to suppress rebellions. Furthermore, the church respected the calling of the warrior, the more so if he used his arms in pursuit of aims of which it approved. The coexistence of the warrior tradition and Christianity is vividly expressed by the imagery on Pictish crosses. At Aberlemno in Angus two winged angels appear on one side of the cross, while the other is decorated with a hunting scene in which horsemen and hounds pursue a deer. In the same county, greyhounds chase a deer on the cross at Eassie, a bowman fires at a boar at St Vigeans, and at Fordoun and Auldbar there are fighting men on horseback, carrying shields and lances.[62]

The importance of winning over kings and noblemen was well understood by the missionaries Augustine, Columba, Ninian and

Paulinus. It was a royal and aristocratic Northumbrian audience that listened to St Paulinus preaching, and afterwards heard a nobleman's moving comparison of the life of a man to the flight of a sparrow from the dark chill of winter through a royal feasting hall and out into the night. King Æthelwealh of the South Saxons was baptised along with his 'principal generals and soldiers' by St Wilfrid, who then ordered four priests to proceed with the baptism of seven thousand families of the kingdom. Æthelwealh's sponsor, Wulfhere of Mercia, made of a gift of land to the royal convert, and the same day, according to Bede, a local famine miraculously ceased.

All the early Christian evangelists possessed magical powers which they used freely. St Columba paralysed a savage boar on the Isle of Skye, once turned water into wine and shared with St Augustine the ability to foretell the outcome of battles. Holy men also had the ability to curse those who offended them. Infuriated by the conduct of King Suibhne, a legendary ruler of Dalriada who tried to stop him building a church, St Ronan Finn cursed him and predicted that he would go insane in battle and wander the land as a naked madman. Unperturbed, Suibhne later killed a priest, but the curse was fulfilled with the king eventually being killed by a spear as St Ronan had predicted.[63]

Prayers offered for victory were considered so efficacious that King Æthelfrith of Northumbria ordered the massacre of Welsh priests who had turned up to a battle to pray for his enemies. They were from the Celtic church which provoked Bede, a follower of Rome, sourly to observe that they deserved to die 'because they had despised the offer of eternal salvation'. Bede also records, without any theological misgivings, the bargain made by King Oswiu of Northumbria before his defeat of the incorrigible pagan Penda in 655. If he won, Oswiu promised God twelve farms for the upkeep of monasteries and pledged his one-year-old daughter to a life of virginity and prayer. St Wilfrid actively encouraged Northumbrian penetration of south-eastern Scotland which, he believed, would extend the influence of the Northumbrian church. This joint expansion of church and state came to grief at the battle of Dunnichen Moss in 685 where King Ecgfrith was killed. Soon afterwards the Picts expelled the Northumbrian clergy and nuns.[64]

Christian kings were the beneficiaries of the supernatural powers that the clergy could harness. Royal power was regarded as a divine gift and the rituals attached to the consecration of a king lifted him above other men, transforming him into a special servant of the God by whose grace he governed. Individual kings of exemplary piety possessed a sanctity equal to that of such holy men as St Augustine; the arm and hand of Oswald of Northumbria, killed in a battle against Penda, became relics that were venerated and once restored to health a man who had been on the brink of death. In the British isles, monarchs became the defenders of the church like the French rulers Charles Martel, Pepin and Charlemagne. With their access to the learning and wisdom of the past, particularly the admired Roman past, the clergy were the natural partners in royal government, providing advice, framing laws and maintaining the records of the state. The church also supported and did all in its power to develop that ideal of political perfection expressed in *Beowulf*: 'each noble is true to the other, gentle in thought, and loyal to his lord; the thanes are in harmony.'

Harmony was still elusive in late eighth-century Britain. Competition between states continued and, with it, intermittent war. In Ireland, the tendency was towards fragmentation, thanks to customs of inheritance that allowed the sons of king and chieftains to partition their fathers' lands, which was a recipe for strife. And yet the elites who regularly fought among themselves were also groping towards some kind of political cohesion imposed by a superior ruler. In Ireland he was known as a high king, a figure who possessed sufficient military muscle to overawe his inferiors and, at the same time, enjoyed a degree of respect by right of his position. In England, too, there emerged the idea of an over-king, the bretwalda, who again was treated with honour, even if his powers were unclear. No permanent political pecking order had been established; in the seventh century, Northumbria had enjoyed dominance, and in the eighth this position was occupied by Mercia, with Wessex as an increasingly strong rival. No single, dominant power had yet emerged in either Wales or Scotland.

How long the power struggles within the British isles would have lasted or how they would have been finally resolved cannot be known. In the final decade of the eighth century, external forces unexpectedly intervened in British affairs and opened a new period of prolonged disruption. In 793, a Viking raiding party made an amphibious attack on the monastery at Lindisfarne, killed the monks, carried off their treasure and burned their church and settlement. Two years later, Iona received the same brutal treatment. The destruction of two of the greatest centres of faith and learning in western Europe stunned contemporaries, and churchmen interpreted these events as signs of the onset of that dark, apocalytic era predicted in the Book of Revelation. For a time, it seemed that they were right.

3

A people accustomed
to be conquered:
800–1100

I

In 1048 Thorfinn Sigurdarson, earl of Orkney, made a journey to Rome where he met the pope and received absolution.[1] A warlord whom his fellow Vikings praised as 'raven feeder' must have aroused much curiosity and, perhaps, unease among the Roman clergy, who were all too aware of how men like Thorfinn had terrorised Christian Europe during the past two centuries. He certainly fitted the popular image of the Viking marauder: aged about forty, he was an ugly, black-browed and sharp-featured man with a prominent nose. His confession was lengthy; of that there can be no doubt.

Over the previous twenty-five years Thorfinn had lived a predatory life. In winter he held state in his feasting hall at Birsay, where 'he furnished all his bodyguard and many other powerful men . . . both with meat and drink, so that no man needed to go into an inn or boarding house.' Each summer he and his companions sailed southwards, coming ashore to raid the coastal regions in Scotland, Ireland and England as their fathers and grandfathers had done, returning home in the appropriate season to tend and harvest their crops. Such exploits were glorified by court poets who satisfied their patrons' penchant for graphic descriptions of violence:

Homesteads then in blaze were blasted,
Danger that day did not fail them,
Ruddy flame o'er reeking roofs
Leapt throughout the Scottish land.

These lines commemorated Thorfinn's harrying of Fife during the 1030s when he was at loggerheads with his overlord and Macbeth's victim, King Duncan I of Scotland. The earl was more than just a pirate; he was a calculating magnate, with extensive lands in Caithness, Sutherland and the Orkneys, who played a political chess game to preserve his inheritance from rivals and his powerful neighbours, the kingdoms of Scotland and Norway. He managed rather well, thanks to a natural shrewdness and some strokes of good luck. Once, an enemy set fire to his hall while his war band were sleeping off their drink and Thorfinn escaped the flames by smashing a wainscot.

Thorfinn survived other scrapes, enlarged his lands and prestige and died in his bed in about 1064. He was buried in the church he had founded at Birsay. His father, Earl Sigurd, had worshipped Odin but had been converted along with the entire population of Orkney by his overlord, King Olaf Tryggvasson of Norway, who adopted the methods that Charlemagne had so successfully employed with the Saxons. 'It is my will,' the king told the earl, 'that you shall be baptised and all the folk that serve you, or else you shall die here at once, and I will ravage all the isles with fire and sword.'[2] To judge by his conduct, Thorfinn found Christianity compatible with the values and activities of his pagan ancestors, as of course did contemporary Irish, Pictish and Anglo-Saxon warlords. His life, as set down in adoring sagas and verses, was in many ways similar to that of other members of that warrior élite that then dominated Britain and western Europe. Conventional piety was blended with the older traditions of the war band and feast hall and the newer arts of dynastic diplomacy.

But Thorfinn was a Viking and a stranger to those novel conventions that would eventually transform the warrior into the Christian knight of the high Middle Ages. Despite his position as a landowning aristocrat, he hankered after the old ways and indulged in those smash-and-grab seaborne raids by which his forefathers had first established their fortunes. Like them, he was a consummate opportunist, always ready to undertake an adventure if it promised to be profitable. It was the Vikings' acquisitiveness and the lengths to which they would go to secure what they wanted that horrified their victims and earned them the opprobrium of the annalists of Christian Europe. 'A filthy pestilence' was how one English chronicler described the Vikings, while the author of the *Annals of Ulster* characterised them as 'fearful, murderous, hard-hearted' and 'impetuous'.[3] Such language reflected the widespread outrage at the Vikings' regular assaults on churches and monasteries, which were naturally attractive targets given that they were undefended and often filled with gold and silver ornaments and jewelled reliquaries. By their destruction of sacred buildings, the theft of their treasures and the murder of clergymen, the Vikings appeared to be uprooting civilisation itself. Moreover, they slaughtered laymen and women indiscriminately, and those they spared were sold into slavery, irrespective of their rank. During one ninth-century Irish rampage, 'Many were the blooming, lively women; and the modest mild, comely maidens; and the pleasant, noble, stately, blue-eyed young women; and the gentle, valiant champions whom they carried off into oppression and bondage over broad green seas.'[4] Some whom they kidnapped were sold to Muslim slavers.

It seemed, and this was the only explanation possible for the Viking phenomenon within the Christian view of the world, that the raiders had been sent by God as a chastisement for the sins of those they tormented. In recent years there has been an attempt to rehabilitate the Vikings, and their unquestioned skills as shipwrights and navigators, their handicrafts and their trading activities (slaving apart) have been placed in the balance to counter their reputation as conscienceless bandits. Nonetheless, it is still hard to imagine that figures with names such as Erik Bloodaxe or Thorfinn Skullsplitter (a tenth-century earl of Orkney) were no more than Scandinavian bagmen on the lookout for a bargain, or that their followers wanted nothing more from life than a chance to grow corn in East Anglia. Of course, overall Viking objectives changed; during the second half of the ninth century Danes and Norwegians established permanent settlements in various parts of the British isles and Ireland. But, as the career of Thorfinn Sigurdarson suggests, old raptorial habits died slowly and hard. Furthermore, the bloodthirsty Viking sagas with their jubilant celebration of violence are evidence of a mindset that exalted war. 'Let us go ashore, before warriors and large militias learn that the English homelands are being traversed with shields: let us be brave in battle, brandish spears and hurl them: great numbers of English flee before our swords.'[5]

The passage contains all the ingredients of a successful amphibious raid: the attackers come ashore swiftly and unnoticed and then proceed inland before their foes are aware of their presence. Wherever possible, the marauders secured horses, the better to move across country. Those forewarned of their approach hurriedly abandoned their homes. The old men and women of Fife 'dragged themselves off to the woods and wastes with weeping and wailing' as Thorfinn's war band descended on their settlements.[6] Improvised resistance by farmers, untrained in arms, was invariably suicidal. When the Hebridean island of Uist was ravaged in 794, 'the peasant lost his land and life who dared to bide the Norseman's stride'.[7] The prospects for those who fled were bleak: Viking arson destroyed crops, storehouses and farm implements, so that those who survived faced starvation.

II

The devastation of Uist occurred at the beginning of the first phase of the Viking onslaught on Britain and Ireland, which lasted roughly until the 850s. This was the time of the lith (expedition) in which one or more boat owners and their war bands crossed the northern seas and raided coastal settlements. Gold, silver and slaves were the prizes on offer and they naturally tempted younger sons and unattached warriors with no obvious prospects of advancement. Their successes encouraged others to try their luck (as they had during the Anglo-Saxon invasions) and they returned home with intelligence which attracted economic migrants. These were the consequence of a rising birth rate, although there is no way of knowing its extent or, for that matter, exactly how many immigrants settled in Britain and Ireland. During the tenth century there was an exodus to Iceland, Scotland and Ireland of Norwegian freemen and their families who wished to escape from the novel, feudal demands of their kings.

Norwegian colonisation in Ireland and Scotland was in all likelihood the immediate consequence of the need for naval supremacy in local waters. The settlements established at Dublin, Wexford, Waterford and Limerick strengthened the Viking grip on the Irish Sea and provided springboards for attacks on the shores of north-western England and Wales. Likewise, the toeholds secured on the Isle of Man, the Orkneys, the Hebrides and the far northern coast of Scotland provided bases for raiders and, in time, the nuclei for communities of immigrants from Norway. A greater expansion westwards gathered momentum in the mid ninth century and encompassed northern Germany, northern France and England. The Danish 'Great Host' of between five hundred and one thousand fighting men landed in Kent in 850, obtained horses and shifted northwards. Within twenty years, this Danish army had overthrown the kingdoms of Mercia, Northumbria and East Anglia. The way was open for the parcelling out of lands to prominent warriors and subsequent peasant immigration.

Resistance centred on Wessex. It was fortunate in having an energetic and imaginative king, Alfred, who ruled from 871 to 899 and, thanks to his will and perseverance, was able to fight the Danes to a standstill. In the process, he laid the foundations of a flexible military system which placed the human and financial resources of the kingdom at the disposal of the crown. What might be called the Wessex war machine was harnessed by Alfred's son, Edward the Elder, king from 899 to 925, and grandson, Athelstan, who ruled between 925 and 939, for a counterinvasion of the territory that had fallen to the Danes. The upshot was the extension of Wessex's power northwards into much of former Mercia and Northumbria and the confinement of the Danes to eastern England. This area became known as Danelaw and its lately arrived inhabitants agreed to accept the rule of the Wessex kings in return for toleration of their peculiar customs and guarantees of property rights. Athelstan's decisive victory over a Viking-Scottish coalition at Brunanburh in 937 extended Wessex's political supremacy over England north of the Humber and secured the acknowledgement of his overlordship of the king of the Scots. With a confidence built upon a string of victories and the submission of his enemies, Athelstan could call himself king of England.

The Vikings had severely shaken the polities they encountered, but had founded no permanent state of their own. In Ireland they 'went native' and threw themselves into the complex power struggles between regional kings, and proved useful allies. Vikings fought on both sides in the battle of Clontarf in 1014 in which the high king, Brian Boruma, defeated the forces of Leinster. Like the Wessex kings, Boruma had done well from the disruption caused by the Vikings. A petty ruler from County Clare, he made a name for himself in a series of campaigns against the Viking colony of Limerick and manoeuvred himself into the high kingship. His assumption of the title *Imperator Scottorum* ('Emperor of the Irish') gave the impression that he was master of a united kingdom, which he was not. He died at the moment of victory at Clontarf defending his pretensions.

In Scotland, Viking pressure accelerated the fusion of the Scots of Dalriada with the Picts, which was finally accomplished in 843 when Kenneth mac Alpin took the title 'King of the Scots'. The exact nature of the process of union is unknown, but it owed something to mac Alpin's success in battle and the increasing precariousness of his power base in the Western Isles, which were being steadily penetrated by the Vikings from the 790s onwards. It was an area with an extended seaboard broken by long, narrow lochs and therefore particularly vulnerable to amphibious attack. Overlooking this coastline there still remain a number of small 'duns', dry stone enclosures which served as watchtowers or the bases for warning beacons which would be lit when alien sails appeared offshore. One, overgrown with ferns and grass but still recognisable and with some of its walling intact, stands above Craobh Haven in Argyll, and commands breathtaking views as far as Jura, beyond which lay the Viking colonies of Islay and Colonsay. Both straddled the sea routes to Ireland which were now effectively severed, forcing the Dalriada Scots to abandon links with their ancestral homeland.

Viking settlement in Scotland was confined to the remote western and northern peripheries, although inland regions suffered intermittent raids. The new kingdom of the Scots did, however, benefit directly from the upheavals in England. The collapse of Northumbria permitted the Scottish crown to extend its authority beyond the Forth valley into Lothian which had hitherto been within the Northumbrian orbit. By 973, Scotland's frontier had reached the Tweed.

While their opponents stumbled towards political unity, and with it centralised governments, the Vikings remained divided. There was intense rivalry between the Norwegians and the Danes, and attempts to forge an axis between Dublin and York foundered because of dynastic tensions. The kingdom of York dissolved in 954, largely as a consequence of internal dissension, and was incorporated into England.

The new strength of England was a consequence of the willpower, energy and organisational ability of the Wessex kings. In 978 the dynasty became a casualty of genetic mischance with the accession of Æthelred, whose name meant 'noble counsel' and was later mockingly rendered as 'Unræd, that is to say 'no counsel'. The king also lacked resolve, foresight and luck. The early years of his reign were marked by an increase in Viking raids which were fitfully and ineffectively resisted. The marauders regularly traversed the countryside at will, killing, stealing and burning as they went. Æthelred's response was a stopgap stratagem that had first been used by the French kings in the ninth century and was adopted by Wessex in moments of crisis: the payment of protection money, known as Danegeld, in return for which the Viking commanders returned home. Between 991 and 1016, a total of £236,000 was paid out in silver pennies (240 to the pound of silver) raised from a land tax.⁰ Like other forms of emergency taxation, the Danegeld was transformed into a permanent levy; in 1018 it raised just over eighty thousand pounds. Buying off the Vikings merely whetted their appetites, and by 1000 the scale of their operations had increased, with the participation of King Olaf Tryggvasson of Norway and King Swein Forkbeard of Denmark. Their intervention marked a new phase in the Viking involvement in English affairs, for the two monarchs aimed to absorb the country into their kingdoms.

The extended struggle for control of England ended in 1016 with the Danish victory at Ashingdon and the accession of Swein's twenty-year-old son, Cnut. The new king secured his position by a division of the spoils between his leading Danish and English supporters; his brother-in-law Erik Haakonsson got the earldom of Northumbria, and Thorkill the Tall (who had once hired his fleet to Æthelred) received East Anglia. A pattern was set by which the victorious candidate for the throne dispensed land to his leading adherents, transforming them into a territorial aristocracy pledged to assist their benefactor in war.

The Anglo-Danish kingdom split in 1042 after the death of Cnut's son, Harthacnut. There followed a peaceful restoration of the Wessex dynasty with the accession of Edward the Confessor. His death in January 1066 marked the beginning of a three-cornered contest for the crown. Harold Godwinsson, whose father had risen to wealth and eminence as one of Cnut's earls, took the crown by a coup d'état with the backing of his powerful kinsmen and the royal council. He was challenged by King Harold Hadrada of Norway, in alliance with Tosti, Harold Godwinsson's exiled brother and sometime earl of Northumberland. The third competitor was Duke William of Normandy. Two battles decided the succession: Stamford Bridge on 25 September where Harold Hadrada was killed and his army defeated by Harold Godwinsson, and Hastings on 14 October where William's forces were victorious and Harold Godwinsson was slain. In 1069, King Swein Estrithson attempted to resuscitate the Anglo-Danish kingdom in coalition with a body of disaffected Northumbrian noblemen. Their revolt was crushed by William and the Danish king agreed to withdraw in return for a bribe. His ambitions were revived by his son, Cnut II, in 1085, but his invasion never passed the planning stage. There were no more Scandinavian irruptions into England.

III

The three hundred years that separated the first Viking raids from the consolidation of the Norman Conquest were a period of innovation in the organisation and waging of war. These changes are vividly illustrated by a fragmentary eleventh-century epic poem, The Battle of Maldon, and the Bayeux Tapestry, a highly stylised but incomplete portrayal of the events before, during and immediately after the battle of Hastings. It was stitched early in the 1080s under the supervision of William I's half-brother, Bishop Odo of Bayeux.

The Battle of Maldon describes an engagement between the Essex fyrd (shire levies) commanded by the local earl, Bryhtnoth, and a Norwegian war band which had landed on Northey Island in the Blackwater Estuary in 991. The 'swift-striking seafarers' may previously have attacked Ipswich, returned to their ships and sailed south for an incursion into Essex. Their mobility owed everything to their seamanship and the versatility of their equally famous 'wave stallions', the longboats. One, the exceptionally well preserved Gokstad ship, may serve as an example for many others. It was clinker-built of oak, with masts and oars of pine, just under eighty feet in length and about seventeen wide amid-ships, and lay low in the water. Propulsion was by a single, large sail, backed by oars, and the vessel was steered by a side-rudder. A facsimile constructed in 1892 crossed the Atlantic and proved itself highly sea-worthy and capable of speeds of up to ten knots. The longboats' nimbleness and the wonder they inspired among those who sailed in them are reflected in a description of Cnut's battle fleet at sea: 'And the prince's dragons had blue sails at the yard as they sailed before the wind, his crossing was magnificent; the ships came from the west and skimmed on the crest of a wave over the Limjord.'[9]

Cnut's navy included English warships. One, presented by Earl Godwin of Wessex to King Harthacnut in 1040 in lieu of 'wergeld' (blood-money) for the murder of his half-brother the ætheling Alfred, included a crew of eighty warriors.[10] 'Each one of them had on each arm a golden bracelet, weighing six ounces, and wore a triple coat of mail and helmet partly gilt, and a sword with gilded hilt gird to his side, and a Danish battleaxe inlaid with gold and silver hanging from his left shoulder; in his left hand he bore a shield, the boss and studs of which were also gilt, and in his right hand a lance, called in the English tongue "Atagar".'[11] To judge from their harness and arms, these soldiers were thegns, perhaps attached to Earl Godwin's household. They and the vessel that carried them would have been paid for by the 'scipfyrd', a levy of men and cash which, in theory, could support a fleet of up to 250 ships. Not all would have been on the scale of Earl Godwin's and, given that the fleet was not permanently at sea, many may have been merchantmen pressed into service.

The English fleet and the wherewithal to sustain it were part of the apparatus of national defence that had been developed by Alfred and his immediate descendants in response to the second wave of Viking incursions. It was designed to mobilise local land and sea forces quickly and concentrate them in areas under threat. At the heart of the system were two legal principles: every free man was responsible for the defence of his country in an emergency; and all land was held from the king who could, therefore, demand such service as a condition of tenure.

Translated into action, the theory was explained by Bryhtnoth in his challenge to the Vikings:

> . . . *there stands here 'mid his men not the meanest of Earls,*
> *pledged to fight in this land's defence,*
> *the land of Æthelred, my liege lord,*
> *its soil, its folk.*

The duties of each of the men who stood behind Bryhtnoth were defined by the amount of land he held. The official unit of assessment was the hide or carucate, the area that could support a peasant and his family and yield sufficient surplus to pay tax. The actual acreage varied from sixty in fertile districts to twice that amount in less favoured ones. The regulations laid down in the reign of Cnut stipulated that eight hides could support one thegn who had to own a horse, a helmet, a byrnie, a sword, a spear and shield, and be prepared to serve with the field army or as part of the garrison of a 'burh' (defended town) for two months. When summoned to a muster, an earl was expected to bring himself and at least four thegns, all mounted and properly armed, and four ceorls. Those who defaulted on their military obligations might expect a fine or forfeiture of their land.

Ceorls were spearmen who went to war on foot. Several appear on the Bayeux Tapestry with swords and shields, but some of those present at Stamford Bridge apparently lacked the latter and were compelled to shelter behind the shields of better-equipped men.[12] The margins of the Bayeux Tapestry show scenes in which ceorls strip dead warriors of their armour, either for their own protection or because it was extremely valuable. And yet even if by some chance a ceorl obtained the equipment of a thegn the law forbade him to enjoy the same status, which was decided by the ownership of land rather than the possession of armour and weaponry.[13] This made good military sense, for a substantial landowner sustained by the labour and produce of others had ample time in which to master the skills of horsemanship, grow accustomed to the wearing of armour and exercise with arms. Revealingly, the ceorls under Bryhtnoth's command at Maldon did not know what was expected from them in battle and required instruction and encouragement:

Then Bryhtnoth dressed his band of warriors,
from horseback taught each man his task,
where he should stand, how keep his station.
He bade them brace their linden-boards aright,
fast in finger-grip, and to fear not.
Then when his folk was fairly ranked
Bryhtnoth alighted where he loved best to be
and was held most at heart – among hearth-companions.

These were men familiar with arms and, like the warriors of earlier generations, were keen to display their skills. They were also the inheritors of older Germanic codes of honour, as one, Ælfwine, reminded them:

Remember the speeches spoken over mead,
battle-vows on the bench, the boasts we vaunted,
heroes in hall, against the harsh war-trial!
Now shall be proven the prowess of the man.

It was a sentiment shared by warrior élites irrespective of nationality. Just before battle was joined at Bourgthéroulde in 1124, a Norman knight steadied his brothers-in-arms by telling them that their resolution and valour were soon to be assayed publicly.[14] Reputation mattered, the more so if those who aspired to it were of noble ancestry. Courage transmitted, as it were, through the blood brought with it a special responsibility, as Ælfwine told his fellow thegns:

I would that you all hear my high descendance:
know that in Mercia I am of mighty kin,
that my grandfather was the great Ealhelm,
wise Earl, world-blessed man.
Shall the princes of that people reproach Ælfwine
that he broke from the banded bulwark of the Angles
to seek his own land, with his lord lying
felled on the field? Fiercest of griefs!
Beside that he was my lord he was allied to me in blood.

The battle was swinging against the English. At its commencement, Bryhtnoth had marshalled his men in the traditional formation of the 'seydburh' (shield fort) or 'wihaga' (war hedge). It is shown on the Bayeux Tapestry with a degree of licence, for the shields appeared to be interlocked, which they were not. Men wielding axes and swords needed room for manoeuvre. In what turned out to be a tactical misjudgement, Bryhtnoth had allowed the Vikings to cross a narrow causeway and rush the shield fort. The battle then dissolved into a mass of individual hand-to-hand struggles in one of which Bryhtnoth was overcome. His death signalled the start of a collapse:

> Then did the lack-willed leave the battlefield;
> Odda's kin came first away:
> Godric turned, betrayed the lord
> who had made him the gift of a good horse.

The bonds of devotion and gratitude were stronger among the surviving thegns whose loyalty to their dead lord compelled them to fight on even though defeat was by now inevitable. They did so gladly in the knowledge that they were vindicating their own and their caste's honour.

The Battle of Maldon provides a valuable insight into the mind of the early medieval warrior. It was a statement of how such a creature *ought* to have behaved in battle, and one that was needed at the time. The heroic constancy of Bryhtnoth and his thegns contrasted with the perfidy and cowardice of Ælfric, the ealdorman of West Wessex, who feigned sickness to avoid leading the Hampshire fyrd against a Viking war band in 1003.[15] There is criticism, too, of King Æthelred's appeasement of the Vikings; when they asked Bryhtnoth for tribute they were offered nothing but 'viper-stained spears and the swords of forebears'. This was how a warlike king treated his enemies.

Bryhtnoth and his thegns showed a relish for war. Its perils were disregarded with a calculated disdain; the earl arrived on the battlefield with a hawk on his wrist as if he had come to hunt the wildfowl of the marshes. His own and his thegns' exuberance for battle was genuine and widely shared by warriors throughout Europe, although today it will strike some people as inexplicable or distasteful. As Christians, fighting men could no longer defile God's image by mentally transforming themselves into wild animals in the former pagan manner. But the old excitement remained; even when mortally wounded, Bryhtnoth is exultant:

> . . . The earl was blither,
> his brave mood laughed, loud thanks he made
> for his day's work the Lord had dealt him.

A similar jauntiness had animated the warriors in *The Gododdin*. Before the battle they cheered each other with laughter and one was heard 'laughing in battle'.[16] Henry I of England was described as 'smiling and jesting' as he encouraged his troops during the siege of Pont Audemer in 1124.[17] Such a lighthearted display of confidence obviously encouraged the fainthearted and fearful. There must also have been occasions when it masked the smiler's inner apprehension.

Command was personal and its effectiveness depended ultimately on a general's ability to generate and sustain optimism, often in the most adverse circumstances. William of Normandy had this capacity, which to a large extent explains why he was the most outstanding commander of his age. During the winter of 1069 to 1070 he led a forced march across the snow-covered hills and valleys of Teesdale and Weardale 'encouraging his soldiers by his own cheerfulness'. Faced with a further arduous campaign in the barren wildernesses of Lancashire and Cheshire and disturbed by tales of the fierceness of their Welsh adversaries, knights from Anjou, Maine and Brittany faltered. They demanded to be discharged, claiming that 'they could not obey a lord who went from one hazard to another and commanded them to do the impossible'. King William showed 'a calmness worthy of Julius Caesar' and resorted to a mixture of invective and persuasion. He branded the waverers 'weaklings and cowards', and promised that the perseverance of the steadfast would be recompensed. He also showed a winning concern for his men: 'The King himself, remarkably sure-footed, led the foot soldiers, readily helping them with his own hands when they were in difficulties.' At the end of the campaign 'lavish rewards' were distributed among those who had stuck it out, while William insisted that the backsliders stayed a further forty days with the army, which was regarded as a mild punishment for such irresolution.[18]

IV

Armoured heavy cavalry were the backbone of the army with which William I pacified northern England and expelled the Welsh from Shropshire and Cheshire. The Norman horseman, familiar from the Bayeux Tapestry, was a novelty in England. Hitherto, horses had been employed to carry armoured warriors to the battlefield; Bryhtnoth and his thegns had ridden them to Maldon, and during the campaigns of 1066 Harold's thegns had travelled to Stamford Bridge and back to Hastings on horseback. The Vikings, too, used horses, which was why Athelstan banned their export to the continent where, it was feared, they might add to the stock available to his country's foes. The enduring love-affair between the English nobility and the horse was already underway. Tenth- and eleventh-century earls and thegns took a deep interest in bloodstock and contrived to breed large, muscular and broad-haunched mounts that could carry an armoured man.[19] In England as in Europe, the ownership of one or more thoroughbred horses was essential for the warrior and had become a token of his status. But the English still preferred to fight on foot as part of the shield fort, although at Brunanburh some thegns had mounted their horses to pursue and cut down their fleeing enemies.

They did things differently in Normandy. Here, the descendants of tenth-century Viking settlers had learned from their French hosts the techniques of fighting on horseback which had been evolving on the continent during the previous four centuries. The knight's charger was a platform that enabled him to tower over infantrymen and thrust down at them with his heavy lance or hack at them with his sword. Or, if he was engaging other horsemen, he rode at them with a lance couched under his arm, a practice that had first appeared in about 1050 and required considerable training to master. One way of gaining the requisite skills and experience was the tournament. That eighth-century innovation, the stirrup, was useful for both forms of mounted combat, but not essential, for the knight had the support of a saddle with a high pommel and back.[20] The warhorses ridden by Duke William and his knights were stallions, full-chested, sixteen hands high and bred for the purpose. A harsh bit added to their natural ferocity.

Between two and three thousand knights and their horses assembled at Duke William's invasion bases at Dives-sur-Mer and St Valéry-sur-Somme during the summer of 1066. From the start, the campaign was meticulously planned. The bulk of the Norman forces came from the modern *départements* of Seine Maritime and Calvados, for it would have been foolhardy to have stripped the duchy's southern frontier of fighting men.[21] Additional contingents came from Brittany, the county of Boulogne and Flanders. All involved were drawn into what was a great and hazardous adventure which, if it succeeded, would secure William a prosperous kingdom and his surviving followers rewards of land. Churchmen were tempted to invest in this enterprise; the abbot of Saint-Ouen paid for ships, as did the almoner of Fécamp whose abbey later received a generous grant of land in Sussex.[22] The largest expenditure of effort and money came from William's half-brothers, Odo and Robert of Mortain, who between them supplied 220 ships as well as knights. The duke's servants, most notably Robert FitzOsbern, his steward and head of his military household, provided men and assisted in the administration of the army.

The preparations for the invasion are depicted on the Bayeux Tapestry. Woodmen cut down timber which is prepared for the shipwrights who construct ships to supplement those hired or supplied by Norman landowners and churchmen. When the invasion fleet is ready, servants carry on board barrels of wine, sacks, swords, helmets, axes and hauberks (mail shirts) for the knights. These vignettes represent a small part of what must have been a remarkable logistical operation. Each day the two to three thousand warhorses would have consumed between fourteen and twenty tons of oats or barley and thirty thousand gallons of water, and required between four and five tons of fresh straw. Furthermore, their stalls would have to have been cleared daily and several tons of excrement removed.[23] Then and later, the maintenance of a cavalry was expensive and labour-intensive.

A Saxon spy who visited the camp at Dives-sur-Mer must have been impressed by what he saw. He met Normans who boasted to him that they were ready to set off the moment the winds were favourable.[24] But nature was disobliging: William's army had to kick its heels throughout August and the first three weeks of September. The delay proved an immense advantage, for during the time the Normans were waiting the English fleet dispersed. Harold's strategy had been to keep his fleet in readiness off the Isle of Wight for an attack on the invading ships as they approached Bosham, which was believed to be their destination. By the first week of September, the ships' provisions were spent and the volunteer crews went home; they had been called up in May and their legal obligations had been fulfilled.[25] On 27 September a southerly wind blew and the seven-hundred-strong Norman armada set sail and disembarked, unopposed, at Pevensey the following morning.

It is still hard to imagine how the cumbersome and high-spirited warhorses were coaxed aboard the ships, secured and calmed during the passage and brought ashore. The Bayeux Tapestry provides few clues. The heads of two horses, stowed amidships and facing each other, appear above the gunwales of one vessel, and another contains four, similarly arranged. A sprightly pair seem to be jumping from one ship into the water, led by a groom. However it was accomplished, the transport of the warhorses was vital for the forthcoming campaign. William's strength lay in his cavalry and its ability to overwhelm or puncture the English shield fort. His horsemen were well disciplined and manoeuvred in small, flexible units, which may have consisted of a lord or a knight of substance with his kinsmen and household.

The English army possessed a similar core of well-trained, professional fighting men: the 'huscarles' (household warriors) of the king and his brothers, and thegns undertaking obligatory military service. Some, perhaps most, of these men had been present at Stamford Bridge and had then ridden the 190 miles from Tadcaster to London in ten days. It was an amazing feat of horsemanship and stamina and there must have been a few who wilted and fell back. Among those who completed the journey some may have been exhausted. 'There was a great slaughter of the English,' the author of a Norwegian saga observed, 'because there were many in that battle who were good for nothing,'[26] He may, however, have been referring to the ceorls of the shire fyrds who joined Harold as he moved southwards from London and who, like their counterparts at Maldon, were ignorant of fighting. And understandably so, for southern England had enjoyed a state of relative peace for the past forty or so years.

There was one indisputable weakness in the English army: its lack of archers. They had been employed by both sides at Maldon, but the poet who described the battle said nothing of the effect of their fire, being primarily concerned with recording the exploits of noblemen. A solitary English bowman crouches between two thegns on the Bayeux Tapestry which, correctly, shows swarms of Norman archers moving ahead of the cavalry. Each carries a short bow, drawn to the chest, and several English shields are peppered with arrows.

Arrow fire could, however, inflict painful, even fatal injuries on horses and so destroy the momentum of a cavalry charge. Dismounted armoured knights, supported by archers, were able to throw back cavalry, and did so at the battles of Tinchebrai in 1106 and Bourgthéroulde in 1124.[27] In the latter, three hundred dismounted knights formed what was the equivalent of a shield fort and, as the battle opened, were charged by forty horsemen led by the impetuous Count Waleran of Meulan. 'Anxious to prove his knighthood' and 'exulting joyously', this young man had jeered at the English who were among his opponents. Expecting another Hastings, he derided them as 'country bumpkins and mercenaries' who would crumble before 'the flower of the knighthood of France and Normandy'. Things turned out otherwise, as they could easily have done at Hastings. The count's charge was thrown into confusion by arrow fire, and, at the end of the day, his forces were thrown back and eighty of his knights captured.[28] It is possible that some of the horses had fallen to crossbow fire. This revolutionary novelty had appeared a hundred years before Hastings, but its use seems to have been largely confined to sieges. It was slow to load and fire, but had a range of over two hundred yards and was accurate. During a raid on Anglesey in 1098, a quarrel from a crossbow fired by the Norwegian King Magnus Barefoot struck Earl Hugh of Chester in the face and killed him.[29] A quarrel embedded in the back of the skull of a casualty of the battle of Visby in 1361 had passed straight through its victim's skull and brain.[30]

After Hastings, William gave several manors in Lincolnshire and the Yorkshire Wolds to Odo the Crossbowman (Odo Balistarius) and it would be tempting to identify him as having had command over the crossbowmen at Hastings. They were certainly deployed alongside conventional archers during the battle and must have added to the overwhelming Norman superiority in firepower.[31] The English deficiency of archers was mentioned by William in a speech he allegedly made before his army advanced. The 'effeminate' English were 'a people accustomed to be conquered, a people ignorant of the art of war, a people not even in possession of arrows'. The words were not the duke's; they were written by a later chronicler, Henry of Huntingdon, who, like so many of his kind, had a knack of flattering the powerful by filling their mouths with brave but fictitious rhetoric.[32] Invented or not, the point was a valid one, for the shortage of archers seriously weakened Harold's army which had to rely solely upon muscle power to repel the Norman cavalry.

In other respects, the two armies were well matched. The professional fighting men wore similar armour: conical helmets with noseguards and hooded mail byrnies or hauberks with sleeves that extended to the elbows. According to the Bayeux Tapestry, thegns and knights wore knee-length mail trousers, which were obviously valuable for the men on foot but uncomfortable for the horsemen. In all likelihood, and this is confirmed by later illustrations and a handful of surviving examples, the Norman hauberk was divided below the waist for ease of riding. Worn over a padded garment, the hauberk weighed up to forty pounds – in a scene on the Tapestry one is carried by two servants. Its weight was more than offset by the protection it provided; Henry I's mail coif protected his neck from what could have been a fatal blow at the battle of Brémule in 1119.[33]

It was superior tactics, combined with the deployment of archers, that decided the battle of Hastings. Harold's forces, probably numbering about eight thousand and expecting reinforcements, occupied a ridge about seven miles from William's camp and adopted the traditional shield fort formation. Some thegns discarded their shields and fought with double-handed, Danish axes – their distinctive triangular blades are quite clearly shown on the Bayeux Tapestry. William, who was slightly outnumbered, placed his men in three divisions, with the bulk of his cavalry in the third, ready to exploit any advantage. None emerged during the first phase of the fighting when mixed units of horse, infantry and archers were thrown back from the shield fort. The Tapestry shows a mass of individual contests with thegns throwing javelins and wielding swords and axes against knights who often stand in their long stirrups to jab over their adversaries' shields.

The impenetrability of the shield fort prompted a retreat by some Bretons and auxiliaries on the Norman left flank who were unnerved by the 'ferocious resolution' of the defenders. A general panic was forestalled by William, who raised his helmet to identify himself and scotched rumours of his death. The incident is shown on the Bayeux Tapestry; Eustace of Boulogne (carrying the duke's personal standard) points to him, and Odo of Bayeux, carrying what is a marshal's baton and not a mace, steadies a group of younger and inexperienced knights. The scene was a deliberate reminder of the crucial parts played by Odo and Eustace, who were both out of King William's favour when the Tapestry was being made.[34] Near-contemporary accounts of the battle naturally flatter William who, like Bryhtnoth at Maldon, demonstrates how a warrior ought to fight. In one charge his horse was killed by a javelin thrown by Gyrth, one of Harold's brothers whom William mistook for the king. 'Reduced to a foot soldier,' the duke 'fought the better, for he rushed upon the young man like a snarling lion, hewing him limb from limb: "Take the crown you have earned from us! If my horse is dead, thus I requite you – as a common soldier!"'[35] In the end, what counted was William's unwavering resolution and presence of mind, which enabled him to sustain his men's confidence in a crisis.

After the flight of the Bretons had been arrested, William regained control of his troops and with it the initiative. Thanks to their training and discipline, his cavalry were able to make two feigned retreats which, like the real one, decoyed substantial numbers of the English from their shield fort. The ruse worked and the line began to fracture. The English continued to fight on and the battle became a series of desperate last stands in which isolated knots of Englishmen were killed as they attempted to defend themselves against their more mobile opponents. Harold died in one of these fights – his death appears on the Tapestry in two vignettes: first he is wounded by an arrow in the forehead (a direct hit in the eye would surely have been fatal), and then is felled by a disabling sword cut to the thigh. As at Maldon, warriors fought on even after the death of their king and his lords.[36] Some took refuge in a nearby ancient hill fort and briefly held off their pursuers; the incident appears on the Tapestry with an animated portrayal of the tumbling warhorses.

V

It was the dogged determination of the Anglo-Danish landowning class that made Hastings a decisive battle. In twelve hours of hard fighting, the Norman army had not only eliminated King Harold, his household and two of his kinsmen, it had severely depleted what until recently had been the political and military élite of England. Further losses occurred during the next four years when some of the survivors attempted an unco-ordinated and sporadic resistance. It failed; the rebels were either killed or driven into exile, and their lands were distributed among William's followers. Not until the First World War would the English ruling class again suffer so many casualties in such a short time.

These losses facilitated a far-reaching revolution in land ownership in which William distributed lands to his supporters, lay and clerical. All land was held from the king and he alone decided who had what and where. Those who invested energy and wealth in the duke's venture gained the returns they had hoped for. William had created a bond between himself and the new dominant class who held land from him and whose individual members would defend the new order, not least because they were its chief beneficiaries. The legal arrangements were familiar: the tenant swore a personal oath of allegiance to the king or his immediate overlord and pledged himself to undertake a fixed term of military service or, if for some reason this was impossible, to pay for a substitute with the appropriate armour, weapons and a horse. The language was that of French feudalism, but the underlying principles of the system had been established in England over the preceding five hundred years. A warrior élite occupied the land in exchange for placing their persons and their skills at the disposal of the crown. For the great mass of the population, Hastings and the subsequent campaigns of pacification meant no more than a change of masters. The new lords spoke Norman French as their first and often only language and would do so for at least the next two centuries, although William attempted to learn some English to help him judge lawsuits. Writing at the end of the thirteenth century, the chronicler Robert of Gloucester observed that in England 'the major part of the high men' were Norman and spoke French.[37]

Those who looked up did so with little affection. In the immediate aftermath of Hastings, 'the English groaned aloud for their lost liberty and plotted ceaselessly to find some way of shaking off a yoke that was so intolerable and unaccustomed.'[38] The folk memory of the coming of unwelcome, alien rule remained strong; early in the fourteenth century the Lincolnshire-born cleric Robert Manning lamented:

> For all the thraldom that now in England is,
> Through the Normans it came, bondage and distress.[39]

A myth was already in the making which would be exploited by left-wing radicals during the Civil Wars of the seventeenth century, when it was alleged that pre-Conquest England was a land where all men enjoyed considerable personal and legal freedom. This had been extinguished by William and his knights who imposed a feudal system and laws that deprived the people of liberty. There is no reason whatsoever to believe that the Anglo-Danish aristocracy were less overbearing than their successors or less exacting in the enforcement of their rights, but in bad times it is easy to re-create the past as a happier age. In fact, William was not an innovator, far from it. He regarded himself as the rightful heir of Edward the Confessor and therefore bound to rule in the manner of his predecessors, using their laws, forms of administration and customs. Moreover, the philosophical basis for feudal society was well understood in Ango-Saxon England. In the 990s, Ælfric, abbot of Eynsham, described the throne resting on three legs, those of workers, warriors and clergymen, each of whom had a specific function to perform. The agricultural labourer provided food, the warrior defended society, and churchmen prayed for it and offered its members the means of salvation.[40] This tripartite division of society was recognisable before 1066, as was the apparatus of feudal obligation.

There was oppression in post-Conquest England, but it was the consequence of William's search for security rather than of novel forms of feudalism. For four years, the king faced a number of attempts to reverse Hastings, of which the most dangerous and persistent were undertaken by the Northumbrian aristocracy. Attacks on Norman garrisons in York and Durham, together with the intervention of King Swein of Denmark, compelled William to move north in the winter of 1069. The military threat evaporated, but the exasperated king was determined 'to pierce the whole of the Northumbrians with a single spear'.[41] The blow was known as the 'harrying of the North', a systematic exercise in retribution designed to punish and deter. Villages and crops were burned and livestock slaughtered. Those who escaped a swift death at the hands of the royal army faced a slow one by starvation. Remoteness was no defence against William's vengeance; his detachments penetrated Swaledale and Wensleydale and did their work thoroughly. The Domesday survey for 1086 recorded that the settlements of Marske, Marrick, Reeth and Grinton were 'waste'. Further south and over the fells, eleven villages between Leyburn and Askrigg were also classified as 'waste', that is without people, beasts or crops.[42] Other areas in Yorkshire were likewise classed as wasteland, although some were probably abandoned for straightforward economic reasons, or had suffered at the hands of Scottish and Danish forces between 1068 and 1070.

When he launched his methodical terror against the north, William was adopting a Norman practice that was normally confined to private feuds between lords.[43] Such behaviour was not tolerated in England; in 1102, Henry I accused Ivo de Grandmesnil, a Leicestershire magnate, 'of waging war . . . and burning the crops of his neighbours, which is an unheard-of crime in that country and can be atoned only by a very heavy penalty'.[44] The constraints of human law were complemented by those imposed by the church. During the eleventh century, continental churchmen had gone to considerable lengths to suppress the feud, a regrettably durable Germanic tradition which consumed too much aristocratic energy and brought suffering to the poor and weak. The result was the 'Peace of God' movement which, its sponsors hoped, would restore to Europe the harmony and stability that was thought to have existed under the Roman Empire. In pre-Conquest England, the church had lacked the strength and structure to restrain a nobility that was still addicted to feuds.

In the eyes of the church, William's indiscriminate harrying of northern England represented an unjust waging of war made worse by the fact that its mainspring was the sin of anger. Ordericus Vitalis, a Norman cleric and annalist, predicted that William, whom he admired, would answer to God for this atrocity. Facing death, the king is acutely aware of the imminence of divine justice, and Orderic has him utter a dramatic confession: 'Oh my friends, I am weighed down with the burden of my sins and tremble, for I must soon face the terrible judgement of God and do not know what I shall do. I was bred to arms from my childhood and am deeply stained with all the blood I have shed.' His conscience is particularly disturbed by memories of his campaigns in England and the persecution of those who resisted him: 'I . . . wrested the kingdom from the perjured King Harold with bitter strife and terrible bloodshed, and subjected it to my rule after killing or driving into exile all his partisans. I treated the native inhabitants of the kingdom with unreasonable severity, cruelly oppressed high and low, unjustly disinherited many and caused the death of thousands by starvation and war, especially in Yorkshire . . . I descended on the North like a raging lion.' This is, in effect, a sermon. The audience is reminded that even the greatest warriors of the age could not avoid God's judgement and would have to face punishment for the infraction of His laws. Expiation was possible; the dying king commanded that churches and the poor should be given the wealth he had accumulated from his 'evil deeds'. He also reminded listeners of his record of lavish generosity to the church, which he had always treated with respect.[45]

This was so; William was a conventional Christian king who set an example by his piety. The knights who followed their overlord in battle also followed him in charity by endowing cathedrals, churches and abbeys. William could have rightly claimed to have done more. He had invaded England with the blessing of the pope, in return for which he pledged himself to regenerate the church in England. He kept his word and, in the years after the Conquest, English spiritual life was revitalised, particularly by the introduction of the standards of the new, rigorous French monasticism. Visible evidence of the church's revival was the programme of cathedral building: between 1070 and 1093 major new work was undertaken at Canterbury, Rochester, Winchester, York, Worcester and Durham.

Other new structures appeared across England: castles. The first was erected within days of William's landing and, to judge by its representation on the Bayeux Tapestry, consisted of a two-storey, wooden tower set on a mound of earth, or 'motte'. This strongpoint was usually surrounded by or attached to a perimeter of palisaded earthworks which enclosed the 'bailey'. Access to the bailey was through a fortified timber gatehouse which was approached by a bridge over an outer ditch, sometimes filled with water. There were many variations in the layout of motte-and-bailey castles, and some utilised existing fortifications. The stone keep at Portchester was placed at a corner of the wall of the Roman fort, and the Ruperra motte on Coed Crag above the River Rhymni was set within an Iron Age earthwork.[46] This adaptation of old strongpoints persisted for the next nine hundred years; part of the Norman motte at Bramber in Sussex was used for a machine-gun trench in the Second World War. Like their predecessors, its twentieth-century defenders left their detritus for the archaeologists to unearth: a beer-bottle top.

A modern machine-gun post set on a Norman earthwork (another was built into the wall of the Roman fort at Pevensey) is a vivid reminder that the early castle builders had a good eye for a defensive position. Political and strategic considerations dictated the overall siting of castles. For King William they were links in a network of chains which bound his new subjects and protected the borders of his kingdom. Durham fulfilled both functions: it overawed an area of persistent disaffection and served as a defence against the Scots. A twelfth-century writer likened it to a monarch: 'the castle is seated like a queen; from its threatening height, it holds all that it sees as its own.'[47] Castles also marked the extension of Norman political influence on the periphery of England. The massive motte at Cardiff, begun by William in 1081 after he had made an agreement with Rhys ap Tewdwr, the prince of Deheubarth, served as the focus of growing Norman power in southern Glamorgan, and, significantly, it housed a mint producing coins in the king's name. Cardiff castle also acted as a springboard for subsequent military penetration of south-western Wales. Northward expansion in the 1090s was marked by William II's castles at Carlisle and Borough in Westmoreland, both overlooking what had been Scottish territory.

VI

Norman thrusts into the lands of the Welsh princes and against Scotland were part of a process of frontier stabilisation which inevitably involved conquest and permanent occupation. The crown gained security, which it paid for by parcelling out the newly acquired lands among those knights who were waging the border wars. Like William I's original companions in his invasion of England, these warriors were partners in a mutually profitable enterprise. The career of one, Robert of Rhuddlan, may stand for many others, and, for that matter, for men of a similar stamp who over the preceding six hundred years had made their fortunes by their swords.

Robert was the son of Humphrey of Tilleul and believed to have been of Danish stock. He was one of the French knights attached to the household of Edward the Confessor and left England, presumably on Harold's accession. He returned after Hastings and took service with his cousin Hugh of Avranches, Earl of Chester, who controlled the turbulent Welsh frontier. Here, Robert was given estates and soon 'he enlarged his territories and built a strongly fortified castle on the hill of Deganwy which is near the sea.' He was tough, ruthless and ambitious, which made him an ideal frontiersman: 'For fifteen years he harried the Welsh mercilessly, invaded the lands of men who then still enjoyed their original liberty and owed nothing to the Normans, pursued them through woods and marshes and over steep mountains and found difficult ways of securing their submission. Some he slaughtered mercilessly on the spot like cattle; others he kept for years in fetters, or forced into harsh and unlawful slavery.'

Such a vigorous life demanded a heroic warrior's death. During the summer of 1093, a surprise Welsh raid caught Robert unawares. Seeing the raiders on the foreshore, he ordered his trumpeters to sound the alarm and then, unarmoured and shieldless, rushed down a slope to set upon the intruders. His followers were less reckless and held back, leaving Robert to be killed by a javelin. The Welsh cut off his head as a prize and returned to their ships. What was left of Robert was conveyed to Normandy and buried in the abbey of St Evroul, where his brother was a monk. The inscription on his grave declared him a paragon of his class:

> *Courteous and warlike, handsome, swift and bold,*
> *While life remained, a true knight in this world.*
> *Most generous lord, faithful and loyal friend,*
> *Obedient ever to Christ's bride and the Church.*[48]

Those who were the losers in the wars of early medieval Britain and Ireland had no tombstones or elegies. Historical literature mentions their sufferings in passing, or not at all. Describing the campaign fought on the border between Normandy and France in 1119, Orderic devotes several pages to the manoeuvres of the armies and the activities of their commanders. As for those unfortunate enough to live on and around the battlegrounds, he has one terse observation: 'in those days the whole region was depopulated by the raging wars.'[49] There can be no doubt that the passage of predatory armies wreaked havoc out of all proportion to their size: villages were burned, crops destroyed and livestock killed or driven off. Those who fled faced starvation, as they do today in those parts of south-eastern Europe and Africa troubled by internecine wars.

The damage was, however, localised. There were areas that were more or less untouched by five centuries of intermittent war. Consider Goltho, once a village and now fields in that uneventful, placid countryside which lies between Lincoln and edge of the Lincolnshire Wolds. The soil is heavy and becomes waterlogged with heavy rain, which was why the village was abandoned in the fifteenth century, when there was more good arable land available than farmers to cultivate it.

Crops were first grown in Goltho just after the Roman occupation, but the settlement was deserted in about 200. Farming restarted in the early ninth century, when Goltho lay within the minor Anglo-Saxon kingdom of Lindsey, a satellite of Mercia. It was the home to a small community headed by a ceorl who built himself a wooden homestead. Forty or so years later, the area witnessed the passage of the Viking Great Army which, according to literary evidence, did great destruction. And yet the excavations at Goltho suggest that it escaped harm. Nonetheless, the owner of the village took the precaution of building defence works along the lines of those that Alfred and his successors were erecting around towns. Construction must have involved a considerable effort for a small community; the earthworks measured 160 by 160 feet and were six feet high and twenty-four wide, and were topped by a timber palisade. Within this enclosure was the rectangular wooden house of the landowner, domestic offices and a weaving shed. Their scale suggested he was probably a thegn. Between 950 and 1000, his successor extended the defence works and built a new, larger hall.

Maybe as a consequence of these measures, Goltho was untouched by the Viking raids that disturbed other parts of the country. Other Anglo-Saxon landowners understood the deterrent value of defensive earthworks; the hall of the thegn who occupied Sulgrave in Northamptonshire was enclosed within ditch and bank defences.

After Hastings, Goltho had a Norman lord, possibly a subtenant of the Bishop of Durham, the Earl of Chester or Ivo de Taillebois. He constructed a new and, by comparison with its predecessors, formidable defence system of timber and earth. Its outer perimeter was a moat, forty feet wide and between twelve and fifteen deep, over which was a wooden bridge which led to a fortified gatehouse. Above the moat was a palisaded bank with a motte in one corner which was revetted with stone, wood and turf. It was surmounted by a three-storey timber castle with a triangular roof. This must have been a defence of last resort, for within the bailey was a hall where the lord of the manor must have lived. Excavated spear, javelin and arrow heads suggest that he possessed the wherewithal and, presumably, men with which to defend his fief.[50] A small-scale castle, Goltho represented a considerable exercise in logistics involving labourers, carters, sawyers and carpenters, all of whom had to be diverted from their regular work. It may also have involved the eviction of men and women from their homes; in nearby Lincoln 166 houses were demolished to make room for the castle, and in Cambridge twenty-seven.[51]

Goltho's experience of war would obviously not have been the same as, say, some equivalent settlement along the Welsh border or in the immediate hinterland of coasts exposed to Viking attacks. Of course, archaeological evidence cannot reveal whether the thegn of Goltho went to the wars or how he fared, or whether freemen from Goltho served with the shire fyrd. Nor can it reveal whether the village was a host to refugees from nearby war zones, or how the inhabitants may have reacted to a French-speaking lord who ordered them to cut wood and shovel earth for his castle. Nevertheless, here and elsewhere archaeology does indicate that conquest was followed by a process of social and cultural assimilation rather than the expulsion of the defeated by the victorious.

The social and political consequences of the war are easier to assess. By 1100, England had emerged as the strongest, most centralised kingdom within the British isles. In response to the demands of war, the Anglo-Saxon monarchy had developed an efficient administrative machine which enabled the crown to mobilise the nation's manpower and wealth in its defence. This system worked well and William I saw no reason to tamper with it; English taxes and English levies helped him and his successors in their wars in Normandy. As part of an Anglo-Norman state, England was drawn into the orbit of France and so became immersed in the mainstream of western European religious, intellectual and cultural life. The Norman connection also made England a partner in the continental dynastic and territorial ambitions of its kings. Moreover, the momentum behind William's invasion of England did not slacken once the English were pacified. It continued with incursions into Wales, which was divided into petty polities whose rulers fought among themselves and, in an emergency, were glad to make alliances of convenience with their Norman neighbours. The Norman grasp reached into Scotland where, in 1072, 1079 and 1091, Malcolm III was forced at swordpoint to acknowledge the overlordship of the English crown. He lost more than face; by the time of the Scottish king's death in 1093, William Rufus had extended his sovereignty over northern Cumbria and pushed the English frontier to the Solway. The expansion of England had begun.

PART TWO

DISPUTED LANDS,
1100–1603

1

Just quarrels: Britain at war, 1100–1603, an overview

I

In 1100 there were four distinct independent polities within the British archipelago. England, now coupled with the duchy of Normandy, was the largest in terms of area, population and economic resources. Wales was a mosaic of principalities of various sizes and already under pressure from land-hungry Anglo-Norman adventurers who were infiltrating its southern and eastern fringes. Scotland had a single monarchy which had yet to assert control over the Highlands and Western Isles whose magnates were free to do as they pleased, which was usually to wage small-scale predatory wars against each other. It was much the same in an Ireland that was fragmented into petty kingdoms and host to the culture of the blood-feud and cattle-raid.

By 1603 the political map of the British isles had been radically changed. Shorn of its French appendages, England had absorbed Wales and Ireland, although its control over the latter was still precarious and rested on force of arms. Scotland had merged with this enlarged English state through the accession of James VI and I, which created a dual monarchy with two legal and political systems under one crown.

War had played a crucial part in what had been a slow and some-times haphazard advance towards unity and, with it, a degree of uniformity of custom. Superior force, rigorously applied, had eradicated the independent Welsh states during the twelfth and thirteenth centuries. Scotland had nearly succumbed to English conquest between 1296 and 1307, but within twenty years had reasserted its sovereignty, largely thanks to a war of attrition waged across northern England. Unlike the Scots, the Irish had never presented anything approaching a united front, but their resistance to English penetration had been as stubborn as it was hopeless. The final phase of the conquest of Ireland was undertaken during the last quarter of the sixteenth century as part of an ambitious plan completely to reshape Irish society. Colonists from England, and later Scotland, were part of this reformation.

War also helped decide how the emerging states were governed, by whom and on what principles. In both England and Scotland, kings had had their powers curtailed and, whether they liked it or not, were forced to listen to the opinions and advice of their subjects. There was some compensation: the legal and moral authority of kings was enlarged to the point where it far outweighed that of its mightiest subjects, singly or in coalition. Ordinary people also gained something: their rights had been both defined and preserved by armed conflict.

Wars within Britain and on the frontiers of its component parts were waged for a variety of reasons. Conflict was accepted, along with other human disasters, such as famines and epidemics, as part of a universe in which, from time to time, God inflicted mass punishment on humankind for its sinfulness. Like the Viking invasions, the civil war between King Stephen and the Empress Matilda, lasting from 1135 to 1154, was interpreted as a divine judgement on a wicked nation. All but a few of the victims of this struggle were the poorest and weakest in society, who became prey for the strong who, in theory, should have been their protectors. Just as the divinely ordained human order was thrown into disarray, so was the natural order: 'Even the wild animals which in former times were preserved peaceably in parks and enclosures throughout the country were now turned loose, and harassed everyone hunting them without reserve.'[1]

War was inevitable in an imperfect world in which humans succumbed frequently and with ease to sin. A fourteenth-century moralist traced the connection between human frailty and war: 'When the Fiend sees love and peace among good men, he is envious and does all that he can or may, with the fury of ire he stirs their hearts to discord and strife . . . After strife comes chiding with great noise and cry. And right as fire first casts up smoke and bursts into flame, right so after ire and evil will come strife and debate; and when one says to another – "It is thus," the other says, "Nay" . . .' And so on. 'Threatenings . . . stir men's hearts to anger so that brawls and wars begin among them and do not cease until one is avenged on the other.'[2] This pattern of rage, harsh words and violence is repeated many times in contemporary legal records. One case may stand for thousands of others. In 1300, Henry Bateman and William de Gamlingey were playing a game of 'penyperch' at Eaton in Bedfordshire. A row broke out, William grabbed Henry by the hair and throat and Henry drew his knife. Hearing the rumpus, Reynold Elys ran from a nearby tavern, attempted to separate the brawlers and was stabbed, probably by accident.[3]

Aristocratic tempers were equally quick. Simmering rivalry between John Cornwall, Lord Fanhope, and Reginald, Lord Grey of Ruthin, erupted in 1439 when they were at the assizes in Bedford, attended by armed followers. Fanhope interrupted the proceedings, placed two fingers in front of his mouth and poked out his tongue at the justices and then leapt on a table, drawing his dagger. A free-for-all followed in which eighteen men were killed, several from a collapsing staircase.[1] This incident might easily have illustrated a sermon on the sins of ire and envy, which were commonly identified as the sources of most human discord. This is not to say that kings succumbed to the same violent passions as animated their subjects and rashly resorted to violence. Rulers had to be more circumspect, not least because their wars were far more destructive in their consequences than the quarrels of lesser creatures.

The miseries inflicted by war on those not immediately involved were all too well known. For this reason alone, wars were never undertaken lightly. 'May I with right and conscience make this claim?' asks Shakespeare's Henry V as he contemplates the invasion of France. 'Yes,' is the unequivocal answer of his clerical councillors and they support their conclusion with sheafs of ancient legal precedents. Together, these provide the foundation for the 'just quarrel' that Henry decides to pursue at great cost to his kingdom and even greater to France. The phrase comes from Christine de Pisan's fifteenth-century handbook on war which, among other things, incorporates the wisdom of the Roman authority on this subject, Flavius Vegetius Renatus. The authoress also paraphrases what had become the commonplace Christian interpretation of the 'just war' as defined by canon law. Perhaps confusing the Old and New Testaments, she declares that: 'Our Lord himself ordained to captains that which they should do against their enemies.' His injunctions could only be followed if the soldier was fighting in a 'just cause'. There are five broad categories of just causes: resistance to oppression; the expulsion of a usurper; avenging the wrongs suffered by the church; the protection of vassals; and the chastisement of those who defy their feudal overlord. Wars fought for these reasons may generate evil, but the rightness of the cause is adequate compensation.

Canon lawyers had remarkably flexible minds and could be relied upon to produce the casuistry appropriate to uphold any quarrel. 'Christ himself will take up arms and shield and rise up and help us,' claimed Walter Espec, a judge and founder of Rievaulx abbey, as he rallied the men of the north against a Scottish invasion in 1138. Abbot Ailred of Rievaulx predicted that St Michael would also be fighting alongside them in the company of other saints whose churches the Scots had desecrated.[5] The defeat of the invaders near Thirsk was unmistakable evidence of divine courage and intervention. Supernatural powers were invoked to enhance a just cause; the banner of St Cuthbert was taken from Durham cathedral together with his relics to raise English confidence before their victory over the Scots at Neville's Cross in 1346. Among those fighting for God's cause was a friar who 'gave no indulgence of days for punishment of sins, but severe penance and good absolution with a certain cudgel'.[6]

It was always deeply reassuring to know that a war had the sanction of God, not least because those who died in it were untainted by the sins associated with war: anger and envy. When Edward III assumed the title King of France in 1340 he went to considerable lengths to demonstrate that he had God's favour. He demanded that his rival, Charles IV, entered a cage full of lions. If he was a true king, then he would survive the ordeal like Daniel. This robust assay of kingship was unnecessary: Edward won a string of victories at Sluys (1340), Crécy (1347) and Poitiers (1356) which provided unshakable proof that God had blessed his cause. This point was enlarged upon in a sermon delivered by the chancellor, Adam Houghton, Bishop of St David's, to the opening session of the 1377 parliament. 'I truly believe,' he said, 'that God would never have honoured this land in the same way as he did Israel through great victories over his enemies, if it were not that He had chosen it as His heritage.' A tableau representing a specific Israelite victory, that of David over Goliath, was among the shows which greeted Henry V on his return to London after his victory at Agincourt in 1415. God's hand had been seen throughout the campaign and was duly acknowledged in two verses of the contemporary *Agincourt Carol*:

> *Our king went forth to Normandy,*
> *with grace and might of chivalry;*
> *there God for him wrought marvellously,*
> *wherefore England may call and cry,*
> *Deo Gracias!*

and,

> *Then for sooth that knight comely*
> *in Agincourt field he fought manly;*
> *through grace of God most mighty,*
> *he had both the field and the victory.*
> *Deo Gracias!*

The French answer to what added up to England's monopoly of divine aid came from the lips of Joan of Arc. Her 'voices', especially that of the Virgin Mary, reaffirmed the traditional belief that France was a nation that enjoyed God's favour. The Virgin, too, cherished France; her symbolic lilies were prominent on the royal oriflamme banner which was said to be of heavenly origin. When Joan appeared at Chinon in 1429 she was widely seen as an agent for the redemption of her country, and her hopeful messages seemed to signal an end to a period during which it had been punished by war for its sins. When she rode with the army to relieve Orléans, she was likened to another Judith or Esther, both female saviours of God's chosen people.[7] No wonder then that when the Burgundians delivered Joan to the English, their inquisitors were so keen to discredit the authenticity of her 'voices'. If they were genuine, then God had withdrawn his support from England's cause, or, and this was unthinkable, He had never approved it.

Rebellion against tyranny was a cause that God would endorse. In 1322, Robert de Clitherow, parson of Wigan, urged his flock to support their liege lord, Thomas, Earl of Lancaster, in his struggle against Edward II. The royal cause was unjust, the earl's just, and for this reason de Clitherow was prepared to give absolution to all who took up arms to back him.[8] Right did not, however, prevail and Lancaster was defeated at the battle of Boroughbridge and subsequently beheaded at Pontefract. Pilgrims were soon beating a path to the site of the execution, where a chantry chapel was built. It housed the earl's hat and belt, which respectively cured headaches and relieved the pains of childbirth. Like St John the Baptist and St Thomas à Becket, Lancaster was the victim of an oppressive and high-handed king. His 'martyrdom' was portrayed on a wall-painting in South Newington church in Oxfordshire.[9]

The miracles said to have been performed at Lancaster's tomb added to the already vast body of evidence of God's regular and direct interference in every area of human activity. His intervention could be deliberately sought, as it was in trial by combat, which was war in microcosm. Whatever the scale of the conflict, God would always uphold justice. How far this belief influenced those engaged in waging war cannot be measured exactly. It was certainly persuasive; an analysis of twelfth-century commanders' speeches delivered on the eve of battle shows all promised divine assistance.[10] Obviously such pledges reassured the individual fighting man and may possibly have taken the edge off his fear. The spectacle of the Yorkshire clergy, armed with bows, arrows and swords, and 'assailing the ears of God and His saints with prayers that His mercy would prosper the purpose of their expedition' must have raised the morale and fighting spirit of the soldiers mustered to resist the Scottish invasion in 1346.[11] By contrast, the Cheshire archers raised to defend Richard II from a coalition of discontented barons lost heart at the battle of Radcot Bridge in 1387. Faced by what they imagined to be the armies of the entire nobility, the royal troops refused to risk their lives in 'an unjust cause' and fled.[12]

II

The concept of the just quarrel may have assuaged some consciences, but there were other equally compelling and more concrete reasons for making war. 'We take up arms for our country, we fight for our wives, for our children, for our churches, driving back imminent danger . . . Necessity urges us on,' Walter Espec told the Yorkshire levies in 1138. In this context 'necessity' was clear enough: it meant the pursuit of security which could only be obtained once the rapacious Scots had been expelled.

The search for security, national and personal, lay at the root of all the wars fought during this period. Security took many, often complex forms. It embraced safety from predators, the elimination of real or imaginary threats to individuals and governments, and the right of the latter to rule without unwanted constraints. No one could ever take security for granted and the prudent were always well advised to prepare for any eventuality, however unlikely. The world was infinitely mutable, which was why human existence was so commonly symbolised by the wheel of fortune. This was perpetually revolving with some people ascending and others tumbling. The many different risks of war made the wheel spin faster and there were some heavy falls. Among the heaviest was that of James IV of Scotland who invaded England in 1513 and was defeated at Flodden where he and a large body of his nobles were killed. The moral was clear and pointed in that baleful Elizabethan catalogue of the downfall of great men and women, *The Mirror for Magistrates*:

> *I was the author of my own woe,*
> *But yet I began it by wicked counsel,*
> *Of my lords spiritual and temporal also:*
> *Which for their merits in field with me fell.*

In his own defence, James could have argued that he had gone to war for the security of Scotland, whose independence had been underwritten by an alliance with France since the middle of the fourteenth century. It was an arrangement that had emerged from the endeavours of Edward I to absorb Scotland into the English state. In 1290, he had been asked to resolve the crisis of the Scottish succession, which he did, demanding that the new king, John Balliol, rendered him homage. Faced with a war with France in 1296 and unrest in newly conquered North Wales, Edward insisted on his feudal rights and demanded military service from King John and the Scottish nobility. They refused and hurriedly made an alliance with Philip IV of France.

Edward was faced with not only a disobedient vassal, but the prospect of war on three fronts: Scotland, Gascony and Flanders. Well supported from the sea, he marched north and swept aside all opposition. King John was deposed and publicly humiliated, and the Scottish nobility swore allegiance to their new overlord, Edward. It was a deceptive and transitory triumph. Nearly all the Scottish landowners who rendered homage did so to save their lands from confiscation and would remain, at best, political weathercocks. English political power was confined to royal strongholds, mostly in the Lowlands, and was thinly supported. Opposition rallied around Sir William Wallace whose sole aim, in the words of his fifteenth-century biographer, was 'Scotland free'.[13] Wallace's revolt began well; in 1297 he surprised and defeated an English army at Stirling Bridge and then took the war across the border with raids into Cumberland.

Edward responded with a second, large-scale expedition in 1298 and defeated Wallace at Falkirk. The pattern of the war was set: the English would enter Scotland in overwhelming force and secure castles and oaths of allegiance and then withdraw, leaving behind a brittle peace. With the rebellion and coronation of Robert the Bruce in 1306 the war entered a new phase. An outstanding strategist, Bruce exploited his own strength (the wish of the Scottish people to be left alone) and his enemy's weaknesses. English power in Scotland was unloved and dependent on strongholds and a handful of collaborators. The situation radically changed whenever a field army crossed the border. Under a commander who knew his trade the English combination of armoured cavalry and archers was incontestably superior to the Scots who relied on phalanx-like formations of spearmen (schiltroms). This had been proved at Falkirk and again at Methven (1306) when Bruce himself was defeated and forced to flee. Henceforward, he stuck to a war of attrition and avoided pitched battles.

Bruce was immeasurably helped by the deteriorating political situation inside England, where Edward II was at loggerheads with his nobles. Unlike his father, Edward II lacked the drive and charisma needed to inspire his soldiers and knew nothing of the art of war. When in 1314 he led an army into Scotland to relieve Stirling castle, the outcome was a disastrous defeat at Bannockburn. It was the battle that King Robert had always endeavoured to avoid. Nonetheless, he chose his ground wisely and stirred the hearts of his outnumbered army with a rousing speech. According to a flattering biography written sixty or so years afterwards, Robert told them they were fighting for 'the freedom of our land'. He also appealed to baser instincts:

> The poorest of you all shall be
> Both rich and mighty . . .[14]

Appetites for plunder were more than satiated during the next eight years when Robert launched a series of devastating counteroffensives into northern England. The incursions in 1315, 1316, 1318, 1319 and 1322 were massive raids in which property and livestock were looted, protection money levied and crops and buildings burned. English countermeasures, including two invasions of Scotland, came to nothing, and in 1327 a peace was agreed in which Scottish independence was recognised.

The war had generated great bitterness. 'Getting rid of a turd is a job well done' ('*bon bosoigne fait qy de merde se deliver*') Edward I quipped when he handed over the Great Seal of Scotland to its new governor, the Earl de Warenne in 1296.[15] King David II of Scotland, captured at Neville's Cross in 1346, was derided by English polemicists who alleged that when he had been christened he had opened his bowels into the font.[16] For their part the Scots reviled their overbearing neighbour who denied them peace:

> Our old enemies coming of Saxon's blood,
> They never yet to Scotland would do good.[17]

There was plenty of racial invective; contemporary Scottish balladeers accused the English of having tails that could conveniently be used to drag them to the scaffold.[18]

The war left a legacy of mutual loathing and an unstable frontier zone. The 'auld alliance' turned out to be more harmful to Scotland than beneficial to France. Bannockburn was never repeated; it was avenged at Halidon Hill in 1333 and diversionary invasions of England by Scottish field armies ended with defeats at Neville's Cross (1346), Homildon Hill (1402) and Flodden (1513).

It is impossible to construct a balance sheet for the cross-border raiding that persisted until the early seventeenth century. The demands of security transformed society on both sides of the Anglo-Scottish border, which was a war zone intermittently disturbed by private-enterprise raiding. These incursions compelled landowners and monasteries to erect and maintain fortified manorhouses or gateways. Of the former the best preserved and most delightful (a dozen or so years ago chickens scurried around the courtyard) is Markenfield Hall, near Ripon. It could not have withstood siege-engines, not that marauding bands would have possessed them, but was a valuable place of refuge for people and livestock. Pele towers, scattered across the valleys on both sides of the frontier, served the same emergency purpose. In Northumberland, farmers built 'bastles' which were thick-walled, barred-windowed dwellings with a byre on the ground floor and living quarters above. Most date from the second half of the sixteenth century; there are clusters of bastles around the village greens at Wall and Chesterwood.

Politically, the borders remained a region of chronic instability. The English and Scottish monarchies were compelled to surrender responsibility for security to the local aristocracy who, with their retinues, enjoyed royal subsidies. These magnates were bound to keep the peace but many, perhaps all, were also part-time robbers or the protectors of thieves. Large areas were outside any jurisdiction. Mid sixteenth-century Liddesdale swarmed with 'hundreds of thieves both of Scotland and England'. Northumberland was plagued by tumults and its inhabitants were 'much given to riot, especially among the young gentlemen and headsmen and divers of them also to thefts and greater offences'. Rules enforced elsewhere were ignored in the Borders. 'It is intolerable,' wrote the Bishop of Durham in 1597, 'that any subject of the Queen should for twenty or thirty years together, stand out against the civil and ecclesiastical authority, and not only withhold themselves, but their wives and children and families &c. from all Christian subjection to their natural sovereign.'[19]

III

Wilful isolation from and indifference to the laws of the state were an affront to the state. From the thirteenth century onwards the English and Scottish crowns had steadily extended their authority and demanded uniform obedience, unqualified by local custom or private inclination. In Wales (before the sixteenth century), Ireland, the Western Isles and the Highlands, attachment to indigenous codes, language and magnates was remarkably durable and was a thorn in the side for the increasingly omnipotent centralised state.

Anglo-Norman propaganda portrayed the Welsh as a disorderly, backward and unproductive race who needed pacification and civilisation. They got both, at a lance's point. Ever since the Conquest, Norman knights, often landless adventurers, had been penetrating the coastal plain of South Wales and advancing up the fertile valleys of the Severn, Usk and Wye. Their progress and the tenacity of local resistance were reflected in the density of castles; twenty-six were built in Glamorgan alone between 1117 and 1147. The competition for land in Wales was not a racial struggle; native Welsh princes entered into alliances of convenience with their alien neighbours, and Welsh archers and spearmen served with English armies. Warfare was seldom distinguishable from brigandage and consisted of ambushes and hit-and-run raids by small parties of lightly armed Welshmen. One detachment formed from the kinsmen and tenants of Hywel ap Catwelan, Maredudd ap Maelgwyn and Dafydd ap Llywelyn ravaged Montgomery in 1249, burning undefended settlements, murdering anyone they met and carrying off livestock. Retaliation was always severe; in 1233, a grateful government paid Richard Muneton one shilling each for the heads of fifty-seven Welshmen he had killed.[20] It is not known whether they were all bandits.

Political conditions favoured an eventual piecemeal conquest of Wales. Its princes were disunited and lacked the resources to expel the interlopers. Nevertheless, the native Welsh were convinced that their past glories would be restored, a faith that rested solely on the belief that their legendary leader, King Arthur, would return. Anticipation of this national resurgence rested on the portrayal of Arthur in Geoffrey of Monmouth's *History of the Kings of Britain* which was written, revealingly, in the 1130s when Welsh fortunes underwent a brief revival. Geoffrey's Arthur had been a warrior king who united Britain through successive wars and, by victories over the Roman emperor, Lucius, and the French, had made his kingdom a power to be reckoned with in Europe. Such triumphs were to be expected from a prince with an illustrious pedigree: Arthur had descended from Brutus, son of Aeneas and nephew of Hector. Brutus and other fugitives from Troy had reached Britain and made themselves its masters, as might be expected from men with heroic blood in their veins.

This was intoxicating stuff which turned Welsh, and later English, heads. The legend coupled with the prophecies of Merlin strongly suggested that history would be repeated and Britain would again achieve its former stature. A new Arthur did appear, but he was not a Welshman. Edward I annexed the Arthurian legend and manipulated it in a cunning and highly effective manner, using it to give legitimacy to his claims over Wales and later Scotland. While in each instance he was waging war justly against defiant vassals, he was also fulfilling events that had, as it were, been preordained. By and large the rest of the world was taken in by this piece of legerdemain. In 1278 there was great excitement when it was rumoured that Edward would attend an international tournament held at Le Hem in northern France. He did not, but a French poet who described the proceedings repeated the tale that Edward was the descendant of Arthur and, through him, the royal dynasty of Troy. In the same year, Edward travelled to Glastonbury abbey and watched the exhumation of the bodies of Arthur and Guinevere. They were reburied under a sumptuous marble tomb before the high altar, paid for by Edward.[21] These solemnities not only identified Edward with Arthur, but reminded the Welsh that he was truly dead and would never reappear as their national saviour.

This psychological warfare prepared the way for Edward's conquest of the rump of independent Wales. The 'just quarrel' was over Llywelyn, Prince of Gwynedd's refusal to perform satisfactorily his duties as a vassal. Edward's purpose was accomplished by four well-co-ordinated campaigns in 1277, 1282 to 1283, 1287 and 1294 to 1295. At the end of the second, Edward continued the Arthurian charade by retrieving Arthur's so-called crown which he delivered to Westminster abbey, now home to the sepulchres of the Plantagenet dynasty. In Wales, the new dispensation of power was marked by castle building, which also provided an opportunity to make a further appeal to the historical imagination of the Welsh. Work on the foundations of Caernarfon uncovered the grave of Magnus Maximus, the father of Constantine the Great. According to Welsh legend, Magnus had had a vision of a great city surrounded by walls of many colours. It lay beside the mouth of a river with hills beyond. This dream achieved substance at Caernarfon: its exterior stonework and overall design were contrived to imitate the walls of Constantinople.[23]

By harnessing legend to his political and military ends, Edward made his conquest of Wales appear both inevitable and desirable. Behind the propaganda was the reality of new laws, bureaucratic efficiency and English settlers with special privileges. Turbulence persisted. Only in the 1530s was Wales fully assimilated into the English state as part of a wider Tudor policy of enforcing legal and administrative uniformity throughout the kingdom.

Another peripheral region in the grip of perpetual disorder was Ireland. A fourteenth-century Scottish chronicler had dismissed the Gaelic Irish as 'a savage and untamed nation, rude and independent' who were 'hostile to the English language and people'. And understandably so given the history of the past two hundred years. In 1170 Draumait Mac Murchada had invited Strongbow, Earl of Pembroke, to help him recover his kingdom of Dublin. He did and established the Anglo-Norman toehold in Ireland. There followed a slow, piecemeal thrust inland which eventually created the English 'pale' which spanned the counties of Louth, Meath and Kildare together with territory to the south-west. Control over this region was always shaky and liable to disruption from outside.

The political and cultural fault-lines of medieval Ireland were dictated by geography. The lowlands were dominated by the English and the wooded, often waterlogged and mountainous regions by the Gaels. Nature provided them with an extensive, near-inaccessible sanctuary into which armies could be lured and sometimes ambushed, as Elizabethan commanders discovered to their cost. At the same time, recourse to isolated, barren fastnesses had its dangers. In 1600, English commanders went to considerable efforts to induce an artificial famine that would deprive the fugitive Irish of supplies for winter.[23]

Within their own areas the native Irish lived according to their own customs, which from the outside seemed a recipe for anarchy. This could not be tolerated by the Tudor state; so long as large tracts of Ireland were out of control it was all but defenceless and could easily become a springboard for an attack on England by either France or Spain. For this reason, in 1541, Henry VIII formally declared himself King of Ireland and the only source of political authority within the island. A moral imperative soon emerged to justify the subsequent campaigns against the untamed Irish. In the words of Edmund Spenser, a veteran of these wars, they were undertaken for 'reducing that savage nation to better government and civility' so that its economic assets might be harnessed to the benefit of the entire nation.[24] He wrote in 1596 when operations were in full swing to uproot 'licentiousness and barbarism' and crush those who embraced them. Among the Irish delinquencies cited by Spenser were the clan vendetta and the habit of paying blood-money to the kinsfolk of its victims. Civilisation could only be achieved if English law was universal. And not just English law; those engaged in the wars detected the hand of the Catholic clergy behind Irish resistance. 'Romish bees' from 'foreign hives' had swarmed to Ireland where they joined local priests in encouraging rebellion, according to an intelligence report of 1600.[25]

By 1603 the Irish rebels were flagging. They needed a breathing space, as Spenser recognised. 'When they are weary with wars and brought down to extreme wretchedness then they creep a little perhaps and sue for grace till they have gotten new breath, and recovered their strength again.' This recidivism could only be prevented by garrisons scattered across the countryside, an imported English landlord class and, in the next century, Presbyterian Scots immigrants who could be depended upon as allies of the government. Ireland would remain a country where a majority of the population was excluded from any say in how it was ruled and where the government's survival depended on military force.

Nonetheless, in London and Dublin it was imagined that a new order, imposed from above, would drive out the old. This astringent recipe for peace was also applied on the peripheries of Scotland where, as in Ireland, traditions of clan feuding persisted. Bonds of blood and tenant-dependency enabled magnates and chieftains to assemble war bands with which to fight each other and defy the crown. Only war could make such creatures tractable subjects. Between 1589 and 1595, James VI of Scotland hammered the Western Isles and the Highland coasts with punitive expeditions. Bruised into submission, the local chieftains accepted the Statutes of Iona (1609) by which they promised to abjure old ways and integrate themselves and their clans into Scottish society. 'Idle men' who lived by the sword were to be excluded from their households, and their eldest sons were ordered to be educated in Lowland academies where they would master English and learn the civilities and duties expected from Renaissance gentlemen. They achieved the latter, but still cherished those old customs and feudal loyalties upon which their status ultimately depended.

IV

Taming one set of noblemen had needed the goodwill and co-operation of another. The Scottish crown could only impose its will in remote areas with soldiers raised from the clients and tenants of loyal lords. The army of intimidation and retribution that hurried the Western Isles in 1530 was raised directly from the dependants of landowners worth over one hundred pounds a year, who also had to pay their levies.[26] Reliance on the aristocracy diluted royal authority and, as in England, led to confrontations in which powerful magnates attempted to impose their will on the crown. Two kings, James I and James III, were murdered, and the death toll among the Scottish nobility was high. John Hepburn, Prior of St Andrews (who died in 1522), sadly characterised his countrymen as 'a violent, fierce people, mutinously proud and knew not whom to obey without the sword were drawn'. He added, 'they were never absolutely governed by their kings.'[27]

Honour and prestige, the lodestars of men of high birth, were the source of altercations which were settled with swords. The murder in 1592 of the Earl of Moray by George Gordon, Sixth Earl of Huntly, triggered a minor civil war in the Highlands into which thousands of clansmen were drawn. Civilians suffered most and by the close of the year some complained to James VI that the commotions had 'so broken the country, that great numbers of honest and true men are in point of present wrack'.[28] Matters deteriorated after the Catholic Huntly invited Spanish help and exposed Scotland to the sort of religious civil war that had recently devastated France. It was prevented by an army raised from loyal noblemen, who also demanded that Huntly made an accommodation with the king rather than suffer punishment for treason. Royal authority and aristocratic independence were simultaneously preserved.

James VI had little choice but to acquiesce. Like other English and Scottish kings before him, he relied upon the co-operation of the landowning classes, who were trained to war and possessed the private resources to wage it. Noblemen and knights were the lions under the throne, councillors to kings and, with them, the defenders of the people. Contemporary political and military theory were combined in the analogy of a ship: 'The forecastle of this ship is the Clergy – prelates, religious [i.e. monks and nuns] and priests; the hindcastle is the Baronage – the king and his nobles; the body of the ship is the Commons – merchants, craftsmen and labourers.' The nobility were endowed with 'bodily might and hardiness' while the king, as helmsman, was guided by virtue and wisdom.[29]

There was no precise or universal agreement as to the nature of these regal qualities, nor were they genetically transmitted. Nor was the nobility capable of setting private ambition above public duty: a class highly conscious of its honour and status never meekly submitted to control, especially when a king did not wholly share its values, or respect its individual members' interests. Unbridled, the nobility had the capacity to cause havoc – this had been proved by the war between Stephen and Matilda. Firm and thorough royal government prevented such disasters, but its implementation provided the source for further dissension. At the heart of all the contentions was the boundary between the rights of the subject and the power of the crown. If the latter enlarged, there was a reaction from those who believed their rights were imperilled. This was what happened in 1215 when a baronial coalition compelled John to accept restrictions on his prerogative laid down in Magna Carta.

'The Charter of Liberties' had been imposed on John by superior force. Subsequent English civil wars revolved around the balance of power between crown and subjects, and the equally contentious issues of who should advise the king and how he should distribute his patronage. Over-influential Poitevins at Henry III's court led to Simon de Montfort's uprising and the civil war of 1264 to 1265. Excessive favour shown by Edward II to his homosexual favourites, Piers de Gaveston and Hugh Despenser, provoked armed baronial opposition in 1312 and two rebellions in 1322 and 1327, the last ending with the king's deposition. Edward II was judged unfit to govern by parliament, but the indictment against him and his minions was presented by men with swords in their hands and the determination to use them if they did not get their way. Aristocratic objections to the personnel and policy of Richard II led to an armed coup in 1399 in which the king was dethroned by Henry Bolingbroke, the Duke of Lancaster. As Henry IV, he justified his actions with promises of good and fair government, but his measures failed to satisfy a coterie of his former supporters. Victories at Shrewsbury (1403) and Bramham Moor (1408) preserved the house of Lancaster.

These contests between crown and subjects had significant consequences for England. From them emerged the foundations of parliament and the principle that all men of property were entitled to a say in the framing of laws, the amount of tax they paid and how it was disbursed. None of these rights could have been established had not those who supported them been willing to use coercion and, as a final resort, war to get their way. According to the theology of the just quarrel, such extreme action was defensible on the grounds that the crown had overreached itself and broken faith with its subjects. Nonetheless, many who engaged in rebellion were also promoting their personal interests. A northern family, the Percys, who had first helped Henry IV to his throne and then became his most persistent adversaries, were driven by private ambition as much as by any concern for the welfare of the kingdom.

Kingmaking was a rewarding, but highly hazardous activity. The Percys had been able to undertake it because, as Border magnates, they could tap a reservoir of well-armed and trained soldiers. Their stronghold at Alnwick was not just another frontier castle, it was the focus of a network of personal retainers, friends and tenants who looked to the Percys for support and remuneration. Raby Castle in Durham served the same purpose for the equally ruthless and acquisitive Neville family which had also hitched itself to the Lancastrian bandwagon in 1399. Unlike their rebellious rivals, the Nevilles flourished. Through the judicious use of patronage and a capacity to inspire a blend of affection and fear, the crown could satisfy all its magnates and contain their local rivalries. If it failed to achieve this equipoise, then there was a danger that provincial power struggles would deteriorate into private wars and, worse still, spill over into the country at large.

This occurred in 1450 at the start of what turned out to be the most prolonged period of civil war in England, the Wars of the Roses. At first, the struggle centred on the practical measures needed to rescue the nation from the consequence's of Henry VI's inadequacies. A naïf and feckless king, he had to be separated from a clique of corrupt and greedy courtiers. His cousin, Richard, Duke of York, offered himself as the saviour of the kingdom and went as far as to enlist mass support through polemic broadsides, just as de Montfort and Thomas of Lancaster had done. The issues were well appreciated at least by some of the lower classes; two shipmen accused of the murder of William de la Pole, the Duke of Suffolk, defended themselves by arguing that they were acting for the whole community in ridding England of a notoriously venal minister.

York allied himself with the Nevilles, who exploited the conflict as an opportunity to pay off old scores and eliminate local rivals. They set the future tone of the wars by singling out and slaying Henry Percy, Earl of Northumberland, and Edmund Beaufort, Duke of Somerset, at St Albans in 1455. Nothing was settled by the first battle of the wars; while well aware of Henry VI's deficiencies, the bulk of the nobility was reluctant to deliver the government into the hands of York and his backers. They finally took it by force in 1461, when York's son, Edward IV, and Richard Neville, Earl of Warwick ('the kingmaker'), defeated a Lancastrian army at Towton.

The last two phases of the wars were the result of private ambition rather than the need to restore efficient and open-handed government, which was achieved by Edward IV. Dissatisfied with his share of power in the new régime, Warwick used his northern forces to coerce the king in 1469, but failed. In the following year, he switched to the exiled Henry VI. The spatchcocked Neville-Lancastrian administration of 1470 to 1471 won few hearts and Edward defeated its armies at Barnet (where Warwick was killed 'somewhat fleeing') and Tewkesbury, which was followed by a purge of Lancastrian sympathisers.

Edward IV's death in 1483 and the accession of his thirteen-year-old son, Edward V, opened a new contest for the throne. The king's uncle, Richard, Duke of Gloucester, stage-managed a coup d'état in London, backed by his private forces rushed from the north and reinforced by those of his crony, Humphrey Stafford, Duke of Buckingham, which were brought from Wales and the Marches. Peripheral, lawless regions again provided the means for local aristocrats to impose their will on the rest of the kingdom. Edward V was deposed on flimsy grounds, and murdered, once it became clear that Richard III's new order would be challenged by Buckingham and a substantial body of disenchanted Yorkists. In the manner of Warwick, Richard had used military muscle in a cause that was plainly unjust; neither Edward IV nor his son had behaved as tyrants, far from it. Dismayed Yorkists and ex-Lancastrians placed themselves behind Henry Tudor who landed in Wales in 1485. Richard was killed at Bosworth Field where a substantial proportion of his troops refused to fight or did so halfheartedly. Popular animus against the dead king was reflected in the abuse of his corpse; hitherto, the bodies of defeated princes had been respectfully treated. A challenge to Henry VII by a bogus Yorkist princeling (Lambert Simnel) was easily overcome at the battle of Stoke-by-Newark in 1487, the last of the wars.

What had been achieved? In 1485, Lord Mountjoy cautioned his sons against the dangers of playing power politics, a game in which the losers lost their lives. Old aristocratic powers were not severely curtailed; the Tudors needed their lions under the throne and, in the vivid phrase of Lyndon B. Johnson, it was better to have them 'on the inside of the tent pissing out' rather than outside and 'pissing in'. The nobility's right to retain men was circumscribed, but it was permitted to keep arsenals of weaponry, armour and artillery. They were held for use in an emergency when, as ever, the crown appealed to its lords for assistance. In 1536, George Talbot, the Fourth Earl of Shrewsbury, raised 3600 men from his friends and tenants for service against the Pilgrimage of Grace, an insurrection confined to the northern shires and aimed at reversing Henry VIII's religious policies. Shrewsbury promised to make 'a breakfast' of the rebels, and his spirit prompted

Thomas Cromwell, the king's chief minister, to praise him 'as the most worthy earl that ever served a prince'.[30]

This ideal was followed by others. Aristocratic retinues were deployed in 1549 against popular uprisings, to forestall the Duke of Northumberland's coup against Mary I in 1553 and to crush Sir Thomas Wyatt's rebellion the following year. They were also instrumental in frustrating a narrowly based and localised revolt by a handful of northern peers bent on deposing Elizabeth I and replacing her with the Catholic Mary, Queen of Scots, in 1569.

Some of those who deployed their retainers and tenants on these occasions did so against their consciences, but their attachment to the old faith did not blind them to the damage that would be inflicted by a civil war. There was the frightening example of contemporary France which was luridly portrayed on the stage in Marlowe's *The Massacre at Paris*. A further, highly persuasive warning of the horrors of civil war was provided by Shakespeare's three parts of *Henry VI* and *Richard III*, which were first performed in the 1590s. Theatregoers watched and heard a vivid account of the Wars of the Roses in which they were rendered as a form of national fratricide and a dire example of what happened when subjects placed private ambition before public duty and disobeyed their rulers. It was as a moral lesson that the Wars of the Roses survived in the national consciousness.

V

Seen in retrospect, the Hundred Years' War against France (from 1337 to 1453) and its continuation during the reign of Henry VIII, was a rarely paralled triumph of hope over experience. During each stage of the conflict, the English crown felt confident that it could detach provinces from a kingdom with twice its population and infinitely greater economic resources. Not only could English kings conquer swathes of France, but it was believed that they could keep them forever. Henry VIII even imagined that his French possessions might, like Wales and Ireland, become integrated with England; Calais and Tournai sent MPs to Westminster. The wars were not just empire building, there was the recurrent fear that France might invade England. A cross-Channel offensive could be frustrated in three ways: by a chain of strongholds along the southern coast; by naval supremacy, and by the occupation of bases along France's northern coastline.

War broke out in the mid 1330s against the background of a squabble over Edward III's right to the valuable province of Gascony. Philip VI of France responded to his cousin's obduracy by threatening a two-pronged assault on England. In 1336 a Franco-Genoese fleet took control of the Channel and made a number of amphibious attacks on coastal towns. At the same time, the French were coaxing the Scots into making a large-scale incursion across the border. Edward looked for allies among disgruntled French nobles and proposed himself as an alternative king of France, basing his claim on the rights of his mother, Isabel, a daughter of Philip V. Henceforward, he was at war to evict a usurper and those Frenchmen who came to his aid could do so with a clear conscience.

Edward's strategy was borrowed from Robert the Bruce whose devastating raids into northern England were a recent memory. Rather than risk encountering the larger French army on the battlefield, Edward's armies pursued a war of attrition through *chevauchées*. Mobile detachments crisscrossed northern and later central and south-western France, stealing what they could carry and burning what they could not. During one of these horrendous progresses, a French cardinal had confidently told Geoffrey le Scrope that England would never sever the 'silken thread' that bound France. When it was dark, the English knight took the churchman to the top of a high tower from where he could see a landscape illuminated by fires. 'Your eminence,' asked le Scrope, 'does it not seem that the silken thread that girdles France is broken?' The cardinal fainted.

The great *chevauchées* demonstrated beyond question the capacity of England to inflict damage on France, but were never decisive. Like the bombing offensive against Germany during the Second World War, they weakened the enemy but did not extinguish either his will or capacity to continue resistance. Victories at Crécy (1346) and Poitiers (1356), both battles the English would have preferred to avoid, did not materially change the course of the war, beyond proving the superiority of English tactics. France showed amazing resilience and, by 1360, Edward was feeling the pinch after funding twenty years of war, and he gladly traded his claim to the throne for Calais and Aquitaine.

War was renewed in adverse circumstances in 1369. Mischance followed miscalculation and English taxes were gobbled up without any compensating gains. The contest continued intermittently and half-heartedly until 1396, when Richard II exchanged peace for Calais and Gascony. The war began again in 1415 when Henry V claimed the French throne and invaded Normandy. The circumstances were highly propitious: France was divided by an aristocratic power struggle which Charles VI could not restrain. In 1419, Philip the Good, Duke of Burgundy, allied himself with Henry who had defeated a French field army at Agincourt and was in the process of occupying Normandy.

As in the previous contest, early English successes were followed by exhaustion and a slow collapse. Signs of overexertion had been apparent before Henry V's death in 1422. He bequeathed to his nine-month-old son, Henry VI, the throne of France, a spiralling debt and a war to which no end was in sight. Just before his death, the king had an inkling that things were going badly and expressed a wish for his claim to the throne to be bartered for Normandy if the worst happened. It did, but the tide turned slowly. The momentum of conquest slackened after Joan of Arc's victories at Orléans and Jargeau in 1429, and within a decade the English were engaged in a desperate salvage operation. After an attempt to keep by negotiation what was being lost on the battle-field, the English war-effort fell apart. Between 1449 and 1453 the English garrisons were expelled from Normandy and Gascony; only Calais remained.

Paying for the war had always been a headache. Henry V had hoped to finance his operations from taxes raised in the territories he occupied, but the sums brought in were inadequate. The English exchequer could not make up the shortfall and parliamentary imposts were earmarked to pay off emergency loans. Royal credit disintegrated in the 1440s and there were clear messages of war-weariness from those whom the government pestered for loans. In 1446 'the wealthy and worthy men' of Northamptonshire pleaded poverty when the king's commissioners came borrowing. Many did not even bother to listen to the appeals.[31] Other pockets were being emptied by the war. The ratepayers of Rye and Lydd had to pay for cannon hurriedly purchased in the late 1450s when it was feared that France would follow up its recent victories with cross-Channel raids.[32]

Nothing had been learned. The repeated experience of defeat and war-fatigue did nothing to dull the glowing memories of Crécy, Poitiers and Agincourt. They passed into martial folklore as memorials of national superiority, demonstrated against the odds by small bodies of heroes. As late as 1803, Crécy and Agincourt were cited on a recruiting poster as examples to inflame volunteers for the army that was preparing to meet Napoleon's invasion.

Henry VIII was mesmerised by old victories and yearned to add to them. Projecting the image of a warlike Renaissance prince, he was less well equipped than any of his predecessors to undertake an invasion of France. Europe had changed in the preceding fifty years with the emergence of two superpowers: the Habsburg block (Spain, the German states, and the north Italian and Flemish provinces of the Holy Roman Empire), and France. Each possessed substantial manpower and revenues to satisfy the demands and expenses of modern warfare, although after a couple of decades both were sliding towards insolvency. For all his bombast, Henry was never more than a bit-part player in a contest in which France and the Habsburgs were the leading actors.

Relative weakness did not dull Henry VIII's appetite for martial glory. Nor was he deterred by the sparse returns on his efforts in 1512 and 1513. The profits from the dissolution of the monasteries reawakened Henry's martial passions in the early 1540s and underwrote the grand design that occupied the last five years of his reign. Security was his first concern and was reflected in the construction of a string of fortifications which stretched from Falmouth to Walmer. These defences, designed to withstand artillery bombardment, were supplemented by an ambitious programme of naval rearmament.

A war with France required a neutralised Scotland. Here, Henry was extraordinarily fortunate. In 1542 a strong but mishandled Scottish invasion was thrown back at Solway Moss and James V died some weeks later, some believed from shock. His successor, Mary, Queen of Scots, was a baby and Henry proposed a marriage between her and his only son, Edward. To press his suit, as it were, an English army landed at Leith and undertook a *chevauchée* in the old manner which cut a destructive path southwards to the Tweed. Under threat of coercion and facing occupation by English troops (many of them mercenaries), the Scottish nobility turned towards France which, in 1545, sent an expeditionary force. Queen Mary fled to France, where she married a French prince, and for the next fifteen years Scotland became a French satellite.

England was by now overstretched and slithering towards bankruptcy. The Scottish war dragged on fruitlessly until 1549 and an assault on Boulogne in 1544 added to the royal debts which, at the time of Henry's death, had passed two million pounds. Overstrained, close to bankruptcy and facing popular commotions in Norfolk and the West Country, Edward VI's ministers abandoned his father's aggressive policies. They were taken up by Mary Tudor in what turned out to be the final round of the Hundred Years' War. As the ally of Spain, England again engaged France and lost Calais in 1558. It was a severe blow to national pride, but compensation came two years later when the French were evicted from Scotland. Their position had become precarious in the face of a powerful faction of protestant noblemen, the Lords of the Congregation, who correctly identified the French garrison as the chief prop of Catholicism in their country. The dissidents allied with England, which provided troops, and by 1560 the French had been expelled. Assistance from home was out of the question, for France was sliding into a religious war.

VI

England had avoided an internal religious conflict and Elizabeth I would have preferred not to embroil her kingdom in other people's. Not all her subjects agreed; the Dutch revolt against Spain and the French Wars of Religion provided opportunities for men of courage and enterprise. They offered their services and their ships to the Dutch and French protestants and, as privateers, probed the Caribbean for profit in defiance of Spain's claim to a commercial monopoly there. It rested on the word of a fifteenth-century pope which meant nothing to English protestants. First as traders and then as corsairs, English mariners encroached on Spain's monopoly and discovered that it was weakly defended. Cargoes of coin, bullion, jewels, sugar and hides were taken from Spanish vessels and their settlements in the Caribbean and Central America were overrun and ransacked.

The scale of these unofficial depredations was stepped up. In 1585, Sir Francis Drake led a fleet of twenty-five sail, including two warships on loan from the crown, across the Atlantic. Among its targets was the city of Santo Domingo which was taken and plundered. According to the Spanish governor, the invaders 'treat the city as any enemy of their religion, of their queen and of themselves'. It was a maritime *chevauchée* with the destruction of whatever could not be carried off. Here and elsewhere protestant zeal was displayed through the desecration of churches, monasteries and convents.[33] Icons were broken by one captain, Thomas Oxenham, who crowned a friar with a chamberpot 'and struck him many fisticuffs upon the head'.[34] For his temerity, Oxenham was later tried by the Inquisition and burned to death.

The undeclared and theoretically private naval war in the Atlantic and Caribbean was a prelude to and cause of the official rupture with Spain in 1585. England could no longer stand by as Spanish power increased to a point where it seemed on the verge of the virtual mastery of Europe. Furthermore, Spain was an active party in conspiracies by English Catholic fanatics to assassinate Elizabeth. Her survival as the ruler of an independent protestant state was vital to the preservation of European protestantism, which was then fighting for its life against the armed forces of the Counter-Reformation, led by Spain.

From the start, England could never have defeated Europe's only superpower. It could and did add to Spain's strategic problems by inflicting pressure on its weak points. English troops stiffened the Dutch in their rebellion and later assisted Henry IV in his campaigns against the Catholic League in northern France. Pressure against Spain's seaborne commerce was intensified. Philip II's counterstroke was the Armada of 1588 which was intended to escort an army of veterans across the North Sea from Flanders for an invasion. It failed, as did its successors, although Spanish troops were landed at Kinsale in 1601 to assist the Irish rebels. Hopelessly muddled liaison prevented them from influencing the outcome of that conflict, but the memory of the incident made future governments aware that Ireland represented a threat to security in event of war with a European power. In the meantime, English warships continued to harass Spain's seaborne commerce and made an amphibious attack on Cadiz in 1596.

There was no decisive outcome to the Anglo-Spanish War. Spain's laborious and costly campaigns in the Low Countries ended in stalemate, its French Catholic allies were eliminated and it was lurching from one financial crisis to another as sources of credit disappeared. England's strategy of sharp pinpricks had worked in that they added to the process of attrition, but, like Spain, it was suffering from fiscal debility and war-weariness. Peace was made in 1605, which, for Spain, provided a welcome breathing space. English energies turned outwards towards the growing Atlantic trade and the colonisation of Ireland and North America and inwards towards disputes over the nature and extent of the crown's prerogatives.

2

So haughty a spirit: Chivalry and command

At the beginning of the twelfth century battlefields were dominated by armoured knights on horseback. By 1600 artillery and muskets were supreme. But the men who fired them took orders from officers who lived by codes of personal honour and gallantry that had their roots in the age of the knight. This was why Renaissance emperors, kings, noblemen and generals appeared dressed in armour on their tombs or in their portraits long after it was worn in action. Even those who never went to the wars were rendered in armour on their monuments, for it announced that the dead man had been a gentleman, a member of that caste that had secured its social eminence through a knowledge of arms and war. That knightly pastime and test of courage, the tournament, flourished and great store was set by the knightly accomplishments of horsemanship and swordsmanship. Tales of past glories entranced Elizabethan paladins. The most celebrated, Sir Philip Sidney, was inspired by the Border ballads of battles fought three hundred years before. 'I never heard the old story of *Percy* and *Douglas* that I found not my heart moved,' he once confessed.

The tale he heard, *The Ballad of Chevy Chase*, was part of the vast literature of chivalry. Chivalry was about horses and the knights who rode them. Its rich and sophisticated culture had a enormous impact on the ways in which men behaved in war and how it was regarded throughout Europe. Above all, it made war glamorous and attractive;

the killing ground was a field of honour where brave men did heroic deeds, for which they were immortalised by minstrels, poets and chroniclers. Listen to one describing an English army encamped outside Caerlaverock castle in June 1300: 'One might observe many a warrior there exercise his horse; and there appeared three thousand brave men-at-arms; there might be seen gold and silver, and the noblest and the best of all rich colours, so as entirely to illuminate the valley.'[1] Life was imitating art. This gorgeous scene might have come from some Arthurian romance written for a contemporary aristocratic audience with a taste for detailed descriptions of pageantry and ornament.

Caerlaverock castle was and is an impressive stronghold. The anonymous herald who had followed Edward I's host into Scotland and recorded its exploits likened it to a 'triangular shield' with a single tower at each of its corners and a pair at the apex, flanking the gateway. This design was retained when the castle was rebuilt a hundred or so years later, with the result that today it looks very much as it did when the siege began. Caerlaverock's strength lay in its inaccessibility. The herald noted that, 'On one side, towards the west could be seen the Irish Sea [the Solway Firth], and to the north a fair country surrounded by an arm of the sea [the Nith estuary]. Looking south, he was faced with 'numerous defiles of woods and marshes, and ditches where the sea is on each side of it'. There is still some thick woodland, close to the castle, but the sea has retreated leaving behind drained land which is now used for the rough grazing of cattle.

Edward's army was compelled to concentrate its operations on the eastern side of the castle where it camped. Trees were chopped down to make huts for the knights and leaves, herbs and flowers were gathered from the nearby woods to lay on floors and sweeten the air. These fragrances did not calm the eighty or so knights who were impatient to display their prowess. A siege offered fewer opportunities for spectacular heroism than a pitched battle, but nevertheless the knights made the most of it, while the herald took notes. The chance came after the infantry had been repulsed by a shower of missiles. Overcome with rage at this setback, the knights surged forward, some running and leaping, to the edge of the moat. The herald was astonished: 'They did not act like discreet people, but as if they had been

inflamed and blinded with pride and despair.' This charge, as impetuous as it was futile, was met with a hail of stones which broke shields
and bowled over armoured men. The barrage was ignored: 'There I
saw Ralph de Gorges, a newly dubbed knight, fall more than once to
the ground from stones and arrows, for he was of so haughty a spirit
that he could not retreat.' No one was killed, it seems, but nothing
was achieved beyond the enhancement of reputations for audacity
and valour.

Within a few days Caerlaverock surrendered, its walls and defenders
knocked into submission by the royal siege engines which had been
shipped across the Solway, unloaded and reassembled. Organisation
and technical expertise had succeeded where purblind courage had
failed. The sixty or so Scottish defenders were either imprisoned or
hanged; Edward I had a sharp way with rebels, as the herald approvingly
observed:

> The King is haughty, dreadful and proud:
> For none experience his bite
> Who are not unvenomed by it.
> But he is soon revived
> With sweet good-naturedness
> If they seek his friendship,
> And wish to come to his peace.

The sixty-year-old king was also the most illustrious knight of his age
and had deliberately cultivated an image of himself as a second Arthur.
A contemporary admirer wrote: 'Of chivalry, after King Arthur, was
King Edward the flower of Christendom.'[2] It was only right and proper
that the knights who rode with him to war should behave as Arthurian
champions, vying with each other in bravery and recklessness. Veterans
added lustre to their laurels, and untested men, like Sir Ralph Gorges,
proved themselves under the discerning eye of the king. Again, reality
was copying art; some of the knights who rushed the walls of
Caerlaverock may well have joined in the pseudo-Arthurian Round
Table festivities that Edward regularly held.

II

Edward I's calculated exploitation of the Arthurian cult was an acknowledgement of the powerful hold it had over the imagination of the knightly classes throughout western Europe. The Middle Ages was a period when, in all things, the wisdom of the past exercised an enormous influence over the thinking of the present. For the nobility, Arthur was a historical figure who, together with his court, offered a model of chivalric correctness which was both admired and imitated. Arthurian literature both entertained and instructed, providing authentic examples of how the gentle classes should conduct themselves in peace and war. 'The flower of chivalry' surrounded a king who was 'gentle and courteous and large of spending'.[3] Knights travelled from every corner of the continent just to listen to Arthur's courteous conversation.[4] Among themselves, his knights spoke of adventures, feats of arms, love-affairs and the finer points of horses, hawks and hounds. Knightly accomplishments included chess, backgammon, singing, dancing and the clandestine wooing of fair ladies; Sir John de Paignel who was present at Caerlaverock was 'well versed in love and arms'.

Men of his stamp possessed two vital qualities. They were 'vaillant', that is courageous on the battlefield and in the lists, and 'curteis', that is gracious in speech and demeanour. Fearlessness and skill at arms were always essential; the younger knights present with Edward II's army at Bannockburn 'yearned to do chivalry'.[5] In this urge to win a reputation for individual valour they were no different from their counterparts at Maldon. Consider Sir Giles D'Argentine whose mettle and taste for fighting matched those of any Arthurian hero. His horse was killed under him at Methven in 1304 and, three years later, he appeared as the 'King of the Greenwood' at a tournament at Stepney where he overcame all his opponents. At Bannockburn, when the tide turned against the English, Sir Giles scorned to join the general retreat. Instead, he spurred his horse straight into the ranks of the Scottish spearmen shouting his warcry 'Argente!' and was killed. Those of his enemies qualified to judge on arcane chivalric matters rated him 'the third best knight that day'.[6] Such a death echoed the fictional boast of Roland: 'my deeds shall never be told as a bad example.'

The heroes of the *chansons de geste* and the knights who strove to copy them were direct descendants of Germanic and Celtic super-warriors. In answer to the question 'Who is the noble young knight?' an unknown thirteenth-century French poet answered with a list of credentials that would have been prized by Beowulf and Cú Chulaind: 'He who is engendered of the sword, suckled in the helmet, and cradled in his shield; and fed on lion's flesh, and lulled to sleep by mighty thunder; he with the dragon's face, the leopard's eyes, the lion's heart, the wild boar's fangs; swift as a tiger, drunk with the whirlwind, making a club of his fist to strike down knight and horse like a thunderbolt . . . Such a man, deserves to hold lands and uphold chivalry.'[7]

The same point was made in a different way in the early thirteenth century in the Scottish Arthurian romance, *Sir Fergus of Galloway*. The son of a farmer, Fergus is determined to be a knight and is rebuked for his ambition by his father in 'language appropriate to a peasant'. 'Son of a whore! Where do you get the idea of asking to be given arms? It is your job to look after oxen and cows like your brothers, who go into the fields every day dressed in sheepskins.'[8] The boy persists, gets his way and proceeds to Arthur's court where, after performing a string of amazing feats of arms, he wins knighthood and a beautiful bride. The hero of the thirteenth-century English poem *Sir Perceval of Galles* is even more disadvantaged for, although the son of a celebrated knight, he has been brought up as a child of nature in the woods. He, too, aspires to knighthood, but his widowed mother (a sister of Arthur) warns him that he lacks the 'nurture' and 'mesure' (moderation) required in 'hall' and 'bower' where rough manners are unwelcome.[9] Nevertheless, Sir Perceval compensates for his bumpkin artlessness by instinctive dexterity with sword and lance, and achieves his ambition and, of course, a fair lady. What his mother had in mind were the attainments of Chaucer's squire, who combined chivalry's warlike qualities with its social graces:

> He knew the way to sit a horse and ride.
> He could make songs and poems and recite,
> He knew how to joust and dance, to draw and write.
> He loved so hotly till dawn grew pale
> He slept as little as a nightingale.

> *Courteous he was, lowly and serviceable,*
> *And carved to serve his father at the table.*

Christianity provided an additional, potent element in chivalry. In their efforts to restrain the violence endemic across large swathes of western Europe during the eleventh century, leading churchmen stressed the Christian responsibilities of knighthood. Men whose power derived from their strength should serve God, protect the weak and uphold justice. The highest expression of Christian knighthood was the crusade, an armed pilgrimage to the lands where Christ had lived and which were beset by His enemies, Muslim infidels. The idealism of the holy war captured the imagination of the knightly class and, simultaneously, exported many of its more turbulent members. From 1096 onwards a steady stream of knights from Britain undertook this journey, including most famously Richard the Lionheart and Edward I.

Knights who took the cross were contributing to their redemption. Death at the hands of the unbelievers raised a knight to that company of martyrs who had been killed for the faith. William Longespee II, who was killed fighting the Muslims at Mansurah in 1250, was exalted as a paragon of Christian chivalry. An epic poem on his life described his uplifting end. With five companions and facing overwhelming odds, Longespee chose to fight rather than flee. 'For the love of Christ here we wish to die,' he declares, adding that an English knight would never run from Saracens.[10]

After the loss of Acre, the last Christian toehold in the Levant, in 1292, knights who sought redemption through the service of God had to seek fresh outlets for their zeal. Driven by unfavourable winds to the shores of Spain in 1330, Sir James Douglas, a Scottish knight, joined in a local war against the Moors, 'to make his manhood and prowess the more known in all parts'.[11] The warrior monks of the Teutonic Order welcomed knights from all over Europe to their regular summer crusades against the pagans of Lithuania. They were joined in 1390 by a contingent of about three hundred men led by Henry Bolingbroke. His force, augmented by Scottish and French knights, took part in the Order's unsuccessful operations against the fortifications around Vilnius.

The knights who assembled for the expedition against Vilnius belonged to a European élite that was defined by its monopoly of the skills of waging war; they rode expensive warhorses and were inured to wearing heavy armour. Their chivalric culture – which embraced common aesthetic tastes, a passion for the chase and precise canons of etiquette – was exclusive. The knightly classes were not superior just because they knew how to fight efficiently, but because of their sensibilities. These were the essence of 'gentleness' which was a virtue of mind, as the Wife of Bath reminded her listeners:

> If you would be esteemed for the mere name,
> Of having been by birth a gentleman
> And stemming from some virtuous, noble clan,
> And do not live yourself by gentle deed
> Or take your father's noble code and creed,
> You are no gentleman, though duke or earl.
> Vice and bad manners are what make a churl.

Nowhere is the paramountcy of the gentle classes more obvious than in parish churches and cathedrals. Look up at the clerestory windows at Tewkesbury abbey. There stand ranks of noblemen and women linked by blood and marriage, and united by their generosity to the monks who prayed for their souls. Names and lineages can be identified by the heraldic devices on their surcoats: there are several de Clares, a Despencer, a Fitzroy and a Zouch. All were powers to be reckoned with in the surrounding countryside and in the kingdom at large.

Perhaps the most eloquent chivalric icon in Britain is the memorial brass to Sir Hugh Hastings who died in 1347 and was buried in the church at Elsing in Norfolk. His career had been spent at court, where he was an official of Queen Philippa's household, and in the field, where he served in the armies of her husband, Edward III. Sir Hugh's figure is the visual counterpart of Chaucer's 'perfect, gentle knight'; his features are unblemished, he wears up-to-date armour and his feet rest on a lion, symbolising strength and fierceness. Over his head is a canopy which contains an image of St George, the warrior martyr whom Edward III considered a worthier patron saint for England than the unwarlike Edward the Confessor. The broad shafts of the canopy contain niches, each filled with elegant figures of knights. In the place of honour on the right and at the top is Edward III, and opposite is his cousin, Henry, Earl of Lancaster, both recognisable from their coats of arms. Below, in descending order of rank, are various noblemen who, like the king and Lancaster, were Hastings's companions in arms during his final campaign, the siege of Calais. He is mourned by an illustrious company of warriors like some Arthurian hero on a tomb which, in a way, is also a war memorial. In its pristine condition the monument's brasswork was gilded and inlaid with jewel-like coloured glass and enamels.

None of this decoration has survived, but there are traces of colour on the equally splendid tomb at Reepham, a few miles away. Sir Roger de Kerdiston, who died in 1337, appears fully armoured with arms and legs crossed and lying on a bed of stones which convey the hard grind of campaign life. Ten years before, English knights had endured such discomforts in the uplands of Northumberland during a campaign against Scotland, and Sir Gawain had done likewise in his quest for the Green Knight. What might be called active knighthood was frequently portrayed on tombs between 1250 and 1340, when effigies were carved in animated poses. Some knights appear to be on the verge of drawing or sheathing their swords, legs are crossed (mistakenly imagined to be a sign of service on a crusade) and torsos twist and turn. One of the most impressive in terms of sculpture (it inspired Sir Henry Moore) is the muscular, mid thirteenth-century knight at Dorchester abbey in Oxfordshire.

III

Strong muscles and stamina were vital for a knight. 'Strength of the body is one of the first fundamentals of battle,' wrote Honoré Bonet, a fourteenth-century cleric whose *Tree of Battles* became a popular guidebook to war and knighthood. But, he added, 'virtues of the body are all subject to virtues of the soul.' Sir Bartholomew de Burghersh, a Knight of the Garter and veteran of Crécy and Poitiers, who died in 1369, certainly possessed the former. He was five feet ten inches tall and sturdily built. Pathologists who examined his skeleton found he had large hands and the muscles of the legs and forearms had been developed by exercise. His right (sword) arm was slightly longer than the left. The coarse fibre in his diet had worn down his teeth almost to the gums, but his bones showed no signs of osteoarthritis of the ribs and vertebrae, those indelible marks of a lifetime of hard labour which frequently appear on peasant skeletons.[12] Sir Bartholomew ate meat frequently and, if one is to judge from the menus of great feasts and private household accounts, in considerable quantities, and, as the same sources suggest, drank plenty of wine and ale. For these reasons, like others of his class, he was larger and stronger than all but a handful of the peasantry – Chaucer's bull-like miller was probably exceptional. These physical advantages would have been reproduced in some, perhaps all, of a knight's off-spring.

Genetic good luck was not enough; the knight needed constant and rigorous exercise to maintain himself as an efficient fighting machine. A 'small belly', straight legs, broad shoulders, wide chest, elegant fingers and 'grim visage' were the physical characteristics of an ideal knight according to two fifteenth-century handbooks on war.[13] These assets were cultivated by a régime of training which began in late childhood. The apprentice knight became familiar with weapons that had been deliberately given extra weight, learned how to run and jump in armour and, interestingly, to swim. He also mastered horsemanship and the handling of a lance which could weigh as much as forty pounds. In readiness for the time when he might have to scale the walls of a castle, the young knight practised climbing a ladder in armour using only his hands. It was said that one, probably exceptional, French knight of the late fourteenth century could accomplish this feat running up the inside of the ladder.[14] The amazing ability to vault into the saddle of a warhorse of perhaps sixteen or more hands wearing full armour was the goal of many aspirant knights. It was achieved by Henry V, among others.

The horse gave momentum to a lance thrust and sword cut. But whether fighting on horseback or on foot, the knight's survival depended on how he handled his weapons and his nimbleness in parrying and dodging blows. Psychological reassurance also helped; a fifteenth-century manual on combat reminded a breathless and exhausted knight that his opponent was probably in the same condi-tion. In hand-to-hand fighting it was best to ' . . . strike almost always on approach, standing firmly on the legs, the body and arm moving freely, the hand holding the sword tightly, and the blow not just sideways, cut not straight down, but obliquely from high to low'.[15] The sword was the favourite weapon of the knight. Fourteenth-century examples in the Wallace Collection in London are between twenty-nine and thirty-three inches in length and weigh between two and just over three pounds.[16] In expert hands such weapons could inflict ghastly injuries; Robert the Bruce once severed an opponent's arm at the shoulder and sliced another through the head.[17] 'Brains burst through burnished helms,' in one fictional Arthurian battle where the blows of swords dented armour and cracked ribs.[18]

Modern forensic investigation has upheld the claims of chroniclers and poets. After examining skeletons of men killed during the battle of Visby in 1361, Swedish pathologists concluded: 'we are astonished at the enormous force with which some of the blows have been struck.'[19] The evidence for this included a right foot severed through the lower leg and two lower legs cut off. One sword stroke had passed through a mail hood and penetrated the skull. Three-quarters of the sword wounds on the head had been inflicted from above and, in some cases, from behind. Sometimes a single blow had crippled the victim who was then finished off on the ground. Medieval inquests confirm this picture of the efficacy of a sword blow; that which killed Robert de Kenilworth in 1277 entered the skull and left a wound two inches deep and three inches long.[20] The nature and extent of the injuries more than justified those stylised illuminated manuscript illustrations of battles that show scattered, bleeding limbs and blood pouring from wounds.

The condition of the skeletons excavated at Visby closely fits with what is known about the actual battle, in which a Danish army led by King Waldemar and well supplied with knights and crossbowmen defeated largely untrained and inexperienced levies raised from the more prosperous peasantry and richer townsfolk of Gotland. This force was also insufficiently equipped. The most sophisticated armour available to the losers was a mail hood and a coat of plates, a poncho-like garment lined with iron plates, which covered the trunk. The pattern of the wounds and the dispersal of the bodies suggest that these defences were inadequate; the Gotlanders suffered from heavy missile fire, chiefly crossbow quarrels, and were then overwhelmed by the Danish horse and foot. In all about 1800 were killed.

Armour greatly increased a knight's chances of staying alive in a battle and gave him an invaluable advantage over an adversary who lacked it. Technical and design improvements during the fourteenth and fifteenth centuries increased its efficiency and effectiveness to the point where it was extremely difficult to kill a fully armoured man. Scottish knights in steel plate armour at Flodden (1513) were all but invulnerable: 'They were so cased in armour the arrows did them no harm, and [they] were such large and strong men, they would not fall when four or five bills struck one of them.'[21]

By this date, armour had reached its zenith in terms of technical efficiency and the balance between protection and flexibility. This had been the objective of armourers since the early 1300s when a revolution in design had begun. Hitherto mail had predominated; the hauberk covered the trunk and arms, and stockings (chauses) the legs. On the head a mail hood (coif) was worn over a padded cap. A thirteenth-century innovation was the helm which covered the entire head. Another was the loose surcoat, worn over the hauberk and often embroidered with the owner's coat of arms. This equipment was not unduly heavy; a fourteenth-century hauberk in the Wallace Collection weighed just under twenty pounds, mail stockings fourteen pounds and a coif one and a quarter pounds.[22] The great helm added a further fourteen to sixteen pounds but would have only been put on immediately before action. In 1327, to the astonishment of the Scots for whom they were a novelty, English knights appeared on the battlefield with crests on their helms.[23] These colourful, elaborate, but impractical ornaments really belonged to the tiltyard, where they added to the pageantry, and on monuments.

Crests appeared at a time when armour was changing rapidly. The 1320s and 1330s witnessed the introduction of iron- or steel-plate defences, which by the end of the century had all but superseded mail. The helm was replaced by the conical basinet to which was attached a snouted visor and a mail mantle (aventail) which reached to the shoulders. Its inside was padded, rather like a modern motorcycle helmet, and, complete with attachments, the basinet weighed between eight and nine pounds. By the time of Agincourt, the knight was completely encased in steel plate. As the fifteenth century progressed, the defences of the shoulders and elbows of the left, or defensive, arm and the thighs were reinforced. A lighter (four to seven pounds) helmet, known as a sallet, was introduced in about 1440, together with the beaver to protect the jaw and neck.

A full suit of armour of the late fifteenth century weighed up to sixty pounds, far less than the packs carried by infantrymen in the Falklands War.[24] Chafing of the skin was prevented by the silk-lined, padded arming doublet, to which leather thongs were attached for securing the armour, and by padded hose and shoes. Every endeavour was made to secure an even distribution of weight, and visors were ventilated although this did not prevent knights from becoming short of breath. This and weariness were why the Second Earl of Douglas was overcome at Otterburn (1388) by a knight who had discarded his visor and could breathe more easily.

Men accustomed to wearing armour were not greatly impeded in their movements and those who fell from their horses could easily get up, so long as they were uninjured. Vision and breathing were restricted and in warm weather armour must have been unbearable. Nonetheless, armour was vital for the knight and he was prepared to pay a high price for it.

The best was manufactured by Milanese craftsmen who, since the thirteenth century, enjoyed a well-deserved reputation for quality. Security was expensive. On the eve of his embarkation for a campaign in France in 1441, Sir John Cressy purchased complete Milanese harnesses for himself and several for his squires. His, obviously of superior quality, cost £8 6s 8d (£8.33), while their suits were priced between £5 10s and £6 13s 4d (£5.50 and £6.67). Given that he was paid two shillings (10p) a day, Cressy's own harness represented eighty-three days' wages. When the political situation seemed threatening in 1468, the Yorkist partisan, Lord John Howard, invested £6 6s 8d (£6.33) in a complete suit of Milanese armour for his son, Nicholas, and eight pounds for another for one of his squires; each came complete with a dashing ostrich-feather plume.[25]

Such armour did not give protection against cannon fire. During fighting at Haddington in 1548 a cannonball killed 'a goodly Frenchman decked in fair harness' and a young Scottish nobleman's thigh was penetrated by a pellet from an arquebus.[26] Henry Barwick, whose career as a soldier began at this time, asserted no armour could stop a musketball, which was denied by a conservative brother-in-arms, Sir John Smythe, who insisted that Sir Philip Sidney would not have been mortally wounded by one if he had worn armour over his thighs.[27] Younger fighting men scorned the wisdom of experience, for Smythe noted with regret that by 1590 more and more captains were discarding all but breastplates and helmets.

The warhorse represented a far greater outlay than armour. Compensation for warhorses lost at Falkirk in 1298 ranged from forty pounds to £46 13s 4d (£46.67), and during the 1306 to 1307 Galloway campaign between twenty and forty pounds. Edward, Prince of Wales (the Black Prince), was prepared to pay £232 18s 4d (£232.92) for a pair for his own use.[28] Some indication of what these sums represented may be gained from the contemporary prices for livestock. Oxen and bulls were worth between seven and eight shillings (35 to 40p), cows between three and five shillings (15 to 25p), sheep between eight pence and 1s 2d (4 to 7p), and a goose threepence (1½p). Carthorses fetched between two and ten shillings (10 to 50p), depending on age and condition, and a good quality riding horse between seven and ten pounds. A warhorse costing fifty pounds was, therefore, the equivalent of five 'trotters' or two hundred cows. Taking £650 as today's market price for a cow, the modern price of a warhorse would be £130,000 and upwards. This sum may be compared with other aristocratic luxury items: the Earl of Salisbury paid eight pounds (sixteen thousand pounds in today's money) for what must have been an Iceland falcon in 1368.[29] And yet there is nothing startling about these figures given today's bloodstock prices, and the cost of the falcon is about the same as that of its modern counterpart, a classic shotgun.

Maintenance of the warhorse was expensive. It consumed at least twelve pounds of oats a day and needed constant attention; grooms working at the Black Prince's stud farm at Princes Risborough were paid twopence and fourpence (1 to 2p) a day according to experience.[30] On campaign, the sustenance of these beasts presented considerable logistical problems, especially in Scotland where grass was often sparse. Of the 550 horses that perished during the Scottish campaign of 1299 to 1300 only half were killed in action; the rest presumably perished from wounds, sickness, undernourishment, or a combination of all three. Warhorses faced starvation during operations in the summer of

1304 when urgent orders were issued for emergency rations of oats and beans to be hurried north.[31] If a horse of any kind was lost on campaign, the crown paid compensation to its owner. Fraudulent overvaluation must have inevitably occurred, which explains why warhorses belonging to knights in the Black Prince's retinue were valued before the beginning of a campaign.[32]

Training a warhorse required time and patience. First, it had to learn how to suppress its natural fearfulness and become accustomed to the bustle and clamour of battle, not least the blaring of trumpets and clarions. At the same time, the warhorse needed regular, daily exercise to develop its wind, heart capacity and overall stamina. In combat the knight faced a rush of sudden emergencies and each demanded a swift response from horse as well as rider. The warhorse had to recognise immediately commands conveyed by leads, reins, spurs and bit and react accordingly. Imparting this knowledge required perseverance and long practice, given that a horse's attention span is between ten and fifteen minutes. At the end of the process, the warhorse could be expected to change pace from a canter to a gallop, to swerve and wheel, and perform such complex manoeuvres as a feigned retreat at the nudge of a spur or a tug on a lead. These exercises survived the warhorse and today form part of the preparation of horses and riders for dressage events.[33] In addition, the warhorse had to become used to the weight of its armoured rider, a padded footcloth and armour for its head, chest and hindquarters. In 1347, John de Warenne, Earl of Surrey, left four warhorses in his will, each with a trapper decorated with his arms and armour; two were trained for battle and two for tournaments.[34]

The tournament was both the training and the proving ground of knighthood. Here the knight proved not only his horsemanship and skills with lance and sword, but his courtliness. Both were amply demonstrated by William the Marshal during a tournament held at Joigny in 1180. After the jousting, he joined in the dancing and singing, and was serenaded by a herald whose impromptu ballad ended with a refrain that asked the knight to give him a horse. William obliged by mounting his warhorse and riding at a party of knights who had just arrived. He unseated one and presented his horse to the herald.[35] A similar spirit of debonair generosity was shown by the Black Prince at a tournament at Bury St Edmunds in 1352 where he presented a warhorse called Morel de Burghersh to a minstrel who had pleased him.[36]

Like William the Marshal, the Black Prince had a reputation for chivalry to maintain and embellish. William's had been established at a time when tournaments were wild and often fatal scrimmages. A younger, landless son, he made his fortune in France by travelling from tournament to tournament where he unseated his opponents and confiscated their horses and armour as custom allowed. Once at Maine, William knocked over three opponents in a day, and in old age he boasted that he had unhorsed five hundred knights. His memory may have been a fault, but his stamina remained formidable. At the age of fifty he clambered up a ladder during the siege of Milly-sur-Thérain and, once on the battlements, overcame the constable.[37] At seventy, William led his forces into action at the battle of Lincoln (1217) and was said to have been so excited by the prospect of a fight that he almost forgot to put on his helmet.

Tournaments at this time were little more than disorderly mêlées and were outlawed by the church which wanted to restrain knightly aggression, or direct it towards, the Holy Land. In one homily a knight is visited by the ghost of his brother, fresh from Hell, who delivers a list of the torments he is enduring on account of an earthly addiction to tournaments. Monarchs were uneasy about gatherings of knights who, in between jousts, might fall to discussing political grievances. The tournament held at Dunstable in 1309 helped coalesce baronial opposition to Edward II, and three years later after the magnates used another tournament as a cover to muster their retinues in preparation for a campaign to overthrow the royal favourite, Piers de Gaveston.

And yet, in spite of clerical and royal disapproval, tournaments flourished, although like other essentially violent pastimes they were gradually neutered. Barriers (lists) were erected to separate riders and save lives and horseflesh, and the proceedings were transformed into highly ritualised entertainments. Accidents still happened; during a tournament held at Nancy in 1445 Gaston de Foix's lance snagged on his adversary's helmet, leaving him dangling in mid air. Lowered, he joked afterwards that he did not know whether he was on earth or in heaven.[38] This misadventure occurred when the theatrical element in tournaments was uppermost. The jousting was now preceded by colourful processions through the streets. In 1348 ladies of Edward III's court appeared dressed in men's clothes and 'with disgraceful lubricity displayed their bodies' at one tournament. Divine disapprobation was expressed by a succession of storms which washed out the event.[39]

By the second half of the fifteenth century, and under the influence of the Burgundian court, the English tournament had become a feature of state pageantry, often produced to celebrate an event such as a royal marriage. Nonetheless, on the eve of jousts held in London in 1467, heralds proclaimed that their purpose was the 'augmentation of martial discipline and knightly honour' for the safeguard of religion and the defence of the crown.

In reality the tournaments held by Edward IV, Henry VII and Henry VIII were contrived to enhance royal prestige through ostentatious shows which advertised the wealth of the crown and the prowess of the nobility. The marriage of Henry VII's son, Arthur, to Catherine of Aragon in 1501 was celebrated by a sumptuous tournament at Westminster. A colourful romantic charade was performed before a vast crowd who witnessed the arrival of the 'Challengers' and 'Answerers' in fantastical costumes. Leading the former was the Duke of Buckingham on a barded warhorse under a pavilion of green and white silk, embroidered with roses and with turrets and pinnacles at the corners. What followed was a visually stunning entertainment which blended romance and ritual. Aficionados were disappointed with the poor quality of the jousting which hardly merited the prizes distributed at the end of play.[40]

IV

In war, as in a tournament, the knight fought for more than personal reputation and honour. However much the chivalric purists regretted the fact, war was also undertaken for personal profit. 'Now honour lies in stealing cattle, sheep and oxen, or pillaging of churches and travellers. Oh, shame upon the knight who drives off sheep, robs churches and travellers, and then appears before a lady,' lamented an early thirteenth-century troubadour.[41] The decay of knighthood continued. In his preface to the *Ordre of Chivalry* (1484) William Caxton complained about knights who preferred to 'go to the baths and play at dice' rather than indulge in manly chivalric exercises. Few, he believed, had ever broken in a horse or had armour ready for use.

This was true enough. Over the preceding three hundred years war had become the preserve of a body of professionals, knights for whom it was a major source of income. This state of affairs had come about gradually and, in large part, as a response to the equally slow erosion of feudal military obligation. Of the eighty-seven knights present at Caerlaverock in 1300, twenty-three were paid for their service and the rest were either members of the royal household or men responding to the traditional feudal summons. Raising knights for forty days of unpaid obligatory service had always been a difficult business and a frequent source of contention between the crown and landowners. Compromises had been arranged with quotas and rewards being introduced to reduce a burden that many found intolerable and attempted to evade. At the same time, the crown exerted pressure on backsliders by compelling those with the appropriate income to accept knighthood and with it the duty to own the necessary armour and warhorse. Substitutes had always been acceptable from those, such as the infirm, widows and churchmen, who were physically incapable of rendering the appropriate service.

The system was stretched to breaking-point by the large-scale wars of Edward I. The feudal summons issued in 1294 after Philip IV had confiscated Gascony met with passive but effective resistance. Edward, his son and grandson relied increasingly on raising armies by contracts, which suited the nobility who profited from wages and allowances. The English armies that fought the first phase of the Hundred Years' War and defended the northern frontier were all raised by contracts between the crown and individual captains. These were noblemen and knights who acted as middlemen. They signed indentures by which they guaranteed to deliver a fixed number of soldiers, all properly equipped, for a fixed period, usually three, six or twelve months. In return, the costs of their transport and wages were paid from the crown's revenues. At the onset of the French Wars in 1337, the rates of pay were 6s 8d (33p) a day for an earl, four shillings (20p) for a knight, two shillings (10p) for a squire, one shilling (5p) for a mounted man-at-arms or hobelar, sixpence (2½p) for a mounted archer, threepence (1½p) for a foot archer and twopence (1p) for a spearman.

These professional forces were often drawn from the existing retinues of the nobility, which consisted of knights and esquires who were bound to an individual peer. One example may serve for many others. In 1319, Sir William Latimer bound himself for life to Thomas, Earl of Lancaster, in return for a substantial annual fee. The agreement required Latimer to undertake military service in Scotland, Ireland or Wales and against all men save the king. Once he joined Lancaster on campaign, Latimer was promised armour, a warhorse and one thousand pounds in wages. This sum covered his own pay and that of the forty men, including a dozen knights, whom he had pledged to bring with him.[42]

Lancaster was an exceptionally rich magnate and through his network of retainers could muster as many as two hundred knights who, in turn, would mobilise their own kinsmen, servants, retainers and tenants. His retinue and those of his fellow peers could be mobilised in a public emergency to provide the crown with a field army or castle garrisons. Faced with growing civil disturbance in the summer of 1549, Edward VI ordered Sir John Talbot 'to put yourself in order with such numbers of men both on horseback and on foot as you shall be able to make of your friends, favourers, tenants and others . . . harnessed and weaponed'.[43] Those who did their loyal duty had their expenses reimbursed. After the 1459 campaign against Richard, Duke of York, Henry VI compensated his followers for their own and their retainers' wages.[44]

Private retinues were a common source of public mischief. They could be called up to promote private quarrels, and they provided the nobility with the forces to defy and, at times, wage war against the crown. Not all retainers would countenance treason. Sir William Skipwith refused to join Richard, Duke of York, on his march to St Albans in 1455 and afterwards lost his annuity and suffered some rough handling from the duke's followers.[45] Henry Vernon ignored repeated summonses to help George, Duke of Clarence, and Warwick the kingmaker during the crisis of 1470 to 1471. In the final request, Warwick added in his own hand: 'Henry, I pray you fail not now as ever I may do for you.'[46] Promises of future favour from the earl did not persuade Vernon; he recognised a lost cause when he saw one. Retainers did not relinquish their political judgement the moment they became engaged to a lord.

Although essentially a military arrangement, the system of private retaining was also a form of social cement in peacetime. Considerable numbers of knights, esquires and gentlemen, who were the backbone of local government, were bound to lords who, in turn, formed the core of royal councils. Retaining, therefore, reinforced royal government throughout the kingdom. In Scotland a similar system obtained, known as 'manrent'. It involved a binding agreement between a nobleman and his retainer in which protection was exchanged for armed assistance and advice. Sometimes a bond was made for a specific purpose. In 1545, Hugh, Master of Eglinton, and others agreed with James, Earl of Arran, to work and, if necessary, fight together to prevent the marriage of Mary, Queen of Scots, to a foreigner. Those who rendered manrent would, if required, serve their lord with a body of their own tenants, servants and kinsmen.

Private and official indentures contained clauses that specified the exact division of the spoils of war: plunder and ransoms. The theft of the enemy's goods, produce and livestock was considered a legitimate act of war, for it hurt his economy. There was no exact line of demarcation as to whose property could lawfully be distrained, although some jurists insisted that all the possessions of noncombatants were inviolate. 'Poor labourers of the cornfields and vineyards and other poor labourers' who toiled for the general benefit deserved to be treated with pity, mercy and charity.[47]

None of these was in evidence during the 1296 invasion of Scotland. Poor folk may have been among the original owners of just under a thousand cattle and oxen seized by Sir Hugh Despenser. These beasts and two captured warhorses were sent south for sale under the protection of Sir William Beauchamp. The livestock were intercepted near Wark and driven into the castle by John Sampson and Robert le Eyr, and only released after Edward I's intervention. The thieves appropriated 166 beeves and one warhorse, valued at fifty pounds.[48]

Men regarded as knightly paragons boasted of their exploits as plunderers. In 1421, Thomas Montagu, Earl of Salisbury, joyfully informed Henry V of his profitable excursion into Maine and Anjou. 'Blessed be to God we sped right well . . . And we brought home the fairest and greatest prey of beasts, as all those said who saw them that ever they saw.'[49] A cold dispassion pervaded the reports of Thomas Howard, Earl of Surrey, who had been ordered by Henry VIII to harry the French coast in retaliation for the burning of Brighton in 1513. His forces landed near Cherbourg and marched through 'as goodly a country and as well builded for small towns and villages as I have seen'. Every house was burned, including those of local gentlemen which were 'well builded and stuffed with hangings . . . of silk'.[50] Many looters must have been deeply frustrated.

Civil wars offered the same opportunities for profit as foreign campaigns. Lords Dudley and Rivers, and Sir Thomas Stanley, commanders of the royal army that suppressed the first stage of Jack Cade's uprising in June 1450, stole cash, silverware, horses and provender from villages in north Kent.[51] They set a pattern that was repeated throughout the Wars of the Roses, which some participants treated as a licence to steal from anyone who had backed the losing side. In August 1483, Edward Redmayne, a Cornish squire, and various other partisans of Richard III descended on Cothele manor house, the home of Sir Richard Edgecumbe, and stole silver utensils, featherbeds, livestock, eggs and hops. Their accomplice was Lord Scrope, a royal councillor, who took a cut of the spoils.[52] What was otherwise a serious civil crime was no doubt justified by the knowledge that Edgecumbe had recently fled to join Henry Tudor in Brittany.

Another invaluable source of wartime revenues was the ransom of prisoners of knightly and noble rank. Quite simply, a living knight was worth more than a dead one. Of the nine hundred knights present at the Anglo-Norman victory over the French at Brémule in 1119, only three were killed. As the French collapsed, their pursuers were 'more concerned to capture than kill the fugitives' and secure their ransoms.[53]

It was not easy to capture a knight, establish his identity and agree an estimate of his value in the middle of a battle. During the last phase of the battle of Poitiers (1356), when the French king, Jean II, and his attendants were in peril of being overwhelmed by superior numbers, there was a helter-skelter rush to snatch him and the fortune his capture would bring. Those who recognised the king from his familiar coat of arms appealed to him to surrender or be killed. Sir Denis de Morbeke, a French knight in the English service, pushed his way through the throng and asked Jean to give himself up, which he did, asking, 'To whom shall I surrender? To whom? Where is my cousin the Prince of Wales?' De Morbeke promised to convey him to the prince, but this was impossible for the king was hemmed in by a dozen or so English and Gascon knights, each shouting, 'I took him.' A scrimmage followed and Jean, now separated from de Morbeke, pleaded to be taken 'in a gentlemanly way'. Luckily, the Earl of Warwick and Sir Reginald de Cobham spotted the fracas and were able to extricate the frightened king and deliver him to the Black Prince. The royal ransom was set at five hundred thousand pounds and a legal row followed as to whether de Morbeke or one of the Gascons present was entitled to a share. It appears that de Morbeke, who was dying by 1360, got nothing from what had seemed an extraordinary piece of good fortune. The capture of William de la Pole, the Earl of Suffolk, at Jargeau (1429) was a more dignified affair, marked by a chivalric punctilio. Just before yielding to his adversary, Suffolk asked his rank and, on hearing that he was a mere squire, insisted on knighting him so that he would be fit to take prisoner an earl. This chivalric charade was somehow appropriate for a knight who whiled away his days in captivity by writing melancholic love poems in French.

Raising ransoms presented considerable problems, not least the liquidising of land assets, and could take several years. Captors impatient for ready cash were willing to sell prisoners at a discount. Sir Thomas Holland delivered the Count of Eu to Edward III for twelve thousand pounds, while Sir Ralph Hastings, who died from wounds received at Neville's Cross, bequeathed his Scottish prisoners to his nephew and a friend.[54] Not all prisoners could raise the money for their release. Thomas Cooley, a professional soldier attached to the garrison of Saint-Laurent-des-Mortiers in Anjou, was captured in the nearby countryside at a date in the 1420s. He was imprisoned at Sablé and, unable to find the ransom of nine hundred saluts (roughly £162), was placed in irons for four months. Three gentlemen agreed to stand surety for him, but after his release he was still unable to raise the money. True to his parole, he returned to Sablé, where his disappointed captors increased the amount to 1100 saluts and he was again shackled and given nothing but bread and water for fifteen days.[55]

Cooley's misadventures were a reminder that war represented a wheel of fortune the turns of which brought extremes of wealth and poverty. 'The first time I fought in battle was under the Captal de Buch at Poitiers, and by good luck I took three prisoners on that day, a knight and two squires, who brought me in three thousand francs between them . . . Sometimes I have been so thoroughly down that I hadn't even a horse to ride, and at other times fairly rich, as luck came and went.' So ran the confession of the Bascot de Mauléon, a professional soldier, whom the chivalric chronicler Jean Froissart met at supper in an inn in Orthez.

There was a way of insuring against the setbacks suffered by the Bascot. In 1421, two English squires, Nicholas Molyneux and John Winter, signed a legal document that made them brothers-in-arms. Friends for some time, they agreed to pool their resources and create a fund for their retirement. If, 'which God forbid', one suffered the calamity of capture, then the other would do all within his power to raise his ransom, so long as it did not exceed one thousand pounds. If it was higher, then the free brother promised to act as hostage for up to nine months to allow the other to find the money. As for their yet-to-be acquired fortunes, these were to be shared and delivered to a coffer in the London church of St Thomas Acon. Irrespective of individual contributions, the total would be divided equally between them once they had retired. On the death of one, the survivor would take all save a sixth which would be deducted to support the dead man's widow and a rent of twenty pounds a year to 'nourish' and educate his children.[56]

What amounted to a comprehensive insurance against the hazards of war was a popular arrangement among men for whom the battlefield was also a goldmine. Among the most successful was an East Anglian knight of moderate means, Sir John Fastolf, whose military career spanned twenty-seven years, all spent in France. Before and after his retirement in 1439, Fastolf made careful arrangements with Italian financiers and English merchants for the investment of his profits. They were impressive: he spent nearly fourteen thousand pounds on land and property in England where, in 1445, his annual rent-roll totalled just over a thousand pounds. He also possessed capital in the shape of plate and jewellery, including a diamond known as the 'White Rose' which had been given him in settlement of a debt of £2666 13s 4d (£2666.67) by Richard, Duke of York.[57] Like many another successful soldier-businessman, Fastolf built himself an appropriately impressive home, Caister castle, a few miles along the coast from Yarmouth.

A hundred years afterwards, local country people told the antiquary John Leland that the castles of Farleigh Hungerford, Ampthill and Sudeley had been funded solely by the French wars of the last century. Certainly their builders, the Hungerfords, Cornwalls and Botelers, had been prominent captains. Whether or not these structures owed their existence to cash brought back from France, it is significant that later generations believed that they did. In the popular imagination, overseas wars had become identified with the creation of private fortunes. The tradition was kept alive during and after the maritime war against Spain. In 1628 a pamphlet urged the youth of a 'Dull and Effeminate Age' to follow Drake's 'noble steps for Gold and Silver'.

V

Like his medieval predecessor, the Renaissance soldier believed that honour and profit were not incompatible, and accumulated both. When the twenty-six-year-old Henry Manners, Earl of Rutland, took command of the royal army in Scotland in 1549, Sir James Croft congratulated him in terms that would have been understood by any knight present at Caerlaverock: 'I hear you are come to the Borders to win honour.'[58] But something more than pure reputation was at stake when a young gentleman took up arms. He was also a commander responsible for his men. Writing at the end of that century, a veteran officer, Sir Roger Williams, emphasised the importance of leadership. 'A multitude without experimented [i.e. tested] leaders, that have [been] to war with expert captains, are to be compared unto a navy in a tempest without masters or pilots.'[59]

Leadership in war came most easily to those who exercised it in civil society. Official instructions, issued in 1586 for the training of the shire levies, specified that they should be commanded by 'ensigns and captains well affected to her Majesty and the state, the eldest sons of the chief gentlemen or of others of like station'. A man accustomed to showing deference to the squire would find no difficulty in taking orders from him or his son. What mattered most was that the officer possessed a natural authority, rather than any experience or technical skill. 'Others more skilful in martial service might be appointed as lieutenants and under-officers.'[60] Birth might qualify a gentleman for command in war, but not all were sufficiently robust. During the great Armada muster at Tilbury in 1588, it was wryly observed 'that those rich men, which have been daintily fed, and warmly lodged, when they came thither to lie abroad in the fields were worse able to endure than any others'.[61]

As well as roughing it, the captain was expected to perform mundane supervisory duties and, above all, to enforce discipline. If he was in any doubt as to how to fulfil his responsibilities, plenty of textbooks became available in the 1590s, all aimed at the young gentlemen taking up commands in France, the Netherlands and Ireland. The ideal captain was 'circumspect, skilful, and expert in the noble art of martial affairs, also hardy and valiant of courage, liberal in rewarding' and vigorous in the suppression of 'drunkenness, common swearing, quarreling [and] defrauding' among his men.[62]

Below the captain was the ensign whose task it was to 'comfort, animate and encourage' the company in battle, where he was always to be alert to the advantages of the ground. If he knew his business, he would have spied out the land beforehand, taking note of potentially useful hedges, banks and hillocks. The sergeant taught the men how to march and handle their weapons, and kept an ear open for 'any mutinous and rebellious words'. A corporal, chosen for his aptitude, helped with training and checked equipment.

Generals kindled the spirits of their soldiers. Before an engagement, the general was expected to deliver a speech to his army. Without his oratory '. . . a whole army is ruined, for his speaking takes away fear, encourages the minds, increases the obstinacy to fight, discovers the deceits, promises rewards, shows the perils threatening, filling with hope, praise, shame'.[63] One is reminded of Shakespeare's Henry V before Harfleur and Agincourt. The reality was more prosaic; in an engagement with a larger force of Irish in the early 1570s, Colonel Edward Randall called on his troops 'to try their valour in that parcel of ground of some advantage, and to show themselves the men they professed to be'. Brave words were no compensation for faulty tactical judgement, for Randall led a charge of horse before letting his infantry fire their arquebuses and lost the fight.[64]

Tactics were also the concern of a general. He was to ride about the battlefield, giving praise to the brave, cajoling the 'fearful' and reassuring 'those that be doubtful and slow'. At the same time, he had to comprehend the overall position and, when necessary, shift men from one place to another and anticipate the moves of his adversary.[65] Although this advice was written in 1590 it describes well enough the conduct of previous commanders. When the infantry at Dupplin Moor (1332) were in danger of being thrown back by a Scottish schiltrom, Lord Stafford shouted out: 'You English! turn your shoulders instead of your breasts to the pikes.'[66] They did and the Scots were repulsed.

On campaign pitched battles were rare, skirmishes between small detachments less so. Inactivity was commonest and provided one of the greatest tests for an officer whose prime duty was to remind bored and sometimes reluctant men of their duty and to see that they were properly fed and equipped. Some managed well. Recommending George Bowes for special favour in 1549, Lord Rutland praised the young man's company who were 'well horsed and well armed' and, thanks to their captain's professionalism, tightly disciplined and reliable. Others shirked their responsibilities. Rutland regretted that his command also contained 'sundry captains, especially such as inhabit Northumberland, [who] neither attend their charges nor have their full numbers; but rather seeking to enrich themselves, lie at their houses, so that when the time of service comes, they either come not at all or bring small numbers of men and those so inexpert and unable that they will not abide in the field or show themselves before the enemy, but fly away to their houses.'[67] A muster of forces in the Netherlands in 1592 revealed that twenty out of forty-two captains were absent from their companies.[68]

As well as the negligent there were the crooked. In 1597, Sir Thomas Baskerville was accused of deducting a groat (2p) from his soldiers' weekly pay on the pretence that it was an insurance against future sickness. Other rackets included filling up numbers with foreign recruits and dishonesty over the supply of clothing and victuals. Traditional methods of wartime enrichment survived. Sir Oliver Lambert, a career officer who 'attained the height of fortune whereat all his hopes aimed' when he was appointed governor of Connaught, fleeced his troops and the local population. He boasted in 1600 that it was 'his resolution to live eternally by spoil'.[69] Sir John Falstaffs and Ancient Pistols were found wherever Elizabeth I's armies campaigned and would have been immediately recognisable to theatregoers.

The old chivalric virtues survived. Proven courage, experience and length of service were the qualities by which Robert Devereux, Second Earl of Essex, judged a captain's suitability for advancement. The phrases 'a very gallant sober captain' and 'a young gentleman, but a captain . . . brought up in the wars' were used by Lord Mountjoy to describe officers he recommended for promotion.[70] In his discussion of the soldierly virtues, Sir Roger Williams argued that 'men of war ought to be more open-handed, more liberal and more affable, than any other profession, although their secrets ought to be but unto few, their hearts must be open to the multitude.'[71]

A soldierly bearing and professional diligence mattered, but birth mattered more when it came to leadership in battle. Chivalry bequeathed to future generations the principle that men of gentle birth and upbringing were natural, and therefore the best, leaders in war. When one of the two gallants in Farquhar's The Beaux's Stratagem (1707) contemplates a military life as an escape from penury, he calls it 'Knight-Errantry' and predicts that he and his companion 'may die as we liv'd in a Blaze'. It is the same careless spirit that animates the young gentleman soldier in Jacques's famous survey of a man's life in As You Like It:

> Full of strange oaths, sudden, and quick in quarrel,
> Seeking the bubble reputation
> Even in the cannon's mouth.

Put another way, such recklessness inspired others. A gentleman commanded because, like the knight, he had cultivated fearlessness, which was a vital ingredient of that quality that distinguished him from the rest of the world: personal honour. It was a virtue that revealed itself at moments of peril. 'The danger grows more worthy of our swords,' shouts the eponymous hero of Sir John Suckling's play Brennoralt (1646) when his men's position is about to be overrun. These words might easily have been uttered at Caerlaverock.

It was not just that the Renaissance gentleman had learned how to ride and had mastered the difficult skills of swordsmanship. Or that he was accustomed to giving orders and expected respect and obedience. Or, and this concept had its roots in feudal society, that he had been taught to feel a moral duty towards his inferiors. Honour gave him the ultimate right to command. Bravery and cowardice were contagious. Men who did not comprehend the niceties of honour were more prepared to risk their lives when they saw those who did hazarding theirs. Moreover, a gentleman was obliged to defend his honour with force, hence the duel which was a public test of his courage in the face of death. All the virtues prized by the medieval knight were cherished by his successor, the gentleman officer.

Early modern British society was hierarchical but fluid. A man acquired the public status of gentleman when he secured that symbol of knighthood, a coat of arms. In Elizabethan England and afterwards, they were freely available to anyone who would pay the heralds' fees and convince them that they lived either by their intelligence, if they were lawyers, or had acquired land, if they were former merchants or, for that matter, a playwright property-owner like Shakespeare. Ancestry was secondary to wealth, but once a family acquired gentle rank, they and their descendants endeavoured to live according to the social and moral code attaching to their standing.

It defined gentlemen as best fitted to command at war on land and at sea and prescribed how they should behave in danger. In essence, this principle had a pedigree that extended back through the chivalric era to the Dark Ages. It would hold sway throughout Europe during the seventeenth and eighteenth centuries until it was challenged by the egalitarianism of the French Revolution. In Britain it persisted and was cultivated in the nineteenth century by the reformed public schools which encouraged their pupils to think of themselves as gentlemen (whatever their fathers had been) and, therefore, leaders. Newbolt's public school subaltern rallying the ranks in *Vitaï Lampada* is the direct descendant of the warriors who laughed at death at Maldon, or Shakespeare's young tyro proving his honour in the cannon's mouth. He was close in temper to Lord Cardigan leading his horsemen into the Valley of Death without pausing either to question his orders or look back and see whether his men were behind him. The ideal of which they were all glowing examples endured until the First World War when the high command was convinced that working-class veterans would follow an unblooded eighteen-year-old Etonian into no-man's-land rather than one of their own kind with battle experience. Chivalry had given birth to an idea that became implanted in the national consciousness and, despite its apparent irrationality, it worked well in practice.

3

The small folk: Infantrymen and Technology

In 1306, Edward I commanded Aylmer de Valence, Earl of Pembroke, to 'burn, slay and raise dragon' in Scotland. Backed by 'a great chivalry', he performed his duty vigorously and caught Robert the Bruce's army unawares near Methven. The Scottish knights fought hard, for they wilful were bound honour', but the 'small folk' fled, since they did not subscribe to a creed that placed reputation before survival.[1] Nor did they have sufficient armour and weaponry, or the knowledge to use them. 'Men untrained in war' who had been hurriedly levied to meet the 1319 Scottish invasion ran from the battle of Myton-on-Swale rather than face the bristling spears of the schiltrom.[2]

The 'small folk' of medieval and early modern warfare were the men and, occasionally, women who carried spears and bills, fired bows and guns, manned ships, constructed castles and siege-engines, supplied and cooked food, dug mines and tended horses. There were also clerks who lubricated the machinery of war with cash and checked that it was spent honestly. By and large, these people were anonymous figures whose activities seldom attracted the attention of the chroniclers of campaigns. Bowmen from Sir Richard Assheton's company which served at Flodden kneel behind their captain on a stained-glass panel of the early sixteenth century in Middleton church, Lancashire. Each has his name written on his longbow and the group must have formed part of a window intended both as a memorial to the battle and as a thank-offering for the deliverance of those who survived it. Not all commanders honoured the rank and file in this way; some saw them as expendable. Sir Roger Williams, reporting on the state of the wounded after fighting near Crotoy in 1592, wrote of one man: 'if he dies it makes no great matter. He was a lackey of mine which carried my headpiece.'[3]

Only in consequence of their misdeeds or shortcomings do the 'small folk' come into focus, and then briefly. There were the Essex levies, mustered at Harwich in 1315 for service at sea, who were found to be 'decrepit, ill-clad men, without bows, arrows, or any other weapons to defend themselves even if they had been physically fit'.[4] These forerunners of the draftees assembled by Sir John Falstaff were no doubt substitutes for stronger fellows with longer purses with which they had bribed the sheriff's underlings who were responsible for selecting men for service. Or there was John Rodowne, a veteran distinguished by a scar just above his wrist which had been caused by a spear thrust, who was wanted for fraud in 1549. He had 'a long visage with a brown beard, and is a broad little man' and had been swaggering around Doncaster in the Earl of Warwick's livery, to which he was not entitled.[5]

Drifting from crime to soldiering and back again was common. William Bucstones, a hobelar (light horseman) from the Carlisle garrison, undertook a spell with a Derbyshire criminal gang and, on apprehension in 1318, was ordered to expiate his misdeeds by further service in Carlisle.[6] Hobelars were then much in demand and Bucstones was of more value patrolling the frontier than hanging from a gibbet. Unlike him, the feeble Essex scarecrows were amateurs who had been forced into their shire levy by poverty, coercion, official fraud, or a combination of all three. The principle that had brought them to the Harwich quayside had remained unchanged since Anglo-Saxon times: free men were obliged to undertake military service for sixty days in a national emergency. It was much the same in Scotland where land ownership brought with it a responsibility either to serve in person or to fund a substitute for the 'common army'. In England local communities footed the overall bill for the transport and wages of the draftees; in Scotland the crown paid.

No one knew for certain the full extent of the manpower available. In 1457 the exchequer calculated that just over thirteen thousand archers could be raised from the English shires.[7] The population then stood at about two and a quarter million, and, assuming a gender and age proportion of four adult men, four adult women and three children under sixteen, there were roughly eight hundred thousand men available for service. Mobilisation would therefore have involved slightly under 2 per cent of adult males. In 1300 the total population was far higher; modern estimates range between four and a half and six million in England, and between seven hundred thousand and one million in Scotland. At full stretch and in a crisis, the English crown raised 31,000 for service in Wales in 1294 to 1295, 28,700 for the 1298 Falkirk campaign, and 32,000 for operations around Calais in 1346 to 1347.[8] A similar all-out effort in Scotland yielded a field army of between seven and ten thousand for Bannockburn. Large as these figures seem, they represented no more than 2 and 3 per cent respectively of those qualified by age to serve.

Several factors inhibited the size of armies. Unfree men were technically debarred from service and, in any case, landowners would have not welcomed the loss of bondsmen who might have been tempted to use military service as a device to secure their liberty. Cash, logistics and administrative capacity also imposed limits on the numbers of men who could be levied. Furthermore, a country that depended on labour-intensive agriculture could not afford to deplete the workforce, especially during the ploughing, sowing and harvest seasons.

Major demographic changes during the fourteenth and early fifteenth centuries severely reduced the available manpower. Famines in 1315, 1316 and 1319 and attendant epidemics halted the growth of the population, which fell rapidly after the bubonic plague pandemic of 1348 to 1349 and the dearths of 1349 and 1350. The poll tax return of 1376 suggests that England's population had fallen to 2.5 million. Losses on a similar scale must have occurred in Scotland and Ireland, and recovery was sluggish everywhere. Only in the second quarter of the sixteenth century were there signs of an upsurge in population. The gradual disappearance of serfdom during this period did, however, raise the numbers of men theoretically qualified to serve in the county levies. It has been calculated that 183,000 fell within this category by 1575, but the local and national authorities could only afford to train, arm and clothe 12,000 and to equip a further 63,000.[9]

In deciding this and subsequent allocations of men and resources, home defence took priority over foreign commitments. An exceptional crisis – the approach of the Spanish Armada in 1588 – provoked an exceptional response. Plans were made to mobilise 140,000 men and concentrate them at various muster points along the south-western, southern and eastern coasts.[10] During the 1590s between two and nine thousand men were shipped annually for duty in Ireland, the Netherlands and northern France, and for expeditions to Cadiz and the Azores.[11] Ireland's security always took precedence; in 1600 there were fourteen thousand men deployed there, and in the next year the threat of a Spanish landing compelled the government to send 12,620 reinforcements.[12] This represented a tremendous exertion by a government that was perilously close to exhausting its manpower, credit and taxpayers' patience. In order to relieve the burden on 'the meaner sort', noblemen were asked in 1601 to raise and equip cavalry at their own expense.[13]

Successive acts had been passed by the English and Irish parliaments that specified when and how county levies were to be raised, the nature of the men's equipment and who was to foot the bill. This legislation was widely ignored. A survey of the men qualified to serve in the hundred of Ewelme, taken towards the end of the fifteenth century, revealed that a third lacked the prescribed armour and weapons. 'Good archers' were plentiful, but some lacked bows and a third of those arrayed owned no armour or weapons whatsoever.[14] Similar shortages were revealed by Scottish 'waponschewings' (weapon showings) in which men liable for armed service presented themselves and their arms for inspection. Only a handful of those who turned up to a waponschewing held by the baillie of Cunninghame, in Ayrshire, in 1532 were armed.[15] No small laird or tenant farmer would waste money on weapons and armour just to provide ill-paid, obligatory and irksome military service. Faced with widespread indifference, the Scottish government abandoned waponschewings in 1599 and chose instead to depend on men directly raised by the nobility from among their circle of clients and tenants.

In England the structure and organisation of the county levies were radically changed in the 1570s to transform them into the backbone of a national army. Modernisation was enforced on Elizabeth's councillors by external and internal threats. On the one hand, there was the worrying possibility of a confrontation with Spain in the near future, and on the other there was the more urgent problem of subversion by English Catholics whom the pope had absolved from their oath of allegiance in 1570. Henceforward, all recusants (Catholics) were treated with understandable if misplaced suspicion; they were excluded from military command in the new militias and, in 1596, those who possessed armouries had them confiscated.

The Elizabethan reforms created a core of twelve thousand part-time soldiers, selected from the county levies, who were given training, armour and weapons and placed under officers drawn from the local gentry who were chosen on account of their devotion to the crown and the Church of England. These trained bands were supported by a reserve of sixty-three thousand men, who were supplied with equipment but not instruction, and three thousand cavalrymen. Overall command was in the hands of the lords-lieutenant of individual shires who were selected for their local standing and loyalty. Equipment was stored locally, like the various pieces of armour that still remain in a room above the porch at Mendlesham church in Suffolk. This collection, probably assembled in the early seventeenth century, includes items that dated back over a hundred years.

The system was primarily devised for domestic security and, where possible, the trained bands were not deployed abroad. The result was that many of those who went on foreign service were instructed as they marched. This improvisation did not always work; in 1592 an officer at the siege of Rochefort complained that the 'most part' of his 1500 men 'cannot tell how to use their weapons' and were no match for professional Spanish troops.[16] Such inadequacies were compensated for by the adventurous spirit of some of the soldiers drafted abroad. A veteran commander, Sir John Smythe, praised the rank and file of the forces he had served alongside in the Netherlands, who were 'young gentlemen, yeomen, and yeomen's sons and artificers of the braver sort; such as did disdain to pilfer and steal, but went as voluntary to serve of a gaiety and jollity of mind, all of which people are the force and flower of a kingdom'.[17]

Traditional obligatory service was never attractive, not least because it disrupted men's lives and reduced their income. Evasion had always been commonplace and was connived at by venal officials who profited from various rackets. Sir Walter de Threekingham, one of the arrayers for hobelars and archers for the 1336 Scottish expedition, extorted a total of 18s 2d (91p) from various villages in south-west Lincolnshire, claiming the money was needed for wages. Bribes for rejecting men were even more lucrative: the villagers of Burton Coggles paid Threekingham 3s 4d (17p) in return for not having to provide a hobelar, and the burghers of Grantham £1 6s 8d (£1.33) in lieu of two archers. Subordinates copied the bad example of their betters. Exemption from supplying two hobelars cost the peasants of Bassingham 13s 4d (67p) which went into the purse of the village constable.[18] Some just ignored the crown's summons to arms. In 1297, Adam de Orton refused to join the forces being hurriedly raised by Adam de Grisedale to resist Sir William Wallace's incursions into Cumberland. Enraged by this lack of local patriotism, de Grisedale drew his sword and killed de Orton with a stroke 'slantwise' across his head.[19]

Desertion was a cheaper and, therefore, more popular alternative to purchasing one's way out of military obligation. In the autumn of 1299, Edward I ordered levies of 22,000 to be assembled for the forthcoming invasion of Scotland, with over half to be recruited in Yorkshire, Lancashire and Durham. The response was disappointing; there were reports of draftees bribing officials and mass desertions. Exasperated, Edward instructed the sheriffs of Yorkshire and Lancashire to arrest and imprison anyone who refused to march north.[20] Locking up draft-dodgers did not solve the manpower problem, but it did assuage the royal rage.

Despite all the practical difficulties involved, the shire levies remained a useful standby for the crown and were frequently used during the Wars of the Roses. During this time, and no doubt with an eye to gaining future royal favours, the cities and boroughs were particularly accommodating. The prosperous weaving city of Coventry sent twenty infantrymen and forty cavalrymen to join Edward IV's army in 1471 at a cost of £13 18s 4d (£13.92) which was raised from a local rate assessed at between twopence (1p) and five shillings (25p) per citizen. Guns were also purchased to defend the city and gunners hired to man them.[21] Uniforms were often provided for the civic contingents; the men from Beverley sent to the Scottish border in 1449 in response to an invasion scare wore white woollen jackets with the traditional red cross of St George and marched behind a banner of blue with streamers of blue and white silk.[22]

II

However well equipped and dressed, drafts of this kind were never a substitute for professional soldiers. These formed the bulk of the contract armies that served in France and elsewhere during the fourteenth and fifteenth centuries. Men were frequently raised on the estates of the commanders; the Black Prince trawled his extensive estates in North Wales and Cheshire for bowmen, instructing his officials to select only the best. Those chosen wore the prince's white and green livery and, wherever possible, were mounted. From among the ranks of such men emerged the first career soldiers, men of often lowly birth who showed outstanding abilities which earned them commands. A Welshman and the son of a bailiff, Matthew Goch, or Gough, rose to secure the captaincies of several French town in the 1420s and 1430s and a reputation for courage among his countrymen. One bard described him as 'An Arthur facing the armies of France' in verses that celebrated his 'great dance' (i.e. raid) through Anjou and Maine.[23] War elevated other humble men; an early seventeenth-century ballad praised the successes of an Elizabethan privateer, Captain Ward, a beneficiary from the war against Spain:

> *A pirate and rover on the sea,*
> *Of late a simple fisherman*
> *In the merry town of Faversham,*
> *Grows famous in the world now every day.*[24]

Wales was a region with strong martial traditions and, like the frontier county of Cheshire, possessed a surplus of young men willing to make their fortunes in war. It was the same in northern England where raid and counter-raid were part of the local way of life, and where a man's survival and part of his income depended on a knowledge of arms. Two hundred borderers were hired by Cardinal Kempe, the Archbishop of York, from 'Tyndale and Hexhamshire and parts towards Scotland' in 1441 to overawe the townsfolk of Ripon with whom he was at loggerheads. All these troops were mounted and wore full plate armour. As the cardinal intended, they made a nuisance of themselves for, as well as taking his wages, they pilfered and uttered 'words of great scorn, rebuke and provoking' to their hosts.[25]

The Irish counterparts of these border horse were the gallowglasses, originally mercenaries from the west of Scotland and the Isles who offered their swords to Gaelic chieftains during the fourteenth and fifteenth centuries. To judge from carvings of them on a tomb in Roscommon abbey, they were well armed and armoured with mail hauberks and helmets. And, importantly for men who lived by their swords, they were robust; a sixteenth-century author described the gallowglass as 'by nature, grim of countenance, tall of stature, big of limb, burl of body, well and strongly timbered, chiefly feeding on beef, pork and butter'.[26] Less physically impressive, but still useful in inter-clan warfare was the kern, a light infantryman who was the direct descendant of the young warriors who had joined the fianna (war bands) of the early Middle Ages. The kern had a reputation for rapaciousness and cruelty, which explains why four hundred were imported for service against Scotland in 1544. The English general, Edward Seymour, Earl of Hertford, told Henry VIII that the kerns were unruly, stubborn and poorly equipped. But they warmed to their work and frightened the Scots by their habit of killing rather than ransoming their prisoners, which ran against 'the custom of the Border'.[27] The kerns were natural mercenaries; in 1599 between forty and fifty of them were employed by Sir Samuel Bagenall who used them to spread terror in the countryside around Newry where they looted, burned down houses and murdered men, women and children.[28]

Such men were criminals by instinct and soldiers by profession. Shortfalls in volunteers and pressed men could always be made up by convicts lured into service by the promise of a royal pardon. Simon le Seler, who murdered a shoemaker in London in 1294, spent four years in Gascony where he proved himself a model soldier, reaching the rank of sergeant of crossbowmen.[29] Just over 1500 pardons were issued to criminals who had served during the 1333 Scottish campaign, including a band of thieves and poachers from Sherwood Forest. A 'Robin Hood' appeared on the muster list of archers who joined the Isle of Wight garrison in 1338. There is no way of knowing whether this was indeed his name or the nomme de guerre of a man who was anxious that the authorities did not know his true identity. If his name was an invention, it was highly appropriate, for the legendary Robin was already celebrated as a skilled bowman as well as an outlaw. A less romantic alternative is that this Robin Hood was the creation of a corrupt captain with a sense of humour who was pocketing the wages of an imaginary archer.[30]

Like their commanders, men like Robin Hood fought for wages and whatever they could get from plunder and ransoms. The prospect of legitimate robbery naturally drew criminals into armies bound abroad. In 1296 four soldiers, William de Ludlow, William de Lucy, John de la Rous and Henry de Brecon, 'formed a company for plundering the King's enemies in Scotland' and agreed to share their spoils equally. Greedy rogues fell out, as they did in *The Pardoner's Tale*, and de Ludlow broke faith by keeping for himself a horse worth £6 13s 4d (£6.67). Men of this type also preyed on each other; booty valued at thirty pounds stolen from Haddington by Adam de Thornhill was afterwards filched by another soldier, Nicholas de Ripon.[31]

The *chevauchées* in France offered golden opportunities for those for whom there was no boundary between brigandage and war. According to a late fourteenth-century preacher, English soldiers 'march not at the king's expense or their own, but at the expense of the churches and the poor, whom they spoil in their path'.[32] For those on the receiving end, the experience was horrific. Towards the end of 1373, two horsemen, one wearing the red cross of an English soldier on his jacket, rode into Saint-Roman-sur-Cher to steal and rape. The frightened villagers knew what to expect and fled en masse into nearby woodland. Perhaps because this fugitive existence became intolerable, or for some other reason, a few of the bolder ones crept back to their homes one night. They found and attacked three men-at-arms. One ran off, another died from his wounds and the third was taken and drowned. Resistance of this kind was exceptional; most French peasants submitted to the troops' demands, which, of course, only encouraged further exactions. A single soldier carried off two draught-horses from Airier in 1368 and returned the following day with twenty of his comrades, no doubt tempted by his report of easy pickings.[33] As a young man, Chaucer had served in France, and what he had witnessed there may have inspired the grim vision of war set down in his description of the Temple of Mars in *The Knight's Tale*:

> And there I saw the dark imaginings
> Of felony, the stratagems of kings,
> And cruel wrath that glowed an ember-red,
> The pickpurse and image of pale Dread,
> The smiler with the knife under his cloak,
> The outhouses burnt with blackened smoke.

Similar images could easily have been conjured up from the second phase of the Hundred Years' War. Again, no one bothered about the distinction between combatant and civilian. Among the 260 people kidnapped and held for ransom during raids into Anjou in 1435 was a young maiden taken by Thomas Paterson, an archer. She must have been of good family, for she was valued at over twenty pounds. The six labourers captured and ransomed by the Pontoise garrison in 1440 suggest that richer victims had either become thin on the ground or more careful about their safety.[34] There was compensation from the *appatis*, protection money levied from towns and villages on the frontier between English and French territories, and, by custom, shared among captains and their companies.

Elizabethan soldiers upheld the predatory tradition. Reporting home on the progress of the amphibious attack on Lisbon in 1589, Sir Francis Drake regretted that the lack of supplies was causing his men to 'droop'. 'But,' he added, 'if God will bless us with some little comfortable dew from heaven or some reasonable booty for our soldiers and mariners, all will take good heart again.'[35] English troops in Ulster resented orders to burn cornfields on the grounds that they were thereby simultaneously deprived of sustenance and profit.[36] Unofficial and therefore uncontrollable looting was discouraged; captains of the expeditionary force sent to the Azores in 1597 were ordered to wage war in a 'Christian manner' and hang any soldier who murdered civilians or desecrated or plundered churches and hospitals.[37] By this date, provost-marshals were attached to large armies with a remit to execute looters summarily, a threat that seems to have made little impression on the ordinary soldier or sailor.

Ransoms, loot and a cut from official or unofficial protection money were windfalls for the ordinary soldier whose basic income was his daily wage. Arrears were normal thanks to administrative delays and the common inability of the crown to find the necessary cash. Unpaid soldiers were always prepared to go to any length to get quittance, even mutiny. Crossbowmen and archers, veterans of the recent Gascon campaign, mutinied at Berwick in 1300 in protest against a four-week arrears of pay. They were encouraged and led by their captain, Sir Ralph Michiel, and threatened to kill and behead any man-at-arms who opposed them. Other commanders sympathised and the matter was only settled when the sheriff of Northumberland appeared with two hundred pounds which was immediately distributed among the mutineers.[38] When their daily ration had been reduced to one biscuit between six men, soldiers aboard a man-o'-war in 1589 mutinied and ordered a Dutch soldier to steer the ship for England. They reached Plymouth and afterwards slipped away and evaded detection and prosecution.

Desertion was a perpetual headache for commanders. Their reports convey the impression that every medieval or sixteenth-century army and fleet was in a state of permanent deliquescence. A local lad, Richard Foster, serving in the army in Northumberland in 1549, took time off to see his mother in Fleetham, took a job in nearby Newham and found time to play cards for an afternoon. Soldiering was obviously not a serious matter for him, nor was it for a comrade who spent a day gambling for 'silk points'. In an effort to set an example, three deserters (including 'a young man without a beard') were sentenced to be hanged at Newcastle. As they were about to climb the ladder, they were told that they were pardoned. Understandably, each promised to 'serve the king truly' in the future.[39] Even the prospect of enrichment could not hold some men to their duty; sailors deserted from Drake's squadron on the eve of the 1587 Spanish expedition and had to be replaced by soldiers. Drake wrote to the local magistrates in the hope that the fugitives would be punished, but it is hard to see how they could have been identified, let alone apprehended.[40] One answer to the problem of desertion and the equally vexatious one of captains falsifying their musters was for a record to be kept of each soldier's age, complexion, colour of hair and distinguishing features.[41] If this procedure was adopted, it had little success.

Discharged soldiers and sailors were a social nuisance. Large numbers congregated in Dublin in the 1590s where some took civilian jobs, others begged and a few, unable to shake off old habits, preyed on the inhabitants. Many were described as 'insolent and licentious' which may be translated as unwilling to accept the disciplines of civil society and the authority of those who enforced them.[42]

III

The fighting man was different from the civilian in so far as he was recognised to have a greater familiarity with extremes of violence and cruelty and, therefore, a greater capacity for them. The ordinary soldier knew better than most how to kill others and defend himself, skills of which he was as proud as any knight.

But the gulf between soldier and civilian was far less than it might have been or would become. Violence and bloodshed were an integral part of everyday life in medieval and early modern Britain; sights that today would be the object of revulsion were commonplace. Livestock was slaughtered and butchered publicly – manuscript and early printed calendars usually show scenes of the killing and evisceration of pigs for November. Bears, dogs and fighting cocks were pitted against each other as a form of entertainment in which the spectator witnessed slow and often agonising death. The theatre of legal retribution offered equally bloody public diversions. Convicted felons were flogged, pilloried and pelted, hanged and beheaded in front of audiences, and those found guilty of treason suffered hanging, castration, disembowelling and decapitation. The corpse was then quartered and its parts, together with the head, were displayed in public places, a practice that endured until the end of the seventeenth century. From 1401 until 1558 those who queried the doctrines of the Roman Catholic church were burned, again in public, a punishment also inflicted on wives who murdered their husbands. War itself attracted spectators. In 1548, Mary of Guise,

Regent of Scotland, and her courtiers rode from Edinburgh to Haddington to watch the siege. Their curiosity to see others die evaporated abruptly after they approached too close to the battlelines and came under artillery fire. Mary fainted, several of her entourage were wounded, and the party hurriedly withdrew.[43]

Whether or not sights of death and mutilation witnessed in civilian life prepared fighting men for what they would encounter on the battlefield or during a raid cannot be known for certain. Commonsense would suggest that large numbers, perhaps the majority, of soldiers and sailors went to war more hardened to human suffering than their modern counterparts. And yet, an Elizabethan officer noticed that his men were unnerved if bodies were left unburied on a battlefield. It was a sight that generated an 'unwillingness in the minds of soldiers to adventure their lives'.[44] And understandably so: the corpses of the slain were a harsh reminder of the inherent risks of war, and the visible presence of the dead made it harder for the living to suppress their natural fear of dying or mutilation. Moreover, the knowledge that death might not be followed by the reassurance of Christian interment added to the soldier's inner distress. Similar disquieting feelings agitated men during the First World War when they contemplated unburied bodies or parts of them in no-man's-land.

There were plenty of men who felt no qualms about inflicting violence on others. Experience or temperament made them callous and willing, sometimes enthusiastic, participants in wars, public or private. 'Slaughterladdes' was the vivid word used to describe the hardcore of Sir William Tailboys's gang of ruffians which terrorised Lincolnshire in the mid fifteenth century. A psychopath and a bully, Tailboys's career of violence and nastiness was remarkable, even for his age. He may well have been the schoolboy 'Tailboys' who 'did most foully browbeat and scold' a monk at Bardney abbey and, within a few years, he and his slaughterladdes had committed several murders and pursued vindictive feuds against his neighbours. Once, he conspired to blow up the London house of his most persistent adversary, Ralph, Lord Cromwell, with gunpowder, then a novel form of assassination. Foreign wars were the natural outlet for men of Tailboys's disposition, but none was available for him and his followers. He did, however, become an ardent and active partisan of the house of Lancaster and was summarily executed in 1464.

Tailboys died as he had lived, for when he was, as it were, run to earth in a coal-hole near Newcastle, it was discovered that he had somehow acquired a large sum of gold from the coffers of the deposed Henry VI.[45]

Men of Tailboys's stamp were more usually found in frontier districts where low-level war was endemic and there was a demand for their services. After the murder of one of his servants in Cheltenham in 1532, Sir John Huddleston identified the killers as 'light fellows out of Wales' who had been hired for the purpose by Sir John Bridges's servants. A known murderer from the Forest of Dean was among the retinue of Anthony Kingston and, in 1538, was seen riding with his master through the streets of Gloucester 'neither regarding God, nor the King, nor any man there'.[46] In 1600 the queen's justices were instructed to punish severely any 'masterless men that live by their sword and their wit' who appeared before them.[47] Such creatures treated violence as if it was a form of fun. 'Would to God the knaves and lads of the [Knaresborough] forest would come hither that we might have a fair day upon them,' shouted the border horsemen as they swaggered through Ripon in 1441.[48] In 1590, when the sheriff of Herefordshire's officers attempted to distrain the cattle of Thomas Wigmore, his servant 'Black Will' promised them that 'they should be very welcome and have good entertainment.'[49] Such provocation, issued lightheartedly in the language of a friendly invitation, has modern resonances in the pre-brawl exchanges between rival groups of 'casual' supporters before, during and after a football match.

Inevitably, since the justices of the peace and mayors were responsible for both public order and the selection of men for overseas drafts, there was a tendency to push troublemakers towards the army. Anthony Wingfield, who commanded soldiers in Flanders and Portugal in the 1580s, regretted the presence in the army of 'slovenly pressed men whom the Justices (who have always thought unworthily of any war) have sent out as the scum and dregs of their country'.[50] Heavy drinkers at home, they became worse abroad where they discovered an abundance of wine to which they were unaccustomed. A practice had been established that would endure for the next three hundred years whereby the army received a steady flow of petty criminals, alcoholics, brawlers, poachers and vagrants of whom civil society and its magistrates were glad to be rid. The armed forces could not cure delinquency, but they could find a use for those who had hitherto vexed society. Needless to say, the margins of society did not yield fit, healthy and willing fighting men. 'Rogues and vagabonds raked together in the streets and kennels of London' compared military service to the gallows. A draft of such creatures shipped from Gravesend to Ireland in 1601 contained only one in ten who could fire a gun and, on disembarkation, a thousand were found to be too sickly for the front line.[51]

However much ministers and captains deplored the presence of the idle, feckless, immoral and infirm in the forces, they had little choice but to accept them. Numbers mattered, for sixteenth-century England faced adversaries (France and Spain) with far larger populations and, therefore, the capacity to field bigger armies. To correct this imbalance, English patriots reassured themselves with racial comparisons from which their countrymen emerged favourably. On stage, Henry V boasted that one Englishman was worth three Frenchmen, and in his military textbooks Sir Roger Williams repeated the calculus with reference to Spaniards. Paradoxically, England was sending its vagrants and cutpurses to the wars at the same time as investing them with superior physical and moral qualities.

IV

During this period the balance of power on the battlefield swung towards the 'small folk'. The landmarks were clear enough: in 1302 French mounted knights were overcome by Flemish spearmen at Coutrai; twelve years later Scottish schiltroms did the same to English cavalry; in 1333 it was the turn of the Scottish knights to be beaten at Halidon Hill, this time by English bowmen; and these did the same to a far larger force of French heavy cavalry at Crécy in 1346. Together, these battles amounted to a revolution in warfare, although admittedly the mounted troops had been badly deployed on each occasion. Nevertheless, the supremacy of the armoured knight had passed. Its end and the reason for it are graphically shown on a misericord of about 1380 in the choir stalls of Lincoln cathedral: a dying knight slumps over his horse, an arrow jutting out from between the joints of his backplate. The piece symbolises, appropriately, the Fall of Pride.

The Lincoln woodcarver was aware of the limitations of the long-bow, for the fatal arrow has not penetrated the knight's armour; it has passed through a gap. For a longbowman to have made such a shot would have been rare, for the purpose of his weapon was to provide heavy covering fire designed to create a killing zone which horses and men entered at their peril. The rate of fire was rapid and the effect must have been unnerving; at Halidon Hill the arrows were 'as thick as motes on a sunbeam', and at Shrewsbury like a 'cloud'. It was the weight of arrow fire rather than its accuracy that broke up the French cavalry formations at Crécy and Agincourt, causing what a later writer described as a 'great disordering of horses'.[52] Human casualties may not have been large, at least among those who were armoured. 'Love shoots with a crossbow not a longbow,' wrote Guillaume le Clerc. 'Love makes his bolt pass directly where he wishes: armour is useless against it.'[53]

Proficiency with both weapons required training and, in the case of the longbow, considerable physical strength, for it was just over six feet in length and had a powerful draw. Mastery of the longbow required constant practice, which was why the English and Scottish parliaments regularly passed laws to encourage archery. They were not heeded; in 1513 English archers were unable to bend bows from a consignment delivered for use in the forthcoming French expedition. At the end of the century, when the longbow was passing into obsolescence, a commander noted that archers wilted under the rigours of campaign life to the point where they lacked the strength to fire their weapons. Conservatives disagreed and continued to extol the longbow as a proven national weapon even though, as in the rest of Europe, the standard infantry weapon was the gun.

Gunfire was first heard in Britain in 1327. The English army that marched north possessed what the Scots later called 'crakys' of war, that is cannon.[54] A contemporary manuscript illustration shows one that resembled a large, old-fashioned soda-water bottle with a large arrow protruding from its neck. This contraption marked the beginning of a far-reaching revolution in warfare.

At first, artillery supplemented the traditional siege-engines. The commonest had been the springald, a large crossbow which fired a feathered, three-foot bolt and was used to attack and defend castles. The trebuchet relied on a counterweight of between four and thirteen tons to throw a rock of between one and two hundredweight over a range of just over three hundred yards. Three of these monsters were deployed against Edinburgh castle in 1296 and hurled fifty missiles a day. Trebuchets were cumbersome and had to be assembled at the site of a siege, or built from scratch. Construction was time-consuming, labour-intensive and expensive; two trebuchets specially built for the siege of Berwick in 1333 at Cowick in Yorkshire required forty oaks, and thirty-seven stonemasons were employed cutting and shaping the missiles. These engines, presumably in parts, and their stones were carried to Berwick in three ships.[55]

Within sixty years, artillery had replaced engines as the principle weapon of siege warfare. Field artillery, that is wheeled cannon or smaller pieces carried in carts, was increasingly deployed in the mid fifteenth century. At the battle of Castillon in 1453 an English army largely made up of bowmen was destroyed by the fire from French cannon which had been laid in previously prepared positions. English commanders were quick to adopt French tactics. In 1457 the government ordered twenty-six cannon 'for the field', and a further three the following year in preparation for a confrontation with Richard, Duke of York.[56] Henry VI's arsenal was also augmented by two dozen 'rebawdekins' or 'great carriages of war', proto-armoured cars which were carts mounted with small calibre guns. Neither they nor the conventional field artillery proved war-winners. At the battle of Northampton in 1460, the royal cannon were deployed in the French manner in trenches, but were rendered useless by heavy rains and the flooding of the nearby Nene. Thereafter, Lancastrian and Yorkist commanders stuck to traditional tactics, although field artillery was used more effectively by Edward IV at the engagement near Empingham in 1470 where its fire utterly unnerved a large body of Lincolnshire peasants who fled without striking a blow. As late as 1544, guns still had the power to scare those unacquainted with them; Scottish borderers were reported to 'love no guns nor will abide within the hearing of them'.[57] Within a generation they had learned to live with these novelties and long-barrelled pistols, known as petronels, were a standard weapon for Border horsemen.

During the sixteenth century the size and weight of a country's artillery became the yardstick by which its power was measured, just as the accumulation of atomic warheads and missiles defined international status at the end of the twentieth century. A loose-tongued peddler who claimed in 1512 that James IV's growing stock of cannon was so formidable that he would have no difficulty marching to London was locked up by the Hereford authorities as a scaremonger.[58] He was also disparaging Henry VIII who was doing all within his power to outstrip his rival's arsenal. In what was an early arms race, cannon were imported and new gun foundries in Sussex, London and Sheffield received royal encouragement.

Some of the cannon made in these foundries were destined for warships. On the continent radical changes in naval architecture during the last quarter of the fifteenth century had produced a new type of man-o'-war. It had evolved first in Portugal and Spain and enabled navigators from those nations to undertake voyages of exploration across the Atlantic and into the Indian Ocean. These armed reconnaissances and the overseas conquests that soon followed were a direct consequence of the new breed of warships. Their increased spread of canvas and enlarged holds for cargoes and stores extended their sailing range, and their hulls provided stable platforms for wheeled cannon which could fire broadsides. Naval warfare underwent a revolution. Hitherto, opposing ships had exchanged missiles launched from springalds and bows, closed, grappled and boarded. Now they could stand off and fire long-range broadsides that could pulverise masts, rigging and hulls. During the engagement with Spanish galleons off Gravelines in 1588, gunfire sank the *Maria Juan* and so damaged the *San Fepine* and *San Mate* that both were abandoned.

From 1500 onwards, the northern powers – France, England, Scotland and Denmark – began a programme of naval rearmament, building warships of up to 1500 tons. James IV was quick off the mark with vessels primarily designed to visit retribution on the 'castles' and oared pirate-galleys of the troublesome backwoodsmen who lived on the Western Isles and the lochsides of western Scotland. His *Michael*, begun in 1506, weighed over a thousand tons and mounted fifteen, locally cast cannon.[59] Henry VIII's jealous response was the creation of a fleet that, by 1547, totalled fifteen 'great ships' and thirty-eight smaller vessels which were manned by eight thousand sailors. A new generation of warships appeared in Elizabeth I's reign with lower castles at the bow and stern and with longer gun-decks. These men-o'-war were smaller and nimbler than their Spanish opponents and their broadsides packed a hefty punch; the forty-two bronze guns of the nine-hundred ton *Revenge* disabled two larger galleons during its famous engagement with a fifteen-strong Spanish squadron off Flores in 1591.

Warships like the *Revenge* maintained the balance of seapower in England's favour in the Channel and western Atlantic. The cost had been heavy; between 1574 and 1605 the government spent £1.7 million on building new ships, hiring merchantmen as auxiliaries and paying for their equipment and the wages of their crews.[60] The effort was not sustained, for, as in earlier periods, the crown recoiled from committing resources to a permanent navy in peacetime. It was a dangerous economy for a nation in the process of extending its trade across the Atlantic, into the Mediterranean and, after 1600, into the Indian Ocean. Moreover, naval victories over Spain had convinced the venturesome that it was possible to flout her New World monopoly and plant colonies on the coasts of North America

v

The largely successive naval offensive against Spain stimulated a pugnacious patriotism which the government encouraged. In a masque written by the Earl of Essex and performed before the Queen in 1595 an actor declared:

> A land there is no other land may touch . . .
> No nation breeds a warmer blood for war.[61]

The English were a godly, and therefore, victorious race:

> O noble England fall down upon thy knee,
> And praise God with thankful heart, which still maintains thee,
> The foreign foes, that seek thy utter spoil
> Shall then through his special Grace be brought to shameful
> foil.[62]

Just what might occur if England was invaded was vividly outlined in another song:

> Our pleasant country, so fruitful and so fair
> They do intend by dreadful war to make both poor and bare:
> Our towns and our cities to rack and sack likewise;
> To kill and murder man and wife, as malice does advise;
> And to deflower virgins in our sight;
> And in the cradle cruelly the tender babe to smite.
> And God's holy truth they mean for to cast down:
> And deprive our noble Queen both of her life and crown.[63]

It cannot be known whether this nightmarish vision made the trained band volunteer or naval gunner more resolute. If he was protestant, he would have had a sense of being among a chosen elect who were defending their faith against one that was in error and an affront to God. Any doubts on this score were dealt with by the growing body of officially appointed chaplains who accompanied armies and were attached to men-o'-war. And yet it would be unwise to assume that the presence of ministers of religion greatly altered the tone of a ship or a company of soldiers or uplifted their spirits. Drake may have taken his protestantism seriously, but there is no reason to believe that his zeal influenced his crew who, like the rank-and-file soldier, came from those sections of society that usually avoided church services if they could, or attended them under pressure from above. Nevertheless, those who regularly hazarded their lives could not avoid thoughts of eternity, as the description of a sailor of the early seventeenth century suggests: 'In a tempest you shall hear him pray . . . Fear is the primest motive of his devotion; yet I am persuaded he shows more than he feels.'[64]

Patriotism inspired by state and church was not new. The Anglo-Scottish and Anglo-French wars generated propaganda from all sides which insisted that whole nations were infected with genetic moral distempers such as perfidy, boastfulness, degeneracy and irreligion. It was probably no surprise to their English opponents that in 1560 some Frenchmen fled from Leith dressed as women and by 'effeminate fashions' (whatever they may have been) captured an English scout and murdered him.[65] The Irish were particularly vilified and, as their resistance stiffened in the 1590s, dehumanised. In 1602, the lord deputy, Lord Mountjoy, likened Ireland to an 'overgrown garden that must be purged of the weeds before it can be planted with good herbs'.[66] To assist this deracination Essex ordered his men to take no prisoners.[67]

War helped define national identity, in so far as it depicted one nation as a repository of virtue and its rival as one of delinquencies. But, while he was conscious of national and later religious differences, the ordinary medieval and early modern fighting man's loyalties were to his monarch, his individual commander and often his region. His totems were the banners under which he went into battle: that of the crown, and those of his captains which were embroidered or painted with their personal emblems. At the beginning of 1460, Henry VI ordered staffs for his personal pennons and 'foxtails', the distinctive Lancastrian devices that had been used in battle by his father, Henry V.[68] The banner advertised the whereabouts of a captain, served as a rallying-point and, by the end of the sixteenth century, had become a symbol of the courage and discipline of those who fought under it. One authority insisted that any company that lost its ensign in battle should be compelled to march behind a black flag until they had redeemed their honour by capturing one from the enemy.[69] Capturing a standard was a deed to be celebrated; two Scottish banners taken at Flodden by Sir William Molineux are proudly displayed on his brass at Sefton church in Lancashire.

Flodden had been a test of endurance, a soldiers' battle in which victory had gone to those who had greater tenacity and stamina. In all likelihood, James IV had wanted nothing more than to retire into his kingdom after an unrewarding incursion across the border, but he was goaded into action by the English commander, Thomas Howard, Earl of Surrey, who provocatively suggested that because 'he was a king and a great prince, he would of his lusty and noble courage' offer battle. Chivalric impulse got the better of military judgement and the Scottish army halted. Rain and wind rendered the exchange of gun and arrow fire ineffective and the battle resolved itself into a slogging match between determined infantrymen. At one stage an English detachment flinched and, for some hours, the outcome of the battle hung in the balance. The stubbornness of the fully armoured Scottish knights enraged their adversaries to the point where lust for blood and revenge overcame greed. 'Many other Scottish prisoners could and might have been taken, but they were so vengeful and cruel in their fighting that when Englishmen had the better of them, they would not save them, though it was so that divers Scots offered great sums of money for their lives.' The English soldiers were already in a sullen humour, for their supplies of beer had run out three days before the battle.[70]

Flodden was exceptional. Wherever possible, commanders preferred to avoid such large-scale pitched battles in which chance played too great a part for the outcome ever to be certain. There were only eight major battles between English and Scottish armies between 1296 and 1346, and seven between the English and French between 1415 and 1453. It was different in civil wars where opposing factions were anxious to secure a swift settlement to their political differences and lacked the wherewithal for prolonged operations. This was why the Wars of the Roses witnessed thirteen battles within thirty-two years. Outside this conflict, the everyday experience of the ordinary soldier was garrison duty, sieges, raids, patrolling and scouring the countryside for food and fodder. Each activity offered plenty of opportunities for contact with the enemy; besieged forces made sallies into their opponents' trenches, patrols clashed and foraging parties were ambushed. Then and afterwards they were known as skirmishes; these scrimmages were the common experience of battle for most soldiers.

An English veteran with a professional eye for such arcane matters praised the quality of the three hours of skirmishing that accompanied the French withdrawal from Edinburgh to Leith in 1560. There was 'never a better and hotter skirmish on both sides, and for my part [I] never saw the like and many were taken and slain on both sides'.[71] More detailed accounts of such actions indicated improvised and often spontaneous engagements for limited tactical ends in which losses were slight. Towards the end of November 1542 a raiding party from Norham crossed the Tweed and fought two skirmishes. At Hilton, corn was burned, cattle seized and thirty-five villagers taken for ransom. Forewarned, the menfolk of Swinton barricaded themselves in the church and held off their attackers for three hours. Twelve Englishmen were badly injured, two Scots killed and sixteen captured, 'whereof the most part of them are sore hurt and six like to die'.[72] As this was the

Borders everyone was well equipped, knew how to use their weapons and was determined to avenge past injuries, to loot, or to defend their home, livestock and winter stores.

The pursuit of comfort, or whatever passed for it on campaign near Dundalk in the autumn of 1600, aroused the courage of an eighty-strong forage party in search of wood. 'Fully resolved to fight for their lodging and purchase themselves cabins and fire', they drove off Irish skirmishers sent to hinder them. The engagement lasted two hours during which a handful were wounded, including William Lovell, a gentleman, who was shot in the face 'serving very daringly'. The official report ended, revealingly, with the remark: 'No other man of note was hurt.' Several men 'of note' were killed and injured, along with twenty ordinary soldiers in a four-hour skirmish some days later. The casualty rate among officers was high: four were killed, including 'two very gallant men', and two wounded. They must have been leading from the front in the manner proper for gentlemen. A cavalry charge over rough ground decided the matter although the horsemen suffered from close-range gunfire. Sir William Godolphin 'had his horse struck under him stark dead with a blow in the forehead' which sent blood and powder spattering across its rider's face, a vivid detail seldom found even in eye-witness descriptions of battle.[73]

Frightening, bloody, close-quarter skirmishes broke the tedium of campaign life, although this does not mean they were welcome. Out of danger, the Elizabethan soldier was often 'mutinous' and 'obstinate', moods that were induced by boredom and shortages of rations and clothing.[74] He made his distress known to his officers, who sometimes reported complaints to a largely indifferent government. Like his predecessors, he was illiterate and his feelings can only be detected through the observations of his commanders. His emotions about such abstractions as country and duty remain unknown, although there may be some general truth in the description of a seaman of the early seventeenth century: 'His familiarity with death has armed him with a kind of dissolute security against any encounter.'[75] If such an optimistic quietism did represent the fighting man's mindset, it was just as well, for, in the words of one of his officers, 'martial men are not accounted of in England longer than their present occasion serves to employ them.'[76] However he performed his duties, the ordinary soldier or sailor could expect little gratitude from the government he had served. He and his sacrifices were soon forgotten.

VI

In some quarters, losses in foreign wars were welcome. According to that commonplace Renaissance conceit that compared a nation to the human body, those who were sent abroad to fight represented malignant humours which could only be expelled through bleeding or purging. War restored the country to health, argued Thomas Digges, who had served in the Netherlands as a muster-master. 'God', he declared, had prescribed 'a perfect remedy' for 'domestic inconveniences' in 'foreign war'. That model of an ideal state, Rome, had cured itself of overpopulation, food shortages, internal discord and social envy by regular wars. England, he approvingly observed, was doing likewise; the 'yearly physic' of the 1580s and 1590s, that is the annual draft of levies for service abroad, was a cathartic that, as it were, cleansed the nation of those who created mischief.[77] Digges's diagnosis and cure were adopted by James VI who rounded up two thousand men from the vexatious Graham clan from the Borders and had them forcibly deported to serve as mercenaries on the continent.[78] War had become an instrument of social policy for governments disturbed by the spread of vagrancy, petty crime and undercurrents of social tension.

The 'small folk' suffered in other ways. The passage of armies disrupted the lives of civilians who lived in their path. Often the arrival of soldiers in an area brought destruction and death, either as a direct result of strategies designed to weaken a country's economy, or from casual looting. A battle could have a calamitous effect on the surrounding countryside; in 1485 Henry VII gave 'of our charity' £51 12s 4d (£51.62) to the villagers of Atherton Wenderby, Atherton, Fenny Drayton and Mancetter for 'losses of their corn and grain' at the time of the battle of Bosworth.[79] Such generosity was unusual, possibly unique.

Suffering and loss were always worst in regions where clan warfare and cross-border raiding were common and where the distinction between the fighting man and civilian was blurred. Beyond these remote, outlying areas of Scotland, Ireland and the Anglo-Scottish border, war was an uncommon and mercifully short-lived phenomenon. In terms of damage and disruption the most wounding periods were those of the systematic harrying of northern England between 1315 and 1322 by the Scots and their incursions in the 1380s. Scotland endured similar large-scale devastation in 1356 ('the burnt Candlemas'), 1385, and during the extended coercive operations between 1542 and 1550. On each occasion, the English copied the Bruce by aiming to inflict as much economic damage as possible and, in the words of one commander, 'to keep the Scots waking'.[80]

How this was achieved on both sides of the border can be discovered from the complaints of the victims. In the wake of Robert the Bruce's depredations the manor of Tirset in Tynedale had become wasteland, its meadows unmowed and its mill dilapidated. No peasants could be found to take over vacant tenancies.[81] Elsewhere, dwindling rent-rolls gave an indication of crops unharvested or destroyed and livestock killed or carried off; particularly hurtful was the loss of seed-corn and plough oxen. The misery was made more intense by the fact that the raids coincided with a period of poor harvests, dearths and famine. In 1380, forty thousand cattle were seized around Carlisle and driven into Scotland, and landowners who wished to keep their stock and crops were forced to pay protection money.[82] Hostages were sometimes taken in lieu of cash; six from Ripon who stood surety for their town in 1319 were still in Scotland five years later, their ransoms unpaid by their ungrateful fellow citizens.[83]

Less painful but still irksome disruptions of daily life and labour came from the wartime demands of the crown. Civilian muscle and property were harnessed to the war-effort by the English state, whose officials could not be refused, although some might be bribed. In 1303, forty sawyers and carpenters were assembled at King's Lynn under Richard of Chester, Edward I's engineer, and Henry of Ryhill, a master-carpenter with orders to construct three collapsible, fortified wooden bridges to span the Forth. They spent 160 days on the project and were joined by sixteen smiths and a boy who produced the necessary ironwork. Timber, iron, nails, coal, hemp, canvas, anvils and anchors were procured by the sheriffs of Norfolk, Yorkshire and Lincolnshire, who had them conveyed by sea to Lynn. When the sections were ready, they were shipped to Berwick in thirty ships manned by 240 seamen. The voyage took twenty-eight days and the whole enterprise cost £938 9s 6d (£938.48).[84]

The raw materials for these bridges were obtained on demand. Other resources could be appropriated in the same way under the excuse of an emergency, and compensation took time and effort to secure. Sometimes it was not forthcoming at all. William of Otford, a keeper of Edward III's horses, brought thirty-four of them to Swinstead in Lincolnshire in 1339. They stayed eleven days and ate well at the villagers' expense, and only departed after William had extracted fourteen shillings (70p) and two cartloads of hay from his reluctant hosts.[85] Redress was obtained, but only after agitation in parliament which insisted on a commission of inquiry in 1341.

Such distraints were spread unevenly; Yorkshire endured thirteen demands for supplies between 1296 and 1307, the western and south-eastern counties seven. In the first decade of Edward III's reign the burden fell most heavily on East Anglia. Direct taxation was an additional drain on rural communities, although in theory those who possessed movables worth less than ten shillings (50p) were exempt. In The Song of the Husbandman of the early fourteenth century a peasant complains that he has had to surrender every fourth penny of his income to the royal war-chest, a calculation that includes a bribe to the tax collector.[86] The poorer classes were asked to contribute directly and disproportionately to the war-effort in 1376 when parliament voted a poll tax. Its extortionate successor of 1380 was widely avoided and efforts to catch the evaders triggered the Peasants' Revolt of the following year. This form of levy was revived six hundred years later with equally disastrous results.

By and large the cost of waging war was born by the mercantile and landowning classes, although there was nothing to prevent the latter from passing on the charges in higher rents and fines. The problem for governments engaged in extended operations was how much they could extract before encountering resistance inside parliament and without. After sixteen years of war taxation, Elizabeth I's councillors noted uneasily that, 'common people grow weary of impositions, and fall into disorder because the best sort murmur underhand that a good peace might be got.' Seventeen noblemen and twelve ladies were among those who had not paid their taxes in 1598, and in the same year a four-hundred-pound loan had to be 'wrung' from the Constantinople merchants and one of five hundred pounds was 'scraped' from those trading with Aleppo.[87] Sulky taxpayers were a symptom of a wider war-weariness that overtook England in the final years of Elizabeth's reign. And yet when unrest occurred, as it did in London and the midlands in the mid 1590s, popular anger was directed not against the war and its burdens, but at high rents and food prices. Both, of course, were indirect consequences of the cost of the war-effort.

There were winners as well as losers among the 'small folk'. In his observations on the conduct of war, published in 1594, Henry Barwick recalled how, fifty-six years before and then aged eighteen, he had been an ordinary soldier, earning sixpence (2½p) a day. Within twelve years he had been raised to captain with a daily wage of fourteen shillings (70p), but he discovered that experience was no substitute for birth. 'In a courteous manner', he suggested to Arthur Grey, the future Fourteenth Lord Grey of Wilton, that the younger man had imprudently sited his camp during operations near Leith in 1560. Grey's response was brusque: 'I could not be charged with these matters, it was his charge and not mine.' With some satisfaction Barwick recorded that soon afterwards the French launched a surprise attack on the vulnerable camp and Grey, caught unawares and unarmoured, was wounded by a bullet.[88]

In Barwick's time, the war at sea offered the man of humble background a better career and greater chances of enrichment than that on land. Michael Geare, a Cockney born at Limehouse in about 1565, made his way onwards and upwards in the egalitarian world of privateering where seamanship, stamina and sheer ruthlessness counted for everything. He began as an apprentice in 1584 and within seven years had undertaken four cruises, three to the Caribbean, rising in the process from apprentice to mariner and then to master. He returned to the West Indies as part-owner and commander of the *John*, of some 120 tons, which was one of a five-strong flotilla financed by, among others, Sir Walter Raleigh. Like everyone else in the privateering business, Geare was a gambler, for there was never any way of knowing whether an expedition would yield any profit. Dreams of riches and the willpower of captains like Geare held crews together during the long, hazardous passage across the Atlantic during which sailors ate poor food and drank stagnant water. When Geare retired in 1603, he had accumulated a considerable fortune. Despite a calculated carelessness in declaring the exact details of his spoils to the prize-courts and customs, Geare was knighted. He lived in Stepney, where his house was distinguished by a dagger hanging outside, and in his will he left an annual rent of five pounds to be shared among indigent sailors and the poor widows of sailors from his native Limehouse. Not all his contemporaries had flourished. Even Geare's profits were a tiny part of a great whole; between 1589 and 1591 the total value of prizes taken by English sailors was £280,000, of which ninety thousand pounds flowed into London.[89]

Most of the 'small folk' who for various reasons found themselves drawn into wars were not so fortunate. Nonetheless, their sometimes unwilling participation in medieval and sixteenth-century wars had important consequences. The English and Scottish crowns depended on their poorer subjects in emergencies and both defined an individual's status in terms of the nature of the military service he could render. In England the Elizabethan militia system created a strategic reserve, admittedly not of the highest quality, in which even the humblest musketeer or pikeman was a partner in the nation's enterprises. This was a necessity; neither the Tudors nor the Stuarts had the wherewithal to support the large standing armies of professional soldiers and technicians that were appearing on the continent. Only rarely did English and Scottish monarchs resort to the costly expedient of hiring mercenaries. Princes without permanent paid forces had to fall back on their subjects' goodwill and muscles.

Although technically at the disposal of the crown, the 'small folk' of England and Scotland who were obliged to bear arms in an emergency were, in practical terms, under the direction of the local magnates who were their officers. Military power in Britain at the beginning of the seventeenth century was devolved, which, together with representative institutions, made it difficult for English and Scottish monarchs to pursue the absolutist policies then being adopted on the continent. Nonetheless, the authority of both was sufficient to impose and maintain religious settlements that worked, in that they contained those passions that led to sectarian wars in France. Only on the periphery, in Ireland, was there an extended religious war.

PART THREE

CIVIL WARS, 1637–1800

1

Sharp sickness: The Wars of the Three Kingdoms, 1637–60

I

From the crest of Edgehill one sees a breathtaking view of a land-scape which is quintessentially English. Below and stretching towards distant uplands is the rolling plain of south Warwickshire, a patch-work counterpane of cornfields, pasture and coppices. Whether or not the tranquillity and richness of this countryside struck the soldiers who marched across it in the autumn of 1642 is not known. Many were acutely aware that their activities would inflict immeasurable suffering on a nation that had not known a major civil conflict since the end of the Wars of the Roses, over a hundred a fifty years before. A contemporary account of the battle fought in the shadow of Edgehill described England as a land that had long enjoyed 'universal and blessed peace'. Another writer predicted that it would soon share the fate of Germany, then in the closing stages of the Thirty Years' War, which had been reduced to a plague-ridden wasteland by the continual passage of the armies. So terrible had been the damage that 'it is credibly reported that a man may travel a hundred miles and not see a town.'[1] Already there were indications that similar misfortunes were in store for Britain. Scottish troops raised to defend the kirk in 1640 had indiscriminately plundered friends and enemies and, during the summer of 1642,

Parliamentarian forces had done the same as they converged on Edgehill.[2]

The Cavalier poet Sir John Suckling had witnessed the wars on the continent and knew better than most their destructiveness. And yet, unlike many contemporaries, he was not repelled by the idea of the civil war. In his play *Brennoralt*, a royal councillor, Miesla, detects virtue in such a conflict:

> *Since War the sickness of a Kingdom is,*
> *And Peace the health: but here I do conceive*
> *'Twill rather lie, whether we had not better*
> *Endure sharp sickness for a time, to enjoy*
> *A perfect strength . . .[3]*

War was a medicine, a severe physic that would purge a nation and leave it healthier and strong. The source of the distemper was an imbalance of humours. Royalists imagined this was the result of three armed challenges to the king's authority by Scottish Presbyterians, Irish Catholics and the puritan bloc in the English parliament. All wished to dilute royal authority and advance their own sectional interests. Kirk, Catholics and Parliamentarians disagreed: the malaise of the three nations had been caused by advisers who had misled the king by persuading him to adopt dangerous innovations in government and religion. Whatever their party, all agreed with Suckling's prescription that an ailing nation could only be restored to health through war, all other cures having failed. Nonetheless, many who marched towards Edgehill did so with heavy hearts.

Charles I ruled over three separate, interconnected but mutually suspicious kingdoms which comprised a comparatively weak state on the periphery of Europe. Its wealth rested on agriculture, although the new commerce in tobacco and sugar from Virginia and Barbados showed promising signs of future growth. Britain's political condition offered no grounds for optimism. The king's policies had isolated him from a large and powerful body of his English subjects, and had provoked defiance in Scotland, which was behaving as if it was an independent nation, and rebellion in Ireland.

England was by far the most settled and prosperous of Charles's kingdoms. Its people were self-confident and pugnacious, believing themselves stronger and braver than other races because of their unique personal freedom. The Roundheads imagined that this freedom was in jeopardy and would vanish if it was not defended. At the end of 1646, when it was feared that Charles I might by subterfuge reverse the verdict of a war that his armies had lost, a Parliamentary propagandist warned:

> He is made lord of all our lives and lands,
> And we our laws and liberties (which cost
> Our fathers so much English blood) have lost.[4]

II

The defence of one freedom, that of conscience, began the procession of crises that culminated in the outbreak of the Wars of the Three Kingdoms. An unwise attempt to introduce the Anglican liturgy and hierarchy into Scotland in 1637 provoked a Presbyterian revolt which effectively detached the country from Charles's control. The rallying cry of 'the faith in danger' raised twenty thousand men for the army of the National Covenant, a tenth of Scotland's adult male population.[5] These volunteers were fulfilling a Christian obligation at a time when doctrinal differences were commonly settled by the sword. During the 1679 Convenanters' uprising Sir George Campbell rebuked a party of country lads, asking them: 'What meant such lusty fellows to stay at home, when the people of God were in arms for their covenanted cause?'[6]

Two successive Scottish incursions across the border caught Charles I's government off balance, exposed its poverty and the extent of the resentment its policies had created. An attempt was made to counter Scottish religious fervour with atavistic English patriotism. The county levies, summoned to resist the invasion in 1640, were reminded of the 'ancient spleen' of the Scots:

> It much imported England's honour
> Such faithless rebels to oppose,
> And elevate Saint George's banner
> Against them as our country's foes.[7]

This appeal was unheeded; everywhere sulky and unpaid militiamen mutinied or deserted rather than fight to impose on Scotland bishops who were equally unloved in England. The hearts of the king's soldiers were not in the matter and, after some minor reverses, Charles was compelled to make an accommodation with the Scottish invaders.

In desperation the king tried to recruit an Irish army of ten thousand for a diversionary attack on the coast of western Scotland. The soldiers never materialised because the Irish parliament withheld the necessary funds. Dublin MPs were following the example set by their counterparts in Westminster who, during a three-week session in the spring of 1640, insisted that no taxes would be voted until political and religious grievances had been satisfactorily settled. A similar deadlock followed the summoning of the Long Parliament which assembled in November.

Distractions and divisions on the mainland offered the native, Catholic Irish an opportunity to overthrow a government that penalised their religion and was delivering their most productive land to protestant immigrants. It was a cause that attracted an Irish mercenary officer, Arthur MacGennis, who was in England in October 1641 recruiting men for the Spanish army. In a Chester inn, he expressed the hope that "ere long the Irish would drive the Scots out of Ireland' and his companion, another Irish professional soldier, raised a glass to the 'confusion' of all protestants.[8] The local authorities interrogated and locked them up. The incident added to the prevalent but groundless paranoia about a vast, hidden, Catholic conspiracy to seize power.

Everywhere customary allegiance to the crown was being overriden by other loyalties. An impecunious king had become the victim of a general backlash against the measures he had introduced during the eleven years in which he had governed without parliaments. His behaviour had convinced the majority of his Scottish and a substantial body of his English subjects that he could no longer be trusted as the guardian of their laws, liberties and the protestant religion. Private freedoms were endangered and the state threatened to intrude between an individual and his God. An authoritarian king was the natural accomplice of the equally domineering William Laud, the Archbishop of Canterbury, and each imagined he was God's servant. Furthermore, the meddlesome Laud was promoting a brand of Anglican ritual that was distasteful to many protestants who believed it smacked of Catholicism. Their anxieties were deep and understandable. In Europe the Catholic church had recently recovered considerable ground and there was every reason to believe that its ambitions extended to the reconversion of England and Scotland by force or subterfuge, or a mixture of both.

In today's Erastian, tolerant Britain it is hard to comprehend the intensity of seventeenth-century sectarian antipathies. For protestants, not only of the puritan persuasion, Catholicism or 'popery' was the creed of Antichrist whose adherents would go to any lengths to overturn that pure religion that provided salvation for the individual and the collective moral strength of the English and Scottish people. These kingdoms were a new Israel, whose inhabitants were specially blessed by God so long as they obeyed His will as revealed in Scripture. If Charles I and his bishops prevailed, it would degenerate into another Babylon:

> The Receptacle of the Common Inn
> Where all Idolatry and Superstition
> Profaneness, Arminianism, and Sedition,
> Atheism, Oppression, Blood and Cruelty
> Extortion, Persecution, Bribery and every sin
> With great applause has been persisted in.[9]

Once the war was underway, Charles's opponents predicted that his victory would deliver his subjects to that 'old Egyptian slavery' which the Israelites had once endured.[10]

England's widening religious fault-lines were revealed during the mobilisation of 1640. Essex militiamen broke into churches, chopped up altar rails (symbols of Laudian innovation) and chased two parsons out of their parishes. The minister at Bocking attempted to divert one company with a barrel of beer, but it fuelled their passions and he too lost his communion rails which were ceremonially burned. Militiamen who reached their destination were warned by Scottish propaganda that their faith was also threatened: 'For when we're slain, this rod comes on your breech.'[11] Conscripts from North Devon were already convinced. Reluctant to fight for what they imagined to be an attempt to foist Catholic bishops on Scotland, they mutinied and murdered an officer whom they suspected of being a Catholic.[12] Once operations began in earnest in the summer of 1642, Parliamentarian troops began to plunder the property of Catholics.[13] For their part, Catholics naturally inclined towards a king who had been sympathetic towards their faith; and they had no intellectual difficulties in accepting the notion of a monarch whose temporal power derived directly from God and, therefore, was beyond human censure.

In a war the initial aim of which was to cleanse England of corrupt and corrupting forces, the enemy was inevitably demonised. Those who took up arms for parliament in 1642 were reassured that not only were they fighting to preserve their historic rights, but to purge the kingdom of moral delinquents. Lurid tales of Cavalier excesses were a stock-in-trade of Parliamentarian propagandists which they exploited for all they were worth. One November night in 1642 a young virgin who was returning to her father's house near Totnes was accosted by a Cavalier who attempted to rape her. She called on 'the Lord of Hosts' and a comet appeared in the skies from which descended a burning sword that struck the would-be ravisher. Wounded, he blamed his injury on 'the perverseness of that Round-headed whore' and died soon afterwards, 'raving and blaspheming'. His fate did not deter a Royalist commander from encouraging his troops to 'ravish' the virgins of Abingdon the following month. Lust satisfied, they were then invited to loot the town. Cornish Cavaliers, 'having filled their ungodly paunches' with food and drink stolen from an 'honest man', reviled him as a 'Rogue, Rascal and Roundhead'. One then demanded from his host a 'sea of drink, a wilderness of tobacco and ten legions of whores' and raised his glass to the devil. A 'damp, fetid air' suddenly filled the room, from which his companions fled leaving the reprobate to die alone, delirious and blaspheming.[14]

A royal court that imported its fashions, morals and religion from Catholic Europe embraced decadent, alien vices. The Parliamentarian news-sheet *Mercurius Britannicus* alleged that the Royalist commander, Charles Gerard, later Earl of Macclesfield, ' has so much of *Sodom* in his conversation, that he turns every place where he comes into a *Gomorrah*'. Such biblical allusions transformed an army into an instrument of divine retribution. The burning of rebel Irish towns, villages and fields by royal troops in 1641 made their commander, James Butler, Earl of Ormonde, think of 'the cities of Sodom and Gomorrah' on which 'God did rain down vengeance'.[15]

Through the inventive imagination of Parliamentarian pamphleteers, the Roundhead army was made to appear a force of godly men, fit for the purification of religion and renovation of the state. Regulations laid down for the Parliamentarian troops under the command of the Earl of Essex in 1642 set a high moral tone: sermons were frequent; those who avoided them were liable to severe censure; and blasphemers were punished by having their tongues pierced by a red-hot needle. Regulations introduced by parliament in 1645 made blasphemy punishable by death.[16] Presbyterian Scotland upheld the same standards; a Scottish militiaman, James Davidson, who remarked in 1680 that 'the Lord that we depended on was a bastard of Joseph', had his tongue impaled.[17] Severe penalties were also given for swearing, which at that time relied on religious rather than sexual imagery. In 1651, three soldiers from the Parliamentarian garrison in Dundee whom an officer overheard cursing ('by God's blood and wounds', 'by God' and 'as God shall judge me') were sentenced to be gagged and set astride a wooden horse for an hour.[18] The shape of this device and the posture into which the miscreant was forced crushed his genitals.

Secretarian animosities were present on the battlefield. On Easter Sunday 1644 the besiegers of Pontefract 'basely stayed wine from coming to the castle' for the Royalist garrison's communion. Soon afterwards, on the eve of an assault on nearby Sandal castle, the Roundheads sang psalms, while the Cavaliers 'dedicated themselves unto God with upright hearts and religious prayers in brief manner'.[19] And of course they were answered. The 'foul night' that facilitated the swift Parliamentarian occupation of Preston in February 1643 was a sign of God's direct intervention in their favour.[20]

The concept of a godly elect which lay at the heart of puritan theology gave the soldier an inner confidence and extra courage when it was needed. At the end of his military career, Sir Edward Harley listed the many mercies he had received from God, including his rescue from drowning as a child, the moral strength to spurn 'evil company' at Oxford, and 'that the shot in my shoulder, August 1 1644, took not away my life, nor the use of my arm'.[21] Oliver Cromwell, who emerged from the war as parliament's ablest cavalry general, believed himself an agent of divine providence whose intentions he could not always fathom, but to which he submitted. He imagined that his soldiers shared his inner conviction. 'It's their joy that they are the instruments of God's glory and their country's good,' he reported to parliament after the capture of Bristol in December 1645. 'It is their honour that God vouchsafes to use them. Sir, they that have been employed in this service know that faith and prayer obtained this city for you.'[22]

Cromwell was right. The puritan frame of mind, in which an individual had a sense of his own uniqueness in God's eyes, made it easy for a soldier to see himself a chosen man. As a result he fought better because he knew he was facing death for a cause that had God's blessing. Some may have moderated their conduct accordingly, for there were no recorded charges of rape brought against soldiers from the New Model Army.[23]

The New Model Army had been formed at the beginning of 1645 to revitalise a flagging Parliamentarian war-effort. Among its recruits were over one hundred Royalist prisoners of war taken at Naseby, a further two hundred captured at Torrington and between 1300 and 1400 from the detritus of Sir Ralph Hopton's West Country army.[24] All had been cast adrift by the collapse of the Royalist cause on all fronts during 1645 and 1646, and either lacked alternative occupations or had developed a taste for soldiering. Some elected to serve with regiments earmarked for the reconquest of Ireland which offered prospects of plunder.

III

The presence of turncoats in the New Model Army was a reminder that there were plenty of ordinary soldiers who lived by a flexible code which placed personal survival before loyalty to a faith or an ideal. They were indifferent to religion and did not understand the political issues which divided king from parliament – facts that distressed their more zealous officers. These soldiers joined up because they were forced to, either by social or economic pressure.

In the summer of 1642 when the shire levies were mustered, a militiaman's choice of side depended on the loyalty of the local magnates empowered to raise men. Lords-lieutenant, sheriffs and magistrates became embroiled in provincial power struggles in which ties of kinship and friendship were employed to secure men and cash. It was assumed that the levies, commanded by local gentlemen or their sons, would fall into line behind their 'natural' masters. They did, in some part thanks to those Anglican clergymen who regularly reminded their congregations that obedience and deference were pleasing to God. This quietist spirit was not universal. In Exeter, where the city authorities had declared for parliament, there were dissident voices. Among them were those of a worsted comber who drank to 'the King and the Cavaliers and to the confusion or condemnation of the Roundheads and the volunteers', an apprentice who considered that 'the Parliament's Laws were not worth a turd' and a locksmith who violently ejected the constables sent to confiscate arms stored in his workshop, cursing them as 'a company of Roundheads and Counterfeits'.[25] For this craftsmen and others like him, the call to arms was an intrusion into their lives that was greatly resented. At South Molton in Devon, the Royalist Earl of Bath's attempts to muster men were frustrated by an angry mob armed with improvised weapons. Whether they favoured parliament, just wanted to be left in peace, or regarded the muster as another irksome imposition by the government is not known.

Squaring private conviction with public obligation was often extremely difficult. This was the dilemma of Sir Edmund Verney, the king's standard-bearer and an officer of his household. 'I do not like the quarrel, and do heartily wish that the King would yield and consent to what they [parliament] desire,' he confided to Sir Edward Hyde. But Verney remained loyal to the king: 'I have eaten his bread, and served him near thirty years, and will not do so base a thing as to forsake him; and choose rather to lose my life (which I am sure I shall do) to preserve and defend those things which are against my conscience to preserve and defend. For I will deal freely with you, I have no reverence for the Bishops, for whom this quarrel subsists.' Verney's decision was automatically that of his tenants and servants, who would have followed him to Edgehill where, as he had predicted, he was killed. There was also a straightforward devotion to the king on the part of gentlemen who saw loyalty to the crown as an integral part of their personal honour.

Supernatural forces were invoked by a Scottish landowner and entrepreneur, Sir John Hope, when he had to choose whether or not to support his countrymen's rebellion in support of Charles II in December 1650. He turned to the Bible and, using the common procedure of 'casting up at adventure', opened it at random. His eyes fell on Chronicles II, chapter 9, verse 4: 'This saith the Lord. Ye shall not go up, nor fight against your brethren: return every man to his house: for this thing is done of me. And they obeyed the words of the Lord, and returned from going against Jeroboam.' This, Hope wrote in his diary, 'did amuse me exceedingly' and his dealings with the king were circumspect to the point where he was accused of running with both hounds and hare. His policy of prudent neutrality was confirmed shortly afterwards when he had a dream in which he saw the camp of the Scottish army consumed by fire.[26] It was a premonition of the subsequent Scottish defeats at Dunbar and Worcester.

As the war progressed, nearly everyone in the country was compelled to play some part in it. Parties of soldiers collected war levies, victuals, carts and the beasts to pull them. Both sides commandeered men as well as goods and money; countrymen living along Prince Rupert's line of march from Oxford to Cirencester in February 1643 were forced to leave their jobs and lead the horses of his baggage train.[27] Coercion was inevitable, particularly when commanders found themselves short of men, which they frequently did. In Lancashire, the Cavalier general Lord Strange threatened to kill anyone who ignored his call to arms and was happy to accept militiamen armed only with pitchforks. On the march, those who straggled, no doubt with a eye to desertion, were to be shot by cavalrymen specially posted in the rearguard. Walter Phillips, who fulfilled his obligation to Charles I by 'trailing a pike' in his army and funding two horsemen, threatened to rob and hang two men for not following his example. They survived and had their revenge by testifying against Phillips to a parliamentary committee investigating assistance given to the king.[28] A dozen Royalist musketeers from the short-handed garrison of Hillesden House in Buckinghamshire ambushed a group of labourers as they returned home one evening in February 1644. The soldiers threatened to shoot them if they did not assist in the construction of defences for the position. The workmen were defiant: 'they bid them shoot if they dared, they would not be made slaves of.' All were released.[29]

It was possible to avoid the militia muster and conscription to the New Model Army because the law exempted certain professions. One was schoolmastering and it was chosen by the scholarly, pious and utterly unwarlike Adam Martindale as a means of keeping out of the war in his native Lancashire. It proved an uncongenial occupation. In those days of constant alarms parents were reluctant to send their sons to school and it was impossible to escape the war. Martindale lodged in Wigan 'in a public house to which many papists and drunkards did frequently resort' and his life was further disturbed 'by the soldiers often quartering among us, to the depriving us of our beds and chambers.' Martindale was accused of being a Roundhead 'and I could not clear myself from it by swearing and debauchery' – Cavaliers clearly lived up to their popular reputation as rakes. After just over four months, Martindale abandoned his job and all hopes of peace and private neutrality.[30] After another stab at schoolmastering, he became a military clerk, a post that left him with plenty of time to pursue his studies. With some satisfaction he recalled: 'I was not by my office either to wear armour or buff coat; to stand upon guard, or to ride out as a scout.' He did, however, have his mare, money and clothes stolen by Royalist soldiers from the Liverpool garrison who had been ordered to fend for themselves after the town had surrendered. At nineteen and after two miserable if relatively safe years of soldiering, Martindale thankfully returned to the schoolroom.[31]

IV

He departed from what had become a highly professional army, which by the end of 1646 had beaten the king. For the next five years its energies were concentrated on winning the peace, that is the making of a political settlement in England and the forceful reassertion of English supremacy over Scotland and Ireland. During this period, and for the first time in its history, Britain possessed a substantial standing army. Moreover, this novelty was an active force in public affairs with the power to make things happen. The trial and execution of Charles I in 1649, the installation of Oliver Cromwell as Lord Protector, and the enforced unity of the three kingdoms within a single republic were consequences of the army's intervention in politics. Army officers (Cromwell's major-generals) were made responsible for regional administration, and army detachments were deployed to discipline the population. In 1659 to 1660 it was a handful of senior officers who organised the coup that restored Charles II, the Church of England and the apparatus and procedures of royal and parliamentary government that his father would have recognised.

An unemployed victorious army was host to all manner of anxieties. How would it be disbanded and when; would arrears of pay be delivered; and, most troubling of all, would its past exertions be squandered by parliament in some compromise with the king? The fighting men who had, as it were, cured the nation of its sickness wondered whether the patient might suffer a relapse. Its symptoms might include the imposition of Scottish-style Presbyterianism, which those of Cromwell's persuasion considered as great a tyranny as episcopacy. Or would the king creep back in the confusion and, helped by the Scots, regain his old powers?

Questions like these and, most important of all, the right of those who won the war to have a say in the final settlement were the subjects of discussion among English soldiers. There were plenty of agitators on hand to whip up alarm and persuade the soldiers to support particular political remedies for their own and the nation's problems. The political press thrived in this atmosphere. Its power was already well established; at the outbreak of the war pamphlets had helped swing the admittedly unpaid sailors of the fleet behind parliament. An officer describing the rash of impromptu meetings, stump oratory and petition-signing among the soldiers in Suffolk in April 1646 noted that: 'Lilburne's books [i.e. pamphlets] are quoted by them as statute law.'[32]

Colonel John Lilburne was one of a loose group of radicals and visionaries, known as Levellers, who were attempting to win support among soldiers who wished to see their efforts rewarded with gains that would benefit them rather than their leaders. If there was to be a redistribution of power, the rank and file wanted to be included. For the radicals who inclined towards the Levellers, the defeat of the Royalists had been the first stage in a remodelling of society. The next would be the dismantlement of the old pyramidal hierarchy of which the king had been the apex and its replacement by an order in which all free men enjoyed the same legal and political rights, including the vote.

The victory of parliament had come from God and was a sign of an approaching millennium in which the old, sinful world would be replaced by one that truly reflected the divine will. The equality of God's elect was more than a mere theological abstraction; if a truly godly society was to emerge from the war, then divisions created by the imbalance of wealth had to be eliminated. Furthermore, the Levellers mistakenly imagined that such a just, egalitarian society had once existed but had been overthrown by the Norman Conquest. The Norman yoke had fallen upon English shoulders and with it a nobility that, in truth, was no more than the officers of William's army. Now, freeborn Englishmen had the chance to reclaim their lost birthright with the army acting as the muscle and voice of what one Leveller called the 'oppressed and distressed commons of England'.[33]

The parliamentary high command had never been revolutionaries. They had waged war to restrain the king, not to distribute power to the masses. The Leveller programme was a recipe for anarchy, claimed Henry Ireton, Cromwell's son in law, who insisted that the nation's health could only be assured if MPs and voters were men with 'a fixed interest' in the country through the ownership of property and the profits of commerce. He was speaking in a debate, held in Putney church in October 1647, between senior officers and Leveller spokesmen. It had been arranged in response to reports that the Levellers were winning support among the soldiers in an army that seemed in the process of being politicised to an alarming degree. As it turned out, the Leveller threat was exaggerated. Leveller doctrines appealed most to urban craftsmen and artisans and had only made converts in a small section of the army, mostly regiments stationed in south-eastern England.

Confronted with determined opposition from above, the Leveller movement crumbled. A month after the Putney confrontation, Cromwell and Sir Thomas Fairfax crushed a Leveller-inspired mutiny at Ware and had the ringleaders shot. Another Leveller mutiny, this time among nine hundred soldiers serving at Salisbury, was broken by the swift intervention of Fairfax in May 1649. Pursued to Burford, 340 survivors surrendered, crestfallen and full of repentance for their 'odious wickedness'. Three were shot as an example. The bonds and habits of military discipline, coupled with the soldiers' affection for two proven generals, Fairfax and Cromwell, proved stronger than visions of a new political order in England. Rich men slept more easily. However much they disliked its impositions or were jealous of its powers, the army had forestalled a social revolution.

Nonetheless, the Leveller phenomenon had been illuminating. Not surprisingly, given its diet of sermons and political pamphlets, the Parliamentarian army had become a politically conscious force. Nothing like this had been seen before in Britain and would not be seen again until 1919 and 1920, when discharged soldiers attempted to organise themselves as a political force to secure a just reward for their exertions and sacrifice. Although often overstated, the existence of a similar radical spirit among British servicemen during the Second World War did much to create the mood of 1945, when the country voted for a Labour government that had pledged itself to create a fairer society. Understandably then, the modern radical left has adopted the Levellers as proto-socialists whose martyrdom is still commemorated every year at Burford.

Isolated within the army, the Levellers were unable to secure victory on their terms. The generals, acting through the Council of the Army established by Cromwell and Fairfax in the summer of 1647, were able to get it on theirs. Backed by a now united army, the high command was the strongest political force within the country, willing to deploy troops to overawe its opponents. When, in August, Cornet Joyce arrested Charles I, the king asked him under what authority. The cavalryman answered: 'the soldiery of the army'.

The emergence of a strong, confident English army gaining political paramountcy created unease in Scotland. It was well known that at all levels this force was openly hostile to Presbyterianism; during the unrest in 1646 disgruntled soldiers in Essex had boasted that they would cut the throats of any Presbyterian minister they encountered.[34] More disturbing was the possibility that the army might be employed to restore effective English control over the rest of the British isles. Ever since the outbreak of the war in England, Scotland had been virtually independent, governed by a handful of aristocrats with support from the kirk. In this condition it had allied with parliament in 1644, delivering rein-forcements which swung the war against the king in northern England.

Scottish Royalism had been extinguished with the defeat of James Graham, Marquess of Montrose, at Philiphaugh in September 1645. Montrose enjoyed subsequent romantic canonisation, although given the cruel nature of the war he waged it is hard to understand why. His uprising the year before had severely shaken Scotland and exposed the tensions among its ruling class. Montrose's part-Irish and part-Highland army was fighting a public war in the name of Charles I and a private one on behalf of the MacDonald clan against its ancient enemies, the Covenanting Campbells, whose head was Archibald Campbell, Marquess of Argyll.

The political crises of the late 1630s had provided a perfect oppor-tunity to reopen clan warfare and settle old scores. An investigation into the murder of fifteen prisoners of war at Ballymoney in 1642 revealed that the victims had been Macdonnells and their captors Campbells, serving with Sir Mungo Campbell's regiment. The 'ancient feud' between these clans dictated that the Macdonnells suffered 'that fate which either sept gave the other coming under their power'.[35] No doubt the Scottish MacDonalds remembered the fate of their Irish kinsmen and added them to the ledger of overdue blood-debts. One anxious to settle this account was Alasdair MacColl of Colonsay, a Gaelic warrior in the old mould who was harrying Campbell lands on Islay in 1640 and fighting alongside the Macdonnells in Ireland the fol-lowing year. Vengeance and the release from captivity of his father and brothers were his causes and he probably knew little and cared less for the issues that separated king from parliament. MacColl's Irish-Highland contingent fought alongside Montrose who gave them the chance to kill Campbells and steal or destroy their property.[36] About three thousand died at the battle of Inverlochy in February 1645 and many more perished from hunger and cold. The slaughter delighted a MacDonald bard, who wrote:

> You remember the place called Tawney Field?
> It got a fine dose of manure
> Not the dung of sheep or goats,
> But Campbell blood well congealed.[37]

MacColl and his clan forces drifted away from Montrose once he had secured the liberty of his kinsmen and wreaked vengeance on the Campbells. He was killed in November 1647. His and Montrose's bloody sideshow did not materially alter the course of the general war, but it did illustrate the gulf between the Presbyterian Lowlands and the Catholic Highlands, and the persistence and venomousness of clan animosities in the west and north of Scotland.

More out of fear of the consequences of what was happening in England than out of conviction, the Scots made compacts with Charles I at the end of 1647 and, after his death, with his son, Charles II. This realignment resulted in the Second Civil War, of 1647 to 1648 and the Third Civil War in 1650 to 1651, in which three Scottish field armies and their English Royalist allies were decisively beaten by Cromwell at Preston, Dunbar and Worcester. These victories vindicated Cromwell's belief that he was the instrument of providence, and transformed Scotland into a province of England. An army of five to six thousand men under General George Monck stayed in Scotland to prevent further Royalist-inspired upheavals and to police the Highlands. One Royalist uprising, a small-scale affair in 1654, was joined by Arthur Forbes who, many years afterwards, recalled that his motive had been the 'freeing of our native land'. Betrayed by some of his countrymen who did not share his patriotism, he fled to the continent where he earned his living as a mercenary.[38]

V

Forbes joined a growing band of mercenaries, mostly Irish and all fugitives from the armies defeated by the forces of the Commonwealth, as the new British republic was called. The reconquest of Ireland had been an objective both of Scotland (which sent an expeditionary force there in 1642 to 1643) and of parliament. The rebels had been spectacularly successful; by 1643, the Scots and Royalists loyal to Charles I were confined to a narrow coastal strip which extended southwards from north Antrim to Dublin. The remainder of Ireland was under the control of the Irish Confederacy. Its cement was religion and a sense of nationhood which was defined in terms of wrongs suffered at the hands of the 'Saxons', a term that embraced English and Scots. This history of abuse was used in a lament for the misfortunes of his people by a Gaelic poet, who asked:

> *Why should punishment be inflicted*
> *Most heavily on one race?*

and,

> *Why should those once free be now enslaved?*[39]

He continued with a catalogue of injustices. Charles I ('He commanded the Saxon speech for all') had been the last in a line of English monarchs who had persecuted Catholicism and edged the Irish out of their country with colonists from England and Scotland. The rebellion of 1641 was nationalist in so far as it aimed to halt and reverse this process.

Jeffrey Barron, taken prisoner after the fall of Limerick in 1651 and sentenced to death, informed his captors that his countrymen 'had been engaged in the same cause as we pretended to fight for, which was the liberty and religion of our country'. He was sharply told that Ireland was a 'conquered country' in which rebellion had to be avenged.[40] Economic, social and religious grievances were combined in the address given to his men by Owen Roe O'Neill before the battle of Benburb in June 1646: 'All Christendom knows your quarrel is good – to fight for your native birthright, and for the religion which your forefathers professed and maintained since Christianity came first to this land. So as now is the time to consider your distressed and slavish condition; you have arms in your hands, you are as numerous as they are; and now try your valour and strength on those that have banished you, and now resolve to destroy you bud and branch.'[41]

Many present at this engagement had had no choice but to take up arms. As in England and Scotland, ties of kinship and tenantry, and bonds between master and servant, drove Irishmen into the Confederacy's army. Others came out of legal obligation. In Clare all between the ages of fifteen and sixty were obliged to join the militia. How they were equipped depended upon their status: men with incomes of less than six pounds a year were to be armed with a pike and dagger; those with between six and ten pounds with a musket; and those with between ten and twenty pounds had to equip an additional musketeer.[42] Like their counterparts on the mainland, Irish conscripts were sometimes unenthusiastic. At Virginia in Cavan in 1642 the accidental burning of a large house convinced some soldiers that the English were advancing. They panicked and 'ran into every corner, and their gentlemen and captains ran after, got them and beat them'.[43] Nonetheless, the overall response of Irish Catholics was remarkable; by 1649 between eighteen and twenty-eight thousand were serving in the army, 2 per cent of Ireland's total population.[44] After the war, a huge body of Catholic veterans chose to remain as soldiers and serve abroad; within two years thirteen thousand of them had left to join the French and Spanish armies.[45] The new régime was glad to be rid of them, for their presence in Ireland would have posed a perpetual threat to the new order established by Cromwell's victories in 1650 and 1651.

The campaigns in Ireland had been far more pitiless than those waged in England and Scotland. Massacres of protestants had marked the early stages of the revolt and they were not forgotten when Cromwell's army began its reconquest. In the middle of anti-guerrilla operations that included crop-burning and cattle-rustling near Clonmel, Colonel Jerome Sankey meditated on the morality of what amounted to creating an artificial famine. Turning to the puritan soldier's vade mecum, the Old Testament, he found comfort for his soul. He was upholding that 'severe justice' of a God who had frowned on Saul and Jehoshaphat after they 'had been sparing when the Lord commanded destroying'.[46] A soldier who ignored an order to give no quarter during the siege of Limerick was court-martialled and Major-General Ireton threatened to demote any of his men who dared to marry a Catholic.[47]

God's war was also a profitable one. Confiscated Irish lands were disposed of to former soldiers (sometimes in lieu of wages) and speculators from England, known as 'adventurers'. In Leinster, Munster and Ulster, 125,000 acres were distributed among veterans.[48] In all, thirty-three thousand soldiers and one thousand adventurers were beneficiaries from this scheme, although only just under a quarter of the former and a half of the latter had their grants confirmed after the Restoration.[49] The rest had lost, sold or abandoned their holdings. Catholics were the losers: their share of the ownership of fertile land dropped from 60 per cent in 1641 to 10 per cent in 1660.[50] Dispossessed, the Catholics of all classes were now marginalised and the foundations were firmly in place for the protestant political and economic ascendancy that remained virtually intact for the next two hundred years.

VI

The cost of the Wars of the Three Kingdoms had been enormous and the suffering they inflicted immense. Ireland was the hardest hit. Rough calculations made soon after their conclusion suggest that 618,000 perished out of a population of 1.5 million, a death rate of 41 per cent. This may be exaggerated, but it accords with contemporary accounts of the epidemics and famines that accompanied and were often caused by the campaigns. English and Scottish losses were also high:

	1639 population	Wartime deaths from all causes
England and Wales	5 million	190,000
Scotland	1 million	60,000

Deaths in battle made up less than half these casualties: in England and Wales they have been calculated at nearly eighty-five thousand, and in Scotland at about twenty-seven thousand.[51] The rest were civilians who perished from hunger or disease, or a combination of both. There were also the thousands of Irish and Scots transported to Virginia and Barbados for forced labour on the tobacco and sugar plantations. Those 'sold by the late usurper [Cromwell] for slaves' who survived the rigours of the Barbados climate were shipped home at the government's expense in 1661.

Although estimates, the statistics confirm anecdotal sources that describe the proliferation of deaths and epidemics that were a direct consequence of the wars. Between 1642 and 1646 the death rate soared in Berkshire, a county squeezed between Royalist and Parliamentarian garrisons and regularly traversed by both armies. Soldiers moving across country carried contagion with them, often into the inns and houses where they were billeted. Infection spread swiftly in the overcrowded garrison towns of Reading and Oxford, where in 1643 there was an epidemic of 'camp fever' (probably typhus) which a physician blamed on 'filth and nastiness' everywhere.[52] Depleted food supplies reduced resistance to disease; food shortages in Ireland in 1648 were swiftly followed by epidemics of plague, dysentery and smallpox.[53] Sieges provided the ideal conditions for diseases caused by human contact or microbes. Preventive quarantine was difficult; human waste could not be removed outside a city or town; the healthy could not flee and food was restricted. Of the 11,817 people who died in Devon during the war, nearly a quarter were victims of disease contracted during the siege of Plymouth.[54]

Sieges also caused widespread disruption of lives and destruction of property. When the defences of Exeter were prepared at the beginning of 1643, houses and gardens were levelled to deprive the enemy of cover. A greater part of the extramural parish of St Sidwell's was razed, much to the secret pleasure of the puritan city fathers who considered it a hive of crime and vice. This was not how the matter was seen by a resident, Richard Lowman, who later complained of 'having lost an estate in four houses . . . burned with fire [in] the late unhappy wars'. Selling off his goods did not prevent him and his sick wife from being reduced to destitution.[55] There were further demolitions in Exeter in October 1645 when its Royalist garrison prepared to resist a Parliamentarian army. Those inside the city were not safe; thatched roofs were torn down because they helped spread fire, and when the bombardment was underway property was damaged by bombs or 'granados' fired from mortars. The homeless, and they appear to have been largely from among the poorest citizens, were shunted off into the neighbouring villages. Here, it was hoped, they would be supported from the parish poor rates. For this reason, they were unwelcome guests.

A woman refugee from Exeter remarked that 'she rather the Turks came into the city than the Parliamentary troops'. It was a justifiable outburst, and similar sentiments were widely expressed. Everywhere, soldiers were a burden to the communities that had to feed, lodge and pay them. From the start, parliament and the king insisted that they had the legal right to levy men, collect the local rates for their wages and commandeer food and fodder. Borrowing methods employed during the Thirty Years' War, commanders commonly attached menaces to their demands. In September 1643 the Royalist garrison at Cirencester used blackmail to extort three hundred pounds from the neighbouring town of Tetbury, promising to loot it if the money was not paid. Defaulting villages in Worcestershire were warned that if they did not pay off their tax arrears they would be pestered by 'an unsanctified troop of horse'. The inhabitants of Swanbourne in Buckinghamshire armed themselves, took refuge in the church and defied a party of Royalist foragers in May 1643. Their commander, Lord Wentworth, threatened to burn down the township if the villagers did not surrender. He did and also ejected them from their sanctuary. In the same year Chinnor in Oxfordshire was twice torched by Prince Rupert for failing to supply his men.[56]

Such examples of terror did not cower the people in an area where sympathies inclined to parliament. Church bells were rung at Long Crendon and Morton on the Oxfordshire-Buckinghamshire border as Royalist scouting parties approached the villages and 'the country arose and beat them all away'.[57] Elsewhere, countrymen and women fended off the foragers with pleas of poverty or claims that the enemy had already stripped them of all they had. The bloodyminded villagers of Wolverton in Buckinghamshire drove their cattle across the border into Hertfordshire where they were sold for below the going price, rather than have them impounded by soldiers.[58]

Compulsory billeting of men and stabling of horses was a further source of loss and distress. On a cold night in December 1651, Richard Walton and six dragoons arrived at the house of Richard Seaton, the laird of Thornton in Fife, and demanded quarters. They ate and, 'full of drink', beat up the servants, who fled in terror. Finding themselves without fuel, the soldiers wrenched doors off their hinges and smashed up other woodwork to light fires. A fortnight later, Thomas Robinson was walking the streets of Dundee in a sullen mood – he was chilled, unpaid and probably suffering from a hangover after a night of heavy drinking. He went to the lodgings of fellow soldier to 'warm himself' and hammered on the door, enraging his reluctant hostess who, he claimed, called him a 'rogue'. According to her, he cursed her as an 'old bitch' and 'Scotch bitch'. Once inside, Robinson became even more objectionable: he suggested that an infant in the house might make a fine broth, and promised that if he and his mates did not get their wages soon they would ransack the town and that he would personally kill the woman who had insulted him. Both drunken dragoon and loutish trooper were punished by court-martial: both got an hour on the wooden horse, and the latter twenty lashes for mutinous language.[59]

These cases and others like them that were dealt with by the Dundee military authorities were not exceptional. In August 1653, Alexander Brodie, laird of Brodie Castle overlooking the Moray Firth, noted in his diary: 'This day came Deal and his troop, and quartered on my land in their march: they destroyed the young oak and birch which I had grown and planted in the little park.' A Calvinist addicted to analysing his own and the world's sinfulness, Brodie wondered whether this act of vandalism was a sign of God's disapproval. Perhaps he cared more for the trees than the kirk, or, and this was equally disturbing, he had taken too much pleasure in their growth.[60] Brodie did not, it appears, seek redress from the military authorities for what he convinced himself had been a well-deserved divine reproof. He was luckier than many of his countrymen who were the victims of that brutal form of economic warfare practised by Montrose and his adversaries. During the summer of 1645, a Covenanting army ravaged the 'fair and fertile country of Atholl'. Unripe corn was fed to the cavalry horses, livestock stolen and the nets of salmon fishermen destroyed.[61]

As well as 'official' depredations carried out as a matter of policy, there were 'unofficial' ones undertaken by soldiers for whom the war offered chances for private enrichment. Soldiering had always been an escape from the routines and restraints of civilian life and it exposed men to novel temptations and opportunities. Sergeant Nehemiah Wharton of the London trained bands appears to have been a respectable figure before he set off across Buckinghamshire in the summer of 1642. His political and sectarian prejudices made it easy for him to condone the looting of Catholics and their property. But there was an element of sheer devilment in his poaching expedition to Hillesden deer park, the property of Sir Alexander Denton, a 'malignant fellow' (i.e. Royalist), where he killed 'a fat buck'. He triumphantly attached its head to his halberd and 'commanded two of my pikes to bring the body after me to Buckingham'. This example may explain why he found it hard to restrain his men from random pillaging.[62] No doubt Wharton would have argued that by depriving Denton of a stag he was hurting an opponent of parliament, albeit to his own advantage. Others who helped themselves to other people's goods did not bother with such casuistry, or discrimination between friend or foe. They just used soldiering as a cover for crime, usually theft, and often of mere trifles like the shirt and apron stolen by a Parliamentarian soldier, Henry Stone, as he tramped through southern Oxfordshire in 1644.[63]

Soldiers existed outside the settled society of city, town and village. Wherever they were posted they were strangers, often anonymous figures whom local people could not identify by name. They were here today and gone tomorrow and, therefore, beyond the reach of the parish constables and magistrates who regulated the communities through which they passed. Evading civilian authority was easy, less so hiding misdeeds from officers who were empowered to try and punish miscreants for civil crimes. Highway robbery, housebreaking and theft from men and women going to and from market seem to have been the commonest crimes among Parliamentarian soldiers in England and carried a death sentence. Nonetheless, small groups of armed men ranging across a countryside where they were not known were tempted to turn highwaymen. One September afternoon in 1651, Andrew Tindall and his father-in-law, James Terry, were returning from Dundee market where they had sold some chickens. They were confronted by two troopers, one of whom pointed his pistol at Tindall's breast and Tindall handed over a Scottish dollar, one shilling and a sixpence. The victims remembered their assailants' appearances and described them well enough for the pair to be apprehended; each was given thirty lashes.[64]

Soldiers stole women as well as money and goods, or so it seemed to jealous rustics who could not compete with martial glamour, dashing uniforms and, at times, full purses. Like American GIs in the Second World War, the fighting men of the Civil Wars were 'overpaid, oversexed and over here'. In Somerset, 'keeping company with soldiers' was synonymous with whoring, and girls attracted to the transient visitors who passed through or were billeted in their communities were subsequently ostracised. Joan Eaton of Doulting spent the night with some Royalist cavalrymen and was afterwards treated as an outcast by the rest of the village. Unable to find any other occupation, she drifted into prostitution. A farmer who noticed one of his female servants strolling with a soldier followed the pair into a barn, where he 'saw the soldier lying upon her and her clothes up so that he saw her naked skin'. For this, she was ducked by indignant villagers. The mere presence of a woman with soldiers was sufficient to provoke a sense of outrage which must have been tinged with envy. When a North Petherton farmer discovered that one of his maids regularly went into the fields milking in the company of Parliamentarian soldiers, he sacked her. 'He would not keep such a slut in his house.'[65] Behind such reactions were fears that soldiers carried sexually transmitted diseases and that the offspring of illicit liaisons would have to be supported by the parish. Furthermore, passing soldiers might lure attractive and marriageable young women away from the humdrum and confined world of the village into the more exciting one of the camp.

Civilians did not always endure passively the exactions of armies. There were plenty of isolated incidents in which foraging parties or tax collectors were manhandled or driven out of villages. At Kempston in Bedfordshire in February 1643, two cavalrymen who had procured fodder for their horses from a frightened Mrs Yarway were confronted by her husband and a crowd of villagers who made 'many threatening speeches' and knocked them about. Reporting this fracas, the soldiers claimed that they had offered no provocation.[66] During the first half of 1645 civilian patience snapped and there was a series of spontaneous demonstrations which spread across western and southern England, the Marches and South Wales. The protesters were called 'club men' and their feelings were expressed in a contemporary ballad:

> And the realm doth groan with disasters:
> And the scum of the land
> Are the men who command
> And our slaves have become our masters.
> Now our lives,
> Children, wives
> And estate
> Are prey to their lust and plunder . . .[67]

The scale of this peasants' revolt at first stunned both sides, but it lacked co-ordination, organisation and any purpose beyond the expression of mass exasperation. The 'club men' movement disintegrated as quickly as it had sprung up with demonstrators scattered by Parliamentarian forces. Ten thousand were dispersed by Cromwell's horsemen at Hambledon Hill in August. He reported a dozen killed, many more wounded and four hundred taken prisoner whom he described as 'poor silly creatures'. They were sent home, having first promised to behave themselves in future.[68]

VII

From the start, there had been well-founded fears that a contest in which men took sides according to personal conviction or loyalty would divide families, father against son and brother against brother. John Lilburne's brother, Henry, died fighting for the king, and there were members of Cromwell's family who sided against parliament. Such fractures within families were comparatively rare. Of the 774 gentry families living in Lancashire, 292 became involved in the war and of them only eighteen were split. In Suffolk there were just under a thousand gentry families of whom 135 took part in the war with just nine divided.[69] What is revealing about these figures is that a large proportion of landowners preferred to remain outside the conflict, although they could not evade paying levies to whichever side dominated the region.

It was impossible for anyone at any level in society to isolate themselves from what, to date, was the largest and most intrusive war in British history. Consider Upton, a prosperous farming community a few miles east of Newark. The parish accounts reveal a constant, sometimes expensive and never welcome involvement in the war. During the summer of 1642, the village armour had to be repaired, gunpowder and match purchased and three horses hired for Upton's militiamen. Soldiers, including a regiment of Royalist cavalry, were billeted in the village inns and food and fodder were regularly requisitioned. In 1644, labourers were pressed to help construct the siege-works outside Newark and two years later were called back, this time to demolish them. An outbreak of plague during the siege of Newark compelled villagers to impose a voluntary quarantine. And then there were the small sums doled out to impoverished travellers and vagrants who stayed overnight. In 1642 to 1643 there were ninety-four, including crippled soldiers, and in 1646 to 1647 ninety-six, among them fifty-eight Irish who were fugitives from the war in their country.[70] Upton's share of this burden may have been exceptional because it was situated within ten miles of a major national thoroughfare, the Great North Road. In other respects, Upton's experience of the war was typical. Those who lived in cities and towns that were besieged or garrisoned were less lucky; they lived, albeit briefly, through something approaching total war in which every resource was at the disposal of the army.

Those who had predicted a national catastrophe in the months before the clash at Edgehill had been correct, although the harm suffered by England and Wales had been less than in Scotland and Ireland. Deaths and damage aside, the most pungent memory of the war was of being pushed around by men in uniform. Peace brought no respite from martial arrogance, for under Cromwell the army had effectively replaced civilian government.

The soldiers' republic seemed likely to continue after his death in September 1658. His son, Richard, succeeded him as Lord Protector, but resigned under pressure in the following spring. A power struggle among the generals followed and it seemed that Britain might succumb to a praetorian form of government. It was a bleak prospect, with political authority concentrated in the hands of a small, exclusive group of ambitious high-ranking officers who were prepared to use force to achieve their ends. Troops bullied members of the recalled Rump Parliament and clashed with Londoners who shared a general apprehension about the direction in which the country was heading.

Under these conditions, the restoration of Charles II seemed the only satisfactory alternative to perpetuating the experiment of military rule or, and this was becoming a distinct possibility in 1659, chronic instability which would lead to a renewal of the wars. Men of property, both former Royalists and Parliamentarians, were alarmed, while supporters of the republic were fragmented and isolated. In February 1660 when General Monck's intervention coalesced the public in favour of the king's return, the Venetian ambassador in London sensed a mood of general relief. The restoration of the monarchy and all that went with it, he told his masters, 'is absolutely necessary if this nation wishes to live in peace; or it can only expect trouble and disaster'. He watched citizens celebrating the news of Charles II's recall with the same soldiers who, three months before, had been jostled and jeered in the streets. Old Royalists were delighted and sang:

> Now the Rump is confounded
> There's an end to the Roundhead,
> Who hath been such a bane to our nation;
> He has now played his part,
> And gone out like a fart.

For 'Roundhead' nearly everyone would have read 'soldier'.

But had the Restoration finally restored the country's health? It had left the patient with a pathological aversion to standing armies, which would endure, and understandably so. The question of the balance of political power was unresolved; the nation's constitution was unchanged, although Charles II took care to steer clear of confrontations that might lead to war. Memories of what had happened between 1637 and 1660 did, however, enable him to foist bishops on the Scots and secure the succession for his Catholic brother, James, Duke of York. Only a few Presbyterians took up arms for their faith and, with a few exceptions, his subjects acquiesced to the idea of a Catholic on the throne. The philosopher Thomas Hobbes might have considered the reluctance of his countrymen to put these issues to the test of war as evidence that they did not want a return to anarchy. His studies of the nature of the state and how it might be perfected, *Behemoth* and *Leviathan*, drew heavily on the experience of the Civil Wars through which he had lived. Only a strong prince could restrain the predatory instincts of his people, who would exchange their freedom for absolute obedience to a ruler who could protect them. Peace, at whatever price, was preferable to perpetual insecurity.

And yet, the instigators of the sufferings, those who had taken up arms against a king, ultimately proved the winners. The war may have generated its own momentum which carried the victors towards Cromwell's unloved military dictatorship, something they had never initially sought, but the ideas they had originally stood for were not extinguished in the process. In terms of institutions, the balance of power within government and concepts of individual liberty, the wars preserved more than they destroyed. Disagreements over the boundaries between the rights of parliament and the prerogative of the king remained to surface again in 1688. If, and this was unlikely given the resources and generals available to him, Charles I had beaten his enemies, then the direction of British history would have been very different. Victory would have given a divine imprimatur to Charles's administrative novelties and would surely have encouraged him to continue and extend his centralising policies. The parliaments of the three kingdoms would have been casualties, either dying from non-use or becoming rubber-stamps for the royal will. Religious dissent might also have withered, depriving Britain of a potent source of political radicalism in the eighteenth and nineteenth centuries. Instead, Charles was defeated and publicly arraigned for his conduct in a trial that was more theatrical than judicial. His execution left in no doubt the principle that in Britain kings were not free agents under God: they were bound by their own laws and answerable to their subjects.

Moreover, the new republican régime laid the foundations for the aggressive pursuit of international trade and overseas colonies. Cromwell's wars against the Dutch and the conquest of Jamaica opened the way for future expansion even though, ironically, they were only possible thanks to the fleet that Charles I had built with taxes which, his opponents claimed, were illegal. The Parliamentarian victory had, therefore, enormous repercussions for the rest of the world, for it set Britain firmly on course towards overseas expansion.

2

The Highland bagpipes mak' a din: Rebellions, 1660–1746

I

The British people were not allowed to forget the Wars of the Three Kingdoms. For generations, loyal Britons celebrated the anniversary of the restoration of Charles II on 29 May 1660. Church bells were rung, bonfires lit and fireworks ignited as reminders that the king's homecoming had signalled a return to peace, stability and everything that was familiar in government. Patriotic protestants soon had further deliverances to celebrate, each an unmistakable sign that a benevolent providence continued to favour Britain. On 5 November the nation annually gave thanks for William of Orange's landing at Brixham in 1688 and the subsequent overthrow and expulsion of the Catholic James II. No day could have been more propitious for the arrival of a protestant saviour, for on 5 November 1603 the Catholic conspiracy known as the Gunpowder Plot had been unmasked. Its anniversary is still celebrated, and at Lewes an effigy of the pope is ceremonially burned in the old style.

William of Orange's bloodless invasion precipitated the Glorious Revolution of 1688 to 1689 and the Bill of Rights, which seemed to settle finally the dispensation of power between crown and parliament and to safeguard the ancient liberties of his new subjects. The new order was secured by William III's Irish campaign of 1689 to 1691 in which James II and his Franco-Irish forces were defeated. Cannon roared from the battlements of the royal castles throughout Scotland after the news of the decisive battle of the Boyne (12 July 1690) was announced. The royal council in Edinburgh decreed that the Sunday after 5 October was to be a day of national rejoicing throughout Scotland with prayers of thanksgiving, sermons and illuminations. Participation was an expression of personal solidarity with the new régime, for the council ordered that 'all persons give punctual obedience thereunto as they will be answerable at their highest peril'.[1] Those who shunned the ceremonies or neglected to place candles in their windows were disloyal and religiously suspect, the two, of course, being synonymous. Prudent men and women everywhere advertised their support for the political status quo by participating in the officially backed festivals. As far away as Boston, Massachusetts, the city fathers provided wine and candles for patriotic colonists to celebrate Queen Anne's birthday and the recent victory over Spain at Vigo Bay in 1702.[2]

On her death in 1714 a new anniversary was added to the calendar of political and religious observances – 1 August – the day on which the Elector of Hanover ascended the throne as George I and preserved the Glorious Revolution. Few houses were lit up in Aberdeen on 1 August 1746, which enraged the garrison soldiers who hurled stones at the darkened and therefore disloyal windows, breaking hundreds.[3]

Aberdeen was a city in mourning and under military occupation. Four months before at Culloden, an army of English and Lowland troops, commanded by George II's son, William Augustus, Duke of Cumberland, had defeated one led by Prince Charles Edward Stuart, whom an infatuated Scottish lady had dubbed 'Bonnie Prince Charlie'. Many who died in the battle and the subsequent pursuit had come from Aberdeen and its hinterland. Local men who had survived, along with Highlanders and a handful of English volunteers, were in gaols and hulks awaiting trial for treason. Some had already been hanged, often summarily, and others were on their way to virtual enslavement on the plantations. Aberdonians were in no mood to illuminate their houses in honour of the dynasty they had hoped to topple and whose soldiers were in the process of hunting down former rebels and delivering them for trial and execution. One officer engaged in these operations in the hills around the city was Captain Hugh Morgan of Fleming's Regiment who 'was very active in ferreting gentlemen who were and are lurking'.[4] Aberdonians were among his bag, which was no doubt why the local authorities attempted to blame him as the instigator of the assault on their windows.

In London, as elsewhere in England and Scotland, they saw things differently. Jubilation and a massive sigh of relief had followed the announcement of Culloden. A supporter of the house of Hanover told a friend in Norfolk: 'the first firing of the Tower guns on Thursday seemed to me the loveliest music I ever heard.' Londoners shared his delight, for there was 'the most universal illumination save for a great part of the Scotch nobles of distinction and some commoners whose sentiments have always been pretty well known'.[5] Darkened windows in Aberdeen and London belonged to Jacobites who had dreamed of reversing the 1688 to 1689 settlement and restoring the Catholic Stuarts. This could only have been accomplished through rebellion and a prolonged civil war. Irrespective of the outcome, such a conflict was bound to have inflicted enormous damage on a nation whose prosperity was increasing rapidly. Dedicated Jacobites appreciated this, but still relished the chance to put their cause to the test of arms. One, an Angus laird called David Erskine, had the saloon of his house of Dun embellished with plasterwork decorations that anticipated the contest and the eventual triumph of the Stuarts. Classically armoured Mars stamps on the union flag (representing the union between England and Scotland) and the British crown, while a lion cowers nearby. Above the god of war's head is a goddess surrounded by the images of war: artillery, pikes and chained prisoners.[6] The civil war Erskine had yearned for was averted in 1746, which was why Londoners were rejoicing.

In June they were also given an object lesson in the consequences of a Jacobite victory by the attorney-general, Sir John Strange, when he made his opening speech in the prosecution for treason of Francis Towneley, a Catholic squire from Lancashire. He had raised a regiment for Prince Charles Edward and his recruits had marched behind a banner embroidered with the slogans 'Liberty and Property' and 'Church and Country', phrases that incensed Sir John. They were:

> Words . . . of the greatest significance if properly applied in the sense every true Englishman and Protestant understands.

But as applied to us they signify the reverse. The word *Liberty* can mean nothing but *slavery*. The word *Property* imports *our being stripped of everything*. The word *Church* could only be meant for introducing the Popish religion and superstition; and the word country . . . must stand for arbitrary Government in opposition to the mild and happy Government under which we live, the blessings of a Protestant succession in his Majesty's Royal Family and in place of these, to the great dishonour of the nation, reducing these kingdoms to a province of France.[7]

The jurymen had probably heard it all before. For nearly sixty years, successive governments had insisted that the Jacobites, in alliance with Britain's most powerful enemy, were bent upon robbing the freeborn Briton of his legal birthright and impoverishing the country in the process.

Jacobitism was inextricably linked with Catholicism. It had contributed immeasurably to James II's unpopularity. Soon after his accession in 1685, he had been challenged by a protestant, James, Duke of Monmouth, one of Charles II's illegitimate sons. Monmouth was strongly supported in the west, where the old puritan tradition was deep-rooted, but his army of ill-armed peasants, weavers and artisans was swept away by the disciplined musketry and artillery fire of a three-thousand-strong royal army at Sedgemoor. Chastisement followed, delivered by that master of mordant judicial humour, Lord Jeffreys, whose 'Bloody Assizes' of West Country folk memory was an exercise in legal terror designed to enforce obedience. Backing for Monmouth had been localised, although there were signs that if his venture had prospered his following would have increased. The Somerset militia defected wholesale to the insurgents and the levies of Dorset and Devon maintained a watchful neutrality. Interestingly, the rebels had many sympathisers in North America and the West Indies, including a body of pirates who, as they admitted, were natural rebels.[8]

James II's throne was preserved by his small professional army. It had demonstrated that in future any popular insurrection was doomed to failure; the enthusiasm of untrained, poorly armed men counted for little against the firepower of regular troops. This was proved again at Dunkeld in May 1689, when the musketry of entrenched soldiers of the Second Earl of Angus's Regiment (all Presbyterians) shattered charges by Jacobite Highlanders armed with bladed weapons.[9]

So long as the army remained steadfast, the crown was safe from popular uprisings. Nothing could protect it from its own folly. During his three-year reign James earned himself the mistrust of the majority of his subjects through policies that favoured Catholics. His tampering with the elected legislatures in the North American colonies indicated an inclination towards centralising absolutism, as did his hamfisted attempts to interfere with the legal system. Anxieties about James's methods and objectives were shared by his soldiers who, like their countrymen, believed that their liberties and protestantism were no longer secure. Sectarian tensions infected the army. Soldiers from the garrison joined in an anti-Catholic riot in Edinburgh's Canongate in February 1686 in which a trumpeter was seized 'by the sleeves of his trumpeter's coat' and called a 'Papist dog'.[10] When William of Orange and his Dutch army of fourteen thousand landed, James II's forces switched sides, leaving the king with no option but to flee to France. A civil war was prevented largely because James II's followers were leaderless, isolated and, in the case of English Catholics, a distrusted minority. In Scotland, there was a brief Catholic reaction. Three thousand Highlanders rallied to the exiled James II under the leadership of John Graham, Viscount Dundee, but the revolt petered out after his death at the battle of Killiecrankie. Only in Ireland did James find substantial support among the Catholics for whom he represented an opportunity to reclaim political and economic power and toleration. Here and in Scotland his forces were defeated by William, whose campaigns were celebrated in a birthday ode for his wife, Mary II, written by Thomas Shadwell and set to music by Purcell:

> *Behold, the God-like Hero goes*
> *Fated and born to conquer all,*
> *Both the great, vulgar and small.*
> *To hunt the Savages from their dens*
> *To teach 'em loyalty and sense.*

An essential ingredient of 'loyalty and sense' was a forthright rejection of Catholicism. The Glorious Revolution, the Nine Years' War, from 1688 to 1697, and the War of the Spanish Succession, from 1702 to 1714, intensified anti-Catholicism in Britain. Catholicism became synonymous with foreign domination, arbitrary government and national impoverishment; in the popular imagination 'brass money, wooden shoes and Popery' were inseparable, Catholics were the 'enemy within' and their loyalty was always suspect. In 1712, when Captain James Richards was accused of cowardice during a naval action against a French squadron off the Guinea coast, his fellow officers also accused him of being a covert Catholic. One wanted to make him undertake that legal assay of allegiance to crown and state, the religious test, by which holders of public offices had to repudiate Catholic dogma in the most forceful language.[11] Catholic malice and deviousness knew no boundaries; in 1714 colonists in North America were disturbed by rumours that Jesuit missionaries were teaching the native Americans that Jesus had been a Frenchman and that his Jewish persecutors had been English.[12]

II

If successive governments' anti-Jacobite propaganda was correct, and on the whole the country believed that it was, then why did men adhere to 'the King over the water' and risk their lives for him? One clue lies in political and religious geography; by far the largest concentrations of active, that is to say, belligerent Jacobites were found in Ireland and the northern and north-eastern parts of Scotland. This is not to say that the entire population of the British periphery was permanently ready to fight for an exiled dynasty. The Highland rank and file of the Jacobite armies during the rebellions of 1715 and 1745 to 1746 did not enlist willingly and a large proportion never comprehended what they were fighting for. They came because tradition demanded that they followed their landlords into battle and, if they did not, they were bullied and occasionally punished. For those who coerced them, the restoration of the Stuarts would offer rewards and opportunities for advancement, as dynastic civil wars always did for magnates who backed the winning side.

Jacobite ideology had a limited appeal. It derived from St Paul's homily on obedience in his Epistle to the Romans (chapter 13, verses 1 and 2): 'Let every soul be subject unto the higher powers. For there is no power but of God: the powers that be are ordained of God. Whosoever resisteth the power, resisteth the ordinance of God: and they that shall resist shall receive to themselves damnation.' Many Catholics, Anglicans and Scottish Episcopalians sincerely believed that rebellion against the crown was rebellion against God and meek submission to the royal will was the only path a Christian could follow. Alexander Lindsay, Episcopalian minister at Corlache in Speyside refused to pray for William and Mary and denounced those who dethroned and killed their kings. A Jacobite by conviction, Lindsay was an old Royalist in temperament, for his detractors complained that he was 'an ordinary drunkard and will sit upon Saturday nights with bagpipes, drinking and playing till daylight'.[13] For men of his inclination, the deposition of James II and parliament's subsequent offer of the crown to William III and Mary broke God's laws. The Act of Succession, which debarred the Stuarts in favour of the Hanoverians, was a further infraction of scripture. Moreover, legislation that transferred power away from the crown to parliament was a denial of the principle that kings governed as agents of God. How much of this political theological creed was understood by the rank and file of the Jacobite armies can only be guessed.

Not all Jacobites saw themselves as supporters of a divinely ordained political system. In so far as it involved attachment to an alternative king, Jacobitism attracted anyone who, for whatever reason, was out of sorts with the governments of William and Mary, Anne and the first two Georges. It represented an unofficial opposition and a weak one, for its adherents came and went according to how they reacted to a particular issue. There were clergymen like Alexander Lindsay who had forfeited their livings for sticking to their principles, overburdened taxpayers (levels spiralled during wartime), Scots who were suffering economically from the Union, and the victims of political power struggles who found themselves excluded from patronage and advancement. Jacobitism existed on the margins of politics as a temporary refuge for the discontented. It never attracted the same following as the established political parties, the Whigs and the Tories, and had it not been for Prince Charles Edward's landing at Moidart in August 1745, Jacobitism might have eventually withered away.

The prince came ashore in the homeland of the Catholic Clanranald where he was safe for the moment. Catholics obviously had much to gain from a Stuart restoration, but the response to the 1715 uprising in strongly Catholic Lancashire had been disappointing, with about 2500 volunteers. Of course, there might have been more there and elsewhere if the rising had flourished, but the waverers were always aware of treason's fatal consequences. They were reminded of them by royal troops which were deployed in potential centres of unrest in Northumberland and the south-west. Outside the heavily armed Highlands, Catholic capacity for insurrection was minimal. Since 1689 they and those who refused to swear allegiance to the crown had been systematically disarmed and deprived of horses worth over five pounds and therefore judged fit to carry an armed cavalryman. After a Jacobite invasion scare in March 1708, a search for arms in the houses of Norfolk Catholics yielded one obsolete matchlock and its ammunition. These preventive measures were effective, for in 1715 Lancashire Jacobites were desperately short of weapons.[14]

None was available for Irish Jacobites thanks to emergency legislation that deprived Catholics of horses, weapons and gunpowder. In 1715 and 1745 the regular garrison was placed in readiness for an invasion that never materialised; had it done so, the leaderless, untrained and virtually unarmed Catholics would have been easily contained. During the 1745 to 1746 rebellion, Sir Stephen Poyntz, a diplomat and sometime tutor to Cumberland, believed that Ulster militiamen ('a hardy race of zealous Protestants') could easily be spared for service against the Jacobites in south-west Scotland.[15]

Most important of all in terms of overturning the government, the Jacobites found few active sympathisers among its armed forces. Officers, like all other public officials, had publicly to renounce Catholicism and provide evidence that they occasionally received Anglican communion. Whenever disaffection was detected, it was treated severely. In 1690, Richard Ravenhill, a sailor serving aboard HMS *Bonaventure* received sixty lashes after the interception of a seditious letter he had sent to one of his friends: '. . . There are two-thirds of the people in London that wish for King James, the seamen are all for him, because King William has no money for them, nor gives them encouragement; there is money to be raised for the States in Holland but not for them which makes them grumble much. Scotland are [*sic*] up in arms . . .'[16]

Ravenhill and his shipmates were resorting to Jacobitism as a protest against a government that refused to remedy what were purely service grievances. In August 1746, Robert Turnbull, commander of Dumbarton fort, complained that 'mutineers, common drinkers, native Irishmen and suspect Papists' had been drafted to his garrison. Their presence had been a danger during the past few months and he hoped that in future honest and trustworthy soldiers would be sent.[17] His anxieties were not entirely without substance. Soldiers from Ireland and the Highlands, where Jacobite sympathies were strong and durable, conspired to deliver a Georgia frontier post to the Spanish in 1738. The Irish plotters had previously served in the Spanish army, to which they wished to return, and one, a Catholic, denied George II's authority over him.[18]

Circumstances rather than conviction drove a handful of British regulars into the Jacobite army during the rebellion of 1745 and 1746. Those who changed sides were the victims of mischance, bewildered and disheartened men who showed no hint of attachment to Prince Charles Edward or his dynasty. Sergeant Hugh Lewis of Lascelles' Regiment (58th) was taken after the rout at Prestonpans (21 September 1745) and held prisoner in Edinburgh. His captors were desperate for trained soldiers and a group of officers approached Lewis, plied him with drink and persuaded him to accept the prince's commission. Afterwards and under trial for his life, Lewis claimed that he had been threatened with incarceration in a Highland dungeon where he was told he would starve to death. Lewis showed his commission in the Duke of Perth's regiment to Private Thomas Blewmines, also from Lascelles', and promised him humane treatment if he joined the rebels. Blewmines 'rejected with scorn' the offer. On 12 October, Lewis, still wearing his red coat, was taken prisoner by a detachment of government troops near Stirling. A witness for his defence claimed that he had drunk King George's health while in gaol awaiting court-martial, but this exhibition of patriotism did not save him from the gallows. NCOs were expected to set a good example.

'Threats and ill usage' forced another sergeant from Lascelles', James Baillie, to join the rebels after they had captured him in Aberdeen. He was insensible after a drinking bout and had missed his regiment's departure from the city. Technically a deserter, he accepted the prince's white cockade and helped drill the rebels. He, too, was executed. John Crabtree, a private from Lascelles' with a record of desertion, alleged that he had enlisted in the prince's army to escape the discomforts of prison and secure clothes and shoes. Given the Jacobite provisions for prisoners of war, this was quite likely. Crabtree was pardoned by Cumberland and sent to serve on the North American frontier, where there was nowhere for him to run save the wilderness.[19]

III

Only in the Highlands could the Jacobites raise a reliable army. In 1724 the government calculated that there were twenty-two thousand clansmen who possessed arms in the Highlands, of whom twelve thousand were judged potentially disloyal. This was at a time when the strength of the British regular army was eighteen thousand, of whom nearly two-thirds were stationed in Ireland. So long as Highlanders were armed and, given their addiction to brigandage and inter-clan feuds, experienced in handling their weapons, they posed a threat to national security. Their capacity for mischief increased immeasurably in wartime when they might receive assistance from Britain's enemies. In 1719, a small Spanish detachment had landed to stiffen a Jacobite uprising, but after a sharp skirmish at Glenshiel the clansmen collapsed and their allies surrendered. George I's government had been extraordinarily lucky, for a squadron carrying Spanish reinforcements was scattered by a storm off Cape Finistère.

This episode convinced the government of the need for a programme of security measures designed to shift the balance of military power in the Highlands in its favour. First, it was essential that any insurrection was contained swiftly by overwhelming force. Major bases were constructed or refurbished at Forts William, Augustus and George (Inverness); fortified barracks were built at strategic points, and over 250 miles of metalled roads laid to expedite the movement of troops and artillery in an emergency. If these precautions failed and the Highlanders somehow managed to break into southern Scotland, it was feared that their success would encourage hitherto passive Lowland Jacobites to show their true colours. To prevent this, a second line of defence was established. Existing royal strongholds, most notably at Edinburgh and Stirling, were reinforced so that they could withstand up-to-date siege-artillery. At Berwick, in accordance with plans drawn up by Sir Nicholas Hawksmoor, a new barracks was constructed guarding the eastern route into England.

At the same time as roads penetrated the Highlands, efforts were in hand to confiscate the arsenals held by clan chiefs and the weapons of their followers. This process went hand in hand with the establishment of detachments of locally recruited troops who served as a police force against bands of marauders. Neither policy proved completely effective and, in 1725, it was suggested that it might be more profitable to recruit large numbers of the hardy and warlike Highlanders and ship them to the plantations where they would serve as a permanent garrison.[20]

The implementation of these ambitious plans was the responsibility of a talented and resourceful Irish officer, Major-General (later Field-Marshal) George Wade. Nothing like them had been seen since the time of the Romans and, revealingly, when a system of armed patrols was being prepared in 1689, it was proposed that Roman precedents should be followed. Garrisons were to be linked by chains of beacons that would be lit as a signal for the militia to mobilise and prepare to intercept Highland raiders.

Major-General William Roy, an officer of Cumberland's staff who continued Wade's work after 1747, was convinced that the problems he faced were the same as those encountered by Agricola in the first century. After all, he argued, the features of the landscape were unchanged and those that Roman commanders had exploited were still the keys to local security. In the course of his road building and perambulations, Roy took time off to search for Roman marching camps, using his military intuition. It was appropriate that in his antiquarian quest for the remains of another colonial power, Roy was accompanied by another enthusiast, Captain Melville of the 25th Regiment, who was later appointed governor of Grenada in the West Indies. Here, as in the Highlands, the native population was unwilling to knuckle down to rules imposed from outside and above. The Highlands became the proving ground for methods of surveillance and control that were afterwards applied in the West Indies, North America and other parts of the

Empire, most notably India's North-West Frontier. Whatever else they achieved, the Jacobites provided the army with valuable training in counterinsurgency techniques in inaccessible terrain.

Men like Wade and Roy were not only concerned with removing the potential for rebellion. Ever since 1660, the administrations in Edinburgh and London had been exasperated by the endemic violence of the Highlands, which frequently spilled over into more settled regions in the form of cattle-rustling, armed robbery and extortion. The Highlands were a magnet for the lawless. In 1666 the royal council decided on a wholesale purge of all 'strong and idle beggars, vagabonds, Egyptians and persons condemned who the magistrates shall think to be punished with banishment, especially in the Highlands, where so many abound and are sheltered that the public laws cannot be executed against them'.[21] How many were shipped to the colonies is not known, but the unending complaints against Highlanders' depredations indicate that most miscreants avoided being corralled.

Twenty years afterwards, it was reported that the 'thieves of Glencoe and Lochaber' were slipping south into Strathearn and the Ochil hills in parties of ten and twelve, all armed. They demanded hospitality ('thigging') 'and if they be denied . . . they steal and rob, so that the gentlemen of the country have not safety or security to themselves'.[22] Old habits were abandoned slowly; in 1747 Major-General William Blakeney was appalled by the 'ingrained villainy and wickedness [that] by long habit is deeply rooted in the hearts of the people' of Rannoch, Glencoe and Lochaber.[23] Andrew Fletcher, Chief Justice Clerk of Scotland, believed that the only remedy for vice was the cultivation of 'manufacture and honest industries' in the region. A revolution in dress would also assist the process of regeneration. The Whig judge wished for the plaid to be made illegal and that, 'like the Lowlanders', the Highlanders should wear only 'cloth without mixture of colours, and not of Tartan'.[24]

Outlandish costume emphasised the separateness of the Highlander and his refusal to become incorporated into an industrious and disciplined society. It was this stubborn attachment to ancient customs and manners that appealed to the Romantic imagination of a later generation. The uncouth, rebellious brigand whose behaviour exasperated ministers and generals in the Age of Reason became the picturesquely clad noble savage, a natural gentleman passionately loyal to his chief, clan and distinctive culture. He lived in a majestic, wild landscape and his ballads and code of honour perpetuated the world of the Middle Ages so dear to the Romantics. With the help of Sir Walter Scott, the Highlander was invested with the same qualities as the paladins of chivalric romance. Revealingly, it was the medieval literature read by Scott's hero, Edward Waverly, that made him susceptible to the archaic but glamorous feudal world of the chieftain Fergus Mac-Ivor.

The clansman's reinvention occurred at the beginning of the nine-teenth century, long after he had been neutered and when Highland lairds were busy recruiting for the army of the house of Hanover. No longer a danger to civil society, the Highlander became its pet. In his new form he was portrayed as a free and noble spirit, fighting hopelessly but bravely against the forces of change in the name of an ideal and led by a gallant and debonair prince.

Reborn Highlanders of this sort populated Scott's *Rob Roy* and *Waverley*, and later Robert Louis Stevenson's *Kidnapped* and *Catriona*. The 'Forty-Five' underwent a metamorphosis: what had been seen as a frightening insurrection that imperilled the stability of Britain became what it had never been, a war to preserve the Highland way of life. Paradoxically, those middle- and upper-class readers who were entranced by Scott's tales were the very men and women who were the beneficiaries of the Hanoverian victory in 1746. Not the least was George II's great-granddaughter, Queen Victoria, who indulged her taste for romantic Highland fantasy at Balmoral.

IV

Bonnie Prince Charlie's rebellion was a calamity for the Highlands. His appearance was not universally welcomed by the magnates, whom it divided, setting clan against clan in what became a regional civil war. Some, like the Macleods of Skye, stayed more or less aloof while others, like the Whig Campbells, remained attached to the Hanoverians. The arrival of the Young Pretender, as Charles Edward was called by his ene-mies, spawned a number of small-scale internecine wars like that in Cromarty. Here, the Earl of Cromarty threatened to kill the menfolk of any village that refused to assist him, and to burn their houses.[25] For ordinary people who wished to be left in peace, neutrality was impossible, for the Jacobite army was forever short of men and supplies and used compulsion to secure both.

Many, perhaps the majority, who joined the prince's army came reluctantly. Or so claimed the survivors when they stood trial for treason. Nonetheless, the frequency with which rank-and-file rebels excused their treachery on the grounds of intimidation, the corroboration of details and the willingness of juries to accept this defence strongly suggest that they were telling the truth. Patrick Macfarlane, a tenant of Margaret, the dowager Lady Nairne, was awakened early on the morning of 21 October 1745 by Andrew Forsythe, one of her servants. He was ordered to rise and go to Five Mile House near Nairn for a muster of her tenants who were to join the prince's army at Perth. When he refused, he was warned that his horses and black cattle would be seized and sent to the Highlands. He agreed to get up and made his way to the gathering, where he found other tenants who had been summoned by Lady Nairne. She was a seventy-five-year-old beldame and an unshakable adherent of the Stuarts, whose husband and son had been involved in the 1715 and 1719 rebellions. She and her daughters distributed white cockades to the tenants while her servants received muskets from a Frenchman. Macfarlane and the rest obtained weapons when they reached Perth, but at the first opportunity he deserted and returned to his farm.[26]

The dowager was a Jacobite by conviction and well aware that if Prince Charles Edward gained the throne, her family would be compensated for the losses it had suffered (including confiscated lands) for their constancy. Equally steadfast in his devotion to the Stuarts was a Gourock factor, John Strachan. 'His youngest son, who was but a boy, he furnished out with Highland clothes, broadsword, pistols &c.,' according to the local Presbyterian minister. His other son, an Episcopalian preacher, played the recruiting-officer, promising lieutenancies and captaincies to local youths if they joined the prince. The father, using his power as a factor, extracted cash and carts from local farmers.[27]

The attentions of such enthusiasts posed a dilemma for the cautious and anyone who just wished to be left alone. When Robert Nairn was approached by Lady Crabstone with a request to raise men for her son, he sought the advice of a friend. He was told: 'it was as much as his life was worth to do any such, and . . . to go and mind his own affairs and not meddle in such matters.' Nairn did just that.[28] He was lucky, in so far as he was not pestered again. Others could not step into the shadows. Charles Gordon, whose father was staunchly pro-government and whose brother was an officer in the royal army stationed in Scotland, was seized at a fair by John Gordon of Glenbucket and forced to serve in his regiment. His sisters wept when they heard the news. Charles Gordon's heart was never in the business and the government agreed, for he was reprieved. So, too, was Alan Cameron, a married man with ten children, who had been a captain in the regiment of Donald Cameron of Lochiel, his landlord. As Alan's counsel explained to the English jurymen, he had no choice because he was a tenant and in the Highlands 'the right of [the] superior [is] always absolute.' Bound by a feudal law abandoned long ago elsewhere in Britain, Alan Cameron was a lukewarm soldier who had attempted to desert and consequently was closely watched by his more committed brothers-in-arms.[29]

John Drummond, Duke of Perth, ruthlessly browbeat his tenants to fill the ranks of his Royal Scots regiment. After ignoring two summonses, James Morrison of Perth was 'surrounded by the Duke of Perth, Lord Strathallan and more than twenty Highlanders and carried off'. Another Perth man, Daniel Macfarlane, was 'carried away' from his house and made to serve in the prince's baggage train. Sergeant Wynne 'was forced by [the] Duke of Perth as his vassal' and, like others, was threatened with the burning of his home if he refused to fight.[30] The duke kept his word: one of his officers was sent to destroy the house and cattle of men who had deserted after Prestonpans.[31] James Burrie, the son of one of Perth's servants, was given the choice of hanging or enlistment. He chose the latter. His mother, seeking to salvage something from her son's misfortune, appealed to the Duchess of Perth for his wages, discovered that he had deserted and went away empty-handed.[32]

The Pretender faced a permanent manpower crisis which his aristocratic adherents attempted to solve by going to considerable lengths to recapture deserters. James Rattray was among the Atholl tenants of William Murray, Marquess of Tullibardine, who were ordered to join the rebels or face death. Rattray gathered his cattle and took them into the hills where, after six or seven days, he caught a severe cold which forced him to return home. Unable to evade his feudal duty, he joined the army, but managed to slip away when it was in England. Rattray was caught, ran off again in February 1746 and concealed himself in the space between the ceiling and the roof of his house. A party of Highlanders was sent to bring him back and they seized his gardener by mistake. The man's wife immediately revealed Rattray's hiding place and he was hauled back to his regiment. He deserted a third time shortly before Culloden, and his story convinced a jury which found him innocent of treason.[33] And with good reason: Chief Justice Wills ruled that all that was needed to prove a man's innocence was proof of his will to desert. If he was restrained, he could not exercise this will. 'All men,' the judge added, 'have not the same degree of courage; fear will work over some more than others.'[34]

Not all the fugitives from the Jacobite army were men who had been terrorised into joining it. The demands of husbandry and hungry families were often stronger than the fear of landlords. During March 1746, Stewart clansmen from Appin had returned to their holdings to sow crops and were pursued by one of their officers who was 'threatening all those who were in rebellion to turn out once more'.[35] 'This is a tempting time of the year to look homewards for ploughing &c.,' observed Lord Glenorchy in the last week of February. His tenants were among the six hundred Campbell levies attached to Cumberland's army and he feared that if they were detained he would lose rents. Nonetheless, he knew his duty as a loyal subject and instructed his steward to prevent his men from drifting home. By the beginning of April at least fifty were back on their farms where, they claimed, their families were facing starvation. Glenorchy was 'extremely angry' at their behaviour but was heartened by the knowledge that they had repented. 'I hear they are mad at themselves for losing the opportunity of sharing the glory of their countrymen.'[36]

There were glory hunters and adventures present in the prince's army. Alexander Mather, a twelve-year-old from Brechin, joined 'out of a childish frolic' and was lucky to escape from the battlefield at Culloden. Barred from his father's house, the boy was hidden by a relative of his mother until the trouble was over. His taste for excitement remained, for he later joined the British army.[37] Like its royal counterpart, the

Jacobite army was also a refuge for misfits and those who had failed in civilian life. The death of his wife, whom he had abandoned, an inability to prosper in business and debts all impelled a James Bradshaw to join the prince's bodyguard. It was said in his defence that he was brainsick and a sleepwalker, but these disorders did not excuse treason and he was executed.[38]

Forget, then, the romantic figure of the brave Highlander, uncovering his hidden claymore and striding boldly to serve his prince. An anatomy of the Jacobite army that marched across Scotland and into England in 1745 and 1746 reveals the presence of a band of sullen, pressed men forced to fight by imperious lairds in the knowledge that refusal would mean destitution for their families. A number of the bolder or more desperate deserted whenever they had the chance rather than risk death in battle or, if they survived, execution for treason.

V

The clansmen were participants in a relatively minor campaign in the global war being fought between Britain and France in Europe, the Caribbean, America and India. Without French ships, cash and a detachment of regular troops, Prince Charles Edward could never have hoped to challenge the Hanoverian state. In the context of the wider war, his uprising was a diversion by which the French hoped to lure British troops from Flanders where, incidentally, they were doing badly. Furthermore, the possibility that additional French forces might be sent to Scotland compelled the Royal Navy to transfer ships from the squadrons blockading the French coast to home waters.

In strategic terms, the French got a decent return on what turned out to be a tiny investment. Rumours of substantial reinforcements en route for Scotland alarmed the British government to a point of panic. South-coast smugglers going about their business at Pevensey were mistaken for French landing parties early in December 1745. The government had a severe fit of jitters; there were not enough troops to defend London and the Jacobites were approaching Derby. The Sussex militia was hurriedly mobilised, but what they could do to throw back French veterans was anyone's guess.[39] During the next three months intelligence reports delivered to the prime minister, the Duke of Newcastle, indicated that an invasion was imminent. He passed on this information to Cumberland to remind him of the urgent need to trap and defeat the prince's army. By 16 March 1746 the danger had temporarily passed; spies had discovered that the French flotilla earmarked for Scotland had returned to Dunkirk.[40]

What scared the government gave hope to the insurgents. Expectations of substantial French reinforcements did much to sustain Jacobite morale and contributed to that unreal confidence that pervaded the prince's high command. There were further grounds for optimism, not least the unlooked-for and spectacular victories that marked the first phase of the rebellion. Luck favoured Charles Edward. There were about three thousand royal troops in Scotland, a high proportion of them inexperienced. Their commander, Lieutenant-General Sir John Cope, initially considered an offensive into the Highlands, but was nervous about being ambushed in unfamiliar terrain with over-extended lines of communication. He fell back to Aberdeen from where his force was shipped to Dunbar. The prince was free to leave the Highlands, enter the Lowlands and advance to Edinburgh unimpeded.

The advantage still lay with Cope, although he was short of trained gunners. His force was surprised at Prestonpans by a sudden dawn attack by the Highlanders who had been guided across a marsh by a local sympathiser. What followed astonished British officers. Their men, recalled Henry Dalrymple, were in the 'highest spirits', but these evaporated with the onrush of clansmen. 'With vast order and incredible celerity', they charged, unnerving their opponents. The dragoons broke first, according to Colonel Peregrine Lascelles, and 'their panic communicated itself to the Foot and all ran shamefully away without making the least resistance, few having fired more than once.'[41] The rout and Cope's precipitate flight from the battlefield were celebrated by a local poet, Adam Skieving, in the jaunty ballad, 'Johnnie Cope':

> Cope sent a letter frae Dunbar:
> Sayin' Charlie meet me an ye daur,
> And I'll learn you the art of war,
> If you meet me in the morning.

Hey, Johnnie Cope are you wauking yet?
Or are your drums a-beating yet?
If ye were wauking, I wad wait
To gang to the coals in the morning.

When Charlie look'd the letter upon,
He drew his sword the scabbard from;
Come follow me, my merry men,
And we'll meet Johnnie Cope in the morning

Hey, Johnnie Cope &c.

Now, Johnnie, be as good's your word;
Come, let us try both fire and sword,
And dinna flee away like a frighted bird,
That's chased frae its nest in the morning.

Hey, Johnnie Cope &c.

When Johnnie Cope he heard of this,
He thought it widna be amiss
To have a horse in readiness
To flee awa' in the morning.

Hey, Johnnie Cope &c.

Fie now, Johnnie, get up and rin;
The Highland bagpipes mak' a din;
It is best to sleep in a hale skin,
For 'twill be a bluidy morning.

Hey, Johnnie Cope &c.

When Johnnie Cope to Dunbar came,
They speer'd at him, Where's a' your men?
The deil confound me gin I ken
For I left them a' in the morning.

Hey, Johnnie Cope, &c.

Contrary to what might have been expected, the débâcle at Prestonpans did not bring Scots flocking to the prince's cause. It was and would remain precarious; royal garrisons held Edinburgh and Stirling castles and Forts William, George and Augustus. Field-Marshal Wade with nine thousand regulars was astride the main route south at Newcastle, and Cumberland with a further ten thousand was moving northwards through the midlands. William Hogarth depicted the departure of one of the duke's contingents in *The March to Finchley* (1750) which upset George II on account of the bustling confusion of the scene even though the imagery was staunchly patriotic. Henry Fielding's Tom Jones ('a hearty wellwisher of the glorious cause of liberty, and of the Protestant religion') briefly volunteered when he encountered another party of Cumberland's soldiers in Gloucestershire during his search for Sophia Western.

Jones's quarrelsome and heavy-drinking companions were on their way to engage the Jacobite army which had entered England in November 1745. It was vital that the momentum of the rebellion was kept up and so Charles Edward with 4500 men shifted south-west towards Carlisle, leaving behind a detachment of three thousand to hold Scotland. As his army trudged through north-west England it met with a frosty reception and volunteers joined at a trickle. The temper of the English showed itself when the Jacobites retired across the border in December. Isolated stragglers were attacked and killed by country people, much to Cumberland's satisfaction.[42]

The Jacobite incursion into England had caused widespread trepidation. That the Pretender had got so far was a source of indignation and fear in equal parts. Seen from the perspective of London, the clansman was a ferocious barbarian bent on pillage. Those who actually had contact with the Highlanders were less fearful. An eyewitness to their arrival in Derby described them as 'a crew of shabby, pitiful-looking fellows, mixed up with old men and boys; dressed in dirty plaids, as dirty shoes, without breeches'. However wretched its appearance, the Highland army had had the temerity to defy the government, defeat one of its armies and spread consternation everywhere.

For this and their collaboration with the French, the Highlanders were marked out for heavy retribution. That bloodthirsty humbug the Earl of Chesterfield (then Lord-Lieutenant of Ireland) urged Cumberland to give no quarter and exterminate the prince's army in September 1745. When the campaign was in its final stage, Chesterfield suggested that victory be followed by genocide in the Highlands.[43] These outbursts reflected in its most extreme form the general view of the British political establishment. Charles Lennox, Duke of Richmond, a grandson of Charles II and sometime captain of George I's Lifeguards, urged Newcastle to use the rebellion as an excuse finally to extirpate Jacobitism from the Highlands: 'I had always much rather the Duke [of Cumberland] should destroy the rebels, than that they should put down their arms, and I hope an example of a great many of them being put to the sword, and I hope a great many hanged may strike a terror in them and keep them quiet, but depend upon it nothing but force can do it, for 'tis vain think [*sic*] that any government can root up Jacobitism there.'[44]

The prime minister needed no prompting in this matter. Three days previously, on 6 March 1746, he had sent Cumberland secret instructions which, he assured him, were endorsed by George II. The duke was to adopt 'such measures as may establish the peace and tranquillity of his Majesty's kingdoms for the future'. He added, significantly in the light of what would follow, that it was imperative that 'the disaffection of the Highlands, at home, may not encourage his Majesty's enemies abroad.'[45] In anticipation of this condign collective punishment, patriotic London theatregoers sang an additional verse to the new and highly popular national anthem:

> *God grant that Marshal Wade*
> *May by Thy mighty aid*
> *Victory bring!*
> *May he sedition hush*
> *And like a torrent rush*
> *Rebellious Scots to crush.*
> *God save the King.*

It was Cumberland rather than the seventy-three-year old marshal who delivered the hammer blow that defeated Charles Edward and, afterwards, supervised the punitive régime devised to prevent the Highlands from ever again becoming a focus for French subversion. The duke's army had trailed the Jacobites back to Scotland, where they gained another fluke victory at Falkirk on 17 January 1746. As at Prestonpans, hopes were briefly raised, but the overall strategic situation was unchanged. By the beginning of March, Cumberland had gained the initiative and the Jacobite army was being nudged back to the only area where it could rely on a degree of popular support, the Highlands. The winter was exceptionally harsh and both armies suffered heavily from cold and hunger. All that could save the Pretender was the arrival of cash and reinforcements from France.

Failing this, the only viable alternative was a guerrilla campaign in the Highlands, which his adversaries feared, preferring a battle which they were now confident they could win. 'A brush would put an end to this cursed and unnatural rebellion,' Colonel the Earl of Albemarle reported to Newcastle at the beginning of March. If a pitched battle did not materialise, 'this affair may be tedious and lasting, for these villains will lead us a dance from one bad country to a worse and through the worst people I ever knew.'[46] The sort of war Albemarle dreaded seemed imminent; a week or so later parties of Highlanders overwhelmed advanced posts on that grim upland, Rannoch Moor, taking their Campbell garrisons by surprise between two and three in the morning.[47]

Rumours that French assistance would soon appear maintained Jacobite morale. A local Presbyterian minister, who, like many of his kind, acted as one of Cumberland's intelligence gatherers, reported the presence of well-known Jacobites in the glens around Brechin where, presumably, they were looking for recruits.[48] Presbyterian clergymen also displayed their loyalty to George II by reading his son's amnesty for surrendered rebels from their pulpits and offering prayers for the king. These were risky gestures; a minister in Elgin was threatened with death and had a pistol thrust against his chest.[49]

Once it was clear that no further French aid was forthcoming (Louis XV did not wish to hazard any more ships or men), Charles Edward had no choice but to offer battle or face the eventual disintegration of his army as men returned to their farms to sow crops. After all, the Highland charge had swept aside regular troops at Prestonpans and Falkirk. But the regulars were different from the men who had fled on those occasions. They had been specially coached to fight in line against men armed with swords, axes and small shields; as the Highlander engaged a redcoat, the man on his right would thrust with his bayonet at the clansman's undefended armpit and trunk. Moreover, the Highlanders had yet to be exposed to sustained and accurate artillery fire from gunners who could manage up to four rounds of round or grape shot per minute.

At Culloden the advantages in terms of firepower and training lay with Cumberland, and he had the bonus of fumbling Jacobite command. The result was swift, decisive and bloody. The Jacobite artillery was silenced by a precise, long-range bombardment from artillerymen who were then free to pound the Highland line with shot. When the charge began, fire was opened with grape which was supplemented by volleys of musketry. The onrush was poorly co-ordinated and the clusters of clansmen who reached the lines of redcoats were repelled by bayonets. Culloden was uncannily like one of those Victorian colonial battles in which steady, confident troops used discipline and firepower to repel tribal armies which, like the Jacobites, relied on bladed weapons. In common with the Zulu and Ndebele, the Highlanders showed an almost suicidal tenacity. During the battle the redcoats were amazed at how wounded clansmen had fought to the death.

VI

Culloden moor is a cheerless place. It is home to rabbits, peewits and linnets which find sustenance among the wiry grass tussocks and heather, and roost in clumps of bushes and crouching rowan trees which seem to have lost the struggle against the sharp winds that blow off the Moray Firth. Today, the battlefield is meticulously laid out. Flags mark the positions of individual regiments and clans, and signs show what happened and where. There is a visitors' centre with relics, models, uniforms, weapons and a video that explains why there was a battle and how it was fought and won. The victor's florid, puff-cheeked Hanoverian features do not figure on any of the many postcards and souvenirs that are on sale. These are decorated with images of Prince Charles Edward and clansmen in war-gear and tartans, for the battlefield museum has become a reflection of subsequent Romantic perceptions of the Highlands. The losers may not have won the hearts and minds of contemporary Scots, but they conquered those of later generations everywhere and the modern heritage industry has responded appropriately.

Modern attitudes to what had happened at Culloden are largely coloured by the events that followed. They earned Cumberland, the original 'Conquering Hero' of Handel's piece, the title 'Butcher'. George II blamed his son's vilification on 'the Scotch, the Jacobites and the English that don't like discipline'.[50] Discipline, as understood by king and duke, meant the pacification of the Highlands that had begun before Culloden and continued with extreme ferocity for several years after. It was a systematic policy enforced by largely Scottish detachments against a background of recurrent fears of a Jacobite resurgence and sporadic reports of an impending French landing. During the first stage of the repression, rumours of a reappearance of the French circulated widely and were believed by both diehard Jacobites and British commanders. The latter were sceptical of the tales of French intervention that surfaced again in February 1747, believing with good reason that they had been fabricated to compel the government to divert troops from Flanders.

By this time, large areas of the western Highlands were facing a famine. Agriculture had been disrupted by the uprising and inter-clan marauding had continued irrespective of the campaign and its outcome. Camerons ransacked and burned Campbell farms in Argyll in March, and crofts on Lord Glenorchy's estates were plundered in June 1746.[51] By far the greatest blow to the economy was delivered officially by troops, commanded first by Cumberland and then by Albemarle, as part of operations designed to neutralise the Highlands. They included the impounding of rebel livestock which was subsequently sold off to entrepreneurs who had come north with an eye to a quick profit.

By the summer of 1746 the British government had fifteen thousand soldiers distributed across the area supported by a flotilla of warships cruising off the west coast and among the Isles, all ostensibly hunting the fugitive Charles Edward. The Highlands had never seen such a concentration of armed power and its presence provided an unprecedented opportunity finally and decisively to resolve the problems of endemic lawlessness and sedition. Moreover, the war with France and the possibility that the French would again exploit the region's Jacobite sympathies justified the measures undertaken. As revealed in the letters of Chesterfield, Richmond and Newcastle, the ministerial frame of mind was unforgiving to the point where it would tolerate any excess so long as its result was permanent security. Cumberland, Albemarle and their officers knew what was required and acted accordingly. As early as February, Cumberland had permitted his soldiers to steal rebels' property so that 'they might have some sweets with all their fatigues'. But there was to be no free-for-all; on the eve of Culloden he ordered that there was to be: 'No plundering on any account except by order, and in the presence of an officer'.[52]

As the army of retribution tramped through the Great Glen to Fort Augustus, parties fanned out to pursue rebels, destroy their property and arrest those who succoured them. The language of the routine reports reflected the harshness of the measures and the temper of those who enforced them: 'Mr Graham of Gartmore seized his neighbour, notorious rebel and thief, either a McGregor or McPherson and sent him here, also a woman who harboured him and his gang and received their stolen goods . . . This man was wounded before he surrendered, and is now confined in the castle [Stirling] and will grace the gallows very well. The woman is confined in the Common Gaol, and I hope will receive the same fate.'[53] Interestingly, this pair were taken by a neighbour, presumably as an act of private vengeance for some past trespass. The pacification of the Highlands provided an ideal opportunity to pursue old feuds and scores, at least for those on the government's side.

In an emergency, legal niceties and procedures were suspended. In March, the Lord Justice Clerk complained to Cumberland about the summary hanging of a spy by the notoriously vindictive Lieutenant-General Henry Hawley. He got a dusty response from the duke's Deputy Judge Advocate, David Bruce. The victim was a 'worthless fellow' who had left the regular army five years before and used his knowledge to drill rebels. 'The Duke,' he added, 'wants to make an example of someone or other, thinking that will strike terror in the country people here.' The excuse was hardly needed, for the judge had already conceded the paramountcy of the 'great law of necessity'.[54] Its application in the Highlands during 1746 included the occasional use of torture, and forcing clansmen and their families to take refuge on the moors and mountainsides where many died from cold and hunger.[55] August was a chilly month that year.

A catalogue of the outrages was compiled by a Jacobite, Robert Forbes, the Episcopalian bishop of Ross and Cromarty, which became the basis for at least one heartrending version of the miseries endured by the rebel clans.[56] Leaving aside Forbes's partisanship, some of his stories are credible because they fit closely with what might have been expected from an army of occupation under orders to punish rebels who were also allies of their country's enemy. Seen from the perspective of a company commander traversing the glens in the summer of 1746, the Jacobites were traitors who, if they had prospered, would have embroiled Britain in a wounding civil war to the advantage of their paymaster, France.

The real tragedy of what occurred during the aftermath of Culloden was that so many of the victims had been coerced into fighting by a handful of harebrained and selfish magnates who ruthlessly exploited ties of kinship and tenancy. Even within Scotland they were a minority; some were cranks and others adventurers who enjoyed cutting a dash in tartan, and all showed the same purblind loyalty to their prince as their dependants did to them, and they too suffered for it, losing lives and estates. The chieftain-landlords were also deprived of their feudal military rights, but they retained enough legal powers to undertake the mass evictions that were a prelude to their adoption of capitalist agriculture, that is sheep farming, in the Highlands fifty or so years later.

Together, the rebels of 1745 had set out to shatter the equilibrium of British society. They miscalculated its strength, the resilience of the plutocracy that dominated it, the steadfastness and professionalism of the army, and the fact that, for all its imperfections, the political system established by the Glorious Revolution, the 1707 Anglo-Scottish Union and the Hanoverian succession satisfied the vast majority of Britons. Their feelings on these matters were summed up in one of the episodes of Tobias Smollet's *Roderick Random* (1748) in which the eponymous hero (like the author, a Scot) disputes political philosophy with a French soldier. Roderick is astounded by the Frenchman's devotion to Louis XV and his willingness to endure every form of misery just so as to add to his monarch's 'glory'. For his part, the Frenchman is angered by the way in which the British treat their kings, creatures whom he considers 'sacred' and beyond censure. 'Every man has a natural right to liberty,' replies Roderick, 'the allegiance and protection are reciprocal; that when the mutual tie is broken by tyranny of the king, he is answerable to the people . . . and subject to the law.' As for rebellions in Britain, about which the Frenchman had been caustic, they were 'no other than glorious efforts to rescue that independence which was their [the British] birthright from the ravenous claws of usurping ambition'.

Roderick offers a brief but nonetheless accurate analysis of what was at stake in the civil wars fought in Britain between 1639 and 1746 – the first to protect and render permanent parliamentary supremacy over the crown and its subjects' legal rights, the last to defend them. What would be called Britain's 'happy constitution' was the product of war, but, as it developed during the eighteenth century, it revealed that political differences could be settled by reasoned debate and a careful balancing of a vast range of individual and corporate interests. Furthermore, as its champions were quick to point out, one of the most valuable consequences of the new system was that it had produced a lasting internal peace. This was why Handel's celebratory oratorio for Queen Anne's birthday in 1713 contained a verse that compared Britain under her rule to Isaiah's vision of paradise:

> Let flocks and herds their fear forget,
> Lions and wolves refuse their prey,
> And all in friendly consort meet,
> Made glad by this propitious day.

The Jacobites were out of step with the times they troubled.

3

A parent's hand:
North America,
1775–83

I

There are Union Jacks and poppies on the mass grave of the British infantrymen killed by the North Bridge at Concord, Massachusetts, on 19 April 1775. An inscription reads:

> They came three thousand miles and died
> To keep the past upon the throne;
> Unheard, beyond the ocean tide,
> Their English Mother made her moan.

One of the dead men had been brutally murdered by a local militiaman as he lay wounded.[1] A few yards away is an obelisk that commemorates the American casualties. On it is written: 'In gratitude to God and in the love of freedom this Monument was erected.' Close by is a statue of a youthful Massachusetts militiaman with a musket, a citizen soldier in his working clothes who symbolises the patriotic courage that was vital for America's emancipation. As in all successful wars of liberation, those who won them were afterwards transformed into true heroes who had risked and sometimes lost their lives for a noble ideal.

Revolutionary propaganda depicted the war as a contest between abstractions: 'Patriotism', 'Liberty' and 'Equality' were struggling against

'Submission', 'Tyranny' and 'Privilege'. This was how it seemed to the twenty-two-year-old Lemuel Smith, a mixed-race Congregationalist preacher who joined in the fighting during the British withdrawal from Concord:

> Oh! Britain how art thou become
> Infamous in our Eye
> Nearly allied to ancient Rome
> That seat of Popery.[2]

Britain had turned its back on its old liberal values and was behaving like imperial Rome, an absolutist Empire which, in the protestant imagination, was associated with the arbitrary power of the pope. Captain William Evelyn of the 4th Foot, who was also present during the retreat from Concord, agreed. He likened the rebellion of the colonists to that of the Jews against the Roman Empire.[3]

And yet he was not absolutely sure as to what was happening around him. He also compared the conflict to a civil war, a view widely held in Britain but less so in America, although George Washington had written about the contest as 'civil discord'. In both countries there was a strong feeling that the colonies were an extension of Britain despite the recent influx of European settlers. The redcoats who fought their way from Concord to Boston must have been struck by the Englishness of the surrounding countryside, although it was less wooded in 1775 than it is today. The local vernacular style of architecture has an East Anglian feel to it, with red brick, weatherboards and classical windows and porticoes on the larger houses. Rustic cherubs and florid rococo lettering appear on the headstones in Concord's churchyard just as they do in English country graveyards. Native Americans of the Iroquois Confederation believed that the English and Americans were one nation.[4] As the crisis worsened in the colonies, the radical Lord Mayor of London, John Wilkes, warned the government that its American policy would 'plunge the nation into the horrors of a civil war'. Once the fighting had begun, opponents of the war repeated the point by their insistence that Britons and Americans shared the same ancestors. In his ode to commemorate George III's birthday in 1775, the poet laureate, William Whitehead, addressed his paean 'To Britain's sons in every clime'.

The Englishness of colonial America can be overstated. By 1775 the thirteen colonies were developing a distinctive culture and society. The southern plantation owner might occupy a colonnaded mansion like that of an English squire, whose tastes, particularly sporting, he shared, but his wealth and prestige rested on the ownership of slaves, not acres and ancestry. The colonies possessed no hereditary aristocracy and no established church, and deference did not intrude unduly into social relationships. Americans 'talk to everyone, whether he be rich or poor', noticed Georg Flohr, a German soldier serving with the French army early in the 1780s. He also discovered with surprised satisfaction that 'all the manners and prejudices' of Europe were absent from America.[5] What pleased a Rhineland peasant infuriated British officers, for whom American egalitarianism was obnoxious. One called the colonists 'a levelling, underbred, artful race of people', with whom it was impossible for a gentleman to associate, for they could not comprehend 'gratitude' and confined their conversation 'to their interest'.[6] No doubt he would have taken some comfort from the fact that the revolutionary army maintained a code with which he was familiar. An officer of the 4th New York regiment who inadvertently introduced an NCO into the officers' mess was reprimanded, and soldiers who struck their superiors were executed.[7]

It was divergent views of the nature of political ties between Britain and the colonies that led to the action at Concord. Having secured paramountcy in North America after the defeat of the French in Quebec in 1759 to 1760, the British government was preoccupied with the consolidation and future security of its Empire. Its maintenance was expensive: the North American garrison cost four hundred thousand pounds per year, 4 per cent of the annual national budget. Efforts to raise a substantial portion of this sum within the colonies provoked widespread and disorderly demonstrations which it was beyond the power of the local authorities to contain. Hitherto, the American governing classes had co-operated with the British crown, but by 1775 their compliancy could no longer be depended upon. Those magistrates and officials who remained loyal were intimidated to the point of utter demoralisation. If the protest movements had proved anything, it was that George III could no longer adequately protect his servants.

Assuming, as they did, that they enjoyed the same political rights as

Britons, the American protesters, or 'patriots' as they called themselves, insisted that only their elected colonial assemblies could levy taxes and those imposed by parliament were illegal. Having enjoyed a considerable degree of political autonomy, Americans suddenly found themselves facing closely supervised and efficient rule from Britain. Extra taxes and restrictions on settlement in what London had designated native American lands alarmed the colonists. The ideological cement for their cause was provided by English political theorists, most notably John Locke, who emphasised that government rested on popular consent. From this emerged the concept of popular sovereignty. Its catchphrases – 'all men are created equal', 'one people', and 'we the people' – littered the declarations of intent issued by the Continental Congress before and during the war. This body, with representatives from each colony, had first assembled at Philadelphia in September 1774 in response to fresh measures from Westminster which, Americans feared, was bent on the destruction of their fundamental freedoms and the introduction of centralised government in which all power flowed downwards. Pressed by an over-assertive British government, its American opponents shifted slowly, and with a degree of reluctance on the part of many, towards a position in which they contemplated detachment from the British Empire.

George III and his ministers could not stop the slide towards revolution and independence without compromising themselves and jeopardising the Empire's future. Any concessions would endanger the entire imperial strategic and commercial system and so reduce Britain's status as a major European power and curtail its trade. The 2.2 million colonists, therefore, could never expect full parity with their kinsfolk in Britain on whom they ultimately depended for their security and prosperity. The Americans were Britain's children, offspring whose subordination would be permanent and from whom gratitude was expected. The king was their benevolent father and his patience was not inexhaustible. In his New Year ode for 1776, William Whitehead reminded Americans of their filial duty:

> *Submissive hear his soft command*
> *Nor force unwilling vengeance from a parent's hand.*

George III would have approved. In 1775 he and his ministers had convinced themselves that a 'smart blow' was all that was needed to bring his wayward children to their senses.[8] It would be delivered against Boston, where they were most obstreperous and unruly.

II

Any attempt to coerce the inhabitants of predominantly rural settlements scattered over a million square miles was a gamble and would have required forces far greater than those that George III had at his disposal. Bluff was the only way in which the Americans could be taught that the government was in earnest, and so it was decided to make an example of Boston. This busy and rich entrepôt had already felt the sting of George III's fatherly chastisement. Ever since the demonstrations against the 1765 Stamp Act, it had been the powerhouse of colonial resistance. Much of it had been directed against the garrison of British troops which was regarded as a symbol of Britain's increasingly minatory policies. Relations between the army and its unwilling hosts were bad-tempered and frequently violent. In July 1769, John Riley of the 14th Regiment rebuked a butcher for striking a boy. A scuffle followed during which the indignant tradesman called the soldier 'a dirty rascal and villain' and, when asked to shake hands, he refused for fear that he would catch 'the itch'. Summoned before unsympathetic magistrates, Riley was fined 13s 4d. (67p) which he did not pay. Recalled before the bench, he and several other soldiers, including his officer, were hustled and reviled by a mob. During the proceedings, one of the magistrates, William Dennie, took the opportunity to deliver 'much invective and abuse' against the army. He urged soldiers to treat his fellow citizens with respect, for they 'carried hidden weapons about them, and they would one day give the troops a crush'. 'We want none of your Guards,' he continued. 'We have arms of our own and can protect ourselves.'[9] Dennie was active in two of the many local associations dedicated to upholding colonial rights and he was clearly convinced that standing armies were a threat to liberty.

His remarks on Bostonian belligerence were not bluster. In the next few months, off-duty soldiers were waylaid, insulted and beaten up. On

23 and 24 October 1769 a crowd congregated outside the fort's guard-room to protest against the demolition and theft of wooden fences by soldiers in search of firewood. A row followed in which the demonstrators demanded entry and were refused. Scuffles broke out and soldiers were pelted with dirt and stones.[10] Tensions increased; at the beginning of March 1770 there was a fracas between Boston ropemakers and thirty to forty soldiers, including a black drummer. His presence infuriated a local magistrate who called him a 'black rascal' and warned him to keep out of 'white people's quarrels'.[11] Then and later, liberty was strictly rationed in America.

On 5 March matters got completely out of hand. Soldiers spoiling for a fight wandered through the streets shouting. 'Where are your sons of liberty? Where are the damned buggers, cowards, where are your liberty boys?' The 'liberty boys' rose to the occasion and there was a series of brawls.[12] William Normanton of the 29th was set upon by a man armed with a hatchet and supported by a mastiff which tore his uniform and bit him. He was rescued by two blacks who were passing by.[13] A night of street-fighting ended in tragedy when an embattled and isolated picket fired a volley into a mob that had been stoning them and killed five. The disaffected called the incident the 'Boston Massacre' and exploited it as an outrageous example of British despotism.

Antipathy between citizens and soldiers whose presence they regarded as a provocation was inevitable. The policy of limited coercion was ultimately unworkable in a country where there was freedom of association and an unfettered press. This was not Britain in 1649 when, using the excuse of an extreme emergency, the army and its nominees could assume political power. Bostonians were not cowed by muskets and bayonets; quite the contrary. And, since the laws of Britain still obtained, they appealed to the courts whenever they were molested by a soldier.

After three relatively quiet years, Boston erupted again in 1773 with the famous 'Tea Party' in which containers of tea were hurled into the harbour in protest against the official monopoly that had just been awarded to the East India Company. This incident, together with regular assaults on revenue collectors, excisemen and loyal Americans, was evidence that the colonies were becoming ungovernable. Intelligence reports indicated that the Americans were organising an underground movement to forestall attempts to disarm the local militias and seize their arsenals. The government's answer was selective intimidation, and the screws were tightened on Boston. Once that city had been calmed and Massachusetts neutralised, then the rest of North America would recognise Britain's resolve and come to heel. At the very least, other colonies would be left in no doubt as to what the future held for them if they persisted in their defiance. In 1774 parliament ordered the closure of Boston, and early the next year declared that all the colonies were in a state of rebellion. These measures were also designed to reassure the unknown number of loyalists who were being bullied by militant patriots.

Statutes alone would not convince either patriots or loyalists. In Boston, Lieutenant-General Thomas Gage, the new governor of Massachusetts, was preparing a coup de main using the eleven battalions of infantry then at his disposal. If his plan worked, his troops would round up the rebel leadership, move swiftly and undetected into the countryside and occupy the militia arsenals. Few hitches were expected. The colonists were not a well-armed people and unfamiliar with the use of guns. Less than 15 per cent of Americans owned firearms and, in 1789, there were under twenty-eight thousand privately owned guns in Massachusetts, spread among a population of 475,000. Many rural militias were short of muskets and were likely to remain so, given an embargo on the importation of powder and firearms imposed in October 1774. Nor did the colonies possess the facilities to arm themselves; during the war 90 per cent of all American powder and 80 per cent of its guns were manufactured in France and Holland.[14]

Even if the colonists had had an abundant supply of weapons, official opinion from George III downwards was confident that they lacked the will to use them in battle against well-trained and disciplined regulars. Concepts of personal courage and honour were alien to men who lived by trade, manufacturing and agriculture, or so some British officers imagined. 'An army composed as theirs is cannot bear the pain of adversity,' observed Francis, Lord Rawdon.[15] When it came to facing lines of redcoats with muskets primed and levelled, American valour would falter and, if it did survive, would surely dissolve after the first volley had been fired.

The events of 19 April 1775 bruised the army's confidence. From the start, it had been impossible to maintain security and the crucial element of surprise was lost. British officers sketching the local countryside and troops regularly undergoing target practice were indications that action was imminent and it was easy to guess Gage's eventual purpose.[16] The timing of the nocturnal march was also revealed and so, as the four battalions began their excursion, messengers, most famously the Boston silversmith Paul Revere, galloped ahead to forewarn the neighbouring militia. After the exchanges of musketry at Lexington and Concord, the troops extricated themselves with difficulty from a series of ambushes by growing numbers of militiamen. Reinforcements, backed by artillery, arrived in time to prevent the retreat from turning into a rout. Their drums and fifes mockingly played what was becoming the rebels' march, 'Yankee Doodle', for which soldiers had written their own words.

> Yankee Doodle came to town to buy himself a firelock,
> We'll tar and feather him and so we will John Hancock.

Hancock was a prominent patriot. Casualties during the day totalled nearly six hundred, a third of the British troops engaged.

After its retirement to Boston, Gage's army was trapped inside the city. An attempt to break out failed at Bunker Hill with heavy losses, and in March 1776, Boston was evacuated by the new commander-in-chief, Lieutenant-General Sir William Howe. The garrison was shipped to New York to open a new front in an area where loyalists were believed to be plentiful. The Boston débâcle, coupled with a daring but ultimately futile incursion into Canada, had damaged British prestige. Britain's military bluff had been called, signal coercion had failed and political control of the colonies had fallen into the hands of local committees co-ordinated by the Continental Congress. It could only be gained when the British army proved beyond doubt that, as had long been claimed, it was invincible. The high command still believed it was, but disdain for the fighting capacity of the American soldier was now tinged with caution.[17]

Political and military objectives were complementary in the strategy for the recovery of North America. The prime minister, Lord North, believed he was facing a 'foreign' rather than a civil war, which in part explains why appeals were made for those customary standbys in European wars, mercenaries. But they and British regulars alone could not reinstate George III; this could only be achieved if America's loyalists were mobilised. For the moment they were inactive, coerced by their patriot neighbours, but the government imagined that in the right circumstances they would come forward in sufficient numbers to swing the military balance against the rebels. Many years afterwards, John Adams, one of the signatories of the Declaration of Independence, estimated that a third of his countrymen were against separation from Britain, the same proportion for it, and the rest unconcerned. An analysis of opinion on Long Island (now Queen's County, New York) indicates that 60 per cent of its eleven thousand inhabitants favoured neither side, 27 per cent were publicly loyal and 13 per cent were rebels.[18] This may be a distorted picture since the district was under British martial law. Nonetheless, these figures uphold the contemporary view that each side had to make special provisions to retain its own adherents and convert the undecided.

Whether myth or reality, the existence of a large body of potentially active loyalists mesmerised the British high command. Both Howe and his successor, Lieutenant-General Sir Henry Clinton, were sure that, in the words of the latter, their strategy had to be based upon the need to 'gain the hearts and subdue the minds' of Americans. For this reason, Howe proposed to George Washington in July 1776 that they should agree to conduct operations in a humane fashion with proper regard for civilians and their property. This principle guided Howe's own subsequent campaign around Philadelphia.[19] Throughout the war, senior British commanders conducted operations on the understanding that they were dealing with wayward subjects of the crown who, if rightly treated, would return to their allegiance. This restraint contrasted starkly with similar wars fought against rebels in Ireland in 1798 and India during the Mutiny of 1857 to 1858. American commanders were also sensitive to the unfavourable political repercussions of all-out war waged by underdisciplined soldiers. 'If we don't give security to the people how can we expect they give support to the army', ran Washington's general orders in April 1780.[20]

Many, perhaps a majority, of the British junior commanders disagreed with Howe and Clinton. Force constrained was force diluted;

America had to be reconquered and not gently coaxed back to obedience. Hammer blows delivered relentlessly were the only means to crush a rebellion that was considered 'unnatural' by officers who were temperamentally inclined to revere the crown and respect hierarchy and discipline. One hardliner, Colonel Thomas Stirling of the Black Watch, told his brother that the war was being prolonged by the refusal to burn and destroy rebel property. There could be 'no neutrality' in this war and John Bull was 'bleeding to death by these ungrateful rebellious rascals'. While he detested cruelty, Stirling believed that only the harshest measures generally applied would pacify America. His views were echoed elsewhere. 'Nothing but the bayonet and torch will ever bring this country's people to reason,' Captain Thomas Davis confided to the veteran general, Lord Amherst.[21]

Private passions often overruled general orders with the result that Americans who wanted nothing more than to be left alone were alienated from the government. Among them must have been the New York farmer who tried to prevent an officer from deliberately grazing horses in an orchard where he had just stacked apples for his cider-presses. The animals went ahead, no doubt relished their treat, and the indignant farmer was cursed by the office as a 'damned old rebel'.[22]

The policy of winning hearts through forbearance and moderation made few converts among the ordinary soldiers. Indiscriminate looting was endemic throughout a war in which troops found themselves scattered about the countryside in penny packets on patrols or picket duties. Temptation was everywhere among the rich agricultural communities and small towns, and pilfering offered some compensation for the perils and discomforts of campaigning. It could, moreover, be justified on the grounds of the hostility of the population. And then there were men who stole and sold their spoils to fund their drinking. Typical of those trapped within the vicious circle of theft and inebriation were two Guardsmen, Robert Hicks and Thomas Burrows. During the 1777 Pennsylvania campaign and 'very much in liquor', they stole out of their camp to burgle local houses and each got five hundred lashes.[23] As his regiment was passing through Edgehill, Rhode Island, in March 1777, Murdoch Macleod of the Black Watch heard a 'noise of people screaming and crying out in a house near the Rising Sun' and moments later met a soldier who dropped his loot and ran off. His spoils included 'two children's frocks, a pair of old breeches, a shirt or shift', all of which would have been sold to one of the American fences who hung around the army. The thief and his accomplices were believed to be Hessians, who were always convenient scapegoats for unpunished crimes.[24]

Civilians were assaulted, like the black Philadelphian woman whom Cornelius Dunn of the 28th Regiment threatened to kill if she did not hand over her ring. A search of his kit uncovered silver and pewter cutlery and a tablecloth, which he confessed to having stolen when his regiment 'was last out', presumably on picket duty or patrol. Three men of the 22nd Regiment, serving on Rhode Island in September 1778, stole, slaughtered and prepared for the pot fourteen sheep.[25] 'The inhabitants of this country are to be pitied,' commented captain John Peebles of the Black Watch after surveying abandoned farmsteads on Rhode Island.[26] As Howe had rightly feared, the victims of robbery and assault and families driven from their homes were unlikely to feel any love for George III.

Allegiance to the crown provided no immunity from plundering. At the end of 1776, when he was acting as a guide to royal troops operating in his former parish of Westchester, New York, the Reverend Simon Seabury found that his former flock had suffered at the hands of both armies. One, Mr Fowler, was pillaged by rebels who took forty head of livestock and told him: 'he was a damned Tory and had gone to the King's troops for protection.' Not long afterwards, a foraging party from the 17th Light Dragoons arrived at his house with empty bags which they filled with Fowler's winter stores of pork, beef and gammon. As they left, one cursed him as 'a damned rebel'. A widow from Westchester who made an official complaint after she was robbed by men from a loyalist unit, the Queen's Rangers, had the satisfaction of seeing the culprits punished. Sometime later she was found stabbed to death by a bayonet; Seabury noted that no investigation followed.[27]

Officers appalled by the extent of the looting wondered whether the army was getting out of control.[28] Brigadier-General John Campbell, the commander at Pensacola, detected a sullen, mutinous mood among his men in March 1779 on account of their being deprived of the rum they had regularly enjoyed in New York. Rather than discipline them, he appeased them by ordering a large and expensive consignment from Jamaica.[29] American officers were vexed by similar problems and efforts to solve them were hampered by the democratic spirit within their army which made men unresponsive to orders. Like its adversary, the American army was also home to soldiers who regarded military service as a licence to help themselves to what they wanted and were undeterred by the many exemplary public floggings of those who got caught.[30] But they were not to blame, loyalists believed, because they were following orders. General Charles Lee was accused of encouraging 'such wanton barbarities as Croats would blush to perpetrate' during the fighting in southern New York in December 1776.[31] Croatian troops, employed by Austria on its frontier with the Ottoman Empire, had become a byword for cruelty and greed during the recent Seven Years' War. It was debatable whether American officers, like their British counterparts, could actually prevent such outrages. In 1780 a lieutenant of the Massachusetts Regiment was dismissed for letting his men break into houses while they were on patrol.[32] Peter Dey, 'gentleman' of Tryon, New York, took wagons with him to bring back his loot when he accompanied a raiding party against Mohawk villages. Dresses belonging to the sister of the pro-British chief, Joseph Brant, were part of his haul and he passed them on to his daughter.[33]

As in the English Civil War, those who lived in areas between the opposing armies could expect ill-treatment from both. The reconnaissance or foraging patrol provided the ideal cover for looting which was undertaken irrespective of the victims' political sympathies. The British army, and with it the government, suffered the greatest harm, for the actions of individual officers and men fatally undermined their generals' policy of firm but gentle pacification. Perhaps such a policy had been unrealistic in the first place. Soldiers could scarcely be expected to treat kindly civilians who might often be their enemies. During operations in New Jersey in 1780, Hessian jaegers found it impossible to take their opponents by surprise. 'Every house that one passes is a warning piquet . . . for the farmer, or his son, or his servant, or even his wife or daughter fires off a gun or runs to the footpath to warn the enemy.'[34]

III

Like every war, the American War offered unexpected opportunities for the ambitious and unscrupulous. There were Americans who believed sincerely in the virtue of their cause and others who carefully weighed the arguments on both sides. Benjamin Franklin's son, William, rejected his father's principles and was a staunch loyalist which was, perhaps, understandable for the last royal governor of New Jersey. His father admonished him by arguing that attachment to family ought to be stronger than to a king, but William was unshaken. His property was confiscated, he was briefly imprisoned and spent some time organising loyalists in New York before travelling to London. After the war, the British government gave him £1800 in compensation for his losses and an annual pension of eight hundred pounds.

There were restless spirits who attached themselves to the rebellion in the hope of advancement and enrichment. One such was William ('Long Bill') Scott, a storekeeper from Peterborough, New Hampshire, and the son of a soldier who had served in the Seven Years' War. Wounded during the fighting on Bunker Hill, Scott explained his motives for joining his local militia: 'When this rebellion was on, I saw some of my neighbours get into commission, who were not better than myself. I was very ambitious, and did not like to see those men above me.' Long Bill refused to serve as a private and secured a lieutenancy in the hope that he would rise as his superior officers fell in battle. 'As to the dispute between Britain and the colonies,' he candidly admitted, 'I know nothing of it, neither am I capable of judging whether it is right or wrong.' Nonetheless, he stuck to his new profession. He escaped from imprisonment twice, raised a company in New Hampshire and served with it on several fronts. Scott was wounded a further eight times; his eldest son died from camp fever; he fell victim to wartime inflation and lost his farm. In 1794 he was rewarded with the post of deputy storekeeper at West Point and a small pension.[35]

Another New Hampshire man, Benjamin Thompson, a farmer from Concord, also used the war to acquire status. He entertained genteel pretensions which earned him the dislike of his homespun neighbours who suspected him of being a covert loyalist. Refused a command in the militia, he offered his services to the British, preferring the company of their officers, and became a spy.[36] Disappointed by the slow pace of his promotion in the American army, John Trumbull resigned his commission in 1779 and travelled to London to continue his career as an artist. His past overtook him and he was imprisoned for six months. Released, he made his way back to America and, the war over, returned to London and the study of painting. When it was completed he became, as it were, the artist of the American War. Among his heroic canvases were depictions of the attack on Bunker Hill and the surrender of Cornwallis at Yorktown.

William Scott's hometown of Peterborough provided a further 170 men for the American army out of a population of 549. Most served for the regulation few months, but some stayed for longer. All were from the poorest section of the community, for whom the army offered regular food and clothing; among them were two blacks, one of whom died as a prisoner of war, a debtor, eight paupers, a suspected madman and two deserters from the British army.[37] It is hard to imagine that creatures from the margins of society were fervent believers in the spirit of liberty, but the army took better care of them than civil society and they stayed for longer than men with farms or jobs to which to return.

Among the rogues who drifted in and out of the American army was Patrick Shehan. Originally a British soldier in the 10th Regiment, stationed in Dublin, he was drafted to the 62nd Regiment at the beginning of March 1775 to bring it up to strength for service in Boston. At the end of the month he deserted, persuaded, so he said, by some friends who reminded him of his responsibilities as a married man. They were not that binding, for Shehan subsequently made his way to Boston where he re-enlisted. He played truant again and joined the rebel army, from which he escaped in the company of a pair of naval deserters. If Shehan had any motive, it must have been the accumulation of recruitment bounties, which explains his severe sentence of a thousand lashes from a British court-martial.[38] He was marginally luckier than a deserter from the Maryland Regiment, who collected his bounty, deserted and then joined the 2nd New York Regiment under the name John Miles. He was sentenced to death.[39]

Americans endeavoured to lure British and Hessian troops into their army with liquor, cash and promises of land. Samuel Dyer, who seems to have been a double agent, confessed to the British that, among other things, he had been employed by the Boston patriot, Samuel Adams, to persuade British soldiers to desert with their weapons in return for land.[40] Thomas Munro of the 26th, who was captured in November 1775 during the fighting on the St Lawrence, was given drink by American officers in an effort to enlist him. He refused and was imprisoned. This convinced him that his best chance of escaping was to join the rebels, which he did. Attached to a party ordered to loot a loyalist's house, he managed to get away. A court-martial accepted his tale.[41]

Another refused to believe the amazing story of Thomas Jones, a private of the 7th Fusiliers whose picaresque adventures would have made an ideal plot for a contemporary novel. In March 1775, when his regiment was part of the tiny garrison of Canada, he made his way to Lancaster in northern New York where he got drunk and was captured by a party of rebellious militiamen. Afterwards, he was spotted in Lancaster with an American recruiting party by Sergeant Gunn of his regiment, then a prisoner of war. Jones defended himself by saying that he had escaped from the rebels at the first opportunity, but had been retaken and was brought before Washington who threatened to hang him. But the Americans needed all the men they could get, so he was given three hundred lashes and sent aboard the American frigate, *Randolph*. This may well have been the merchantman *Randolph* which was lying in the James River in May 1775. He jumped ship, was seized by a press-gang and forced to serve on another rebel vessel from which he also contrived to escape in April 1776. Jones then somehow managed to re-enter the service of George III as a seaman on HMS *Perseus* which was cruising in the Caribbean. He was transferred to one of *Perseus*'s prizes, which he helped sail to New York where, in August 1777, he was recognised by Gunn, now restored to his old regiment. If Jones is to be believed, and his account of his punishment at the hands of the American army was verified by a woman with whom he had been lodging, he had been a resourceful and durable soldier. Nevertheless, his subsequent misfortunes did not compensate for his original desertion and he received three hundred lashes.[42]

Some soldiers made a habit of switching sides. Cornelius Nix twice deserted to the Americans in New Jersey and, in March 1780, absconded a third time, taking a British prisoner of war with him, for which he was executed.[43] Men from the British garrisons at Mobile and Pensacola were deserting to the Spanish army at New Orleans, tempted by offers of land. 'The greater part [were] Irish vagabonds (deserters from the rebels),' remarked the local commander, who was also troubled by a haemorrhage of soldiers from the 60th which he thought unavoidable given that it was 'composed chiefly of Germans, condemned criminals and other species of gaolbirds'.[44] Captain Peebles noticed that a high proportion of American deserters were Irishmen, some of whom had their passage home paid by the army.[45]

Men of brittle loyalty made bad soldiers. Better to recruit those whose allegiance to the crown was proven and who, in the face of patriot violence, had often been driven from their homes and had their property confiscated in the name of the sovereign people of America. The Tories, as Americans called the loyalists, had had their morale severely damaged during the first phase of the war when they had been systematically persecuted. In November 1775 a New York Anglican clergyman lamented that 'we begin, one and all, to be convinced the nation is united and greatly incensed against us.'[46] During the following year, the government took the military initiative in New York and began preparations to create an army of loyalist auxiliaries. Heartened by Howe's reoccupation of New York city and Washington's retreat northwards, the War Office ordered equipment for ten thousand Tory volunteers. The officials had calculated correctly; by 1780 there were roughly ten thousand loyalists serving with the army.[47]

Not all, however, were Americans. Officers of the New York Loyalist Volunteers in 1782 included eight ex-sergeants from the British army, and Americans were outnumbered by Scots and Irish. Of the thirty-two officers of the Loyal American Regiment, twenty-four were American and the rest of British origin, including a former midshipman and an Irish cavalry sergeant.[48] The occupations of the Americans included a farmer, a surgeon and a merchant's clerk, despite injunctions that commissions should be restricted to men of 'rank and wealth'. George III, a stiff partisan of the gentleman's monopoly of military command, was apprehensive about the new corps which, he feared, would serve to elevate ambitious men of unsuitable birth and background.[49] Regular officers shared their king's reservations. A New York loyalist noticed the jealousy of junior officers against their volunteer colleagues. 'The men he sees passing him with fierce cockades and swords, with full pay as generals, colonels, majors &c. who the other day was his humble servant as Honest Parchment the lawyer, Thrifty the farmer, Brush the hatter &c.'[50] These amateurs were attracted to the new corps because they could obtain commissions according to how many recruits they could find.

This inducement made them indifferent to the quality or background of their volunteers. In 1779 the Inspector General of Provincial Forces complained that as a result of this system, 'Negroes, Mulattos, Indians, sailors and rebel prisoners are enlisted to the disgrace and ruin of the provincial service.'[51] Recruits of higher social status, including farmers from Long Island and New Jersey, formed the King's Military Volunteers in order to fight what was tantamount to a private war against rebel detachments who had been marauding their lands. They planned to take hostages as insurance against future raids.[52]

The most controversial of Britain's American allies were the native Americans of the six-nation Iroquois Confederation. While not averse to employing them themselves, Americans deplored their use, as did the Earl of Chatham, although as William Pitt and prime minister he had welcomed native American auxiliaries during campaigns against French Canada in the 1750s. They were again welcomed by the British twenty years later. On hearing of their participation in the war, Captain Francis Sill of the 63rd wrote: 'I am glad to find they have begun for they are like foxhounds [and] need blooding.'[53] The hunting analogy is revealing: the native American was perceived as an instinctive killer whose ferocious nature could, as it were, be tamed and usefully directed like that of a hunting-dog. Native Americans also made their prisoners undergo excruciating ritual torture before killing them, a habit that American propaganda exploited. However repellent this custom was, it was an integral part of native American culture in much the same way as that standard punishment for loyalism, tarring and feathering, was part of the colonists'. British officers, too, had qualms about native American mistreatment of prisoners during the war and that of 1812 to 1815 against the United States, but they were often forced to suppress their feelings rather than risk antagonising their allies.

Native American participation on Britain's side owed much to the persistence and persuasiveness of the mission-educated Joseph Brant, who was Britain's ambassador to the Iroquois Confederation. He argued that native American lands and freedom would be endangered if the colonists won, and his words were accompanied by a dazzling and generous collection of gifts, including rum and ostrich feathers imported from Africa. He convinced a substantial body of native Americans to abandon neutrality and join the British, although some Senecas and Tuscaloras sided with the colonists. The outcome was a sequence of pitiless raids and counter-raids at various points along the north-western frontier in which native American often fought against each other or as part of improvised units. One of these, engaged at Cobleskill, New York, in May 1778, consisted of black loyalists, white Tories and native Americans.[54]

The wider conflict was largely unaffected by these frontier campaigns. In 1779 a large expeditionary force commanded by Major-General John Sullivan penetrated Iroquois territory in an attempt to knock the native Americans out of the war, but failed. It did inflict considerable economic damage on their agriculture, but did not deter further raids which continued until the end of the fighting in 1782. Atrocities were commonplace and committed by both sides, often wantonly. Native Americans proved to be the ultimate losers from the war. Diehard white loyalists were able to flee to Britain or Canada, where they were resettled with government assistance, but the native Americans had to stay and live alongside the colonists whose independence some had tried to prevent. They had a foretaste of what the future held in store for them in March 1782, when an American militia detachment slaughtered over a hundred Delawares, all Moravian Christians, pacifists and neutral.[55]

The War of Independence split the colonies: native Americans fought against native Americans, and Tories fought against rebels, often in localised campaigns where the larger issues were lost from sight. Black Americans joined both armies. They gained nothing from their efforts; slaves who fought for George III were promised their liberty, but when the war was over many who survived were shipped to the West Indies and renewed servitude.

IV

After 1778, the scale and nature of the war were transformed. The failure of the British army to make headway in America during the previous year persuaded France, then Spain and the Netherlands, to enter the conflict in the hope that they could recover overseas territories lost in the Seven Years' War. The American struggle was now one part of a world war in which Britain was friendless and overstretched on every front. Thrown on to the defensive in the Atlantic and Caribbean and, in 1779, threatened by a French invasion, Britain had to divert ships and men to new theatres of war. Inside America, the British army stuck to the hope that the loyalists could be mobilised in sufficient strength to secure an outright victory. From the end of 1778 the centre of operations shifted to the southern colonies which were believed to be lukewarm towards independence and home to many loyalists. Whatever opportunities did exist were lost, for, as on other fronts, field commanders followed contradictory strategies, some adopting a hard line, others a milder one. In 1781, the Royal Navy temporarily lost control of American waters and this precipitated the surrender of General Sir Charles Cornwallis's army to a Franco-American force at Yorktown. Two years later, a peace was signed in which the British government acknowledged American independence.

Few wars have had such far-reaching repercussions for world history as that waged by the British to regain North America. The colonists' victory created the United States, a republic whose government was framed along democratic lines and where a man's place in society depended upon his talent and energy rather than his parents' rank. The war had guaranteed that all white American citizens enjoyed those civil and legal liberties that they had always insisted belonged to all Britons. For the next hundred years the American republic existed in a world dominated by absolutist monarchies and, for European liberals, became a beacon which both enlightened and encouraged. The United States was a shining example of what a free people could achieve within a just society where their collective will shaped the laws. America was the future, and it appeared to work.

It was also an expansionist state, driving its frontier westwards and, simultaneously, attracting an increasing number of immigrants from

Britain and the continent. All believed that the American system offered them a better chance of advancement than existed in their homelands. And for many it did; a hundred years after the shots at Concord the United States was well along the path that led to unequalled global economic power and, in the twentieth century, worldwide military supremacy.

The nature of the war against Britain had in large part defined American citizenship in terms of popular participation in government at all levels and the right to carry arms in defence of the citizen's natural rights. It was therefore fitting that the first free man of what would become an experiment in government should have been portrayed at Concord as a man holding a gun. When one contemplates him and the prosperous countryside in which he stands it is easy to picture the war as a contest between 'village Hampdens' and an overbearing tyranny, which is what it has become in the American popular imagination. Appeals to the values of the 'Founding Fathers' still provoke a positive political response in the United States, although in many respects they were more appropriate to the rural communities of Massachusetts than to a complex, multiracial, industrial superpower. Moreover, American perceptions of liberty coexisted uneasily with a savage intolerance that had expressed itself in the persecution of the loyalists. Fear of the 'enemy within' is another legacy of the war, and one that has periodically resurfaced in predictably ugly forms. Senator McCarthy's denunciations of suspected communists in the early 1950s were a form of tarring and feathering.

The war had extensive consequences for Britain, where successive governments came to appreciate that it was imprudent and impractical to deprive Britons of legal and political rights once they left home to settle overseas. Within a hundred years of America's independence, Canada, the Australian states, Cape Colony, Natal and New Zealand were all self-governing, and educated Indians were beginning to talk about self-determination in terms that would have been immediately recognised by Boston patriots in the 1770s. The War of Independence had dictated the future form and, for that matter, the eventual fate of the British Empire.

By Jesus, we have dirks and arms a-plenty: Ireland, 1798–1800

I

Dr William Kirk was frank with the British officer who interviewed him in Carrickfergus castle during the second week of September 1798. There was no point in evading the questions, for his own record was well known to his captors. The previous June he had led a body of Antrim rebels, riding a horse that was said to have been stolen, and with forty men had overwhelmed the garrison of Ballyclare, seven miles away. His questioner wanted to know the present mood of the people, in particular how they would react to the French invasion that was expected daily. Kirk was sure that popular support for a republic was still strong because the Irish believed that this form of government was 'most conducive to their comfort and happiness'. Among its benefits were fewer taxes and the disappearance of tithes rendered to the heretic Anglican church. 'Some of the better sort', he continued, were frightened that conquest by France would be followed by anarchy and the destruction of their property. Only the appearance of the French would trigger another rebellion because the people lacked the 'fortitude' to act on their own.

This observation puzzled his interrogator, who had witnessed the bravery of the insurgents in the face of overwhelming odds, and so he asked Kirk to be more explicit about this lack of 'fortitude'. 'He replied in comparison with the efforts made by the people of France and

America.'[1] Kirk's analysis of the temper of the Irish revealed what the army already suspected; general orders in the event of a French landing insisted that every effort be made to prevent the invaders from having any contact with the Irish. An anonymous letter sent to Colonel Robert Anstruther, the officer in command at Carrickfergus, warned of a spontaneous uprising in which yeoman cavalrymen would be slaughtered in their homes and their weapons seized. Afterwards, the insurgents would shift into the hills and wait for the French.[2]

No one could predict when or where the French warships and transports would arrive, and so the defences of Carrickfergus were being hurriedly strengthened in case they appeared in Belfast Lough. It was ironic that Kirk and other rebel prisoners were confined within an Anglo-Norman stronghold, built at the beginning of the English ascendancy in Ireland. As he had explained, it was again under challenge from below, and by men and women animated by the same dreams, if not the same resolve, as the American rebels and the French revolutionaries.

Irishmen had been moved by the example of the Americans, but recent events in France proved their greatest inspiration. The 1789 French Revolution had laid the way for an egalitarian state governed by the general will and abolished aristocratic legal privileges and, in 1792, the monarchy. If Frenchmen could create a perfect state, then why not the Irish, who were also burdened with what many considered an equally unjust and oppressive ancien régime. The implications of what was happening in France were eagerly discussed by Irishmen who joined the political clubs that suddenly mushroomed and in which traditional sectarian animosities were temporarily suspended.

The political ferment was greatest among the middle classes. Professional and businessmen, manufacturers and shopkeepers were the backbone of the United Irishmen, a nationwide association founded in 1791 to agitate for parliamentary reform and the removal of restrictions on Catholics in public life. During the next four years the United Irishmen were transformed into revolutionaries dedicated to overturning the Irish government and founding a democratic republic on the French model. This change of direction was to a large extent dictated by events in France. Members who had enthusiastically celebrated Bastille Day as the birth-day of Liberty became increasingly disturbed about how France was changing and why. Louis XVI's execution, the Terror of 1793 to 1794, the persecution and impoverishment of the church and the erosion of property rights dismayed Catholics and men of substance. Whatever its reason, disillusion with France produced a fall in the United Irishmen's membership. At the end of 1794 the organisation was withering. Within a year it had revived and was shifting leftwards. In its new, radical form the United Irishmen cultivated a mass appeal, attracting artisans, labourers and peasants with a revolutionary programme designed to create a democratic Irish republic. Hitherto hostile to any alliance with France, the United Irishmen were now prepared to invite the French army to assist them in what would be a violent revolution.

Even with French support, the revolutionaries would need as many men as they could get. Anyone with even rudimentary military knowledge was most welcome, and efforts were made to subvert Irish militiamen and yeoman cavalrymen. By the middle of 1796 the United Irishmen's leadership imagined they had converted over two thousand militiamen (almost a tenth of those in uniform) and that as many as one hundred thousand civilians were ready to rise in Ulster alone.[3] In all likelihood, these figures owed more to optimism than arithmetic, and a pledge of active support, even when backed by an oath, did not guarantee that a man would appear in arms when summoned. To make sure that he would, and to provide a command structure, the United Irishmen created an underground organisation that extended throughout Ireland. The highest priority was given to procuring arms and instructing members in drill.

For the Tory Sir Richard Musgrave, the United Irishmen were traitors who had learned the arts of seditious organisation from the Americans. The movement's leadership was driven by envy. Linen drapers 'who made immense fortunes' were jealous of the nobility and gentry 'on account of their superior weight and respectability'. To swing the balance of political power in their favour, such men were prepared to proselytise peasants, labourers and craftsmen and teach them 'to think themselves amply qualified to dethrone kings and regulate states and empires'.[4]

In crude terms, he was describing the new philosophy of the United Irishmen and its alliance with a very different organisation, the

Defenders. They belonged to an older Irish tradition of resistance, which was rural, clandestine, nocturnal and violent. Its targets were landlords, their agents and anyone who exercised official power in the countryside. Assassination, arson and the mutilation of livestock were its methods. Secrecy was essential in this furtive and nihilistic war; each Defender was bound by an oath of loyalty to his brothers and to a cause that, if it ever succeeded, would return the land to the native Irish and re-establish the Catholic church. Notwithstanding the secularism of the French Revolution, the Defenders were able to persuade themselves that French soldiers could liberate their country and deliver them the land that had been stolen from their countrymen over the past eight hundred years.[5] An oath found on a Defender hanged at Carrick-on-Shannon said it all: he had sworn 'To quell all nations, dethrone all kings and plant the true religion that was lost since [the] Reformation'.[6]

Men travelling in the course of their work or in search of it acted as recruiters, both for the United Irishmen and the Defenders. A flat joke circulating among army officers in 1798 described the arrest of a Dublin organ-tuner in Wexford who was discovered to be an agent of the United Irishmen. A wag remarked he had been 'sent down to organise the country'.[7] Persuading men to pledge themselves to the cause was a hugger-mugger business even in tightly knit and remote rural communities. Michael McMully, a carpenter and agent for the United Irishmen, took the oath of Paddy McWilliams in his cowshed. The farmer promised to help the French and destroy all gentlemen and clergymen, and was shown a sealed document from Belfast which listed all United Irishmen, including himself. These proceedings were overheard by Mrs McWilliams who was standing by the slightly open byre door, a flimsy structure of 'woven broom and twigs'. Three months later, in January 1797, she denounced her husband and son, John, to the Tyrone magistrates. She also declared that James McGuinn, a deserter from the Tyrone Militia, had drilled United Irishmen at her husband's farm and that Patrick Glasse of Tambiskenny had boasted to her about his narrow escape from a party of soldiers looking for arms. 'By Jesus,' he confided to her, 'we have dirks and arms a-plenty.'[8]

What made Mary McWilliams betray her husband, son and neighbours? On the surface it was an extremely dangerous act, for which she would have faced at the very least ostracism by her community and at the worst assaults on herself, her property and livestock. She may have been compelled by terror (soldiers regularly extracted confessions by flogging), unbearable domestic tensions, frustration, or the offer of a reward. More easily imagined were the motives of an Enniscorthy schoolmaster and committee member of the local cell of the United Irishmen. He saved himself from transportation and his dependants from the poorhouse by revealing the whereabouts of a store of pikes in return for a passage to America for himself and his family.[9] Hundreds of men and women were forced to make similar decisions, choosing between survival and loyalty to kinsmen, friends and a cause.

From 1794 onwards, the testimonies of informers and spies, together with suspects' statements made to magistrates, presented a picture of a widespread, underground movement dedicated to violent revolution and willing to collaborate with the French. Intelligence reports of covert drilling, thefts of firearms from gentlemen's houses and the manufacture of pike staffs and heads indicated that the creation of the military infrastructure for a revolutionary army was well in hand. There was no way of knowing how far the preparations had advanced, the precise number of those involved, or whether the French would co-operate. One thing was certain: the authorities in London and Dublin would do everything in their power to crush the revolutionaries and deprive them of leaders and arms.

II

Since the beginning of 1793, Britain had been at war with France. The prime minister, William Pitt the Younger, and his cabinet quickly realised that victory would require an unparalleled mobilisation of the nation's manpower, capital and resources in what turned out to be Britain's first 'total' war. Ireland had to deliver its full share of men, money and matériel; by 1799, 78 per cent of its annual revenue was being spent on the war.[10] So desperate was the government for Irishmen in the forces that Kirk's fellow prisoners in Carrickfergus were offered army service in the West Indies as an alternative to transportation to Australia.[11] Many former rebels accepted the bargain, although they must have known that their chances of survival were slim in an area infamous for its torrid climate and fevers.

The direction of recruitment and the Irish war-effort was in the hands of successive lords-lieutenant and their staff who ruled from Dublin Castle. Their power was immense; more than half the MPs in the Dublin parliament were controlled through patronage, and a web of spies and informers watched over the rest of the population. Coercion and policing were provided by a garrison of just under ten thousand regular troops who were scattered across the country. This vital prop of a widely unloved administration was gradually removed during the first three years of the war as more and more soldiers were drafted to the Low Countries and the Caribbean.

To replace these men, Dublin Castle had to win over the Catholic majority, so long excluded from any form of public service. In an attempt to secure the loyalty of the richer Catholics, the vote was granted to those with freehold land worth more than two pounds per year, although they were still debarred from standing for parliament and continued to be excluded from the higher echelons of the administration. In return, Catholics, mainly from the poorer classes, were made liable for militia service. The 1793 Militia Act prompted serious riots in which over two hundred were killed after regular troops were called in to suppress protests.

Nevertheless, the measure worked and, by January 1798, over twenty-two thousand Irishmen were serving with the militia regiments which performed the same internal security duties as the former regular garrison. Asking the poorer Catholics to police their own kind was a gamble, and the government did all it could to protect the militiamen from any external pressures that would test their loyalties. In January 1797 the commander-in-chief ordered every officer to take pains 'to know the character of every man in his company', which presumably included his political sympathies, if any. At the end of the year, and for their 'safety and tranquillity', detachments were always to be accompanied by an officer whenever they were more than a mile from their quarters.[12] Isolated bodies of men could find themselves ambushed for their arms or, and this was just as likely, approached by subversives. It was assumed that in either case they were incapable of acting on their own initiative.

In February 1798, and against a background of growing unrest, all militiamen were paraded and addressed by their officers who relayed an appeal from the government. 'Let them never forget they are British and Irish soldiers, a name to which Honour, Courage and Fidelity has ever been attached, which has rendered them the terror of their enemies and secures to them the affection and confidence of their country.' But each soldier needed to be wary, for, unable to beat them in battle, their foes would overcome them by 'means of corruption'. Any man who succumbed to subversion could expect no mercy; listeners were told that two soldiers from the Dublin Militia had recently been hanged for mutiny and sedition, and five given between five hundred and a thousand lashes. Each had been found guilty of urging their colleagues to take the United Irishmen's oath. Old sectarian antipathies also strained a soldier's loyalty. Just over a week later, militia officers were ordered to be vigilant for any hint that their men were forming clubs 'under the denomination of Orange Men'. Officers were reminded of the 'impropriety of such associations' and were to 'impress in the minds of the soldiers that no distinction should exist among his Majesty's loyal subjects and that the character of a soldier rests on the faithful discharge of his duty and the obedience he pays to the orders he receives.'[13]

The expansion of the militia had occurred at a time when religious acrimony was becoming more bitter and threatened to split both the revolutionary movement and the armed forces. Seen from any perspective, the protestant ascendancy in Ireland was showing signs of severe strain in the early 1790s and clearly could not survive in its old form. Laws relaxing the legal restrictions on Catholics, however limited, indicated that henceforward they would enjoy a degree of political power. Protestants from the lower classes resented these developments, sensing that their reassuring superiority was being diminished and might be further reduced. They were also alarmed by the spread of Defenders who were viciously sectarian and whose terrorism was often directed against protestants. A Defenders' secret password, ELIPHISMATIS, was alleged to have been based upon the initial letters of 'Every loyal Irish Protestant heretic I shall murder and this I swear'.[14]

Religious tension was most acute in Armagh, a densely populated county where people of Scottish, English and Irish descent were in competition for scarce land. Secret societies were common and resorted to forms of intimidation that in many ways resembled the 'ethnic cleansing' undertaken in Yugoslavia two hundred years later. In 1795 and 1796 thousands of Catholics were expelled from Armagh to Connaught, most in fear of their lives. It was against this background and in reaction to the Defenders' outrages that the Orangemen emerged in September 1795. They were as bigoted and bloodthirsty as their adversaries, which was clear from Orange papers that fell into the army's hands in May 1798. Noviciates pledged themselves to exterminate Catholics and were expected to respond to the question, 'Can you swim?' with 'Knee deep in Roman Catholic blood'.[15]

The rhetoric of murder prepared men for the deed. Growing sectarian tension led to brawls which military discipline could not prevent. A row over an Orange cockade displayed on a hat led to a fracas in which eight Catholic Kerry militiamen lost their lives fighting with Orangemen and the yeomanry at Stewartstown in County Tyrone in July 1797.[16]

This was just the sort of mayhem that the military authorities had endeavoured to prevent and which added to their anxieties about the trustworthiness of Catholic militiamen. Similar apprehensions were felt about the yeomanry, first raised in 1796 specifically for internal security. Within a year, thirty thousand Irishmen had volunteered, of whom eighteen thousand were mounted, and they were distributed throughout the countryside in small troops, usually of less than a hundred. Units inevitably reflected the local religious balance, with Kerry's yeomanry being almost entirely Catholic. Nonetheless, and to a large extent as a consequence of atrocities committed during 1798, the yeomanry was regarded as a predominantly Orange force in subsequent nationalist demonology.

Like the militia, the yeoman cavalry might easily become a Frankenstein's monster, capable of wounding, even destroying, its creator. It was impossible to foretell which way the new, amateur soldiers would jump in an emergency. Would Catholic militiamen fire on men and women who shared their religion and condition in life? And it was the spirited daughter of 'the Captain of the Yeos' who rallied the 'brave United Irishmen' in that rousing rebel song 'The Boys of Wexford'. It took a woman to remind men of where their duty lay, but this is not to say that her father, like many other yeomanrymen, was not fighting for the crown. Many did in 1798, both Catholic and protestant, as did a majority of Catholic militiamen.

III

The pro- and anti-government forces in Ireland in 1798 were unevenly balanced. The revolutionaries had the power to frighten the government; of that there was no doubt. But Dublin Castle would not surrender control of the country and jeopardise the national war-effort without a struggle in which it was fully prepared to go to any lengths to crush every form of dissent. Its resolution was its greatest strength. This was not America, where ministers and generals felt the need for restraint and waged war accordingly. The Irish situation was more akin to that in the Highlands in 1746; Britain was engaged in a war in which it was performing disappointingly and, to use a modern term, the Irish dissidents were an armed fifth column. Their potential for mischief was demonstrated in the last week of 1796 when French men-o'-war and transports carrying 14,450 soldiers appeared off Bantry Bay. This armada had slipped past the naval blockade, which could no longer be relied upon as Ireland's first line of defence. Only extraordinary good fortune in the form of severe weather and storms which scattered the fleet prevented a landing. Had the French come ashore, then government forces would have been stretched to breaking-point fighting both the invaders and Irish rebels.

The Bantry Bay episode was followed by another, greater shock. In the early summer of 1797 there was a general mutiny throughout the Channel Fleet which stunned the government. Irish sailors had been involved and there were fears that the mutineers had been influenced by domestic agitators who wanted a revolution in the French manner. Ministers may have been unduly alarmist, but given the intelligence they were receiving their fears of uncontrollable sedition were understandable, as was their determination to root it out. A government that imagined its position was precarious was willing to condone any measures that enforced loyalty. These considerations shaped the savage policies adopted in Ireland during the second half of 1797 and in 1798.

Repression on the scale needed required substantial and dependable reinforcements. The backbone of the drafted units were English, Welsh and Scottish fencibles, who were volunteers whose terms of service confined them to the British isles. In some cases they were recruited by landowners from among their tenants and their loyalty was beyond doubt, as the Irish soon discovered. The pugnacity of these troops was advertised by public announcements issued by some units on their arrival in Ireland. The NCOs and privates of the Midlothian Fencible Cavalry announced to the people of Dundalk that they would remain loyal 'as long as life exists'. The 'infamous and dastardly scoundrels who call themselves United Irishmen', who were too scared to meet them in the field, were promised rough treatment, as was anyone who dared attempt to subvert the cavalrymen or insult George III. The fencibles also assured the discontented that they would 'make example' of any traitor they captured before delivering him to the law.[17] Once the rebellion was underway, a poet attached to the detachment (he was either a trumpeter or farrier) added a couple of verses to the triumphant yeomanry song 'Croppies Lie Down':

> You Croppies of Wexford, I'll have you be wise
> And go not to meddle with Midlothian Boys
> For the Midlothian Boys, they know and declare
> They'll crop off heads, as well as your hair.
>   Derry, down, down.
>
> Remember at Ross, and at Vinegar Hill
> How your heads flew about like chaff in a mill
> For the Midlothian Boys when a Croppy they see,
> They blow out his day-lights, or tip him cut three.
>   Derry, down, down.[18]

The 'Croppies' were United Irishmen who cut their hair short in what was taken to be the fashion in Revolutionary France. It was an unwise advertisement of political affinity because some soldiers made paper caps, filled them with molten tar and, as it were, crowned their victims. The grisly result was burnt hair and blistered flesh.

Tar-cropping was one of the many torments inflicted by troops carrying out orders designed to terrorise dissidents into submission. The Midlothian Boys told the people of County Louth to expect 'acts of rigour' from their nocturnal patrols in search of United Irishmen and their arsenals. Unnerved by the near-miss French invasion at the end of 1796, Dublin Castle sanctioned a reign of terror in which troops were free to do as they pleased so long as they hauled in rebels. The Irish parliament provided the necessary legal apparatus, and individual officers were left to select their own methods. If there was a model for this systematic brutality, it was, paradoxically, that of the *colonnes infernales* of the Vendée, where the forces of the French republic had criss-crossed the countryside inflicting summary and savage punishment on royalist and Catholic insurgents during 1793 and 1794.[19]

The security forces made little effort to discriminate between the disaffected and the neutral. Suspects were regularly flogged until they revealed the names of United Irishmen and where their arms were hidden. It required superhuman devotion to a cause or friends for a man to stay silent as his flesh was torn apart, and many succumbed to pain, telling their interrogators what they wanted to know. Weaponry was confiscated and the United Irishmen's organisation was fractured in many areas. Its members now lived from day to day, often as fugitives, and, as the pressure intensified during the first quarter of 1798, many saw that an uprising was the only way in which they could escape from their tormentors. The possibility that the coercive measures would prove so unbearable as to compel the United Irish to rebel precipitately was welcomed in official quarters. Dublin Castle had the initiative and, as time went by, was bound to secure the upper hand. If, and there seems to be little doubt that this was the case, Dublin Castle had set out to provoke a revolution the better to crush it, then it had succeeded. The odds were shortening in its favour during 1798; the garrison had more than doubled to 77,600, of whom just over a half were yeomanrymen, and there were now 22,360 Irish militiamen and 12,600 fencibles. In theory, and assuming that the French navy did not break the blockade a second time, this force was thought sufficient to cope with the rebels whose numbers were estimated at around two hundred thousand.

Official arithmetic did not include any assessment of the quality of the troops, which was giving grounds for concern. Contact with various militia units in early 1798 convinced Major-General Sir John Moore

that their officers were 'profligate and idle', displayed their protestantism arrogantly and, not surprisingly, earned no respect from their
men.[20] Discipline was dissolving among the hundreds of small, isolated
detachments as soldiers supplemented official torments with their own;
allegations of rape, robbery and arson were widespread and substanti-
ated. Major-General Sir Ralph Abercrombie, who took command early
in 1798, was shocked by the reports of his army's crimes and attempted
to soften the measures, which displeased the hawks in Dublin Castle.
They warmly welcomed his successor, Lieutenant-General Sir Gerard
Lake, whose recent disarming of Ulster showed that he had no qualms
about applying martial law with the utmost severity.

The pace and rigour of the government's counterinsurgency measures
directly reflected growing anxieties about French intervention. For the
past six years the United Irishmen's leadership had cultivated close
relations with successive Revolutionary régimes in Paris. Lord Edward
Fitzgerald and the brothers Henry and John Sheares had joined the
Paris Jacobin Club and, while serving in the city's National Guard,
had watched the trial of Louis XVI. Their appeal to the French was
largely on ideological grounds; liberating Ireland would represent a
blow in a war that the Revolutionaries had represented as a struggle for
the emancipation of Europe from crowned tyrants. There were also
good strategic reasons for a diversionary campaign in Ireland. The uprising in the Vendée and the counter-revolutionary *chouannerie* in
Britanny had taught the French how a domestic guerrilla war could
soak up men, money and energy. Britain had actively assisted the enemies of the republic and there was a desire to retaliate in kind. In a
sense, the 1796 expedition to Bantry Bay was a response to the British
landing at Quiberon Bay in support of the royalist Breton *chouans* the
previous year.

But by early 1798 French strategic objectives had changed. Ireland
took second place to the grandiose coup de main planned against Egypt
by an army commanded by the up-and-coming Napoleon Bonaparte.
The *Armée d'Angleterre*, earmarked for a seaborne attack on Ireland,
dwindled as men were drafted to other fronts. After operational delays,
the Irish expedition sailed early in August with just three thousand men
and, given British dominance of the seas, slight chances of reaching its
destination.

Ignorant of the condition and mood of their fellow countrymen, the leading Irish émigrés in Paris, Theobald Wolfe Tone and Napper Tandy, were unaware that the United Irishmen were facing the worst crisis in their existence. The army had shifted its operations from Ulster to the middle counties and everywhere the situation of the Catholic population was becoming desperate. Rumour ran that Dublin Castle was about to unleash an Orange terror in which Catholics would be massacred. At the top, the United Irishmen's leadership procrastinated. They believed that they could mobilise 280,000 men, but co-ordination was bound to be difficult thanks to Dublin Castle's intelligence and the army's elimination of much of the movement's local infrastructure. As soldiers traversed the countryside, leaders became fugitives. In County Carlow, 'All were obliged to quit their houses and hide themselves the best way they could.'[21] With the lower echelons in disarray, those at the top were facing a dilemma: was it wiser to move only when the French were ready, and risk a further splintering of the organisation's framework, or to rise at once? To some extent the question became academic during the second half of May when Fitzgerald and the Sheares brothers were arrested. There was now only one way forward; thrown on the defensive and facing gradual extinction, the United Irishmen had little choice but to play their hand.

IV

Dogs barking throughout the night were a feature of life around Wexford during May 1798. They had been alarmed by the noises of bodies of men drilling and cutting down ash trees to make staffs for pikes. During the day, yeomanrymen and soldiers strutted through the town provocatively singing 'God save the King' and loyalist songs, accompanied by what would become the instruments of future Irish discord: fifes and drums.[22] These sounds were the overture to an insurrection that from the beginning was unco-ordinated and improvised. It was suppressed within six weeks in one of the nastiest wars ever fought in the British isles.

The first districts to rise were Kildare and Carlow where, during the final week in May, the insurgents were swiftly overwhelmed. The victory at Carlow was followed by a massacre of fugitives which concentrated minds in County Wexford, where the population swung towards the rebels as much to protect themselves from the army as to free Ireland. Wexford was seized at the very end of the month, but efforts to extend the uprising north-eastwards and into Waterford failed when the insurgents were defeated at Arklow and New Ross. Thereafter, the momentum of the rebellion slackened and the twenty-thousand-strong insurgent army encamped at Vinegar Hill. In Ulster the local leadership prevaricated and when it came, the uprising was botched. The Antrim United Irishmen rose, unsupported, on 7 June, and were resoundingly beaten four days later at Ballynahinch.

It was also a victory of religious over political convictions. On the eve of Ballynahinch, there was a row over who should be in command between a Catholic officer, John Magennis, and a Presbyterian, Henry Munro. The matter was settled by tossing a coin and Magennis won, which enraged Munro, who 'drew his sword and did cry aloud his intention was to establish a Presbyterian independent government'. This was not the goal of Magennis and the Catholic contingent, who slipped away to their homes during the night.[23] The sense of common purpose that had originally been achieved by the United Irishmen six years before dissolved and ancient tribal and sectarian passions reasserted themselves. The rebellion became a religious war, an extension on a larger and more brutal scale of the conflict between Defenders and Orangemen that had been simmering during the previous three years.

There was something approaching a pogrom of protestants in the Kildare and Wexford sectors of the rebellion where old hatreds and frustrations boiled over and men hit out wildly. Unable to catch its master, a protestant revenue officer, one mob killed his dog.[24] Revenge was the chief motive and it was random. Servants of, and the real and imagined supporters of, tyranny were shown no pity. Victims of the government's terror, some with the scars of tar-cropping, arrived at Vinegar Hill and 'claimed the right of vengeance' on the towns where they had suffered.[25] In Dublin it was said that a lady's maid had told her: 'Mistress, you had better go to mass; for the pikemen will soon come into the city and pike all the Protestants.'[26] On both sides the fear and hatred had reached such a pitch that such tales were taken as gospel. The rebels who massacred protestants at Wexford and elsewhere had nothing to lose save their pent-up anger and despair as their opponents gained the upper hand. As insurgents, their lives were already forfeit; Lake had ordered no prisoners to be taken and his men were glad to obey. In defeat, there was some visceral satisfaction in retaliation against anyone who could be considered an enemy and, for the rebels of 1798, all protestants were so by definition.

Defeat came swiftly to the rebels. Their standard weapon was the pike, which could repel cavalry charges and did so on several occasions, but was useless against artillery fire and musket volleys. The largest concentration of rebels, in County Wexford, was hampered by a lack of firearms, powder and gunsmiths.[27] When the camp at Wexford was attacked on 21 June, heavy casualties were suffered from cannon fire, with columns of pikemen torn apart by howitzer shells and round and grape shot.[28] Counterfire from the insurgents' few cannon was poorly aimed, because they possessed few trained gunners. Nevertheless, they had some inspiring leaders. According to the rebel Miles O'Byrne, they were 'young men, sons of gentlemen farmers, and the farmers' sons . . . whom the people looked up to with confidence in this perilous struggle'.[29] Even in an uprising whose goal was an egalitarian republic, command in battle remained the prerogative of those who dominated society, as it did among the government's forces. But not always; one cell of United Irishmen elected as its commander a man whose qualification was his repertoire of rebel songs.[30]

As for the ordinary rebels, civilians in arms in coats, shirts and countrymen's flowerpot hats, their purblind courage astonished their adversaries. The Reverend Thomas Hancock, rector of Kilcormick, who was prepared to defend George III and the Thirty-Nine Articles with a blunderbuss with a spring-loaded bayonet, praised 'the extraordinary degree of intrepidity' displayed by the Wexford rebels who grabbed bayonets with their bare hands and hurled themselves against the muzzles of loaded muskets.[31] When it was all over, onlookers were struck by the nonchalance with which condemned men faced the gallows.[32]

By the beginning of July, the surviving insurgents were all fugitives, occasionally capable of winning small-scale rearguard actions against their pursuers, but little else. Isolated guerrilla units would continue fighting in remote areas for months. In December, three men of the Loyal Tayside Fencibles were ambushed near Ballymena and robbed of their muskets. Their commanding officer suspected, probably rightly, that they had been drinking at a local fair, which explained their feeble resistance.[33]

Promiscuous and ferocious retribution followed. Callousness had become habitual among the security forces during the preceding three years. The newly arrived Captain Thomas Hodges of the West Kent Militia discovered how ingrained it was when a gaoler complained to him: 'I hate this dribble, dribble work, I shall soon have my own gallows and I can hang thirty at least at a time.' The Kentish soldiers had just arrived in Ireland and were soon infected with the prevailing mood. After watching a mass execution at Kilkenny, Hodges observed: 'our soldiers seemed overjoyed at the proceedings, in fact were execution-ers.'[34] Such deterrent exhibitions were needed, for the threat of French intervention remained. No one knew for certain when, where and in what strength they would arrive, but it was assumed that, unless thor-oughly intimidated, the population would welcome them.

When the French did appear, they were too late and too few. Less than two thousand, commanded by General Jean Joseph Humbert, came ashore at Killala Bay, County Mayo, on 26 August. He immedi-ately called for a levée en masse of Irishmen against 'the tyrant of Anglicised Ireland whose destruction alone can establish the indepen-dence of Ancient Hibernia'. Green uniforms were available for volunteers, but the response was lukewarm. Nonetheless, the benefi-ciaries of 'Anglicised Ireland' trembled. James Little, the Anglican parson of nearby Lackan, feared, as did many others of his kind, that Ireland was about to be plunged into an abyss by the forces of 'atheisti-cal liberalism' and Catholic fanaticism.[35]

At first, the French did very well. Four thousand militiamen were scattered by eight hundred French at Castlebar in a skirmish that was mockingly called the 'Castlebar Races'. This fiasco proved beyond doubt that partially trained and undisciplined amateurs were no match for veterans. And yet what was a Concord in reverse did not send a signal to the rest of Ireland, although it unnerved the government. Dublin Castle may have splintered the organisational framework of the United Irishmen and killed or driven into hiding its leadership, but it was still jittery and dared not risk any further humiliations. Reinforcements poured in from England, and Humbert surrendered on

8 September rather than fight on against overwhelming odds. Once again the government had had a stroke of good luck, for just over a month later, the Royal Navy intercepted and captured a second French flotilla carrying reinforcements and arms off Tory Island.

By the end of 1798, Ireland had been pacified. New problems had been created in the process by the policy of drafting dissidents and captive rebels into the armed forces. The victims of this diaspora did not shed their opinions and followed events in Ireland through the newspapers. Reports of coercion so enraged Thomas Darbyshire of HMS *Defiance* that, 'With a pipe in his mouth, much the worse for liquor, he expressed the words, there has been injustice done to my country, I will be revenged for it if it cost me my life.' Former United Irishmen on board *Defiance* and three other line-of-battle ships of the Channel Fleet, *Caesar*, *Captain* and *Glory*, conspired to extend the Irish uprising to the navy. In each ship, they planned to overwhelm their officers and the loyal men and steer their ships into French harbours during the summer and early autumn of 1798.

Recklessness was the common feature of all these plots. Those involved made no secret of their intentions. An Irishman on the *Caesar* declared to his English shipmates that he was 'no Briton but a true Irishman' and 'a true Catholic'. As for the protestants, he announced: 'By the Holy Ghost, I never will be easy but I've washed my hands in their blood.' On *Defiance*, William Lyndsey, a United Irishman, assured one of his wavering protestant countrymen that, 'there are many Jacobin Protestants in the ship who to get free of their slavery and confinement will as soon go there [Brest] as any where else to get quit of the service.' United Irishmen oaths were sworn, illicit meetings held and efforts made to subvert other sailors. Too much rum and its consequence, too little discretion, were the plotters' undoing, for their rash and bloodthirsty boasts alerted their patriotic colleagues who informed their officers. The culprits were arrested, tried and either hanged or transported to Australia.[36]

Thereafter, Irish resentment expressed itself through isolated, individual protests. They are interesting in so far as they indicate the depth and persistence of nationalist passions, and the willingness of a handful of men to make themselves martyrs. Robert Powell, a seaman on *Repulse*, interrupted his captain's address to the crew with a cry of 'Vive la République, bogre le Roy!' in April 1799 and got one hundred lashes for his temerity. Equally imprudent was Walter Tanton, a former United Irishman and captain's clerk on board HMS *Magicienne*. While it was cruising off the Cayman Islands in November 1805, he interrupted a general political discussion in the mess with the announcement: 'Damn the King and all kingly government, I wish to see a republican form of government established throughout the world.' In his defence, Tanton claimed that his views were well known and had earned him the nickname 'Mad Pat the United Irishman'. He was sentenced to 150 lashes and two years in gaol.[37]

Ultra-nationalism also crossed the Atlantic, where it would flourish for the next two hundred years. In Nova Scotia and Newfoundland the authorities detected 'much disaffection, and a strong tendency to republican principles' among Irish settlers at the end of 1799. If the colonies were attacked, no reliance whatsoever could be placed upon the militia. Two-thirds of the Newfoundland Fencibles were suspected of being United Irishmen and could not be trusted if called upon to suppress the 'mob' in districts inhabited by the 'worst sort' of their countrymen.[38] Eighteen men from this regiment and five artillerymen, led by Sergeant Kelly, deserted on a stormy night in April 1800, carried off arms and ammunition and headed off into the countryside. What followed was one of the most incompetent rebellions of all time, for the fugitives had forgotten to take any food with them. A boy was sent to St John's to fetch some and was captured by the local commander, Major-General William Skerrett. A veteran of the fighting in Wexford in 1798, he knew just what to do. A noose was placed around the neck of the boy who, to save his life, led a party of loyal troops to the insurgents. A few shots were exchanged and most were rounded up; the survivors took to banditry. Skerrett blamed the incident on a 'strong Roman Catholic faction' within the Fencibles.[39]

V

At the same time as the Newfoundland United Irishmen were mounting their tiny insurrection, the governments in London and Dublin were putting the finishing touches to the process that would fully integrate Ireland with the rest of Britain. The Dublin parliament disappeared and Irish MPs were returned to Westminster, which henceforward would make Ireland's laws. The Act of Union was an immediate consequence of the 1798 rebellion and the wider global war in which it had been a minor incident. Britain could no longer afford a partly detached and strategically vulnerable province whose grievances could so easily be exploited by a hostile power.

Neither the desire nor the will existed to appease the discontented, but at least Ireland could be tied more closely to Britain, which needed tighter control over an invaluable nursery of fighting men. By the end of the war, Ireland had provided the British army with a third of its manpower. Irish soldiers were welcomed, but the authorities took care to keep them under surveillance, particularly when they were close to a Catholic population, as in Gibraltar and Lower Canada.[40] Inside Ireland, the militia was reduced and the losses made good by British regulars who were isolated from the population in the new barracks which sprung up in the 1800s.

The rebels had been demonised by the British press. On 11 July 1798, *The Times* reported that the Wexford insurgents, with 'the thirst of cannibals', had licked the blood of murdered protestants. Irish militiamen stationed at Wellington in Somerset and Sunderland were called 'Croppies', 'Irish Rebels' and 'Irish rascals' by the townsfolk. The presence of Irishmen among a party of recruits travelling through the midlands in 1807 'aroused all the little brats and blackguards', who jeered at them as they passed.[41] Racial antipathies were the cause of brawls between the people of Nottingham and the Kilkenny Militia which was stationed in the town in June 1813. Catcalls from locals drew 'dreadful imprecations' from the Irishmen, who later assembled armed with cudgels on the streets where they looked for and found plenty of scraps.[42] Such behaviour fitted closely with the stereotype of the volatile, quarrelsome and irrational Irishman that was in the process of creation and, thanks to British cartoonists, would gain in colour and substance as the century progressed.

Within Ireland, the consequences of the 1798 rebellion were baleful. The Anglo-Irish ascendancy had been shaken, but still remained in power, ruling over a people with whom it had nothing in common save a shared interest in horseflesh. The Orange Order became a permanent force in politics, widening the religious rift and constantly reminding protestants that their survival depended on watchfulness and militancy. Traditional, confessional loyalties had proved more durable in 1798 than attachment to radical political programmes. After 1800, the protestants in Ulster regarded the Union as the guarantee of their identity, and when its abolition seemed imminent in 1886 and 1912 they were prepared to fight to preserve it.

The Catholics, too, had been unable to free themselves from ancient grievances, and so the 1798 uprising had become an extension of the sixteenth- and seventeenth-century contests for land and religion. Catholic emancipation and reform of the land tenure laws came slowly and grudgingly during the next century and against a background of mass protest and rural terrorism. The secular republicanism of the United Irishmen survived in new forms, as did the tradition of underground political organisation with its apparatus of oaths and stockpiling of weaponry. The 1848 rising and the Fenian conspiracies of 1866 to 1867 were reminders that there were still Irishmen who were prepared to wage war to detach their country from the British state.

Divergent political cultures produced divergent histories. The Orange men remembered the Boyne as the moment when they had been delivered from popery, and still celebrate it with a defiant exuberance. Catholic nationalists recall with bitterness Cromwell's campaigns, William III's war and the crushing of the 1798 revolt, with each serving to remind them of their enemies' malevolence, misdeeds and the need to keep faith with past martyrs. Memories of heroism are kept evergreen through songs like 'The Croppy Boy', the tale of a youth who died on the gallows, deserted by his family but true to the cause. Protestants, too, have their legacy of distant suffering; in 1798 two lines of 'Croppies Lie Down' recalled previous Catholic atrocities:

> Remember the steel of Sir Phelim O'Neill
> Who slaughtered our fathers in Catholic zeal . . .

Interwoven folk memories of war have become embedded in the Irish political consciousness. They are also part of the landscape, as Gerald Seymour shows in his thriller *Journeyman Tailor*, which is set in Ulster in the 1980s. The hero's tour of the countryside is turned into an historical explanation as to why Ulster is presently fighting another civil war. As his guide says:

> History doesn't go away here. Stories lose nothing by the telling. Stories are handed down, father to son, family to family, close as frogs in a drain here. Listen . . . This cross-roads, anyone'll tell you, was where the Auxiliaries shot the Catholic postman in 1922 . . . The Protestants came to burn down the R.C. chapel here, there was a hell of a fight and about a dozen Catholics were beaten to death. They call it the battle of Black Bridge. They know it like it was yesterday, but yesterday was 1829 . . .

In mainland Britain the practice and language of politics followed a different course. The nineteenth and early twentieth centuries witnessed the evolution of a system by which elected bodies and reasoned debate provided the means to settle political differences. Neither solved Ireland's problems and so the Irish stayed attached to the methods they had used in 1798. Violence appeared to offer to Catholic nationalists a divorce from Britain on their own terms, and to Ulster protestants the right to remain in the Union on theirs. 'Ulster will fight and Ulster will be right' was a phrase coined by a Conservative politician, Lord Randolph Churchill, in 1886, but Ulstermen hardly needed any prompting to adopt what they had long seen as their ultimate resort. In April 1914, British military intelligence was certain that armed Ulster volunteers would attempt a coup d'état the moment Home Rule became law and seize public buildings.[43]

This was exactly what Sinn Féin did in Dublin in 1916. The nationalists accepted force as a legitimate political weapon and believed that individual self-sacrifice was essential for the regeneration of a nation. According to Padraic Pearse, war would simultaneously secure freedom for Ireland and redeem its people. Taking back by force what had once been snatched by force would both eliminate past shame and complete the work for which so many had given their lives. This was the message of the Easter Rising of 1916, which, like its counterpart in 1798, occurred when Britain was doing badly in a world war. Again, the Irish sought assistance from Britain's enemy, this time the Kaiser's Germany.

Another lesson from 1798 was applied by the Irish Republican Army (IRA) in 1919 when, on Michael Collins's instructions, it struck at Dublin's already overstretched and fragile intelligence services. Once this prop had been knocked away, the IRA turned its attentions to the Irish police and the British army and, at considerable cost to itself, managed to fight both to a standstill by the summer of 1921. The IRA's campaign against the British army, the Royal Irish Constabulary and its auxiliary gendarmeries was not a civil war, as Sinn Féin repeatedly made clear. It was fighting a colonial war against an oppressive imperial power.

No one in 1798 could have predicted the persistence of violence in Irish life. The contemporary view was that the rebels had been misled by giddy French ideas. 'Do not, my lads, suffer yourselves to be deluded by the deceitful sounds of Liberty and Equality,' Admiral Waldegrave told three Irish sailors found guilty of sedition and mutiny in August of that year. 'They are only held forth to deceive and betray you into the sacrifice of all the real blessings and comforts you now enjoy.'[44] As understood by the admiral and the government he served, these benefits were the constitution and the freedoms enjoyed by the king's subjects.

All had been won and preserved by civil wars. And yet, as the events of the preceding months had clearly demonstrated, a substantial body, probably the majority, of Irishmen were convinced that they had been excluded from these advantages and were willing to join Britain's enemies to secure not only liberty but separation from the British state. Why they felt this was explained by that humane general, Sir John Moore, who after a few weeks touring Ireland observed in his diary: 'Every man is oppressed to whom the privileges of his fellow citizens are denied.'[45] This principle, in various forms, had been at stake during Britain's civil wars and the American Revolution. It was among the casualties of the 1798 rebellion; Ireland was integrated into Britain as a wartime emergency measure, literally at gunpoint. It was an arrangement that satisfied neither the Irish nor the rest of Britain, which had to live with a dissatisfied and sullen partner.

PART FOUR

OVERSEAS WARS, 1660–1870

1

You fight for a good cause: Patriotism and the pursuit of power

I

'Whosoever commands the sea, commands the trade of the world, commands the riches of the world, commands the world itself.' Sir Walter Raleigh's formula for national prosperity and global supremacy was applied by Britain's rulers from the middle of the seventeenth century onwards with spectacular success. The relentless pursuit of power and profit demanded national unity and strong nerves; faltering or a loss of momentum could mean disaster. Wars were unavoidable. Other European powers with similar ambitions, most notably France, would not stand by and allow Britain to engross the world's commerce. Nor were they willing to permit Britain to extend its tropical Empire at the expense of theirs and so forfeit markets, raw materials and the revenue they generated. This being so, it was vital that the whole country was convinced that defeating Britain's rivals was in everyone's interests, the more so as the costs of the war and the demands for fighting men increased.

The wars that made Britain's overseas expansion possible were not the product of a carefully prepared, long-term strategy. Rather, they were the outcome of official responses to various international crises in which British interests were perceived to be in jeopardy. When rivals appeared to be on the verge of securing some strategic or commercial advantage, Britain intervened, guided by the general principles outlined by Raleigh. With hindsight and in the knowledge of the eventual outcome of the mainly Anglo-French conflicts between 1688 and 1815, it is tempting to depict Britain as singlemindedly bent upon a course whose goal was the global mastery described by Raleigh.

Nothing so far-reaching was ever envisaged by eighteenth-century ministers, admirals and businessmen, who were primarily concerned with immediate security and, on occasion, exploiting unexpected opportunities. Resolution, self-confidence and imagination were abundant and there were plenty of chancers like Robert Clive ready to gamble against the odds if the stakes were attractive enough. War was and is one of the most unpredictable of human activities and there were hesitant spirits who feared that the nation's luck was bound to run out. After the astonishing victories between 1757 and 1763 which gave Britain control over Canada and Bengal and, for a brief time, Cuba and the Philippines, sibylline voices warned that the nation was over-stretched and could never maintain such an unwieldy, vast Empire. After the loss of the North American colonies in 1783, pessimists predicted that British power had entered a period of irreversible decline. Those of them who survived to witness Waterloo and the eclipse of France would have been astonished by the speed and extent of Britain's recovery.

Britain's wars during this period were dominated by the struggle with France, usually in alliance with the decrepit Spanish Empire. France fought Britain in the Nine Years' War (1688 to 1697), the War of the Spanish Succession (1702 to 1714), the War of the Austrian Succession (1738 to 1748), the Seven Years' War (1756 to 1763), the second phase of the American War of Independence (1778 to 1783) and the Revolutionary and Napoleonic Wars (1793 to 1815). Save in the American conflict, Britain was compelled to send expeditionary forces to various European fronts, although wherever possible the government preferred its continental commitment to take the form of subsidies to allies. This was partly out of necessity, since Britain lacked the population to raise mass armies equal to those of France, Prussia, Austria or Russia, and partly out of choice. Unlike her allies, Britain wanted no part in the ritual redrawing of boundaries and transfer of provinces that marked the end of every continental war. It measured its war-dividend in terms of bases that extended and reinforced maritime supremacy; overseas lands for settlement; colonies that produced sugar, tobacco, textiles and spices for sale at home and re-export to Europe; and markets for slaves and domestic manufactures.

Naval paramountcy depended upon bases which had to be guarded. By 1815, British troops were stationed at Halifax, Bermuda, Gibraltar, Malta, Cape Town, Mauritius and St Helena, where they were also Napoleon's gaolers. Permanent garrisons were needed to provide internal and external security for fledgling colonies. During this period, British armies fought against native Americans on the frontiers of North America, rebellious slaves in the West Indies, Xhosas in Cape Colony and Maoris in New Zealand. On a larger scale, an Anglo-Canadian army with native American auxiliaries defended Canada against an invasion by the United States and launched a series of counterattacks on the American coast between 1812 and 1815.

The largest concentration of British manpower and martial exertion was in India. Since the early 1750s, the East India Company had hired British regiments to augment its British-officered, locally recruited army. Between 1757 and 1849 this miscellaneous force extended the company's control over the entire subcontinent, successively expelling the French and defeating the armies of Bengal (1757 to 1760), Mysore (1792 to 1798), the Maratha Confederacy (1803 to 1805 and 1817 to 1918), Nepal (1815), Lower Burma (1824 to 1825), the Scindian amirs (1843) and the Sikh state of the Punjab (1845 to 1846 and 1848 to 1849). Paramountcy in India was preserved in 1857 to 1858 with the suppression of the localised and mainly military rebellions known as the Indian Mutiny. These campaigns were all financed by British investors in the company and the Indian taxpayer.

Supposed threats to India's external security drew Britain into the geopolitics of the Middle East and Asia and an extended confrontation with a new rival, Russia. In 1838 an Anglo-Indian army occupied Afghanistan to keep it out of Russia's orbit, and a Russian attempt to alter the balance of naval power in the Mediterranean in 1853 led to an Anglo-French invasion of the Crimea and naval operations in the Baltic and against Vladivostok. Anglo-Indian forces were used in 1840 to 1842, 1856 to 1857 and 1859 to 1860 to compel another Asian power, China, to accommodate British traders.

The number and magnitude of the wars required an extraordinary expenditure of money and manpower. They also demanded the participation of more and more of the population, either passively as taxpayers or actively as soldiers, sailors and reservists. Statistics provide a gauge of the nation's efforts. From 1692 onwards, Britain's war-effort was largely funded by long-term credit, that is cash loaned to the government which paid fixed rates of interest to investors. The sum raised was known as the National Debt, and it rose steeply:

1697	£16.7 million
1748	£76.1 million
1783	£242.9 million
1815	£744.9 million

By the last date there were half a million holders of government stock. Interest payments took an ever-increasing slice of the annual budget, rising to 56 per cent by the 1780s. Britain's ability to borrow ultimately depended upon a constantly increasing revenue from regular and emergency taxation. Yields from these sources, in particular customs and excise, were contingent upon the growth of trade. Commercial expansion was essential for procuring credit and, in so far as they opened new markets and released new sources of raw materials, Britain's wars helped in part to pay for themselves.

Nonetheless, taxpayers had to dig deep into their pockets. In the final phase of the American War they were paying two and a half times as much as their French counterparts, and three and a half times during the Napoleonic Wars.[1] The main sources of revenue were import and export duties, charges on landed income, and levies on wines, spirits and such luxury items as wigs and carriage-horses. As perceived by the public, the system was onerous but fair. Moreover, cash raised on the money-markets cut the need for astringent emergency taxation which could have provoked unrest. When eighteenth-century crowds rioted, which they did often, it was rarely in protest against taxes. Fiscal policy was supervised by parliament which scrutinised the nation's accounts, and the officials responsible for collecting taxation (whose number more than doubled during the eighteenth century) were by and large regarded as honest servants of the state. In France they were not.

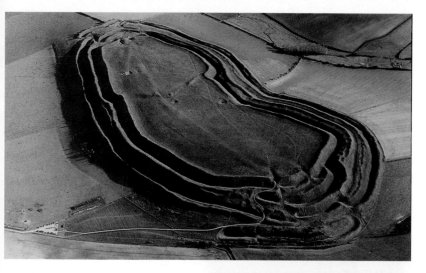

No impediment: the earthworks of Maiden Castle, Dorset, captured by the Romans in AD 45 after a brief fight.
CROWN COPYRIGHT NMR

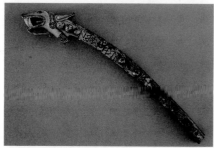

Wargear: a Saxon sword, appropriately decorated with the head of a wild beast, and the Sutton Hoo helmet which was embellished with images contrived to protect the wearer from fate in the form of the Valkyries. Weapons and armour advertised the prestige of the warrior as well as fulfilling their utilitarian functions.
BRITISH MUSEUM

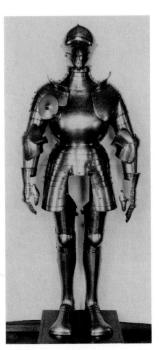

Master of the battlefield: armour for knight and war horse, manufactured in Germany in about 1500. Such equipment was expensive, but similar suits would have been worn by Scottish aristocrats at Flodden (1513), which was why they proved so difficult to kill. WALLACE COLLECTION

Siege craft: a donkey operates a trebuchet of the kind Edward I used against Scottish castles [*left*] while a fox prepares to fire a crossbow [*centre*]. Apes hurl down rocks on the assailants, which include a foxy knight [*extreme right*]. Maastricht Hours, *c.* 1300. BRITISH LIBRARY

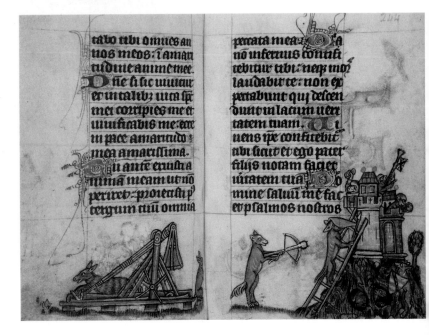

Evolving efficiency: church brasses reflect new fashions in armour, introduced to give added protection [*left*]. Sir Nicholas Dagworth, 1401, Blickling, Norfolk [*centre*]. Sir Simon Felbrigg, 1416, Felbrigg, Norfolk [*right*]. Simon Norwich, 1476, Brampton-by-Dingley, Northants. Elaborate, crested tournament helms are shown behind the heads of Norwich and Dagworth, who, like Felbrigg was a veteran of the Hundred Years War.

[*right*] For King and Parliment! Thomas Fairfax, a Parliamentary general in conventional heroic pose, behind, masses of pikeman and musketeers await his command. AKG

[*below*] Crown and Constitution preserved: George II's infantrymen repel Jacobite clansmen at Culloden, 1746. THE ROYAL COLLECTION © HM QUEEN ELIZABETH II

How a hero should die: a print of Benjamin West's 'The Death of General Wolfe' at Quebec in 1759. NATIONAL ARMY MUSEUM

Broadside: British and French men-o'-war exchange fire at close range, c. 1780. NATIONAL MARITIME MUSEUM

Fighting deck: HMS *Victory* in close engagement at Trafalgar. Nelson falls wounded, while around marines and gunners return French fire, each man concentrating on his immediate task. NATIONAL MARITIME MUSEUM

Cold steel: an infantryman overcomes an Indian adversary, c. 1840. Contemporary generals believed that the British soldiers' capacity for such hand-to-hand fighting gave them a unique superiority over all their enemies. NATIONAL ARMY MUSEUM

Contrasts: James Gillray shows the brainsick, starving Revolutionary feasting on grass, snails and crackpot idealism, while John Bull tucks in to roast beef under the protection of King, Constitution and the Royal Navy, 1792. BRITISH MUSEUM

Discipline upheld: flogging on board a warship during the Napoleonic Wars. This punishment was considered distasteful by many officers, while others believed it was the only way in which obedience could be imposed on crews which contained criminals and press-ganged men.

Cash in hand: a general counts his prize money from West Indian campaigns while petitions for widows of soldiers killed in the fighting lie discarded on the floor; a cartoon of 1797 highlights both the profits made from the war and the inequity of their distribution. NATIONAL ARMY MUSEUM

In a mess: a drunken militia officer surrounded by the detritus of his carouse, c. 1800. Mass mobilisation against invasion and high wastage on campaign had led to commissions being granted to men who were unaware of the traditional codes of honour of officers and gentlemen. This officer may soon discover them for public inebriation was a court-martial offence. NATIONAL ARMY MUSEUM

Boney beware! An elegantly uniformed Scottish volunteer rifleman prepares to engage the French invader, *c.* 1803. NATIONAL ARMY MUSEUM

Officers and gentlemen: artillery officers relax at Edinburgh, *c.* 1842: unlike their colleagues in the infantry and cavalry, they would have received professional training. COURTESY OF ST ANDREWS LIBRARY

Revenue collection was privatised, with officials enjoying the right to siphon off sums for themselves, and there was a range of exemptions that placed the heaviest charges on those least able to afford them. On paper, France's economic resources were superior to Britain's, but venality and bad management ensured that they were never fully exploited.

II

A breakdown of Britain's war-budgets reveals strategic priorities. The navy always came first; it had to. It was the nation's principal defence against invasion and, incidentally, spared it the expense of maintaining a large standing army in peacetime. Warships protected the sealanes and escorted convoys of merchantmen whose cargoes generated the cash that powered Britain's war-machine. The navy was the most important component in Britain's offensive strategy: the neutralising or elimination of the enemy's battlefleet and the extinction of his seaborne commerce. 'The destruction of the commerce and colonial possessions of the enemy' was Britain's overall aim, the secretary of war, Henry Dundas, told the Commons in 1801, as it had been in previous wars. This policy made economic sense, for the markets gained compensated for those temporarily lost in Europe.

Attrition was the key to maritime supremacy. The enemy was denied access to the sea by a blockade that strangled coastal and ocean-going trade and bottled up fleets. In the process, the morale and fighting efficiency of the enemy's navy deteriorated, for there was no substitute for training sailors at sea. If and when French and Spanish fleets escaped, they had to be hunted down and engaged immediately, whatever the odds or weather conditions. For this strategy to succeed, the Royal Navy had to have enough ships to cordon the French and Spanish coasts and, if challenged, to engage the combined fleets of both nations, as well as maintain a superior presence in the Mediterranean, Caribbean and Indian Ocean. The upshot was a naval race, which lasted throughout the eighteenth century, in which Britain always managed to keep ahead, although the margin narrowed dangerously during the American War. The total number of battleships mounting seventy-four or more guns rose from sixty-three in 1714 to 193 in 1809. There was an even greater increase in the number of frigates, which undertook the donkeywork of the inshore blockade, protected merchantmen and disrupted enemy shipping. By 1815 the navy possessed 574, of which 206 had been captured in battle and 217 had been constructed over the previous twenty-two years.[2]

The new frigates had cost the country £4.26 million, a small fraction of the funds allocated to the navy. At the end of the seventeenth century, naval expenditure averaged about £1.8 million per year; a hundred years later it stood at over fifteen million pounds. Extra ships needed more men and the navy's strength rose from forty thousand in 1697 to 140,000 in 1809.[3] They required feeding and medical treatment, and their ships constant maintenance and repair, and therefore as the fleet expanded so did its administration, dockyards, storehouses and hospitals. The Royal Navy became the largest single employer of civilians in the country. In 1700 the staff of its logistical departments totalled 6500, and in 1814 it stood at 17,300, nearly all of whom worked at Deptford, Woolwich, Chatham, Portsmouth and Plymouth.[4] These vast complexes contained the first modern factories where ropes and wooden pulleys were mass-produced using the most up-to-date industrial technology. The steam-driven pump introduced for draining a Portsmouth dry-dock in 1799 was the first of many, and between 1802 and 1812 steam-engines were introduced to drive sawmills and the machine-tools that turned out 130,000 pulleys a year.[5]

These innovations saved money, reducing labour costs and, incidentally, making redundant several hundred sawyers and blockmakers. Economies were always welcomed by ministers and MPs who, while agreeing that the navy was an irreplaceable asset, were nevertheless anxious that it should not become too burdensome. At the same time, the Admiralty was acutely aware that overseas traders wanted the maximum return from their taxes which were, in a sense, indirect investments. If this was not forthcoming, then commercial lobbyists made a clamour that could not be ignored by ministers whose survival depended upon alliances of interest-groups in the Commons.

A plea for ships and men from Georgia and South Carolina to help repel native American incursions in 1738 concluded with a pointed reminder to the government that the latter alone annually exported goods worth £150,000 to Britain.[6] In 1760, Jamaican merchants and plantation owners accused the local commander, Admiral Charles Holmes, of not safeguarding their vessels and failing to prevent the kidnapping of slaves by French privateers. Instead, he was deploying his warships in such a way as to promote 'his private advantage' from prize-money for captured enemy vessels, of which he was entitled to a share. He vehemently rejected this slur on his honour and demonstrated that between November 1760 and October 1761 all ships under his command had been employed on operations against privateers and on convoy duty.[7] Likewise, in 1808 there was disquiet among ship-insurers after the loss of several merchantmen in the Caribbean, and pressure was put on the Admiralty Board. It censured the local commander, Admiral Sir Thomas Cochrane, who was ordered to 'consider the protection of trade as of the first importance'.[8]

Embattled colonial governors and indignant merchants were upholding the prevalent economic orthodoxy: Britain's colonies and overseas commerce were of universal benefit, directly and indirectly providing employment to all classes. By the mid eighteenth century, 40 per cent of Britain's trade consisted of the re-export to Europe of colonial products. These commodities — tobacco, fabrics, coffee and tea — were steadily becoming cheaper and were available to all save the destitute in every corner of the country. Wars in which competitors' fleets were swept from the oceans and colonies annexed were, therefore, a form of long-term investment for the benefit of everyone.

III

The majority of Britons were aware that foreign wars fostered trade and added to their country's prosperity. Prospects of profit were useful inducements for the sacrifice of blood and money, but they lacked the persuasive power of visceral patriotism. Success in war was a vindication of national honour and proof of the pugnacious faith in the Englishman's physical and moral superiority that had emerged during Elizabeth I's reign. It was as robust as ever in 1666, when an anonymous balladeer looked forward confidently to a war with three powers:

> *The* Heavens *look big with wonder and inform*
> *Our expectations of some present storm.*
> French, Dutch, *and* Dane *too, all at once? Why then*
> *'Tis time to show that we are* English *men.*
> *They say, at Football three to one is odds;*
> *But 'tis nothing, for the cause is Gods.*
> *Have at 'em all, we care not where we come.*[9]

Of this trio, France became the focus of vilification and ridicule. Francophobia was a constant in popular ballads, verses and cartoons throughout the eighteenth and early nineteenth centuries. The Frenchman was mocked for his pretensions of grandeur, his Catholicism, his fripperies and mincing manners which bordered on degeneracy. Haughtiness and Popery were the vices of the Spaniard who, therefore, needed regular reminders of his place in the scheme of things:

> *For to humble the proud Spaniards British courage must be*
>   *shown,*
> *Or those haughty proud villains will never know what is their*
>   *own,*
> *Their men-of-war we'll make rattle; Spain shall tremble at the*
>   *sight;*
> *Haste, brave boys, way to the battle; the French nor they could*
>   *never fight.*[10]

Jack Tar, of course, could, and was distinguished by courage, manliness, resolution and an apparently limitless capacity to thrash anyone who crossed his path. Or, in the words of a poem of 1799:

> *Invention I need not, their deeds are enough,*
> *Like their own native oak, they are hardy and tough,*
> *No foreign material, but true British stuff*
>   *O the brave tars!*[11]

Fops and runagates were no match for such fellows, as a ballad of the late seventeenth century, 'The French Dancing-Master and the English

Soldier: or, the difference between Fiddling and Fighting', explained:

> *'Tis true, at dancing you do us excel*
> *But can you, as the English, fight as well*
> *When Mars unsheathes his sword and cannons roar,*
> *And men lie welt'ring in their purple gore,*
> *When towns are burned, and cities destroy'd*
> *To what use will your dancing be deploy'd.*

The soldier seals the argument with a list of French defeats stretching
back to Crécy.[12] Fresh victories were added to this catalogue and new
heroes to the English pantheon:

> *The Lilies of France and the fair English rose*
> *Could never agree as old history shows;*
> *But our Edwards and Henrys those Lilies have torn,*
> *And in their rich standards have born,*
> *To show that old England beneath her strong lance*
> *Had humbled the glory of France.*

> *What would these Monsieurs? Would they know how they ran?*
> *Why look at the annals of Glorious Queen Anne,*
> *We beat 'em at sea, and we beat 'em at land,*
> *When Marlborough and Russell enjoy'd the command;*
> *We'll beat them again boys, so let 'em advance,*
> *Old England despises the insults of France.*[13]

'With words we govern men', observed Disraeli. A great many were
written and uttered to foster patriotism and national unity throughout
the eighteenth and early nineteenth centuries. Most of this output
came from independent wordsmiths, songwriters and printers, and its
sheer volume suggests that they knew exactly how to cater for popular
tastes and sympathies; if they had not done so they would have gone out
of business. Victories abroad and tales of heroism obviously had a powerful appeal at all levels; the rich man purchased his print of Benjamin
West's 'The Death of General Wolfe', and the poor his penny broad-
sheet that told the story in verses that could be sung in taverns.

A graver, but still compelling patriotism was declared from the pulpits of the Church of England, whose clergy were mouthpieces for the government. In essence, the Anglican vision of the nation derived from that older and by now deep-rooted image of a new Israel: England and, after the Act of Union, Britain as an elect nation whose protestantism qualified it for divine blessings, so long as its people remained staunch in faith and morals. Listen to the Reverend Simon Lavington preaching on the amazing sequence of victories of 'that glorious year', 1759, in which Britain won the battles of Minden, Quiberon Bay and Quebec: 'We count it our duty to take a delight in ascribing our success to Divine Providence, because it endears and sweetens our victories to consider them as proceeding from God, and as being an eminent and signal display of Divine Favour.' He then produced impregnable proof of the dispensation of providence: in each engagement the weather had favoured the British forces.[14] In 1797, when invasion threatened and taxation was soaring, Dr Munkhouse mingled patriotism with self-interest in a sermon delivered at Wakefield in a service of thanksgiving for recent naval victories. Grumblers should pay up, for, it was 'better to advance to the government a part of our possessions in defence of the whole, than reserve the whole as a prey to the enemy: to submit even to the heavy burdens of our own imposing, than take upon us the yoke of a foreign power'.[15]

The conviction that God favoured a godly people grew stronger after Waterloo. Adding his voice to those congratulating the army for its victory over the Sikhs in 1846, the Tory MP Sir Robert Inglis noted approvingly that Sir Hugh Gough had attributed his success to providence. He reminded members that Marlborough had done the same after Blenheim and Collingwood after Trafalgar, quoting the latter's thanks for God's 'constant aid to us in the defence of our country's liberties and laws'. Imperial Britain was surely destined to equal, if not surpass, the glories of Rome, for the Whig member John Cam Hobhouse detected in the recent events in India 'something . . . that reminds one of Roman grandeur'.[16]

British victories had long been celebrated in Roman manner by public celebrations, which were sponsored by the civic authorities and anyone of substance who wished to advertise his or her loyalty to king and country. Bells were rung at Nottingham after the announcement in

March 1793 of some relatively insignificant naval success. Afterwards, bonfires were lit, crowds sang the national anthem in the streets, the houses of pro-Jacobins were pelted and an effigy of Tom Paine, the radical who had defected to France, was ceremonially hanged.[17] Sir Walter Scott was delighted by the news of Wellington's victory at Salamanca (1812) and immediately invited all the craftsmen working on Abbotsford to a party where a bonfire was lit and an 'ocean of whisky punch' was on hand. 'The banks of the Tweed looked very merry on this glorious occasion', and as the September evening wore on there was dancing to the sound of fiddles and pipes. Neighbouring patriots had lit bonfires which reminded Scott of the time when hilltop fires had signalled the approach of raiders from across the border.[18]

These patriotic diversions were always welcome. They were a chance to have fun, kick over the traces, eat and get tipsy at someone else's expense and be rowdy without risking prosecution. Boisterous assertions of national superiority not only reinforced that popular fancy, but contributed to national cohesion. Unity was vital during wartime, not only among classes but among the different peoples of Britain. Each had to take its share of the war-effort in a spirit of co-operation which was described in a Scottish popular ballad on 'The Battle of Vittoria' of 1813, in which English, Scottish and Irish regiments had fought.

> *The English Rose was ne'er sae red,*
> *The Shamrock waved where glory led*
> *And the Scottish Thistle raised its head*
> *And smiled upon Vittoria.*[19]

Verses such as these contributed to the cultivation of a sturdy sense of Britishness which was so vital to the ambitious military, commercial and imperial enterprises of a state that had only been united in 1707. The new British identity subsumed, but never wholly eradicated, Welsh and Scottish peculiarities. One, the Celtic warrior tradition, was extremely valuable to the state and was encouraged in order to tempt Scottish and Irish recruits, particularly during the Napoleonic Wars. 'All Scotsmen of true patriotism and spirit who love their native country, and feel animated with the noble determination of protecting it against an implacable foe' were invited to join the Banffshire militia in

1803 and so help confound the 'Tyrannical Corsican usurper and his bloodthirsty army of desperadoes'.[20]

To some extent, the fabrication of a British identity was an imposition of English culture and values which found expression, then and later, in that common but revealing linguistic slip of speaking of 'England' when 'Britain' was intended. 'I do not in the least doubt you will behave like Englishmen,' General Howe told his army, which included Welsh, Scots and Irish on the eve on the assault on Bunker Hill.[21] Scots were guilty of the same lapse. 'I must own Old England never was in such a ticklish situation,' Captain Ralph Dundas wrote to his family during the invasion scare of 1779.[22]

Within the armed forces former national rivalries were occasionally resuscitated, as they were among the Shropshire Fusiliers on St David's Day 1746. The regiment was stationed at Cirencester and its Welsh soldiers wore their leeks in their caps, which vexed their English colleagues who attempted to seize the offending vegetables. Scuffles followed and during the evening a body of Welshmen, led by 'King Jones' and a fiddler, poured on to the streets in search of more fights. The commotions that followed owed as much to alcohol as to national sentiment.[23] A more tolerant mood prevailed among troops stationed in Canada in the early 1760s when Englishmen would take night guard duties so that their Irish comrades could enjoy the traditional St Patrick's Day carouse.[24]

IV

A patriotism that was a compound of xenophobia and racial superiority needed some fresh ingredients during the Revolutionary and Napoleonic Wars. France was no longer populated by weaklings and poltroons. Its people were raised to an unprecedented and alarming pitch of martial animation by the political ideology of the Revolution. Its theories impassioned many Britons, especially those who were excluded from political life by religious denomination or economic circumstances. Nonconformists, shopkeepers, craftsmen and labourers looked to France as a model for reform at home. From 1790 onwards they formed networks of clubs which met regularly to discuss and disseminate doctrines of equality, natural rights and republicanism. Seen from above and in the light of the war that began early in 1793, bodies such as the Corresponding Societies, Friends of the People and the United Englishmen appeared as subversives who could fracture national unity and hamper the war-effort.

Like Catholics in Elizabethan and Jacobites in early Georgian England, the British Jacobins were considered an 'enemy within', at best fellow travellers and at worst potential traitors. Official apprehension was confirmed by intelligence reports of the circulation of seditious handbills and pamphlets, meetings where glasses were raised to the armies of the Revolution and the king damned, and riots in which demonstrators howled slogans such as 'liberty, equality and no king!' Patriots wrote to ministers with their own, sometimes highly imaginative accounts of restlessness and insubordination. 'The devil is there are a cussed set of bad subjects, seditious and democratical' in some Ayrshire parishes, complained the Earl of Eglinton, who believed that the remedy was to billet troops among them. In the same year, 1798, an 'Allegiant Fencible Volunteer' warned that in his district 'nine men out of ten are rank Jacobins'. None could see the error of his ways: 'You may just as well attempt to give life to a dead cabbage or a turnip as to give right understanding to the common people whenever their noddles are distempered.'[25]

Irrespective of the extent or depth of Jacobin sentiment, it was imperative for the government to do all in its power to instil 'right understanding' among all classes, everywhere. As the war unfolded, it was clear that a hitherto unequalled mobilisation of manpower was required. It was therefore necessary first to quarantine soldiers from seditious influences, and then to eradicate them so that the enlarged militia would not become contaminated.

Regular troops were drawn from the poorest sections of the working class which played little part in pro-Revolutionary movements. Desultory and fruitless efforts were made to suborn servicemen. In 1796, a local newspaper exposed the visit to Portsmouth of John Binns of the London Corresponding Society, whom it branded as an 'incendiary' intent upon subverting the 'brave soldiers and sailors'. He angrily denied this, claiming he had come to 'instruct them in their political rights' for, on entering the forces, they should not forget 'their characters as men'.[25] An insurance against this sort of interference was the construction of barracks where soldiers could be closely supervised; previously most were scattered across town and villages in billets, usually inns. From 1792 onwards, the government adopted a crash programme of barrack building which was also designed to counter political unrest. Six were erected in the industrial cities of Birmingham, Coventry, Manchester, Norwich, Sheffield and Nottingham.

Wider sedition was contained by emergency legislation, which in many respects was a prototype for that introduced in the First and Second World Wars. Traditional legal forms were temporarily suspended and new offences created to catch those whose words might undermine loyalty or injure the war-effort. Juries and jurists were on the whole compliant; the formidable Lord Justice Clerk, Lord Braxfield, interrupted a trial of radicals in Edinburgh to lecture the defendants on the virtues of restricting the vote to property owners. All this may have been unduly alarmist. Unlike the United Irishmen, British sympathisers with the French Revolution never prepared for a rebellion, although they freely resorted to violent language.

Ideas were best fought with other ideas. An ideological offensive was launched that aimed to redefine patriotism, encourage it and, above all, demonstrate to the poorer classes that they were an integral part of the nation's war-effort, the failure of which would bring them nothing but woe. At the heart of the new patriotism was the contrast between Britain and Revolutionary France. One was the antithesis of the other. Britain was a godly, stable, prosperous kingdom ruled by a benevolent king whose subjects enjoyed tranquillity and freedom under the just laws provided by the constitution. France was a chaotic state whose people had been driven to collective lunacy by the reckless pursuit of airy dogmas which had reduced them to poverty and the tyranny of godless demagogues and bloodthirsty mobs. As for the moral claims of the Revolution, they were blown away by the breezy commonsense of the sailor in a ballad of 1800:

> Why what's all this nonsense they talks of and pother
> About Rights of Man? What a plague are they at?
> If they mean that each man to his messmate's a brother,
> Why the lubberly swabs, every fool can tell that.[27]

At times, particularly when fears of invasion and subversion were greatest, the rhetoric of patriotism, like the emotions behind it, was hysterical:

> *And thou, whose sable pinions, wide outspread,*
> *O'er all the west cimmerian darkness sheds,*
> *Known by the phrenzy'd eye, thy blood-stain'd vest*
> *The Gorgon horrors gleaming on thy chest,*
> DEMOCRACY![28]

The cartoons of James Gillray and Isaac Cruikshank repeated this image. Revolutionaries were depicted as diabolical creatures with manic eyes, performing grotesque and often murderous antics. Furthermore, and this was repeatedly emphasised, French liberty brought universal destitution. In one famous cartoon, the skeletal Frenchman eats grass and frogs' legs in his ramshackle hovel whilst an overfed, ruddy-cheeked John Bull drinks ale and feasts on beef and plum-pudding, the nourishing staples of the freeborn Englishman. Bull and his diet outlived the war and became a lasting image of the whole British nation.

Serious invasion threats between 1795 and 1798 and again in 1803 to 1805 made a powerful focus for patriotism. The safety of the nation and its people was at stake, which made it easy for the government to rally the country. Indignation and defiance mingle in the final verses of a poem written in the spring of 1795 by Robert Burns, a radical by inclination but also a patriotic volunteer. Britain is likened to an old and somewhat imperfect pot:

> *The kettle o' the kirk and state,*
> *Perhaps a clout may fail in 't;*
> *But de'il a foreign tinker loon*
> *Shall ever ca' a nail in 't.*
> *Our fathers' blood the kettle bought,*
> *And who would dare to spoil it,*
> *By Heaven the sacrilegious dog*
> *Shall fuel be to boil it!*

The wretch that would a tyrant own,
And the wretch, his true-born brother,
Who'd set the mob aboon the throne –
May they be damn'd together!
Who will not sing 'God save the king!'
Shall sing as high's the steeple;
But while we sing 'God save the King!'
We'll not forget the people.

The people were needed as never before to fill the ranks of the expanded militia, volunteers, fencibles and yeomanry which were being mustered as a mass reserve army. Those who joined these corps were constantly reminded of why they were in uniform and the part they would play in saving their country. A crowd estimated at twenty-two thousand gathered at Stroud in August 1799 to watch the Frampton Volunteers receive their colours. Drink, the lubricant of patriotism, was abundant and the atmosphere was that of a fair. It was also the opportunity for Mary, Countess of Berkeley, to say a few robust words of encouragement. She was a local girl, the daughter of a butcher/innkeeper from a nearby village, but as the wife of an earl she spoke with the voice of the ascendancy. She denounced the 'infernal' French 'New Philosophy' which denied God and His law and praised Britain's 'happy Constitution'. Britain had 'like a spark of electric fire, diffused an universal spirit of patriotism throughout Europe'. She concluded with remarks for purely local consumption, urging 'drunken and profligate characters' to embrace 'habits of industry'.[29]

Notwithstanding her origins, snobs with an eye to raising themselves within society would have been overwhelmed by the chance to enjoy, even at a distance, the company of a figure who was the local equivalent of Jane Austen's Lady Catherine de Burgh. For this reason, they applauded her sentiments and boasted about the occasion afterwards. Public displays of patriotism temporarily broke down the social barriers between the middle classes and the landed gentry. Likewise, those of lesser status but substantial means could add their names and subscriptions to those of the nobility on the lists of contributors to various charities for the widows and orphans of soldiers and sailors. These records of patriotic generosity were published in national and provincial newspapers.

The poor, too, had to pull their weight in the national effort. They were the backbone of the militia and volunteers and were left in no doubt that they were fighting for their homes and families. In 1798, the Bishop of Llandaff instructed his clergy to warn their parishioners of what might befall them if the country was overrun by swarms of robbers and atheists. Parsons were to describe 'the cruelties which the French have used in every country which they have invaded'. Despite their promises of protection for the poor, the armies of the Revolution would 'strip the poor of everything they possess', rape their wives and daughters and burn their cottages. Welsh churchgoers were also to be on their guard against traitors in their midst, creatures 'of so base a temper, so maddened by malignity, so cankered by envy, so besotted by folly, so stupefied as to their own safety, as to abet the designs of the enemy'.[30] In various forms, this message was delivered from the pulpits of the established churches and by teachers in the new Sunday Schools.

Napoleon's grand design for the invasion of England and the *Grande Armée*'s muster at Boulogne concentrated minds and efforts to an unparalleled degree between 1803 and 1805. Bonaparte's ruthless rise to power, his autocratic style of government and coronation as emperor provided a bonus for British propaganda, which underwent a significant change. Britain was now unquestionably the champion of liberty, France a despotism and her people slaves to a belligerent monomaniac with a shady background. Sussex volunteers were warned by their captain that if he conquered Britain, 'Boney' would enslave them, pay them a pittance and send others to 'distant climes, there to perish of disease, misery and hard usage'.[31] The better informed may have been puzzled by this, given that during the preceding ten years thousands of British soldiers had been killed by fatigue and sickness in the West Indies.[32] 'Boney' the bogeyman was also a figure of derision. Cartoonists rendered him as a preposterous cockalorum, swaggering around in an oversized cocked hat and brandishing a sabre. The emperor added to the fun by formally complaining to the British government about these pictorial affronts to his dignity.

Jeering at Napoleon may have relieved some of the tension that was inevitable as the nation prepared for invasion. Everywhere there were disturbing signs that a country that had not experienced warfare on a large scale since the mid seventeenth century might do so again. Newspapers reported troop movements, the construction of Martello towers, and the government's emergency measures. In the counties along the southern and western coasts plans were laid for the evacuation of civilians, the removal of wagons and livestock from the path of the French army and the destruction of bridges. These were the tasks of the army of reserve, a body of men who were to be mobilised once the enemy had established a bridgehead. Press accounts of Napoleon's activities and descriptions of the camp at Boulogne added to the sense of alarm and urgency. It was not universal; the response to the call for volunteers was cool in Wales and Scotland, where it was imagined that distance from the invasion area gave some security, and in urban Yorkshire where there was little love for the government.[33] Elsewhere, there were understandable objections to detaching farm labourers for military service at crucial times in the farming year.

Trafalgar removed for ever the threat of invasion. Thereafter, the war reverted to the familiar global struggle against France and its allies, but with one important difference. The British army that fought in Portugal, Spain and south-western France between 1808 and 1814 was depicted as waging a war of liberation in alliance with Iberian patriots. This popular and justifiable portrayal of the conflict was set out at length by a fourteen-year-old poetess, Felicia Browne (better known under her married name, Felicia Hemans), two of whose brothers were campaigning in Portugal. Her 'England and Spain; or, Valour and Patriotism' was an appeal to other young men like them:

> Ye sons of Albion! first in danger's field,
> The sword of Britain and of truth to wield!
> Still prompt the injured to defend and save,
> Appal the despot, and assist the brave;
> Who now intrepid lift the generous blade,
> The cause of Justice and Castile to aid!

Expansionist imperial wars were also seen in favourable moral terms. Sergeant Bingham of the 1st Bengal Europeans considered the 1845 to 1846 war against the Sikhs as a crusade for civilisation. He saluted his comrades who had died as martyrs:

They breath'd their last – in Britain's cause!
For Britain's Empire! Britain's laws!!!

In explanation, he added a paean to the blessings of British rule in India and the order and tranquillity it had created, which no doubt pleased his employers, the East India Company.[34] It would also have satisfied his countrymen at home who were deeply conscious of Britain's unique position within the world as a progressive, industrial nation with enlightened values, not least of which were respect for individual liberty and the rule of law.

The image of a free country selflessly going to war to defend the freedom of others was resuscitated at the outbreak of the Crimean War in the spring of 1854. Like Bonaparte's France, Russia was portrayed by politicians and journalists as the antithesis of Britain. Its ruler, Czar Nicholas I, was a despot with absolute control over a barbaric and backward nation of serfs who were little more than slavish automata. He was the enemy of progress whose armies had crushed Polish and Hungarian patriots, and his invasion of the Ottoman Empire, the immediate cause of the war, was clear proof of a megalomania equal to Napoleon's.

The moral contrasts were highlighted in 'Hoist the Flag', a poem written to celebrate the departure of the fleet for the Black Sea:

In freedom and for right
Our heroes man the deck,
To punish pride they fight,
And wild ambition check.
Shall despots madly bold,
Their barbarous hordes array,
And like the Goth of old,
With ruin pave their way,
Must Europe bend the rule
Before the Northern Bear,
And nations brave and free,
His serf-like livery wear.[35]

The new humorous weekly *Punch* followed in the patriotic footsteps of

Gillray with cartoons of the czar, a grotesque figure in an overtight uniform surrounded by an army of wooden marionettes who were quickly dealt with by British soldiers and tars. But defeating him was not just drubbing a village bully; another cartoon showed an armoured, virginal Britannia kneeling and presenting her sword to an altar. Again, Britain was acting as an agent of divine providence. Sergeant Timothy Gowing of the Royal Fusiliers had clearly seen this material. About to embark for the Near East, he wrote: 'We are about to face in deadly conflict the strongest and most subtle nation of the civilised world, that could bring into the field one million bayonets, swayed by despotic power.'[36] Russian might did not perturb William Gibbs, who concluded a letter to his parents with, 'So no more at present from William Gibbs, gunner, Royal Marine Artillery, and a Briton every inch, able to tackle any three Russians that will stand before him.' His proud family passed on these stirring words to the press, whose readers were reassured that their fighting men possessed the right spirit, and, as always, the odds did not matter.[37]

V

Poems, songs and images conveyed a patriotism that was largely for civilian consumption, designed to present war in persuasive and comforting terms. But did they inflame those who had to fight? There is no clear answer. The letters, diaries and memoirs of individual fighting men are abundant, the majority written by officers who were more likely to be literate and had the time to set down their experiences. Nearly all of what they and the other ranks had to say was concerned with the exterior world of military and naval routine, the weather, rations, the landscape of the countries where they were serving, the peculiarities of their inhabitants, anecdotes about colleagues and camp or shipboard gossip. Boredom apart, few analysed their emotions or revealed much about their patriotism. What was unsaid was not necessarily unfelt.

Whenever servicemen took the risky step of seeking the redress of a grievance, they were careful to prefix their demand with a fulsome affirmation of their patriotism. In 1793 the crew of the *Alfred* declared themselves, 'Men who are proud to serve in the defence of their King, Constitution and Country'.[38] Men from the Inniskilling Dragoons expressed their devotion to king and country by wrecking Norwich pubs where Jacobin sympathisers assembled. Like civilians who menaced those suspected of sedition, they were no doubt glad to enjoy some licensed rowdiness.[39]

Everyone took for granted British superiority in fighting. 'We long to meet the French to show them how much British troops are superior to them,' the newly commissioned Ensign William Bell of the 89th told his family in 1808.[40] 'We can fight better than other nations,' insisted Lord George Paget of the 4th Light Dragoons. He added, sadly, for this was the Crimea during the winter of 1854 to 1855, 'but we have no organisation'.[41] Not only were the British the best fighters, they claimed an inner moral superiority which was reflected in the propriety of their conduct. Signalman Robert Mercer Wilson was horrified when a fellow sailor was charged with theft at Corfu in 1807 and called the crime a 'disgrace to the character of an Englishman'.[42] In the same year, during the retreat to La Coruña, Sir Henry Paget warned soldiers that their drunkenness and plundering 'was compromising the honour of their country'.[43] Such admonitions cut little ice with hungry men, or those for whom soldiering overseas was an opportunity to help themselves to whatever they could. Nonetheless, some sense of national honour did exist, both in the minds of officers, who were more susceptible to the concept, and among the better-educated rankers.

This reservoir of patriotism was tapped whenever men went into battle. That acute observer of the Peninsular War, Sergeant Joseph Donaldson, was particularly struck by Colonel Cadogan of the 71st's mastery of 'the art of rendering his men invincible'. 'He knew that the courage of the British soldier is best called forth by associating it with his country, and he also knew how to time the few words which produced magical effects.' So did that testy Welshman, Lieutenant-General Sir Thomas Picton, who, on discovering that they had been looting, castigated the 94th Highlanders: 'You are a disgrace to your moral country, Scotland.' His rebuke had the intended effect, for Donaldson remembered that afterwards he and his comrades felt deeply ashamed.[44]

The ancient tradition of commanders addressing their men before a fight remained strong. Generals and colonels had to produce the rhetoric that would stimulate the fighting spirit of their men and, at moments of extreme danger, draw from them extra reserves of energy and stamina. A love of country and knowledge of what the country expected from them were powerful stimulants to courage. On 1 June 1794, as the British fleet was closing with the French, the captain of the battleship *Defence* called his crew to prayer and then toured the ship, urging all gun-crews 'to fight for their country'. The response was heartening: 'The noblest feelings of patriotism were proclaimed, with expressions of the warmest enthusiasm: in short, a determination to conquer prevailed throughout the ship.'[45] At Salamanca in 1812, Brigadier-General Sir James Leith employed a lighter touch. Waving his cocked hat, he told the 38th: 'Now, my lads, this is the day for England: they would play at long ball with us from morning to night, but we will soon give them something else.'[46] Practical advice was blended with patriotic exhortation by Lieutenant-General Sir Robert Craufurd before the storming of the fortress of Ciudad Rodrigo in 1812: 'Soldiers! the eyes of the country are upon you. Be steady, – be cool, – be firm in the assault. The town must be yours. Once over the wall, let your first duty be to clear the ramparts, and in doing this keep together.'[47]

A patriotic voice from below, that of Private John Haime, a literate and articulate Methodist serving in the Queen's Regiment of Dragoons, was heard before Fontenoy in 1745, animating his fellow-horsemen: 'I exhorted them to be ready at all calls, and to obey those who had rule over them; and if called on out to battle, to stand fast, yea, if needful, fight up to the knees in blood. I said, "You fight for a good cause, and for a good King, and in defence of your country."'[48] This appeal from a private soldier may have been exceptional although, like other Methodists in the army, Haine never missed a chance to harangue his comrades on their moral lapses, the virtues of quietism and hopes of salvation.

A contempt for the enemy was an element of campaign patriotism, although less so than at home. Most commonly he was treated with condescending amusement. In the Napoleonic Wars the French soldier was 'Johnny Crapaud' ('Toad' – from the alleged staple of his diet) which was sometimes shortened to the more insulting 'Craps'.[49] In the Crimea, the foe was 'Johnny Rooskie', and his generals' names were a source of lower-rank humour: Gorchakov was known as 'Got such a cough' and Dolgororski as 'Dog of Rooskie'.[50] Americans were disdained, at least by officers who detested their democratic spirit. In 1776, one described them as 'psalm signers' who spoke with a 'Godly twang through the nose' and were not gentlemen. 'We know that honour is little practised by the American government or people,' regretted the *Naval Chronicle* in February 1814.[51]

Gallant opponents were respected because soldiers saw in them reflections of their own virtues. During the battle of Sabraon in 1846, men of the 9th spared a Sikh gunner with a wooden leg because he appeared a 'true patriot', while his able-bodied and equally determined comrades were slaughtered.[52] Like many other soldiers in the Peninsula, Sergeant Donaldson learned to admire the French and made friends with several. 'How different were our feelings in this respect from many of our countrymen at home,' he remembered, 'whose ideas of the French character were drawn from servile newspapers and pamphlets, or even from so low a source as the caricatures in print shops.' 'Instead of pygmy wretches who fed on nothing but frogs and beef tea,' he encountered 'stout and handsome fellows, who understood the principles of good living as well as any Englishman among us; and whatever may be said to the contrary, remarkably brave soldiers.'[53]

Unpatriotic sentiments were rarely heard; military and naval disci pline saw to that. In June 1805, on the quarter-deck of HMS *Prince George*, a drunken marine, John Daniels, was overheard 'damning the King and the bloody country . . . the service and every bugger that was in it'. This outburst was in effect an attempted suicide as he admitted afterwards, for he hoped that it would get him hanged, because he could not endure a flogging. He was spared noose and cat: a court-martial considered his words so intemperate as to be evidence of clinical lunacy and ordered him to be shipped home for confinement in Bedlam.[54] Those who had come within an inch of death were some-times sceptical of the value of patriotism and glory. During the battle known as the Glorious First of June (1794) a midshipman cried out: 'Never mind the honour and glory of the Country. Give me back my leg again!'[55] Having survived two hard-fought battles against the Sikhs in which he had been engaged in hand-to-hand combat, Private Baldwin of the 9th confided to his cousin: 'Some persons have said "it is sweet to die for one's country", but I am not quite sure of that; I think it is sweeter to live . . .'[56]

2

A wild rattling man: Recruitment and discipline

Men entered the strictly regulated and disciplined worlds of the eigh-teenth- and nineteenth-century army and navy for a variety of reasons, most of them negative. A survey undertaken in 1846 revealed that two-thirds of the army's recruits enlisted because they were destitute, a fifth foolishly imagined that they would be paid for loafing, and a twelfth took the queen's shilling because they were bored or wished to spite their parents.[1] Between a half and two-thirds of those who joined up were unskilled labourers, usually dependent on casual industrial or agricultural work. When the demand for men exceeded supply, as it always did in wartime, the services were grateful to accept petty crimi-nals under sentence of transportation, Highland bandits and former Irish rebels. Emergency expedients were also employed in peacetime. In 1824, 150 convicted smugglers were drafted into the navy, which no doubt put to good use skills acquired evading revenue cutters.[2] Not even the infirm were excluded; in March 1801, fever-stricken merchant seamen were pressed aboard HMS *Achille*, where they promptly infected the rest of the crew.[3]

Those who joined the services of their own free will were refugees from an uncongenial world. Samuel Hutton, a runaway apprentice turned vagrant odd-jobman, was overwhelmed by the 'unceasing' drudgery and precariousness of his existence. He joined the 12th Regiment in the 1750s accompanied by one of his former employers, a whip-maker who 'heartily weary perhaps of his wife and weary perhaps of beating her . . . had undertaken to beat the French'.[4] Both were victims of the fickle casual labour market and were the natural targets of recruiting parties, who normally concentrated their efforts in areas where trade was stagnant and unemployment high. From the late eighteenth century onwards, recruiting-officers hovered around the growing industrial centres which were magnets for unskilled men seeking work. During the summer of 1814, when it needed to find men to make up for losses in the war in North America, the 85th Light Infantry's recruiting-sergeants were trawling Manchester, Birmingham and Glasgow.[5] In the last city they faced competition from the Scottish regiments whose recruiters looked for their prey in the Lowland industrial towns which attracted jobless Highland migrants.[6]

Hungry, derelict men were easily tempted. At a stroke they gained the security of a regular wage, a permanent home and an assured, if sparse, diet. The recruiting-sergeant's patter also attracted bored youths with a fancy for travel and adventure. 'An inclination to see the world' propelled a farmer's son from the backwater of Nailsworth in Gloucestershire to the Indian Ocean, where he served as a marine on board an East Indiaman.[7] 'A compound of fire and life', George Sladford escaped from the stifling routines of small-town life in Lincolnshire by volunteering for the army during the Seven Years' War.[8] Others of similar temperament snatched at a chance to liberate themselves from parents who had forced them into tedious occupations. Apprenticed to a Cork attorney, John Magrath broke his indentures, fled to London and enlisted as a marine in July 1791. Two years later, when his ship the Medusa was docked at Cork, he deserted and, spurned by his outraged family, set off to seek his fortune in America. 'The boy was very wild,' explained his father in a petition for his son's pardon.[9]

Another harum-scarum lad on the run from middle-class parents, Joseph Donaldson, ran off to sea in a Greenock merchantman and, still afflicted by what he called a 'melancholy and restless' spirit, joined the 94th Highlanders on his return.[10] 'A roving and a restless spirit' led Edward Costello into the 95th Rifles in 1807. His taste for war's excitement and glory had been whetted by the tales of a workmate, a veteran who had lost his leg but not his enthusiasm for soldiering during the 1801 Egyptian campaign.[11] Newspaper reports of heroic deeds in the Khyber Pass in 1842 caught the imagination of John Baldwin, then employed in a shop in North Walsham in Norfolk. He asked a workmate whether he wanted to be in India playing 'rough sport'. 'I should,' Baldwin continued, 'for in our confined sphere, we know literally nothing of the world and are dying of ennui.'[12] Soon after, he abandoned stocktaking, joined the 9th and within three years found all the 'rough sport' he could desire in the First Sikh War. The glamour of a soldier's life, as revealed in poetry and books on war, had first turned the head of James Pindar, a twenty-two-year-old Fife miner who enlisted in the Royal Scots in 1858 after a recruiting-sergeant had promised him tiger and lion shooting in India.[13]

All these young men were exceptional: they were literate and capable of rationalising their actions in retrospect. They enlisted as the result of a conscious decision. Others, the majority of the recruits, did so accidentally in an alcoholic haze. Public houses and inns were favourite hunting grounds of recruiting-sergeants, and strong drink and tobacco their accomplices. Enticement went hand in hand with intoxication. The process was outlined in an eighteenth-century ballad that described the methods of a captain scouring Ayrshire for volunteers:

> And with very good will he proffered the lads
> A pint of Scots ale and a gill
> And some bits of silver he slipped to them
> And then he drew them in with his pauss [purse].
> Some need took on for to get bread
> And some came in for good cause
> Till in a short time he had enlisted them
> The number of twenty and two.[14]

William Lucas found a recruiting party from the Inniskilling Dragoons in a Westminster pub early one morning in 1845. 'As soon as I sat down gin was called for,' he recalled, but he refused, only accepting a half-pint once he had enlisted.[15] Half-pints of whisky, paid for from his bounty money and shared with his new comrades, marked Joseph

Donaldson's reception into the 94th Highlanders. John Ryder, the son of a Waterloo veteran and a former manservant, met his fellow recruits in the Bull's Head in Nottingham in 1844. 'I was ashamed of being among them; for they were a dirty, ragged lot of blackguards – some of them nearly drunk.'[16]

Once he had sobered up, the rookie realised that he had signed away the rest of his life, for most recruits were induced to pledge themselves to unlimited service, which until 1829 usually meant twenty-one years in the infantry and twenty-four in the cavalry. What had seemed a good idea at the time suddenly became a nightmare and some new recruits panicked, taking the only way out, flight. If the absconder was lucky, he might still possess some of his bounty money and there were a few who played the system by joining up, pocketing the cash, deserting and then enlisting again. Most deserters drifted back into their old habits, and as vagrants they were always liable to scrutiny by poor law officers, parish constables and magistrates to whom descriptions of deserters were routinely sent. Marine George McKenzie fitted a pattern that was all too common. He signed on at Coventry in November 1823, changed his mind in a few days and ran off. McKenzie was identified two months later when he was in Leicester gaol, under arrest for vagrancy. He was returned to the naval authorities and given twelve months imprisonment and, like all other deserters, had the letter D stamped below his left armpit and made indelible with gunpowder. If he tried to enlist again he would be instantly recognised and rejected.[17] The histories of men who joined on impulse and deserted on impulse confirmed the general view that the services were home to the fickle and feckless.

Part of the recruit's bounty went to the officer, NCO or soldier who had persuaded him to sign on. The full amounts reflected the government's need for men. During the Napoleonic Wars the army bounty rose to between sixteen guineas (£16.80) and twenty-three pounds, although the navy's was restricted to five pounds, which helps explain why it had to rely so heavily on impressment. Newly joined men got little of this cash; in 1793 a recruit to the Dragoon Guards received £2 18s (£2.90), and the officer who had persuaded him to join got five pounds. In peacetime bounties fell dramatically to the point where the sum delivered barely covered deductions for uniform and equipment. In the mid 1840s a Light Dragoon's kit cost £8 3s (£8.14), and his bounty was £6 17s 6d (£6.75), leaving him to borrow the difference from an officer who would deduct it from his pay in instalments.[18]

Soaring wartime premiums attracted private contractors, known as 'crimps', who specialised in procuring men. The government chose not to inquire too closely into the methods of these entrepreneurs from the urban underworld. Their victims came from the poorest sections of society and their methods included kidnapping. In 1813 a radical joiner, John Leonard, whose son had been 'trepanned' (abducted) by a notorious Newcastle crimp, Johnson Reed, protested in verse:

> Behold the girl with face of clay
> Where blooming roses late did play
> Alas her lover's torn away
>   By J——R—d

The local authorities supported Reed, and Leonard was put in gaol. Unbowed, he composed a new ballad denouncing another crimp.[19]

II

In a crisis, the state could compel men to join the services. Since the sixteenth century the navy had had the legal power to impress sailors, and during manpower emergencies in the Revolutionary and Napoleonic Wars the government drafted militiamen into regular regiments. The navy suffered most from manpower shortages; between 1793 and 1815, 103,660 sailors died, 84,440 of them from various diseases.[20] Every form of inducement and coercion was required to provide a steady flow of men to compensate for these losses.

Naval officers in command of press-gangs pocketed a payment for each man they seized which, of course, encouraged them to be ruthless in pursuit of their quarry and none too choosy about whom they collared. The rewards never matched the sums that an officer could gain from prize-money, but they were not to be sniffed at. Between 1793 and 1795, Lieutenant John Newton pressed just over a thousand men in Devon and received £1589 6s 8d (£1589.33) from the Admiralty, which praised his 'zeal and economy'. Not all officers were so cost-conscious and premiums of up to thirteen pounds per man were paid in other areas.[21]

Figures like Newton and their bands of sailors were universally detested in ports throughout Britain and the colonies. Wherever they went, their activities were the cause of thousands of human tragedies. Breadwinners were snatched, leaving wives and families destitute and forced to live off parish relief. There were other, equally distressful domestic disruptions. In 1695 the Admiralty received a plea from 'two pretty young seamen's wives' who 'only desire the enjoyment of their husbands for a month'. The pair promised to return their spouses to their ship once the extended honeymoon was over.[22] Careers were disrupted and prospects destroyed, although John Stevens tried to gain some advantage from his misfortune. 'I was chief mate of the *Neptune* scow from Georgia bound to London,' he informed the Admiralty in 1755, 'and was pressed by the occasion of my captain's ill behaviour to the officer of the *Elizabeth*'s tender who boarded us in the Channel.' He asked if he could be promoted to midshipman in light of his experience, 'otherwise [I] hope your lordships will not detain me, as I have many offers in the merchant service.'[23]

A system that plucked men from merchant vessels was loathed by shipowners and businessmen. Commercial interests overrode public ones, and officers in charge of press-gangs faced hostility whenever they arrived at a port. At Yarmouth in 1776, local shipowners and merchant captains helped sailors dodge the press-gang which was pestered by jeering crowds.[24] A mob attacked a recruiting party when it came ashore at Greenock in 1795, but the officer in command persisted and within eight months secured over seven hundred men.[25]

Snatching men for the navy was an occupation that attracted bullies and anyone who enjoyed the high-handed exercise of petty authority. During the summer of 1804, Poole was terrorised by the irascible Lieutenant Osmer, who browbeat the local magistrates and their officers, and grabbed apprentices and yeoman farmers who were legally exempt from the press. When one victim protested, Osmer snapped: 'Damn me, if you were a younger man I'd wring the nose out of your face', and others were threatened with the lieutenant's stick.[26]

As the Admiralty constantly complained, the trouble was that

Osmer and his colleagues were denied access to large numbers of eligible men. Hundreds of South Devon farmers who undertook seasonal work in the Newfoundland cod fisheries and six thousand Cornish inshore fishermen were legally beyond the reach of the press. Exemptions designed to protect commerce drove the navy to look for recruits among casual workers and the unemployed. Accompanied by a fifer and drummer, one officer appeared in Devon towns on market days, hoping to lure jobless farm labourers. He failed, largely because the rustics had flocked to the militia where they were safe from the press and had the bonus of a bounty. The Devon militia was also a haven for naval deserters, and Fife fishermen obtained immunity by enlisting in the local fencibles.[27] This was frustrating for the Admiralty, which in 1795 demanded that all seamen were discharged from the militia and volunteers, but the War Office was unsympathetic.[28] It, too, was strapped for men.

Faced with these obstacles and desperate to make up crews reduced by sickness, fatigue and desertion, the navy turned to criminals. Felons under sentence of transportation preferred the hazards of service at sea to those that they might encounter in Australia and exploited the navy's manpower problems. During the Revolutionary and Napoleonic Wars the Admiralty received a steady flow of petitions from convicts. The sentiments of a request presented by thirteen felons on board the aptly named prison hulk *Retribution* in 1805 were typical. All promised to 'conduct themselves as British seamen and by their future behaviour convince your Lordships that they have renounced depravity and are determined to persevere in the jocund paths of Virtue, and again become useful to society'.[29] This was wishful thinking; men who flouted the laws of civil society did not knuckle down under the far tighter régime of a man-o'-war. They tended to become sea-lawyers, mischief-makers who spread discontent, and many turned out to be recidivists who could only be constrained by the lash.[30]

Moreover, like all pressed men from on shore, criminals were ignorant of the sea and had to learn the complex skills of seamanship and gunnery on the job. This education was often slow, difficult and sometimes painful. Naval surgeons faced a steady stream of men with accidental shipboard injuries such as fractures from falls, contusions and powder burns which were the consequence of the landsman's inexperience and clumsiness. Unaccustomed exertion strained the feeble recruit to breaking-point. In 1756, Nathaniel Eardly, who described himself as 'no seaman but a broken tradesman', requested his discharge from the Admiralty on the grounds of his debility. He had been pressed on board the *Culloden* in the West Indies, served on two other ships and succumbed to various ailments which had confined him to the sickbay. Despite his failure in business, Eardly possessed the wherewithal to hire a healthier and more adept substitute and offered the navy what was a good bargain: 'a stout, able and good sailor about 5 feet 10 inches high [who] had used the sea 30 years'.[31]

Foreign birth did not disqualify a sailor from impressment. What mattered above all was a knowledge of seamanship, which was why men were taken from interned Dutch merchantmen after Britain went to war with the French-occupied Netherlands in 1795. Continental, American, African and Afro-Caribbean sailors were pressed at sea for the British service, although it prudently tried to distribute them in such a way that they never outnumbered their British shipmates. Unable to replenish crews with pressed men from Britain, the Mediterranean Fleet relied on men taken from foreign vessels during the 1790s, with the result of an imbalance of nationalities on some smaller warships. 'There were few Englishmen on board,' claimed an officer from the bomb ketch *Albanaise*, which explained why the crew had been able to seize the ship and steer it to the Spanish port of Malaga in 1800. The mutineers were chiefly 'Italians, Danes and Swedes', all of whom had been pressed.[32] There were defections, too, by French prisoners of war who joined the Canadian forces during the war against the United States, although, as might be expected, they proved unreliable. Among the deserters was Jean Chauvin who was recaptured and sentenced to transportation for life, but pardoned by the Prince Regent in 1814 on the grounds that he could not reasonably be expected to show loyalty to a foreign power.[33]

Accepting men who were in effect mercenaries was a necessity forced on the War Office and Admiralty in dire emergencies. German mercenaries were hired by contract from their rulers during the American War, and others were recruited from the crown's Hanoverian territories and elsewhere during the Napoleonic Wars. Another shortfall in manpower in 1855 led the government to consider raising foreign units, promising survivors land on the frontiers of Cape Colony as a reward for their services. Like ex-Roman legionaries who were allocated farms on the fringes of the Empire, the Crimean veterans were expected to serve in defence of their property.

Manpower crises in the fledgling North American colonies, where there were not enough whites to fill the ranks of the militia, led to the recruitment of blacks. Slaves and European indentured labourers joined the Virginia volunteers in 1711, although the local authorities were nervous.[34] Drill, discipline and a familiarity with firearms might easily engender a self-confidence and sense of independence that would make it hard for the volunteers to resume the servility demanded from them as civilians. Similar misgivings had to be put aside in 1714 and 1715 when South Carolina was all but overwhelmed by a native American invasion. Two hundred blacks, paid the same wages as white men (four pounds per month), were among the scratch forces raised to meet the threat.[35] As the European population rose, the need to enlist blacks diminished, although between 1775 and 1776 the governor of Virginia proposed raising black regiments from the dominion's slaves, much to the horror of the plantation owners. Black slaves from nearby estates flocked to the British during operations on the Chesapeake in 1814; their masters' enemies were automatically their friends and a few acted as guides to British units.[36]

Anxieties about teaching blacks the arts of European warfare were strong in the West Indies, where the white population was heavily outnumbered by slaves. The dilemma was always the same: could these men be relied upon to point their muskets in the right direction, or might they turn them against the oppressors of their race? Arguments of this kind were raised in 1795 when it was proposed to raise black regiments in the West Indies for garrisons and seaborne attacks on the rich French, Spanish and Dutch sugar islands. Pragmatism and the urge for profit prevailed. Britain's strategy of conquest and annexation in the Caribbean was in danger of collapsing because of the alarming death rate among white soldiers. Between 1795 and 1801, 42,250 out of eighty-nine thousand British soldiers drafted to the region died from local sicknesses, and an unknown number were invalided home.[37] The only solution to this problem was the recruitment of black slaves, who were imagined to be more resilient to the climate and indigenous distempers.

Rather than take slaves from the plantations, whose sympathies would be with their kinsfolk and workmates, the War Office decided to purchase blacks newly arrived from Africa. Ten per cent of all slaves imported into the British West Indies were bought by the army, and by 1808 the black regiments mustered 13,400. Efforts were made to find new recruits in Africa. In March 1812, Sergeant Nuanda was employed by the 1st West India Regiment procuring men in West Africa, no doubt instructed only to take recruits from those tribes like the Coromantee who had an aggressive reputation.[38]

Whether obtained in Africa or at quayside auctions in the Caribbean ports, black soldiers were given a new, warrior identity by their officers. Among the men of the 1st West India Regiment were 'Ajax', 'Boatswain', 'Columbus' and 'Buonaparte', perhaps a soldier who had struck his white officers as possessing extraordinary military potential. Or maybe he was one of the awkward squad whose name conveyed an irony he would never understand. The experience of such men was dismal and their sufferings as great as the white soldiers they had superseded. In 1808 an inspection of the 5th West India Regiment, then stationed near Belize, revealed that they were 'lodged in miserable huts' by a swamp and commanded by officers most of whom were on extended furloughs in Britain. An exceptionally high proportion of the men were aged and sickly.[39] There were compensations, for in that year the government, having just outlawed the slave trade, promised its black soldiers freedom on the expiry of their service.

III

Whether he entered the services by accident, coercion or of his own free will, the new recruit found himself immersed in a world utterly unlike the one he had left. Some accepted the novelty with equanimity. William Richardson, an apprentice mate who was pressed from a slaver off Beachy Head in 1791, recalled: 'I was young and had the world before me, did not fret much, and was willing to go to any part of the world.'[40] Benjamin Harris, an illiterate Dorset shepherd, likewise surrendered to forces beyond his control when he was drafted from the local militia in 1802. 'As I had no choice in the matter, it was quite as well that I did not grieve over my fate.'[41] His resignation goes far in explaining why the army preferred simple countrymen who submitted to their lot without demur.

Quietism was the best philosophy for the serviceman. If he thought otherwise, he was soon made to change his mind. Shortly after he had been pressed in 1803, John Wetherell, a merchant seaman, was warned that henceforward he was subject to 'the martial laws of my country and must use every means to obey my superiors' and 'to be sober, silent and submissive'.[42] Joseph Donaldson learned the same lesson in the 94th Highlanders. 'Damn you, sir, *you have no right to think*: there were people paid to think for you – do what you are ordered sir, right or wrong', was one officer's response when Donaldson protested against what he considered an injustice.[43] 'Obedience, temperance and clean-liness' were the virtues the young soldier ought to cultivate, believed Thomas Quinney, who embraced all three and rose to the rank of staff-sergeant.[44]

Wetherell, Donaldson and Quinney existed within a rigidly con-trolled and structured society with its distinct codes and patterns of behaviour, many of which would have been unrecognisable to out-siders, and some repugnant. Since 1689 the armed forces had been controlled by parliament which, through the annual Mutiny Act, apportioned the yearly budget for the army and navy and set a limit on the number of men they could employ. From 1713 onwards, the Mutiny Act also defined military and naval law, fixing the penalties that could be imposed by every level of court-martial. So that no one was in any doubt as to what these laws were and what lay in store for those who broke them, ships' captains would regularly stand on the quarter-deck and recite the Articles of War to their crews.

What emerged from this catalogue of misdeeds and punishments was that the sailor, and, for that matter, the soldier, had forfeited his right to a trial by jury and was liable to be punished for a range of offences unknown to civil law. In one sense, the serviceman was worse off than the civilian, in that he could no longer exercise his legal rights and free will. This deprivation could not have been heart-breaking for men who had had few opportunities to do so, since their lives had hith-erto been dominated by the need to acquire money, food and shelter. All were available, if in disappointing measure, from the services which, in return, expected total submission. As Joseph Donaldson ruefully observed, the recruit was drawn into a 'vortex of abject slavishness and dissipation', the latter a reaction to the constraints of the former.[45]

Many were aware of the contrast between their subservience and the patriotic ballads that extolled the 'liberty' that was the Briton's birthright. The line from 'Hearts of Oak' – 'For who are so free as we sons of the waves?' – must have provoked some sour gibes below-decks. In 1796 the crew of the frigate *Shannon* asked the Admiralty to remove their 'tyrant of a captain' whose severe régime was 'more than the spirits and hearts of true Englishmen can bear, for we are born free but now we are slaves'.[46] He remained and the *Shannon's* crew continued to suffer. Between February 1797 and February 1798 eleven men were flogged.[47] The commonest offences were drunkenness, insubordination and brawling, crimes that might reasonably be expected in a ship of this type with a high proportion of pressed men.

The frequent use of the cat-o'-nine-tails characterised military and naval discipline. Many officers were disturbed by corporal punishment and a few resorted to it with extreme reluctance or not at all. Eleven-year-old Midshipman Dillon was 'touched to the quick' when he witnessed his first flogging in 1790, but soon appreciated that it was the only effective way of controlling 'bad characters'.[48] One such, a deserter who had been pressed aboard the *Unité* in 1805, jeered at shipmates who read religious tracts that had been distributed by an officer and immediately got twenty-four lashes for insolence. Another pressed man of a pious nature approved and noticed that the miscreant was a rogue who gambled and got drunk on Sundays and so deserved his chastisement.[49] A seaman who watched the regular floggings on board the battleship *Albion* in 1852 noticed that 'the plucky ones used to consider it a feather in their cap' if they suffered in silence, and their standing among their shipmates was subsequently enhanced. Nonetheless 'bad characters' had a huge capacity to make a nuisance of themselves within an enclosed community, often by throwing their weight about, and for this reason private soldiers and seamen approved of the occasional use of the lash.[50]

Punishments that simultaneously degraded and deterred were performed in public. Great emphasis was set on the spectacle of retribution which was contrived to overawe. At eight o'clock one May morning in

1746, all the regimental pickets drew up in ranks before the gallows in Inverness to witness the execution of three deserters. A fourth received a thousand lashes and was then 'drummed along' both the lines with a halter about his neck.[51] A yellow flag was hoisted on a warship immediately before an execution, a gun was fired, and before the smoke had cleared, his shipmates hauled the condemned man up to the yardarm from which his body would hang for an hour.[52] A boatswain found guilty of the attempted buggery of two ship's boys in 1808 had a halter placed around his neck and was put in a boat that was rowed around all the warships anchored at the Nore. As he came alongside each, his crime and sentence were read out, which no doubt provoked jeers and a pelting from the listeners, for his offence was particularly loathed by sailors.[53]

The public rituals associated with the punishment of crime were common to both the forces and civil society. Until 1868 executions were public and drew large audiences in London and the provinces, and the treatment of the boatswain was little different from the contemporary practice of pillorying convicted homosexuals, an event that attracted noisy and vindictive crowds. And yet long after civil punishments had been withdrawn to the privacy of the prison, the army insisted on executions in public during wartime on the grounds that onlookers would be left in no doubt as to the consequences of cowardice and desertion. For this reason, one company of the Dorsets and another of the Cheshires were ordered to witness the shooting of Thomas Highgate, found guilty of desertion early in September 1914.[54] The practice lasted until 1919.

Highgate's trial was little different from those conducted by military and naval courts-martial over the previous two hundred years. The accused was tried before a panel of officers and, in wartime conditions, without any kind of legal representation. For serious offences on land, sentences were confirmed, reduced or remitted by the crown, acting on legal advice. In the field and at sea, the local commanding officer undertook the same duty. Such procedures were reserved for grave infractions of military law. Minor crimes were handled by ships' captains and regimental colonels or, in their absence, the most senior officer available.

There were plenty of quirky officers who had their own ideas of how best to uphold discipline or what constituted a breach of it. The captain of the *Minerva*, an outstanding practical seaman, had an aversion to noise, especially that of the human voice. His crew performed their duties in complete silence, instructed only by whistles or the boatswain's pipe. Bad language, unavoidable given the number of petty but painful mishaps that occurred, was banned. Those who swore had their names taken and were each given seven or eight lashes the next morning.[55]

Other officers adopted other forms of corporal punishment for minor shipboard misdemeanours. The commonest was 'starting', by which a petty officer struck an offender with a knotted rope until the officer considered the man had been corrected. How often and how severely this punishment was used depended on the temperament of a ship's commander. 'Starting' was frequent on board the *Cyane* during 1822 when it was cruising off the West African coast looking for slavers. The captain had devised his own astringent, which was a yard-long stick, wrapped in twine, with a musket ball at the tip. On one occasion it was used on one miscreant by a marine sergeant who recalled: 'I hit him over the back and every place I could get at him and drew the blood through his clothing.' The offences were all trivial and a court martial reprimanded the captain for his severity and for not listing his punishments in his log, as the law required.[56] Such practices were not exceptional. James Scott, who saw service at sea between 1803 and 1814, recalled approvingly that 'infamous characters' were unofficially chastised with wet swabs wielded by ships' boys.[57]

By the second quarter of the nineteenth century, legal limits were imposed on the number of strokes that could be imposed by courts-martial. After 1807 the upper limit was set at one thousand, and over the next forty years it fell to fifty in the army and forty-eight in the navy, where summary sentences of up to a dozen lashes were still common on many ships during the 1850s. As ever, the commonest offences were insolence and drunkenness. Serious military crimes still received heavy sentences. In 1839 two men from the 71st received two hundred lashes each for rape and burglary and, during the next six years, the same number was given to soldiers guilty of striking NCOs and officers.[58] The alternative sentence was seven years' transportation, which tempted a few desperate men to hit their officers as a means of escaping the army and getting to Australia. A lancer who tried this method of securing a discharge was executed in India in 1847 to deter others similarly inclined.[59]

Whatever the circumstances, assaulting a superior could never be condoned: it was a blow against the whole system of discipline and was treated accordingly. In 1805 a midshipman discovered a sailor in a drunken stupor in the fo'c'sle of the *Russell*, shouted at him and, when this failed to wake him, pulled him up by his shirt. 'What did you do that for, you bugger!' the seaman shouted and then threw his assailant against the taffrail. Whether or not he was aware who he was striking, and it seems unlikely he was, the man got three hundred lashes.[60] The same sentence was imposed on John Vanperson who in January 1807 had stolen a loin of mutton from the captain's steward on the *Impeteux*, which he boiled to make himself some broth. It was bubbling away in a pot when he was apprehended and the meat retrieved. He had hoped at least to keep the broth, but this was not allowed. Deprived of a change from the monotonous shipboard diet, he violently resisted arrest, shouting at a lieutenant, 'I will be buggered if I don't knock your bloody brains about the deck you bugger, rascal and villain.'[61]

Forbearance was unevenly distributed among servicemen. The demands of discipline and the caprices of some of those responsible for its enforcement built up frustration and anger, especially in men who had become soldiers and sailors unwillingly. Drink could and did bring relief, but, as often as not, it deepened discontent. It also stiffened resolve, dissolved inhibitions and encouraged recklessness, particularly when several men gathered together and chewed over their grievances. Individual challenges to authority, like that of the sailor on the *Russell*, were commonly the result of intoxication.

By contrast, civilians could express their feelings against their employers and risk nothing more than dismissal. Furthermore, this was an age during which crowds rioted in protest against food shortages, price rises, militia service, lockouts, wage cuts, evictions, disputed outcomes to prize fights and the efforts of those in authority to enforce unpopular laws. Even such an illustrious figure as the Duke of Wellington was not immune from the mob's insolence and brickbats, both of which he suffered for his opposition to political reform. Such behaviour was deplored by governments, magistrates and judges, and when disorders got out of hand they were suppressed by force, but the right to demonstrate was never questioned.

Such activities were not tolerated within the services. Passive submission was the cement of discipline. Swift, unwavering obedience to orders was vital if the soldier and sailor were to perform their duty, which was to kill their country's enemies as efficiently as possible. The mechanics of eighteenth- and early nineteenth-century warfare demanded instant responses to orders. The Royal Navy's achievements rested on superior seamanship and gunnery, which enabled British men-o'-war to outsail, outmanoeuvre and outshoot their adversaries. Whether aloft handling spars and rigging or below manning guns, the sailor had always to be alert, dexterous and prompt in doing what he was told. On land, battles were determined by the deployment of mass firepower. Like the sailor, the individual soldier was obliged to function as part of a machine, moving in formations that had to change front or pace at the word of command. The loading, priming and firing of muskets had to be undertaken with clockwork precision to produce the synchronised volleys that shattered Highlanders at Culloden, French infantry in the Peninsula and at Waterloo, and native armies throughout India.

Minor infractions of service regulations such as a dishevelled uniform, a fouled musket, mislaid items of kit, or a routine chore undertaken sulkily or not at all were symptoms of a wider contempt for discipline. Habits of obedience had to be cultivated in every area of the serviceman's life. There was no borderline between war and peace; orders not to smuggle whores into barracks had equal force with those for an assault on a French position. Slovenliness and insubordination were contagious and diminished fighting efficiency. Exasperated by the debilitating effects of drink on his crew and tired of flogging drunks, one captain warned them: 'You are now on the enemy's coast, and who knows how soon our utmost exertions may be required to defend ourselves.'[62] Men who failed to control themselves could not hope to handle their ship in battle.

Doing so to perfection and winning victories offered compensation. Those who learned to think and act like soldiers and sailors saw themselves as distinct from the rest of society. They were proud of the achievements of their regiment or ship and the values of the fighting man: loyalty to comrades and unit, regularity, dutifulness, courage and honour. 'I am a man of Honour,' declared Sergeant Kite in Farquhar's *The Recruiting Officer* (1706), 'Besides I don't beat up for common soldiers; no, I list only for Grenadiers, Grenadiers, Gentlemen – Pray Gentlemen, observe this cap – This is the cap of Honour, it dubs a man a Gentleman.' Uncommon soldiers wore an uncommon dress, in this case an elaborately embroidered mitre cap. Kite's fictional sense of honour was shared by a contemporary soldier, a sergeant, who in mitigation for killing a man who had insulted him, claimed that he wore 'the Queen's cloth' which he was honour-bound to defend.[63]

Articulate soldiers expressed satisfaction and pride in martial virtues and their value in the scheme of things, and there is no reason to believe that their sentiments were not shared by their unlettered colleagues. Sergeant Quinney, who served in India during the 1820s and 1830s, believed that the soldier was the 'protector of the institutions of his country' and 'though a man of war, is also a keeper of the peace'.[64] Moreover, those who accepted their peculiar conditions could find contentment within the armed services. 'I am very pleased in the station of a soldier now,' Andrew Phillips, a gunner stationed in Gibraltar, told his father in 1806. His satisfaction with army life survived his experience of war. In 1812 he wrote from Spain: 'although I am a soldier I am no discredit to my family. I know very well that a soldier is disdained at home, but he be very happy.'[65]

IV

Those who were dissatisfied with their lot had only two means of legitimate escape: death from disease or enemy action, or a discharge because of persistent illness or debility. For the fit man, desertion was the only other alternative. It was a risky enterprise; the fugitive gambled on his ability to submerge himself in the crowd and so elude pursuit and detection. The odds were finely balanced, which may explain why, when apprehended, deserters frequently claimed that they had acted upon a drunken impulse. This was the excuse of George Dallas of the 60th who ran off from picket duty and drank himself to sleep during counterinsurgency operations in Ireland in August 1798. He was probably scared; several of his comrades had been killed in recent skirmishes and his detachment was expecting an ambush. On waking, he changed his mind and decided to return to his unit, but took the road to Dublin. The court-martial was unimpressed and sentenced him to death.[66] Drink and a belief that he could start a new life in the United States impelled Francis Toole to slip away from a landing party which had come ashore at Cape Cod Bay to collect ballast in December 1813. He spent five hours wandering along the Massachusetts shore before he was retaken by a search party that had been alerted to his whereabouts by an American woman.[67]

Had he got further, Toole would have assimilated easily in English-speaking North America and had little difficulty in finding work. Faced with labour shortages, New York colonists had been enticing soldiers and seamen with promises of high wages in 1711.[68] In the Revolutionary War and that of 1812, Americans tempted deserters with bribes of cash and land. During the summer of 1813, the 103rd Regiment lost sixty men who deserted to the enemy, the 8th forty-seven and the 49th fifteen. Only a small number were subsequently caught.[69] Prisoners of war, particularly sailors, also came under pressure, for like its adversary the American navy was permanently short of trained seamen. Those who rejected inducements to join were bullied. Prisoners from merchantmen captured by the frigate *Essex* were carried to the Marquesa Islands in 1813 and forced to undertake hard labour in chains. 'American seamen were placed with whips over the English prisoners, and practised the greatest cruelty on them,' which drove some to desert.[70] Others did not, despite incentives. A rifleman of the 95th on outpost duty shot dead the American who tried to lure him away with a hundred dollars.[71] John Nicholes, a prisoner of war, spurned bribes and the rank of boatswain in the United States navy.

Later, Nicholes was exchanged, and deserted in Hamilton, Bermuda. He did so with another sailor and a marine, like him desperate to escape the torments of Lieutenant Johnson of the *Ruby*, who threatened them with flogging and threw stones at men working the capstan or aloft on the spars. Nicholes's behaviour was uncharacteristic, for he was 'a quiet decent man', which earned him a remission of a third of the 150 lashes of his sentence.[72] Even a man of Nicholes's temperament could be driven to desertion by a sadistic officer, and there were quite a few in the navy.

One such repulsive creature, Lieutenant Charles Leaver, commander of the sloop *Martial*, was dismissed from the service after a court-martial heard a harrowing account of his calculated and systematic cruelty to the sixteen-year-old John Ansell while the vessel was cruising off the Basque Roads between July 1812 and March 1813. The victim had been of decent character but simple mind and incapable of controlling his bowels or bladder. The rest of the crew treated Ansell kindly, but Leaver was determined to cure him of his affliction through illegal thrashing with a wooden plank, incarceration in a coal-hole and repeated floggings. The boy's condition deteriorated as wounds from the beatings turned septic and he became deranged; during one imprisonment he sang about his mother. Warned by the ship's doctor that Ansell would not survive another flogging, Leaver remarked that 'he would rather kill him than keep such a dirty brute' and the punishment went ahead with the boy dying as a consequence.[73] The matter was brought to the attention of the authorities by members of the crew. In some respects their tale of Ansell's persecution resembles that of Billy Budd in Melville's eponymous novel.

Captain Hugh Pigott of the frigate *Hermione* displayed a similar but fickle sadism which extended even to his officers. One, Midshipman David O'Brien Casey, was favoured one moment and reviled the next. After castigating the young man for a trifling misdemeanour, Pigott demanded that he publicly knelt before him and apologised for suggesting that the reproof had been unmerited or be flogged. Casey refused and was whipped – a punishment considered unfitting for a gentleman. It was commonly used by Pigott on the rest of the crew, whom he treated with vicious contempt; after three hands had fallen from the spars, he ordered their bodies to be thrown overboard. Not long afterwards, in September 1797 when the *Hermione* was cruising off Puerto Rico, a small body of men mutinied and murdered Pigott and nearly all his officers. Afterwards, the mutineers steered the ship to a Spanish American port.[74] In 1806 a similar attempt at mass desertion by the crew of the brig *Ferret* was frustrated by its captain, George Cadogan, another exceptionally brutal officer.

What is intriguing about the *Hermione* episode is that one of the ringleaders, David Forrester, was later pressed into the navy, where, having prudently changed his name, he served for three years with an exemplary record. He might have done so for longer had he not been recognised in Portsmouth. Was he, like Nicholes, a man of good character, who had snapped when he could endure no more? Both knew that they would be pursued relentlessly, Forrester the more so because he was also a mutineer and murderer. All that they could hope for in the West Indies, where unemployed white men were conspicuous, was to find work using the only talent they had: seamanship. This was not too difficult, as there were always merchant and privateer captains looking for experienced hands. If he did secure such a berth, the deserter faced a fresh hazard: being pressed at sea. William Bowen, a *Hermione* fugitive, managed to evade capture for five years as a seaman on board various American vessels before he was pressed at Malta and identified. William Burke of the 9th Regiment, then stationed at Brimstone Hill, St Kitts, fled to the nearby Basseterre Island in 1792 and earned his living as a sailor until his discovery six years later. He was pardoned by George III.[75]

A royal pardon was also extended to Thomas Taggart of the 59th, a veteran of the siege of Gibraltar of 1782 to 1783, who so liked army life that he signed on again at the expiry of his service.[76] One night in October 1786 he was found with an injured leg and cut hands at the foot of a bastion. A rope dangling from the parapet and the absence of several men from the 25th indicated that he had taken part in a mass desertion. He denied this and claimed that the runaways had asked him to join them and escape to Spain, but he had refused and been attacked, which did not quite explain why he was found under the wall. What is interesting is that all involved imagined that they could somehow invent a new identity in a country the language of which they could not speak. This obstacle did not deter soldiers during the Peninsular War, where 1800 deserted between 1811 and 1813.[77] Many may have tried to steal back to Lisbon in the hope of getting a ship home; others may have turned to brigandage. A few, mainly German mercenaries, crossed over to French lines, as did John Prince, a light dragoon and 'a unworthy character', who took his horse, saddle and weapons as well.

Wartime desertion was a headache for the military and naval authorities, already short of men, and considerable efforts were made to retrieve the fugitives so that they could be given condign and exemplary punishment. In 1798 the captain of the *Melampus* asked the authorities at Carrickfergus to watch out for a local man who had deserted from his ship. He offered a guinea of his own beyond the normal two pounds reward to whoever caught the man, for 'the example of attempts of that nature is so pernicious that I am certainly anxious to hook him again.'[78] Fear of the lash made a deserter from the 25th – 'a wild rattling man' – plead for a posting to a febriferous station in 1778. The army did not bargain with men who had broken faith: he received one thousand strokes and then was posted to temperate Gibraltar.[79]

Desertion was safest in Britain, where the truant had the best chance of finding refuge and anonymity. If he was traced at all, it was by his appearance. Tattooed sailors were always vulnerable; Thomas Byrne, a deserter from the battleship *Bellerophon* in 1797, who had turned to forgery, was identified by a crucifix on his right arm and a nautical mermaid and anchor on the left. Under sentence of death in Dublin, he claimed that he had been on board his ship when his offence had been committed; a flogging was obviously preferable to a hanging.[80] The descriptions that were circulated of other deserters present a melancholy, sometimes touching, picture of men who were either inadequate or misfits, or both. A twenty-five-year-old light dragoon who ran off at Dorchester in 1812 was 'hard of hearing and stoops in his walk, speaks rather effeminately'. George Clemenson, a rifleman who deserted from his regimental camp in Kent in the same year, 'has a pock-marked woman with him, stoops in his walk, clownish look'.[81] Both were easily distinguished, but neither appears to have been apprehended.

V

Desertion was essentially the act of an individual undertaken for personal reasons. It could be combined with mutiny, a mass protest, as it was when a section of the *Bounty*'s crew seized control of the ship off Tahiti in 1787 and expelled its commander, William Bligh. He was not an exceptionally spiteful officer and the rebels' main objective was to start a new and, they imagined, easy life in a remote region, where they mistakenly believed they would be immune from the navy's retribution. It was a notorious incident and encouraged imitation by sailors on active service, whose only means of escape was to commandeer their vessel and take it to a port where they might be welcomed. In 1798, William Timmings, still smarting from a flogging he had received for insolence, approached a messmate on the *Haughty* and proposed a coup to commandeer the ship and take it to France. He may not have been sober for he was 'a troublesome man when in liquor', and his confidant warned him that he endangered the rest of the crew by such talk, that he could never subvert enough men to cover the hatches and, if the mutineers reached France, they would not be well treated, which was true.[82]

Sober men could assess risks, drunks could not. When over a hundred men from the line-of-battle ship *Adamant* tried to excuse their noisy protest against poor food and delayed wages in June 1798, they asked the Admiralty to pardon them, for they had been drunk. 'It was owing to our being too much intoxicated or else we should not have gone aft and your Honours knows the ways of seamen when they are in liquor, that they are always [a] very unruly set of men.'[83] No doubt the admirals did, only too well. Sailors who had illicitly stored their daily rum issue would gather furtively in the fo'c'sle for a weekly beano during which they vented their grievances. As the drink was consumed, the language became stronger and threats of vengeance followed.[84]

If words turned to action, as they did on the *Hermione*, the faint-hearted were swept along, as John Hayes, one of the mutineers testified: 'I was a boy in my fourteenth year with all the disadvantages of education and moral example. Necessity drove me to sea in my ninth year. Driven by the torrent of mutiny, I took the oath administered to me on the occasion. The examples of death which were before my eyes drove me for shelter amongst the mutineers, dreading a similar fate with those who fell, if I sided with, or showed the smallest inclination to mercy.'[85] This would not do. The Articles of War enjoined every sailor to do all within his power to frustrate a mutiny, and for this reason Hayes was executed.

The large-scale mutinies that convulsed the Channel and North Sea Fleets during the spring and early summer of 1797 were altogether different from the nihilistic jacquerie on the *Hermione*. To a large extent these rebellions were the result of the influx of thousands of pressed and drafted men into the navy, many with radical or Irish nationalist sympathies. William Pitt's effigy hung from the yardarm of the battle-ship *Nassau*, and on board the *Sandwich* Coxswain Charles Chant declared: 'Damn and bugger the King. We want no King!'[86] Such sentiments were largely confined to a sprinkling of the ringleaders at the Nore and Yarmouth, where the protests were Jacobin and republican in tone.

The original outbreak at Spithead was solely concerned with increases in pay, improvements in the quality and quantity of rations and the expulsion of a number of overbearing officers. The ringleaders were political animals with a knowledge of organisation and an ability to present their case in a persuasive manner designed to enlist public sympathy. Throughout what was in effect a four-week strike, the muti-neers asserted that they were loyal patriots; indeed, much of their propaganda highlighted the irony that the rights of freeborn Britons were being defended by men who were being treated as slaves. After prevarication, the government sent the sailors' darling, the gouty seventy-one-year-old Admiral Lord Howe ('Black Dick') to Portsmouth to negotiate with the ships' delegates. Pay was raised, better victuals promised, two hundred unloved officers and petty-officers were removed from their ships, and pardons issued for the ringleaders.

Events at Spithead and Plymouth had discountenanced William Pitt's government, which suspected that the mutiny had been fomented by French agents. The phantom of revolutionary conspiracy assumed a frightening substance at the Nore, the anchorage north-west of Sheerness. Here the mutiny followed a more threatening course, with the mutineers forming committees on the contemporary French model, which busied themselves with drawing up regulations for the running of the ships. Unpopular officers were evicted and overall control of the mutiny passed into the hands of a vain, failed schoolmaster, Richard Parker, who proclaimed himself 'president' of a floating 'republic'. Its demands were radical and designed to introduce a democratic element into the day-to-day running of the navy. Crews were to have the right to vote on the return of expelled officers, a general indemnity was sought for deserters who re-enlisted, and alterations in the Articles of War proposed that would have curtailed the authority of captains.

The Admiralty refused to dilute its authority and an ill-tempered confrontation followed during which the mutineers blockaded the Thames and themselves came under siege. Isolated, their will began to crumble once it was clear that the government would not budge. A handful of mutineers fled to France, while the rest snatched at the chance of a pardon, leaving Parker and his committee men to face punishment. Fifty-nine of them were hanged.

The unrest spread to foreign stations, carried by the crews of the men o'war that had been at Spithead and the Nore, and newspaper reports of what had occurred there. Commanders were urged to show no tolerance whatsoever to any form of protest, passive or otherwise. The view from the Admiralty and the quarter-deck was that slack discipline lay at the root of the disturbances, even though then and a few years later mutinies like that on the *Hermione* were a direct consequence of severity. Furthermore, excessive use of the lash did not notably improve a crew's fighting efficiency. This was one of the conclusions of the official investigation into the surrender of the frigate *Africaine* during an action in the Indian Ocean in 1810. Her commander, Captain Corbett, was a notorious flogger and his crew were known to be disaffected to the point where it was rumoured that he had been shot dead by one of them early in the engagement with two French frigates. Over-zealous in resorting to the cat, Corbett neglected routine gunnery practice, which explained why his fire inflicted little damage.

As both Napoleon and Wellington observed, bad or indifferent commanders were invariably responsible for the shortcomings of their men. Fear of punishment alone did not make a soldier or sailor braver, nor was it possible to instil a fighting spirit in men whose own spirits had been broken by excessive chastisement or the fear of it. Those who had entered the services by choice, or for whom no other alternative existed, accepted subservience more readily than those who had been recruited against their will. The mutinies of the 1790s were an unintended consequence of the mass mobilisation that drafted into the navy a body of men who clung to the belief that they retained some of their civilian rights. This did not weaken their patriotism; when the Spithead mutineers declared they would die for their country, they meant it. They were dimly aware that they had become, as it were, partners in a national enterprise and deserved to be treated with humanity and justice. After all, Britain was at war to defend its people's unique freedoms.

The same mood, with more pronounced egalitarian undertones, was present among the large numbers of servicemen who mutinied during the winter of 1918 to 1919 when demobilisation procedures broke down. There was a limit to the patience of the civilian in arms.

3

Honourable danger: Command, courage and rewards

I

One afternoon in the early spring of 1803, Lieutenant-Colonel Robert Montgomery of the Household Cavalry and Captain James Macnamara, RN, were riding in Hyde Park accompanied by their Newfoundland dogs. These normally benign creatures suddenly started a scrap and the colonel's dog got the worst of it. He dismounted, separated the pair and angrily asked, 'Who's dog is this?' 'It is my dog,' answered Macnamara. 'If you don't call your dog off, I'll knock it down,' warned Montgomery. A rancorous exchange followed as the two rode towards Piccadilly. Incensed by Montgomery's tone, Macnamara asserted; 'Your declaring me to call off my dog was arrogance and not such language as should be used to a gentleman, or by a gentleman.' The outcome was a duel – the customary procedure by which a gentleman vindicated his honour and status. On the following morning the two officers exchanged pistol shots in a secluded part of Chalk Farm and each was wounded, Montgomery fatally.

Three weeks afterwards, Macnamara stood trial for manslaughter at the Old Bailey. He justified his actions and the code that dictated them: 'I am a Captain in the British Navy. My character you can hear from others; but to maintain my character, in that station, I must be respected. When called upon to lead others into honourable danger, I must not be supposed to be a man who had sought safety by submitting to what custom has taught others to consider a disgrace.' This speech had resonances that would have been appreciated and applauded by the Renaissance gentleman, the medieval knight and the Dark Age warrior. They were accustomed to danger and separated from the rest of the world by their honour. 'Mine honour is my life . . . Take Honour from me, and my life is done,' declares Mowbray in *Richard II* when he promises to repudiate charges of treason by fighting his traducer, Bolingbroke. But the moral climate of early nineteenth-century Britain was very different from that of Plantagenet and Elizabethan England, as Macnamara acknowledged. Slaying a man in a duel was repugnant to 'general feeling' and 'Religion and the Law'. Nevertheless, the circumstances in which he found himself that afternoon left him with no choice but to ignore conventional restraints. He explained why: 'It is impossible to define in terms, the proper feelings of a Gentleman; but their existence has supported this happy country for many ages, and she might perish if they were lost.'

He expanded the last point in his final appeal to the jury: 'I hope to obtain my liberty through your verdict, and to employ it with honour in defence of the liberties of my country.' These words must have weighed heavily with the jurymen at a time when Britain was facing invasion. A galaxy of illustrious naval commanders, including Nelson, attested to Macnamara's affability and acute sense of personal honour.[1] He was acquitted and eleven years later was promoted rear-admiral.

Edmund Blunden used the episode for a poem which concludes with the two Newfoundlands meeting again in Hyde Park and playing together. The moral is obvious: the beasts show a greater wisdom and sense of proportion than their masters. Or so it appeared to a subaltern who had served on the Western Front under the command of men who, like Montgomery and Macnamara, were slaves to outmoded precepts and irrational traditions. There was some truth in this, and it was also true that Blunden's brother officers would have considered themselves gentlemen, qualified by social standing, education and shared values to command. Admittedly, they no longer fought duels to defend their honour, for these had been outlawed under the pressure of largely bourgeois public opinion in the 1840s. Nonetheless, like Montgomery and Macnamara, First World War officers complied with unwritten rules of probity and decency in their dealings with each other and the world at large. Social pressure exerted in mess and wardroom was supported by naval and military law; if an officer defaulted as a gentleman, he was disqualified for command. Unpaid mess bills, coarse language, rough manners, indecorous conversation, drunkenness and over familiarity with other ranks were grounds for a court-martial and dismissal in 1914 as they had been in 1815.

Officers of Macnamara's generation would have interpreted his words and actions favourably. He had eloquently defended the creed by which gentlemen both defined themselves and prescribed how they should treat each other. Most important of all, as he reminded the jurors, gentlemen had to be allowed to exist in their own moral universe because the nation's security rested upon their courage.

II

Macnamara had been correct in that the duel was, as it always had been, a practical test of that personal bravery that was essential for every officer who led men into battle. By deliberately facing death in a nonchalant manner, the duellist proved his capacity to suppress that most deeply implanted of all human impulses: the urge for self-preservation. If he surrendered to his animal reflexes or his reason, he would simply run away and reveal himself a coward. Cravenness was inexcusable in a gentleman and automatically disbarred him from the company of his equals. When officers shirked their duty in the Crimea and returned home feigning sickness, they were cold-shouldered by ladies and one was 'cut' in Whites.[2]

It would be impossible to analyse precisely the nature of individual courage. It varied from person to person and was inconstant and unpredictable: men who were brave on one day were chicken-hearted the next. A surprise American resurgence threw the 71st and a cavalry unit into confusion during an engagement at the Broad River, South Carolina, in January 1781. The horsemen eventually rallied and the 71st fought gallantly at the subsequent battle of Guildford Court House.[3] A stupid commanding officer, muddled orders, clouds of dust and quick thinking by Sikh horsemen who exploited their misfortunes threw the British cavalry brigade at Chillianwala into chronic disorder. Some light dragoons galloped off to safety behind the lines where they announced that the battle had been lost, which it nearly was. A handful of officers contained the panic and the regiments involved behaved admirably during the battle of Gujarat a month later.[4] Like bravery, fear was contagious; that was beyond question.

Apart from invoking atavistic patriotic stereotypes, there was no way of foretelling how soldiers would behave in battle, especially if the odds were long or an unlooked-for emergency occurred. Colonel Dundas, the author of a widely used drill manual published in 1788, gave a candid diagnosis of the problem. 'It is not sufficient to advance with bravery,' he insisted. Soldiers would certainly falter 'if they don't trust the ability of those in command'. Even if they did trust their officers, the men still needed the 'prospect of success' to make them fight. It was absent at Chillianwala, which was why the cavalrymen took to their heels.[5]

Dundas accepted the conventional wisdom that held that a prime ingredient of the ordinary soldier's courage was an urge to emulate brave men. The officer who had mastered his own fears could, therefore, persuade others to suspend theirs during that terrifying period of waiting before a battle when soldiers and sailors had time to dwell morbidly on what might befall them. Once the action had started, the officer faced a harder task. For his men, death was no longer an abstraction, but a reality in the form of whistling cannonballs, exploding howitzer shells, musket volleys and advancing lines of bayonets, sabres or lances. This was a crucial moment, when the primal urge for self-preservation was strongest. Afterwards it was relatively easy for the officer, for as battle was joined, he had only to harness his men's inborn will to survive.

All this was possible so long as the officer had conquered his own apprehension. This process was deceptively simple, according to the instructions given by their colonel to newly commissioned officers of the 82nd on the eve of their embarkation for Copenhagen in 1807. The testing time for officers and men was when the regiment first came under fire:

> ... the whizzing of the balls is apt to cause a disagreeable sensation; but this, gentlemen, arises from a mistaken idea, for

the moment you hear that sound, the danger is past. You will not, therefore, show a bad example to the men by ducking your heads and flinching your bodies, for that is unsoldierlike, and may cause panic in the troops; but always keep the head up, the body erect, and even in danger show a pleasing and determined aspect, which may command respect and admiration in your men, and animate them to that glory which Britons have a right to expect.

One listener, George Wood, recalled these words a year later when, for the first time, he led his men into battle in Portugal. He behaved as instructed, but once the French opened fire he found it impossible to banish anxiety from his mind. 'I must confess it caused a little imperceptible tremor, notwithstanding the brave and manly admonitions of Sir George [his colonel].'[6] This was uncommonly frank, for officers seldom confessed to nervousness before battle.

The psychology and practice of leadership were straightforward: 'I can overcome my fear, you must do likewise.' This precept was admirably suited to warfare at a time when battles were won by soldiers and seamen who could keep their nerve under often extended bombardment or musket fire. Joseph Donaldson, who had experienced both in the Peninsula, was convinced that courage was latent in every soldier and could be elicited by the example of gallant officers who led from the front.[7]

And so it was. During an assault on American fortifications near New York in October 1778, Sir Henry Clinton's 'active and intrepid spirit and his exposing himself in the most dangerous places' had 'the desired effect on the troops' who pressed home their attack successfully.[8] Admiral James Hope, commanding a flotilla of gunboats in the attack on the Peiho forts in 1859, showed the same composure in the face of danger. Badly wounded in the thigh, he transferred from his flagship, the *Plover*, to the *Opossum*, and then passed between the ships in his barge 'to show the crews how cheerfully he shared the full dangers of their position'. He sent his congratulations to a marine gunner for particularly accurate shooting and an eyewitness reported that everywhere his presence encouraged the crews of vessels under heavy fire. 'Even the wounded were more patient and enduring owing to such example.'[9]

Hope died from loss of blood after the operation, having displayed in a classic manner how an officer should behave in battle.

Interestingly, the same style of leadership was also found in the merchant service. When the slaver *Mary* came under attack from what was imagined to be a pair of French privateers in 1806, her captain, Hugh Crow, addressed his men: 'Commend yourselves, my brave fellows, to the care of Providence: let us have no cursing or swearing.' He used 'cheering language' to his gun-crews and when one man left his post, exclaimed: 'What, is it possible that we have a coward on the *Mary*?' The chastened gunner returned to his duty.[10] It must have been a severe shock when Crow discovered that his assailants were two British men-o'-war that had mistaken the *Mary* for a Frenchman.

Outstandingly brave officers could make their men do the impossible. Praising the battalions of his Light Division which stormed the Kourganè Heights during the battle of the Alma in 1854, Lieutenant-General Sir George Brown singled out those who led them forward. 'Nothing,' he reported in his official dispatch, 'could be more admirable than the conduct and spirit of the troops throughout the transactions, unless it was the example set them by their officers, which throughout the day was characterised by a gallantry and devotion which was most distinguished.'[11] This was just as well given the nature of the attack, which solely depended on what Brown called 'the spirit and individual courage of the troops' whom he had ordered to charge uphill into concentrated and accurate artillery fire and storm Russian earthworks. A French officer who was watching was astonished by the cold, drill-book manner in which the British moved forward.[12]

Those advancing were not immune to emotions, even if they were not apparent to onlookers. Each soldier's trepidation reached its highest pitch when he entered the twin killing zones, the first created by artillery fire, the second by musketry. Timothy Gowing, for whom the Alma was his first battle, recalled his terror. 'Presently, they began to pitch their shot and shell right amongst us, and our men began to fall. I know that I felt horribly sick – a cold shivering running through my veins – and I must acknowledge that I felt very uncomfortable.' It was a momentary spasm and Gowing recovered to proceed with what he later called 'very exciting work'.[13] A few of his comrades reacted instinctively, or reckoned the odds against them were too high and sheltered in ruined farm buildings, where they stayed until the battle was over. Other fainthearts were urged forward by their efforts with straightforward commands: 'Forward! First Company!' and an appeal to pride, 'Second Company, show them the way!'[14] It was the same a few months afterwards when the Light Cavalry Brigade mistakenly charged Russian batteries at Balaklava. As the shot tore the ranks apart, officers were heard to shout matter-of-fact orders: 'close to centre', 'keep up Private So-and-so' &c.[15]

At sea, the eerie silence as warships sailed into range raised tension. It was made more intense by that tactical device favoured by British captains by which fire was open at the closest and therefore deadliest range. Sailors had to endure a brief but nerve-racking period during which they came under fire without the satisfaction of hitting back. The body's chemistry provided some relief, as the naval surgeon Sir Gilbert Blane observed during the battle of the Saints (1782). After watching the sailors manning their guns under French fire, he remarked: 'It would appear that there is something in situations of exertion and danger which infuses a sort of preternatural vigour. When the mind is interested and agitated by active and generous affections, the body forgets its wants and feelings, and is capable of a degree of labour and exertion which it could not undergo in cold blood . . .' He wondered whether the thirst, hunger, heat and smoke endured by the sailors was a form of therapy that restored the health of invalids and malingerers. 'The future health of those who survive unhurt by external violence is so far from injured that it is sometimes mended by this violent, but salutary agitation.'[16]

Although he did not know it, Blane was describing the effect of what modern medicine recognises as adrenaline. The strange effects of emergency supplies of adrenaline pumped into the bloodstream were noticed by another naval surgeon, Henry Banks, who served on the frigate *Hussar* during the invasion of Java in 1812. After a number of seamen had taken part in an amphibious attack on a fort, he treated fourteen who had been wounded in the foot by caltrops and two who had been stabbed with spears. Those who had previously been 'in a state of debility' were suddenly 'overcome by the great and powerful stimulus of the hope of conquest', by which he meant plunder, and 'all the most exhilarating powers of the system' had manifested themselves when the men rushed forward.[17]

A mood verging on hysteria prevailed among soldiers before and during the battle of Bladensburg, near Washington, in 1814. 'The feelings of those engaged are delightful; because they are in fact so many gamblers playing for the highest stake that can be offered.' Nervousness was disguised by 'careless faces and rude jokes' which Banks likened to the 'false hilarity' of criminals before their execution.[18] There was black humour on board the *Defence*, where a gunner confidently announced that he was too small to be a target for a cannonball. Soon after, one sliced off the top of his head. 'His sudden death created a sensation among his comrades,' Midshipman Dillon remembered, 'but the excitement of the moment soon changed these impressions to others of exertion.'[19]

As any battle unfolded, men who were striving to overcome their fear of death and mutilation were forced to witness them in all their most hideous forms. At Chillianwala Lieutenant Daniel Sandford led his men past '. . . poor fellows lying the ground and writhing in agony and no doctor or a drop of water to be got. One poor fellow in my company was mortally wounded and lay bleeding to death; another had his leg struck off and the quivering of his frame was fearful.'[20] Neither Sandford nor Gowing, who glimpsed similar horrors at the Alma, had the time to pause and ponder on what they were seeing or to contemplate their own fate. The battle was underway and everyone's mind was focused on survival and killing their enemies.

By the early nineteenth century it was commonly believed that British fighting men possessed an inbred psychological advantage over their adversaries. Its constituents were a phlegmatic resilience, stubbornness and tenacity. During the 1759 campaign in Canada an officer had been struck by the coolness of the troops. 'If they advance to engage, or stand to receive a charge, they are steady, profoundly silent and attentive, reserving their fire until they have received that of their adversaries.'[21] This stoical resolution was recognised as a token of superior strength of character, that 'steadiness' that British soldiers always showed in the face of danger. This word and its variants became the standard accolade for fighting men in both services. The squares at Waterloo in 1815 displayed 'a steadiness almost inconceivable' as they prepared to receive the massed charge of French cavalry. The same eyewitness was also struck by 'the cool and quiet steadiness' of the horse artillerymen.[22] Both qualities were just what was needed in a battle that Wellington afterwards described as 'a pounding match'. Never promiscuous with praise, he added: 'I never saw the British infantry behave so well.' They showed their mettle in India too. In his semi-official account of the 1817 to 1819 Maratha war, Colonel Valentine Blacker digressed on the intrinsic virtues of the British foot soldier which, he thought, reflected those of the country as a whole. 'Infantry best succeeds among a people with robust bodies and obstinate minds.' No wonder Maratha gunners and horsemen crumpled before the advance of the British line – they lacked the moral ballast to withstand it.[23]

A well-founded confidence in the 'natural' doggedness and willpower of the British regular tended to absolve generals from exercising their brains. 'No troops in the world will withstand the assault of British troops, if made with the bayonet and without firing,' declared Lieutenant-General Sir Charles Napier. He had proved this beyond doubt at the battle of Miani against Baluchis armed with swords and matchlocks in 1843. This Peninsular War veteran forgot, perhaps conveniently, the part played by his horse artillery. Technology, old and new, was regarded with deep suspicion by Napier, who strongly objected to the introduction of the rifled musket with its longer range which, he predicted, would 'destroy that intrepid spirit which makes the British soldier always dash at his enemy'. Access to superior weaponry might weaken the soldier's confidence in himself and his officers.[24]

There was no fear of this with men of Napier's kidney in command. During both Sikh Wars, Lieutenant-General Sir Hugh Gough scorned tactical chicanes and placed his faith in the capacity of his men to make headlong advances against Sikh fieldworks and artillery. Despite heavy losses, it worked, but only just. A similar spirit pervaded the high command at the Alma when flesh and blood were again pitted against earthworks and artillery. There was, however, a limit to the soldier's capacity to risk his life in bull-headed offensives. In June 1855 justifiable anxieties about the assault on the Redan, a well-defended Russian stronghold outside Sebastopol, led to at least one regiment refusing to advance. Officers leapt on to the trench parapets waving their swords in the traditional manner and, when gestures failed, they belaboured their men with the blades, but to no effect.[25] Other regiments followed their officers and were repelled by the weight of Russian fire in what in many ways was a dress-rehearsal for similar offensives sixty years later on the Western Front.

III

Like the army, the navy believed in the inherent fitness of gentlemen to command. A good pedigree was not enough, given that a naval officer needed a mastery of the arts of seamanship and navigation. These added immeasurably to his authority, as Peter Cullen, a naval surgeon serving on the *Agamemnon* in 1800, observed:

> The common seaman knows his officer to be a well-instructed man, competent to work in a ship, or manoeuvre a fleet, which he himself is incapable of doing; he therefore, as it were from instinct, obeys him at once, without hesitation, as a superior being, more intelligent than himself. A seaman looks up to his officer, as a son to his father, whom he knows to be more wise, more experienced, and more skilful than he can possibly be, because scientifically taught. A seaman knows himself to be but a handicraftsman, and his officer a master who must direct him.[26]

Technical competence was crucial, as Nelson acknowledged in his routine advice to midshipmen, although he pointedly added: 'you cannot be a good officer without being a gentleman.'[27] Most of his listeners were gentlemen, for the Admiralty's entry procedures were designed to see that as many as possible found their way on to the quarter-deck. The prospective midshipman needed a letter of recommendation from a naval officer or some figure of public standing. Sometimes he faced an interview by senior officers and an entrance examination, which was often a formality. In 1844 the fourteen-year-old Clements Markham was asked to write out the Lord's Prayer, which was no hardship for the son of a canon of Windsor. Young Markham enjoyed the sponsorship of Rear-Admiral Sir George Seymour, the recently designated commander-in-chief of the Pacific station, who had invited him to learn the theory and practice of navigation and seamanship on board his flagship, the *Collingwood*.[28]

Shipboard instruction and examinations ensured technical expertise, but the pace of an officer's promotion largely depended on his or his kinsfolk's social and political connections. There were some notable exceptions; the humbly born James Cook and William Bligh were promoted because they were outstanding navigators and the navy needed technocrats. And then there were those fighting officers whose exploits captured the public imagination. Nelson was by far the most celebrated. His victory at Aboukir Bay in 1798 made him a national hero, who after Trafalgar was revered as his country's saviour. Never diffident about his genius, he was a wayward figure whom the establishment barely tolerated, not least because he questioned his superiors and held politicians in contempt. He was also a notorious adulterer.

All this might raise eyebrows, but what mattered was that Nelson always beat the French, and died in battle. His exploits and simple code of selfless patriotism were set down by the poet laureate, Robert Southey, whose *Life of Nelson* appeared in 1813 and became an immediate bestseller. It was more than an encomium; Southey hoped that his book would impel young men to follow Nelson's path to glory in the service of their country. For this reason, the book was recommended by the future prime minister, Sir Robert Peel, to his midshipman son, William.[29] His subsequent distinguished career suggested that he had thoroughly understood Southey's message.

Patriotism of Nelson's passionate intensity was found among a large number of naval officers who were deeply aware that their country's safety ultimately depended on the service. In May 1805, when the fear of invasion was greatest, Lieutenant Robert Fernyhough, RM, watched spellbound as the twelve three-decker battleships of the Channel Fleet set sail. It was a brave show and he was overwhelmed by patriotic emotion. 'What a fine and glorious sight! An Englishman might well be proud of this tremendous force. Our spirits were high, our hearts panting for a trial of strength . . .'[30] Ideals of personal honour were as strong at sea as they were on land. They were nowhere better or more movingly expressed than by the seventeen-year-old Lieutenant Thurnham, serving on board the *Illustrious* in 1805, in what turned out to be his last letter to his father.

> I am going this evening on a dangerous enterprise . . . If I escape, nothing will give me so much pleasure as to think that I have neither disgraced my commission nor my father, and to have it said that I am an honour to my family; if I die, I die an honourable death – God bless you all! and may the next son you have die as honourably as I do! Do not blame me for volunteering my services, as while the blood of the Thurnhams circulates in my veins, I could not bear for it to be said *that he is a coward*.[31]

How Nelson would have applauded. At the end of the American War in 1783, he wrote that: 'I have closed the war without a fortune . . . True honour, I hope, predominates in my mind far above riches.' What he meant was that he had enhanced his reputation but failed to pick up much prize-money. Captured warships and merchantmen were prizes of war which were sold with their fittings and cargoes and the cash divided among the crews of the ships that had taken them. It was a tradition that stretched back to the Middle Ages and made a naval career attractive to young men whose pursuit of fame went hand in hand with a desire for enrichment. The 1708 Prize Act regulated the business which, at the outbreak of war in 1793, was handled by twenty-five officially recognised prize-agents, whose number doubled within twenty years. The sums involved were immense; the total value of prizes seized by British warships and privateers between March 1744 and April 1745 was £4.92 million, and between 1803 and 1810 reached seven million pounds.[32]

Once the prizes and their cargoes had been sold and the agent's 5 per cent commission deducted, the money was shared out according to rank. First in line was the local senior commander who took one-sixth; between November 1799 and July 1800 Nelson received £3344 of the prize-money collected by ships under his command in the Mediterranean.[33] The residue was split among the crew of the ship that had made the capture, with three-eighths of the total going to the captain, three-eighths to the officers and petty officers, and the remaining quarter to the hands. The captains of men-o'-war on blockade and patrol duties were best placed to intercept merchantmen; between April and September 1813 the squadron based at Halifax seized eighty-four vessels, mostly under two hundred tons and engaged in the American coastal trade and fishing.[34]

These vessels were, so to speak, minnows, although they had a cumulative value. Occasionally, officers had a stroke of luck and netted a bigger catch that would literally make them a fortune. In October 1799 the frigate *Naiad* sighted and gave chase to two Spanish frigates carrying specie and bullion from Mexico valued at six hundred thousand pounds. Three other British frigates joined the pursuit and the two Spaniards were engaged and boarded close inshore. It had been a risky affair with three of the British ships narrowly avoiding being grounded on the rocks, but the gamble was worth it. The captains involved received £40,730 each (enough to purchase an estate), and the ordinary seamen £182.[35] William Dillon, serving on the battleship *Defence*, was jealous of his colleagues on board frigates which were seizing prizes during 1793 when the navy was driving French commerce from the seas. He did not fare too badly, picking up £105 for the capture of a French Indiaman, and eighteen guineas (£18.90) for the French warships taken on the Glorious First of June.[36]

Spending prize money was a matter of temperament, with thrifty and family-minded men investing their windfalls. The less encumbered enjoyed a beano. On receiving his share of £140 for the capture of a French frigate in 1812, Peter McIntyre, a marine lieutenant, chose to blow the lot on three weeks' indulgence in London. He was a likeable, cultivated Highlander who was curious about the high life: 'I never had any money before; I may never have any again; I never have yet lived luxuriously; I may never more have an opportunity of doing so: I'll do so now.'[37] He had no regrets afterwards.

McIntyre was lucky in that he had no difficulties in getting what he was owed. Despite Admiralty supervision, the prize-agency business attracted crooks who defrauded their clients. In one case, Samuel Judas and Daniel Jacob were discovered to have cheated a midshipman out of seven hundred pounds of the £1005 due to him. In another, in 1803, a gunner successfully sued Judas Jacob, a Portsmouth slop-seller and prize-agent, for £251 which he had dishonestly retained.[38] These and other

instances of malversation, together with pressure from indignant officers, compelled the Admiralty to tighten its control over prize-agents.
Nonetheless, as one official noticed, it was hard to fathom how such
shysters as Jacob had managed to secure their positions in the first
place. Some disgruntled officers suspected it had been through the connivance of venal officials.[39]

There were also profits to be made from soldiering, but the sums
were smaller and the opportunities less frequent. Military prize-money
came from the sale of captured enemy equipment, and stores and property seized when a fortress or town were taken by storm. In principle,
the procedures employed by the army were similar to the navy's, but the
official machinery was slow and cumbersome. There were long delays;
the widow of John Steele of the Royal Scots received the 3s 9d (19p)
due to her husband for the battle of Nagpur in 1817 twenty-six years
later.[40] As in the navy, rank dictated how much a man received.
Brigadier-General Robert Brereton, commander of the land force
engaged in the capture of St Lucia in 1803, got £66 8s 8d (£66.43), and
the privates of the 64th and the 3rd West India Regiment (including
'Puny, 'Tipperary' and 'Hannibal') 3s 11d (20p) each.[41] The original
spoils included ships taken in the harbour, merchandise, and ninety-
eight male and female slaves who were auctioned in Trinidad for
£2940.[42]

Rather than wait years for trifling amounts, soldiers preferred to do as
they had always done, loot. Despite the severe penalties for plundering,
they stole whatever they could carry. After the taking of Vigo in 1702,
one provost-marshal recovered eleven silver spoons, two silver forks,
various trinkets and 130 silver dollars from the pockets of men he had
intercepted. The canny surrendered choice items to their officers for
cash; Robert Ackerley, a grenadier from Columbine's regiment, got five
guineas (£5.25) for a gold ring set with seven diamonds and obviously
worth much more.[43]

Prospects of acquiring treasures for a bagatelle attracted entrepreneurs. After the fall of Lucknow in 1858, a quartermaster who acted as
a regimental translator exchanged valuables for bottles of rum and
cigars, which were of greater value to soldiers on campaign than jewels,
silks and precious ornaments.[44] During the march to and occupation
of Peking of 1860, sharp-witted pillagers learned how to identify a

pawnbroker's shop, which was distinguished by a painted dragon's head. An officer with an instinct for business procured some carts and sent a consignment of stolen tea to the base at Tientsin for export. This fiddle was uncovered and he was ordered to return the goods by Sir James Hope Grant, the commander-in-chief. Grant also intervened to forestall another piece of shifty legerdemain. Several officers had stripped gold worth nine thousand pounds from a building and carried it off for distribution among men of their own division, which Grant considered unfair. The gold was deposited in a general pool of spoils which was auctioned and the money raised distributed among all British and Indian troops. Much of the cash was soon exchanged for alcohol and tobacco.[45]

Some soldiers kept what they had pillaged and arranged for it to be shipped home to their families. Ingham Britcliffe, a private in the Bengal Fusiliers, had a good haul from the capture of Delhi in September 1857. He sent a catalogue of his spoils to his parents: 'I have several little things which I sent home to my brother and sister; I have some nice purses and several beautiful stones; I have a gold ring with diamonds in a setting, which I wear regularly myself, and a cashmere shawl worth five pounds, which I should like to give to mother, a double-barrelled fowling piece worth quite as much, some handsome silks, and about two hundred rupees [about twenty pounds].'[46] Interestingly, Britcliffe had had some of his items valued, presumably by one of those dealers who hung around armies during the Indian Mutiny. How he managed to carry all these articles on the march can only be guessed at, although another consummate looter, Lieutenant Kendal Coghill, obtained a cart to carry his booty from Delhi.

Indian towns and cities were an Aladdin's cave. Indians of all ranks kept their wealth in jewellery, coin and artefacts of precious metals which, in an emergency, they hid, usually by burying. Experienced looters knew this and at Delhi and elsewhere excavated likely sites, or, if they could not be bothered, used threats of torture or death to find out where the goods had been buried. At Delhi, the local commander, Sir Archdale Wilson, attempted to curtail freelance plundering by demanding that all loot should be collected, sold and the cash distributed. He was taken at his word by some who surrendered goods whose total value was calculated at about £350,000.

Honesty did not pay. A few weeks after the sack of Delhi, the governor-general, Lord Canning, forbade the distribution of prize-money for goods stolen from British subjects, which the Indians legally were. Instead, the 'heroes of Delhi' had to be satisfied with the East India Company's customary campaign allowances ('batta') which worked out at thirty-six rupees and ten annas (£3.60) for privates and 450 rupees for lieutenants (£45). Hopes were dashed, and fighting men who had endured fatigue, sunstroke, hunger and thirst and won battles against overwhelming odds were understandably enraged. 'Delhi taken and India saved for 36 rupees and 10 annas' was the bitter graffiti which appeared on buildings during the subsequent campaign around Lucknow. Not surprisingly, during these operations soldiers took whatever they could: a rupee in the knapsack was worth more than a general's promise. In the end, the Indian government caved in, not least because of domestic protests, and the cash was distributed in 1860. A private received one share worth seventeen pounds, almost equivalent to a year's wages, a captain and a major-general £912.[47] Without question, hopes of reward helped make soldiering in India bearable.

IV

Such windfalls were uncommon. No one ever joined the army to make money, declared Lord Elcho, which was why the commercial classes considered buying commissions for their sons 'a very bad investment'.[48] He was addressing the Lords in a debate held in March 1855 over the future of a system by which the majority of cavalry and infantry officers paid for their commissions and promotion. The system naturally favoured gentlemen, and the arguments in its favour were the same as those used to defend the gentleman's monopoly of command. 'The sergeant drills the men, but the officer fights them,' was an army maxim produced by one speaker. Another quoted remarks recently made by envious French officers in the Crimea, who claimed that British soldiers were more tractable than their French counterparts simply because their officers were gentlemen.[49]

Purely pragmatic arguments were put forward to uphold an arrangement that had been introduced during the early eighteen century as a means of raising money for the Treasury. Purchase was never applied to the Royal Artillery and Royal Engineers, where technical proficiency had to be the criterion for entry and advancement. Other officers, or their families or patrons, paid for commissions and promotion to the rank of lieutenant-colonel according to an official scale calculated by rank and the prestige of the regiment. At the lower end were the line infantry regiments, where an ensigncy cost £450 and a lieutenant-colonelcy £4500. Next came the cavalry, where a cornetcy was £850 and a lieutenant-colonelcy £6175. The highest rates were for the socially exclusive Horse and Foot Guards, where all commissions and promotions were by purchase. In fashionable regiments it was a seller's market in peacetime and there were plenty of rich, vain and ambitious men willing to pay well above the odds. For an outlay of twenty-eight thousand pounds Lord Cardigan leapfrogged from a cornet to lieutenant-colonel in six years, and his future antagonist, Lord Lucan, was said to have handed over twenty-five thousand pounds for command of the 17th Lancers.

A commission, like a medical practice before 1947, was a piece of property that could be sold or exchanged. Command of a regiment offered some return on capital, in that a colonel clothed his men. If he was astute and none too particular as to the quality of the cloth, he could make at least four hundred pounds per year from this perk. During the manpower crises in the 1790s, Highland magnates contracted to raise regiments for the government in the knowledge that they could make a profit. In August 1793, Donald Cameron of Erracht proposed to recruit a regiment and invested eight thousand pounds in the project to cover inducements, which included £12 8s 3d (£12.41) for sixty gallons of whisky. Cameron's family were partners in the enterprise; his five-year-old son, Ewan, already an ensign in the 9th Regiment, was transferred to his father's as a lieutenant.[50] One of the anomalies of purchase was that age was no hurdle to entry or promotion, although a regulation of 1795 banned schoolboy officers from exercising command in the field.

Like other lairds who blended patriotism with profit, Cameron faced stiff competition for recruits in Scotland and was driven to cast his net beyond the border. Of the 454 men raised by Sir James Grant, the chief of Clan Grant, for his 97th Highlanders, over one-third were from

England, and some had been provided by crimps. Their work had not been easy because English working men disliked having to wear a kilt.[51]

Wartime exigencies, in the form of the heavy death rate among officers and the supply of candidates failing to meet the demand, led to a dilution of purchase. During the Peninsular War, 70 per cent of officers owed their position to promotion by seniority or merit, 20 per cent to purchase, and the rest to family or political string-pulling.[52] Nevertheless the army continued to be dominated by the relatively small landowning class. Statistics based on the backgrounds of officers receiving commissions suggest that this dominance increased during this period:

	Aristocracy/gentry	Middle class
1780	40%	60%
1830	53%	47%

It must be remembered that the middle-class category would include the sons of men engaged in those professions considered fitting for a gentleman: the higher civil service, the army and navy, the established church and the law.[53]

As Jane Austen appreciated, those from outside these circles could penetrate them through a commission. For George Wickham, a factor's son with no discernible gentlemanly instincts, the officers' mess offered 'a prospect of constant society and good society', and for this reason he procured a commission in a county militia battalion which was reputed 'a most respectable, agreeable corps'.[54] Married to Lydia Bennett, his future is assured by the patronage of his brother-in-law, Mr Darcy, who will buy him a commission in a regular regiment and provide the wherewithal for his promotion. But Wickham would need to tread carefully if he wished to win the approval and friendship of his brother officers. In the mess of the 87th in 1807 a newcomer observed that officers whose conduct revealed 'the want of politeness, good address and propriety of speaking' would face 'most unpleasant consequences'.[55]

More than elegant manners and decorum were demanded in fashionable regiments. Having purchased his commission, the parents, guardians or patrons of the young ensign or cornet would have to provide the cash to buy his uniforms, settle his mess bills and maintain an appropriate stable, none of which would have been possible on regulation pay. In messes where lordly extravagance was the rule, the burden was considerable. One can only pity the papa of Thackeray's young cavalry officer: "'Gad!" says he, "our wedgments so *doothid* exthpenthif. Must hunt you know. A man couldn't live in the wedgment if he didn't. Mess expenses enawmuth. Must dine at mess. Must drink champagne and claret. Ours ain't a port and sherry light-infantry mess.'"[56]

The languid drawl and affected lisp were not satirical exaggerations. These were the unmistakable tones of the early Victorian cavalry officer and were overheard by Mr Jorrocks when he encountered a pair in a hotel coffee-room, relaxing after a day's hunting. One asks the other: "'what shall we have to dwink?" "Do us no harm, I des-say," replied his companion, ". . . 'spose we say clart?'"[57] Speech marked out officers from men, although some of the older generation retained provincial accents. Gough, born in 1779, had an Ulster twang ('Saiks' for Sikhs') and Sir Colin Campbell, born in 1792, spoke in his native Glaswegian.

Speech, along with bearing and a self-confident authority, distinguished a gentleman. Common opinion held that servicemen instinctively recognised a gentleman and for this reason assented to take orders from him. The author George Borrow, who was not a noted snob, was emphatic on the subject. 'Soldiers and sailors will bear any amount of tyranny from a lordly sot, or the son of a man who has "plenty of brass" – their own term – but will mutiny against the just orders of a skilful and brave officer who 'is no better than themselves".'[58] This was why Captain Bligh, the son of a customs collector, lost control of the *Bounty*. His experience with the transport corps during the China war of 1859 to 1860 convinced Lieutenant-Colonel Garnet Wolseley, the future field-marshal, that it was possible for commissioned rankers to command respect and obedience so long as they 'gradually acquire the tone of habits of those with whom they associate'.[59]

This was not easy, for ordinary soldiers were discriminating in their assessment of which of their officers were gentlemen and were quick to detect revealing deficiencies. A 'brave and manly' officer from an Indian regiment placed over British regulars during the siege of Delhi was unable to secure any authority over his men. One, an Irishman to judge by the spelling, scrawled on a wall: 'Sind him back to his ould mutinous saypoy rigiment.' It was just possible that this officer was accustomed to the more easy-going atmosphere of an Indian battalion where discipline was enforced by NCOs and the sepoys were more docile. Or, and this is just as likely, he did not possess the gentlemanly qualities with which the British soldier was familiar.[60] East India Company offices did not buy their commissions and could live off their pay, although their families had to give them money for their kit and passage out.

It requires considerable mental effort for anyone today to appreciate how important social distinctions were to our recent ancestors. This century has witnessed the slow erosion of these distinctions and the simultaneous spread of an egalitarian spirit that cannot comprehend, let alone accept, the concept that one section of society should be uniquely qualified to lead. Even more puzzling is the fact that everyone else more or less willingly consented to this principle. The words 'élite' and 'élitist' have become terms of abuse and today it would be unthinkable to extend the idea of superior 'breeding' beyond the world of animals to that of humans. And yet, 'thorough-bred' was the adjective applied by an officer to two colleagues who, off their own bat, hurried with their men to support the 93rd Highlanders at Balaklava.[61] The pair had behaved like gentlemen who knew what was expected from them. And it was not just a matter of upbringing: Tom Jones and Oliver Twist, separated by a century, shared a gentle background which became apparent only through their behaviour in often extremely adverse circumstances.

An age that set great store by pedigree and upbringing was also one in which the balance of political power was tilting towards the middle classes. After the 1832 Reform Act men who lived by their talents (manufacturers, retailers, bankers, attorneys and doctors) shared power with the landowners. The middle classes were also intruding into another aristocratic preserve as arbiters of artistic and literary taste. Bourgeois moral values, strongly influenced by evangelical protestantism, were also making headway, although slowly. There had been predominantly middle-class protests against flogging in the army (though not the navy), and it had been the weight of mainly middle-class opinion that had led to the disappearance of duelling by 1850. At the same time there was assimilation, a process expedited by the post-Arnoldian public school which introduced boys of middle-class background to the old values and codes of the gentleman overlaid with a heavy varnish of evangelicalism.

For all the shifts in political power, the landowning classes and their offspring continued to dominate the armed forces. Their position in the army was strongest, despite parliamentary and press rumblings against purchase during the bleaker moments of the Crimean War. Its battles offered ample proof that the country was still right to entrust gentlemen to command its armies and navies, as the prime minister, Viscount Palmerston, enthusiastically declared to the Commons in February 1855: 'Talk to me of the aristocracy of England! Why, look at that glorious charge of cavalry at Balaklava – look to that charge, where the noblest and wealthiest of the land rode foremost, followed by heroic men from the lowest classes of the community, each rivalling the other in bravery . . .' What better evidence could there be that in Britain all classes 'enjoy in common those noblest qualities which dignify mankind. I would appeal to that gallant charge as immortal proof of the glory of the country.'[62] MPs with long memories and a sense of irony would have recalled that the officer who led the Light Brigade into the 'Valley of Death' was Lord Cardigan, whose only previous experience of hostile fire had been when he had fought a duel fourteen years before.

4

Duty must be done:
Killing, dying and
surviving

I

During operations near Washington in 1814 an unknown but resource-ful British soldier was captured by the Americans. Soon afterwards, he cut his bonds with a knife, grabbed a musket from one of his guards, brained him, then shot another and made his escape. His story impressed a naval officer, Edward Codrington, who related it to his wife. Anticipating her distress, he pointedly added: 'You may think this, however soldier-like, a sort of legal butchery; but it is an act of well-performed duty, nevertheless, and were it not so estimated England would not be what she is.'[1] Never a man to mince words, Codrington was saying something that contemporaries sometimes and conveniently chose to forget: war was all about what Brigadier Ritchie-Hook would call 'biffing' the enemy, that is killing him by every available means and in the largest possible numbers. Doing so in a just cause need not burden the conscience and was not considered unnatural.

Pioneers investigating the mysteries of the brain accepted that the urge to fight in war was deeply rooted. One, writing in 1856 against the background of the Crimean War, insisted that: 'The love of glory is a passion inherent in the breast. It is not easy to define it. To love danger, and to delight in peril and woe is a contradiction in terms; but then it is the pleasure of peril past and danger overcome.'[2] It was possible for

someone in the grip of this passion to separate himself from its consequences, death and maiming. Many soldiers were genuinely shocked by
the sight of a battlefield, but did not consider how their own actions
had contributed to the horror. 'A more bloody and dreadful field of
battle was never seen,' Captain Edward Kelly of the Life Guards told his
wife after Waterloo. As for his part in it, he observed in a matter-of-fact
manner that he had led a charge against French lancers and 'had the
good fortune to kill their Colonel myself and one of the privates when
our Corporal Major came up just in time to save my life'. Kelly also cut
down a cuirassier colonel, dismounted and cut off his epaulettes as a
trophy.[3] Killing a man in single combat with a sword was obviously a
matter of great satisfaction to him, and he must have taken a considerable
risk securing this memento in the middle of the mêlée. The same feeling
must have animated a marine officer who shot dead a Chinese general
during the storming of the Taku forts in 1860 and afterwards plucked
the peacock feather from his hat as a souvenir of the encounter.[4]

The psychology behind such gestures was timeless. The medieval
knight took the horse or armour from a defeated adversary, and soldiers
in the wars of the twentieth century would accumulate objects taken
from enemy corpses, even parts of their bodies. These tokens were proof
of having been in and survived combat, irrespective of whether the collector had slain their original owner. They were irrefutable evidence of
daring and prowess, much like the skulls, horns, tusks and skins of
Asian and African animals brought home for display by sportsmen
throughout the nineteenth and early twentieth centuries. Or, for that
matter, the shrunken heads and testicles collected by Dyak headhunters
and Ethiopian warriors.

Attitudes did not change with the coming of modern weapons which
killed at a distance. 'You knocked him over, my man, in good style and
deserve something for the shot,' an officer told Benjamin Harris after he
had killed a French sharpshooter whom he had encountered on a
Spanish hillside. He then advised Harris where to look for his victim's
valuables, and the rifleman found a purse of coins in the lining of the
Frenchman's tunic.[5] In another, similar incident during the fighting
near Lexington in 1775 a British infantryman singled out an American
and shouted: 'You are a dead man.' 'And so are you,' came the reply.
Both were killed in what must have been a close-range exchange, for

the smoothbore musket was not an accurate weapon.[6] Killing men with muskets was usually an anonymous business with volleys fired at masses of infantry and cavalry who were often half obscured by smoke. Likewise, artillerymen could seldom distinguish their targets as individuals, although many must have known from experience what effect their fire would have on human bodies.

Nonetheless, soldiers and sailors throughout this period were expected to kill at close quarters if necessary. Harris, the former Dorset shepherd, admitted that if his victim had been wounded he would have finished him off with his sword-bayonet. Battles still resolved themselves into thousands of individual contests in which men were expected to kill their enemies face to face, using brute force and skill. No one doubted that British manhood was up to the task. Its capacity for such fighting was a source of national pride and, as Edward Codrington had reminded his wife, something for which to be thankful. The soldiers who were repelled from New Orleans in 1815 fought with musket butts, bayonets and even fists with what an eyewitness described as the 'savage ferocity of bulldogs'.[7] Like the Dark Age warrior, men of the early industrial age still possessed the power to transform themselves into animals, in this case an exceptionally pugnacious beast which was already well on its way to becoming a popular symbol of national aggressiveness. 'Our warrior race' had displayed all its ancient mettle in the Crimea, The Times's war correspondent assured his readers after Sebastopol had fallen.

There had clearly been no dilution of the British combative spirit. Generals and admirals could take it for granted, and did, and no one was aware of those mental disorders that could undermine the fighting spirit. Nor did medicine comprehend, let alone diagnose those traumatic stress syndromes that had become almost a pandemic by the end of the twentieth century. This is not to say that battle fatigue and shellshock did not exist. Among the invalids from the Crimea admitted to the military hospital at Portsmouth in 1855 was James Micklethwaite of the 34th Regiment who hid under his own or other patients' beds. He died soon afterwards and no explanation was sought for his behaviour. Another man showed the symptoms of what the receiving doctor called 'raving madness' and had to be restrained with a straitjacket and chloroform. He subsequently recovered.[8] Had he not, he would, like other soldiers and sailors who were considered insane, have been discharged and sent back to his parish which would arrange for his detention in a local lunatic asylum. There, his condition, like other nervous illnesses, would have been attributed to alcohol, heredity or moral degeneracy, or a combination of all three.

That there were soldiers who could suffer clinical shock as a consequence of battle would have surprised many contemporaries at a time when the working class was believed to be becoming increasingly violent. From the second quarter of the eighteenth century onwards, there were outbreaks of public jitters about the seemingly unstoppable rise in crimes of violence, invariably committed by those at the bottom of the social pile. If these panics were anything to go by, 'natural man' with his primitive instincts was very much alive. Moreover, his numbers were increasing in the expanding industrial centres where, undisciplined, his capacity for mayhem was growing. Evidence for the crimewaves that alarmed the respectable was to a large extent anecdotal, but nonetheless frightening for that. Those who felt threatened were willing to take severe measures to safeguard themselves and their property. In many households firearms were kept, and in September 1854 they were used by the villagers in Lauderdale against three hundred Irish casual workers who had been terrorising them. Shots were fired, but no one seems to have been hurt.[9]

Cruelty and violence as public entertainment disappeared gradually. The 1835 Cruelty to Animals Act outlawed bull-baiting, dog- and cock-fighting, although the last persisted in the north-east mining communities well into the 1850s. So did those bloody spectacles, prize-fights; and executions remained public until 1868. Denied the opportunity to see bloodshed and suffering at first hand, the man in the street could still sample it at one remove through newspaper reports of murders and assaults, which left nothing to the imagination, and the equally lurid penny broadsides which sold in millions. Among their readers were creatures whom Dickens characterised as 'savages', inhabitants of the half-secret and infinitely scary world of the slums. They emerged menacingly as the mob in *Barnaby Rudge* and singly in the form of Bill Sykes in *Oliver Twist*.

As well as making the flesh creep, such creatures could also stir the heart when they stormed Sikh earthworks or charged Russian batteries. Victorian attitudes to violence were always ambivalent and a permanent source of anxiety to those pessimists who feared that the veneer of civilisation was paper-thin. Blood-curdling reports of atrocities committed by mutineers and their allies in India aroused vengeful passions at home and at the front which threatened to plunge the country into moral chaos. 'Barbarism must not gain or hold the ascendant,' a physician warned. 'The intelligence, the science, and the prowess of England, as well as of Europe, must not succumb.'[10] He suspected that events in India had uncovered a 'hidden licentiousness' among his countrymen.

Others suspected that old primitive passions were on the verge of extinction. As early as 1855 a surgeon was wondering whether 'the high pressure excitement by which we now live' was weakening the collective mental resilience of the nation. He was thinking of the pace and competitiveness of industrial and commercial life which were destroying the 'natural' man.[11] By 1900, there were fears that the working classes were losing those primordial, violent impulses that were vital if they were to become soldiers and sailors. Music halls, spectator sports and materialism were killing off the old warrior strain.

This was nonsense. So-called deracinated and pampered industrial man was just as capable of killing as his remote forebears. They would have appreciated the distinctively heroic tone of an account of the 17th Lancers' charge against the Zulus in 1879, set down by one of them, Miles Glissop, a former Leeds clothworker. At the onset of the action a chance shot had killed a popular officer, adding a 'fierce yearning for revenge' to the cavalrymen's 'warlike ardour'. 'A moment more and the bristling line of steel meets the black and shining wall of human flesh rent and pierced and gashed by a weapon as death dealing and unsparing as their own assegais . . .' As ever, encounters between men armed with bladed weapons provided opportunities for individual displays of strength and skill: 'One officer cut a stalwart Zulu warrior completely in half, another officer, after narrowly escaping . . . [an] assegai thrown with such force and precision as to go through his cloak and into the wallet of the saddle, severed the head from the hapless fellow who threw it . . .'[12]

II

Cavalry charges were by their nature highly dramatic incidents, although rare after the 1850s, and Glissop had adopted an appropriate style which sounds somewhat overblown to our ears. Nonetheless, his narrative seems authentic; single sword strokes sliced off the heads of two rioters during the 1831 Bristol demonstrations.[13] Such details would not have been forgotten easily, but what is striking is what Glissop chose not to remember. He makes no mention of his own emotions: was he afraid, or exhilarated, or a mixture of both? Did his lance kill a Zulu and, if it did, how did he feel about it, then and later? Was he sickened – there must have been fountains of blood spurting from wounded men and horses.

John Baldwin was less reticent about the mechanics of killing. At Sabraon in 1846 his regiment charged a Sikh battery. 'Compassion is swallowed up in the wild uproar of fierce passion and deadly animosity,' he recalled as he squared up to his adversary, a gunner who appeared to be at least six feet tall. He thrust his bayonet into the man's chest and pulled it out. It was a tricky business, for around him dying Sikhs were finding the strength for sword blows that struck off their antagonists' heads. Baldwin was lucky and astonished: 'Till now I was unconscious of having spilt the blood of any of the enemy, though I fired at them enough times at Mudki.' There was a moral gulf between killing indistinct figures a hundred or so yards away with a musketball and slaying a man face to face. Baldwin did not believe that he had done wrong. 'I hope,' he wrote to a friend afterwards, 'I shall not be reproached for barbarity, as it was solely in self-defence, and you know "self-preservation is the first law of nature."'[14]

Private John Pearman of the 3rd Light Dragoons, who fought in six battles against the Sikhs, was in single combat twice. The first time a Sikh gunner swiped at him with a sponge staff, hitting the hindquarters of his horse. 'I cut a round cut at him and felt my sword strike him but could not say where.' He was slightly wounded when he had his second, near-fatal encounter. A Sikh would have shot him, for his horse was plunging and he had his sword in his assailant's shoulder. A sergeant appeared and cut off the back of the Sikh's head, allowing Pearman to disengage and ride back to his lines.[15] Thirty years later and a policeman in Buckinghamshire, he regretted what he had done: 'I verily believe man was not made to kill his fellow men.' By then, he had become a radical and regarded himself as 'a hired assassin' who had been employed to take the Sikhs' country away from them. He had not thought that way at the time, when his chief concerns had been satisfying thirst and hunger, acquiring alcohol and mourning the deaths of comrades.

Lieutenant-Colonel Edward Elers Napier had no inhibitions whatsoever about killing Xhosa tribesmen on the frontiers of Cape Colony during the 1830s and 1840s. For him it was an extension of hunting, which was why he chased them on horseback armed with a spear designed for pig-sticking. He wrote with relish of driving it 'right between the shoulder blades' of one native, and on another occasion was delighted by the sabres of the 7th Dragoon Guards 'inflicting well-merited chastisement' on 'the skulking, treacherous foe'. As for those who escaped, Elers Napier was glad that their backs showed 'deep and bloody characters marking "retribution"'.[16]

This candid confession of the pleasures of killing would have struck early students of psychiatry as prime evidence of the existence of 'blood lust' as a clinical condition. Its pathology was frightening: the victim became 'unconsciously infuriated with a sense of this diabolical thirstiness' at the sight of fresh blood and surrendered to the passions of 'fury and alarm . . . ardour and revenge'. These, in turn, generated a destructive energy which was expressed through plundering and promiscuous lust.[17] Although this doctor preferred to 'drop the veil over this lurid glimpse of hell', some at least of his readers would have recalled the rapes that occurred after the storming of Badajoz in 1812 and, though this was not so well known, after the taking of Multan in 1849.[18] Only motive separated the soldier from the murderer, the author gloomily concluded.

He had correctly identified revenge as one of the prime impulses behind killing in battle. Looking over the 'blood, brains and mangled limbs' of comrades during the defence of Cadiz, Sergeant Donaldson felt 'no visible feeling but revenge'. '"Now for the retaliating shot" was the word; every nerve was strained to lay the gun with precision.'[19] During operations in the Khyber Pass in 1842, William Hall of the 41st was astonished to watch a soldier tie a turban around the neck of a wounded Afghan and drag him down a hillside. He asked the man for an explanation and was told 'for the satisfaction of my comrade' who had been killed three days before.[20] The sight of wounded comrades killed or tortured by Afghans, Pathans and Sikhs enraged British troops to the point where they also slew at random and without mercy. The Russians were also notorious for killing the wounded, and at Inkerman they fired on an improvised field hospital.[21]

There was repayment in kind. A press report of the battle of the Alma recorded that 'a villain with a redcoat' had been seen killing wounded Russians.[22] During the Charge of the Light Brigade, Lord George Paget had to prevent a private from killing a dismounted and unarmed Russian officer. In similar fashion, a Russian officer saved the life of Captain Lord Chewton of the Scots Guards who had been badly injured at the Alma.[23] It would be dangerous to generalise on this point, but it appears that officers were expected to restrain men in the grip of blood lust.

Both interventions and official protests against Russian outrages by the commander-in-chief, Lord Raglan, assumed that there were rules in warfare, at least when it was between the forces of civilised, European powers. The diplomatic agreements that defined international law on such matters as the treatment of the wounded and prisoners were a feature of the early years of the next century. Hitherto, the observance of conventions of humanity had rested with individual commanders, who were expected to behave as civilised, Christian gentlemen. Indeed, the parole system by which prisoners of war were released on condition that they did not fight again rested upon a universal acceptance of a solemn oath.

From at least the early nineteenth century, the British prided themselves on their humanity which had its roots in a respect for fairness. In his encomium on boxing written in 1812, the sporting writer Piers Egan praised that peculiar 'generosity of mind' and 'humanity of heart' that prevented the British soldier and sailor from ever taking an unfair advantage in war.[24] The growing popularity of boxing exemplified these qualities, in so far as the otherwise bloody shambles of a prize-fight was regulated by rules. There was an element of smug, self-congratulation in Egan's analysis, which also assumed that, unlike his own countrymen, the knife-wielding Italian would always fight dirty. And yet there were British soldiers who appeared to agree with him, as Gleig noticed during the 1814 campaign near Baltimore. American riflemen who had concealed themselves in trees, for 'securing good aim and avoiding danger' were thought to have sought an 'unfair' advantage and, therefore, were shot when captured.[25] Interpretation of the code of so-called 'fair play' was elastic. On one occasion during the retreat to La Coruña in 1808, Sir Edward Paget offered a guinea to any rifleman who could pick off a French general. One did, and added to his purse by hitting a trumpet-major.[26] Perhaps the use of a long-range and accurate firearm was not considered unsportsmanlike.

Applying, in an admittedly flexible fashion, the rules of the game to war was a reminder that for many participants it had close affinities with sport. Referring to a cricket match in which his local eleven had been trounced, John Baldwin told a friend in Norfolk: 'we have a finer match here between the Sikhs and British . . . we did not get licked like you Swaffhamites.'[27] An unknown rifleman told his family that skirmishing near Balaklava provided some 'very good sport'.[28] Neither writer was blind to the suffering of war, far from it, but they were acknowledging its excitement, competitiveness and that sense of achievement that followed a good innings or a successful shoot.

A passion for sport crossed social barriers. It was most intense among officers, for whom sporting language and metaphors came easily and which they increasingly used to describe battle. On hearing that the Russian general, Prince Menschikov, had fled to Sebastopol, Sir John Astley of the Scots Guards compared him to 'a rabbit with an old dog-ferret behind him'. Astley was mad about sport; he had played and hunted hard at Eton and Oxford and continued to do so in the Crimea whenever the opportunity presented itself. For Astley, the battlefield became, as it were, an extension of the cricket pitch. When a cannon-ball passed through his company at the Alma, he called out to a soldier 'who was our best wicket-keeper' to take it. Rising to the occasion, the man replied, 'No sir! it had a bit too much pace on. I thought you was long stop, so I left it for you.'[29] Soon after, the wicket-keeper was killed, but no doubt such badinage about what was familiar would have briefly distracted men's thoughts from the terrible reality that was encompassing them. In just the same way and more famously, the Royal West Surreys kicked their football as they advanced from their trenches sixty-two years later.

A more compelling restraint on killing than any sporting rules was the divine commandment: 'Thou shalt not kill.' Those of a religious frame of mind who contemplated it before battle were able to absolve themselves from guilt by reference to what they took to be a higher duty. An unknown private of the 38th recalled the text that began 'They that take the sword' as he advanced into action at Salamanca in 1812. He would have heard it many times in the chapels he had frequented before enlistment, but, as he wrote afterwards, 'I knew that I was bound by the law to do my duty as a soldier. I knew that if I did not my own life was liable to pay for it.' He therefore placed himself in the hands of providence.[30] The equally God-fearing Private Pindar of the Royal Scots stiffened his resolve before facing Pathans during the 1863 Umbeyla expedition by reading over 'the glorious deeds before performed by my countrymen upon the field of battle'. When the tribesmen charged, 'an indescribable thrill' passed through him, which was repeated when the man in front of him was killed and 'I had to step into his place to keep the "thin red line" unbroken.' 'All finer feelings gave way as I saw at what cost "Duty must be done" and how true was the exclamation of the Psalmist when he said: "Come see the desolation war has wrought."'[31]

By and large, soldiers and sailors came from that class whose godlessness and resistance to the doctrines of organised religion were a source of perpetual concern to the pious. The Reverend Edward Mangin, sometime of Balliol College, despaired of achieving anything as a naval chaplain in the 1790s and concluded that clergymen were redundant aboard a man-o'-war on active service. His main task had been to rebuke swearing and blasphemy, but he failed miserably.[32] Another naval chaplain, attached to the *Hercule* in 1802, took his moral duties seriously and remonstrated with the officers for bringing Brixham prostitutes into the wardroom. Incensed by this interference with their pleasure, they retaliated by accusing him of drunkenness and intemperate language, charges of which he was acquitted by a court-martial.[33]

Those of Methodist inclination who served in the ranks of George II's armies concentrated on saving individual souls and delivering impromptu sermons against the everyday vices of soldiers. 'I preached against swearing, whoring and drunkenness,' declared dragoon John

Haime, and he did so well, attracting congregations of up to three hundred or so, which peeved Anglican regimental chaplains.[34] Another Methodist, Sampson Staniforth, found his faith gave him great strength and protection under fire at Fontenoy in 1745 and in other battles. It was heartening, he noted, how many 'profane spirits' who had been wounded converted easily, including a man who had lost his legs and died praising God.[35] Sermons given by Anglican chaplains to troops during the 1842 Afghan campaign concentrated on the familiar theme of moral regeneration. Soldiers were asked to trust in Jesus as they would their commander and to fight depravity as they would the Pathans. If the preachers touched on preparation for death and salvation, it was in terms of redemption through the repudiation of the soldier's favourite sins. 'Flee fornication', 'Swear not at all' and 'Be not drunk with wine wherein is excess' were texts recalled by one listener.[36]

III

This emphasis on repentance as the way to salvation, rather than easing consciences about killing, reflected prevalent evangelical views. The assumption that soldiers and sailors recognised that they did not break God's injunction against killing was accepted unquestioningly. What mattered to Methodist rankers, chaplains and the growing number of evangelical officers who were concerned with their men's spiritual health was that the souls of those who faced death were properly prepared.

On one level, death in battle was noble, a form of self-sacrifice for a greater good. Perhaps the most familiar icon of the uplifting death from this time was Benjamin West's rendition of the last moments of General Wolfe at Quebec, which was first exhibited at the Royal Academy in 1771. Its realism disturbed some; Sir Joshua Reynolds and George III would have preferred the figures to have been dressed in classical dress rather than contemporary uniforms.[37] Pitt the Elder (whose own death in the Lords would later be heroically portrayed by West) complained that the onlookers' faces were too glum – they ought to have been glowing with triumph at the moment of victory. He had missed the point: the cost of national victory was the private sacrifice of a brave man. West himself compared Wolfe to a martyr and portrayed him facing death calmly. The patriotic public agreed; the scene and genre it established gained immediate and widespread popularity, and copies and prints of West's picture sold briskly.

Nelson was deeply moved by 'The Death of General Wolfe' and once remarked to West that he would be happy to die in battle if he could be immortalised in such a grand manner.[38] His wish was fulfilled. There were objections that West's 'Death of Lord Nelson' of 1806 was untrue to life in so far as he succumbs on the deck of the *Victory* rather than in the ship's cockpit. West rejected them. There was, he asserted: '. . . no other way of representing the death of a *Hero*, but in an *Epic* representation of it. It must exhibit the event in a way to excite awe and veneration . . . Wolfe must not die like a common soldier under a bush, neither should Nelson be represented dying in the gloomy hold of a ship.' Revealingly, he concluded that: 'No boy would be animated by a representation of Nelson dying like an ordinary man. His feelings must be roused and his mind inflamed by a scene great and extraordinary.'[39] And so it was: as perceived by West, the hero's death at the moment of victory was a posed, theatrical tableau with few signs of pain or any emotion beyond grief.

Such scenes were not completely detached from reality. There were plenty of examples of lesser men dying in a heroic manner which, in various ways, emulated Wolfe and Nelson. James Hawkings, a young naval officer who fell mortally wounded during the boarding of a French schooner in 1813, cried with his last breath: 'Carry on if you can, I am no more.'[40] Of course, such information would have been relayed to the press or to the deceased men's families and may, therefore, have been deliberately comforting. Yet there is occasional evidence to indicate that some were prepared for such a death. For instance, in 1802 when a landing party on Dominica found itself cut off and without victuals, a marine volunteered to fetch them. 'I will go to the village and bring them – I know I must go and re-pass the enemy's fire, and my life is not mine, it is at the constant command of His Majesty's service.'[42]

Perhaps he was one of those who had previously fortified themselves with a belief that they were under some special supernatural protection in battle. There were also fatalists. Captain Glanville Evelyn spoke for many when, at the commencement of the American War, he wrote in the prefix to his will, 'As all men who have taken upon them the profession of arms, hold their lives by a more precarious tenure than any other body of people'.[43] His mind may well have been concentrated by what he had recently witnessed after the skirmishes near Boston. A battlefield was a chilling sight. Those engaged in the fighting had little or no time to spare for those who were dying around them, but afterwards they could pause and contemplate death. Gleig noticed that those who had been killed instantaneously by musketballs to the heart and head appeared to be asleep, while those clubbed, stabbed or sabred to death had the 'most savage and ghastly expressions'.[44]

The sight and sound of the wounded aroused the greatest horror and pity. After the battle of New Orleans in 1815, Gleig came across a field hospital full of men suffering 'excruciating agonies', some shrieking, others groaning, gibbering or praying – the last he took to be a sure sign of imminent death.[45] Sergeant Bingham was glad that the smoke hid the dead and dying from sight at Firozshah in 1845, for he feared that their plight would have unnerved younger, unblooded soldiers.[46]

Wounds were dreaded more than death, understandably given the risks of surgery in the era before anaesthetics and antiseptics. John Colbourne, later Field-Marshal Lord Seaton, was haunted by the memory of the first man he had seen lose a leg. 'The poor fellow screamed so,' he recalled, and thereafter he had a special fear of leg wounds and their invariable consequence, amputation. Hit in the shoulder at Ciudad Rodrigo in 1812, he rejected the suggestion of amputation after the surgeon's probes had failed to find the ball. Some months later, when he had returned to England, it was removed in an operation so painful that it was undertaken in stages with five-minute breaks for Colbourne to recover.[47]

It is difficult today to contemplate, let alone imagine, the agony, discomfort and despair endured by those who underwent surgery during or after a battle. It is harder still to read the notes taken by army and naval doctors and then to believe that some of their patients recovered. That they did so is testament to good fortune, the dedication and perseverance of physicians, and sheer stamina. The last was probably the greatest source of recoveries. It alone must explain the survival of a seaman from the *Racoon* who was one of twenty severely injured by an accidental explosion of gunpowder in October 1813. The surgeon all but gave up hope for a patient who had suffered massive burns to the body and head and presented 'one of the most melancholy pictures of human distress'.[48] He recovered within nine months, although he must have been grossly disfigured. Routine treatment for burns involved doses of opium to relieve the pain and the application of either linseed oil, sometimes mixed with lime, or carbonate or hydrate of lead.[49] As usual with such concoctions, physicians were never quite certain which ingredient, if any, had brought about the cure.

Two medical breakthroughs in the middle of the nineteenth century transformed battlefield surgery, but only gradually. The introduction of chloroform as a general anaesthetic, first used by Sir James Simpson in 1847, extended the scope of surgery. Twenty years later, Lister's application of Pasteur's study of germs produced antiseptics and a reduction in postoperative infections. Anaesthetics were initially denounced in some quarters of the medical profession, which was a host to prejudices, mainly conservative. The boneheaded John Hall, the army's senior medical officer in the Crimea, instructed surgeons to revert to the old ways and not resort to chloroform when treating gunshot wounds. 'The smart of the knife is a powerful stimulant,' he insisted, 'and it is much better to hear a man bawl lustily, than to see him slip silently into his grave.'[50] This order prompted a public outcry and Hall sulkily rescinded it. Among the beneficiaries of his change of heart was a casualty of the Alma who had been hit by an iron canister ball weighing three ounces which had lodged to the left of his nose. Only by using chloroform was a surgeon able to extract it.[51]

The greatest value of chloroform lay in its use for amputations. These were the standard clinical response to the commonest battlefield wounds, those caused by missiles. Musketballs, round and grape shot and shell splinters produced fractures of the limbs, often compound, which were beyond the capacity of surgeons to repair. Those who treated wounded Russians in the Crimea discovered that the conical bullet fired by the new British Minié rifle shattered rather than cracked bones, leaving no alternative but amputation. Moreover, experience strongly indicated that removal of a limb could check or prevent the onset of infection.

Before anaesthetics, the amputee's chances of survival were increased if the operation was performed swiftly while he was still traumatised by the initial shock of his injury. In this condition patients were uncon-scious of pain, like two officers at the assault on the Redan in 1855 who 'had their limbs carried away at the knee by round shot, and, so slight was the pain at first, that one hopped about for some time on the unwounded leg' and the other refused to believe that he had been wounded.[52] Here, the sailor was marginally luckier than the soldier, since he could be quickly taken below-decks to the surgeon in an anal-gesic state of shock.

The army's arrangements recognised that swift treatment of the wounded was imperative. Each regiment had one surgeon, three assis-tants and thirty-two stretcher-bearers, most of whom were bandsmen. At the start of an action an assistant accompanied the regiment into action and supervised the evacuation of casualties to the unit hospital. Regular procedures could rarely be followed in the confusion of battle. Assistant-Surgeon Ludovick Stewart rode forward with the 29th at Chillianwala followed by a dozen Indian dooly (palanquin) bearers and some bandsmen to look for wounded and soon found himself immersed in chaos. Smoke reduced his vision to ten yards and he collided with a body of retreating horsemen. Their panic unnerved the dooly bearers who ran off, despite blows from Stewart's sword. Frustrated of his pur-pose, he left the pandemonium, returned to the hospital and helped his fellow-'sawbones' who had plenty of work.[53] In the Crimea at least one regimental surgeon despaired of the stretcher-bearers, who were uni-versally regarded as 'the greatest blackguards in the army'. Another found that the hospital orderlies were 'drunken old prisoners, all subject to delirium tremens'.[54] Reports such as these impelled Florence Nightingale to raise her company of nurses and lead them to the Scutari base convalescent hospital on the outskirts of Constantinople.

There she found men who, after field surgery, had been shipped across the Black Sea for observation, additional treatment or convales-cence. Their case histories were often a testament to the extraordinary toughness of the human body and, in some instances, the skill of sur-geons working in haste under the most unfavourable conditions. And there was good luck. A twenty-one-year-old private from the 33rd recovered from a Russian musketball, fired at six yards' range, which struck his nose, passed through his cheek and exited by his ear. It had missed arteries and left nerves and tissue untouched. Less fortunate was a private of the 93rd Highlanders who had been struck by a ball fired at two hundred yards' range which hit him by the left eye and left through his neck, just below his left ear. The impact knocked him insensible and his body was found, stripped, the following day. No artery had been severed and the cold may have lowered his blood pressure, preventing a fatal haemorrhage. He regained consciousness after thirty days (presumably he was given liquids, perhaps by the intravenous techniques then in their infancy) and was found to have suffered damage to his optic nerves. Blind in his left eye and with the sight of the right impaired, he suffered from pain in the right side of his face. 'He cannot read or apply his mind for many minutes at a time; feels stupid and dull,' noted the doctor who examined him on his return to England.[55]

Between September 1854 and December 1855, 8809 wounded men entered various military hospitals, of whom one thousand died and 4414 were discharged to their units or sent home as invalids. Among the dead must have been a high proportion of men with gunshot or splinter wounds in the chest or abdomen where, despite anaesthetics, surgeons were reluctant to probe. The remainder of the dead were the victims of postoperative infections; the death rate for amputations from the hip was 100 per cent, from the upper thigh 76 per cent, from the lower thigh 63 per cent and from the ankle 20 per cent. Contemporary civilians who underwent amputations, and nearly everyone who suffered limb injuries in industrial or rail accidents did, had an average survival rate of 58 per cent.[56] Allowing for the problems that attended operations conducted under extreme pressure and often in makeshift hospitals, the army's record was quite remarkable.

IV

The efforts of the field surgeons were applauded by a doctor treating Crimean invalids at the military hospital at Portsmouth in the summer of 1855. Patients who had been successfully treated for wounds appeared 'stern, martial and *healthy* looking'. Their vitality contrasted with the debility of the diseased: 'Boys of eighteen bore the haggard, time-worn aspect of men of seventy or eighty, with sunken, glazed eyes, prominent jaws, and an expression of utter prostration, painful to look at. Their bodies were crawling with vermin, and their skin encrusted with filth, even excrement.' Several of these wrecks collapsed and died between leaving the dockside and reaching the hospital.[57]

Microbes killed far more fighting men than their human enemies. The statistics say it all: of the 103,660 sailors who died between 1793 and 1815, 6540 were killed in action, 12,680 were lost in shipwrecks, and 84,440 died from illnesses contracted during their service.[58] Many, perhaps a majority, of these were the victims of contemporary clinical ignorance, which was why the surgeon and his sickbay were feared by sailors. 'I should hesitate long before I submitted to the command of a medical gentleman,' wrote Lieutenant Scott, who had seen them in action many times. In 1797 the crew of the battleship *Ramillies* protested at the excessive use of 'blisters' (hot cups) on sores and flesh wounds by the surgeon, who used them 'with no other view than to torment the men who unfortunately fall into his hands'.[59]

The odds of a sailor surviving a battle were far greater than those of his recovering from a fever or serious wound. Losses in major fleet engagements were comparatively small; 4 per cent of those who fought at the Saints in 1782 were killed. A comparative analysis of losses in ship-to-ship encounters strongly suggests that the Royal Navy's superior gunnery and dexterity of manoeuvre paid dividends in terms of lives saved. Only one man was killed and eleven wounded in the two-hour encounter between the frigates *Phoebe* and *Africaine* off Gibraltar in 1801, while French losses were two hundred dead and 143 wounded, all from cannon fire. The French casualties were distorted by the presence on board of four hundred soldiers packed closely together. Likewise, in the duel between the *Endymion* and the USS *President* in 1815, British shots aimed at the hull and gun-decks accounted for 105 casualties, 20 per cent of the American ship's crew. Its counterfire, directed against masts and rigging, produced a smaller tally of dead and wounded. The *Endymion* suffered twenty-seven killed and injured, just 7 per cent of its complement.[60] A brisk and unequal twenty-minute fight between the mail-packet *Marlborough* and the French schooner *Josephine* in 1808 resulted in the former losing spars and being holed below the waterline. Neither vessel suffered any losses, which may have embarrassed John Bull, the commander of the *Marlborough*. He assured his superiors that his twenty-three-man crew, ten of whom had never been to sea before, fought 'in a steady and manly fashion'.[61]

Casualties in land battles were considerably higher. At Talavera in 1809, 11 per cent of the Anglo-Portuguese army of fifty-four thousand were casualties, and the same proportion was killed and wounded at Salamanca in 1812. Losses at Busaco in 1809 and Fuentes del Onoro in 1810 were under 5 per cent, a testament to Wellington's ability to choose defensive positions that spared his men punishment from artillery. The casualty rate during the four-day Waterloo campaign was exceptional, with just over a quarter of the 32,418-strong British contingent killed or wounded. Such heavy losses were a reminder of the scale and ferocity of the operations and were in keeping with those from the similar massed battles fought by Napoleon against continental armies. Allied losses at Austerlitz in 1805 amounted to 20 per cent, Prussian losses at Jena in 1805 were 29 per cent, and Russian losses at Borodino in 1812 may have been as high as 40 per cent. During the Revolutionary and Napoleonic Wars, the British army came off rather lightly.[62]

But like the sailor, the soldier could not overcome bacteria and micro-organisms. Of the forty thousand men landed on Walcheren peninsula at the mouth of the Scheldt in 1809, four thousand died from fever and intestinal distempers and a further twenty thousand had to be shipped home as invalids. Physicians could not discover precisely what had infected them, so their ailments became known collectively as 'Walcheren fever'. Worse than the stagnant, malarial marshes of Walcheren was the Caribbean. Its reputation as a soldiers' graveyard was so grim that men of the 105th and 106th preferred to mutiny and risk the firing squad rather than be posted to the West Indies in 1795.[63] When Captain Thomas Browne stepped ashore at Bridgetown, Barbados, in 1808, he was hailed by a half-naked black woman with the words: 'Ah Massa Johnny Newcome go back to shippy, too hot here for him, kill him.' On hearing that he was from the 23rd Regiment, he was told, 'Ah me show you plenty of twenty third in churchyard here.'[64]

Within a few days, two of his brother officers had died. On St Lucia 1588 men of the 68th died between 1801 and 1806, just over 60 per cent of its total strength, including drafts sent out from Britain.[65] The killing time was the wet hurricane season which lasted from midsummer to October. Dr George Pinckard, deputy inspector-general of West Indian military hospitals in the 1790s, remembered it as a period of intense melancholy, induced in part by the regular army funerals. A soldier's interment, against the sound of slow drumbeats and Handel's 'Dead March', was 'one of the most awful ceremonies that the age can contemplate'.[66] A similar fatalism pervaded the troops besieging Sebastopol during the winter of 1854 to 1855, when a familiarity with funerals also bred a resigned indifference to death.[67]

The British experience of mass losses from sickness was not exceptional. In spite of inexact diagnoses of the cause of death which were common throughout Europe, it has been calculated that during the first phase Napoleon's invasion of Russia in 1812 at least 150,000 men died from an epidemic of intestinal disorders. During the Leipzig campaign of 1813 the French and their allies lost 105,000 from enemy action and 219,000 from disease. Of the 118,000 Russian casualties during the Russo-Turkish War of 1828 to 1829, three-quarters died from fevers and bowel infections.[68]

Whether in the Caribbean, Eastern Europe or the Balkans, the high proportion of wastage through sickness was the direct result of fundamental medical ignorance. No one had yet identified the organisms responsible for the commonest fatal illnesses, nor discovered how they were transmitted. Insects carried yellow fever, malaria (mosquitoes) and typhus (lice) into the bloodstream. Water was the source of typhoid fever (commonly confused with typhus), cholera, dysentery and diarrhoea. Without this knowledge, prevention and remedy were matters of chance.

Gaps in clinical understanding were filled with conjecture. It was widely assumed that major infections were the result of human contact, which they were only when lice were the agents of transmission. The deaths of eight sailors from 'fluxes' (probably dysentery) on the *Racoon* in 1814 were attributed to homeward-bound invalids who had been picked up at Lisbon and brought the disease onboard with them.[69] As to the origins of contagion, there was a general consensus that it was the product of putrefaction which released infectious vapours into the atmosphere. Florence Nightingale and many others explained the prevalence of cholera among the troops in the Crimea as the consequence of miasmas from decaying animal and vegetable matter, which was abundant around the camps and in Balaklava harbour. Others proposed alternative causes. One doctor attributed the first cholera outbreak to the over-consumption of fruit and vegetables during the early phase of the campaign.[70] Those who imagined cholera to be contagious blamed the French army which, they believed, had become infected at Marseilles and then carried the disease to the Near East. Guesswork easily became dogma; it did not strike a naval surgeon as odd that a cholera victim who had picked up the disease in a South American port in 1855 did not infect any of his shipmates.[71]

Doctors were fumbling in the dark. An inability to trace the sources and processes of infection inevitably led to hit-or-miss treatments, or doctors falling back on remedies based upon the ancient theories of the internal balance of hot, cold, dry and wet humours. Occasionally a quantum leap was made, as in 1747 when Dr James Lind, surgeon on board HMS *Salisbury*, was impressed by the rate of recovery of scurvy patients whose diet included oranges and lemons. He published his results six years later and in 1795 the navy officially added citrus juices to its rations. The disease was all but eradicated within a year. Since no one knew of the existence or nature of vitamins, a precise clinical explanation of this phenomenon was impossible. As late as 1854 some army doctors were inclined to blame scurvy on eating too much salted meat and prescribed fresh meat as a remedy.[72]

Empirical observation enabled physicians to establish a rough-and-ready correlation between disease and climate. In cold and temperate regions, servicemen were prone to colds, catarrh, rheumatism and pleuritic disorders. The entire crew of the *Cerberus* suffered from all these complaints during a cruise in the Baltic during the summer of 1809. The ship's surgeon blamed the 'wild damp north-east wind' for a sharp increase in inflamed eyes among the crew. Sufferers were treated with purgatives, emollients, poultices and unspecified 'Formulations' of his own devising.[73] A night of fog and rain during which all hands on board the *Achille* worked hard to get their ship off rocks near Cape Ushant transformed an outbreak of catarrh into an epidemic.[74] Rheumatism and respiratory ailments were inevitable and plentiful with men constantly on deck and aloft in rain and wind, and living in damp, chill and airless conditions below.

Shipboard accidents were common, especially among drafted and pressed men. Sailors slipped on wet decks, fell from spars, stumbled into bulkheads, suffered hernias from carrying over-heavy loads and grazed their flesh on ropes. Inexperience no doubt caused the seventeen-year-old Samuel MacDowell to fall from the rigging of the *Cerberus*. The surgeon diagnosed concussion and immediately prescribed a purgative. After this had done its work, MacDowell's head was shaved and a blister applied to his scalp. He recovered. Untreated, minor injuries became septic. A seaman transferred to the *Cerberus* at Chatham had to be treated for contusions of the finger suffered months before in the East Indies which had become 'ulcerated'. His ligaments were reset and he was discharged for duty after four days' recuperation.[75]

Fever, a term that embraced malaria, was the scourge of servicemen in the tropics, although it also existed in temperate zones. There were 109 fever cases on board the frigate *Hussar* during a tour of duty in the Indian Ocean and off the Malayan coast from 1812 to 1813. Ninety-four patients recovered, although the surgeon's log makes no mention of those who may have suffered recurrent bouts. Another 210 men suffered attacks of 'dysentery' (a term that often included other bowel diseases) and two died, one a soldier whose failure to respond to treatment was blamed on his having pickled himself with pure arrack before his embarkation from Madras.[76] Of course, many who were pronounced fit and sent back to their duties suffered relapses, especially fever cases. One, a thirty-seven-year-old seaman serving on the *Racoon*, was found by the surgeon to possess 'a weakly habit of body' and a 'constitution [that] had suffered much from the West Indies climate'. His symptoms were dejection and listlessness, which suggest a recurrence of an old fever, possibly malaria.[77]

Chance was always an important element in any cure. Consider William Chatton, a twenty-two-year-old cavalryman, who had contracted dysentery in the Crimea. Shipped home as an invalid, he reached the military hospital at Portsmouth on 8 January 1855. His first treatment consisted of draughts of a mixture of chalk, acetate of lead and opium. This would have had the effect of soothing by neutralising the stomach acid, although opiates could cause constipation. By 10 April he was still 'frightfully emaciated' and appeared on the verge of death. New medication was tried in the form of a solution of morphia, spirit of nitric ether, peppermint water and two gills of brandy and spiced wine. Doses were administered three times daily with a miraculous effect. Within five days, Chatton was showing signs of improving; on 20 May he walked for the first time, and on 1 July the doctor pronounced him fully recovered. What had happened? The nostrum was a 'ferocious drug' for the stomach and the kidneys, but had the virtue of compensating for fluid loss. Vital rehydration had been achieved by accident.[78]

Of equal and perhaps greater importance for patients were rest, warmth, dryness and a better diet than they had been used to. Fresh food, particularly greens, vegetables and fruit, was universally recognised as a key to recovery, and rightly so, for they strengthened the body's natural resistance. At the Royal Navy's hospital at Haslar, three diets were prescribed in the 1790s. The 'low diet' consisted largely of liquids (water broth, milk pottage, gruel) and bread, and was presumably consumed by the very feeble. Half a pound of mutton, bread-pudding or greens and a pound of bread, together with three pints of weak beer, was the menu for the 'half diet'. Those on a full diet ate milk pottage for breakfast, followed by a pound of meat, a pint of broth, a one-pound loaf and two quarts of small beer. For those suffering from dehydrating bowel complaints the liquids would have been invaluable. Standards of cleanliness, necessary for the elimination of lice, were poor. Nurses changed patients' sheets once a fortnight and 'body line' every four days. Men were encouraged to wash daily, but were admonished for scrubbing their trousers in the lavatories.[79]

V

It was regretted that seamen discharged from Haslar made straight for nearby sutlers, got drunk and were utterly incapacitated by the time they returned to their ships. Dr Thomas Trotter, physician to the Channel Fleet, deplored 'avaricious spirit-dealers and distillers' who purchased licences and opened public houses to cater for sailors with full pockets. These were also the haunts of thousands of whores. 'The wretches,' he wrote in 1802, 'flock to the naval sea-ports for the wages of prostitution, after having been debauched in the interior of the country by the idle and dissolute soldiery.' Plymouth docks, he lamented, had become 'a huge brothel'.[80]

So, too, was Portsmouth. In 1795, Dr Pinckard found it 'crowded with a class of low and abandoned beings, who seem to have declared open war against every habit of decency and decorum . . . The riotous, drunken, and immoral scenes of this place exceed, perhaps, all others.' As for 'Sweet Poll of Portsmouth', the sailor's sweetheart, she was an awesome trollop, of 'Amazonian stature, having a crimson countenance, emblazoned with all the effrontery of Cyprian confidence, and broad Bacchanalian folly; give to her bold visage, the warlike features of two wounded cheeks, a tumid nose, scarred and battered brows, and a pair of blackened eyes, with deeply reddened balls, then add to her sides a pair of brawny arms, fit to encounter a Colossus . . .'[81]

After weeks or months at sea, sailors were none too particular and the Portsmouth Polls and their counterparts elsewhere in Britain and across the globe did good business. Too often, and to the permanent despair of the Admiralty and ships' commanders, the immediate result was infection by sexually transmitted diseases. When *Cerberus* was acting as a receiving ship at Chatham for sailors awaiting posting, the surgeon complained about the 'great number of venereal cases' that were crowding his sickbay.[82] All responded to treatment, or at least the symptoms were suppressed, but recovery usually took eight weeks. Those wary of the ship's surgeon could choose private treatment from a 'pox doctor'; they charged fifteen shillings (75p) for a 'cure' in Portsmouth in 1795.[83] However they might be remedied, sexually transmitted diseases meant that infected sailors were not performing their duties and the navy was getting nothing in return for their wages, a source of considerable irritation at a time when governments were deeply cost-conscious. The scale of the problem was enormous in both services; a survey undertaken between 1839 and 1846 revealed that in Britain alone 8072 soldiers went sick with sexually transmitted diseases. One man in thirty-one was infected with 'true syphilis' and one in eighteen with gonorrhoea. It was marginally worse in the navy, where 2880 out of 21,493 men stationed in the British isles were annually diagnosed with some form of sexually transmitted infection, and the proportion was higher on foreign stations.[84]

Sexual abstinence could not be expected, let alone enforced, among men aged predominantly between sixteen and forty. Waging war was considered a celibate occupation, and when a regiment was ordered overseas only a small number of married men were allowed to take their wives. When the 55th was ordered to Canada in 1757, distraught soldiers' wives and their offspring were provided for by a Cork private charity on the grounds that husbands were unlikely to be able to send money home.[85] More usually, servicemen's wives and families were forced to make do on grudgingly given parish relief.

The young sailor or soldier parting from his true love was a common and often poignantly expressed theme in contemporary ballads. In one from the 1760s, a sailor bound for the Caribbean takes leave of his sweetheart:

> Then a ring from off her finger she instantly drew,
> Saying, 'Take this dearest William and I will go too,'
> And as they embraced, tears from her eyes fell,
> Saying, 'May I go along with you?'
> Saying, 'May I go along with you?'
> Saying, 'May I go along with you?'
> 'Oh no my love, farewell.'

A few army wives were allowed on active service at the discretion of regimental commanders. Like their husbands, these women faced a precarious existence. If made widows, they immediately looked for new husbands, not a difficult task, given the abundance of unattached men. Against stiff opposition William Hutton of the 12th secured the hand of a recently widowed soldier's wife who, like Mother Courage, ran a sutler's business. Their first child was wrapped in a soldier's cloak and put with its mother on a baggage wagon.[86]

Wives of men of the 23rd who followed their husbands to Spain in 1812 quickly learned the soldierly arts of survival. 'All ideas of conduct and decency vanished', and they became adept at plundering the dead of both sides. Close and continual contact with death made some callous. One recent widow was overheard to spurn a suitor with, 'Nay, but thou'rt late, as I am promised to John Edwards first, and to Edward Atkinson next, but when they two be killed off, I'll think of thee.'[87] Nearly all, like the sutleress whom William Hutton married, supplemented their husband's income by cleaning, washing and cooking, mostly for officers who could afford to pay them. A handful turned to prostitution. Among the charges proved at the Lucknow court-martial of Lieutenant Lewis Edwards of the 67th in 1814 was that he had 'associated' with the wife of Sergeant Tankard for three months on nights when he was on duty. Given that the sergeant called her his 'baggage', her adultery may be forgivable.[88]

Officers in India and the West Indies found no difficulties in procuring mistresses. A black slave concubine was 'an object of envy, and is proud of the distinction shown her' in the West Indian garrison towns during the 1790s.[89] In Guyana, concubines could fetch up to £150 at auction, as much as a skilled craftsman, but some purchasers got more than they bargained for.[90] Rose, a black woman, who he assured the buyer was 'flawless', was sold by Quartermaster John Goode of the 14th to Captain Charles Portier of the 12th West India regiment in 1802. Afterwards, he discovered that she had run away from her former master in Martinique and 'he could never get any good of her'. Aware of her 'faults', Portier angrily raised the matter with Goode. The upshot was a duel in which Goode was shot dead; a court-martial could find no evidence against Portier and he was acquitted.[91] What became of Rose is not known. Perhaps she joined those slave women who were officially provided as prostitutes for the other ranks in the West Indies, with lighter-coloured, mixed-race women proving the most favoured.[92] Authorised brothels, under medical supervision, were allowed by the army in India.

Women were actively discouraged aboard warships, although some illicitly followed their husbands to sea. A heavily pregnant woman was smuggled aboard one man-o'-war by her lover and gave birth the following day. She was given two guineas by the ship's officers and put ashore with her child.[93] In the unlikely event of her presence being overlooked, she would have been in the curious position of being an official non-person, that is to say unrecognised by either officers or the Admiralty. One such creature, a seaman's wife on board the battleship *Tremendous*, gave birth during the Glorious First of June in 1794 to a son, who was christened Daniel Tremendous Mackenzie. He and his mother were alive in 1847 and were, therefore, qualified to receive the medal belatedly issued by the government for service at sea in the French Wars. Employing that unreason of which only bureaucrats are capable, he got the medal and she was refused it on the grounds that she did not officially exist and could not, therefore, have been on the ship during the battle.[94]

Homosexual acts were bound to occur within the closed, masculine world of the warship. Whenever revealed, they were treated with the utmost severity as outrageous infractions of the laws of God, man and nature. In the words of one court-martial indictment buggery was 'in derogation of God's honour and corruption of manners', and another described the act as 'a situation disgraceful to manhood'. Whether those who engaged in homosexual practices at sea did so because of prior inclination or frustration is not known; courts-martial were solely concerned with what occurred and not why.

Fear of opprobrium and punishment meant that homosexual behaviour always had to be furtive and hidden from sight in many dark corners of a ship. Lorenzo Greenard and Thomas Fuller were found playing with each other's genitals at night under the launch of the *Vengeance* in 1802. Both were sentenced to death. In the same year, John Holland and John Reilly of the *Trident* were so drunk on rum as to abandon any attempt at subterfuge. Their behaviour disturbed their messmates who summoned the master-at-arms. He caught them in flagrante, prised them apart, and later declared to the court-martial that he had examined the penis of one and found it 'fit for action'. Both men had a reputation as 'bad characters' and Reilly had once kissed another sailor when drunk. His record was reflected in his sentence: he got six hundred lashes, his companion three hundred.[95] Both had suffered because their conduct had been intolerable to those living close by.

There was some degree of tolerance among sailors towards homosexuals who were discreet. Sergeant George Pewtrer, a marine with fourteen years of service, and Michael Millard, a marine drummer, on the *Defiance*, were accused of indecent acts in 1808. Their hammocks were adjacent and one marine reported that they had been cuddling, and another had come across them embracing and kissing under a gun. No one appeared unduly perturbed by this; one witness to their activities observed, 'I never formed any opinion upon it.' This pair was acquitted.[96] In a singularly nasty but mercifully rare case an officer was charged with using his rank to procure sexual favours from a subordinate. The incidents occurred on board the *Sapphire* during a voyage from Portsmouth to Cape Town towards the end of 1807 and involved

Lieutenant John Brown, who was already in trouble for being repeatedly drunk on duty. He was in this state when, at midnight, he sent a midshipman for Francis Evans, a ship's boy. 'He put his yard up my backside and told me not to say anything,' Evans testified. This occurred several times, once when Evans was reading a book, and he admitted afterwards, 'I did not know the meaning of it.' Brown was dismissed with ignominy.[97]

How much he was driven by alcohol or by lust is not known. What was known, only too well, was that a drunken sailor was unable to perform his duties and, in so much as he required time in which to recover, could be considered as evading them. Overindulgence was sometimes fatal. Dr Outram, the surgeon of the La Nymphe, recorded that three seamen from ships anchored off Spithead had died from drinking spirits in April 1797. Four men from this ship were brought on board blind drunk and one died. The rest recovered, including one resembling 'a man dying from apoplexy', whose life was saved by a drastic purge in the form of a mixture of oil and warm water pumped into his stomach and rectum. Afterwards, he complained of 'universal pains and soreness and extreme languor' and needed several days to recuperate.[98]

All these drunkards had no doubt been recently paid. On reaching Port Royal in Jamaica in 1702, sailors used their wages to buy 'strong liquor' and 'throw themselves into distemper'.[99] Intoxicated men were easy prey to tropical infections. These, and a massive spree by troops and seamen newly landed at Barbados in the same year, prevented the invasion of Guadeloupe. Christopher Codrington, the governor of the Leeward Islands, blamed the fiasco on rum distributed by local planters. 'Strong liquor which will scarce warm the blood of our West Indians, whose bodies are like Egyptian mummies,' he observed, 'will most certainly dispatch the newcomer to the other world.'[100] Ironically, rum became the standard issue drink for sailors, which lined the pockets of the West Indian sugar-growers and, presumably, prepared the sailor's constitution for what was on offer when he visited their islands.

Soldiers also tended to drink as much as they could buy, cadge or steal. The surgeon of the Connaught Rangers, stationed in Jersey in 1797, was appalled by the 'great intemperance' of his patients. 'To procure gin they would part with provisions, necessaries and every comfort,' he complained during an epidemic of what he diagnosed as typhus. Since his treatment included thorough purges and 'James's anti-monial powders', the resort to gin was understandable.[101]

In a sense, the inebriate was like the man with a self-inflicted wound and no better than the malingerer who could somehow fake symptoms to secure a place in the sickbay. Naval and military surgeons were no doubt brisk with malingerers, or else deterred them with rigorous treat-ment or unpleasant physics – there were plenty available. Maybe Dr Outram was more forbearing than most of his colleagues, for he took seriously the phantom illnesses that afflicted a seaman on *La Nymphe*. 'There is a singularity in this man's complaint that I cannot account for, otherwise than he is attempting to impose upon me, in order to get clear of the service,' Outram noted. A second opinion was invited from a doctor at Haslar who declared the man fit for duty. A month and a diagnosis later, the perplexed Outram observed: 'This man makes still a variety of complaints and says he is much debilitated and distressed.'[102]

This sad creature came from a society in which various forms of debility and distempers were a common feature of life for large sections of the population. Thanks to those Gradgrindian accumulations of sta-tistics made by early Victorian public inquiries, the perils of military and naval life can be seen in the perspective of a civilian world in which survival was equally, if not more, precarious. In terms of infirmity and the dangers of infection, men who exchanged a civilian existence for the services would scarcely have noticed the change. Micro-organisms did not distinguish between the barrack-room and the cottage. In some respects, soldiers and sailors were better off than civilians, for at least they had constant access to free medical treatment and hospitals. In 1854 there were roughly 17.9 million people in Britain, of whom three million were solely dependent upon doctors employed by the poor law authorities, who were paid the minimum possible rate for their ser-vices. If they took sick, the poor often refused to seek treatment. A doctor's visit cost at least five shillings (25p), just over a half a farm-worker's weekly wage, and anyone who sought free medical attention under the poor law could automatically became a pauper.[103]

Civilian death rates from accidents and disease were as high as those in the services. Between 1848 and 1856 there were 237,488 deaths from cholera, dysentery and diarrhoea, with two major epidemics in 1849 and 1854 accounting for 116,246. Total losses from intestinal and respiratory illnesses in the Crimea between March 1854 and March 1856 were 16,297, and the survival rate for cholera at the front was much the same as in the 1853 Tyneside epidemic, which killed two thousand. In all, 4516 men were killed in action and died from wounds, while at home the average yearly death rate from what the authorities classified as 'violence' was fourteen thousand. This category included all types of accidental injuries at home and work; a thousand died annually from mining accidents and, astonishingly, 1800 children died from scalding. The everyday perils of civilian life were equal to those on the battlefield. Of the male children born annually in industrial Liverpool, 15 per cent did not reach their fifth birthday, while in more salubrious, rural Caernarfon the loss rate was 6 per cent.[104] A British soldier who charged the Russian batteries at the Alma had twice the life expectancy of an infant born in the industrial slums. Of the thirty-six thousand engaged in the Crimea, 7 per cent (2002) were killed or died from wounds.[105]

Furthermore, the forces did learn from their mistakes. Out of twelve thousand British and Indian troops who invaded Abyssinia in 1868 only 330 died from local sicknesses, thanks to well-organised facilities for treatment and recuperation on hospital ships. It could not have been otherwise: a public more enraged by the sufferings of the nation's heroes in the Crimea than by similar distresses at home had clamoured for and got a thorough reform of the army and navy's medical departments.

5

Each honoured name: Memories and attitudes

I

Mid Victorian Britain was an exceptionally proud and belligerent nation. Behind the façade of a country devoted to universal moral improvement, industry and trade was a self-assured people who never flinched from asserting their rights and interests with force. If Britain's patience was exhausted, or its will thwarted, then warships sailed and armies marched. The country was richer and stronger than ever. In 1852 the *Edinburgh Review* declared: 'her people are and always have been hardy, robust and brave; her resources are inexhaustible.' Xenophobia was commonplace. A guide to France, published in 1843, politely suggested that British tourists might refrain from 'talking loud, laughing and stamping with their feet' during Catholic services and suppress their 'pugnacity' when dealing with foreign officials.[1]

Bad news from the Crimea momentarily jolted the country's self-confidence. 'Are we so demoralised by a long peace – so soaked and soddened in the fat of commercial speculation – that we have lost the robust manly virtues of our ancestors?' asked the *Illustrated London News* in February 1855. The country soon recovered its old hubris and the national mettle was proved beyond question by the suppression of the Indian Mutiny and the defeat of China in 1860. A few dissident voices, like those of the cotton-manufacturers, Richard Cobden and John

Bright, lamented the way in which their countrymen equated national greatness with a capacity to win wars. Both dreamed of a time when Britain would forsake war, which, they predicted, would eventually be abandoned once the world adopted free trade. Thereafter, all human energies would be concentrated upon making money.

This vision was ignored or ridiculed by a public that was conscious that their country's present stature rested upon past victories and present strength. A barometer of the nation's temper was the immense popularity of prints of Maclise's 'The Death of Nelson' and 'The Meeting of Wellington and Blücher after Waterloo'. Twenty thousand of each were distributed by the Art Union of London in the 1840s, most for display in middle-class houses.[2] Those who were doing well from manufacturing and commerce were fiercely patriotic. It was with profound sadness that John Bright heard how theatre audiences in London and his native Manchester had cheered when the news of the death of Czar Nicholas I was announced.[3]

For him such outbursts were shameful in a Christian country. Yet most of his contemporaries and the clergy of the established churches sincerely believed that waging war was not incompatible with Christian principles, far from it. Cathedrals and churches were becoming filled with memorials to those who had died in wars, erected to perpetuate the memory of self-sacrifice and to render thanks to God who had delivered victory to a godly nation.

Both themes appear side by side on two memorials of the late 1850s on the wall of the north chancel aisle in York Minster. The first, a brass, commemorates officers from the 19th Regiment who died in the Crimea. It was designed in the heavy-handed Gothic style of the time, which suits its symbolism. Men who died in Russia are celebrated as Christian warriors: figures of armoured knights fill the panels which frame an image of the resurrected Christ. Those who died had followed His teaching, in that they had laid down their lives for others. A few feet away is an elaborate marble monument to the soldiers and sailors who died when the transport *Europa* caught fire and sank during its passage to the Crimea. A carved scene shows the ship's final moments and, again, the imagery is of inspirational self-sacrifice. In the centre stands an officer, who is comforting a seated soldier, while on the opposite side another soldier reassures a dejected comrade, placing one hand on his shoulder and raising the other to heaven. Behind, in semi-relief, stand calm sailors and beyond them the flames that were engulfing the steamer. This group might well be martyrs awaiting death, which in a sense they were, for they lost their lives in the service of a godly, Christian nation. Less than ten years after they died, the Reverend Sabine Baring-Gould would liken all Christians to warriors:

> *Onward, Christian Soldiers!*
> *Marching as to war,*
> *With the cross of Jesus*
> *Going on before.*

There is something distinctly Roman about the memorial to a young officer of the Bombay Horse Artillery killed at the battle of Miani in 1843, now unforgivably relegated to the crypt of Christ Church cathedral, Dublin. It is on a grand scale, classical in style and unashamedly heroic. The young officer stands, ready for battle in full-dress uniform with a helmet like that of a centurion. The inscription pays tribute to his zeal and bravery which were praised by his commander-in-chief, Sir Charles Napier. Less florid, but equally eloquent memorials to fighting men are found in parish churches and kirks everywhere. Some include scenes of battle. At Radway in Warwickshire, the monument to Charles Chambers, a sometime naval surgeon who died in 1854, shows a landing party in a small cutter. As the inscription explains, he had taken part in coastal operations in the Baltic forty-six years previously, something of which he and his family were clearly very proud.

Although they often conveyed uplifting public sentiments, these were all private monuments, paid for by families or comrades. Governments preserved the memories of greater men whose achievements were more spectacular. Under the terms of a wartime measure, introduced in 1795 and intended as propaganda, the Treasury was permitted to allocate funds for memorials to illustrious commanders which were placed in St Paul's, transforming it into a national pantheon. In their lifetimes, these immortals were also rewarded with titles, gratuities and pensions. Admiral Cuthbert Collingwood, the son of a Newcastle merchant who had entered the navy at the age of eleven, received a barony in 1805 together with a pension of two thousand pounds, and an annuity of one thousand pounds for his widow. After his death in 1810 he had his statutory memorial in St Paul's and another in Newcastle cathedral. Local pride generated the wherewithal for a statue at Tynemouth which sits on a fifty-foot-high pedestal and was erected in 1847.

A thriving, industrial seaport had every reason to revere the memory of a naval commander whose exertions had helped uphold and extend British seapower. For this reason, Glasgow merchants paid for a memorial to Nelson in 1808 with a triumphant inscription: 'To NELSON, The scourge of France, the Avenger of his Country and of Europe; who, wielding the Naval Thunders of EMPIRE, poured Destruction on the terrified foe . . .'[4] The man who saved the nation from the threat of invasion was more elaborately commemorated by the monument in Trafalgar Square. A public subscription was opened in 1838 and designs were judged by a committee headed by Lord Anglesey, who had lost a leg at Waterloo. The sum raised (just over twenty thousand pounds) was disappointing and the committee was forced to substitute a stone for a bronze statue. When it was at last placed on its column in November 1843, the operation was conducted 'in a quiet manner' and went almost unnoticed by passers-by.[5] Four panels showing scenes from Nelson's battles were added to the column's base in 1849 and 1850. Landseer's bronze lions were installed in 1867 after considerable production hitches, not the least of which was the death of the beast who had served as a model.

Public settlement of the nation's debt to its other saviour, Wellington, was first made by Lavinia, Countess Spencer, who proposed a statue to be paid for solely by women. They raised ten thousand pounds which purchased a figure of Achilles, naked save for shield and helmet, executed by the fashionable sculptor, Richard Westmacott. When the bronze was set up in Hyde Park in 1822, its nudity provoked the inevitable ribaldry which the committee was obliged to deflect with a fig leaf, adding to the mirth.[6] Conventional, uniformed and equestrian Wellingtons appeared at the north end of Edinburgh's Prince's Street and opposite London's Royal Exchange during the 1840s. The duke was honoured by Manchester in 1856 with a statue in Piccadilly which showed him in the frock-coat of an elder statesman with figures of Mars and Britannia below. Sadly, the composition has been defaced by supporters of local football clubs.

The Mancunian Wellington provides a valuable clue as to why he and Nelson were so extensively and expensively remembered. A figure of Britannia looks upwards at the duke with a gesture of gratitude. Manchester, the city that believed itself to be the powerhouse of economic change, was joining the rest of the nation in thanks to the general whose victory at Waterloo had ended an era of protracted war and opened one of unparalleled prosperity and progress. Writing not long after his visit to the battlefield, the poet laureate Robert Southey predicted that Britain was about to become a beacon of enlightenment throughout the world:

> *The virtuous will she hath, which should aspire*
> *To spread the sphere of happiness and light;*
> *She hath the power to answer her desire,*
> *The wisdom to direct her power aright;*
> *The will, the power, the wisdom thus combined,*
> *What glorious prospects open for mankind!*

Waterloo had been the key that had opened the door to a golden age.

Moreover, victory had been the springboard for overseas expansion. An ode written shortly after Wellington's death in 1852 portrayed Britain as a global superpower without equal:

> *Britannia's power, respected by the world,*
> *Sails on the wave with banners bright unfurled.*
> *Her thunder roars on every land and sea,*
> *Acre and China fell, once more agree,*
> *The Burmese trembling, own Britannia's sway,*
> *And powerful Sikhs submit and homage pay,*
> *Australia opens wide her fields of gold,*
> *For ages hid; but now all eyes behold*
> *Those hidden treasures blazing in the light,*
> *The Koh-i-noor shines forth in splendour bright*
> *Great Queen Victoria's glorious fame resounds,*
> *The greatest Queen that sat on England's throne . . .*[7]

Behind these and many other flattering expressions of national self-congratulation was the knowledge that Britain's recent spectacular advances had only been made possible by success in the French and Napoleonic Wars. They had amply vindicated the older notion of the British as a protestant people specially favoured by God. It was resuscitated during the gloomier phases of the Crimean War and Indian Mutiny, which were marked by days of national prayer in which clergy of all denominations and their congregations begged forgiveness for the country's sins and asked God for victory. If Britain ever faltered in war it was because of domestic moral waywardness.

In political and economic terms, Britain occupied the same position in the world as the United States did in 1945. Its agricultural, manufacturing and transport infrastructure were undamaged and it possessed a disproportionately large share of the world's industrial capacity and capital reserves. Furthermore, and this became clear during the next thirty years, Britain had a head start in the development of new technologies. Despite some dicey moments and the temporary loss of continental markets, the British economy had grown during the war years. The momentum of expansion increased after 1815, although the Industrial Revolution based upon steam-driven machinery and factory production was a slow and uneven process. Rifles used to suppress the Indian Mutiny were produced at Enfield by machine-tools while their ammunition was assembled by hand at Woolwich, where over eight hundred children aged between eight and twelve were employed.[8] Although a paddle-steamer had been used in the 1824 Burma War, only fifty-nine of the navy's 303 warships were steam-powered at the outbreak of the Crimean War.[9]

Businessmen had always acknowledged the connection between maritime supremacy and access to overseas markets and raw materials. Both had been secured at Trafalgar which was why the steam-engine manufacturer Matthew Boulton had medals cast and given to every sailor who had been present at the battle. Hitherto, medals had only been awarded to officers, but in 1815 the government was persuaded by Wellington to give one to each soldier who had been at Waterloo. This precedent was followed after the 1838 to 1842 Afghan War, although veterans of the French and Napoleonic Wars had to wait until 1847 for their campaign medals. The named, silver medal given to the private or the ordinary seaman was the equivalent of the statue erected to the general: a token of the nation's appreciation. It also endowed the recipient with honour, for, as Lord Ellenborough, the first lord of the Admiralty, observed in 1847, a medal was proof that a man had shown 'good conduct under fire'.[10]

Front-line soldiers were not always grateful for the country's favours. 'Half a crown and a pennyworth of ugly ribbon [it was sky blue and yellow] from a grateful nation' was how one officer greeted the news that every soldier of the Crimea was to receive a medal.[11] He was no doubt delighted by a *Punch* cartoon that showed two frozen soldiers dressed in rags. They have just heard that they are about to be awarded campaign medals. One remarks: 'That's very kind. Maybe one of these days we'll have a coat to stick it on.' These men deserved more than a medal for what they had endured. At the beginning of 1855 there was agitation for a memorial to all who had died in the Crimea; the ordinary soldier was to receive the same permanent recognition as the great commander. Pious and patriotic emotions were blended in a verse suggested for this monument:

> For us they fell, lest our free necks should feel
> The foul reproach of Russia's despot's heel.
> Now doth their country on her loving breast,
> Inscribe their deeds, and consecrate their rest:
> And cry, while pointing to each honoured name,
> 'Read, youth of England, read – and do the same.'[12]

II

The nation that fought in the Crimea was freer and more liberal than that which had defeated Napoleon. Of course, during the French Wars government propaganda had repeatedly and forcefully insisted that the British constitution was the most felicitous form of government ever devised, a view not shared by radicals who saw it as a device that preserved the power of a narrow, landowning class. A public emergency was not considered a suitable time for altering the balance of political power and so the French and Napoleonic Wars effectively postponed any reform of parliament or extension of the franchise. Conservatives believed that neither was desirable and took comfort in the fact that if war was the ultimate test of a political system, then Britain's unique ancien régime had successively triumphed over a republican democracy and a populist military dictatorship. But the institutions that defeated Napoleon were extensively overhauled; parliamentary and local government reforms in the 1830s shifted the balance of power away from the landowners towards the commercial and professional classes and set the country on the path to democracy.

There was a loose connection between the transformation of the political landscape and the war that had ended in 1815 and whose memory was still fresh. Thomas Hardy, born in 1840, based much of *The Trumpet-Major* (1880) on the 'recollections of old persons' who had been alive 'when the landing was hourly expected'.[13] Dorset farmworkers were among the poorest people in the country, but like everyone else they had been expected to play a part in the national war-effort. Farm labourers, servants, a gamekeeper and a dog-breaker were among the Seal and Tongham Volunteers who drilled each week in preparation for Boney's invasion in 1804.[14] Even criminals were enrolled. In 1803, Lord Sheffield had proposed to raise a jaeger corps from the smugglers, poachers and ruffians who infested the North Pevensey area. 'The worst looking and worst made men often made excellent skirmishers,' he rightly argued, for they had mastered the necessary fieldcraft by dodging parish constables, gamekeepers and revenue officers. In all 1100 men from the Sussex underworld joined; whether they did so for the bounty or because they loathed the French is not known.[15]

A desperate state could not afford to be choosy. By 1814, 890,000 men were under arms, five hundred thousand as part-time soldiers in the reserve militia, volunteers, fencibles and yeomanry, 250,000 in the regular army and 140,000 in the navy. In Scotland 20 per cent of all adult males were in the services, a proportion marginally less than that mobilised throughout Britain during the First World War. Nearly a third of the young men of Cambridgeshire were militiamen or volunteers in 1803.[16] To winkle out shirkers, the government ordered a register of all able-bodied men to be compiled in 1798, and three years afterwards the first national census was taken in order to quantify manpower available for wartime service.

Strategic necessity had driven the government to seek the partnership of all ranks in society, including hundreds of thousands whose incomes and status placed them outside political life. Care was taken to exclude anyone with radical views from the militia and volunteers. The removal of large numbers of labourers from the militia after the invasion threat had disappeared in 1805 suggests that ministers appreciated the hidden dangers of arming and drilling the masses. If, as the Americans insisted, the rights of citizenship were a reward for bearing arms for the nation, then the measures adopted in desperation in the late 1790s and early 1800s were bound to have political repercussions. 'To teach the people military tactics' was a 'dangerous experiment' a left-wing journal claimed in 1831, which was why militia training was so poor.[17] Yet advocates of parliamentary reform and an enlarged franchise were oddly quiet about the well-known fact that thirty years previously everyone had been expected to share in the war-effort. Perhaps it went without saying.

The concept of national defence based upon part-time militiamen was appealing to those of all political complexions who believed that standing, conscript armies were the chief supports of continental tyrants. In the eighteenth century, there had been an antiquarian fancy that the armies of the Ancient Britons had been the prototypes of the militia, free men trained in arms and ready to defend their homes and homeland against Roman aggression.[18] This was far-fetched nonsense and, in any case, Britain's first and most formidable line of defence was always the navy. Nonetheless, in political terms, the militia was infinitely preferable and far cheaper than a standing army on the European or, more importantly, the Cromwellian model of infamous memory.

The 1757 Militia Act had established a reserve filled with unmarried men aged between eighteen and twenty-three, and over five feet two inches in height, who were chosen by ballot. They were provided with uniforms, basic training and were mobilised in an emergency. Each militiaman received a ten guinea (£10.50) bounty, which represented over twenty weeks' wages for a farm labourer and was sometimes recklessly spent on alcohol when the unit was assembled. The crises in the 1790s broadened the age and height qualifications, and in 1797 Scotland was required to provide its own militia. This measure was widely resisted in the southern part of the country where village schoolmasters, who supervised enrolment, were manhandled by mobs.[19] Here, as in England, exemptions were granted to married men with more than three children, clergymen and Quakers. Christopher Grieg, a divinity student and intended minister, pleaded to be excused his local ballot. 'The military life,' he suggested, 'is not quite the proper school for acquiring those habits and ideas which a clergyman ought to possess.'[20]

It certainly was not. Separated from the disciplines of their own communities, militiamen were fractious and unruly. In Sunderland in 1796, Westminster militiamen killed the goat that served as the mascot for the Lowland Fencibles and brawling followed. When the Northumberland militia's pug thrashed the Warwickshire's in a prize-fight at Norwich, rival supporters began fighting and bayonets were drawn and used. Cheshire militiamen, encamped near Eastbourne, poached rabbits from a neighbouring estate and, when the landowner protested, the men marched to his house and advised him to purchase a coffin.[21] There were political undertones to some disorders. In 1795, soldiers seeking to purchase meat were sniffily treated by a Bristol butcher. 'With an erect nose of visible contempt', he told them 'I don't deal in meat for soldiers!' 'Fierce and menacing', the men responded that they 'would have meat for the poor and for themselves at a fair price'.[22] In the same year, local people and soldiers joined forces at Wells in Somerset to prevent market traders from overcharging for butter.[23]

Subversion was an ever-present danger, particularly during the late 1790s when food prices rose and war-weariness was increasing. Both produced popular commotions which, on occasions, were suppressed by militia and volunteers, a duty that some civilians turned soldiers found distasteful. In 1800 the Wolverhampton Volunteers declared that they had never joined 'to give security to the inhuman oppressor, whilst the poor are starving in the midst of plenty'.[24] Such opinions were unlooked-for from this quarter since the volunteers tended to be drawn from the better-off, who ought to have been upholders of the rights of property. 'The suppression of riots and tumults' was specified as among the duties to be undertaken by the mounted yeomanry when they were first raised in 1794. They did so repeatedly and, next to the regular army, were the most dependable force available to handle civil unrest.

The South Nottinghamshire Yeomanry were deployed against local bread rioters in 1795, 1796 and 1800.

Part-time soldiering was usually an agreeable diversion. 'Interest and Happiness for the Rest of Life' were promised to anyone who enrolled in the St Anne's, Westminster, Volunteers.[25] Like the yeomanry, the volunteers made their own terms with a government grateful for their services and could insist on performing their duties close to home. Nothing but 'the presence of the enemy' on the East Anglian coast would have induced the Cambridgeshire and Hertfordshire Volunteers to cross their county boundaries.[26] The impetus behind the creation of these detachments was often the local squire, whose tenants formed their backbone. This was so of the Frampton Volunteers, first formed in 1798 at the instance of Nathaniel Winchcombe, which, when they reached full strength, included forty-eight local farmers, shop- and innkeepers, two pig-slaughterers, an accountant and a schoolmaster. They devised their own code of discipline which enjoined officers 'to behave as gentlemen to every member of the corps' and established a scale of fines for petty misdemeanours – swearers paid a shilling (5p) for each oath.[27]

With a preponderance of gentleman officers, it was assumed that discipline would present few problems among men who had been brought up to respect and obey their landlords and social superiors. Nonetheless, compromises had to be made. When Nehemiah Wimble, a Lewes ironmonger, collected sixty-five local men for a volunteer company, the Lord-Lieutenant of Sussex, the Duke of Richmond, resigned himself to granting him a commission. 'I should have preferred an independent gentleman, but as there is none to be got, we must be content with Mr Wimble.'[28] Another shopkeeper who styled himself 'esquire', a banker, a schoolmaster and an attorney's clerk were among the officers of the various Cambridgeshire volunteer corps.

Aspirants to gentility did not have the same authority as those born to it. When the commanding officer of the Sutton Volunteers remonstrated with his men for passing round a quart mug of ale during a parade, he was jeered at and threatened with bayonets.[29] Obviously these fellows were not taking their duties too seriously, but trouble occurred elsewhere when militiamen refused to knuckle under to what they considered unjust treatment. In 1810 the West Mendip militia mutinied after the cost of their trousers was deducted from their one pound marching allowance. Wearing the king's uniform did not deprive a man of his rights.

The tradition of amateur soldiering largely lapsed after 1815, but was resuscitated in 1859 in a fit of national fury that followed exaggerated rumours of an imminent French invasion. Tennyson, always vigilant when it came to threats from across the Channel, drummed up support for the new volunteers with a poem which was published in *The Times* in May 1859:

> *There is a sound of thunder afar,*
> *Storm in the South that darkens the day!*
> *Storm of battle and thunder of war!*
> *Well, if it do not roll our way*
> *Storm, Storm Riflemen form!*
> *Ready, be ready against the storm*
> *Riflemen, Riflemen, Riflemen form!*

The tempest did not come, but the rifle volunteers remained and became a permanent feature of British life. Small units proliferated, attracting those in search of congenial companionship who were able to afford the entrance fees and the dashing uniforms. The 32nd Middlesex Rifle Volunteers wore scarlet tunics adorned with black braid and black-plumed helmets. Such finery helped make the volunteers immensely popular; between 1859 and 1877, 818,000 men served with the volunteers, roughly 16 per cent of the adult male population.[30] Most were from the middle class or skilled craftsmen; membership of a volunteer corps counted for something in local society and enhanced a man's prospects. It advertised loyalty, reliability and a willingness to accept discipline – qualities that appealed to employers. One volunteer, Alexander Smith, a Glasgow businessman who raised himself from private to colonel, founded the Boys' Brigade in 1883. It was inspired and guided by the values and spirit of the volunteer movement which, he hoped, would protect the young from immorality.

III

Free Britons in arms of their own free will and ready to defend their country were peculiarly British. A satirical account of three Englishmen abroad, published in 1854, showed one squaring up to a dwarfish Prussian sentry, complete with pickelhaube. The caption reads: 'Jones expostulates with that freedom of Speech which is the birthright of every Englishman.'[31] The confrontation was symbolic: in Prussia and elsewhere on the continent, the soldier represented the coercive power of the absolute state over its subjects, while in Britain the army was the politically neutral agent of a government that ruled by consent.

It was an enduring paradox in the nation's public life that while the British never shrank from boasting of their soldiers' prowess, they remained deeply suspicious of the army as an institution. The evolution of its administration reflected this apprehension. Authority was decentralised and divided among a multiplicity of separate boards in charge of command, provisions, equipment, quarters, ordnance and medicine. Ministerial responsibility was split between the War, Foreign, Home and Colonial Offices, whose ministers were answerable to parliament. The result was a complex, often bewildering machine which easily became snagged in red tape and moved ponderously; it took eleven years of interdepartmental correspondence to repair a barracks in Trinidad.[32] Unable to take the pressure of emergencies in the Crimea, the administrative apparatus buckled and fell apart, as it was bound to do. Its purpose had never been to foster efficiency, but rather to prevent any single figure from securing control over the army, which was still regarded as a potential threat to liberty.

This was not too far-fetched, seen from the perspective of the second quarter of the nineteenth century. In the 1840s, France had a largely conscripted army of 348,000 men distributed among eighty-nine garrison towns. It had been the ladder by which Napoleon had climbed to power, and had intervened in political crises in 1830 and in 1848 to 1849 when it helped his nephew, Napoleon III, to the throne. Russia had a standing army of just over a million drafted men, which had been deployed to suppress the Polish national uprising of 1830 to 1831 and, on behalf of the Austrian emperor, the Hungarian rising in 1849. At the same time, the conscripted armies of Austria and Prussia crushed liberal and nationalist revolts in Vienna, northern Italy and Germany.

The far smaller British army was detached from political life. Its total strength rose from 109,000 in 1829 to 138,000 in 1847, but it was scattered. On average the domestic garrison was forty thousand, with about the same number serving in India and between fifteen and twenty thousand in Ireland. The rest were distributed in Canada, the West Indies, Gibraltar, Malta, Corfu (until 1860), Cape Colony, Mauritius, Ceylon, Australia and New Zealand. On occasion, troops from the home garrison were deployed to deter or suppress unrest, usually in small detachments. From 1840 onwards, the railways made it possible to shift troops to trouble-spots quickly. A battalion of the Guards and a Royal Horse Artillery battery were moved overnight by train from London to Manchester during the Chartist disturbances in 1842. These and other political tumults never presented the army with any difficulties. Nonetheless, successive governments did not take any risks. During 1848, the prospect of further Chartist unrest and the Young Ireland insurrection prompted Lord John Russell's ministry to increase the British and Irish garrison to sixty-five thousand.[33]

By this date, the new civilian police manned the front line in any riot. Bringing in soldiers was a last resort, although jumpy magistrates were inclined to call for them at the first hint of demonstrations. Cavalry were usually preferred on the grounds that if called upon to disperse rioters they could use the flat edge of their sabres, reducing the chances of deaths and serious injuries. In general, both infantry and cavalry showed extraordinary forbearance under bombardment from brickbats and any missiles rioters could lay their hands on. Firing into a mob only occurred when matters were completely out of control and after a magistrate had read the Riot Act. The highest casualties, perhaps as many as two hundred, were at Bristol in 1831, but most of these were drunken looters trapped in burning buildings.

Radicals naturally exploited these incidents. The most famous was at St Peter's Fields, Manchester, in 1819, when the sixty-thousand-strong crowd demanding political reform was broken up by the 15th Hussars, who had been called in after the Manchester and Salford Yeomanry had become entangled with the demonstrators. Men from both units panicked; a Hussar officer had to restrain some of his own troopers and yeomanrymen from slashing at people who were attempting to escape from the press.[34] Eleven protesters died and many more suffered cuts, bruises and broken bones in the crush. The incident was called 'Peterloo', as a parody of Waterloo where the 15th Hussars had served with distinction. A contemporary cartoon showed cavalrymen charging the crowd with the caption 'Britons strike home' – an ironic reference to a popular patriotic song of the French Wars. The inference was clear: a tyrannic ministry had, as it were, declared war on the people and was attacking them with soldiers.

Comparisons with continental despotisms were commonly made by those on the left who depicted the army as the defenders of property owners and the Tory and Whig ministries which placed their interests first. In November 1835, *The Poor Man's Guardian* expressed apprehension at the possibility that London's Millbank prison was about to be converted into a barracks. 'All oppressive Governments place great confidence in the military, and like to have large bodies of them near the seat of Government, to overawe; and all governments are oppressive that are not representative.' The writer then launched a hysterical diatribe against all soldiers who were 'idle, dissolute, having nothing to do – commanded by licentious, immoral officers, seducers of women, absorbents of public money, swaggering about in regimentals'. Even the glance of a frisky soldier could discompose a modest woman. Martial vices aside, this was a distorted picture, but understandable given the part that the army had recently played in smothering popular agitation for the Reform Act.

It was a different tale in Ireland. There, the government was still alienated from the majority of the population, for whom the Union delivered few, if any, benefits. In Ireland, the British army was an army of occupation. The police force, which, unlike its mainland counterpart, was an armed gendarmerie, was never able to cope with the endemic restlessness unaided. Soldiers had to escort men to and from gaols, protect officials and be present at public hangings (as they were in Britain whenever crowd trouble was expected) and other occasions, such as elections and fairs, where large bodies of people assembled. The army also had to support Ireland's bloodsuckers. Small detachments guarded the bailiffs who evicted smallholders who had failed to pay their rents, poor rates or the tithes squeezed from the Catholic peasantry to pay the stipends of the unloved clerics of the protestant

Church of Ireland, which quite literally rested on bayonets and sabres. Officers and men loathed these duties, which they considered to be political and, therefore, no concern of the army.[35]

The navy also played a part in coercing Ireland. Fifteen steamships were ordered to Irish waters during the summer of 1848, when an uprising was expected. Some were equipped with launchers for Congreve rockets, which it was thought would prove an efficacious weapon against large bodies of insurgents. At the same time, battleships were anchored off Cork to intimidate its inhabitants.[36] Sailors were also used to intercept smugglers. In the early 1820s, three thousand were patrolling the Kentish coast. One party was fired upon by a sixty-strong gang near Margate, wounding the midshipman in command. A ten-minute engagement followed during which the smugglers were heard shouting 'Kill the buggers', but no one died. The miscreants escaped with their contraband, but several were later arrested, tried and sentenced to death by a judge, who rebuked them for 'assisting the enemies of the country and favouring the commerce of other countries'.[37] Such activities in part gave the lie to the conventional wisdom that the navy was the natural complement to the freedom it safeguarded for it could never intervene in politics.

What was beyond question was that both army and navy were entirely subordinate to civilian government. As institutions, they were apolitical and MPs and peers with service backgrounds never acted in unison as a pressure-group, like, say, the manufacturing or agricultural interests. The army and navy isolated themselves from political faction. Invoking the spirit of Nelson, Captain Harris reminded the Commons in 1850 that his fellow sailors embraced 'The pure example of his generous spirit of patriotism'. 'To serve our country with individual zeal and energy' was the desire and 'duty' of every Jack Tar.[38]

IV

Harris's sentiments were directed towards a public that knew more about how sailors and, for that matter, soldiers performed their duties than any previous generation. Since the mid eighteenth century newspapers had proliferated; during the Seven Years' War of 1756 to 1763 the total national circulation passed ten million.[39] There were two far-reaching consequences: the gradual creation of a national consciousness, and a far greater awareness of exactly what was happening on distant battlegrounds. Admittedly, press coverage of war was largely restricted to official dispatches, extracted by London and provincial papers from the government's news-sheet, the *London Gazette*. These reports were sometimes vivid and full of exciting detail. That sent by Captain Lord Cochrane of the sloop *Speedy* describing its engagement with a more heavily armed Spanish frigate in 1801 may stand for many others: 'The great disparity of force rendering it necessary to adopt some measure that might prove decisive, I resolved to board and, with Lieutenant Parker, the honourable Mr Cochrane, the boatswain, and crew, boarded; when, by the impetuosity of the attack, we forced them instantly to strike their colours.'[40] As was customary, there followed a list of casualties.

Accounts like this were good for morale and helped turn figures like Cochrane into national heroes. The public was now becoming acutely aware of the mechanics of warfare and, through the regular publication of casualty lists, its human cost. The reality of war came into sharper focus after 1815 with the publication of a flood of memoirs, diaries and letters written by those who had served in the recent wars. For the first time the voice of the ranker was heard, for some of the authors were ordinary soldiers and sailors. Some of this material was graphic and evocative with descriptions of the discomforts of campaign life, the struggle to secure rations and the nature of death in battle. The reminiscences of veterans from Indian and colonial campaigns added to this growing war literature in the 1840s and 1850s.

War reporting in the modern sense began in the early 1840s, when the London and provincial press printed passages from the letters home of soldiers on campaign in India, Afghanistan and South Africa. Some appeared in the *Illustrated London News* (founded in 1842), which also produced prints of campaign scenes and engagements based upon on-the-spot sketches by officers. During the 1845 to 1846 Sikh War, *The Times* supplemented the official dispatches with extracts from participants' letters and reports from Indian newspapers. *The Times* also employed a 'correspondent', but to judge from his copy he relied on eye-witness accounts of the fighting sent to him by officers whom he knew.

This material took as much as six weeks to reach London, being carried by steamer from Bombay to the Suez isthmus, then overland to Alexandria and by another steamship to Marseilles, from where it was carried overland to Calais.

On 31 March 1846, *The Times* secured a scoop which it announced with a banner headline: 'India: Another Victory Over The Sikhs'. This was all that was known, for the information had been conveyed by telegram from Marseilles via Paris. Close behind came further information, carried in official and private mail, and the next day *The Times* presented a full story of the battle of Sabraon as set down in Sir Hugh Gough's dispatch of 24 February. On 1 and 2 April several columns were filled with first-hand accounts of the fighting, some of them forwarded by the paper's India correspondent.

Readers were given a vivid and stirring picture of the battle. One officer observed that it was 'a beautiful sight, shot and shell playing and tearing up the ground around us'. Most impressive of all was the demeanour of the British infantrymen: 'Nothing could surpass the steady way in which our fine fellows advanced; not a step was quickened, not a turn left or right, but all pressing onwards.' And there were dramatic vignettes of men dodging cannonballs and hand-to-hand combat. No attempt was made to hide the horrors of war. After the capture of Multan in 1849, a soldier of the 32nd wrote: 'I wish never again to see a sacked city with its heaps of slain and of wounded, and dying all around; and its crowds of poor old men, and women, and children crowding together in fear on the corners of the streets.'[41] Nor did editors suppress criticism of superiors. An account of the fight at Ramnuggar in December 1848 frankly admitted that the British force had been lured into a trap. One officer in the Punjab hoped that his caustic remarks on the cheeseparing policies of the government and the East India Company would be publicised in the press.[42]

These communications set the tone of future British war reporting. It satisfied a broad range of emotions, appealing to the patriotic pride of readers, exciting them with thrilling stories of brave deeds, and moving them to pity with accounts of the anguish of the wounded – 'Captain Alexander, 5th Cavalry, was shot through the right arm and has since had it taken out of the socket.'[43] And there was anger whenever letters revealed mismanagement or slipshod generalship.

Front-line reports printed in one paper were reproduced in others, with the provincial press borrowing heavily from the metropolitan. At the same time, many families offered dramatic passages from home letters to their local newspapers. The knowledge that their words would appear in print tempted a few writers to elaborate or invent. This may explain a communication from an amazingly resilient private in the Scots Fusiliers which described his misfortunes during the battle of the Alma:

> The balls were coming thick as hailstones. My front rank man was shot dead. I took his place and was firing away as fast as ever. In a few minutes a musket ball went through my right arm. It was just like a pin touching me at the time. I continued firing about five minutes: then I got a ball in the left breast. I never fell, but thank God the ball passed as quick as lightning through my back just below my shoulder. I fired thrice after this; then I reeled like a drunk man. I could scarcely stand for lack of blood.

He was struck again in the thigh and finger, and had to wait four hours for medical assistance.[44]

This new publicity aroused jealousies. Servicemen had always been prickly about getting appropriate and fair public recognition. There was umbrage whenever a unit's contribution had been neglected in an official dispatch or the formal parliamentary vote of thanks that followed a victorious campaign. Major Alexander Robertson of the Bengal Artillery was sour about the newspaper coverage of the 1852 to 1853 Burma War in which too little was written about Indian detachments while the navy was given undeserved prominence. The 'toady press' had praised the local commodore and his men, who were 'selfish, marauding buccaneers'.[45]

Fiercer passions were aroused a year later by the newspapers' treatment of the Crimean War. It witnessed the appearance of professional war correspondents whose stories augmented the flow of letters from servicemen. Much of this material was highly and, on the whole, justifiably censorious of senior officers and the army's bureaucracy. One staff-officer, Colonel Sir Anthony Sterling, believed that the blame for this criticism could be split between the public and the amateur and professional writers who satisfied its craving for 'perpetual information about military movements and perpetual gossip about the routine of the camp'. The British, he thought, were 'not naturally a military people' and, therefore, were unaware of the harm done to officers' pride by carping press reports. Officers who wrote them were no better than spies, and it was alleged that the Russian commander, General Gorchakov, had claimed that *The Times* was worth a dozen agents.[46]

Sterling did not and probably could not explain the value of two-month-old newspaper reports to Russian intelligence. Nonetheless, an indignant French officer accused *The Times* correspondent, William Howard Russell, of assisting the enemy and undermining morale at the front. Such things would not happen in France where editors did what they were told.[47] In Britain they did not and although the censorship of soldiers' correspondence and journalists' copy would certainly have saved the army embarrassment, it ran against the grain. Gentlemen did not read other gentlemen's letters and any attempt to muzzle the press would have been political suicide. After all, Britain was upholding liberty against despotism.

Unfettered, Russell was able to uncover and minutely chart the disintegration of the army's logistical and medical services, and to name those responsible. He went further and queried the tactical judgement of the commander-in-chief and the professional competence of several of his senior officers. This was bad enough for an army that had not delivered the victories the public had been led to expect, what was more galling was that sheaves of letters from officers confirmed his impressions and upheld his conclusions. The upshot was a public and parliamentary outcry which toppled Lord Aberdeen's ministry and prepared the way for the more energetic Palmerston. It was a signal demonstration of the power of the press and a warning that the public would show no mercy to governments and commanders whose operations went awry. For the first time, the people had become active partners in the conduct of warfare and the newly enfranchised middle classes were not willing to leave it to aristocratic generals who did not know their job. Issues of class, most notably the purchase system, surfaced during the parliamentary and press debate on the war.

Sombre newspaper descriptions of the privations at Balaklava hindered enlistment. A recruiting party touring Sussex, adorned with ribbons, accompanied by a small band playing 'Rule, Britannia' and well supplied with cash to stand rounds, made little headway. One potential recruit explained why: 'It was only last night when we stood the parish clerk drinks to read how the war was going on in the East and we heard there was no beer, and wonderful little to eat for the sodgers out there, that we made up our minds that men couldn't fight on an empty stomach, and we ain't going to try.'[48]

Press accounts of the Crimea were radically altering the public perception of the fighting man. He was no longer just a name singled out for congratulation in an official dispatch, but an individual whose character, feelings and exploits could be intimately known. Consider Captain Edwin Richards of the 41st, killed in a skirmish in November 1854, whose letters were sent to the *Illustrated London News* by his family. In the last he had written breezily of night-time picket duty: 'being out all night agrees with me very well, and I feel as fresh as I used to after a ball.' A brother officer related how he died: 'Refusing to surrender himself a prisoner, he shot four of his opponents, and killed two with his sword: thus dying the noblest and most glorious death a man can die – without pain – shot through the body, and stabbed by several bayonet wounds, he suffered no pain, as death must have been instantaneous.'[49]

No doubt the forensic details comforted his family, as they would have been intended to, and the manner of his death would have inspired manly respect and womanly compassion. A contemporary *Punch* cartoon showed a family's reaction to the first report of the Charge of the Light Brigade: an ebullient papa brandishes his poker as if it was a sabre, while the features of mama and her daughters appear drawn as they force back their tears for the dead and wounded. Soon their mood would change to rage as the family read how the miseries of the nation's heroes were being intensified by imbecile bureaucrats and inept generals.

Every household following the course of the war would have been equipped with maps supplied by stationers and booksellers, and many acquired prints showing Russian fortifications, Crimean landscapes, battles and portraits of Allied commanders. The public demanded authenticity and the printsellers obliged. Artists were sent to the front, and one firm offered a prize of a hundred pounds for the best sketches forwarded by an officer. That novel art form, photography, offered the most perfect verisimilitude; the army employed a pair of photographers, but they and their plates were lost when a ship capsized in Balaklava harbour in November 1854. Two accomplished commercial photographers, Roger Fenton and James Robertson, followed them and the latter's pictures were used for engravings that appeared in the *Illustrated London News*. Fenton's photographs were exhibited in London in the autumn of 1855 and showed a variety of scenes of camp life, individuals including private soldiers, and views of Balaklava harbour. Many of his pictures were commissioned by officers who sent them to families anxious to have a likeness of a loved one, in some instances the last they would ever possess.

Prints and photographs of the war presented images of glory and pathos. An exhibition of war pictures held in London in the summer of 1855 drew large crowds anxious to see reproductions of scenes of which they had read so much. A reviewer sensed their mood and reactions: 'All looked with painful interest at views of the spots . . . where the flower of England, unscathed by fire, unsmitten and unhurt, rotted away, with their faces turned towards England. For them, there will be no victory, no rejoicing – for them, no open arms and happy faces, no flags waving or jubilee of bells – but in their stead, cold, narrow graves, in an enemy's country . . .'[50] These were the victims of maladministration. Then and later, popular views of death and burial in a foreign land involved different and sometimes contradictory sentiments. A contemporary ballad that told the story of the Charge of the Light Brigade spoke of 'that fateful death vale enriched with English blood'.

Between the invasion of the Crimea in the autumn of 1854 and the fall of Sebastopol a year later, the war dominated British life. It filled newspapers and magazines and offered every form of diversion; dioramas showed what the battlefields looked like, and wax figures of the commanders were displayed in Madame Tussaud's. Songs with triumphant and sorrowful themes were written and sung on stage and in parlours. The highlight of Monsieur Jullien's promenade concert at Drury Lane in January 1855 was the first performance of the 'Allied Quadrille'. It was played by musicians in British and French uniforms while schoolboys waved Union Jacks and tricolours; above the auditorium was an illuminated sign which read 'Alma'. Never before had a war so infiltrated popular culture. A pattern was set that would be reproduced during the Boer War at the end of the century and the First World War at the beginning of the next.

V

There was a minority for whom the 'Allied Quadrille' and all the hulla-baloo generated by the war struck a sad, discordant note. They were the Quakers and a handful of Christian pacificists for whom war was never justified on any terms. The Quakers were the followers of George Fox (1624 to 1691) an eccentric, errant and persuasive preacher who believed that he had a monopoly of truth. At his death there were estimated to be sixty thousand Quakers, but their numbers plummeted during the next century, during which they abandoned their pentecostal quirks, plain wardrobe and exclusiveness. The 1850 denominational census revealed that there were fourteen thousand Quakers attending weekly meetings – there were 2.3 million Anglicans, 694,000 Methodists and just over half a million Congregationalists. Quakers were pacifists by principle and, for this reason and the smallness of their numbers, were excluded from the militia draft. Some Quakers were by no means united on the issue of war; a few armed ships hired by the government during the French Wars and some supported the Crimean War.[51]

Quakers were prominent in the Society for the Promotion of Universal Peace which had been founded in 1816 with the intention of printing and disseminating pamphlets against war. Their arguments were based upon Christ's teaching and a conviction that war was an outdated and uncivilised means of settling disputes between modern states. A sequence of tracts issued in 1839 outlined the theological case against war. It devalued human life and the 'war spirit' encouraged ambition, malevolence and vengeance.[52] All that Christ had preached on forbearance and forgiveness was incompatible with waging war, and this had been recognised by the early fathers and, more recently, Erasmus.[53] Christian compassion was set aside during wartime when the deeds of heroes were exalted and 'the sufferings of the wounded are lost in the animated description of the pomp of battle; the tears of the widow and orphan are unnoticed in the enunciation of its idealised glories.'[54] Just how hideous these sufferings were was presented in a pamphlet full of eyewitness accounts of the havoc and miseries inflicted on Russia in 1812.

The Peace Society, as it was usually called, was one of those earnest and well-meaning bodies that mushroomed during the 1830s in support of various causes such as temperance and the abolition of the corn laws which were dear to the evangelical, nonconformist heart. Pacifists, in particular, were inspired by the success of anti-slavery agitation which had, with divine guidance, aroused the nation's conscience.[55] Quaker businessmen gave the Peace Society its cash, and Richard Cobden and John Bright provided its parliamentary voice. Both hated war from the depths of their souls, and condemned it on economic as well as ethical grounds: armies and navies ate up taxes. If these fell, then trade would expand, to the benefit of manufacturers and employees, according to current dogma. The strong argument that pared-down naval and military budgets would imperil Britain's security was deflected by the Peace Society's attempts to promote international disarmament. There was a further, less high-minded element in Cobden and Bright's pacifism: both resented the armed forces because they were a bastion of that aristocratic influence that still held the levers of power and denied it to men like themselves from commercial backgrounds.

What amounted to a two-man campaign against war and those who waged it achieved nothing, save that military and naval budgets were clipped in the late 1840s with disastrous results in the Crimea. Just before hostilities began in April 1854, the Peace Society's secretary, Joseph Sturge, made a last-ditch personal attempt to avert them. With a couple of fellow Quakers, he rushed by train to St Petersburg, but failed to convert the czar.[56] The anti-war protests of Cobden and Bright (whose moral opposition to the war did not stop him from buying government stock when prices fell on its eve) had no impact whatsoever on events.[57] Adversaries of Cobden and Bright characterised them as humbugs for whom the ledger was gospel and who were devoid of any patriotism or honour, qualities that neither would have prized.

To some extent this was unfair but, like so many politicians in the grip of rectitude and dogma, Cobden and Bright were out of touch with the feelings of the majority of their countrymen. These remained convinced that the army and, in particular, the navy were vital for the nation's security. Anyone who had second thoughts had their minds concentrated by the war scares of 1847 to 1848, 1851 to 1852 and 1858, when fears of a French cross-Channel invasion gave the country the jitters. Invasion scares were a reminder that an otherwise overconfident nation could become the host to all kinds of disturbing phantoms, not least the fear that its present good fortune could be suddenly reversed.

VI

Over the preceding one hundred and fifty years, wars had not only delivered Britain an Empire and prosperity, they had helped bind the nation together. Wartime unity, fostered by successive governments, was a national cement that strengthened the Union. Ireland still nursed ancestral grievances, and yet it was one of the paradoxes of the Union that its least enthusiastic members, the Irish, gave a disproportionately large number of men to the army:

	England and Wales		Scotland		Ireland	
	% of UK population	% of army	% of UK population	% of army	% of UK population	% of army
1830	58.2	43.2	9.5	13.6	32.2	42.2
1870	72.1	60.3	10.5	9.6	17.4	27.9[58]

The shift is in large part explained by two demographic factors: the 1845 to 1848 Irish potato famine, and the rise in emigration before and after it. Nonetheless, as the century progressed the trend was towards an army dominated by recruits of English origin. Within that army, there were strong particularist identities owing to patterns of local recruitment. The 18th, 27th, 86th and 87th Regiments and the Connaught Rangers were almost entirely Irish; the Black Watch, the 71st, 79th, 92nd and 93rd were Scottish, although Sassenachs were enlisted to keep up numbers. All regiments adopted indigenous traditions: tartans, kilts, bonnets and bagpipes. 'No one – at least, no Scotsman – can read the record of their service without feeling "his pulse beat quicker" and his heart "warm to the Tartan", declared the *Aberdeen Chronicle* after reports of the local regiment's courage at the Alma.[59]

On St David's Day, officers of the 23rd Royal Welch Fusiliers ate a leek. Like Ancient Pistol, they found the vegetable unpalatable; a subaltern recalled that new arrivals were given large ones and 'day after day passes by before the smell and taste is fairly got rid of.'[60] Just over a hundred years later, in 1914, Robert Graves, who joined the same regiment, recalled the pride associated with the old-fashioned spelling of its name: '"Welch" referred us somehow to the archaic North Wales of Henry Tudor and Owen Glendower and Lord Herbert of Cherbury, the founder of the regiment: it dissociated us from the modern North Wales of chapels, Liberalism, the dairy and drapery business, slate mines and the tourist trade.'[61] In Wales, as well as Scotland, military customs harked back to martial traditions that predated the Union.

Graves was aware that the fighting man's values and preoccupations were different from those of the society he served. In particular they looked backwards. Consider John Maddocks, a Light Dragoon officer of the 1840s, who not only represented all that was cherished in his profession, but who might easily have served with Prince Rupert or the Black Prince. According to an admiring brother-officer, he was '. . . the picture of soldier and a gentleman, very good looking and strong as a horse, about 5 ft 11 in., like Prince Albert, but more manly looking and more expression. A first-rate horseman, capital cricketer, could run like a stag, full of fun, very popular with everyone.'[62] These were, perhaps, not the qualities that distinguished a contemporary banker, lawyer or businessman, who set greater store by sobriety, diligence, thrift and piety.

Nonetheless, these men would have had nothing but praise for the manner in which officers like Maddocks exercised their authority over their men. In 1849, a reviewer of two manuals of dog-training noted with some interest that both had been written by army officers. 'Both alike,' he wrote, 'advocate drill, discipline, order and obedience; both denounce unnecessary flogging and extravagance; and assuredly mercy, a quality of the brave, and economy, the soul of efficient armies, ought also to animate well-regulated stables and kennels.'[63] Dogs and soldiers responded to and learned their duties from a mixture of fatherly patience, firmness and moral generosity. Nearly forty years previously,

Sir Walter Scott had paid tribute to Colonel Cadogan of the 71st who had hugged his soldiers after the victory at Arroyo Molinos. 'Such an officer will be followed to the jaws of death,' he commented, 'and our army has many such, now that the cold, iron-hearted system of German discipline has, thank God, given way to the Moral management and that a soldier is reckoned something better than the trigger of his gun.'[64]

The paternalism that still held sway in mid Victorian Britain was mirrored in its army and navy. 'Her crew was like one happy family,' a newspaper announced after the *Frolic* had completed a four-year cruise in 1847 with only two desertions and one flogging.[65] Camped before Sebastopol in January 1855, the 63rd Regiment was neither happy nor efficient. An inspecting officer reported that it was 'in a miserable condition' with underfed, dirty soldiers whose rifles were fouled. Tents were untidy and everywhere was evidence of slack discipline. The commanding officer, Colonel Robert Dalzell, protested that he had just taken over 'an easy-going regiment' in which bad habits had been made worse by an influx of young recruits who were 'the very scum of Dublin'. The excuses were dismissed and Dalzell was superseded for failing in his moral and military duty.[66]

Like Dalzell, his superiors were working under adverse conditions, not the least of which was the knowledge that their shortcomings would be exposed in the press. People at home, who were better informed than ever about his deeds and sacrifices, demanded humane treatment for the fighting man. He was the embodiment of the nation's ancient heroic virtues and was now being endowed with those emotions dear to a sentimental age. In a poem written at the start of the Crimean War, a young soldier takes his last glance at the village where he had grown up:

> *Beside the cottage porch,*
> *A girl was on her knees,*
> *She held aloft a snowy scarf*
> *Which fluttered in the breeze.*
> *She breathed a prayer for him*
> *A prayer he could not hear,*
> *But he paused to bless her as she knelt,*
> *And wiped away a tear.*

He turned and left the spot,
Oh! do not deem him weak.
For dauntless was the soldier's heart,
Though tears were on his cheek.
Go watch the foremost ranks,
In danger's dark carer,
Be sure the hand most daring there,
Has wiped away a tear.[67]

PART FIVE

TOTAL WAR, 1914–19

1

For civilisation: The nature of total war, 1914–18

I

The human cost of the total war waged by Britain between 1914 and 1918 can be measured by the war memorials that are found in every city, town and village. The names of local men and women who died in the conflict are listed, occasionally with their units. Sometimes, one surname will appear several times as a reminder of how modern war has cut swathes through families. In all, the death toll was between 702,000 and 740,000, and many more were maimed in body and spirit. Nearly all the casualties were suffered in France, where, at the end of the war, 2.3 million servicemen and women were deployed.

Many were a new breed of soldier: technicians and engineers attached to specialist units which operated wireless sets and telephones and maintained and repaired the machinery of industrial war. Among them were the railwaymen whose names are listed on memorials at all the London terminuses. At Baker Street the dead of the Metropolitan Railway Company are remembered on a now rather dingy white marble slab set in a wall. Above the names of former porters, guards, firemen and signalmen is a carving of a roaring lion crushing a monstrous serpent – this was a war in which good was perceived as triumphing over evil. The inscription says that 'at the call of King and Country' those who died 'left all that was dear to them, endured hardness, faced danger and finally passed out of sight of men by the path of duty and self-sacrifice, giving up their lives that others might have freedom'. This epitaph must have been familiar to many passengers, for it was composed by M. R. James, the writer of ghost stories, and appeared on a scroll sent in George V's name to the next of kin of every man and woman who had died in the war.

Similar sentiments were expressed on other monuments whose form followed closely those to the victims of Victorian wars. Christian themes predominate in words and images, with the cross as the commonest motif.[1] That, and the image of Christ crucified, are deliberate reminders that those who had been killed in battle had followed His example of sacrifice for others. Those who died in a modern, scientific war are often, paradoxically, commemorated by icons from the age of chivalry. Figures of St George and armoured knights abound; at Sledmere in the East Riding of Yorkshire the war memorial is embellished with brasses of mailed crusaders. Their weapon and the symbol of knightly honour, a sword, was placed on the coffin of the Unknown Warrior at George V's instructions in 1920. Public grief and private sorrow converged at this ceremony at which the message was unmistakable: the 'glorious dead' had lost their lives in an elevated and hallowed cause.

By contrast, the reality of the war of machines and chemicals is powerfully portrayed by Charles Jagger's Royal Artillery memorial in Hyde Park, which was erected in 1925. It shows a massive howitzer surrounded by gunners in steel helmets and carrying shells filled with high explosive or gas. There is also a corpse, shrouded in a blanket, which was a controversial and rare feature. On the whole, it was thought more appropriate to commemorate mechanised and mass-produced death by images from the age of heroic warfare.

The dead are remembered by more than stone and bronze. In the past few years the tradition of the two minutes' silence at 11.00 a.m. on 11 November (the month, day and hour of the armistice agreed in 1918) has been revived with remarkable success. Mourning and recalling the dead still provides a source of national unity when others have decayed. This is evident throughout the country each Remembrance Sunday when ceremonies are held in which prayers are said, wreaths of Flanders poppies laid at memorials, the national anthem sung and the

Last Post sounded. Afterwards, veterans march past in honour of old comrades. Whether in a village churchyard or before the national shrine, the Cenotaph in Whitehall, the proceedings are somehow very moving.

This is because the experience of total war, particularly as it was fought between 1914 and 1918, has become deeply embedded in the national consciousness. The emotions aroused by the war are ambivalent and uncomfortable: there is pity at so many killed and profound unease as to why and how. There is a prevalent and largely justifiable feeling that the war was grossly mismanaged at the top. Generals, who were national heroes during the war and showered with coronets and cash when it was over, have now become villains. Profligate with soldiers' lives but sparing with their own brains, their collective lack of flair and imagination swelled the casualty lists. Worse still, the First World War settled nothing and, with hindsight, can be seen as a hideous prelude to the Second. In *Death of a Hero* (1929), Richard Aldington, a Western Front veteran and an 'angry young man' of his generation, rebuked the dead in terms that would have been blasphemous during the war but that rang true afterwards. 'You the dead, I think you died in vain. I think you died for nothing, for a blast of wind, a blather, a humbug, a newspaper stunt, a politician's ramp.'[2]

Little had been achieved by the sacrifice. A conflict that, according to the medal issued to all who took part, was 'for civilisation' destroyed much of that European civilisation that had flourished in the previous century and which was showing every sign of further and greater achievements in 1914. Postwar Europe was distinguished by erratic economies and societies that became hosts to monstrous phantoms that intensified old social, racial and political animosities. Russian state communism, Italian fascism and Nazism were all direct consequences of the war.

II

The phenomenon of total war, which appeared to end half a century of progress and enlightenment, was one of its products. It is possible to trace the genesis of total war back to the end of the eighteenth century when Revolutionary France attempted to mobilise all the nation's resources to defend the beleaguered republic. The concept was premature in that the French state lacked the administrative and economic capacity to support mass armies in the field for long periods. The soldiers of the Revolution went hungry, marched barefoot and were driven to plunder the lands they overran in order to survive.

Nineteenth-century industrialisation, a revolution in communications and the spread of popular nationalism made total war a practical proposition. The steam revolution opened the way for a new kind of warfare; railways and steamships carried mass armies to the front and kept them supplied with food, clothing and weapons which were the products of the latest technology and science. The American Civil War of 1861 to 1865 provided an alarming glimpse of how war was evolving. The Confederate States of America raised between 750,000 and 850,000 men out of an available total of a million, and one in three of them died in battle or from disease. Losses were also high among United States soldiers: 2.2 million of them were in action, roughly half the adult male population, and one in six was killed. Both sides resorted to conscription and in the Confederacy men's jobs were taken by women. One told a British visitor that Southern women 'won't let a man capable of carrying and handling a rifle stay round home. If he can walk he must be off.'[3] As in the First World War, both sides were driven by a passionate nationalism which, in the Confederate case, made it possible for the fledgling republic to fight on despite crippling casualties, invasion and the destruction of its economic infrastructure. Those at home felt bound to keep faith with their soldiers, whose suffering and courage became symbols of the national will to persevere and win.

The pattern was set for future wars between modern nation states. Within two months of Britain's entry into the First World War, the secretary of state for war, Field-Marshal Lord Kitchener, cited the example of the Confederacy as evidence that the conflict would continue for a further two or three years. Like the Confederate states, Britain would need to raise armies in haste and be prepared to replace enormous losses.[4] He was right and, as in the American Civil War, former distinctions between fighting men and civilians soon vanished. Already, the emergency Defence of the Realm Act (DORA) had curtailed or suspended cherished individual freedoms and provided the government with extensive coercive powers. As the war progressed, state agencies took control over the production and distribution of food and manufactured goods. Everyone, regardless of sex or age, was considered to be at the disposal of the government.

Unthinkable in peacetime, such measures were the inevitable consequence of total war. Modern transport systems had vastly extended the scale and size of military operations and eliminated the logistical problems that had hampered commanders in the past. By 1900 advances in medicine, surgery and hygiene had reduced the number of those epidemics that had previously run havoc through armies in the field. The power to save lives was more than offset by inventions that made it possible to kill soldiers in larger numbers than ever before. During the last forty years of the nineteenth century, developments in chemistry and metallurgy had produced a revolution in firepower. Prototype machine-guns had appeared during the American Civil War and, by the 1890s, infantrymen were armed with bolt-action, magazine rifles that were accurate at ranges of up to a mile. A new breed of artillery appeared that fired explosive shells faster, further and more accurately than ever. Modern machine-tools and mass-production techniques meant that factories could manufacture limitless supplies of the new guns and ammunition.

No one could doubt the lethality of the new weapons, for it had been abundantly demonstrated on colonial battlefields. One onlooker noted how the Burmese defenders of a stockade 'were mown down in masses by a machine gun' as they fled through the main gate in 1885.[5] At Omdurman in 1898 a combination of British artillery, machine-gun and rifle fire killed or wounded over sixteen thousand spear- and sword-armed Sudanese within four and a half hours. Among the spectators was Douglas Haig, who would command the British Expeditionary Force (BEF) in France between 1915 and 1918. Neither he nor any other witnesses to similarly unequal contests in Africa and Asia speculated as to how British troops might react in the face of such firepower.

The British army did have a foretaste of modern warfare in South Africa during the Boer War of 1899 to 1902. Although lacking a manufacturing base, the Boers were equipped with the most up-to-date armaments imported from France and Germany. The result was a nasty shock for British soldiers who were stunned by the sheer weight of Boer rifle and artillery fire. During the battle of Modder River in November 1899 an unknown NCO of the Loyal North Lancashires sensed that the air was 'humming and throbbing' with bullets. When they fell to earth they left the 'sand mottled like a pool in a shower'. A rainstorm again came to his mind at Spion Kop in January 1900 where he faced 'a continual driving shower' of Boer shell, machine-gun and rifle fire.[6] The only way in which to avoid being struck was to dig a trench and lie in it.

By the standards of recent wars against native Indian and African armies, casualties were distressingly high and some soldiers wrongly convinced themselves that each Boer was a marksman. Colonel Sir William Lawson, Bt, commanding the 10th Imperial Yeomanry, was more percipient. After one prolonged exchange of fire during a skirmish in June 1900, he observed: 'what a lot of lead it takes fired by both sides to do any damage.'[7]

This was indeed the case, both in South Africa and during the First World War. It was the intensity and volume of fire that sent casualty figures spiralling and, given the need to mass-produce weapons and missiles, transformed war into a test of the belligerents' industrial capacity. This connection between productivity and firepower had been made by British military observers during the war in 1904 and 1905 between two industrial powers, Russia and Japan. The land operations around Port Arthur in North China had involved three million troops and centred on an artillery duel between Japanese besiegers and Russian besieged. If such conditions prevailed in a European conflict, and some analysts predicted they would, then it was of paramount importance to maintain a steady flow of ammunition.[8]

Vast numbers of men would be needed to fire the new weapons, keep them in good working order and service the transport systems that sustained armies in the field. The easiest way to fill the ranks and provide reserves was conscription, which had been adopted by France, Germany, Austria-Hungary and Italy. In each country, young men underwent a period of military training and absorbed those qualities that generals prized: discipline, patriotism and the suppression of the individual will. On completion of his training, the conscript returned to civilian life but remained part of the army of reserve, ready for mobilisation in an emergency. The system was expensive and costs rose steeply as more complicated weapons were introduced; Russia was spending 50 per cent of its income on its armed forces in 1885, and 56 per cent in 1913.

Mobilising and transporting the new armies required precise staff-work and an administrative machine to make them move efficiently and swiftly. Staff-college orthodoxy insisted that the state that deployed its troops in the greatest numbers and with the greatest speed had a considerable advantage, in that it could deliver a decisive hammer blow against its rival. This had happened in the Franco-Prussian war of 1870 to 1871 when German forces had been able to concentrate quickly and in sufficient strength to overwhelm the unprepared and disorganised French. German planners imagined that they could repeat this coup in 1914, but they underestimated the resilience of France and Russia. Like the antagonists in the American Civil War, both nations showed an unexpected capacity to absorb crushing defeats and heavy losses and fight on with as much resolution as ever.

Britain rejected conscription. It was pointless, since the navy remained the basic defence against invasion and there were strong moral objections. The historic antipathy to over-large standing armies remained, and there were plenty of willing amateurs to fill the ranks of the volunteers. Between 1882 and 1904, 953,000 men passed through various local volunteer units.[9] A manpower crisis during the first phase of the Boer War was solved by appeals for men from the white dominions and for young Britons who could ride and shoot to join a new volunteer force, the Imperial Yeomanry. The older yeomanry and the volunteers were merged into the new Territorial Army in 1909, a body that was intended to provide troops for imperial garrisons in the event of the regular army being required to fight on the continent. If this occurred, then substantial reinforcements would be needed from Canada, Australia, New Zealand and South Africa, where a quarter of the Empire's white population now lived. There was every reason to believe that these volunteers would be forthcoming, given that in 1912 the foreign secretary, Sir Edward Grey, had warned dominion prime ministers that their countries' security would be endangered if Germany was allowed to dominate Europe.

In persuading the dominion leaders to throw in their lot with Britain in the event of a war with Germany, Grey had portrayed Kaiser

Wilhelm II as Napoleon reincarnate. How far this was so and to what extent Britain's interests would have been threatened by a German and Austro-Hungarian victory over France and Russia in 1914 are still hard to assess. What is beyond question is that during the final week of July and the first few days of August, the Liberal government needed a cause that would unite the country and swing it behind a war with Germany. There was a strong isolationist element among backbench Liberal MPs and the Labour party, which argued that British interests were not at stake in what in essence was a confrontation between Russia and Austria-Hungary over the latter's perfectly reasonable request to root out terrorist cells inside Serbia.

Public opinion now counted more than ever, not least because in the event of war the government would make unprecedented demands on the entire population. Furthermore, since the reform and redistribution acts of 1884 and 1885, Britain had become a democratic nation, although women were still excluded from the franchise. Since 1870, basic primary education had been made compulsory and the new, largely literate electorate was served by mass-circulation dailies and weeklies which gained considerable political muscle. It was, therefore, vital that national support for a war was as widespread as possible.

As in the Napoleonic and Crimean Wars, Britain needed to appear on the side of moral righteousness. This had also been the case in 1899, when the government claimed that it was fighting the Boers as champions of the uitlanders, foreign workers in the Transvaal who had been denied the vote. In fact, the Boer War was fought to consolidate British paramountcy in southern Africa and naval supremacy in the southern oceans. Important though these were from the perspective of desks in the War, Foreign and Colonial Offices, they did not constitute a cause with any popular emotional appeal, whereas taking up cudgels on behalf of an oppressed minority did.

On 2 August 1914, the German high command solved the cabinet's dilemma by invading Belgium. Britain was offered a welcome moral pretext for intervention, for it could pose as the defender of a weak nation whose neutrality had been underwritten by the great powers, including Germany. This was humbug, but the press and public were taken in and, during August and afterwards, the wrongs of Belgium were a potent rallying call.

The real issue was Britain's security. As the crisis had unfolded, ministers were primarily concerned with what might happen if Britain stayed neutral and Germany won. France would certainly be eclipsed as a great power and Germany would be free to impose its will on central Europe and the Ottoman Empire and possibly annex parts of western Russia. Germany would become a superpower, economically supreme across a huge swathe of the continent, and there was every likelihood that it might absorb parts of France's tropical empire. A German defeat offered an equally bleak scenario. France and Russia had been bound to Britain by ententes agreed in 1904 and 1907, which had concluded fifty years of bickering over competing territorial claims in Asia and Africa. Britain had offered no military commitment beyond a promise not to let German warships approach the French coast, but there had been secret discussions with the French high command about British forces occupying positions on the Franco-Belgian border in the event of a war with Germany. If Britain remained aloof and France and Russia won, then they would be free to reopen old disputes with a former friend that had so conspicuously let them down. Whichever way the war went, a neutral Britain would face a precarious future in the postwar era.

In the short term, there was the frightening prospect of German occupation of the Belgian coastline and perhaps the French Channel ports. An eight-year naval race with Germany had just ended with the Royal Navy achieving a comfortable margin of superiority in home waters. This was not as reassuring as it might have been, for the navy was powerless to defend the country from airships and aeroplanes which, if the Germans occupied Belgium and northern France, could easily reach and bomb targets in eastern and south-eastern England and London. The sea was no longer a moat and, in the prophetic words of H. F. Wyatt, a writer on imperial defence, the British people's 'immunity to personal peril is gone for ever'.[10] This was understood by the government which, in 1912, ordered the construction of a chain of sixteen air stations along the east coast from the Orkneys to the Lizard. The day war was declared anti-aircraft guns were mounted on the roofs of the Admiralty, War Office and Charing Cross station. Four months later, the first lord of the Admiralty, Winston Churchill, admitted to the war cabinet that the Germans were preparing for Zeppelin raids on London which, for the moment, could not be prevented by the infant

Royal Flying Corps (RFC) or the Royal Naval Air Service (RNAS).[11]

The potential of aerial warfare had already been recognised – in 1914, Churchill was considering imitating the Italians in Libya and using airships against tribal rebels in Somaliland. If technical developments were to proceed along current lines and at the present pace, it was more vital than ever that Britain forestalled any German occupation of the Belgian and French coasts. Since the eighteenth century both had been treated as strategically sensitive areas since they were obvious springboards for a cross-Channel invasion. No invasion materialised, but as the war progressed Zeebrugge and Ostend became bases for U-boats which preyed on Channel and North Sea shipping.

Immediate preoccupations about security and long-term apprehensions about Britain's vulnerability and isolation in a postwar world swung the cabinet towards declaring war on Germany. Strategic and political considerations were laid before the Commons by Grey, leaving it to the prime minister, Herbert Asquith, to state the country's moral position. We were fighting, he declared, to safeguard the integrity of small, weak nations and uphold international law. *Punch* caught the mood of the country with one cartoon: on 12 August it showed Belgium as a defiant schoolboy facing a stout Prussian bully. The nation's conscience was clear. 'I hate war, I detest it,' declared Cosmo Lang, Archbishop of York, but his congregation in the minster were reassured that their country was engaged in a 'righteous' conflict in defence of 'honour'.[12] Real and invented German atrocities in Belgium during the next few weeks reinforced British rectitude.

III

In 1914, Britain was primarily a naval power with a relatively small army whose main functions were to guard India, the Suez Canal and various naval bases, and to support the police in Ireland. At the outset of the war, the government adopted a grand strategy which followed lines that had been laid down during the French and Napoleonic Wars. Maritime supremacy came first and had to be upheld come what may. Without it, the Allies would have lost the land war in which the German army was superior to those of France and Russia. As Churchill once remarked to Admiral Sir John Jellicoe, the commander of the Grand Fleet, he was the man who could lose the war in an afternoon.

This was true: the Royal Navy won the war. Command of the sea guaranteed that Britain would survive economically and harness her manpower and industrial capacity to the Allied war-effort. Both were vital after mid 1917 when the Russians had been defeated and the French reduced to exhaustion. Maritime supremacy gave Britain the ability to draw reserves from the dominions and India and to deploy large armies in northern France, the Middle East and East Africa and keep them supplied with all they needed. Early in 1918, when reinforcements were urgently required to meet what turned out to be the fiercest and most persistent German offensive on the Western Front, they were shipped from Egypt and Palestine. Had it succeeded and the severely shaken French army disintegrated, then plans were ready for the navy to cover the evacuation of what was left of the BEF from Dunkirk.[13] If the British army in France had been expelled, Britain would not have been defeated, although in those circumstances it might have had to accept severe German terms.

From the moment it had embarked for France in August 1914, the BEF had been completely dependent on the navy's control of the Channel. Regular patrols by warships and aircraft in search of U-boats, anti-submarine minefields and continual sweeps for German mines kept the narrow seas open. Every tin of bully beef, every bullet and every boot used by the army on the Western Front was transported by ship; and command of the sea permitted that welcome novelty for some soldiers serving on the Continent, regular home leave. Even the French trains that conveyed men and matériel to and from the front line relied on coal imported from Britain, for the Germans controlled three-quarters of French coal production. After the German U-boat campaign was stepped up at the beginning of 1917, the vital Calais–Paris–Marseilles line was down to a week's stock of coal; had it not been replenished, the BEF's logistics would have collapsed.[14] Without naval supremacy there would have been no BEF or Western Front.

Most important of all, but now overlooked, control of the seas gave the Allies access to foreign credit and with it the wherewithal to fight on. The blockade that denied the Germans food also cut them off from the world's money-markets. From mid 1915 onwards, when

Anglo-French dollar reserves had been exhausted, each power was free to sell their overseas investments and secure loans from American finance houses. Deprived of this vital source of income, Germany had to depend on domestic taxation, which the state assemblies did not offer in sufficient amounts, and internal credit raised in the expectation of victory.

Much of the cash raised in the United States was spent there on food for Britain's population and armed forces. Since the 1840s, domestic agriculture had been unable to feed the nation and so Britain had had to depend upon imported food, which was paid for by exports and the returns on overseas investments. In 1913, 75 per cent of the grain, half the eggs and margarine, two-thirds of the butter and four-fifths of the cheese consumed in Britain came from abroad. Forty per cent of Britain's meat supplies were shipped, frozen or canned, from Australia, New Zealand and Argentina. It was the same for petrol and raw materials; the millions of yards of the army's khaki cloth was spun and woven from imported wool. Only in February 1917, when Germany launched a concerted U-boat campaign in which British, Allied and neutral merchantmen were sunk without the hitherto customary warning, was the flow of supplies seriously interrupted.

Resort to a novel and far from reliable weapon appeared the only way in which the Kreigsmarine could challenge the navy's monopoly of seapower even though, as pessimists had foretold, unrestricted U-boat warfare would nudge the United States into the war. The price appeared worth paying: in the first four months of 1917, German submarines sank 2.36 million tons of Allied and neutral shipping, twice the tonnage built in British yards during the entire year. During the late spring and summer, food stocks fell to dangerously low levels. Emergency measures, including tightened domestic rationing and the reallocation of scarce raw materials, staved off disaster. Escorted convoys, barrages of mines in the Channel and North Sea and aerial patrols slowly swung the balance against the U-boats. During 1918, sixty-nine were sunk by Allied action, of which twenty-one were destroyed by depth charges and twenty-two by mines.

The war against the U-boats was a close-run thing. Only in the summer of 1918 did the tonnage of merchantmen launched from British yards exceed that lost to submarines, and then only briefly. The

Germans, too, had difficulty replacing lost U-boats since the high command placed them near the bottom of the national pecking order for matériel and skilled workmen. At the end of September 1918, there was a shift in priorities and a new programme was started to increase the numbers of what Admiral Reinhard Scheer, the former commander of the German battlefleet, called 'the only offensive weapon at our disposal'. In November there were 226 U-boats on the stocks.[15] Had the war continued, Allied navies would have faced a renewed submarine campaign of greater intensity.

The Royal Navy's economic strategy was traditional. By the end of August 1914, a cordon of patrolling warships extended from the Orkneys to the Norwegian coast, cutting off German trade through the North Sea. The Channel was likewise sealed off, and Germany's seaborne trade withered. The consequences were not felt immediately, for Germany was nearly self-sufficient: it grew nearly all of its potatoes and sugar, 90 per cent of its cereal, and produced 60 per cent of its fats, fish and eggs. The shortfalls could have been made up by raising production, although this was hampered by the disappearance of imported organophosphate and artificial nitrate fertilisers and an unbroken sequence of indifferent to poor harvests. Nonetheless, the impact of shortages might have been less damaging if the German government had imposed a system of rationing and food distribution that was perceived to be equitable.

It was, up to a point, but in the mind of ordinary Germans privation appeared unequally distributed. The 'Turnip Winter' of 1916 to 1917 was followed by further dearths which increased social tension at a time when wages were either static or falling. The Royal Navy's blockade did not starve Germany to death, but it substantially contributed to that widespread hunger which ultimately corroded the national will to fight and expressed itself in growing restlessness in the large, urban, industrial centres. This might have been contained if the German army had delivered the long-awaited breakthrough in France, but it failed to do so in the spring of 1918, leaving the German people to face more suffering and sacrifice. This slow war of attrition never attracted headlines and the public then and afterwards never wholly comprehended its crucial effect on the outcome of the war. British prisoners of war, unwilling victims of the shortages, did. One remarked drily that, by the middle of 1918, 'The officer prisoner who receives his parcel is living better than the German.'[16]

Naval paramountcy allowed amphibious forces to converge on German colonies in Africa, the Far East and the Pacific, all of which, with the exception of German East Africa (Tanganyika), were quickly occupied. Seapower also permitted Britain to wage subsidiary but large-scale campaigns against the Turks in Palestine, Syria, the Lebanon and Mesopotamia (Iraq), all of which were occupied by the end of the war. Like the assaults on the German colonies, these sideshows were intended to pay postwar territorial dividends in the manner of their eighteenth-century counterparts. Imperial ambitions, coupled with the mistaken belief that Turkey would crumple easily, lay behind the massive seaborne assault on the Straits in the spring of 1915. Before and during what became known as the Gallipoli campaign, Britain, France and Russia were negotiating agreements for the future partition of the Ottoman Empire. The assumption was that if, as seemed extremely likely, the stalemate in France would continue, then the Allies would be compelled to seek a peace-settlement with old-style bargaining and annexations.

Britain dominated the seas throughout the war because the German High Seas Fleet chose not to seek another Trafalgar and engage the Grand Fleet. And with good reason, for the Royal Navy's battleships outnumbered the Kreigsmarine's by five to three. On occasions, German dreadnoughts did leave port for hit-and-run raids against east coast towns, which provoked considerable popular outrage but did not materially influence the course of the war at sea. In an attempt to even the odds, the High Seas Fleet put to sea on 31 May 1916 with the intention of luring units of the Grand Fleet into a U-boat trap. Signals intelligence provided an indication of German movements and a fleet action was fought off Jutland. After inflicting heavier losses than it sustained, the High Seas Fleet turned tail and dashed for its bases. The balance of seapower remained in Britain's favour; the North Sea and the Channel were virtual British lakes and the blockade was intact. Two subsequent sorties for the High Seas Fleet came to nothing: one at the end of April 1918 miscarried after an accident to a battleship, and another scheduled for 29 to 30 October 1918 provoked a mutiny.

The Royal Navy had won the war, in as much as without maritime paramountcy Britain could never have engaged the German army on the continent with any hope of success. The decision to commit a small, professional army to assist in a continental land war was very much in the strategic tradition that had been established in the eighteenth century. It was not enough, as Kitchener was quick to conclude. Like the Confederacy, Britain would have to improvise a mass army and adapt its economy to transport, feed and equip it for what was going to be a long contest. His presentiments were upheld by the casualty rates; between 22 August and 31 December 1914 the BEF and Indian reinforcements had suffered nearly ninety-six thousand losses, of whom 16,900 had been killed. This period had also revealed a deficiency in ammunition; the allocation of shells to guns had been unrealistically low and, throughout 1915, the BEF was outgunned.

The upshot of the first six months of fighting in France was a stalemate. Static warfare replaced mobile as the antagonists occupied a mesh of well-defended trenches and fortifications which stretched 475 miles from the Belgian coast to the Alps. These works soon became more and more complex, often extending for as much as twenty miles behind the front line. A deadlock followed with defenders enjoying enormous advantages over attackers. For the next three years strategists searched for a method to break this impasse, and the result was trial-and-error generalship.

A decisive victory on the Western Front proved elusive. At the highest level doubts grew as to whether it could be achieved at all, and it was feared that the deadlock would lead to a compromise settlement. Whatever the war's outcome, just to keep fighting would require huge numbers of men, weapons and munitions, and a resolute nation united behind its leaders and willing to overcome the physical hardships and emotional traumas of total war.

IV

There is no better general introduction to the nature of total war, its impact and how people coped with its demands than reading the weekly issues of *War Illustrated*. It first appeared on 26 August 1914 with the pledge that its readership would experience the 'living reality' of war. They got a mixture of photographs, vivid drawings, eyewitness accounts of the action and analyses of events, often written by eminent experts. *War Illustrated* cost twopence (1p) and was designed to attract a lower-middle-class and working-class readership. These were the sections of society that were bearing the brunt of the war. Their young men filled the ranks of the 'new' army and, when the flow of volunteers began to dry up, as it did during 1915, were conscripted. By the beginning of 1917, there were 3.8 million Britons in the services at home and abroad. Their letters were censored and so their families had to rely upon the press to discover what they were doing and how the war was progressing.

Like every other journal and newspaper, *War Illustrated* had to do all in its power to promote unity, a sense of purpose and confidence in the country's leadership, particularly its generals, and to persuade the public that victory was both certain and imminent. Looking through the issues for the spring of 1917 one is struck by the relentlessly optimistic tone. Glancing at such captions as 'The Glorious Battle of Arras', 'Victorious Canadians Who Captured Vimy Ridge' and 'War-Weary Bavarians in their Barbed-Wire Cage', it is hard to believe that the fighting would last for a further eighteen months. There was also stirring but overblown coverage of the achievements of Britain's allies, France, Russia and Italy, all of whom were faltering and on the brink of exhaustion. These stories were contrived to alleviate the war-weariness which intensified as the casualty lists lengthened and the population faced food shortages and rationing. By its nature, total war was bound to resolve itself into a test of national willpower and stamina. After three years of fighting, it was crucial that the public remained unaware of the fact that victory was not preordained and that defeat was a distinct possibility.

At the top, ministers and commanders agonised over the manpower deficit. Throughout the year, the War Office and the Department of Trade were desperately attempting to contrive a formula by which industrial production could be raised without depleting the pool of men available for the Western Front. On the eve of the 1917 Passchendaele offensive, the BEF was calculated to be eighty-three thousand men under strength, and pessimists predicted that the situation would get progressively worse. Less and less help could be expected from Britain's allies; Russia had all but withdrawn from the conflict and France was wobbling. She recovered her equilibrium, but for the remainder of the war British troops had to replace the French in some sectors of the line. Nothing of these crises was revealed in *War Illustrated*, beyond appeals for everyone to make greater exertions and sacrifices. As photographed in its pages, Allied politicians and commanders appeared self-assured and determined.

While those directing the war strove to avoid defeat, *War Illustrated* and the rest of the press did their bit in keeping civilian morale at a high pitch. Never before had there been such demand for buoyant propaganda, for the current U-boat campaign was having repercussions for the housewife's shopping basket. Using emergency legislation, the government responded by banning what were considered unnecessary imports, among which were oranges, bananas and grapes, whose nutritional value was considered to be negligible.[17] The cargo space released was largely filled with frozen meat and cereals, but not enough to prevent rationing. At the close of the year, government agencies had taken charge of the meat trade at every level and soon afterwards imposed limits on how much could be eaten. What previous generations would have considered a gross infraction of personal freedom was accepted because nine-tenths of imported meat was diverted to feed the soldiers at the front.

The nation was asked to feed itself. *War Illustrated* offered reassuring photographs of public schoolboys with spades preparing to dig potato patches, but not, it seems, on their playing fields. These pictures were clear evidence that all classes were pulling together and that the better-off were not shirking their duty, contrary to rumour. In Leicester, 'council schoolboys' dug up local parks for potato planting and everywhere women were undertaking work that had hitherto been done by men. In Chester they swept the streets, in Glasgow they heaved sacks of coal, and elsewhere they were firefighters and factory hands; one photograph shows a group holding the steel helmets they had just produced. While the women worked, men trained and held the line in France.

There was some compensation for these inconveniences in the reports that the Allied blockade was causing extensive privation throughout Germany. Prices for horseflesh were rising, seal meat was being offered and spurned, eggs were scarce, there was a dearth of chickens and ration quotas for staples were being cut. Advertisements were said to have appeared in some newspapers requesting dogs for cooking.[18] While hungry Germans contemplated eating dogs, some hungry Britons were demanding a wholesale slaughter of dogs to make their food available for humans. No dogs were killed, although in France military policemen attached to the provost-marshal's department of the Royal Navy Division were inexplicably shooting dogs in September 1916.[19]

Official censors made sure that the public did not read about this execution of dogs, which was just as well for the news would have provoked fury. The dog was regularly portrayed as the front-line soldier's companion, sharing with his master the discomforts and perils of the trenches. Such reports of canine fidelity were just what the government wanted civilians to read. An undated Christmas card sent by the Press Bureau showed two girls in bathing costumes, one scantily clad, representing 'Publicity' and the other, prim and well covered, representing 'Censorship'.[20] There was no better summary of what the government expected from newspapers: stories that would boost morale, and suppression of information that might cause despondency and panic or assist the enemy's intelligence services.

Dependent on newspapers for their knowledge of the war, the public succumbed easily to alarms. On 30 August 1914, The Times broke two of its conventions by publishing on a Sunday and placing news stories on the front page. They made disturbing reading, with references to 'Broken British Regiments', the German 'Tidal Wave' and 'terrible' losses suffered by the BEF. According to the parson of Yoxford, the 'Sabbath peace' of rural Suffolk was broken by this terrible news and his parishioners put in a fluster. The arrival of the special edition turned the Shropshire village of Tenbury 'into a terrible state of alarm and caused untold misery and alarm'.[21] F. E. Smith, the former Tory firebrand and director of the government's new Press Bureau, had officially censored the piece but gave it his private blessing. City and town dwellers appear to have kept their composure.

D-notices, which survive to this day, warned editors not to print stories that might help German intelligence, particularly any relating to the movements and dispositions of ships and men. Infringements occurred. On 12 September 1914, the *Burnley Express and Advertiser* proudly announced the departure of the East Lancashire territorials with details of their route and eventual destination, Egypt. The editor was upbraided and, chastened, he published an apology which, of course, drew further attention to the story.[22] Rumours were always a nuisance, especially if they were close to the truth. The 'Londoner's Diary' of the *Evening Standard* made a speciality of leaking stories that appeared to come from high-level sources. At the height of the U-boat crisis in May 1917, the columnist confided that: 'I was talking today to a man who professed to know the real position,' who claimed that German submarine losses were no more than three a week which equalled the number launched.[23]

Contrary to what is so often assumed, the British people were not shielded from the forensic realities of death at the front. Officially approved stereoscopic pictures of front-line scenes showed British and German corpses.[24] An eyewitness newspaper report of a gas unit in action during the Somme offensive in July 1916 described how it came under artillery fire. 'In other bays men are struck by flying shell pieces or their limbs fly from them, for flesh and bone are but poor weak stuff against high explosives.' But the enemy was suffering as well. 'Over in the German trenches hundreds of men are choking and gasping in agony for an hour before they die, Fritz has been made to quaff his own medicine.'[25] Official censors and editors supposed that civilian grief and privation were somehow diminished or relieved by the knowledge that things were worse for the enemy.

As for our soldiers, they were doing their duty in a manly and cheerful fashion. This was plain from the official film, *The Battle of the Somme*, which was shown in cinemas throughout the summer and autumn of 1916. It was a box-office success and was shown in nearly all the 4500 cinemas in Britain, earning thirty thousand pounds. The material was presented in that sombre, factual manner that characterised official British war films. Hysterical Hun-hating was absent and one sequence highlighted comradely humanity; the caption read: 'British wounded and nerve-shattered German prisoners arriving. Officer giving drink and Tommies offering cigarettes to German prisoners.' Death was frequently shown and many were upset by footage that showed a unit going over the top and one man falling dead – actually one of the film's few faked sequences. Herbert Henley Henson, the Dean of Durham, protested to *The Times* 'against an entertainment which wounds the heart and violates the very sanctity of bereavement'. This was cant coming from a cleric who had spoken at recruiting-rallies to persuade young men like the one in the film to join up.[26] The film of the Somme was an enormous success; for the first time civilians got an authentic impression of the nature of front-line warfare and some of its horrors. Perhaps it was all too much for audiences, for *The German Retreat and the Battle of Arras* of 1917 contained fewer images of death and wounded men.[27]

Death in battle ought not unduly to have disturbed cinema-goers in 1916. Wounded men convalescing and the permanently maimed were an everyday sight. The national and provincial press printed reports and letters from soldiers that did not shun the nastiest aspects of the battlefield as they had done in previous wars.

What mattered was that every sacrifice could be justified. Families who received the War Office telegrams that announced the deaths of loved ones were repeatedly assured that they had died fighting an inhuman foe who was bent on overturning civilisation. A largely invented abstraction – 'Prussian militarism' – was identified as the principal enemy, an aggressive and amoral force that threatened to overwhelm Europe and reshape it in the interests of Germany. Churchmen damned militarism as demonic; in 1915, Dean Inge comforted Easter Sunday worshippers in St Paul's, many of them in mourning, with the assertion that British men fought with 'a pure and elevated patriotism' against dark forces.[28] Manifestations of this militarism were plentiful and took the form of atrocity stories that illustrated German arrogance and callousness. The press and government propaganda agencies exploited such incidents for all they were worth to create a picture of a ruthless and barbaric adversary who would stop at nothing to get his way. The Kaiser was represented as a second Napoleon, a bloodthirsty and vainglorious megalomaniac.

Demonising the Kaiser could not entirely mask the fact that Britain's ally, Russia, was the most oppressive and vicious tyranny in Europe. The deposition of Czar Nicholas II in March 1917 and his replacement by a parliamentary régime offered British propagandists a glimmer of hope, which became a flame when the United States entered the war the following April. President Woodrow Wilson's pleas for self-determination throughout central Europe gave Britain the opportunity to announce itself as unequivocally on the side of democracy. 'We are fighting for freedom and for nations to decide for themselves how they are to be governed,' Rudyard Kipling proclaimed at a Folkestone war-rally in May 1918. Like the clergy, sympathetic authors and poets were expected to do their bit in a total war, most notably in easing the nation's conscience.

In the earlier absence of a plausible moral cause, British propagandists had fallen back on the barbarism of the 'Hun' (the expression had first been used by the Kaiser in 1900 when he urged German troops suppressing the Boxer uprising in China to behave like 'Huns'). The barbaric resonance of the word remained and made it easy for the British press to portray the individual German soldier as a loathsome and contemptible creature. Whereas the emaciated Frenchman of the cartoonists of the Napoleonic War had been a comic figure, the German was an uncouth, menacing monster. In an article entitled 'Cultured Kameraden: Study in Hun Physiognomy', the *War Illustrated* for 24 February 1917 showed a series of snapshot-sized photographs of German prisoners of war. Each had been selected for his coarse features and the result was a sequence of ogreish, battle-weary, shifty and sullen faces. They revealed 'truculence, cunning, meanness and criminal hostility', while several were 'marked by features associated with criminality', and 'some approximate to the idiot type'. 'Men of this low type' were presently occupying lands from which the male population had departed and 'they are encouraged to treat the women and children as they please'.

Contrived racial hatred formed a powerful bond of national unity. It was widely promoted at home, where it was most passionate, and at the front, where it was far less so and needed cultivation. An eighteen-year-old volunteer remembered how he was prepared for combat at Etaples training camp in 1917. Ordered to thrust his bayonet into a stuffed figure, he was told he was a 'Bloody Boche'. 'You hate him,' the instructor would bellow, 'kill the bugger.' A half-hearted jab at the dummy provoked rage: 'You must kill the bastard or he will kill you, come on and hate the bugger and put some thrust into the bayonet.'[29]

The bayonet charge was highly popular with *War Illustrated* because it exemplified the superior will and strength of the British fighting man and presented the opportunity for plenty of stirring, dramatic pictures. Taking their cue from the propaganda photographs, artists portrayed the German infantryman as a lumpish, crop-headed creature who was always flinching, running away or staring with wide-eyed horror as he was about to be bayoneted. Early in 1917, a series of small-scale cavalry actions provided illustrators with a rare chance to depict war's ancient glory, and they responded with scenes of horsemen galloping pell-mell at a terrified foe.

Images from the past were outnumbered by others that showed the awesome apparatus of modern, industrial warfare: battleships, submarines, aircraft, armoured cars, tanks and mighty artillery pieces. Not only did Britain possess brave men capable of killing their enemies face to face with cold steel, it could contrive and manufacture an impressive range of deadly and potentially war-winning gadgetry.

V

Technology now dominated the battlefield. This was clear from the calculus of death: the infantry suffered one casualty for every 0.5 they inflicted, the artillery one for every ten, and gas units one for every forty.[30] Most of the technology was relatively new; telephones, bicycles, motor-cars and lorries, wireless telegraphy and aircraft had all appeared and been developed during the thirty years before the war. Other inventions were a direct response to the war. Armoured cars appeared in the autumn of 1914; chlorine gas was first used by the Germans at Ypres in April 1915; flamethrowers were introduced (again by the Germans) at Hooge the following July; and a British invention, the tank, made its debut at the battle of Flers-Courcelette in September 1916. Each new weapon took the enemy by surprise, briefly unnerved him and was immediately copied. A crash, seven-week research, production and training programme enabled the British to launch a gas attack at Loos in September 1915. In June 1917, George V watched a demonstration of a new flamethrower which astonished attendant journalists. One reported that, 'A battalion of men would be charred like burnt sticks if it touched them for a second.'[31]

After watching a gas attack, another newspaperman compared the contraptions that delivered it to the inventions of H. G. Wells.[32] The readers would have known exactly what he meant. Over the preceding twenty years, Wells's futuristic writings had suggested how war might evolve through the application of current scientific and technical knowledge. His mind leapt ahead to a time when biological, chemical and possibly atomic weapons would be introduced, although he was uncertain of the pace of this progress. Where it could end was revealed in *The War of the Worlds*, in which a parallel but far more advanced civilisation on Mars invades the Earth with a superior and irresistible range of armaments.

Henceforward, science would dictate how wars were fought; of this Wells had no doubt. Writing in 1902, he predicted that soldiers armed with accurate, quick-firing rifles would transform the battlefield into a 'deadlock of essentially defensive marksmen'. Complex networks of entrenchments would be excavated behind the front line and artillery fire would be directed by observers in 'great multitudes of balloons'. There would also be 'flying machines', but Wells dismissed the submarine as impractical.[33] Moreover, and this form of collectivism appealed to Wells the socialist, 'the State will be organised as a whole FN AUTIC as a whole, it will have triumphantly asserted the universal duty of its citizens.' In the process, the old 'privileged' army officer (i.e. the ex-public school amateur) would be superseded by a technocrat, whose qualification to command was his mastery of the new machinery of war. All this showed remarkable foresight, although Wells was drawing a picture of warfare in the middle of the century.

Once the war was underway, Wells recognised that it was fitting the pattern he had foretold. In a letter to *The Times* in June 1915, he demanded the 'mobilising' of our 'inventive and scientific forces' into a 'Bureau for Inventors'. 'A modern politician,' he urged, 'has no more special aptitude for making war than he has for diagnosing diseases or planning an electric railway system. It is a technical business.'[34] This was fair, in that most ministers, civil servants and commanders (the navy excepted) had a limited knowledge of the principles of the science, but unfair in that they were susceptible, often to the point of impetuosity, to any idea that might yield war-winning weapons. Speed was vital, for Germany had a head start. Before the war there had been close co-operation between its armed forces and the chemical, electronics and metallurgical industries, which were outpacing their British counterparts in terms of research.[35]

Wells's plea caught the popular imagination, and the press and the public clamoured for new gadgets. During 1915 and 1916 there was an official 'mobilisation' of scientists for the war-effort. 'Inventions were rather the fashion,' remembered Brigadier-General John Charteris, Haig's intelligence chief. In consequence, the inventor of a 'death ray' was officially permitted to demonstrate his device, which appeared to work, given that its animal 'target' had previously been given strychnine.[36]

The promotion of new ideas inevitably led to tension between commanders, who thought they knew best how to wage war, and politicians and journalists, who believed that the professionals had closed and narrow minds. Differences over the application of science to war added to the undercurrents of suspicion between ministers and the army's high command, which were close to the surface throughout the war.[37]

Both Churchill (minister for munitions from 1917 to 1918 and secretary of state for war from 1918 to 1921) and Lloyd George (minister for munitions from 1915 to 1916, secretary of state for war in 1916 and prime minister from 1916 to 1922) were keen advocates of the tank, and later claimed that its potential as a decisive weapon had never been realised by the generals who, in Churchill's scathing words, had been 'content to fight machine-gun bullets with the breasts of gallant men'. Preliminary work had begun on the tank at the beginning of 1915 and, by the close of the year, Churchill had been able to persuade Haig of the weapon's viability. The field-marshal asked for 150 to be ready for the Somme offensive in July 1916, but production snags delayed their delivery until September.[38] Brilliant concepts alone were useless. New weapons had to be carefully designed and tested before production, which was a slow process. It took between seven months and a year for a new aircraft to pass from the drawing-board to the stage when full-sized prototypes were ready for flight-trials.[39]

Although the value of aerial photography had been appreciated from the first months of the war, it was only at the beginning of 1917 that techniques had been perfected that exactly correlated aerial images with maps, making it possible for pilots and gunners to identify enemy positions and batteries.[40] Accurate aerial surveys required air superiority over the sectors to be photographed, which needed fast, nimble fighters armed with machine-guns. Adapting aircraft for combat and bombing presented a rash of problems, which were slowly solved. Primitive bomb-sights appeared in 1915, and machine-guns specifically designed for mounting on aeroplanes a year later. Synchronising these guns with the aircraft's propellers so that they could safely fire through them was the greatest hurdle of all. It was overcome for the Germans by the Dutch engineer, Anthony Fokker, in the summer of 1915. For the next twelve months this technical advantage gave the Germans aerial supremacy over the Western Front.

The British response to Fokker's breakthrough was a device contrived by a Russian naval aviator and the ingenious F. W. Scarff, an RNAS warrant-officer and engineer who had previously developed a bomb-sight and machine-gun mounting for aircraft. Their invention was fitted to British machines in time for the Somme offensive, during which the RFC re-established aerial parity. George Constantinesco, a Romanian mathematician, produced a more sophisticated and efficient engine/machine gun synchroniser which was adopted by the RAF (the Royal Air Force, formed in April 1918 by the amalgamation of the RFC and the RNAS) in the closing months of the war. It is revealing that each of these inventors came from outside the traditional military and naval élites; Scarff, though an NCO, fitted closely Wells's picture of the future technical officer. So, too, did William Bentley, a young motor-car engineer who joined the RNAS and applied his knowledge of aluminium and light alloys to aircraft engines, thus reducing their weight.[41]

The ultimate and most demanding test of all new technology was on the battlefield, where unforeseen technical faults were exposed. In the three weeks after the BEF's first use of gas, over two thousand British soldiers were accidentally injured by leakages or unpredictable shifts in the wind direction that blew the chlorine back across their own lines. A similar mishap occurred at Messines on 1 September 1916 when nineteen were killed.[42] Practical problems emerged during early tank actions. They moved at a slower pace than the infantry, were conspicuous artillery targets, and their eight-man crews laboured in cramped conditions and were nauseated by carbon monoxide and petrol fumes.

Tanks were heavy and therefore functioned only on firm ground, a fact that did not prevent the BEF's high command from deploying them during the Passchendaele offensive, when 190 were abandoned after being immobilised in the mud.[43]

Over-hasty development, improvisation and the inability of many component makers to standardise their products caused mechanical defects which were exposed in campaign conditions. Pilots of the splendidly named Bristol Bullet biplane discovered that the petrol-supply pipes on the Gnome engine regularly became detached because of a manufacturing flaw. Other engines possessed their own, equally dangerous idiosyncrasies.[44] Nothing like this happened in Wellsian science fiction where gadgets never appeared to go wrong; in reality they did, and frequently. When it worked, technology was the commander's servant. But what understanding did he have of what it could or could not do? The answer was very little, before 1917, unless he was a persistent man with an inquiring mind. In that year GHQ (general headquarters) of the BEF began issuing pamphlets, for circulation among officers commanding armies, divisions, brigades and battalions, that explained how they could apply new technical developments. Thereafter, these handbooks were regularly updated.[45]

Progress in communications was one the subjects covered. Given the expanded area of the battlefields and the numbers of units deployed, advances in this area were surprisingly few and haphazard before 1917. Marconi wireless transmitters and receivers had been employed in the Boer War and operations against the 'Mad Mullah' in Somaliland in 1902 and 1903. Detachments of wireless signallers were attached to the BEF in 1914, but front-line communications at corps, brigade and battalion level relied heavily on telephones, which the Germans were expert at tapping and whose lines were easily snapped by shell fire. The organisation of signals detachments was chaotic and there was an unwise dependence on old methods. Messages were regularly delivered by pigeons, cyclists, runners and dogs. Basic training in 'communications' for new recruits to the Middlesex Regiment in 1915 consisted of 'shouting to officers across the Parade Ground in a loud and clear enough voice to be understood'.[46] How this might be accomplished against the noise of shell and small-arms fire was never explained.

In September 1916, Flight-Lieutenant P. S. Jackson-Taylor of the

RFC was detached for signals exercises with cavalry units, held with unintended historic irony near Crécy. Trials were undertaken with flares, semaphore flags, an Aldis lamp, wireless telegraphy and messages attached to weights. Jackson-Taylor was well aware of the demand for an efficient communication system; on a recent mission he had been sent in search of a unit of Indian lancers that had got 'lost' behind German lines.[47] By this time, research was underway in wireless telephony; in February 1916, Kitchener had put on headphones and listened to the voice of a pilot flying overhead during a snowstorm at St Omer.[48]

This demonstration and the Crécy experiments were part of a wider programme contrived to expedite the transmission of intelligence between commanders of all levels. Wireless was an obvious answer, but it had its drawbacks. Transmitters and receivers were cumbersome and fragile and, when installed in aircraft, had to be able to cope with engine noise and turbulence. On the ground, the heavier pieces of equipment could only be carried in lorries, while the smaller ones, which were used in forward positions, had to be manhandled along with their batteries. Aerials made conspicuous targets, and the Germans were good at intercepting and decoding messages.[49] These disadvantages were outweighed by the value of wireless in providing quick intelligence of tactical developments, enemy movements and the sites of his batteries. All this emerged during the last phase of the war on the Western Front between August and November 1918, when British forces began a campaign of movement as the Germans fell back.

Revealingly, the fullest understanding of technology's applications was among the specialist technical élites that had emerged alongside the new weaponry: the Tank Corps and the RAF. In July 1918, officers from 8 Squadron and the Tank Corps worked in harness, each training with the other and together endeavouring to contrive the means to transmit spoken wireless messages between aircraft and tanks. After a month, they had found a way in which air-to-ground signals could be exchanged at ranges of up to six miles. The scheme was not tried out under battle conditions, for it was feared that if aircraft carrying the new and highly secret radios crashed they would fall into German hands.[50] It was from the cockpit of a crashed Gotha bomber that the British had discovered about German oxygen-masks.

Close air-to-ground co-operation using wireless was employed by reconnaissance aircraft and artillery during the battle of Bapaume on 8 September, when 80 per cent of German batteries destroyed by British fire were pinpointed by aerial reconnaissance.[51] To correlate this flow of wireless information, an intelligence unit was established (Wireless Central Information Bureau) which distributed it, identified targets for bombardment or bombing and contacted available squadrons.[52] The final weeks of the war witnessed the first step towards the electronic battlefield of the late twentieth century.

Wireless gave a general the capacity to co-ordinate as exactly as possible all the arms at his disposal and deliver rapid responses to changing tactical situations. That this was so in the summer of 1918 owed much to a greater mental rigour and flexibility among the high command, which was first detectable during 1917.[53] In his *Memoirs of an Infantry Officer* Siegfried Sassoon recalled an exchange that followed his and his colleagues' chance encounter with a staff officer during 1916: "'I suppose those brass-hats [staff officers] do know a hell of a lot about it all, don't they Julian?' I queried. Durley replied that he hoped they'd learned something since last autumn when they'd allowed the infantry to educate themselves at Loos, regardless of expense. "They've got to learn their job, as they go along, like the rest of us," he added sagely.'[54]

VI

They did, with painful slowness, and in time a new army emerged to fight a new type of war. The most striking change in its composition was the growth in the numbers of men employed in technical, logistical and medical services.

	August 1914	November 1918
Royal Artillery, Royal Horse Artillery, Royal Garrison Artillery	92,920	548,780
Royal Engineers	11,700	234,370
Royal Army Medical Corps	18,400	134,400

In 1914 the strength of the Royal Army Service Corps (RASC) attached to the BEF was 6400; by November 1918 it had risen to 159,000, of whom over half drove or maintained the fifty-seven thousand lorries, vans, ambulances, cars and motorbikes then in France. And yet the BEF was still far from being mechanised. Horses and mules continued to undertake much of the army's transport work. In August 1918 there were 305,670 horses, including cavalry mounts, and eighty-one thousand mules in France. Their wellbeing was in the hands of 50,500 RASC men and a further 27,300 from the Royal Army Veterinary Corps.[55] Animal losses were high throughout the war, with a wastage rate of between 12 and 28 per cent; stocks were mainly replenished from North America which supplied the army with 428,600 horses and 275,000 mules.

The new technical units had mushroomed. The Tank Corps, formed in May 1916, grew from 1200 to 28,300 by November 1918 and the Machine-Gun Corps, created the following month, from 576 to 119,990. The RFC detachment in France in August 1914 had consisted of sixty-six aircraft and 1430 men; by 1918 the RAF's strength was 150,000 and there were 1364 machines in France alone. During 1917 the shortage of skilled fitters and riggers had led to the recruitment of women. By the end of the war the fledgling Women's Royal Air Force (WRAF) contained 8400 women employed as clerks, cooks, drivers and storekeepers.[56]

The simultaneous appearance of the Queen Mary's Auxiliary Army Corps (QMAAC, later the Women's Royal Army Corps, WRAC) and the Women's Royal Naval Service (WRNS or more commonly 'Wrens') performing similar duties, was a reminder that total war embraced the entire population. Women typing and filing, tightening the struts of aeroplanes or driving staff-cars were undertaking tasks that released soldiers for the front line, which was where the Germans would be beaten, or so the generals convinced themselves.

2

Their officers' example: Preparation for command and civil war postponed, 1870–1914

I

One evening towards the end of October 1897, in the middle of a long and laborious punitive expedition against the Pathans of the North-West Frontier, the officers of the Seaforth Highlanders dined formally. Their meal was continually interrupted by Afridi snipers, who wounded one officer. Unperturbed, his brothers-in-arms proceeded to finish their dinner at the correct pace and according to hallowed protocol. Captain Aylmer Haldane was struck by the nonchalance of the Indian attendants: 'The native servants were very calm while waiting on us and, as they were standing up and we sitting on chairs, I admired their courage.'[1] One hopes that the mess silver had been well polished and the port properly decanted.

Depending on one's prejudices, this incident was a shining example of either the composure and casual gallantry of the late Victorian and Edwardian officer caste, or its addiction to absurd ritual and carelessness with other men's lives. At the time, the Seaforths' conduct would have been applauded by officers everywhere and, if it had been reported by any of the war correspondents present, would have been portrayed as a glowing example of those qualities that underpinned the Empire. Today, the whole affair appears slightly ridiculous, drawing to mind a scene at the end of an early 1970s comedy film, *Carry on up the Khyber*.

Haldane, who recorded the dinner in his diary, was then in his thirty-sixth year, a career soldier who would successively serve in the Boer War, where he was in charge of the armoured train whose ambush led to Churchill's capture, and the First World War, where he commanded at brigade and corps level. Afterwards, and like many other generals, he became a proconsul ruling over the newly annexed province of Iraq. A native uprising there in 1920 was his undoing and he passed out of public life, carrying with him a conviction that his talents had never been acknowledged by his contemporaries. A gaunt, dignified figure, he volunteered for employment at the War Office at the outbreak of war in 1939. There were no jobs for seventy-seven-year-old veterans and he was rebuffed, which greatly hurt his feelings. He reprimanded the officers and men he encountered during his visit for the slovenliness of their appearance, departed and eventually became an air raid warden.[2] His treatment was similar to that of another game but elderly veteran, General Wynne-Candy, the hero of the 1944 film *The Rise and Fall of Colonel Blimp*.

The 'Colonel Blimp' of the title was a figure of ridicule. The original Blimp was the interwar invention of the cartoonist David Low, who rendered him as an overweight, retired officer with the obligatory walrus moustache and reactionary opinions. The likeness between him and generals of the First World War was obvious, unflattering and deliberate. The caricature became a stereotype of that generation of officers who had sipped port and chatted about past polo chukkas under the fire of Pathan jezails, and ended their careers presiding over the mass slaughter of civilians turned soldiers in the trenches.

Posterity has been unkind to the First World War generals. Their vilification began once a country stunned by the losses had recovered and started analysing what had actually happened. Disillusioned junior officers with literary talents dealt the first blows. Robert Graves's and Edmund Blunden's memoirs presented themselves and the men they had led at the front as the helpless victims of distant, Olympian generals. The growing revulsion against the horrors of war embraced those who had allowed it to be waged in such a harrowing way. The public gained a further insight into the realities of war through the sombre film of Remarque's *All Quiet on the Western Front* which was released in June 1930. 'No film has yet depicted the horror and waste of war more forcibly,' wrote the *Spectator*'s critic.

The publication, from 1933 onwards, of the six volumes of Lloyd George's political memoirs challenged the judgement of the generals, who were wrongheaded and deceitful. On one occasion the prime minister suspected that a 'weedy lot' of German prisoners of war had been corralled for his inspection in 1917 to demonstrate GHQ's dubious claim that the German soldier's morale was plummeting. After Passchendaele, Lloyd George was repelled at the manner in which the generals blamed everyone but themselves for the offensive's setbacks. Given the recent losses, there was something deeply unpleasant about a corps commander, General Sir Ivor Maxse, alleging that wounded men on leave were broadcasting stories of his colleagues' shortcomings.

After the war, the generals continued to protect their own reputations with falsehoods. Brigadier-General Sir James Edmonds, compiler of the official histories of the campaigns in France which began appearing in 1922, was niggardly with the truth. 'I have to write of Haig with my tongue in my cheek,' he once confessed to Captain Basil Liddell Hart. 'One can't tell the truth. He was really above the average – or rather below the average – in stupidity.'[3] Liddell Hart, a former infantry officer and military guru of the interwar years, felt no such inhibitions and his books and articles slated the incompetence of Haig and his subordinates. Liddell Hart warmly endorsed Alan Clark's indictment, *The Donkeys* (1961), which took its title from the alleged remark of a German general that the British soldiers were 'lions led by donkeys'. Clark's polemic was the inspiration for the musical *Oh! What a Lovely War* and its film version of 1969, which presented Haig and the rest of the high command as a band of snobbish incompetents, breezily indifferent to the sufferings of the ordinary soldier. This image has stuck and recent generations, whose knowledge of the war has been largely gained through the writings of a handful of soldier-poets, have been hostile and unforgiving towards their generals.

For some, the assaults of historians did not go far enough. In 1998 a press campaign to have Haig's equestrian statue prised from its plinth in

Whitehall gathered a brief momentum, and there are persistent demands that his portrait should be removed from the walls of two venerable Scottish institutions.[4] Blimp has recently resurfaced in the form of General Melchett in the television comedy *Blackadder Goes Forth*. There, he is a brigade commander, a rotund, moustached figure who sits behind a desk in a château far from the trenches and thinks and speaks in the clichés of the public school playing field. A glance through the memoirs of many actual Melchetts suggests that the parody is not too remote from reality.

What is revealing, and infuriating to the guardians of the generals' reputations, is that their systematic denigration has been widely accepted by the public, and understandably so. Between the wars, the high command provided a scapegoat for losses that could only have been justified, if, as official propaganda had alleged, they had died in 'a war to end wars'. It did not, as events in Europe and Asia soon made clear. The dead, and, for that matter, everyone who had done their duty, appeared to have been cynically manipulated by politicians and generals who had exploited their sense of duty, bravery and patriotism. The country had learned a painful lesson, which was why in 1933 members of the Oxford Union voted not to 'fight for King and Country'. For the first and only time in British history pacifism became a political force to be reckoned with.

Of course, there had been manic flag-waving during the Napoleonic, Crimean and Boer Wars, and to a large extent the frenzied outburst of popular patriotism in 1914 was a revival of this. John Bull was alive, as pugnacious as ever and itching to lay into 'Kaiser Bill'. But there was a difference; three years of enormous casualties, no victories and increasing domestic privation made it impossible to sustain the early patriotic euphoria. By 1917 it had been superseded by a mood of defiance and stubbornness; both at home and at the front Britons would 'see it through' come what may. After the war there was a sigh of relief rather than the triumphal blaring of trumpets. The fruits of victory were sparse and sour-tasting. Economic instability, unemployment and industrial unrest at home, and popular insurrections in Ireland, Egypt and India, were the bleak features of the immediate postwar world. Nor was there the consolation of a heroic leadership that exemplified national virtues and won battles. No Nelson or Wellington emerged from the First

World War. Its survivors revealingly turned to someone from outside the traditional, aristocratic martial caste, a civilian-in-arms, Colonel T. E. Lawrence, as a national hero. He, too, condemned the performance of the generals: 'they did their best, but it was a poor best.'

And yet, like Wellington, the generals who had led armies would have agreed that command in war was their birthright. Haig (the son of a prosperous whisky distiller with gentry pretensions) and the rest of the 'brass-hats' had severely bruised the nation's faith in gentlemen as natural leaders. It was left to Churchill, the grandson of a duke, to follow Wellington's example and restore national confidence in his class, in what turned out to be the last and most illustrious display of aristocratic wartime leadership.

II

Nonetheless, faith in what by now was an ancient principle remained strong after the war. John Birley, a Wykehamist neurologist who had served with the RFC/RAF, was convinced that the experience of war had strengthened the concept of gentlemen making the best officers. He explained why to an audience of medical men in 1923. Gentlemen were 'accustomed to rule as lords of the land, they had been wont to indulge their leisure in vigorous and dangerous sports and pursuits, and to cultivate the spirit of adventure with a strict if inelastic code of class discipline.'[5] The pilot, who had often been described as a 'knight' of the skies, required the same qualities as distinguished his armoured predecessor or, for that matter, Nelson's or Wellington's officers. Readers of John Buchan will recognise the close similarity between the characteristics of Birley's ideal airman and those of Brigadier-General Sir Richard Hannay and his companions in adventure.

And, of course, there was the old paternalism. 'I cannot desert my men, it would be awful to do so under such appalling circumstances, I must return to them,' Colonel F. H. Neish repeated several times as he wandered blindly through the darkness near Bertry on the night of 25 to 26 August 1916. His men, the 1st Gordon Highlanders, were lost, isolated and outnumbered by pursuing Germans to whom they eventually surrendered.[6] Nearly five years later, those present had to relive that night when a formal inquiry investigated whether the colonel, his brothers-in-arms or the battalion had been compromised by this misfortune. Personal and regimental honour were sacrosanct to an officer. Professional ineptitude or a lack of initiative were unforgivable, as Lieutenant Ommaney discovered when he was severely reprimanded for his failing to go on board the captured U-39 (a rare prize) in February 1917 and then allowing it to sink.[7]

The code and values of officers had remained constant since 1815, and there had been little change in their social background. In 1870, Gladstone's Liberal administration had fulfilled its pledge to open up all levels of government to men of talent by abolishing the purchase of commissions. The old hurdles of low pay and costly, obligatory outgoings remained and so, if they were to live in the manner of gentlemen, officers had to depend on family subsidies. In 1912, 9 per cent of newly commissioned officers were from titled families, 32 per cent were the sons of country landowners, and the rest were from the upper sections of the middle class, a group that encompassed army and naval officers, lawyers, clergymen of the established churches and physicians.[8] More than half of the senior ranks had been brought up in the country at a time when most Britons lived in towns and cities. Fashionable regiments maintained their exclusiveness; over four-fifths of the Guards and Household Cavalry officers were from the aristocracy. When the latter advanced at Arras in April 1917 officers were heard singing 'The Eton Boating Song'.

Whatever their parentage, officers were invariably the products of the post-Arnoldian public schools. It would be impossible to overestimate the influence of these institutions which shaped the thinking, not only of generations of army and naval officers, but of the entire ruling élite of Britain from the late nineteenth century to the mid twentieth. If, in the forty years before the outbreak of the war, a father had been asked what he expected for his son from a public school, he would have answered: 'I want him to be taught the morals and manners of a gentleman; I wish him to play games; and I hope that he will make friends who will be useful to him in after life.'[9] The modern public school would do all in its power to accomplish this by a mixture of example and intimidation.

The reformed schools were very different places from their chaotic but freer predecessors. A naval officer who had attended Harrow in the 1840s recalled pitched battles with local boys which had all 'the excitement of war' and an absence of 'close supervision' which encouraged 'self-reliance' and 'codes of honour' among pupils.[10] The latter were still fostered thirty years later, but in a restrained atmosphere and under the tight control of a hierarchy of prefects and predominantly clerical headmasters. There were considerable variations in approach and methods among the reformed public schools, but a general agreement as to the qualities that were to be encouraged. If they did their job properly, the public schools would produce a Christian gentleman. He was a sturdy chap, pure in thought and possessed 'character'; that is to say he was truthful, felt a responsibility for the less fortunate, was daring and endured adversity without complaint. This stoicism, together with a love of fair play, was learned from long hours on the rugger pitch or the cricket square where he also absorbed lessons in self-discipline. The interests of the team always overrode private feelings and ambitions, and the rules of the game were inviolable.

When he left school, this young Spartan carried with him the knowledge that his peculiar virtues were those that his country respected and needed. 'British manliness and pluck' were regularly extolled by the headmaster of the Jesuit Beaumont College in the 1880s, and he wrathfully told an American pupil who howled after a beating that his conduct was 'UnBritish'.[11] According to one of their Edwardian school songs (still lustily sung annually on the day of a gruelling cross-country race, the 'Long Run'), Sedbergh athletes were expected to 'laugh at pain'. This was how officers should behave in adversity. Writing in 1918, a gunner observed that his comrades did not expect officers to 'grouse' publicly, although he guessed that they did so in private.[12] Above all, the officer had to be a man who could command respect. Just before the outbreak of war, the ageing national hero Field-Marshal Lord Roberts of Kandahar told the Reverend Edward Lyttleton, the headmaster of Eton, how many rankers had told him of their admiration for public school officers as 'men', which was evidence that the public schools had the right formula for teaching leadership.[13] 'Training, character and ability and the powers of leadership' distinguished the Oxford and Cambridge blues and public school alumni who were flocking to the Public School Battalion, declared a Unionist

MP in March 1915. It went without saying that these young men were destined for commissions; a recruiting advertisement for the battalion promised suitably qualified volunteers that it offered a 'short and pleasant way to promotion'.[14]

Since the 1870s, hardy games players with prefectorial experience had been directed by headmasters towards Sandhurst and Woolwich and coached for their entrance exams in special classes. Brighter pupils were segregated and prepared for Oxford and Cambridge. The two military academies were extensions of the public schools; former Beaumont College boy Harry Ross discovered an already familiar world at Sandhurst in the 1880s. There were cold baths in the morning and plenty of games, and mess bills for drinks were strictly regulated.[15]

Aspirant naval officers, sent to Dartmouth at the age of twelve, found themselves immersed in a public school atmosphere with plenty of games to fill their spare time. Not long after he had left, the seventeen-year-old Midshipman Hamilton Allan was posted to the Far Eastern station in 1900 and played football and golf in Hong Kong, which he found 'simply ripping'. At the Wei-Hai-Wai naval base there were facilities for fives, tennis and hockey,[16] Other, less pleasant features of public school life were found in the navy. Midshipmen in the gun-room of the battleship *Benbow* in 1916 were bullied and beaten. One victim, the son of a captain, complained and the matter was investigated at the highest level. The officer responsible, Lieutenant Athelstane Doelberg, was reprimanded, forfeited seniority and posted to another ship. He blamed the trouble on 'badly brought up' middies who had been transferred from the *Canopus*, which was no excuse for it was an officer's prime duty to exert authority.[17]

Once commissioned, the new army officer could expect plenty of sport, particularly if he was posted to India, which was a sportsman's paradise. In the early and bleak days of the Second World War, the septuagenarian General Sir George Barrow recollected the bliss of Indian soldiering at the beginning of the century, when he had commanded the 2nd Royal Lancers. 'The regiment was one united family and my year in command passed happily and all too quickly. In the summer there was the individual training, polo, a little pigsticking, bathing in the Commissioner's swimming bath, the long, long Indian days, the weary nights and the howling of dogs, the siesta, the burning heat and dust . . .'[18] It was a world away from his present occupation, serving in the Home Guard in rural Buckinghamshire.

Young and energetic officers under Barrow's command would have played tennis and hunted in the cooler season. For many, war was an extension of sport because it offered exercise and excitement. On his return from the 1891 Miranzai expedition on the North-West Frontier, a satisfied Captain William Maxwell of Hodson's Horse reported to his family: 'I have got stale, anyhow I feel younger and twice as fit.'[19] He admitted he had been 'lucky' to get attached to the force, for he secured a medal with a clasp which helped his chances of promotion. But above all, frontier force service was a hazardous and, therefore, stimulating hunting trip. Or so it seems from the language he used to his father to describe the fighting. After one skirmish, he wrote of the Ghurkas 'slipping away' like hounds in pursuit of Pathans.

Sporting language and metaphors litter the correspondence and memoirs of late Victorian and Edwardian officers. In December 1899, during the fifth week of the siege of Ladysmith, old Etonian Captain Rudolph Jelf asked his parents how the public judged him and his fellow defenders. 'Do they look on us in the light of "rotters" or "heroes" . . . I must say personally that I think we "played the game" in keeping the Boers busy with us here.'[20] The Ladysmith XI had clearly saved the follow-on. Pursuing mounted Boer Kommandos across the veldt during the following year was 'just like a good fox hunt', according to an Imperial Yeomanry officer, which it was in a way.[21]

Memories of Perthshire shoots must have returned to Lieutenant John Crabbe of the Royal Scots Greys when he examined some shooting books in a château near Lumigny where he spent a night in September 1914 during the retreat from Mons. They contained 'some really large bags of pheasants and partridges'. Soon afterwards, his unit engaged some Germans who put up a feeble fight and surrendered. 'We had some quite good shooting,' he recalled, 'although I was not bloodthirsty enough to fire on such poor game.' A German officer apologised for his men's performance: 'These men are pigs . . . most of them hid in the cellars. You will not find the whole German army like them.'[22] Once trench warfare had set in, boxing metaphors sprang more readily to mind. Colonel Charles Fitzgerald of the Northumberland Fusiliers reported that he had 'biffed out' the Germans from a position, and elsewhere officers wrote of them getting 'a good shaking' and a 'good thump'.[23]

Those doing the biffing had learned about war in India and Africa. The last quarter of the nineteenth and the first decade of the twentieth centuries had provided ample opportunities for instruction. Driven by an anxiety that other European powers might occupy 'empty' areas or install themselves permanently in regions where, hitherto, it had exercised a loose control, Britain entered a new phase of imperial expansion. The search for security in southern Africa led to wars against the Zulus in 1879, the Boers in 1880 to 1881 and 1899 to 1902, and the Ndebele in 1893 and 1896 to 1897. Most of the fighting was undertaken by white troops, supported by large bodies of black auxiliaries. Egypt was invaded in 1882 after an upsurge in local nationalism which threatened European investments and the Suez Canal. The occupation of Egypt dragged Britain into two wars against the Mahdist state of the Sudan (in 1884 to 1885 and 1896 to 1898), and the extension of British power in East and West Africa spawned a series of small-scale campaigns against local polities, which were largely fought by native and Indian troops under British officers. India's peripheries continued to be a battleground, between 1885 and 1889 British rule over Burma was consolidated, and chronic instability on the North-West Frontier required campaigns of pacification, the largest being between 1897 and 1898, and 1919 and 1924.

III

Imperial campaigns offered little in the way of preparation for war against modern industrial powers. Many were tiny in scale, employing detachments of less than a thousand men, always well equipped with the most up-to-date weapons. At times the disparity of arms caused moral disquiet. After what he called a series of 'funny little fights' at Gyantse during the invasion of Tibet in 1903, Captain George Preston told his wife: 'It was a weird sight – the whole place strewn with dead bodies. I hate it Ciskins – these poor Devils are brave men and they haven't the weapons we have. They fight to the bitter end. It's my first show and I feel awfully sorry for these poor fellows.'[24] 'Burning farms and bullying women' were distasteful to Captain Ballard during the second phase of the Boer War, as he and thousands of others rounded up the families of Boers who had joined the Kommandos. 'I'm afraid we are fighting for the benefit of a lot of money grabbing German Jews,' he added, referring to the owners of the Transvaal goldfields.[25] Ballard had succumbed to the current left-wing Liberal and socialist view of the war as one being waged to safeguard and expand the interests of financiers, notably Cecil Rhodes, and shareholders in the gold-mining corporations. If they shared his misgivings, his brother officers largely kept them to themselves, although many found anti-guerrilla operations frustrating and tedious.

On the whole, army and naval officers accepted the current imperial ideology; it could hardly have been otherwise for men who risked their lives as the Empire's pathfinders and policemen. A knowledge that he was part of the advance guard of his country's predestined civilising mission offered some compensation for what a Highland officer in the Sudan summed up as endless 'heat, dust and blazing sun'. A fortnight later, he complained that 'I have not had my kilt off for days except to bathe.' As the campaign came to its conclusion he confessed he was 'dead sick of it'.[26]

Others thrived fighting the wars of Empire and could not get enough of them. Sports fanatic Midshipman Allan had the time of his life fighting Boxer rebels in north China in 1900. At first he had felt 'rather shaky', but soon got into the swing of things: ' . . . the best fight I had was coming into Tientsin as that was at close quarters and we could see the brutes. I managed to shoot two to my great satisfaction and was most anxious to slay one with my cutlass.'[27] Another fire-eating sailor was Walter Cowan, a veteran of the 1897 Benin expedition and the 1898 Sudan campaign, who was described in 1918 as the 'only officer in the Grand Fleet who was sorry that the war was over'. Retirement some years later as an admiral did not dull his appetite for action and, aged sixty-nine, he somehow managed to be appointed as a naval liaison officer with No. 11 Commando and joined in the unit's rigorous training programme. He subsequently attached himself to an Indian cavalry regiment with which he served in North Africa. Afterwards, he returned to the commandos and secured a bar to a DSO (Distinguished Service Order) that had been awarded over fifty years before.[28] This was a spirit whom Brigadier Ritchie-Hook would have admired.

Thanks to their experiences and fluency in local languages, some officers stepped sideways and became colonial administrators. It was automatically assumed that a British officer's character fitted him for the firm and even-handed exercise of authority over races that were characterised as childlike, fickle and liable to spasms of insubordination. After the relief of the European legations in Peking in 1900, George Barrow was made temporary police commissioner for the city, responsible for six hundred thousand Chinese. Backed by 121 British and Indian soldiers and just over five hundred Chinese detectives, constables and nightwatchmen, and a couple of interpreters, he diligently set about his task. He was immensely proud of his performance particularly in cross-examining suspects who took a flexible view of truth and delivering judgements based upon 'natural justice'.[29]

Imperial service reinforced the ideal of the officer as adaptable, tough, adventurous, aggressive, ready to snatch the initiative and lead from the front. Although the technology at his disposal was very different, the officer fighting the Pathans in 1897 needed the same qualities as his predecessor who was pitted against the Sikhs fifty years before. Cleverness was not essential and, in some circumstances, was a handicap. At the beginning of the twentieth century, the commandant of Woolwich declared a preference for a public school classicist rather than a scientist as a potential gunner officer. 'We want them to be leaders in the field first . . . Power and command and habits of leadership are not learned in the laboratory.' Even Sir W. S. Gilbert's 'model of a modern major-general', Field-Marshal Lord Wolseley, with his string of intellectual attainments, disliked officers who read too many textbooks. He sincerely hoped that the British officer would never 'degenerate into a bookworm'.[30]

Absurd as such a statement might sound to modern ears, it made sense a hundred years ago. The junior officer in command of a company of askaris in Somaliland or a mountain battery on the North-West Frontier needed grit and audacity more than a mastery of military theory. The trouble was that as these men approached middle age they were asked to fight an utterly different kind of war for which few were mentally prepared. Poring over staff-college analyses and field exercises on Salisbury Plain suggested how war might be organised, but could give no indication of what it would feel like to be under that concentrated artillery, machine-gun and rifle fire that had annihilated the Dervishes at Omdurman. Nor, and this is a testament to the imaginative shortcomings of the British army officer, did anyone realise that a war with a European power would expose the British soldier to such an ordeal.

In 1914, naval and army officers formed a closely knit élite. Its members were bonded by common experiences of schooling, sporting recreations, professional training and imperial campaigns. The ingredients of their collective philosophy were loyalty to the crown and the Empire (but not always to each other), a faith in their own natural powers of leadership, courage, teamwork and modesty. As in the past, officers had always conducted themselves as gentlemen, whatever the circumstances. In 1918, one senior officer was dismayed by the behaviour of some young officers who had discarded the army's 'customs' during their imprisonment in a German prisoner-of-war camp. They 'squander money on any unobtainable luxury, drink to excess (the Germans purposely throw facilities for this in their way), gamble beyond their means', and so discredit the Allies. In another camp an officer kept a 'black book' with the names of such reprobates.[31] In normal conditions such misdemeanours would have invited a court-martial and possible dismissal.

Jealousies and rivalries were inevitable. The ambitious officer needed to catch the favourable attention of his superiors and so secure their patronage. Captain Ballard congratulated himself in 1900 on being part of 'Kitchener's ring', for there was 'nothing like having a bit of connections'.[32] Competition for promotion created tensions at every level, especially at the top, where senior officers felt obliged to prefer their own friends and protégés. Cavalrymen such as Haig imagined themselves as ideal leaders for the purely atavistic reason that men who rode at the enemy with sword and lance possessed plenty of killer instinct. Aggressiveness would be a vital asset for a general even in an age of long-range and quick-firing small arms and artillery. And yet, cavalry charges were now rare occurrences, even on colonial battlefields. The 21st Lancers had charged at Omdurman, and there had been a single opportunity for a charge during the Boer War at

Elandsgaate in 1899. A few heretics in the artillery and infantry thought that lances and sabres were obsolete, although cavalrymen had some value as mounted infantry. Nevertheless, a few days after the declaration of the war in 1914 the people of York were given the spectacle of the Royal Scots Greys practising charges against infantry on the Knavesmire racecourse.[33]

In the face of outside censure or interference the ranks of the officer caste closed swiftly, if temporarily. As always, officers submitted to civilian control, although many instinctively distrusted their political masters. Like Coriolanus, they despised men elected by the people and swayed by popular feeling and, from the 1890s onwards, the views of newspaper proprietors and editors. The politician was driven to abandon integrity in the interests of vote catching and expediency. By temperament conservative and reverential towards established authority, the majority of army and naval officers were Conservative or Unionist in sympathies. 'The Army is an aristocratic body, impregnated with the bitterest hatred of the Government and all it stands for,' declared the former diplomat and Liberal MP Sir Arthur Ponsonby in April 1914.[34] Events of the preceding few weeks had proved this beyond doubt. For the first time in over two hundred years, a knot of army and naval officers had abandoned their traditional, dispassionate political role and thrown themselves into partisan politics in a provocative and, some believed, extremely dangerous way.

IV

In March 1914 the government faced a tricky situation in Ireland. Dependent for their parliamentary majority on the votes of Irish Home Rule MPs, the Liberals had conceded self-government for Ireland, without, it must be said, much enthusiasm. The Tories and Unionists in the Lords had exercised their right to suspend the Government of Ireland Act for two years, so that it became law in the summer of 1914. The Ulster Protestants reacted as they had done in 1886, when the first home rule measure had been proposed. With the slogan 'Ulster will fight and Ulster will be right' they formed the Ulster Volunteer Force

(UVF) which, by the beginning of 1914, numbered one hundred thousand and was being armed with smuggled rifles and machine-guns. The UVF's aim was to start a civil war if London imposed home rule. Neither they nor the nationalists were prepared to countenance partition. Tories and Unionists on the mainland fervently encouraged the UVF's embryonic rebellion. In the south, Irish nationalists followed suit and joined the Irish National Volunteers (INV) which were estimated to be eleven thousand strong at the end of March 1914. Like its counterpart in the north, the INV was drilled by former soldiers.

The calculation of the UVF's strength had been undertaken by the army's Special Intelligence Section in Dublin which had been hastily set up on 21 March. Its purpose was to uncover the intentions of the two organisations and how far they were prepared to go if the government chose to fulfil the terms of the Home Rule Act by force. This was now a distinct possibility, given that the Royal Irish Constabulary lacked both the manpower and the willpower to intervene. Ten days of intelligence-gathering revealed that the UVF might take precipitate action and attempt a coup d'état in Belfast with the occupation of public buildings. The INV were less well equipped, armed largely with revolvers and shotguns, but an observer who had watched them drilling noted that they seemed 'very happy and keen'.[35] There was an underlying fear that heady talk of action and preparations for a fight would exacerbate social tensions. In the event of disturbances, the Special Intelligence Section suggested the use of mobile columns, and analyses were made to find out whether workers on the Great Northern Railway (Ireland), who were largely Orangemen, would co-operate in moving troops and supplies, which was, of course, unlikely.

This collection of intelligence was part of a programme of tentative measures agreed by the cabinet in anticipation of resistance. At first, the objective was the security of arms depots within Ulster which, it was feared, might be raided by the UVF. During the second week of March, small detachments had been transported by warships to reinforce the Ulster garrison. At the same time, the 3rd Battle Squadron was ordered to steam from Spanish waters and take up its station off Lamlash on the coast of Arran, where it arrived on 23 March. The Conservative press depicted these measures as minatory and suspected that Churchill, the first lord of the Admiralty, was trying either to provoke the UVF or to launch a pre-emptive strike against them. Comparisons were made with the attempt by the army to disarm Massachusetts militiamen in 1775.[36]

Against a background of rumour and an imminent and possibly bloody confrontation with the UVF, the commander-in-chief in Ireland, General Sir Arthur Paget, met senior officers to discuss future security policy in Dublin on 20 March. All present knew where most officers' sympathies lay. They were Unionists who no doubt recalled that Irish Home Rule MPs had cheered the news of Boer victories fifteen years before, and that the chancellor of the exchequer, Lloyd George, had been a prominent pro-Boer. And then there were men who were Ulster Protestants by birth. Paget attempted to forestall any assay of their loyalties by exempting them from any future service in the north. Those whose convictions made them averse to such services were told that they could resign their commissions and, in the process, forfeit their pensions, which was tantamount to dismissal.

Sixty officers resigned the next day at the Curragh, led by Brigadier Hubert Gough, commander of the 3rd Cavalry Brigade, a cocksure and ruthless careerist from Ulster landowning stock. Further departures followed and more were expected. The mood of the wardroom was the same as that of the mess, although the former sailor George V had hoped that the navy would show greater discipline than the army. It did not, and among those who threatened to resign was Admiral Sir George Callaghan, the commander of the Grand Fleet, whose family came from Cork.

In defence of their conduct, the protesters alleged that Paget's ultimatum had impugned their honour and demeaned that of the services, which were being compelled to act as agents of an autocratic government determined to pick a fight with the UVF. Given that officers had been perfectly happy to undertake policing duties during recent strikes in Britain, this was twaddle. In reality, the officers who resigned did so because they objected to Irish home rule on political grounds. Six junior officers of the 7th Destroyer Flotilla, based at Devonport, declared that if they were forbidden to resign, 'we would steam our ships into Belfast or Londonderry and place ourselves under the orders of Sir Edward Carson [the Unionist leader].'[37] Less than a month after the crisis, Gough told a colleague that the 'jobbers and gasbags' (i.e. politicians) had brought the country to the 'brink of civil war'. If it broke out, he would not stay neutral. 'We will not wage war on our own flesh and blood merely as a blind tool. If we have to do so, we claim equal rights with every other citizen to choose which side we will fight on.'[38] His followers were of like mind. 'Goffy is splendid,' a captain in the 1st Fusiliers told his family, and added, revealingly, that, 'If there's any fighting now it will be the Army and UVF nationalists.'[39]

Such outbursts were mutinous and a flirtation with treason, but the right-wing press treated the protesting officers as heroes who were defending their caste and the establishment as a whole from a government of radical extremists. 'The Liberal, Labour men have wrecked the House of Lords; they now purpose to wreck the Monarchy and the Army, leaving us with an autocracy of Ministers who are prepared to shoot down resistance . . .' shrieked the High Tory *Saturday Review*. In a bad-tempered Commons debate on the affair, the Conservative leader Andrew Bonar Law compared the officers' defiance with that of their counterparts who had refused to become accomplices in the tyranny of James II in 1688.[40]

The intemperate language of civil war and references to such conflicts in the past gave a sinister quality to what, according to prejudice, became known as either the 'Curragh Mutiny' or the 'Curragh Incident'. After a compromise had been cobbled together and the dissidents reinstated, Gough and his supporters within and outside the forces boasted that they had prevented a civil war. This was very wide of the mark, since it had been the UVF that had been set on starting one, and its resolve was strengthened by the knowledge that neither the army nor the navy would ever disarm it or prevent an armed coup in Ulster. The message from the Curragh to the Ulster Protestants was that they could continue preparing for war without fear of interruption. On 24 April a large consignment of weaponry and ammunition was smuggled into Larne; seventy years later the ship used for the gun-running was restored under the patronage of the Unionist firebrand Dr Ian Paisley.

As was to be expected, the officers of the Curragh were soon lionised in Unionist folklore and were celebrated in a song, 'The Saviours of Ulster':

General Paget gave the order, cried Gough 'Can it be true?
Are we to shoot down loyal men? Why this we cannot do.
We remember, Sir, when England stood in danger grave
These very men had shed their blood our noble flag to save.'[41]

A copy was sent as a Christmas card to the 3rd Cavalry Brigade, some of whom may have noticed a similarity between its tune and the words of those of 'Balaklava', a popular ballad of sixty years before which had described the Charge of the Light Brigade. For Irish nationalists, Gough was a villain and they were delighted to hear of his sacking from the command of the Fifth Army after it had crumpled under German attack in March 1918. The *Drogheda Argus* declared that the general 'who allowed the Germans to break through has been dismissed the service', and, piling on the bile, added that the Ulster division, which included ex-UVF men, was 'the first to be "bent in"'.[42]

A minority of officers were unwilling to jeopardise their careers for the UVF. Commander William Goodenough of the cruiser *Southampton* admitted that if he was ordered to, he would shell Belfast.[43] Brigadier-General John Headlam, a gunner, speculated on how the rank and file might interpret their officers' defiance. He wondered whether soldiers would follow their officers' example and refuse to serve against strikers 'of their own class and with whom their sympathies lie'.[44] This awkward point was raised by the Labour leader, Ramsay MacDonald, in the Commons when he observed that officers who felt qualms about shooting 'rioting Ulstermen' did not feel the same inhibitions when it came to trade unionists.[45] An officer from the Gordon Highlanders rebuked him privately for this remark: 'The King, Empire, & the Flag which are everything to us are little or nothing to any of you.'[46]

Sentiments that animated officers were under attack in the country at large, as Captain Savory sadly admitted after mutiny aboard the cruiser *Leviathan* in 1909. There was, he reflected, a 'general feeling' throughout the country against 'discipline in any shape or form', and sailors were being exposed to 'socialist doctrines'.[47] Soldiers were immune from this contamination, or so their officers believed. Second-Lieutenant Eric Miles of the King's Own Scottish Borderers imagined the ranker was not a political animal and would do what he was told. 'The man we get has no feeling beyond his pocket and his stomach, the reasons being that he is uneducated and unintelligent.'[48] Interestingly, a memorandum drawn up in August 1911 for the future use of troops in industrial disputes suggested that when it came to collecting local intelligence it would be unwise to employ officers whom the people at large mistrusted. The job of spying was best undertaken by NCOs and privates in plain clothes, chosen from battalions that recruited in the disaffected districts.[49] So strong was the War Office's faith in the habits of discipline that it was assumed that these soldiers would offer no objections to snooping on former friends and neighbours.

Ordinary soldiers were never put to the test, nor would their officers have another chance to pick and choose which orders they obeyed when in Ireland. The outbreak of war overshadowed events there and postponed the civil war that had seemed unavoidable. With the agreement of the Home Rule party, self-government was suspended until the end of hostilities. The UVF volunteered to join Kitchener's new army – as self proclaimed 'loyalists' they could do little else – and some elements of the INV did likewise, encouraged by John Redmond, the chairman of the parliamentary Home Rule party.

The rancour of many officers remained. Captain Roger Keyes, whose family owned land in Donegal, reproached Churchill for his party's Irish policy when the pair were being driven from the fleet anchorage at Loch Awe in September. The first lord of the Admiralty was conciliatory and predicted that the present war would dissolve Irish animosities. When it had ended 'and Ulster had fought for the Catholics in Belgium and shed their blood with that of the nationalists all the trouble will be over', he wrongly prophesied.[50]

The Curragh affair was an aberration in British political life, but an extraordinarily illuminating one. Contemporary comparisons of events in Ireland with those in Britain in the seventeenth century and North America in the eighteenth were a reminder that all the participants were ready to employ violence to secure their political goals, even if the consequence was a civil war. The UVF would fight to prevent Irish self-government and the INV to impose it across the whole of Ireland, while a substantial body of army and naval officers were ready either to stand aside, irrespective of their orders, or intervene on the side of the Ulstermen. The elected government was effectively hamstrung and could only hope to patch together a political compromise, something that neither the Unionists nor the nationalists were inclined towards. There is no way of knowing what course events would have taken if Britain had not intervened in the European war in August, but given Ireland's past and the depth of passion on both sides, bloodshed was extremely likely. Irishmen had never had much faith in reasoned political debate and its inevitable outcome, compromise. Their history had created a peculiar political culture in which violence, or threat of it, was acceptable because it yielded results, which it did between 1919 and 1923 and for that matter, between 1969 and 1998.

As for the army and navy, their élite had turned its back on its apolitical tradition, which was something that went against the grain among men who revered custom, form and obedience. That they did so explains the depth of their animus. It was directed towards a government that appeared bent on destroying the influence and interest of the class that officers either came from or aspired to – in the previous five years there had been increased taxation targeted on the rich and dilution of the powers of the House of Lords. Naval and army officers counted themselves among the losers in what they saw as the cynical manipulation of social envy. There was a limit to their forbearance, and the language of some of the protagonists hinted that they might go further than just resigning if pressed by the government.

The rhetoric of violence was frequently heard in the decade before the outbreak of war. It was employed by ministers who used the vocabulary of class conflict, by socialist and trade unionists who urged working men to flex their muscles and sometimes spoke of revolution, and by the suffragettes who backed words with actions. Prewar politics were particularly venomous, and in 1914 showed no sign of changing their nature, rather the contrary. One historian of this phenomenon has suggested that the nation as a whole was in the process of abandoning old peaceful methods of settling its differences and resorting to more aggressive ones.[51] If this interpretation of the national psyche is true, then the officers were just following the crowd.

There is a tendency to portray prewar Britain as a lost bourgeois Arcadia, a land of parasols by the seaside, croquet and Rupert Brooke, blissfully unaware of the horrors about to overwhelm it. Against this not altogether make-believe image is another of a nation riven by deep political and social fissures. An unexpected war terminated the golden post-Edwardian sunset and provided a powerful sense of national cohesion and purpose which healed internal rifts, if only for a time.

By and large, officers greeted the war with elation, and many felt that they were about to embark on a great and glorious adventure. It was an opportunity to test their courage and professional competence, and the smooth operation of the mobilisation plans was a cause for early satisfaction. Bernard Montgomery, then a lieutenant in the Warwickshires, shared the common illusion that it would be over quickly. 'A modern war would not last very long,' he told his family, 'and would be such an awful affair that there would be no more war for 50 years.'[52] He was mistaken on both counts and, like every other officer, had only the vaguest idea of what lay ahead of him, or what would be expected from men like him in a war that would prove utterly unlike any other they had experienced. This was also true for French, Russian and German officers, and so all armies would have to learn on the job. This process of self-education would demand imagination and mental flexibility, qualities that had never been fostered by the institutions that had shaped the minds of British officers. And yet, at the trench level, young men stamped by the ideals of the late Victorian and Edwardian public schools made excellent and often inspiring leaders who, in some part, redeemed their fumbling and purblind superiors.

3

The stern business of war: Command and discipline

I

Incredible as it may seem, British and continental officers spent the decade before the outbreak of war agonising as to whether the masses they would command could withstand the mental and physical strains of modern warfare. Conclusions were largely pessimistic. While the officer class retained its ancient, selfless patriotism, urban industrial man had become less receptive to this ideal. The warrior spirit seemed on the verge of extinction, killed off by materialism, individualism and socialism. Factory workers and the growing number of office clerks were now enjoying greater comforts than their parents and grandparents and had more for which to live. The urge for self-preservation was growing stronger.

Soft living had not diluted the courage of the Japanese soldier who followed the medieval bushido warrior code. It was admired by Colonel Philip Repington, *The Times*'s correspondent during the Russo-Japanese War, who observed that the Japanese fighting man 'looks death calmly in the face and prefers it to ignominy'.[1] At the same time as military men lamented the apparent devitalisation of the European working man's nerve, there were fears that he was progressively becoming weaker.

Of this there was no doubt, at least in Britain, where army doctors had turned down a third of recruits on grounds of debility during the Boer War. Independent surveys confirmed these diagnoses and persuaded governments to introduce public health and welfare programmes. Moral decay could be arrested by regeneration through youth movements which advocated manliness as the antidote to loafing, masturbation, cigarette-smoking, watching football matches and left-wing agitation, all identified by Major-General Sir Robert Baden-Powell as prime sources of decadence. His Boy Scout movement was designed to stop the rot by promoting self-discipline, love of country and toughness among Edwardian schoolboys. The Scouts wore uniforms modelled on those of the British South Africa Company's police and the principles of 'scouting' derived from Baden-Powell's experiences during the Matabele War of 1896 to 1897. In Germany, the 750,000 members of the Jungdeutschland Bund were encouraged to recover the old Teutonic warrior spirit.

Fears about national degeneracy did not evaporate once the war was underway, despite the fact that modern man proved beyond doubt that he could endure the stress of battle. Once huge losses had to be made good through conscription, the army authorities became nervous about accepting men who were physically and psychologically incapable of fighting and had instinctively resisted the pressure to volunteer. Among them were the malingerers and valetudinarians who passed through the wards of the 1st Eastern Military Hospital in Cambridge during the second half of 1916. The senior medical officer, Lieutenant-Colonel Frederick Burton Fanning, noticed that the majority were of 'stunted, weedy growth' with 'a natural lack of constitutional vigour' which made them prone to 'drooping spirits' and 'a sense of comparative unfitness'.[2] Such men frequently deserted, like Private T. Keegan of the 11th Royal Scots who gave up soldiering in France in June 1917. He was aged seventeen, five feet four inches tall, of 'poor intelligence' and 'in a childish way is easily frightened when spoken to' according to the wanted list circulated to the military police.[3] Men like Keegan were a headache for Major-General Sir Wyndham Childs, the assistant adjutant-general, who after the war candidly admitted that it was 'a horrible crime . . . To send out to the front men really incapable of doing their duties as soldiers owing to their mental make-up'.[4]

The erosion of physical standards for recruits was both a product of necessity and a response to the determination of miners to volunteer, despite their value to the war-economy and short stature. Their persistence earned them a place in the special 'Bantam' battalions, one of which so dismayed Aylmer Haldane that he proposed weeding out 'degenerates' from his division in November 1916. 'I am sorry,' he wrote in his diary, 'for the poor little devils for it is positively cruel to put them against the sturdy Germans.'[5] Appearances were deceptive, for the 'Bantams' performed gallantly in battle. Gordon Dean, an officer in the 8th York and Lancaster Regiment, had nothing but praise for the miners: 'a gamer, tougher, friendlier crowd of men than those in that battalion it would be hard to find.'[6] Another Western Front veteran and former prime minister, Harold Macmillan, recalled the pitmen's wartime bravery during the 1984–5 miners' strike after Mrs Thatcher had vilified them 'as the enemy within'.

Macmillan's admiration for the working man in khaki was shared by many other junior officers. In a flight of forgivable romantic fancy, a subaltern in a London battalion claimed that its men had shown the same robustness and courage as their ancestors who had fought in the Barons' Wars, the Wars of the Roses and the Roundhead trained bands. Those pre-war Jeremiahs who had predicted otherwise had been utterly mistaken: 'They scoffed at the idea of the young draper's assistant or bank clerk putting on khaki and taking a rifle and bayonet to fight the trained men of Continental armies. They argued that the undersized youths from our poorer quarters would be physically incapable of fighting the hulking peasants of Brandenburg.' With their Cockney humour and 'philosophical calm', the Londoners had proved themselves more than the equal of their German counterparts, whom, it must be said, were in all likelihood former Berlin insurance clerks or salesmen.[7] Haig agreed; after the BEF's victories in August 1918, he proudly affirmed that 'none of the fighting qualities of the Anglo-Saxon race' had been lost.[8]

Just as commanders suffered spasms of unease about the stamina of their troops, the other ranks sometimes questioned the wisdom of their superiors. In his novel *The Middle Parts of Fortune* (1931), the veteran Frederick Manning describes an exhausted unit waiting for orders to go into action. One man rails against those distant figures upon whose decisions his life hangs: 'Bloody swank. They don't give a fuck what 'appens to us 'uns.' Manning detected the rationale behind such grumbling: 'It does not harm a man to know that he may be sacrificed with some definite object in view . . . but no man likes to think that his life may be thrown away wantonly, through stupidity, or mere incompetence.'[9] Officers sensed this too. That wayward martinet, Brigadier-General Frank Crozier, remarked in his memoirs that 'it is not a question of how many soldiers were killed, but have actual lives lost been worth it.'[10] This neatly summed up the great dilemma of command on the Western Front. Of course, not everyone, whatever their rank, agreed upon the definition of what was worth dying for and what was not. But since soldiers did what they were told, this question was academic.

Private A. V. Conn, a sometime London dock labourer and taxidermist, was one of thousands who occasionally paused and queried the judgement of his superiors. He had enlisted aged seventeen in August 1914 and a year later was contemplating an imminent trench raid. 'Some brass hat sitting miles away and after having his breakfast in bed mornings had decided to liven things up a bit, after all there was a war on. So we organised trench raids and wiring parties, patrols out in no-man's-land. Of course this sort of thing brought retaliation, unfortunately for us poor sods in the line the enemy had more and better artillery.'[11]

He was quite right. In February 1915, Sir John French had insisted that, while the BEF remained on the defensive, local attacks were to be made to 'relieve the monotony and improve the morale of our troops'. Details of these sallies and, as it were, the scores were to be publicised to stimulate a 'keen spirit of rivalry and emulation' between units.[12] Trench warfare had been reduced to an inter-house sporting contest with prizes in the form of gallantry medals and mentions in despatches. Commanders who preferred not to enter the competition and thereby preserve the lives of their men faced unpleasant sanctions. 'Unless we advance and undertake enterprises, we are sure to be given some costly attack to carry out,' Aylmer Haldane noted in his diary. He despised French, whom he characterised as 'a thick-headed, conceited creature'.[13] This was true enough, but the commander-in-chief had to be obeyed.

The cost of compliance was heavy. Early in March 1915 four companies drawn from the 1st Wiltshires and 3rd Worcesters were ordered to seize four lines of German trenches near Kemmel in one of these raids. The preliminary bombardment had been ineffective and the attackers faced rifle and machine-gun fire that was so intense that 'only a few isolated parties' managed to reach the German wire. After fifty minutes, the survivors were falling back. In all, thirteen officers and sixty-seven other ranks were killed and just under two hundred wounded or reported 'missing'.[14]

The tactics of attrition were pursued by French and Haig, the successive commanders of the BEF. They fostered the 'offensive spirit' which both believed was essential to keep amateur soldiers on their toes. To sustain morale and prevent that lassitude that would infect soldiers if they just undertook routine chores, a policy of 'nibbling and gnawing' at the enemy's line was adopted. It was a disaster. The Neuve Chapelle, Aubers Ridge and Festubert offensives between March and May 1915 failed to penetrate the outermost German defences. Nor did they achieve their secondary objective, which was to grind down the enemy by killing him in greater numbers. In May alone the British suffered sixty-six thousand casualties, including thirteen thousand dead. Then and in all further offensives German losses were smaller.

Calamities on this scale never shook Haig's faith in attrition. Rather the contrary, for he and his staff talked themselves into believing that success was bound to follow if the scale of the attack was increased. A massive bombardment (shells were now abundant thanks to increased production) was followed by a large-scale frontal infantry attack on a twenty-five-mile front. This formula was tested on the Somme in July to November 1916 and failed with hundreds of thousands of casualties. Haig's champions have alleged that this offensive and its equally wasteful repeat performance at Passchendaele in July to December 1917 taught the army invaluable lessons. Perhaps so; but these battles were never intended as training exercises.

II

While the high command learned lessons in pragmatism, those who carried out its orders had to learn quietism. Whenever operations miscarried, as they did so often, those at the bottom got the blame. Brigade and battalion commanders were in an invidious position since their first-hand knowledge of conditions on the ground and the state of their troops counted for very little with their superiors at divisional, corps and army level. These officers and their staffs were responsible for strategic planning, imposing timetables and objectives. Once these had been formulated, their implementation was in the hands of brigade and battalion officers who were responsible for devising the appropriate tactics. Irrespective of their validity, objections from below were invariably interpreted as evidence of a lack of 'fighting spirit'. This amalgam of pugnacity and blind faith in the offensive was the touchstone by which a field commander was assayed. Dissent was intolerable and best kept to oneself. 'Let's rejoin our battalions,' one colonel remarked after hearing staff-officers outline the plan for the Arras offensive in April 1917, adding, 'the more we look at it the less we shall like it.' Another gloomily observed: 'the attack looked all right on the map, but viewed from the actual ground it was hopeless.'[15]

Refractoriness went against the grain among men schooled in unquestioning obedience. And yet, a handful of officers risked careers and reputations by criticising and even rejecting battle plans. Objections were based upon impracticality, flawed or slipshod intelligence assessments and humanity. Over ten years after the war, Lieutenant-Colonel Frederick Flanagan's conscience was still agitated by an incident during the Somme offensive. An attack had been planned against Morval at the end of September 1916 and his brigade commander, Brigadier-General Lord Esme Lennox-Gordon protested that his men were 'quite unfit' for action, which was so. He was overruled, but Colonel Harold Fargus of the 1st Duke of Cornwall's Light Infantry displayed 'great moral courage' and successfully demanded the withdrawal of his fatigued and sickly battalion from the offensive. Flanagan's 1st East Surreys were similarly cut up, but he lacked the nerve to follow suit. 'I have often regretted that I did not save the remnant of my battalion by taking similar action,' he recalled. It lost twelve officers and two hundred men out of four hundred during a day of pointless attack.[16] Both Lennox-Gordon and Fargus were regular officers with gallant records.

Fear of superiors smothered criticism and was a vital prop to divisional, corps and army command structures. Lieutenant-Colonel

Hubert Morant confessed that he had ordered an attack by the 10th Durham Light Infantry at Flers-Courcelette on 15 September 1916 'to save my reputation and not, as you say, owing to "desperate gallantry"'. 'I was more frightened of my superiors than even the Germans,' he added.[17] A few bold spirits spoke out. Lieutenant-Colonel Laton Frewen of the 8th King's Royal Rifle Corps told Major-General Sir Percy Skinner that his plan for attacking Delville Wood was the equivalent of walking into a 'hornet's nest'. A row followed in which Skinner finally gave ground, revising his plan. Not that this changed much, for the assault on 21 August came to nothing.[18] Both Morant and Frewen informed the official historian of their conduct, but were ignored. Robert Graves secured a change of mind when he pointed out the unfeasibility of the proposed attack during a brigade level conference. Another officer backed him and the assault was called off. 'That night,' Graves remembered, 'I went up with rations as usual: the officers were much relieved to hear of my stand at the conference.'[19]

Those who vented their apprehensions jeopardised their chances of promotion and sometimes their careers. A junior officer in Egypt who criticised his superiors in a letter was sent home after it had been read by the censor.[20] Gough, the arch-intriguer at the Curragh who later took command of the Fifth Army and whose faith in the doctrine of the 'fighting spirit' was more slavish than even Haig's, scared some of his subordinates.[21] The tubby, avuncular Lieutenant-General Sir Herbert Plumer, commander of the Second Army, was intimidated by Haig. 'Poor old Plum,' Edmonds recalled, 'was in deadly fear of Haig at that time [1916], Haig twice had him on the carpet, threatening to send him home.'[22] It was impossible to shrug off such warnings. Lieutenant-General Sir Charles Barter was dismissed from command of the 47th Division by Haig after what he considered its poor performance during an engagement at Flers-Courcelette in September 1916. He was replaced by Lieutenant-General Sir George ('Blood Orange') Gorringe, who was instructed to teach his men 'Discipline and Digging'.[23] After he had expressed growing scepticism about the continuation of the Arras offensive, the commander of the Third Army, Lieutenant-General Sir Edmund Allenby, was removed by Haig. Previously a staunch adherent to the 'fighting spirit' philosophy, 'Bull' Allenby was transferred to the Middle East where, unburdened by GHQ's dogma, he proved himself a highly capable commander.

Whatever its foundation, contradiction bruised a commander's vanity. Philip Landon, a lawyer who later became an Oxford don, was a staff-officer involved in the planning of the calamitous Fromelles diversionary offensive of July 1916. He bitterly recalled the ' . . . reckless extravagance in expenditure of life which ruled the minds of some of the subordinate commanders, like General Haking [Sir Richard 'Butcher' Haking], at this stage of the war.' Not understanding its purblind faith in the 'fighting spirit', Landon wondered why GHQ did not stop a commander bent on 'attempting to win glory for his Corps by a spectacular success'.[24] In East Africa, there was continual tension between 'Base' and 'Front', and ambitious officers in pursuit of medals and promotions 'played for self and not for side'.[25]

Major George Lindsay, a regular and a staff officer, was horrified by the sheer inflexibility of his superiors' minds. ' A feeling was created amongst those in the front line that to tell unpalatable truths . . . was unpopular with those above, and led to one being considered not to have the right amount of "the Fighting spirit". This undoubtedly led people to hesitate to tell the whole truth.' Deception resulted in ' . . . the useless waste of life and material, and the destruction of moral[e] that inevitably results from those in command disregarding the advice of those who know, not taking into proper consideration the actual conditions, human and material, that exist, and ordering human beings to do things that are not humanly possible.'[26] One of the few brave spirits who placed lives before strategic orthodoxy was Haldane. He spoke up against 'thick-headed asses' who demanded hopeless, headlong assaults that squandered 'valuable lives'.[27] His prospects may well have been blighted, but he was a first-rate commander and, therefore, indispensable.

What peeved Haldane and many others was the carping of superiors who blamed anyone but themselves for failure. 'There are several Generals in our army,' he wrote in February 1916, 'who, the moment anything goes wrong, search for a scapegoat without going thoroughly through the mishap.'[28] Among them was Sir Henry ('the Cad') Rawlinson who singled out the East Lancashires as culprits for a reverse at Aubers Ridge in 1916. They 'did not advance with the dash they might have done . . . it is doubted they tried very hard.' Given that the battalion lost 454 out of a thousand men it is hard to imagine what Rawlinson would have considered a determined effort.

Private jealousies and clashes of ambition were inevitable at every level in an army that was groping towards a way in which to break the deadlock and, in the process, making catastrophic miscalculations. For better or worse, the BEF was held together by a commander who saw himself not as a generator of ideas but as a sheet anchor. Haig fervently believed that he was a servant of that providence that had always been generous towards Britain and its Empire, both of which were in dire peril and had to be saved whatever the cost.[30] Not perhaps since Cromwell had a general been so acutely conscious of himself as an instrument of God's will. It manifested itself through the sermons of George Duncan, a Scottish minister, whose words were what his latest and best biographer calls 'a powerful stimulant to Haig's spirit'.[31] One wonders what comfort he drew from one of Duncan's pulpit assertions: 'We lament too much over death. We should regard it as a welcome change to another room.'

Whereas Nelson and Wellington had depended on their intellects, which were outstanding, Haig, whose was not, fell back on his singleness of purpose and willpower. He disliked contradiction and had a stubborn faith in attrition and 'fighting spirit' as the keys to victory. Intelligence tended to confirm dogma and encouraged wishful-thinking. Accounts of disheartened German soldiers surrendering and rumours of the privation and unrest created by the blockade were eagerly seized on by Haig as proof that his strategy was working. At the close of 1917 he was convinced that the Passchendaele offensive had left the Germans severely shaken.[32] If this was so, then their resilience was astonishing, for a few months later the British were reeling under an offensive of such force that Haig told his men that they were fighting 'with their backs to the wall'.

Those who consider themselves as infallible discount anything that suggests the contrary, and this was true of Haig. Looking through the intelligence analyses, often based upon the interrogation of dispirited prisoners of war who were anxious to please their questioners, it is hard to understand why anyone should have believed that Germany was on the verge of defeat during 1917 and much of 1918. 'You

English are such damn fools,' a German told Sergeant F. Ward of the 20th Liverpools after he had been taken prisoner during the Somme offensive. 'We see you go over this morning, yes, in the dark, we do hide in the ground, then we get up and are all around you, and we shall have you all.'[33] During the battle of Arras a soldier's letter was found with an equally succinct summary of what was actually happening: 'the Englishmen have attacked several times, but to no purpose.'[34]

Over-optimistic intelligence analyses of the state of German morale were vital ammunition in Haig's secondary campaign: his struggle against those politicians who doubted his judgement. Throughout the war, and in accordance with constitutional custom, all commanders were subject to cabinet and, ultimately, parliamentary control. It was an arrangement that was bound to promote tensions, for in a war in which the gap between expectation and performance was so wide there was a constant search for excuses and whipping-boys. Lieutenant-Colonel Fred Lawson of the Royal Buckinghamshire Hussars, then serving at Gallipoli, vented his spleen against Churchill, one of the architects of the campaign: 'I should very much like to have Winston tied to the end of the Pier here every morning at 9 o'clock, when the shelling commences, and watch him from the seclusion of my dugout.'[35]

Botched operations were systematically scrutinised by parliamentary committees, as they had been during the Napoleonic and Crimean Wars. Parliament and, with the confines of official censorship, the press probed every aspect of the management of the war without mercy. On the eve of the publication of the official investigation into the disastrous 1914 to 1916 Mesopotamian campaign, one of the generals responsible, Sir Beauchamp Duff, was believed to have taken his own life rather than face its findings.[36] Commanders fought back and attempted to win over public opinion by using their social and personal contacts at court and among politicians, newspaper proprietors and editors. If necessary, they were prepared to leak information and propose subjects for partisan articles.

Peacetime political animosities did not vanish in August 1914. Lloyd George, the prewar radical and scourge of the rich, never forgot that he had been the champion of the poor and weak, or that the generals came from the class that had exploited them. They still did, but in other ways. 'Haig does not care how many lives he loses, he just squanders the lives of these boys,' the prime minister privately observed in January 1917. 'I mean to save some of them in the future. He seems to think they are his property. I am their trustee.'[37]

These revealing remarks touched upon one of the major sources of contention between the high command politicians: priorities in the allocation of manpower. The other and closely related cause of friction was the overall thrust of grand strategy. On one side were the 'Easterners' who believed that victory or a satisfactory peace could only be achieved by exerting pressure on the enemy's weak periphery in the Balkans and the Middle East. The 'Westerners' claimed that the war could only be won in France, where the Germans were strongest. The failure of the Gallipoli landings and the débâcle in Mesopotamia discredited the 'Easterners', although Lloyd George pressed for and secured resources for the Palestine offensive in 1917. For the 'Westerners', led by Haig and his London-based ally, Field-Marshal Sir William ('Wully') Robertson, the Chief of the Imperial General Staff, operations outside France were trifling 'sideshows' which squandered manpower. The continental commitment had to take precedence over imperial expansion, a reversal of traditional British global strategy.

Lloyd George was unpersuaded, but he was in no position to override the generals. Unlike Churchill in 1940, he was not a supreme warlord with a commanding say in strategic decisions. His political base was shaky in so much as he headed a coalition that included Tories and Unionists, who were sympathetic towards the high command, and faced opposition from the pro-Asquith Liberals and Labour in the Commons. The prime minister also had to contend with the right-wing press, most notably the Morning Post, which favoured the generals. Moreover, and this is easily forgotten today, debates over war policy occurred against a background of uncertainty: no one could predict how events would turn out. After 1943 it was clear that Germany could not win the war, but as late as the summer of 1918 well-informed ministers and commanders believed that an Allied victory was not predestined, far from it. There were serious fears that France and Italy would follow Russia and implode and that the new Turco-German advance through the Ukraine towards the Causcasus might endanger regional imperial interests and open a new Asian front. If events followed these courses, then American assistance would merely avert defeat rather than secure outright victory.

Considerations like these influenced the dispersal of troops. During 1917 and early 1918, Lloyd George was reluctant to release men for service in France on the grounds that Haig would deploy them in another prodigal and ultimately futile offensive. The field-marshal and his followers argued that the prime minister was starving the BEF of men. Running political battles over aims, priorities and the details of strategy were an inevitable consequence of democracy; they had occurred during the Crimean, Zulu and Boer Wars, but with one significant difference. The earlier conflicts had been fought by professionals in distant lands; between 1914 and 1918 the whole country had been drawn into the war and was paying a heavy price in terms of casualties and the disruption of everyday life. Sacrifice had to be justified and so, to keep morale high, the people had been given unrealistically high expectations. But the flow of blood and effort failed to produce the promised result. Victory was proving elusive and, from late 1916 onwards, the nation was increasingly impatient with its leaders.

III

The voice of the people and the men in the ranks could not be ignored. It was heard at its most strident through the words of their self-appointed tribune, Horatio Bottomley. His twopenny (1p) weekly paper, John Bull, was immensely popular; it spoke vehemently and sometimes cheekily for 'us' against 'them' and was frightened of no one. Reading John Bull, one is constantly aware of a style and tone that are the same of those of the modern tabloid press, of which it was the progenitor. Here is Bottomley inveighing against governmental lethargy and half-measures at the beginning of 1918: 'In God's name, when will it be realised that we are at war; the blood of the firstborn is spattered on the lintel of the doors of the people. Stop this fooling: conscript, commandeer – I care not what term you use – everything essential to the life and health of the nation.'[38] However distasteful they found this journal and the rogue who owned it, politicians could not disregard Bottomley or those for whom he spoke so forcefully.

John Bull was widely known as the 'Tommy's Bible', which pleased Bottomley who saw himself as the champion of servicemen's rights. Each week, the 'Tommy and Jack' column exposed the misdeeds of neglectful or overbearing officers whose injustices had been reported by their men. The tempers of gunners based at Newark were 'almost at boiling point' because of abuse by a foul-mouthed officer, and the sailors on the Admiralty tug *Universe* were down to their last pennies as they had not been paid for several months. Why, asked Bottomley, was a major reprimanded for striking a soldier when a private in the East Lancashires had been imprisoned for five years for hitting an officer?[39] Military discipline, like strategy, was now dissected and debated in public, and social antagonisms were never far from the surface.

It would have been interesting to have known what Brigadier-General Crozier would have made of these letters from disgruntled servicemen who clearly had no faith in the orthodox procedures for airing grievances. Not much, one suspects, for he had a simple philosophy towards the men he commanded who, he imagined, were receptive to old-fashioned methods of discipline. Volunteers of the 'New Army' created between 1914 and 1916, and the conscripts who followed them, were compared with retrievers. 'Your troops are like dogs,' Crozier advised. 'They require careful handling before being gradually shot over, and led up to the point of more serious work.'[40] There were other, equally effective techniques and Crozier approvingly singled out a colonel in his brigade who enforced 'public school discipline' in his battalion.[41] In the heat of battle, Crozier resorted to draconian measures; he once threatened to shoot 'a funker' on the spot and actually shot dead a subaltern who was running away during a German attack in April 1918.[42] Reports of Crozier's quirks filtered back to his superiors, for his divisional commander vetoed his promotion 'owing to his roughness and the ruthless way in which he handled his men.'[43] Unperturbed by criticism, Crozier boasted that his brigade always held the line.

His views on discipline were firmly rooted in the prewar era when the army still depended upon poorly educated, unskilled and casual labourers for its recruits. Despite addiction to drink, these men were biddable and knuckled down when firmly handled. The volunteers of the New Army were very different in their backgrounds and outlook.

One, a prewar yeomanryman who eventually became an RFC officer, recalled that, 'The mind of the average territorial soldier of 1914 was more enquiring, more susceptible to reason, and often less inclined to obedience than that of the prewar regular.'[44]

The army had had a brief encounter with soldiers who were used to thinking for themselves in the men of the Imperial Yeomanry who had volunteered during the Boer War. The 37th Squadron of the 10th Imperial Yeomanry (Royal Buckinghamshire Hussars) was typical. Farmers were predominant, with a sprinkling of innkeepers, blacksmiths, corn merchants, an auctioneer, a veterinary surgeon, and Robert Southby, an 'art student', who shamed his unit by stabbing a horse, for which he got fourteen days' field punishment.[45] This procedure had replaced flogging in 1881 and involved the miscreant being shackled to a wagon wheel or other convenient object for two hours a day for up to three weeks.

Like their successors in 1914, these young men were inspired by patriotism and a taste for adventure. None appears to have had any idea of what was in store for him, and disillusion soon spread as a consequence of the chores of service life, periods of inactivity and the shock of coming under intense fire. The mood of the Royal Buckinghamshire Hussars was gauged by their commanding officer who told his wife that, once in South Africa, they soon became fatigued and discontented. As a consequence the numbers reporting sick rose rapidly. He did not imagine that the volunteering spirit would reappear in any future war.[46] One regular thought that the volunteers would have stayed at home if they had known what it was like. 'I have had enough of fighting. Three hard fights in a week ugh! how I hate the sound of these beastly bullets.'[47]

'Beastly bullets' fired in vast numbers combined with tactical ineptitude produced a handful of headlong flights and surrenders during the war. At Spion Kop in January 1900, junior officers begged, kicked and even threatened to shoot soldiers who refused to advance; several regiments were on the verge of disintegration, and nearly three hundred men threw in the sponge after their position had become untenable. Watching this spectacle, Captain Henry Jourdain of the Connaught Rangers wondered if the British soldier had lost his old 'fighting spirit'.[48] There were investigations into the circumstances behind the surrenders and, when evidence of faintheartedness emerged, those responsible were tried and either imprisoned, or in the case of officers, dismissed. Individuals were also arraigned for cowardice. A yeomanryman, whose unit was surrounded and outnumbered, and who refused to mount, burst into tears, and was taken prisoner, received one year's hard labour. Another who fell behind after relieving himself and was captured got the same sentence, as did an unlucky regular who was seized by the Boers as he slept on the latrine.[49]

Given the axiom that cowardice and valour were contagious, the army was determined to prevent any repetition of these displays of timidity. Perhaps the most demanding test of collective and individual nerve was in the third and fourth weeks of the war in 1914 during the retreat from Mons. Popularly portrayed as a glorious rearguard action, it was actually a period of chronic confusion in which the morale of many units all but dissolved. Although the BEF was a professional army, incidents occurred that appeared to confirm prewar apprehensions about the unbearable pressures of modern warfare, particularly fears that prolonged artillery bombardment would snap the nerve of the hardiest soldier. On 14 September, when the crisis had passed, Haldane wrote of his 10th Brigade: 'I feel uncertain whether they would stand really heavy shellfire, but might run to the rear.'[50]

During the previous three weeks he had watched the Royal Irish Rifles waver under bombardment and had had to threaten some of its men with his revolver when they became fractious and disorderly. Their own and other officers seemed unable to exert any authority over disorientated, weary and dismayed soldiers as they trudged across northern France.[51] At the start of the withdrawal, the 5th Division was diagnosed as 'shaky' by its commander, Major-General Sir Charles Ferguson, who feared that 'it would not stand for much longer'.[52] There were jitters at the top: on 29 and 30 August, Field-Marshal French was anxiously investigating the possibilities of a march through France for re-embarkation from some western port, possibly La Rochelle.[53] It was rumoured that the commander-in-chief had only stiffened his resolve after a visit from Kitchener who had warned him he would be sacked if he did not pull himself together.

Lower down the chain of command, officers faced agonising decisions when their severely mauled battalions got lost or were cut off and enveloped. There was a clash of personalities near Clary on the night of 26 to 27 August when remnants of the 1st Gordons and the Royal Irish Regiment stumbled through the darkness, using signposts to find their way. Isolated, exhausted and unfed, they collided with a superior force of Germans who quickly surrounded them. Colonel F. H. Neish of the Gordons concluded that nothing more could have been expected from his men. 'I call this slaughter,' he declared and proposed surrender. 'The whole thing was like a dream,' recalled an officer of the Royal Irish, who 'scarcely knew what they were doing, nor where they were'. Despite this, he felt confident that resistance was still possible: 'British soldiers . . . would have made a show of it if one could have got in touch with them.' Colonel William Gordon, a North-West Frontier VC, rejected Neish's pleas about a prevention of a 'useless waste of life and slaughter' and wanted to fight his way out of the trap, although he was unsure of his own men's and the enemy's exact whereabouts.[54] The Gordons surrendered. Yielding was the option chosen by the commanding officers of the Royal Warwickshires and Royal Dublin Fusiliers after their men had been severely hammered at St Quentin on 27 August. As it turned out, both battalions escaped their pursuers and the two officers were tried for cowardice, found guilty and dismissed. Only the vote of one of their judges saved the pair from the firing squad.[55]

No such good fortune intervened to save Private Thomas Highgate of the Royal West Kents who was executed on the morning of 8 September 1914 in the presence of detachments from the Cheshires and Dorsets, who were thought to be in need of a salutary warning. Highgate was nineteen and had enlisted in Dublin nearly eighteen months before. His battalion had been in action at Crepy-en-Valois on 1 September. Five days later, as it was moving forward for the Marne offensive, he was discovered in civilian clothes lurking in a barn on the estate of the banker Baron Edouard de Rothschild at Tournan. His discarded uniform was nearby and he told his captor, an English gamekeeper: 'I have had enough of it, I want to get out of it and this is how I am doing it.' At his court-martial, Highgate claimed he had lost touch with his unit after he had left it to ease himself. He bequeathed 'all I have to come from the government for my services' to Mary MacNulty of 3 Leinster Street, Phibsborough, Dublin.[56] In March 2000, the villagers of Shoreham in Kent voted to overlook Highgate's lapse and add his name to their war memorial.

Few aspects of the war have aroused such morbid curiosity or provoked such public indignation as the execution of 322 servicemen on the Western Front. Eighteen had been found guilty of cowardice and nearly all the rest were deserters. A considerable proportion of these absentees were recidivists who had escaped punishment under the terms of emergency legislation introduced in 1915, which permitted a suspension of capital sentences. A soldier in the trenches was more valuable to the army than one in a detention compound. The total number of deserters during the war was 39,060, of whom most absconded in Britain, and just over three thousand death sentences were passed for other crimes, not all of them military. Of these, a little over 12 per cent were carried out.[57] The army has always been cagey about these executions and the trial transcripts were only made available in the last decade. In 1992 a Labour MP presented a private member's bill extending a posthumous pardon to all those shot, whatever their crimes. This bill made no progress and in 1998 the armed forces minister, Dr Reid, stated that such a measure would be impractical.

Of course, there were enormous variations in the nature of the offences and the conduct of the trials. Like Highgate, some of the accused had no representation, and others were never medically examined to discover whether they were victims of shellshock or some other condition that might have impaired their judgement. A generation that accepts unquestioningly the clinical existence of mental disorders caused by trauma and treats them as seriously as the loss of a limb or a sense when it comes to compensation, finds it hard to understand why this was not so in the past.

By present standards of justice, many of the courts-martial were conducted in a rough and ready manner with inadequate arrangements for the accused's defence. This partiality was sometimes deliberate, for senior officers exerted pressure on their subordinates to secure guilty verdicts. Acquittals displeased Major-General Bertram Mitford, commander of the 42nd Division, who warned officers that leniency would encourage disobedience and desertion.[58] A confidential caution against softheartedness in capital cases was circulated among officers in the Third Army by its commander, Allenby, in October 1916.[59] Such admonitions were needless: nearly 90 per cent of courts-martial ended with convictions.

The prevention of desertion and insubordination overrode any considerations of equity. Severe sentences were deliberately awarded to deter. Executions were public and details of the accused, his crime and sentence were announced at morning parades throughout the BEF. The prevalence of 'very bad' discipline among the 1st Royal Scots justified the shooting of two privates from that battalion, Joseph Byers and Andrew Evans, for desertion, according to the assistant judge-advocate. Byers, aged sixteen, had enlisted in November 1914 and deserted the following January, while Evans had fled two days before his battalion was due to enter the line.[60] 'It is necessary to make an example in order to prevent cowardice in the face of the enemy as far as possible,' Haig minuted on the file of George Ward of the 1st Royal Berkshires. On 14 September 1914 he quit his post after two of his comrades had been killed by a shellburst, falsely claimed that he was wounded and then deserted.[61] He was shot, and a corporal who was 'not the last to leave' a forward position during the same action was given two years' hard labour.

Reflecting on these and similar cases, Haldane concluded: 'I do not regard a momentary lack of self control or brief absence and then return as nearly so serious as the case of a man who deserts on service.' After the execution of two privates from the Royal Fusiliers in May 1916, he observed that such men were 'not really cowards and they all face being shot calmly'. Courage was unevenly spread among soldiers: 'It is the uncertainty of life which affects their nerves, I think. The unknown has terrors for some much more than others. I can only feel sorry for the poor beggars, as there are so many shirkers at home and conscientious objectors it is doubly hard on men here to suffer.'[62] It is easy to sympathise with Haldane's good sense and humanity. It was, however, far from universal. 'There is only one thing to do with a fellow who says he is or seems to be shell shocked and that is to give him one on the point,' asserted Colonel A. D. M. Browne, who was appalled to find men so afflicted in his brigade.[63]

Generals who had convinced themselves that 'fighting spirit' was the cement of the army were bound to reject out of hand the suggestions that shellshock might dampen or even eliminate it. For Gough there were no grey areas when it came to courage. At the end of 1916 he had been angered by signs of a decline in the aggressive spirit among officers in his Third Army and decided on a sharp remedy, shooting one of them.[64] His victim was Sub-Lieutenant Edwin Dyett of the Royal Naval Division, a young man of nervous temperament, who had been found wandering behind the lines in a dazed state after the Ancre offensive. He was shot on 5 January 1917 by a naval firing squad which had been prepared for its task the previous August, when they had watched the execution of another man 'for instruction'.[65]

Valid questions about the lawfulness of Dyett's trial were raised in *John Bull* and in the Commons by the Liberal MP Philip Morrell (the husband of Lady Ottoline), who was disturbed by stories of men having been executed for a failure of nerve. While the death penalty was essential 'in the stern business of war', he suggested that court-martial procedures needed revision in the interests of justice. The under-secretary of state for war, J. Ian Macpherson, acknowledged that public concern in these matters was creditable in a civilised nation where human life was respected. Not long afterwards, he assured the House that a man's chances of acquittal in a court-martial were greater than in a civilian court, which was a lie.[66]

IV

Contemporary and subsequent disquiet about the iniquities of military justice reveal much about new attitudes towards the fighting man. He was no longer a creature from the margins of society, driven into uniform by economic and social pressures, but a civilian who had bravely and selflessly responded to a national emergency. He deserved decent treatment and had not forfeited the rights he had previously enjoyed. Those who volunteered or were drafted by and large recognised and accepted the necessary demands of service discipline, but they were not prepared to endure injustice passively. If soldiers came from the urban working classes, as most did, they were part of a culture shaped by trade unionism and the nascent Labour party. The collectivism of one and the socialism of the other had encouraged the working man to believe that he was no longer a helpless creature whose future was in others' hands. He had sympathetic allies among Labour MPs who would lay his complaints before the Commons. In July 1918 the pacifist Independent Labour Party (ILP) MP Philip Snowden asked why compassionate leave had not been given to an unfortunate soldier whose wife had been committed to a lunatic asylum and whose children were in the workhouse. He also spoke up for men from the 82nd Labour Company who had not had leave for a year, and protested about the shocking conditions at Ranelagh Camp, Barnes, where the Welsh Guards were stationed.[67]

Between 1914 and 1918 the total membership of trade unions rose from 4.4 to eight million. Many entered the services as craftsmen and technicians, often applying the same skills they had employed in civilian life. An advertisement for butchers, foremen, railway guards and stevedores placed in an Irish newspaper (there was no conscription in Ireland) in September 1918 claimed: 'You will . . . be able to do your bit for the fighting man as a working man.' Another guaranteed postwar employment for the air mechanic who had served with the RAF.[68]

It would have been impossible for men from this background to discard civilian habits, especially as they were undertaking the same work in uniform as they had been doing in civilian employment. Over 170 greasers, turners and firemen from the merchant navy serving on the repair ship HMS *Teutonic* momentarily forgot where they were in March 1916 and went on strike over poor rations. The eight ringleaders were court-martialled for mutiny and each given two years. In mitigation they pleaded: 'we have been in the habit of settling our grievances or disputes in the same lamentable manner as we have on this occasion.'[69] In October 1918, after a row with their captain over leave, about a hundred ratings from the battleship *Leviathan* defied him and spent several days ashore in Liverpool, coming and going as they pleased. An eighteen-year seaman who wished to have no part in what was a mutiny was reviled as a 'blackleg'. This use of the language of an industrial dispute may have prompted the officer investigating the disturbances to enquire as to whether the sailors had been encouraged by local shipyard workers.[70]

Both the army and navy were worried about the prevalence of the collectivist spirit among servicemen. It was manifested by the suspected presence of obstreperous and malcontented men whom Haig feared might easily foment unrest. 'Men of this stamp are not satisfied with remaining quiet,' he warned the minister of war, Lord Derby, at the beginning of October 1917. 'They came from a class which like to air real and fancied grievances, and their teaching in this respect is a regrettable antidote to the spirit of devotion and duty of earlier troops.'[71] Haig may well have had in mind a disturbing episode of a fortnight before during which several thousand soldiers had been involved in a six-day outbreak of rowdiness at the base camp at Etaples. It was the only serious mutiny among British troops during the war, but it was nevertheless alarming since it occurred at a time when war-weariness was spreading through the army. Moreover, during the summer forty-nine battalions of French troops had mutinied, many expressing fervent anti-war sentiments. In Russia the collapse of morale had been total; by the autumn the mutineers were forming 'soviets' and demanding an end to the war.

Virtually nothing remains of the vast sprawl of railway sidings, stores, depots, Nissen huts, canteens and training grounds that formed the Etaples camp. It lay just beyond the dunes that have nearly been covered with holiday homes for Parisians in search of sea and sand, and was close to the fashionable resorts of Paris Plage and Le Touquet. These fleshpots were out of bounds to the soldiers who came to Etaples, some to recuperate and others for strenuous battle-training in the 'Bull Ring' while they waited for allocation to new units. Then, as now, Etaples was a forlorn, unlovely place where grievances festered. The camp's spiteful military police were an obvious target for pent-up rage, not least because they prevented soldiers from leaving camp in search of diversion, and enforced bans on popular estaminets which offered cheap wine and unsupervised brothels. On 9 September a trigger-happy military policeman fired at random to scare off a crowd that had gathered in protest against the arrest of a New Zealander and killed a Highland soldier and wounded a Frenchwoman. This incident provoked six days of spontaneous demonstrations which temporarily paralysed the authorities.

The troubles died out without the need for condign measures and did not unduly disrupt the routine of the camp. To judge from the memories of participants and spectators the commotions were no worse than those that sometimes occurred at weekends in industrial cities after the pubs had closed, or at fairgrounds and sporting fixtures. If anything united the rioters, it was an urge to kick over the traces and create an uproar, although afterwards one wrote to a left-wing journal and alleged that the whole thing had been an anti-war protest. There were, however, raids on field punishment compounds, and the military police were withdrawn for their own safety, which suggests that fury was concentrated against army discipline and its agents. There was a nasty moment when an officer remonstrated with a band of rioters and a corporal exhorted them to kill him. He was arrested, tried and executed for mutiny – the second and last fatal casualty of the affair. Elsewhere, some officers managed to bring their men to heel. One soldier recalled: 'Our camp commander . . . appealed very strongly to the men from this camp to report back and like true Scots we did.'[72] Others, separated from their units and familiar officers, ignored calls to duty and cheerfully joined in the mischief.

Australian and New Zealand troops were prominent in the disturbances, as was to be expected. All were volunteers and aggressively democratic in their attitude towards officers (their own were appointed from the ranks) and notoriously indifferent to saluting. These soldiers closed ranks in the face of the military police, whom they regularly defied; a week before the Etaples ructions, an Australian pioneer had appeared outside an assistant provost-marshal's office and sung the 'Marseillaise'.[73]

The victim of this revolutionary serenade later complained that Australian personnel were automatically blamed for nearly all crimes committed by soldiers in France.[74] At Etaples, Aussies and Kiwis lived up to their reputation and confirmed Haig's fear that their insubordinate attitudes might lead British soldiers astray. This did not occur, nor was there anything to suggest that the restlessness at Etaples was an expression of political grievances or pacifism. The novelist R. H. Mottram, whose Spanish Farm trilogy refers to events at Etaples, spoke of them as manifestations of a widespread change of mood throughout the BEF. 'From this time there developed a new spirit of taking care of one's self among the men . . .'

Whether this had not always existed is a moot point; what is not is the claim that the Etaples disorders were a political statement that proved that the generals could no longer expect obedience from their men.[75] If there was a new spirit abroad, its principal ingredient was war-weariness, and this was apparent from the censors' reports. But men tired of war and, in the words of an analysis made at the end of 1917, infected by 'an almost universal longing for peace', were not prepared to throw in the towel. The rankers' letters made it plain that they were determined to see it through and beat the Germans. At the beginning of 1918, GHQ assured the war cabinet that the men at the front were against a premature peace.[76]

V

This determination to persevere was evidence of the remarkable cohesion, devotion to duty, stoicism and discipline of British fighting men. Their mental and physical stamina amazed their officers, not least because for the most part they were amateurs, often with less than six months' training. Drill, which had long ceased to be a means of teaching soldiers how to manoeuvre in the field, had a new importance in as much as it inculcated automatic obedience to the words of command. Discipline was very important and it was largely accepted as a necessity, however tiresome, which was why wounded men would sometimes seek an officer's permission before falling out to seek treatment.

Adherence to the strict military codes and the fear of punishment do not explain why soldiers were prepared to suffer the unending noise of artillery fire, sleeplessness, cold, rain, mud, lice, rats and sudden death or mutilation. These torments did, however, have a limit. A life of peril and unpredictability alternated with another of comparative safety during periods behind the lines, although base camps were bombed and strafed by German aircraft. Time spent recuperating was in large part consumed by routine chores, drill and combat training, and, for officers, courses in such subjects as anti-gas precautions and the deployment of the Lewis gun. Four-fifths of the infantryman's life was spent away from the trenches. At the front, daily existence was dominated by sentry duty and fatigues such as carrying supplies and repairs. This routine was interrupted by often capricious bombardment and moments of extreme danger during raids and offensives. Whatever he was and whatever he was doing, the soldier was always closely supervised; there were twenty-five officers per battalion compared with eight or nine in the

German army and, at the end of the war, one military policeman to just under three hundred soldiers.[77]

Sophisticated soldiers attempted to rationalise their circumstances. Private Ivor Gurney, a musician turned poet serving with the 5th Gloucestershires, believed that he was on the side of good in a contest against a 'huge evil'. 'Cold feet and mud' were among the 'prices' he was paying for some as yet undefined but desirable reward.[78] Whether or not he had the intellectual capacity to make satisfactory sense of the hostile universe into which he had been thrust, the soldier always had to concentrate on staying alive. In doing so, many, perhaps the overwhelming majority, subscribed to the prevailing mood of the army which was a blend of defiance, fatalism, resignation and mordant humour. It was reflected in the common catchphrase:

> *Are we downhearted?*
> *NO!*
> *Then you damn soon will be!*

In the same vein, and sung to the tune of Heber's hymn 'Holy, Holy, Holy', was a marching song which went:

> *Raining, raining, raining,*
> *Always bloody well raining,*
> *Raining all the morning,*
> *And raining all the night.*
>
> *Grousing, grousing, grousing,*
> *Always bloody well grousing,*
> *Grousing at the rations*
> *And grousing at the pay.*[79]

There was plenty of grumbling, some of it tearful, among members of the Queen Mary's Auxiliary Army Corps stationed at Aldershot in the summer of 1918. Olive Taylor, a girl who relished bucking authority, told the moaners to 'shut up'. They were 'lucky' to be in a 'lovely camp' and, after her appeal, 'they pulled themselves together and made the best of things.'[80] There was nothing else they could do; in the often repeated phrase of the contemporary cartoon figure, that archetypcal soldier-survivor 'Old Bill': 'If you know a better hole, go to it!'

Those patriotic impulses that had inspired men to join up flickered and died in France. While French troops sang the 'Marseillaise' as they marched, and the Germans 'Deutschland über alles', the British avoided patriotic songs. Rather, their sentiments were coarsely parodied:

> I don't want to be a soldier,
> I don't want to go to war,
> I'd rather stay at home,
> Around the streets to roam,
> And live on the earnings of a well-paid whore.
> I don't want a bayonet up my arse-hole,
> I don't want my ballocks shot away,
> I'd rather stay in England,
> Merry, merry England,
> And fuck my bloody life away.[81]

Domestic Hun-hating jingoism was rare in the trenches save among newly arrived subalterns, according to Robert Graves. Ivor Gurney observed that there was 'no hate for Germans' among his comrades, but rather 'a kind of brotherly though slightly contemptuous kindness – as to men who are going through a bad time as well as ourselves'.[82] Such feelings were not universal; prisoners and men on the verge of surrendering were often shot or bayoneted out of hand. But there were officers who behaved like the heroes of contemporary boys' adventure yarns, not surprisingly since many of them would have been brought up on such books. Lieutenant J. W. Reynolds of the 8th Lincolns recollected an exchange between himself and a German officer after he had been wounded and taken prisoner in September 1915:

> I [Reynolds]: 'Drink, drink, give me a drink.'
> Hun Officer: 'What are you, Englander?'
> I (proudly): 'Yes.'
> Hun Officer: 'All right, swine, die.'

His captor then shot him in the hand.[83]

Another patriotic officer was dismayed to discover that when he talked to his men about the Empire, they imagined he was referring to a music hall. Loyalty to such a remote abstraction was far less easy than to comrades, the battalion and its officers. During the early phases of the war these were young public school men who were accustomed to giving orders to their inferiors. Major Christopher Stone, MC, DSO, the son of an Eton master, who had passed through Eton and Christ Church, and in 1927 became the BBC's first disc-jockey ('the first gentleman of the gramophone'), is a perfect representative of these young men. He enjoyed command in the trenches: the 'comradeship, good feeling and taking everyone's evaluation of their capabilities, regardless of their social position, are delightful'. His paternalist principles would have won the approval of Wellington and officers in his army. Stone saw it as his duty to set standards in his company and he always placed his men's welfare and comfort before his own.[84]

By 1918 heavy losses had driven the army to commission more and more men from the ranks, like the fictional gamekeeper Mellors who became Constance Chatterley's lover. At the end of the war 40 per cent of officers came from working- and lower-middle-class backgrounds.[85] Their social superiors were often uncomfortable with officers who were disparagingly known as 'TGs' ('Temporary Gentlemen') and suspected that they lacked the sense of responsibility that came naturally to those who were gentlemen by birth and upbringing.[86] Hampshire squire and old Rugbeian, Colonel Sir Morgan Crofton, remembered that numbers of TGs, sometimes shellshocked, were posted to East Africa to command native troops. 'They were very troublesome in Nairobi and other towns, many not having the faintest idea how to behave like gentlemen. The askaris noticed the difference at once. They used to call them the "Shensi B'wanas" (low class masters). One NCO wanted to know which tribe they were from.'[87]

Tribal differences were not dissolved by shared danger. The junior officer faced the same perils as those he commanded, but enjoyed greater comforts, not the least of which were a servant and freer access to alcohol. Christopher Stone imagined that he had somehow got close to his men, whose lives and opinions fascinated him in much the same way as those of Pacific islanders would excite an anthropolgist. Wilfred Owen thought that 'Animal Sports and Mortal Danger' broke down social barriers, but never completely.[88] If he was to lead effectively, the officer had to isolate himself from his men, for familiarity would undermine his authority. It was different in the Australian army where egalitarian traditions of 'mateship' were strong. On the eve of an inspection, an Australian officer told his men: 'Now boys, these English officers are coming to size us up today. So look smart . . . And look here, for the love of Heaven, don't call me Alf.'[89]

The bonds that held together the BEF were many, complex and remarkably strong: they had to be. There certainly were officers and men who were frightened of their superiors and the apparatus of army discipline. But fear alone could not sustain an army and make its individual parts perform so well and for so long, often against hopeless odds. There was a far stronger and more durable ligature whose strands were bloodyminded pride, duty to comrades and a nihilistic spirit of resignation which was expressed in a popular marching song, chanted to the tune of 'Auld Lang Syne':

> *We're here*
> *Beeause*
> *We're here*
> *Because*
> *We're here*
> *Because we're here.*

4

The intensity of
the moment: Survivors
and casualties

I

Stamford is one of the most elegant and pleasing towns in England. Its skyline is undefiled by glass and metal boxes, its churches, houses, shops and public buildings are made of local limestone and in various Gothic and classical styles. In all, the town looks very much as it did on 4 August 1914. Like the rest of the country, Stamford was then in a state of expectant excitement, with people poring over the latest editions of the newspapers and discussing the war that was breaking out. Forty local territorials hurried to the drill-hall and signed on for overseas service. Three days later and now in khaki, these young men were driven to Lincoln in motor-cars provided by better-off local patriots. The vehicles were festooned with Union Jacks and, as they moved off through crowded streets, a band played 'The Lincolnshire Poacher'. As the motorcade passed through villages, people gathered to cheer and labourers abandoned their harvest work to wave the soldiers on their way. Similar scenes were witnessed across the country and older men and women would have remembered bands playing and crowds cheering as soldiers had departed for South Africa, the Sudan and even perhaps the Crimea.

For the Stamford lads the carnival ended abruptly. The day after their arrival in Lincoln they heard a lecture on discipline, in particular the need to salute officers. They probably did not find it too hard to adapt to a new hierarchy since they had been brought up in a world in which social deference was still customary. A period of training followed at a camp near Luton and early in March 1915 the Terriers were on their way to France. One, Ralph Clark, placed his fate in the hands of providence and, like everyone else, he was eager to see what the trenches were like and how it would feel to be close to the enemy.

First, Clark encountered death in the form of a corpse being brought back from the front line. 'All felt the intensity of the moment and the awfulness of war came close to many who never before had realised the fact until the tragedy was under their gaze.'[1] The sight of a dead British soldier was something that few would have contemplated during their drive through familiar countryside seven months before. Nonetheless, their morale was unshaken. In May, when Clark and his companions were about to go into action, he 'felt an intense joy with the thought of coming to hand-grips with the enemy at last. We longed to see their heads rise above the parapets . . .' When it came, the experience of battle drained Clark's enthusiasm and afterwards he felt pity for fresh troops who came into the line to replace the dead. He was killed that summer, less than a year after he had left Stamford.

Ralph Clark's reactions to war were common enough. First, there was the impulse to join. Its roots lay in that emotional intoxication that infected the country during the first weeks of the war. Thousands of men succumbed to or were swept along by a mood that verged on hysteria. Its ingredients were a passionate patriotism mingled with a sense of outrage at Germany's treatment of Belgium, a desire for adventure and the example of friends and workmates. Danger was ignored and, in any case, everyone imagined the fighting would be over quickly, which was why employers were guaranteeing payments to the dependants of men who joined the colours. Similar feelings had animated the thousands of Americans who volunteered during the first months of the Civil War.

This euphoria did not last long at the front. The introspective volunteer found himself beset by bewilderment, regret and resignation. 'The great adventure was no adventure,' concluded one volunteer, Hiram Sturdy, after a year in France.[2] Like Ralph Clark and thousands of others, his mind was now wholly concentrated on doing his duty and surviving, or in the common phrase of the time, 'making the best of it'.

The rush to volunteer had taken the government by surprise and for a time the administrative machinery had been paralysed. No enlistment forms were available at Chester on 7 September when Joseph Shields, a Birkenhead dock labourer, arrived to join the Cheshires. He was billeted with sixty other volunteers in a single hotel room without pillows or blankets. After two days of waiting, Shields' enthusiasm wilted and he drifted home to his wife and five children.[3]

He was one of just over three thousand volunteers who came forward during the first four weeks of the war. Like others who had come with him to Chester, Shields hoped to join the 'Wirral' battalion of the Cheshires where he would be among men with whom he had grown up and worked. The army soon recognised the value of local attachments and, for that matter, rivalries, and encouraged the creation of battalions that had their roots in the volunteers' communities. Bonds created in the workplace or during recreation provided a basis for that regimental loyalty that had always been considered one of the greatest strengths of the army. This theory lay at the heart of the 'Pals' battalions which translated the comradeship of work and shared interests to the battlefield. Employees of Mitchell and Butler's brewery and the Birmingham Small Arms Company comprised the 5th Warwickshires, while workers from the Glasgow tramways formed the 15th Highland Light Infantry, and so on. When such units were heavily engaged and suffered heavy losses, as many did, whole towns would be thrown into mourning.

By far the largest group to come forward were men from commercial, banking and professional backgrounds. In all, 41 per cent of men employed in these sectors of the economy volunteered, followed by 40 per cent from the food, drink and tobacco industries, and 33 to 34 per cent from mining and construction.[4] What the *Saturday Review* called 'the old splendid martial spirit' of the nation was strongest among middle- and lower-middle-class white-collar workers and the aristocracy of labour – in 1914 bricklayers earned up to £2 2s 10d (£2.14p) a week and miners £1 19s (£1.95).[5] Those who had passed through that nursery of manly patriotism, the Boys' Brigade, provided several battalions. As might be expected, the response from public schoolmen was massive and a testament to the influence of chapel, playing field and classical texts which elevated patrician self-sacrifice for the good of the nation. At Downside, photographs of old boys killed in the war are still displayed in a corridor, the number indicative of the feeling of many Catholics who believed they were under a special obligation to prove their patriotism.[6] During the first half of the war at least, there was no shortage of officer material.

Other pressures nudged men into the forces. There were posters – fifty-four million were distributed during the war – which ranged from the emotional 'Women of Britain Say Go' to the grim stare and accusatory finger of Kitchener singling out those who were shirking their duty. Reproach worked, particularly from women who prowled public places and handed out white feathers, a sign of cravenness, to men in civilian clothes. Equally nasty was arm-twisting by social superiors. In Wotton in north Lincolnshire 'the gentry of the village were making it very clear to them [the young men] that it was their duty to join the forces.' The elder brother of Olive Taylor, a farm servant, had a mind of his own and insisted he would go 'when he was ready'. He eventually joined the Lincolnshire Yeomanry, inspiring his father to enlist, even though he was beyond the official age limit.[7]

Thousands of recruiting-rallies were held to keep up the flow of men. On Sunday 18 April 1915 an audience of three thousand at Newport in Monmouthshire heard local worthies declaim on liberty and denounce German atrocities. Union Jacks were flourished and the bands of the Salvation Army and the local tramway company played patriotic tunes. The Reverend Thomas Richards invoked God's aid and declared that Britain was fighting for 'the Christian soul of Civilisation'. 'I rejoice,' he went on, 'that the Newport Free Churches have provided 1000 men for their King and Country. These men will prove worthy successors of Cromwell's Ironsides – men of courage, self-control and enthusiasm.'[8] Twenty volunteers stepped forward. Ancient warrior traditions were also invoked at Macroom, County Cork, in April 1916 where Colonel The O'Donovan reminded a recruiting-rally that: 'Every young Irishman is half a soldier already.' Three of his own sons were presently engaged in the struggle of 'humanity against tyranny'.[9]

Recruiting-rally sentiments were sourly recalled by Hiram Sturdy in 1915 after he had witnessed a comrade's death: 'The top of his head lifted off, a clean swipe . . . one (his chum I expect) holds his hand, and I see him die. The first for me to see die, as they say, for his country and it might be glorious, noble, brave, heroic and all the rest of those beautiful words that sound so well on a platform or toasting your toes by the fireside, but it is certainly not a glorious sight to see a young fellow, with his face covered with blood, stiffening out in a hole dug out of clay.'[10]

II

Others experienced similar shocks and expressed the same feelings of anger and despondency. After taking part in his first attack in May 1915, Hugh Munro, a subaltern in the Argyll and Sutherland Highlanders, could not bear to tell his mother 'the horrible parts'. Resting behind the lines, but still under fire and 'in a state of high nervous tension', he wrote to her that 'it is not easy to get used to the ever present menace of high explosives dropping in, and you are defenceless'. Nor could he come to terms with the sights and smells of death: 'I shall never return to France again. I am weary forever of the ruins, the trenches, the graves, the desolation . . .'[11] Even professionals despaired. A trooper in the 4th Dragoon Guards wrote to his sister in April 1915: 'I had a good experience of warfare, so called, but this is not warfare, it is science against science, or deliberate murder.'[12]

This letter was published in a local newspaper and could not have helped recruiting. Extremely gruesome descriptions of fighting and injuries did find their way into the provincial press, so that by mid 1915 the volunteer knew something of what was in store for him. In October 1914 the Cork Eagle reproduced extracts from a letter by a medical officer that described the wounds of soldiers who had been brought to his dressing station: 'The fragments of the shell are burning hot, and they tear and crush. Even the doctors, with their trained eyes can hardly see them [the wounded] without shrinking . . .'[13] Terror and chaos were evoked in an account of an ambush written by a reservist from the Gloucesters for publication in the South Wales Weekly Argus: 'The pitiful cries for water were enough to shake the stoutest hearts . . . We were like rats in a trap (or the grip of a Newport policeman) calmly awaiting death.'[14]

Potential volunteers gradually became aware of the chasm that separated patriotic rhetoric from the reality of the battlefield. It was not the backdrop for adventure, and death there was not endowed with a peculiar, ennobling virtue. Whether this knowledge or the publication of ever-increasing casualty lists contributed to the dwindling numbers of volunteers during 1915 is not known. The reactions of one conscript, Henry Firth, a civil servant from Bradford, suggests that many draftees were all too conscious of what might befall them. On hearing that he was about to be called up he made considerable efforts to find a place in the Pay Corps, Royal Army Medical Corps (RAMC) or RNAS. The last offered glamour and he mistakenly imagined that the first two might secure him a post away from danger. As he told his fiancée, an infantry private was 'not a very enviable position'.[15] He ended up as a sapper attached to a light railway unit in France.

Like millions of others, Firth had to come to terms with an uncomfortable and precarious existence. 'If we have to fight,' observed an RFC squadron commander, 'let us fight in comfort when we can, for we fight better when we are comfortable.'[16] No one, wherever he was or whatever his rank, would have quarrelled with that, although the squadron's smallholding with its several cows and over fifty chickens might have raised a few eyebrows. The provision of fresh milk and eggs was one way in which a fundamentally unkind world could be made tolerable, even agreeable. Hugh Munro's dug-out was furnished with chairs, tables, chests of drawers and flower boxes, and a wire-pull for summoning orderlies.

Other officers' quarters were similarly furnished and hung with pictures. There were photographs of loved ones and, in one billet, illustrations cut from magazines including 'female lights of musical comedy'.[17] Coquettish, flimsily clad ladies from French journals also served as 'pin-ups'. Racier material was available in Egypt where an indignant missionary collected a sheaf of 'dirty postcards' that were being sold to servicemen and presented them to headquarters in Cairo with a demand for them to be banned. No action followed; by today's standards the material was innocuous.[18] The familiarity helped render a grotesque environment bearable and reminded men of the world they had abandoned and to which they hoped eventually to return. Otherwise anonymous trenches were called 'Petticoat Lane', 'Lowndes Square' and 'Edgware' and alien names were anglicised. Ploegsteert became 'Plug Street' and Ypres, 'Wipers'. It seems that French pronunciation was retained by officers, which enabled one nurse to identify them in hospital.[19]

Important diversions kept alive memories of former pleasures and were a sort of bulwark against the all-encompassing madness and dislocation of trench warfare. Football, by now the nation's most popular sport, was the serviceman's favourite pastime. A match is being played by figures incongruously dressed in shorts and team shirts behind the line of blinded casualties in Sargent's famous painting 'Gassed'. Maybe this was a deliberate irony, for during the first year of the war the Football Association had promoted the idea of volunteer battalions of players and supporters. Chelsea fans were confronted by a poster that invited them to 'follow the lead given by your favourite Football Players' and become 'a Chelsea Die-Hard' by joining the 17th Middlesex. Two-fifths of the five thousand professional footballers did enlist, but there was some disquiet about those who did not. A patriotic poet appealed to them:

> Come, leave the lure of the football field
> With its fame so lightly won,
> And take your place in a greater game
> Where worthier deeds are done.[20]

Famous among these deeds was that of Captain Nevill of the East Surreys who had purchased four footballs before his battalion went into action at the Somme. On the first day of a battle he kicked one forward and promised a reward to whoever got it into a German trench. He did not live to see the goal scored.

Soccer was played so often behind the lines and with such energy that Haig wondered if it was responsible for so many men returning to the front fatigued and prone to doze on sentry duty. Blighty's delights were also reproduced in the form of impromptu concert parties which derived from the music halls. Amateur singers mimicked Sir Harry Lauder and George Robey and comic recitations were performed. Understandably popular was the robustly vulgar 'The Showman':

Ah, now the rhinoceros, the richest animal in the world. To those familiar with the Classics, the derivation of the name is interesting: *rhino*, meaning money, *soreass*, meaning piles. There you have it, ladies and gentlemen: piles of money. And next the leopard, one spot for every day of the year. 'What about Leap Year?' Bill, just lift his tail . . . Here is the Wild Man of Borneo. He has no cock. 'How does he fuck, guvnor?' He can't; and that's what makes him so bloody wild. I will now show you the camel. This peculiar animal eats mud, shits bricks and has a triangular arsehole. Hence the Pyramids.[21]

Chaplin imitations were also in vogue. His films had a special place in the serviceman's heart, because he was a humble figure forever beset by misfortune and at loggerheads with authority. His afflictions and misadventures also struck a chord with African soldiers who attended army cinemas in East Africa.[22] Over a quarter of the divisions in France possessed cinemas and, towards the end of the war, those of the Fourth Army were entertaining forty thousand men a week.[23]

A few cinemas were funded by the Young Men's Christian Association. The YMCA was the largest of several voluntary organisations that provided behind-the-lines canteens, concert halls, billiard- and rest-rooms and filled them with pianos, gramophones and stationery. These establishments offered cut-price tobacco and cigarettes, hot meals and snacks. At Etaples the YMCA dispensed an average of two hundred thousand cups of cocoa each month. Similar facilities were offered by the Roman Catholic Women's League and the Church and Salvation Armies. The latter was quick off the mark and had a detachment in Belgium by the end of August 1914. Some of its members were taken prisoner, escaped and 'rendered invaluable service' during the retreat from Mons by distributing 'coffee and buns, and in spreading cheer'.[24]

All these charities were amply supported by the public. During the winter of 1917 to 1918 the YMCA invited British companies to match the generosity of United States businessmen who had raised ten million pounds for its American counterpart. The response was impressive, with Imperial Tobacco, the West Yorkshire Coal Association and the biscuit makers Peake and Frean and Huntley and Palmer each subscribing five thousand pounds.[25] Schoolchildren in South Wales were urged to give their coppers to a welfare fund for local soldiers; those who were generous with their pocket-money were told that sixpence (2½p) purchased two ounces of tobacco or thirty-five cigarettes for a soldier in the trenches.[26] A pipe, tobacco and cigarettes were among the gifts placed in a specially designed box as a Christmas present from Queen Mary to all men at the front in 1914. A further supply of cigarettes was included along with a scarf, a pair of mittens and notepaper in a parcel received that Christmas by Sergeant A. V. Reeve from the daughters of the Duke of Richmond.[27]

The donors' priorities were right. Tobacco, especially the easily lit cigarette, was a universal stimulant and narcotic, easing tension and promoting a sense of wellbeing. Official photographs showed wounded men being given an obviously welcome cigarette. Writing paper, too, was essential for the fighting man, for whom letters to and from home were a lifeline to family and friends. While some vividly described life at the front, most related everyday but nonetheless vital matters such as the availability and quality of rations and the prospects of leave. And there were always requests for news of the writer's kinsfolk and friends. Like the inter-company soccer match or concert party, chronicles of domestic trivia were something to hold on to and, if only briefly, to distract the reader from a world of capricious violence. Delays in letters from home were always deeply resented.

What had before been taken for granted acquired a new significance. Hugh Munro was struck and probably puzzled by a swallow that, inexplicably given the surroundings, chose to roost in his dug-out. Private Conn was astonished when he heard the birdsong in no-man's-land. The birds' exuberance angered a surly colleague who shot at them, shouting: 'What the hell have you got to sing about?'[28] In June 1916, Siegfried Sassoon was preoccupied with the world he had left behind: 'I'm thinking of England and summer evenings after cricket-matches, and sunset above the tall trees, and village streets in the dusk.'[29] Everywhere, men on foreign service had similar reveries. Literature became therapeutic, a sort of antidote to despair which extracted the reader from his surroundings and transported him to another world. Books were also a source of nostalgia. Those that had been well loved or had agreeable associations offered the comfort of the familiar and were a welcome distraction in moments of extreme stress. This was why the romantic medievalist T. E. Lawrence kept a copy of Malory's *Morte d'Arthur* in his saddlebag when he crossed the desert. A mission over, he withdrew to a self-contained world of chivalric make-believe.

III

On the surface, Malory's knights and their codes of honour appeared utterly detached from a world in which killing was largely impersonal and carried out by machines and chemicals. And yet, paradoxically, the appearance of a Fokker monoplane in the skies over the Western Front in the summer of 1915 revived the ancient concept of war as a contest between honourable men of exceptional skill and prowess. Designed as a fighter and representing the most advanced military technology of the time, the Fokker was like a sword, a weapon whose effectiveness depended solely on the training, dexterity and nerve of its user. Pilots on both sides understood this and felt themselves elevated to the status of, say, Achilles or the Black Prince. 'It was like the lists of the Middle Ages,' Cecil Lewis recalled, 'the only sphere of modern warfare where a man saw his adversary and faced him in mortal combat, the only sphere where there was still chivalry and honour.' Looking down on the trenches, he was filled with revulsion: 'That was not fighting; it was murder. Senseless, brutal and ignoble.'[30]

German aviators shared these sentiments. J. E. P. Howey, an observer who had been taken prisoner after his aircraft had crash-landed in November 1915, was visited by his recent antagonist. The two men shook hands, and, after hearing that anti-aircraft fire had forced down Howey's machine, the German pilot expressed his regret. 'He was sorry we could not have another fight together, as he was certain he would be able to put up a better show next time.' He then promised to get in contact with Howey's family and inform them that he was safe.[31] RFC officers reciprocated these chivalric courtesies. Shortly after their arrival in France, pilots of 13 Squadron issued a challenge whose tone would have been admired by any of Arthur's paladins: 'A British Officer pilot is anxious to meet the redoubtable German Captain Immelman[n] in fair fight.' The rendezvous would be above the trenches near Hebuterne where the challenger would wait between ten and eleven each morning from 15 to 30 November. Anti-aircraft batteries were to be ordered not to distract the duellists.[32]

This showed considerable audacity by inexperienced fliers on their first posting. Max Immelmann was the best the Germans had: he was a consummate pilot who manoeuvred his Fokker deftly and had achieved seven victories within seven months. Whether any machines from 13 Squadron were added to Immelmann's tally is not known. He was killed over the Somme in the following June.[33]

Among the earthbound spectators who watched Immelmann's aerial acrobatics may have been Trafford Leigh-Mallory, an officer in the Lancashire Fusiliers who found 'the limitations of life in the trenches rather irksome'.[34] He transferred to the RFC; the sky offered excitement and freedom. The pilot was master of his own fate which depended upon his vigilance, skill in handling his machine and, above all, quickness of reaction. Every mission, whether reconnaissance, photography or escorting machines engaged in these activities, was a gamble. Fuel ran out, engines stalled, machine-guns jammed and the enemy could appear suddenly from clouds, mist, or, most dangerously, the sun, leaving his opponent dazzled and helpless. These hazards could appear singly or successively, as they did for a pilot and observer from 15 Squadron who were undertaking a photo-reconnaissance flight over Bourlon on 15 January 1918. The camera jammed and, while the observer tried to fix it, seven German machines attacked, diving out of the sun. After firing two drums, the Lewis gun seized up and the aircraft went into a spin with a German on its tail. The pilot recovered control after falling two thousand feet, evaded his pursuer and made his escape. One of his opponents had been hit and made a forced landing.[35]

Aerial scrimmages were brief moments of intense but often inconclusive activity. A German might suddenly appear, fire a few rounds and vanish into the clouds. Mêlées were confused and it was often difficult to assess their outcome. Surprised by a Fokker biplane on 30 October 1918 a pilot from 16 Squadron fired back and saw his assailant 'going down out of control over Rieux de Condé'.[36] The flier had escaped, but could he claim a 'kill'? Like Chaucer's knight ('Thrice in the lists, and always killed his man'), the pilot's tally of victories was a source of pride and a measure of his reputation among friends and adversaries. A high-scoring aviator became an 'ace', a word that derived from 'as',

French slang for a top sportsman. The ethos of competitive sport permeated the air forces of all protagonists and, as might be expected, RFC officers applied the language of the playing field to combat. 'I consider this a very good effort,' declared the commanding officer of 12 Squadron after hearing how two of his officers had beaten off an attack by eight or nine Pfalz scouts during a reconnaissance patrol, shooting the tail off one.[37] He could have been a first-eleven captain congratulating a batsman after an impressive innings.

Such praise was shrugged off. Nonchalant understatement was the rule and was nowhere better exemplified than by Lieutenant Pattinson's terse description of his machine being struck by anti-aircraft fire: 'a piece of shell passed through the side of the nacelle and lodged in the pilot's leather trousers.'[38] Dramatic and terrifying moments were recollected unemotionally. Pursued by a Fokker monoplane over Cambrai, unable to return fire, targeted by anti-aircraft guns and with a stalled engine, Captain Charles Darley took a bullet through his left arm which nearly severed his thumb. 'This did not inconvenience me much,' he commented, and then reported how he glided down to earth, destroyed papers that might have assisted German intelligence and then tried to set fire to the plane by firing his revolver into its fuel tank. Afterwards, he sawed off his shattered thumb with a pocket knife.[39] He was taken prisoner, then later exchanged and rejoined the air force where he rose to the rank of wing-commander.

Fortitude of this kind was almost unbelievable. Before the war, physicians had wondered whether the human body and mind could ever adjust to the pressures of flying, which, according to one, imposed 'the most intense strain to which the human nervous system can be subjected'.[40] Even the strongest man was bound to succumb to a combination of mental stress, extreme cold, lack of oxygen at high altitudes and, if his aircraft spun out of control, the effects of centrifugal force. Mind and muscle would be affected by these disorders and the aviator would lose the co-ordination that were vital for steering his machine. After 1915 he faced new traumas with the onset of aerial combat which required swift responses and precise judgement.

There could be no respite, given the imperative to maintain at least aerial parity over the front. Pilot losses soared and, as on land, had to be made good as quickly as possible. There was no choice but to replace the dead with young men fresh from flying schools and with minimal flying experience. This expedient raised the casualty rate; during 1917 a novice flier had an average life expectancy of two months and eighteen days from the moment he reached his squadron. Just over a third of those killed had spent less than four weeks at the front.[41] It was a Darwinian universe in which only the fittest and most adaptable survived, for after three months the loss rate fell to one in nine. Of those killed, a high proportion died in crashes caused by pilot error, which was to be expected among pilots who were still learning on the job.[42]

Aircraft with speeds of between sixty and a hundred miles per hour were highly vulnerable to ground fire. Tactical, low-level bombing and strafing raids therefore produced high casualties; forty-five machines were lost and fifty-seven pilots killed in twenty-four hours during operations against German troops, batteries and communications during the first day of the Amiens offensive on 8 August 1918.[43] A formation approached its target and then, one by one, the aircraft peeled off and attacked. 'Each machine must sit tight in its place and wait its turn,' one pilot recalled. This gave time for anti-aircraft gunners to get the range and, he concluded, it was 'inevitable' that the nerve of some fliers broke.[44]

Mental breakdowns happened frequently and in many different circumstances. Loss of nerve, and with it fighting efficiency, was the overriding concern of medical officers attached to the RFC and RAF. Whatever the reason, the officer who fell victim to some neurosis could no longer function and was as much a casualty as his colleague who had been wounded by a bullet or shrapnel fragment. With proper treatment, the latter could recover and return to his duties; but was it possible to repair a damaged mind? If it was, could the patient ever be fit for further service? These questions had to be addressed by doctors who were under pressure to return as many men as possible to duty. For the first time in the history of war, the psychology of the fighting man was scientifically explored.

The physical symptoms of pilot stress were easily detected. Weight loss, insomnia, abnormal pulse and excessive drinking and smoking were signs of dissolving confidence. Most revealing of all, there was a tendency for a pilot to calculate the odds of his own survival. If he

continued flying his behaviour could swing between extremes of caution and recklessness.[45] Once the likelihood of a breakdown was
apparent, medical officers withdrew the pilot from service and packed
him off to Britain and a period of curative rest. In some quarters it was
suggested that a régime of relaxation and sport offered the best hope of
recovery.

Clinical procedures for treating nervous conditions were in their
infancy and there was no consensus as to their cause or how they might
be cured. Before the war, the prevailing view had been that all forms of
mental instability were the consequence of heredity, some physical
malfunction inside the brain, or a hidden obsession. For these reasons,
medical officers concentrated some of their efforts on weeding out
potential pilots who might crack up. The ideal flier had what one
doctor described as 'a sporting and fearless temperament' and he warned
selectors to look out for 'delicate hands', which indicated interior weakness.[46]

A flier was 'no use . . . unless he has got guts', declared Dr L. E.
Stamm who served with the RFC and RAF between 1917 and 1919.
Recounting his experiences to a professional audience after the war, he
concluded that outdoor pursuits such as riding, shooting and hunting
fostered the qualities needed for flying, together with the killer
instinct.[47] 'The emotion of anger with his foe' had to be cultivated by
a pilot if he was to achieve a 'fighting spirit'. His listeners were divided
over this point which, incidentally, ruled out the chivalric element in
flying. One colleague warned that passion would impair technical
judgement and that the pilot's survival depended on the cold calculation of a hunter. Another RAF doctor emphasised inherent racial
characteristics as the key to domination of the skies. 'The Huns made
their mistake when they made pilots out of NCOs with officers as
leisured passengers. They lacked our pride and our spirit of devotion
and self sacrifice and that power of individual adventure which flowed
in the blood of the British race.' This opinion might have been
expressed about British servicemen at any time in the preceding two-
hundred years. It was comforting that ancient, racial qualities still
counted in the age of technical war.

IV

A common symptom of impending breakdown was the recurrence of a
nightmare in which the flier imagined himself suffering the most agonising of deaths: plummeting to earth in a blazing aircraft.[48] No doubt
many who were disturbed by such dreams had watched their comrades
perish in this way. From the start of the war it was discovered that the
most hideous experiences of battle were making indelible imprints on
the minds of fighting men. Early in 1915, a medical officer noted how
what he called 'neurotic subjects' in his hospital would sleepwalk in
search of their regiments and were tormented by dreams in which they
heard shells explode close by, were suddenly called to arms and found
their equipment deficient, wandered down unending trenches and,
most commonly of all, imagined themselves to be lost and isolated.
One patient convinced himself there was an unexploded shell in his
bed.[49] Other symptoms included temporary loss of sight, speech and
hearing, often after the explosion of a shell. All were indications of a
condition that doctors and the public came to know as 'shellshock'. Its
most famous victim, Siegfried Sassoon, was disturbed by recurrent
nightmares in which dark memories would invade his consciousness
such as that of a brother officer who had failed to get his gas-mask on in
time. Daytime brought no respite, for particular noises, sights and smells
could trigger flashbacks.[50]

Shellshock was thought a novel condition that resulted directly from
conditions on the modern battlefield, and it aroused an enormous
amount of interest in the medical and lay press and in parliament.
Journalists and MPs were concerned as to what, if any, measures were
being taken to alleviate or cure it. Between 1914 and the end of 1917,
over twenty-eight thousand cases of shellshock were diagnosed by army
doctors, well over half during the period covered by the Somme offensive. Numbers rose sharply with the influx of conscripts and, by the end
of the war, it was estimated that at least eighty thousand men had suffered some form of shellshock. Many suffered long-term disorders: in
1921, sixty-five thousand victims of shellshock were receiving disability pensions, a total that had fallen to thirty-two thousand by 1930, of
whom twenty-eight thousand were diagnosed as beyond treatment.[51]

The War Office contemplated the sudden upsurge in shellshock cases with dismay. A wholly unexpected drain on manpower had appeared and the army's first reaction was to pretend it did not exist. Suggestions that neurological units should be established were rejected on the grounds that they would attract soldiers with 'insufficient stoutness of heart' who would outnumber genuine victims and open 'the floodgates of wastage'.[52] In the end, the sheer volume of cases during the Somme campaign forced the authorities to cave in. At the close of 1916, specialist units were set up in France where cases could be examined, sifted and treated. The object was always to restore the patient's equilibrium as quickly as possible so that he could be sent back to the front.

An effort was made to separate patients according to their symptoms so that they could be prescribed the most appropriate therapy. Using definitions based on prewar psychiatric practice, the shellshock victim was categorised as suffering either from neurasthenia (depression and anxiety) or hysteria. By and large, hysteria cases were confined to the other ranks and neurasthenia to officers who were often disturbed by their inability to show the courage expected from them. Treatment varied and was often of a hit-or-miss type. A soldier suffering from what had been categorised as 'mental confusion' underwent a course of daily hot baths, soporific drugs which calmed and helped him sleep, and laxatives. The state of the patient's bowels was considered to have a considerable bearing on the state of his mind. Massage, exercise, mild hypnosis and 'faradism' (electric shocks) were also tried, the latter being very popular with French doctors. One sufferer from delirium was given a 'stiff whisky' and promptly became violent. All these therapies assumed that the condition was in some way the consequence of a physical malfunction of the brain which could be corrected or controlled. Psychoanalysis was only resorted to in the most obstinate cases.[53]

Statistics suggested that these methods were succeeding. Out of the one thousand men admitted to neurological clearing stations during the last ten days of November 1917, just over nine hundred were returned to their units. It was, however, noted that two hundred had been treated at least once before.[54] Those who failed to respond were referred to one of the twenty-one neurological centres that were established in Britain between 1916 and 1918. There were seven for officers and fourteen for other ranks, with a total capacity of six thousand beds. More were required; in 1921 nine thousand shellshock casualties were still in hospital and receiving therapy.[55]

The purveyors of tonics and quack panaceas were quick to move into what was bound to be an expanding market. In an advertisement of October 1915 two naval gunlayers proclaimed the restorative powers of Phosferine which they had taken before and after the battle of the Dogger Bank: 'After the engagement [we] were as fresh as daisies . . . but there were some fellows who did suffer headaches.' 'Your soldier and sailor will be better for Phosferine,' this puff concluded, in the hope that anxious families would buy bottles and send them to servicemen. As well as steadying nerves, this concoction was a prophylactic for 'Premature Decay', 'Brain-fag' and backache. 'Brain stress' and 'nerve strain' could also be relieved by, among other potions, Sanatogen and Bynogen.

Shellshock had far-reaching repercussions for medicine and the army. Old clinical orthodoxies were thrown into question as pioneering doctors probed victims to discover how and why they had succumbed. Most perplexing was the fact that many sufferers came from backgrounds with no history of madness, had revealed no previous instability and were not hosts to secret obsessions. Some patients were ashamed of their disorders, which they imagined to be the result of personal shortcoming. Faced with 'big, healthy-looking young men' who were reduced to spasms of 'hysterical neglect', the prominent neurologist Sir George Savage resorted to 'sympathetic but judicious neglect'. He told them that their behaviour stemmed from 'a nervous disorder' rather than hysteria, knowledge that 'reassures the youth that he is not feminine'.[56] Whatever his other tribulations, the patient had the comfort of knowing that he was not homosexual.

Dr Burton Fanning detected 'a pre-existing neurotic temperament' among his patients. Few ex-public schoolboys broke down, but the 'overwrought and sensitive' did, frequently.[57] Old notions of the sources of nervous illnesses appeared to be confirmed. The postwar official committee that investigated the clinical nature of shellshock heard from witnesses who still insisted that its origins were genetic or environmental. Jews, Irish, 'artistic types', 'the highly strung' and 'imaginative city-dwellers' were all identified as liable to mental collapse in the face of battlefield stress.[58] The presence of the last group suggests that prewar anxieties about the interior stamina of the working classes were still prevalent.

Sir Frederick Mott's treatment of shellshock cases reaffirmed his belief that many of them were predisposed to it by some other nervous incapacity – one of his patients was obsessed with sex – which incidentally upheld the assumption that mental illness had a moral dimension. After performing autopsies on soldiers whose bodies revealed no surface wounds, he conjectured whether the shockwaves from an exploding shell had dislocated neurone pathways or that the men had been killed by the carbon monoxide released as the missile detonated. Mott also discovered the therapeutic value of informing a shellshock victim that he would not be returned to the front for at least six months or, in some instances, never.[59] From this, it might have been deduced that what the patient had experienced on the battlefield was directly connected to his present condition.

This line of inquiry was pursued by Dr W. H. R. Rivers of Craiglockhart Hydro, Edinburgh ('Dottyville' to some inmates), where Siegfried Sassoon and Wilfred Owen were treated in 1917. Rivers regarded shellshock as a mental wound caused by a soldier's past experiences and that widespread sense of utter helplessness that had overwhelmed soldiers in the trenches. Inclining towards the still professionally suspect Freudian concept of neuroses and their exposure, Rivers encouraged his patients to unburden themselves of their most terrifying memories, which otherwise only emerged from the subconscious when they slept. All suffered nightmares in which they were haunted by images of death, mutilation and decay. Mingled with partially repressed sights, sounds and smells were anxieties induced by the knowledge that they had failed as officers, for they had failed to overcome fear.[60] What we now know as psychoanalysis uncovered the sources of the patient's neurosis and could help restore him to stability. There was a bitter irony in all this, for having been 'cured' the shellshock victim was returned to the very environment that had caused his breakdown.

Getting men back into the line was what the army, the RFC and the RAF expected from their medical staff. However embarrassing they found it, the services could not ignore the implications of this unlooked-for consequence of modern warfare. In 1920, when the

Lords were discussing the public inquiry into shellshock, Lord Horne, who had commanded the First Army during the Somme, admitted that, 'Courage is merely a form of nerve control.' This was now harder than ever to accomplish, for 'under the novel conditions that are met on a modern battlefield there is no man who does not suffer from fright.'[61]

This being so, was there a need to redefine cowardice? Had many of those shot for desertion or running away from the enemy been victims of unpreventable mental breakdowns? How, for instance, were the authorities to handle the case of a Royal Marine battalion that had fled during fighting near Murmansk in September 1919. Most were nineteen-year-olds who had been in Russia for less than a month as part of an Allied force sent to stiffen the anti-Bolshevik armies in a war that turned out to be as futile as it was unpopular. The marines endured dilapidated and dirty billets, inadequate clothing and poor rations. Sent into action, they came 'streaming back' after an ambush, ignoring appeals to their 'better natures' and threats of shooting. One officer, a veteran, was described as being 'in a state of collapse and was talking the utmost nonsense and not trying to exercise any self control'. Under fire, his men had 'bunched' together in fear.[62] All showed symptoms of shellshock, but a court-martial sentenced thirteen to death for cowardice. No one was executed, and in the end, and after public and parliamentary pressure, those convicted were released after a few months' imprisonment. The war had uncovered much about the nature of fear and, as a result, there was a willingness to forgive the lapses of those who were simply unable to cope with constant exposure to terror. In 1930 cowardice and desertion ceased to be capital offences, much to the irritation of the War Office.

Fear had always been present in war and men had tried to suppress it with varying degrees of success. There was one important difference between the modern soldier and his counterparts in, say, the Crimea or the Peninsula. They experienced relatively few pitched engagements and spent long periods out of contact with the enemy, although often suffering considerable privations. The First World War soldier was better cared for, but a far greater part of his time was spent within range of the enemy's artillery, and aircraft could strike anywhere. Concentrated and random shelling was an essential ingredient of attrition and, despite weeks spent away from the front, fighting soldiers faced more intense and persistent dangers than their predecessors. Men did, of course, break down in the past, but in smaller numbers, and the psychological reasons for their behaviour were not understood. A temporary nurse in Tientsin during the Boxer campaign of 1900 saw something akin to shellshock when she witnessed sailors and marines return to the city after heavy fighting. 'The poor fellows drank as if they had never drunk before – some bursting into tears, like children.'[63]

A new type of war had produced a new type of casualty. Not everyone was willing to concede this and, as ever, the pigheaded clung to old shibboleths. Lieutenant-Colonel Viscount Gort, VC, told the shellshock committee that it was a regrettable weakness and never present in crack units (he was a Grenadier Guardsman) which could be remedied by extra drill and tighter discipline. Henceforward, officers would have to learn to master their men as they did their horses.[64] Charles Moran, an RAMC officer, who later wrote a pioneering study on the pyschology of fear in battle based upon his experiences, was of similar mind. 'Those who succumbed to shell-shock were in essence unmanly and degenerate.'[65]

Men whose minds had been thrown out of kilter by the war got scant sympathy from a government that did not consider mental injuries as wounds when it came to pensions. Whether or not the permanent victims of shellshock received a disability pension was the concern of Sir John Collie, a doctor who had gained a reputation as a specialist in detecting medical insurance fraud and persistent malingering. As consulting medical officer to the Ministry of Pensions he employed his talents in sniffing out valetudinarians and shirkers, and assessing what, if anything, shellshock victims deserved. Very little, he concluded, since he was clinically sceptical of shellshock as a condition; tribunals of ex-RAMC doctors and retired practitioners were, therefore, encouraged to dismiss non-organic symptoms such as tremors and amnesia when making their assessments. Needless to say, and this had no doubt played a crucial part in Collie's appointment, the Treasury saved a lot of money.[66]

V

Although his nerves sometimes frayed and even snapped, the First World War infantryman was never short of the killer instinct. He unflinchingly killed Germans and Turks in face-to-face combat just as his recent ancestors had Zulus, Russians, Sikhs and Frenchmen. As a Guards sergeant bellowed at new arrivals at the base camp, they were there for one purpose: *'To fight, to kill Germans.* You've left the gals and pictures and the pubs behind in England. This here is WAR! D'you know what WAR means? I'll tell you. War means that if you don't kill the other fellow first, he'll blooming well kill YOU.'[67] This was a prelude to bayonet drill. No one was exempt; officers listened, sometimes appalled, to the lectures of the master of the bayonet, Colonel Ronald Campbell, who explained its mysteries and how to arouse that vital animosity needed for the fatal thrust. The mind had to be purged of pity. If a German cried for mercy and claimed to have ten children, Campbell's instruction was: 'Kill him! He may have ten more.'[68] Death was the invariable outcome of bayonet fighting, for the medical authorities noted that it was very rare for anyone to appear at the casualty station with a bayonet wound.

The hatred needed to kill in this way came easily. It was a compound of the urge to survive, the encouragement of officers and NCOs, and the wish to avenge dead comrades, friends and kinsmen and pay back the enemy in kind for such outrages as the sinking of the *Lusitania* and, from 1915 onwards, the air raids on British cities and towns which slaughtered women and children. Revenge was random. After a patrol had found a French farmhouse in which a pregnant woman and her daughter had been bayoneted, the sergeant in command took German prisoners to the sight of the outrage. They were shown the corpses, lined up and shot. As he pulled the trigger, the sergeant yelled: 'You bastards.'[70] Those who killed with the bayonet or, more rarely, sword or lance, described what they did in a calm, matter-of-face manner. A yeomanry officer who charged a Turkish position at El Maghar in 1917 recalled: 'One missed and missed again until the odd Turk wasn't quite quick enough . . . one instinctively leaned well forward to offset the jerk as the sword comes out.'[71]

In all likelihood many of these Turks were about to surrender. Not that this made much difference to the cavalrymen who, having faced intense fire and seen their comrades shot down, were in no mood to spare those responsible. Passions generated in battle did not evaporate the moment a man who had spent the last few seconds doing all in his power to kill you raised his hands and mumbled 'Kameraden' or whatever. There were rules on how prisoners were to be treated, set down in the 1907 Hague Convention, but legal procedures were the last thing on the minds of soldiers in the middle of a pitched battle, sometimes fighting for their lives. Horrible though they might seem to us, there were practical reasons to kill men about to give themselves up. Prisoners of war were an encumbrance as troops advanced, and a dangerous one for they might escape, find weapons and cause mischief behind the lines. There were many instances of prisoners being shot or bayoneted where they stood, rather than being conducted to the rear – a chore that, incidentally, diverted soldiers from where they were most needed, in the attacking units.[72]

Justifying such expedients, a Highland officer (Scots had a bad reputation for killing their prisoners) argued that it was merely trouncing the Germans at their own game. 'Being more Prussian that the Prussian' was necessary if the Allies were to win.[73] Furthermore, and this was common knowledge in the trenches, the Germans regularly killed British prisoners and wounded, and so it was a matter of tit for tat. Since the first days of the war, allegations of all kinds of atrocity against prisoners and civilians had been levelled against the Germans, and many proved genuine.[74] Authentic or not, newspaper reports of German barbarities hardened soldiers' hearts; indeed, many had been urged to enlist in order to avenge these crimes.

Whenever prisoners of war were repatriated, intelligence officers interviewed them to discover how they had been treated. These inquiries revealed plenty of instances where wounded men and prisoners had been killed, confirming trench rumour.[75] And yet the former prisoners' narratives also testified that German attitudes towards them swung between bewildering poles of kindness and spite. Captain T. B. Butt of the King's Own Yorkshire Light Infantry was wounded at Cateau in August 1914. An 'extremely gentle and kind' German officer dressed his wound under fire. Soon after, a German private appeared and grabbed his sword with which he performed a 'fearful war dance', lunging and parrying, and then moved off.[76] Alexander Reid of Buckie, a Gordon Highlander also captured in August, was shoved with other prisoners into filthy cattle-trucks that had just been used to transport horses. 'Being the only Highlander, I had to stand out at every station and show myself,' and at one a German civilian stepped forward with a knife, to cut a piece off my kilt.' A guard stopped him 'from doing further mischief'. At every stage of their journey, Reid and his companions were cursed by officers and soldiers as well as civilians.[77] Then and throughout the war, 'Englander schwein' and 'Englander schweinhund' were the commonest calumnies.

There were other instances of sheer vindictiveness. Anthony Loftus, a former corporation labourer from Huddersfield, who had been taken during the early days of the fighting, remembered a German Red Cross girl who responded to his plea for water by throwing it in his face. Variations on this refusal of water to a thirsty invalid cropped up elsewhere.[78] What makes this tale interesting is that a report of a similar incident formed the basis for a propaganda poster which showed a shrewish-looking German nurse pouring water on the ground in front of a wounded soldier. The message was that no British woman would ever behave like this and none would ever forgive such callousness.

On the whole, German medical staff behaved with that universal humanity common to their profession. An exception was the doctor who treated Albert Wilkins of the Buffs after his capture in April 1915. He was hit with a whip and sent to hospital with a label with read: 'This man had shot two German wounded.' It was removed by an orderly. The officer who interviewed Wilkins was sceptical, but had to admit that he was a 'fairly intelligent and reliable witness'.[79]

During the early phase of the war, when the fighting was fluid, it was possible to escape capture and find sanctuary among sympathetic Belgians and French. The remarkably composed and resourceful William Phelan, a medical orderly from Tipperary farming stock, was taken by Uhlans on the last day of August 1914 and conveyed to Chauny, from where he managed to escape. He walked about eighteen miles in an attempt to rejoin his regiment, was overtaken by advancing Germans and returned to Chauny. Here he found four other men who had been cut off from their units. The locals kept the five hidden, despite notices that warned civilians that they would be shot for harbouring enemy soldiers. In November 1915, Phelan left Chauny and, with the help of a black American electrician who was married to a Frenchwoman, acquired papers that said he was an American. The Germans did not believe him and he was arrested and imprisoned. He got away by using a hot poker to burn away the wood around the screws that held the shutters of his cell and made his way to St Quentin, where he met Monsieur Bommaire, whom he had encountered during the 1914 retreat. Bommaire secured him a faked pass and Phelan stayed in St Quentin until March 1917. He believed that there were many British and French soldiers in a similar predicament.[80]

An inkling of what might befall them if they surrendered, and a knowledge of how they sometimes dealt with their German captives, discouraged British soldiers from throwing in the towel. Men taken prisoner comprised 6 per cent of British losses; the German proportion was 9 per cent, the French 12 percent and the Russian 52 per cent.[81] Those British servicemen who survived capture noticed that once in prisoner of war camps they were singled out for harsh treatment, whereas the French were favoured, in part because they grovelled to the Germans.[82]

At their rare best, German prisoner of war camps were spartan. Their inmates' existence depended upon caprice and they lived in perpetual uncertainty as to supplies of food, clothing and fuel. Whether or not a prisoner shivered, went hungry or was overcome by tedium depended on the temperament of his camp commander. His whim was law and there were malevolent German officers who contrived to make life as unpleasant as possible for their charges. At Bad Colberg, the commandant was a caricature who might have been invented by British propaganda. One prisoner recalled him as 'A brute, detested by his men, by trade a schoolmaster or a crammer', who 'fancied himself as Sherlock Holmes', 'loathed the English' and was 'a fearful snob'.[83] The complainant was an officer who shared a common feeling that the privileges of rank should have meant they were spared distasteful chores. At Torgau, officers were furious when a shortage of German orderlies compelled them to clean latrines and drains.

Camp régimes varied enormously. Lieutenant-Colonel Charles Andersson of the 8th North Staffordshires and a veteran of the Jameson Raid experienced every kind between his capture at Grandcourt in

November 1917 and his exchange five weeks later. Medical attention given to his wounded arm varied from good to indifferent, as did his food. At Mainz it was 'very coarse and inferior' and at Gleissen 'plentiful and nourishing' with regular fresh milk and eggs, but a wholesome diet was offset by severe restrictions on daily exercise. Heidelberg represented perfection, thanks to a commandant who 'did all in his power' to provide comforts and diversions, including concerts, lectures and facilities for gymnastics. Clausthal in the Harz mountains was a bleak contrast: the accommodation was overcrowded and stuffy, the food poor and, to everyone's distress, German orderlies could not be made to understand that water for tea had to be boiling.[85]

Camp regulations were a perpetual source of contention. Collective punishments were imposed, exercise curtailed, and bans were placed on football and boxing (too brutal!) and smoking inside huts. Nothing galled so much as deficient and unpalatable rations which, together with interference with the flow and contents of Red Cross parcels, was the commonest source of rancour.[86] Pottages, mostly vegetable, were the prisoner of war's staple, eked out with black bread. When Gerard Mills of the 7th Liverpools complained about some fish ('vile, full of ammonia') guards 'blamed it on our Navy', which was in a way true.[87] Austere menus and shortages were a direct consequence of the blockade which was gradually reducing the food available for the whole of Germany. The Reverend L. N. Fox, a chaplain captured at Givenchy in April 1918, was served nothing but boiled swedes at Rastatt and survived on two platefuls of soup with a small loaf each day at Pforzheim. He heard that some prisoners had died of starvation.[88] After seven months, the guards announced 'Kaiser Willy kaput, gut' and opened the gates.

VI

At each camp, Fox had conducted regular services for prisoners. He was among the many brave and conscientious chaplains who fulfilled their spiritual and charitable responsibilities to their flocks. When he had been captured, Fox was in a front-line clearing station, comforting the injured, taking down the letters of the dying and giving them the last rites. Fox's task as God's representative was extraordinarily difficult; many soldiers had never been exposed to Christian teaching and some regarded Anglicanism as the religion of 'them' rather than 'us', understandably since the chaplains of the established churches messed and lived with officers. Those with faith were prone to despair and abandon it in the contrived hell of the trenches. Frightened and perplexed Christians asked how could a loving God permit such pain and misery?

It was a question that M. S. Evers, a chaplain attached to the Loyal North Lancashires, heard from soldiers at his Christian Union meetings. Some found immense comfort from what he called their 'personal religion' and were able to rationalise their situation and its part in the divine scheme of things. 'God did not plan this war,' one remarked to Evers, 'but is nevertheless using it to bring men back to himself.'[89] Imminent death concentrated the minds of those who were about to face it or had just escaped it. 'War is a rough school and makes rough men,' observed a Church of Scotland chaplain, 'but there are times when the most hardened and callous are as clay in the potter's hand. Such an occasion is after a battle, and poor indeed is the preacher who cannot evoke a response in such conditions.'[90] Those who had been delivered were truly thankful to a protective God and, having seen others die, mindful of their own mortality and sinfulness.

The dead were promised salvation. Congregations of soldiers heard how they had been individually elevated because they were serving God's purpose. This was the message of Dr Wallace Williamson, an energetic and passionate Church of Scotland preacher, who regularly addressed men in the trenches. 'Remember,' he told one group in April 1915, 'there is only one way to peace in this dread hour of history: it is through the bloodstained path of war.' 'You are the peacemakers,' who, like Christ, would shed their blood for peace. Williamson also preached absolute submission to God's will: 'You and I have but one life, one death to die. Let us live the clean life while we live and be sure of this, wherever and whenever it may please God to call us, we shall die a noble death.'[91] Such a death was a certain prelude to redemption and eternal life. A. F. Winnington Ingram, Bishop of London, sometime chaplain to the London Territorials and a trenchant apostle of Christian manliness, quoted with warm approval the words of a colonel who had lost two sons in the war: 'Christ will welcome his comrades in arms as they come into another world.'[92] The image of Christ receiving the body of a soldier was one of the most potent icons of the war, expressing hope both for the dead fighting man and for those who grieved for him.

A simple theology comforted the serviceman. He was exempted from the Mosaic injunction against murder, for he was fighting in a righteous cause that had divine sanction and, for this reason, would be rewarded with salvation. It was a doctrine that made some chaplains uneasy. Charles Raven, a former dean of Emmanuel College, Cambridge, detested his colleagues who played the recruiting-sergeant, offering eternal bliss for all who were killed in action. Other Anglican chaplains found it intellectually convenient to push to the back of their minds any misgivings about the war's implications for their faith and its future, choosing to devote themselves to a ministry of good works. 'Take a box of fags in your haversack and a great deal of love,' advised Theodore Hardy, who died of wounds in 1918. Geoffrey Kennedy was unhappy about this 'Woodbine Willie' image of the chaplain, a hearty fellow who distributed cigarettes to men in canteens or as they marched into the line. 'For the men to whom I owed God's Peace, I put off with a cigarette,' he ruefully commented. A soldier observed: 'The Church of Rome sent a man into action mentally and spiritually cleaned. The Church of England could only offer you a cigarette.'[93] Nonetheless, a free smoke was always welcome.

5

Same as the lads: Women, work and wages

I

The First World War was all-pervasive. Everyone's life was touched by it in some way, which made it quite unlike all previous wars. One can imagine that it might just have been possible for an incurious, reclusive individual to have remained detached from the French and Napoleonic Wars, particularly if he grew his own food, never read a newspaper and paid no taxes. Such isolation would have been inconceivable between 1914 and 1918. No one could have avoided the inconveniences of food shortages, rationing, higher taxation, rising prices and having to register themselves for war service. Nor could anyone who walked abroad ignore men in uniform, training or home on leave, or the blind and limbless in their distinctive blue suits. And then there were the posters on hoardings and in post offices, exhorting fit men to enlist, which the public found either boring or irritating.[1] Above all, there were discontinuity and disruption as men and women abandoned the familiar patterns of their lives, some to go abroad and fight, others to make weapons. Families were changed for ever as men went away, many not to return, and women found jobs, often far from home.

Millions of lives were permanently transformed, not always for the worse. The war opened as many doors as it closed. It offered individuals the opportunity to abandon the familiar and humdrum, propelled them into new worlds and in directions that they would never have contemplated. Consider Olive Turner, who was born in 1898 in the village of Wootton just beyond the northern edge of the Lincolnshire Wolds. It was then the back of beyond, so much so that Olive did not hear the news of the outbreak of war until November 1914. She was a general maid on an isolated marshland farm where no newspapers were read and where the farmer's wife only spoke to her to give orders. Contact with the outside world, if it can be called that, was the service each Sunday in the chapel of one of the glummer and more self-contained nonconformist sects. In many respects, her situation and horizons were scarcely different from those of a girl holding a similar post a hundred years before.[2]

The widespread shortage of domestics provided her with promotion to cook-general in the household of a doctor. Frustrated by the restrictions of domestic service, she volunteered to work in a munitions factory towards the end of 1916. Her wages would have been considerably higher, which was why middle-class housewives were finding it increasingly hard to entice and keep servants. In March 1918, a lady wrote to that sounding-board for bourgeois disquiet, the *Saturday Review*, to complain that 'temps' (temporary servants) were demanding between fifteen and thirty shillings a week and 'do as little work as they dare'.[3] Olive Turner may well have been lured by the money, but she was developing an independent trait: 'Though small [just over five feet] I consider myself equal to any man, having carried occasionally sacks of wheat weighing eight stones.'

She was sent to a factory in Morecambe, where she filled shells for twenty-five shillings (£1.25) a week. Her pay rose to thirty-three shillings (£1.65) a week, not far short of the prewar rate for a skilled craftsman, which she considered a fair return for 'boring and laborious' work in which she snagged her fingers and sometimes fainted from the stench of the chemicals. Shell production was fiddly and, if you were not alert, dangerous work. Edith Airey, a former farm girl from Euston in Suffolk, recalled the routines she undertook in Lowestoft where she worked making shells in a converted engineering workshop. 'We each had a die in which we placed the brass caps and proceeded to make the screw end. It was tough going. Small bits of brass seemed to be a target for my eyes and I was forever at the first aid post.' The night-shift brought a fresh hazard. 'I was always tired, especially about midnight. I would find that I could not keep awake and would suddenly come to life with a start with the foreman shaking me and my head a hair's breath from the spinning fly wheel.'[4]

In October 1917 there were a fire and several explosions in Olive Turner's factory, but she was unharmed. She was lucky; in the Silvertown factory explosion in January 1917, sixty-nine women were killed and hundreds injured. Contact with high explosives brought other risks. Women who handled TNT, phosphorus and nitroglycerine were distinguished by the yellowing of their hair and skin and were called 'Canaries'. Nonetheless, they were jauntily patriotic. One of their songs ran:

> *Same as the lads*
> *Across the sea,*
> *If it wasn't for the ammunition girls*
> *Where would the Empire be?*

From the middle of 1915 onwards, Canaries and other munitions workers in factories on the shores of the Thames estuary found themselves sharing one of the perils faced by the 'lads across the sea', air raids. The range of Zeppelins and bombers confined them to eastern and southern-eastern England, but coastal areas everywhere were vulnerable to sudden bombardment from the sea. These attacks were eccentric and seemingly pointless. On 16 July 1916 a U-boat surfaced off the Durham fishing village of Seaham, fired between twenty and thirty shells and then disappeared. One woman was killed and a bungalow and a pigsty damaged.[5]

During the late afternoon of 16 August 1915, while sailing off the Cumberland coast, John Bennewith, the skipper of a fishing smack, was puzzled by a 'black object' in the water some distance from his boat. He also heard explosions, which he took to be blasting somewhere on shore. On his return to harbour, he discovered that he had witnessed a U-boat shelling a coke works near Workington. A cottage, home to a miner, his wife and nine children, was hit, but the only casualty was a dog which was slightly hurt. The official view was that this had been an attack against a specific industrial target and there were murmurs about the involvement of the German wife of one of the mine's directors. Sir Vernon Kell, the head of MI5, recommended that she be sent to some other part of the country under DORA's regulations for aliens and potential troublemakers.[6]

Nothing better illustrated the disappearance of the distinction between servicemen and civilian than the air raid. Over eight thousand bombs were dropped on English targets between December 1914 and October 1918. They killed 1570, injured over four thousand and destroyed property worth three million pounds. These totals would have been substantially higher if the war had continued, for the Germans were stepping up the scale of their attacks; a raid by twenty-two machines against Margate and London in July 1918 left fifty-seven dead and 193 wounded.[7] By now, the RAF was regularly bombing industrial sites in the Rhineland where over seven hundred Germans were killed.[8] Both sides employed comparatively crude sighting devices and bombing was indiscriminate. Ten bombs aimed at Faversham and Sittingbourne in August 1915 killed one blackbird, and after a raid on Freiburg an RAF pilot remarked that his colleagues 'were probably quite satisfied if they hit any part of the town'.[9]

Unlike her fellow workers in the south-east, Olive Turner was spared air raids, although her factory might have been a tempting target for a U-boat commander audacious enough to enter Morecambe Bay. She left Morecambe at the end of 1917 and returned home, restless and looking for new experiences. 'I had always wished I had been a boy,' she remembered, and the chance to remedy fate came when she saw a poster for the Queen Mary's Auxiliary Army Corps. She enlisted at Doncaster in January 1918 and was sent for training at Aldershot.

At her first parade, a recruit appeared with her umbrella and, when reprimanded, calmly remarked that she never ventured into the rain without one. For a former munitions worker, the pay was poor, ten shillings (50p) a week. From this Olive had to find cash to buy Brasso, show-brushes, cap-badges, underwear and corsets. These may have been lest constricting than those she had grown used to, for one manufacturer was currently advertising corsets designed to cope with the needs of active women. Next to a picture of a busy landgirl was the slogan: 'The modern woman demands comfort.' During the next few weeks, Olive would have probably been tightening her stays, for she had little to eat. Lunch consisted of two potatoes, gravy, boiled rice and stewed prunes. Everyone was on short commons in 1918. What food was available was distributed in a manner designed both to husband resources and to give the lie to persistent and not altogether false rumours that the better-off did not go without. Ration books issued in July 1918 fixed the weekly allocation per person at eight ounces of bacon or twelve of ham, eight of sugar, five of butter or margarine, and two each of lard and tea.

Perversely, army discipline brought out a streak of rebelliousness in Olive Turner. It may have been fostered by her fellow-workers in the munitions factory or her new intimates in her army hut. Common discomforts and the need to conform to what appeared irrational regulations generated a camaraderie that was strengthened by shared resentment. 'We always hated the officers and anyone in authority,' she recalled. Her camp was enclosed within a network of trenches for use in air raids which the 'more daring' used for nocturnal assignations with soldiers. When the women's huts were checked, NCOs would be told that the absentees had gone to the lavatory, which gave their friends time to warn them to be back for the next inspection, ten minutes later. Windows were kept shut in summer to deter intruders, even in the hottest weather. Officers were given the comfort of tents, which aroused a mood of envy among Olive and her friends who, one stifling night, crept out, cut the guy-ropes and fled back to their huts by way of the trenches. During the winter of 1918 to 1919 she was posted to a camp near Woolwich where she shivered in an unheated hut and joined in a protest march, chanting 'No coal, no parades'. Five years before, she had knuckled down to the commands of farmers' wives.

In March 1919, Olive Turner left the army to marry a soldier, a clerk who had been wounded, whom she had met at Aldershot. Some nights they met in the hut where he worked and slept, but the proprieties were observed. She had listened to cautionary lectures in which, among things, the QMAAC girls were told that sexually transmitted diseases could be passed on by a kiss. Olive was also aware of soldiers' instincts and where they led: 'What did it matter to them if a girl lost her character and ended up in the workhouse with a baby.' Sex had been a mystery to Olive Turner before she entered the munitions factory. Back in Lincolnshire she had 'walked out' with a young soldier who 'wanted to touch me where I had always been taught to keep covered'. Her fellow workers soon enlightened her on these matters and, to their amusement, she insisted: 'My mum and dad would never do that.' She was nicknamed 'Old Molly never had it'.

II

The moral safety of girls like Olive had been a constant and often extremely worrying preoccupation of the civil and military authorities throughout the war. At its end, there was a widespread feeling that it had somehow corrupted those whom it had touched, in particular women, who were considered easily susceptible to bad influences. 'War brings excitement', declared a doctor in September 1919, 'especially in women' which 'easily runs over into sexual manifestations'. He singled out mixed bathing, scanty dress and jazz as evidence of a 'lowering of the moral tone' across the country.[10] Her experience with the new women police convinced Mrs Creighton, a bishop's widow, that the war had produced 'a new type of girl'. She was '. . . absolutely independent, very often wild and undisciplined. She laughs and screams about the streets and is ready to defy authority; she has shown herself addicted to petty thieving of many kinds; she is eager for any fun and nonsense. But she is good-natured, responsive to affection and kindness shown in the right way. There is splendid material in her.'[11] Treated correctly, her slide into crime and prostitution could be halted.

Lamentations about moral decay and the imminent collapse of the social fabric have been a constant in British history for at least two hundred years. The evidence has always been the same: forwardness and insolence from those from whom passiveness and respect were demanded, and sexual licence. It would have been surprising if the nation's immersion in a total war had not aroused alarms about social disintegration, and those who assumed authority in these matters had plenty of anecdotes to support their fears. One may speak for many. 'An elderly gentlewoman of a type of *grande dame*' entered a Regent Street store in May 1918 and asked the girl assistant for an article. 'It can't be got now,' was the answer, but on the approach of the shop-walker, the girl went off in search of it. 'Passing a long mirror, she stopped to arrange a curl and to steady a rebellious collar' and started chatting to another salesgirl. Overwhelmed by this casualness, the besom walked out of the shop in a huff and doubtless spent the rest of the day complaining about the 'new' girl.[12]

This creature had been around since the beginning of the war and it was not just her impudence that aroused concern. In November 1914, the chief constable of Huntingdonshire was disturbed by the sudden appearance in the Fens of flighty girls who 'appear to run after [the soldiers] in a most indecent manner'. Lax mothers were to be blamed, he thought, and he considered it a good idea to send the culprits' names to their local clergyman.[13] In the end, it was the policeman, not the parson, who had to cope with what rapidly became the national problem of amateur and part-time prostitutes and its consequence, an epidemic of sexually transmitted diseases. Both had existed before 1914, but it took the war to expose their extent and for the authorities to seek remedies. They did so for pragmatic rather than moral reasons: an infected serviceman was out of action for at least two months and, as it proliferated, the disease became a prime source of manpower wastage.

Various measures were undertaken to curtail the transmission of infection. They included addresses, like that heard by Olive Turner, and patrols of streets, parks and even hospitals by Woman Police Volunteers (including former suffragettes) and members of the National Union for Women Workers. Both groups were simultaneously concerned with saving women from degradation and publicly demonstrating that women were responsible citizens, capable of making what was turning out to be an important contribution to the war-effort. It was not a popular one. Patrols accosted embracing couples and warned them of where their activities might lead; impromptu cautions along the same lines were delivered to 'highly painted teenagers', and Jezabels who smoked in the streets were admonished. Reactions were frequently hostile.

In France, the military police did their bit by seeking out infected women and extracting details about them from soldiers who had contracted sexually transmitted diseases. They were asked when, where and by whom they had been infected and, if the woman was French or Belgian, to reveal her name, describe her appearance and name her other clients.[14] This information was passed on to the local police for action. Investigation among New Zealand soldiers between November

1917 and September 1918 indicated a high incidence of casual inter-course and a large number of infections by prostitutes in England. Of seventy-eight men interviewed during 1918, sixty-six had contracted the disease while on leave and only thirty-one could identify the women they believed responsible.[15]

This information confirmed what the army authorities already knew. Dominion soldiers, who were paid considerably more than the British, were a prime target for prostitutes. Early in 1918, inquiries made around Seaford in Sussex, a Canadian base, revealed the existence of a body of whores who had got the better of the authorities. The waiting-room attendant at the local railway station told a woman police investigator that 'these women brag openly of their trade, their earnings and how they dodge the Military Police.' The more cunning alighted at Bishopton and walked a couple of miles to avoid the patrols. Eighteen had been arrested during the previous two months, one, aged twenty-two, 'a mass of sores from head to food'. Another, Dorothy C—, aged seventeen and from Marylebone, was discovered on the esplanade with a Canadian private who had had sex with her twice before. Her rate was five shillings (25p) (a day's pay for a dominion serviceman); she had fifty shillings (£2.50) on her, all in half-crowns (nearly twice a muni-tions girl's weekly wage), and 'was dirty and has a most offensive odour'.[16] Annie B— had three previous convictions and was found to be badly infected when she was arrested in the company of an uncon-scious Canadian soldier. Punishments were clearly ineffective.

As it stood, the law was failing to cope with an emergency that no one had foreseen. In desperation, the government introduced section 40D of the Defence of the Realm Act in March 1918, making it an offence for a women to pass on sexually transmitted diseases to a ser-viceman. The punishment was either a fine of one hundred pounds or six months' imprisonment. Almost immediately, the senior naval offi-cer at Grimsby demanded the arrest of Miss B. D— of Grimsby, who had infected five ratings with gonorrhoea, and of Mrs W—, a soldier's widow. Her address was unknown, although one of her clients said she was often at the Duke of Wellington and the Fountain public houses and lived on the same side of the street as the Paragon cinema. He added that, 'She is tall, with a cast in her right eye.'[17] After consulting a local solicitor, the police decided not to prosecute and gave each woman a discreet warning. There was a similar lukewarm attitude towards making arrests in London, where large numbers of prostitutes were congregating around Waterloo and Victoria stations on the look-out for men travelling to and from the front. An official report of February 1917 blamed the phenomenon on the 'abnormal conditions and excitements' of war, slackening parental control and the easy money that could be made. Many of the women involved were not habitual prostitutes, or from the 'prostitute class', and wherever possible the police preferred to warn rather than to arrest them. Nonetheless, there had been some successes: Piccadilly underground station had been clear and there had been a decline in immoral behaviour in the parks.[18]

There were sixty thousand cases of sexually transmitted diseases ('sick through negligence') in the army during 1918, a figure that the War Office deliberately kept secret.[19] Nonetheless, the sheer scale of the epidemic could not be hidden. What the medical profession had known for years was now a subject of national concern, which was aired in the press and parliament with a candour that would have been unthinkable before the war. Open discussion and analysis were the first, vital stage in addressing a social and medical problem that had long existed more or less out of sight. In acknowledgement of it, the government set up a committee of inquiry in June 1918 with members drawn from the higher clergy and representatives from the Allied forces. No women were chosen.

III

It is extremely unlikely that Gabrielle West would have known of such things in August 1914. She was the daughter of a parson of Selsley, a parish on the western edge of the Cotswolds. Her upbringing and education at Sherborne school for girls had provided her with that sense of public service that animated so many upper-middle-class women of her generation and found abundant expression during the war in various kinds of voluntary work. During the last part of 1914 and all of 1915 she worked for the Red Cross, first with Belgian refugees and then tending wounded soldiers at a nearby convalescent hospital.[20]

In January 1916, she took charge of a canteen for girls working at the Royal Aircraft Factory at Farnborough. Three months later she was moved to Woolwich, where she found the cockney factory girls 'very rough', but 'amiable' so long as they were not 'rubbed the wrong way'. The dirt and noise were overbearing so, at the end of the year, she joined the new Women's Police Service, which was being formed to supervise munitions workers. Gabrielle West was given a fortnight's training and received two pounds per week, from which she had to pay for her uniform. It was dark blue with an ankle-length skirt, a jacket identical in cut to those worn by army officers, a white shirt with a black tie and a peaked cap. Officers and NCOs wore Sam Browne belts.

Her level-headedness and ability to handle unruly munitions girls were ideal qualifications. Her colleagues included women with similar experiences, nurses and former domestic servants, although over two-fifths of the one thousand policewomen recruited during the war had private means. General Sir Nevil Macready, the Metropolitan Police commissioner, was particularly anxious to attract the 'broad-minded sensible woman' rather than 'the vinegary spinster' or 'blighted middle-aged fanatic'.

Gabrielle West's first post was at a factory near Chester, where she searched women for matches, cigarettes and spirits and kept an eye open for 'larking or slacking'. In January 1917, she was promoted sergeant and, two months later, was transferred to a factory, three and a half miles from Pembrey on the Carmarthen coast. The workforce was 3800 strong, 'very rough', and included girls from the country who spoke only Welsh and mixed-race girls from Swansea, one of whom was a fine singer who performed at works concerts. All detested the police; Sergeant West and her assistant were threatened on their arrival, but after they advanced with determination their would-be assailants backed off, full of praise for 'a bit of pluck'. Soon after, a lesbian sergeant turned up and disconcerted everyone, although Gabrielle had no notion as to why she behaved as she did. The newcomer was a 'most peculiar person' with 'hair cropped like a man', a 'thickset' figure apparently without a waist, with a disconcerting tendency to kiss and stroke the hair of other women, whom she called 'darling'. The factory girls sensed something odd and were unwilling to be searched by her.

Women from mining districts were 'full of socialistic theories' and a source of strikes. Gabrielle West experienced one at her next factory, at Hereford. The girls broke windows, shrieked and attacked a 'well reared' timekeeper's clerk who had turned up to work. A fire-hose was played on the strikers, which calmed them down. Further tumults were caused by Irish workers who sang Sinn Féin songs and made provocative jibes about British soldiers. During one fracas, an Irishwoman chanted: 'Will we be trampled on? No!' As a consequence of this brawl, which spilled on to Hereford railway station, the Irish were sent home. They were replaced by girls from the Midlands, the 'roughest of the rough', who proved as combative as their predecessors. Aggression seems to have been contagious, for when Sergeant West was patronised by a part-time police inspector who called her 'my dear lassie', she told him he was 'a nasty little cad', walloped him and threw him out of her office. After the war, she moved to Dorset where, with a friend, she ran a tea-shop.

Like everyone else in Britain, Gabrielle West and Olive Turner had submitted themselves to forces that were largely beyond their control. And yet each had the opportunity to make choices in a wartime world where accident and chance seemed the only constants on human existence. If there had been no war, each would have lived a life constrained by the circumstances of their birth and upbringing in which their independence of spirit might never have been revealed or their resourcefulness tested. If there had been no war, then Mrs W— of Grimsby would not have been widowed and become a prostitute; or did chance perhaps make her one of the victims of the all-too-common delays in settling her ten shillings (50p) a week widow's pension and drive her on to the streets? Or did she find this pittance inadequate? After all, local women doing war-work were getting much more and acquiring luxuries that could have only been dreamed of before the war. Just before Christmas 1916, *Carry On*, the journal for workers at Armstrong's of Newcastle-upon-Tyne, carried advertisements for a dia-mond necklace with a coral pendant costing thirty-five pounds and a 'Fashionable Skunk Opossum Cape' which cost sixty-three pounds.[21] It was wryly observed that regular employment and high wages were marked by a steep rise in drinking, better-fed children and increased sales of gramophones and pianos.[22]

IV

Pianos in working-class parlours were one small consequence of what we now call a command economy. The sacred dogmas of free-market capitalism which had largely guided governments and businessmen for the previous hundred years were suspended for the duration of the war. That upholder of prewar orthodoxy, the *Economist*, disapprovingly summed up the period as one of 'restriction of industrial freedom, the limitation of opportunity, and the rise in prices'.[23]

Mining, inland transport, shipping, manufacturing and the allocation of raw materials and finished goods were placed under state control, and, after December 1916, agriculture and food distribution. The principal agency for the direction of the economy was the Ministry of Munitions which was founded in May 1915. During the next four years it disbursed two thousand million pounds and employed sixty-five thousand men and women. The Munitions Acts passed between 1915 and 1917 and amendments to DORA provided the legal and coercive apparatus with which the state supervised every aspect of production and the labour market. Strikes were made illegal, management and trade unions had to submit their differences to arbitration, wages were fixed by law, skilled craftsmen lost their privileges so that unskilled workers, including women, could do their work. Barriers were erected to prevent hands from leaving one employer for another. These regulations were universal, for the law defined 'munitions' as anything that was of value in waging war, from jam to wool for soldiers' socks. As in the Napoleonic Wars, everybody capable of contributing to the war-effort had to register and be ready to accept whatever tasks they were assigned.

In 1914, Britain's manufacturing industries were ill equipped to fight a total war. They were uncompetitive, underfunded with both cash and ideas, and suffered from intermittent and often bitter warfare between employers and labour. Most worrying of all, given the nature of the conflict ahead, British industrialists had neglected the opportunities offered by the new technologies. In 1913, British car makers produced 15,800 vehicles, a high proportion for the luxury market, while American firms turned out 376,000.[24] An official conference on the future of aviation held in 1911 regretted that Britain was lagging behind Germany, France and Italy in this field. British aircraft manufacturers were dependent on continental suppliers for engines and plans were in hand to purchase an airship from Germany.[25] The War Office found the native chemical industry 'backward' when it was asked about facilities for poison gas manufacture in the spring of 1915.[26]

The four years before the war had been marked by stagnant wages and slowly rising food prices which had led to a wave of strikes in which there had been strong undercurrents of class antipathy. In an attempt to forestall social tensions, the Liberal government had passed a Trades Disputes Acts which weakened the authority of management and added immeasurably to the power of the unions by giving them immunity from civil actions. The growing strength of organised labour hindered the introduction of the new production techniques that were being developed in the United States, which relied on standardised parts, automation and assembly lines, and where there were no differentiations of pay and status between skilled and unskilled hands. In Britain, the craft unions were jealous of their members' privileges, which is why they objected to the methods introduced at Henry Ford's Model T factory at Manchester in 1911.[27] This defensive conservatism impeded innovation and often gave union representatives greater power than production managers on the shop-floor.

The catalyst for the reorganisation and modernisation of British industry was the shell shortage that became apparent early in 1915. From the start, Lloyd George recognised that the only way to prevent labour problems was to assimilate the trade union leadership into the national and local committees and boards that would henceforward regulate the economy. Many found their elevation flattering, but in return for a hand on the levers of power trade union leaders were expected to exercise authority over their members.[28] The railwaymen's leader Jimmy Thomas appealed to craftsmen in midlands munitions factories on the eve of a strike in July 1918 in terms that had become familiar: 'Don't forget the nation's difficulty. Don't forget what is due to our soldiers at the front, and, above all, remember that loyalty to your executive is a fundamental of unionism.'[29] The strikers were not persuaded and here, as on other occasions, stump oratory by union bosses and politicians, including Lloyd George, was ignored.

And yet, like nearly everyone else on the left, trade unionists at all levels were fiercely patriotic and believed that Britain was on the side of liberty and democracy.[30] West Midlands munitions workers who pledged themselves to enlist when called wore khaki armbands to advertise their patriotism. Those of their workmates who refused were stripped of their boots and socks, dumped in wheelbarrows and trundled along to the recruiting office to make them change their minds.[31] One reason for the collapse of the Clydeside engineering strike in February 1915 was the hostility of local public opinion.[32] In May 1915, would-be strikers in Sheffield were lampooned in a doggerel with included a reminder that craftsmen were often exempt from conscription:

> Take all the — labourers, but for God's sake don't take me.
> You want men for a soldier? Well that can never be:
> A man of ability, and in the A.S.E.[33]

The ASE was the Amalgamated Society of Engineers which had always been trenchant in protecting the advantages of its members.

The Clydeside strikers had been disowned by the ASE. Its action demonstrated why the government needed the backing of influential trade unionists; the mass-production demanded by wartime needs required the suspension of the old distinctions between skilled and unskilled, the acceptance of novel technology and production techniques and diversification. There were demands for new products such as benzol, tungsten for machine-tool drills and electromagnets for generators, and techniques used for making old ones were adapted. In Sheffield, cutlers made surgical instruments and spades, but failed to meet the army's demand for cut-throat razors, which eventually had to be imported from America. Large-scale steel technology was transformed with electric arc furnaces introduced to speed up production and make the alloys for aircraft engines and motor-car frames. A relatively new and previously undeveloped product – stainless steel – was used for making gun barrels and, after the war, cutlery.

By far the greatest demand was for projectiles which required metal casings and fuses, both of which had to be standardised and precision-made. Existing factories were converted and even small workshops, such as garages and bicycle repair shops, were adapted for the manufacture of components. On Clydeside the modern production lines of the American Singer sewing-machine works were adapted to produce bombs, grenades, aeroplanes and fuses, as well as shells.[34] At the end of the war this complex employed twelve thousand women. Overall, British industry underwent four years of forced modernisation which raised output to the levels needed to win the war. Afterwards came the intractable problem of overcapacity when industry found itself unable to find markets at home or abroad.

Technical flexibility was not matched by mental flexibility, on the part of either employers or labour. Each possessed considerable reservoirs of patriotism and they were never shy of saying so, but at the same time they considered the war an opportunity to prosper as never before. Old animosities were never suspended and broke surface frequently. The influx of new machine-tools, automation and unskilled labour were deeply unnerving for members of the ASE and other craft unions, who saw the changes as nothing more than the forceful imposition of what they had been resisting before the war. At the same time, and like everyone else's, the skilled worker's wages were lagging behind the rise in the cost of living. And then there were men who were temperamentally disinclined to take seriously the new demands for efficiency and maximum output. In October 1915, a Glasgow shipbuilder noticed 'no less than about 50 lads playing football' in the streets while not far away warships were waiting for urgent refitting.[35] Such fellows, he thought would never be shamed into action by the words of imported 'Parliamentary Orators', or, for that matter, their union leaders. And not surprisingly, since there were local employers who were keen to use the pretext of the wartime emergency to pursue those sweeping changes in production and shop-floor discipline they had been planning before 1914. Some would go to any lengths, even requesting the government to impose martial law.[36]

Strikes continued throughout the war. There were just over 2500 between August 1914 and March 1918. Invariably, the impetus came from shop-stewards who usurped the function of the official leadership, which from the perspective of the factory floor appeared to have sold out to the government and to support its new coercive machinery. This was used sparingly and with some reluctance, the cabinet not wishing to provoke disharmony. Moreover, as Gabrielle West knew, strikes were disorderly affairs that could easily get out of hand. In July 1918 striking women tramway conductresses in Liverpool stopped trams carrying munitions workers, dragged colleagues from their platforms, hurled mud at drivers, smashed windows and scratched the face of a passer-by who intervened.[37]

Under the terms of DORA and the Munitions Acts, these women could have been arrested, fined, locked up, or, if they were identified as troublemakers, exiled to another part of the country. The same measures could be applied to strike organisers or anyone who appeared to impede the flow of production. To many trade unionists, these laws smacked of oppression. When the chairman of one industrial tribunal questioned the patriotism of some unco-operative Birkenhead shipyard workers, one shouted out: 'It is time the Germans were here if this is how British working men are to be treated. We are here, not as slaves, but as workmen, and we can do our work.'[38] To deflect such allegations, the tribunals had to be appear equitable and conciliatory, and to a considerable extent they succeeded; over two thousand disagreements were settled by negotiation during the war.[39]

The government could be firm. Those held responsible for a spate of strikes on Clydeside in the spring of 1916 were prosecuted, imprisoned or deported. This reaction was in part the consequence of mistaken fears that the Clyde shop-stewards' movement was somehow being organised and manipulated by German intelligence.[40] This suspicion forms the background to an episode in John Buchan's *Mr Standfast* (1919) in which Hannay visits Glasgow incognito and discovers German agents helping to foment industrial unrest and pacifist agitation. Such revelations would have come as no surprise to the former suffragette, Christabel Pankhurst, who publicly declared after a walkout by munitions workers in July 1918 that: 'Berlin had ordered this strike.' She added that the Kaiser's hidden hand was also guiding pacifist and Bolshevik agitators.[41]

Traffickers in conspiracy theories would have made much of the misfortunes of G. Salaman, a garment manufacturer who was one of the thousands of small contractors undertaking work for the forces. He owned three inner London workshops that produced clothing for the army and, early in December 1916, was fulfilling an urgent order for leather jerkins which were needed in the trenches with the onset of winter. A row flared up among his workforce of eastern European Jewish immigrants over whether or not only skilled hands should operate machines; there were scuffles and work was held up. In exasperation, Salaman sacked two members of the Amalgamated Society of Tailors and Tailoresses, which called a strike. The next day a pair of pickets (the men who had been dismissed) appeared outside Salaman's Marylebone workshop. The police were called in to deal with an infraction of DORA, the pickets were arrested and the union organiser, Faivel Alexandrovitch, appeared to protest at the police station. In the end, the authorities transferred the dispute to official arbitration and the pickets were discharged on sureties of fifty pounds each. Alexandrovitch disappeared and turned up in Russia in June 1917, no doubt to lend a hand in the Revolution.[42] The case was typical in that the government had achieved an accommodation that maintained deliveries of vital matériel through coaxing, rather than coercion.

V

In some form or other, the inexorable rise in the cost of living lay behind wartime industrial unrest. Between 1914 and 1918 the average weekly working-class family budget more or less doubled.

Status:	Skilled		Semi-skilled		Unskilled	
	1914	1918	1914	1918	1914	1918
Food	27s	49s 10d	23s 5d	46s 3d	20s 7d	42s 9d
Total (including fuel and clothing)	49s 3d	82s 4d	41s 2d	73s	36s 4d	65s 10d

Inflation on this scale had worrying implications for the war-effort. Its chief sources were increases in the prices of grain and meat and the poor harvest of 1916. If the free market in food continued, social tensions could become acute. A hint of what might happen occurred in industrial Cumberland during December 1916 and January 1917 and involved munitions workers. In the previous year, the cost of a stone (fourteen pounds) of potatoes had soared from sixpence (2½p) to 2s 3d (11p) and there were well-founded rumours that local farmers were ignoring nearby markets and selling their produce wherever they could get the highest price. In response to charges of profiteering the farmers blamed the middlemen.

The upshot was a series of disturbances. Using their lamps to see, Maryport miners dug up potatoes at night and, when one was charged before a local magistrate, the defence claimed that the farmers deserved to be robbed, since they withheld food and their sons were shirking their duty by securing exemption from conscription. One sympathetic JP observed that farmers ought to consider soldiers and sailors who were risking their lives for a shilling a day.[44] Housewives made the biggest fuss; at Maryport market there were scuffles after farmers had refused to lower prices, and at Whitehaven they were jostled and forced to sell potatoes for a shilling a stone. At Carlisle market, women warned farmers: 'A shilling a stone, or we'll give you a Maryport do.' Others threatened: 'A shilling a stone or over goes your cart.' Soldiers on leave joined housewives and overturned carts at Keswick market.

Spontaneous and small in scale, these commotions were a reminder of what might easily happen elsewhere as a result of perceived inequalities of sacrifice. 'My father is fighting in France: We are fighting against Huns at home' was the message of a placard carried by a child during the October 1915 rent strike in Glasgow. The government saw the point and hurried through legislation to curb grasping landlords who jacked up rents in areas where the inrush of munitions workers meant that the demand for lodgings outstripped supply. On her arrival in Morecambe, Olive Turner found boarding-house owners were charging twenty-five shillings (£1.25) a week for a shared room with bread and margarine as the main meal of the day.

National unity had to be preserved at all costs and so the laws of supply and demand were suspended. In December 1916, the new Lloyd George coalition introduced the Ministry of Food with far-reaching powers to fix prices and to determine what was grown and where it was marketed. At the close of the war this ministry and its network of local food committees controlled over four-fifths of the food eaten in Britain. Its responsibility had been extended partly as a consequence of the 1917 to 1918 U-boat campaign, and partly because of fears of social friction. As a rule, the poor queued for food while the better-off had it delivered, and hearsay alleged that many retailers were hoarding food-stuffs that were sold at high prices to the better-off.

Rationing staples was the only answer, since it was a socially fair method of guaranteeing everyone basic sustenance. It came into operation in July 1918 and, given that the war was expected to last at least another year, it offered a solution that would take the edge off social tension, which it did, for the queues vanished. Rationing was supplemented by practical measures. People were encouraged to grow their own vegetables on allotments made available by local authorities (there were 1.4 million allotment owners in July 1918) and to eat at the new state restaurants which offered cheap, nourishing and hot food at subsidised prices. Official fuel restrictions during the particularly severe winter of 1917 to 1918 had prevented many poor families from cooking food.

Food production was geared to national needs and the ministry ordered farmers to give priority to cereals and potatoes. Between June 1917 and June 1918, 1.2 million acres were converted from grass to arable crops. The final year of the war saw the largest area under corn since 1879, when production had begun to decline in the face of American competition.[45] To cope with the 1918 harvest farmers were given assistance from eleven thousand Land Army girls, seventy thousand soldiers and thirty thousand German prisoners of war.[46] Fraternisation was forbidden; in September 1918 three Lincolnshire farmworkers and a girl were each fined one pound for giving prisoners three silver sixpences which they promised to make into rings. One magistrate remarked that this money might have helped the recipients to escape. In Cheshire, care was taken that prisoners were never conveyed to the fields in lorries driven by Land Army girls, a wise precaution given the propaganda image of the lustful Hun.[47]

Every source of nutrition was exploited. Early in September 1918, Scottish schoolchildren were given a welcome holiday to go into the countryside and gather blackberries for jam-making. In the home counties, Boy Scouts and Girl Guides joined in this pleasant contribution to the war-effort and were paid three pence (1½p) a pound. A curmudgeonly Sussex farmer failed to enter into the spirit of the occasion and ordered the blackberry-pickers off his land and destroyed their baskets with blasts from his shotgun. His bad temper put him in the way of prosecution by the local food committee on the grounds that he had deliberately wasted food.[48] Like its Munitions counterpart, the Ministry of Food had powers of compulsion which it freely used to chastise black-marketeers, traders who overcharged and anyone who was profligate with food. In May 1917 the case of Louisa Heritage of Bromley in Kent was widely reported: she was found to have thrown four pounds of bread into her dustbin and was fined five pounds. Unrepentant, she told the magistrate: 'Pooh! It was not stolen property. I can do as I please with my own.'[49] A Falkirk farmer's wife who was accused of selling butter at over the official price pleaded ignorance of the regulations in September 1918. The sheriff fined her two pounds and urged her to read the newspapers more carefully in future.[50]

There were other, private protests against constraints on eating. My late mother-in-law once recalled refusing to eat a bloater for her breakfast and her dismay at seeing it reappear on her plate at luncheon and tea. She was told that consuming it was a blow struck against the Kaiser, a message no doubt regularly delivered to children who were fussy about what they ate. Not only the young were pernickety; Welsh miners objected to eating margarine rather than butter, and during a royal tour of the Windsor food committee's office Queen Mary grumbled about 'state' bacon which was too salty for her taste.[51] Rationing had indeed eliminated social barriers.

Brewers were peeved by successive cuts in the amount of sugar allocated for beer production. In June 1917, Cork brewers held a meeting to protest against a measure that would weaken their stout and possibly ruin their industry. 'Unreasoning Puritanism' and an 'egregious body of kill-joys and cocoa drinkers' were blamed, presumably the nonconformist, teetotal element in the Liberal party.[52] Abstainers were delighted and hoped for a total prohibition on the selling of alcohol. 'Children are being robbed of Bread and Sugar' declared an alliance of Ulster temperance groups during 'Prohibition Week' in February 1918. The plight of hungry children was contrasted with that of plump brewers who were doing well from the war.[53] Strong drink sustained the working man, as it did the fighting man, but while it could help the latter, it handicapped the former. With more money in his pocket, he drank more and needed more days off to recover from his hangovers. Ministers and managers wrung their hands; and in May 1915, Lloyd George melodramatically announced that 'drink is a more dangerous enemy than Germany and Austria.' It did prove far easier to beat; licensing regulations were introduced in 1915 and statutory closing times were imposed, which endured for over seventy years. Chronic drunkenness among Carlisle munitions workers led to the nationalisation of local pubs, which remained state-controlled until the 1980s when, along with many other public enterprises, they were sold. Increased duties and the progressive weakening of beer also helped reduce the scale of the problem. But a glance down the newspaper reports of the police courts indicates that throughout the war those who wished to get drunk always found the means to do so.

State controls hurt other interests. Fuel restrictions introduced in the autumn of 1918 prevented commercial greenhouses from growing strawberries and asparagus during the winter for what was a luxury market. Covent Garden wholesalers, who handled half a million tons of potatoes annually, were annoyed when they were ordered to buy from central stocks rather than from farmers with whom they had been doing business for years. Farmers suffered a small drop in profits, which had risen spectacularly during the first two years of the war with a farmer's annual return on capital rising from 2.75 to 11. 5 per cent. Government controls meant a slight cut and during 1917 and 1918 returns averaged 9 per cent. Overall, the annual national income from farming grew from £175.6 million to £344.3 million.[54] Agricultural affluence was reflected in higher prices for farms and the large number of tenants who were able to purchase the freeholds after the war.

VI

Farmers' profits might have been higher, but, like other employers, they had to pay wages fixed by the state. On the whole, wages had lagged behind the cost of living until 1917 and 1918, when the official bodies that assessed pay conceded a number of rises, including one to farm labourers who were given twenty-five shillings (£1.25) a week. There were no hard and fast rules for wage growth, although obviously those employed in activities with a direct bearing on the war-effort did well. Women's wage rates were set lower than men's, with the munitions workers whom Gabrielle West policed in 1918 getting thirty-five shillings (£1.75) for a forty-seven hour week. This was well under the £2 10s (£2.50) to three pounds per week earned by 'white-blouse' workers in banks and offices, but well above the twenty-eight shillings (£1.40) obtained by dressmakers and the rates for domestic service.

The aristocracy of labour prospered. The average weekly wage for a miner in 1914 was 36s 3d (£1.81) with skilled coalface workers earning forty-six shillings (£2.30); by the end of the war the sums were ninety-three shillings (£4.65) and 115 shillings (£5.75).[55] Anecdotal evidence suggested that far higher rewards were being secured. In September 1918, the *Economist* reported that coal-tippers were getting up to eight pounds for a four-and-a-half-day week, and the Clydeside shipwrights were demanding a minimum basic weekly wage of five pounds.[56] Of course, such figures ignored bonuses and extras for overtime and night work.

Perhaps the best yardstick of pay rises was the growth in the number of income-tax payers. In 1914 the tax threshold was £160, a figure that remained unchanged throughout the war, and there were two million payers. Between 1916 and 1918 a further two million became liable.[57] A substantial number were farmers and skilled workers; in 1918 tax inspectors had to be sent into the Welsh valleys to instruct miners on how to fill in their returns. By then, the basic rate had risen to six shillings (30p) in the pound which, while it enabled the government to recover some of the additional wage bill for war-work, gave workers a fresh reason for demanding higher pay. A further indication that working-class families were more prosperous was the increase in savings accounts. During the war, the number of accounts at the Glasgow savings banks rose from 877,500 to 1.25 million and the value of their deposits increased from three to thirteen million pounds.[58]

Improvements in living standards were unevenly spread. The new prosperity was brittle because it depended on an artificial economy, created by the wartime needs of the state. This was nowhere more apparent than in the explosion of company profits. By 1916 those of shipbuilders, foundries, engineering works and coal mines were up 32 per cent over their prewar levels. The shipmakers Cammel Laird reported an increase of 74 per cent, and there were similar gains made by oil and chemical firms.[59] Company results like these gave substance to the popular image of the war-profiteer: the caricature capitalist with paunch, brandy in one hand, cigar in the other and the sneer of a man who cynically enriched himself while others sacrificed blood and sweat.

Apprehensive of the effect war-profiteering would have on class ani-mosities, the government hastily imposed a levy on excess profits which progressively rose from 20 to 80 per cent. It continued until the collapse of the postwar boom in 1921, after which companies that made a loss could reclaim the wartime profits tax.

Clipping the dividends of the better-off was a reminder that national unity and cohesion could only be preserved if the burden of sacrifice appeared to be shared as equally as possible. It was impossible to eradi-cate social jealousies or those between servicemen and civilians. Suspicions that certain groups were not pulling their weight or that others were out for what they could get also surfaced in contemporary newspaper reports, letters, diaries and memoirs. In 1916, a quartermas-ter told Seigfried Sassoon that: 'This war is being carried by the highest and the lowest in the land – the blue-blooded upper ten [thousand], and the crowd that some silly b[ugge]r called the "submerged tenth".'[60] Alfred Bradburn, a Bristol munitions worker, confided to his brother that factory hands now 'work less, are more independent and get more money'. His workmates were looking forward to a postwar world in which they would do even less work and paid even more. He was appalled by striking miners in South Wales and thought they ought to be shot.[61]

In January 1918, a chauffeur who also worked at an army camp told his mistress that the soldiers in France 'were grumbling about having their wives and children starve at home', a piece of information she thought was worth passing on to General Sir William Robertson. Naval ratings and petty-officers were envious of the money earned by dock-yard and munitions workers and in October 1918 were muttering about holding mass meetings and forming unions.[62] They were following a precedent set by another body of disciplined men, the Metropolitan Police, who believed themselves losers in the race for higher pay. The formation of a police union and threats of a strike early in September 1918 forced the government to concede a weekly pay rise of thirteen shillings (65p) to all ranks, bringing a constable's wages to forty-three shillings (£2.15).

The total of working days lost by strikes in 1918 was 5.9 million, over twice that for 1914. Some sensed that these figures were a barometer of waning patriotism, which was true in so far as the ebullient jingoism of the first months of the war had been killed off by the casualty lists.

Henceforward, government and people understood that they were engaged in a gruelling endurance test. Technical and managerial improvisation, together with a willingness to forgo familiar freedoms, enabled the country to mobilise all its resources. Although it came late in the war, rationing neutralised that social rancour that did so much to undermine the Russian and German war-efforts. A sense of equality of sacrifice was a vital ingredient in the national will to win, whatever the cost. Inflation, shortages and personal discomforts were all faced and overcome and, paradoxically, millions of civilians found themselves richer. For women, the war provided a form of emancipation, a degree of independence and a chance to prove themselves fit to be full citizens.

6

Ramsay MacDonald and his German comrades: Objections to war, 1914–19

I

Throughout the war there was a powerful unity of purpose in Britain where the population was almost entirely in favour of the war and determined to win it. In Ireland, a substantial number were of a different mind; they were republican nationalists who wanted to detach their country from the Union and, as in 1798, were prepared to use force to gain their ends. On the mainland, opponents of the war were a tiny, persecuted and powerless minority who were treated as outcasts. They were reviled by the press which portrayed them as either perverse eccentrics or the Kaiser's stooges. Being out of step with the rest of the country was a risky business, and whenever pacifists or anti-war socialists voiced their opinions publicly they were invariably howled down and sometimes roughly handled. Their sense of rectitude was unshakable and they persisted against the odds.

One of the most tireless peace-campaigners was Philip Snowden, an Independent Labour Party MP. In December 1916, he was on the stump in Wales and, addressing an audience in Swansea's delightfully named Elysium Hall, he produced an astonishing statistic: 99 per cent of the soldiers at the front were against the war. 'Why don't the 99 walk home?' shouted a heckler.[1] Snowden had no answer to a question that was a source of anguish and puzzlement to all pacifists. They supposed that every rational and humane individual would abhor war and refuse to have any part in it. For the Christian, it breached Mosaic law and Christ's teachings. For the socialist, it was a contrivance of capitalism, designed to further its greedy aims and fracture the international brotherhood of working men. And for those who believed in humanity's capacity for enlightened advancement, the war was a lurch backwards towards barbarism.

During the final week of July and the first week of August 1914, socialists had hoped that prewar ideals of class solidarity might check the belligerent powers because working men would recoil from killing each other in obedience to the state. They did not; international socialism dissolved in days as millions of British, French and German workers placed country before class. Even the ILP was split, with over four hundred young men from its Bradford branch enlisting.[2] 'We simply don't count,' concluded the veteran Labour MP, James Keir Hardie, who within a year had joined Asquith's coalition as a junior minister.[3]

Others resisted the tide of patriotism. The ILP's Stop the War Committee tried to persuade the workers that they had failed to identify their true interests and had been tricked into fighting by imperialist politicians, armaments manufacturers, financiers and newspaper owners. A handful on the left, like the quixotic Marxist schoolmaster John McLean, declared that the war was distracting the working class from its real purpose: revolution. He appealed for the creation of 'a Socialist army' and vilified the worker in khaki as 'a hired assassin and a murderer'. McLean's views got him three prison sentences for sedition and the post of Soviet consul in Glasgow in 1918. He died five years later from pneumonia after giving his overcoat to a poor West Indian immigrant.[4]

Many consciences, including Rupert Brooke's, were troubled by Britain's fighting alongside the cruel and expansionist czarist Russia.[5] As the war progressed, its left-wing critics became alarmed by emergency legislation that suspended traditional liberties and stripped working men of their bargaining rights. In June 1916, Snowden told Welsh miners that the Munitions Acts had transformed them into 'colliers with iron collars, the Bond Slaves of Lloyd George'[6]. 'Starvation and coercion threaten us at home,' warned Sylvia Pankhurst's *Worker's Dreadnought* in December 1917.[7]

Few cared to listen, although what anti-war groups had to say was heeded by the Press Bureau, the police and MI7(a), whose job it was to monitor dissent and, when it seemed dangerous, stifle it. During 1916 these agencies scrutinised thirty-eight thousand articles, twenty-five thousand photographs and three hundred thousand private telegrams.[8] The public was happy to co-operate with the security services. North country newspaper editors rejected advertisements for anti-conscription meetings. Printers and booksellers sought the advice of the Press Bureau whenever they were asked to produce or stock journals and pamphlets that might be judged seditious. In January 1916 a London printer submitted copy for an anti-conscription circular to the Press Bureau and asked whether he should print it. Despite its assertion that DORA would 'enslave England', the bureau gave him permission, much to the irritation of the War Office which wanted to suppress any material that could hamper recruiting.[9] The editor of the *Western Mail* delivered to the local police his reporter's verbatim account of one of Snowden's speeches.[10] At the end of 1916, a film company concurred with the Russian embassy's suggestion that a proposed film of the life of Ivan the Terrible was inappropriate at the present time'[11] At times, the authorities had to resort to nudging. In June 1916, an Abertillery police inspector warned the proprietor of the Palace Picture House that he would be held responsible for any disorders that might follow if Snowden was allowed to hold a meeting there. The cinema owner caved in and the rally was transferred to Blaina Park.[12]

Providing premises for anti-war gatherings was a chancy business, for they usually degenerated into brawls in which windows got broken and chairs were used as bludgeons. Pacifist sentiment provoked rage and violence in a population that found the peacemongers' message intolerable. If what they said was true, then the public had been duped and hundreds of thousands were being killed and maimed for no reason. All over Britain there were families in mourning, in some streets small shrines were erected in commemoration of local men who had been killed in action, and everywhere there were wounded servicemen, some discharged because of their injuries and others recuperating. According to the anti-war propagandists, all this suffering was futile, a possibility that was as unthinkable as it was grotesque. It was understandable that those who expressed such opinions were assailed with words and blows in much the same way as Jacobin sympathisers had been in the 1790s.

Those, like Snowden, who were shouted down or manhandled by furious patriots imagined that what he called 'hooligan elements' had been surreptitiously egged on by the authorities. Official connivance was also blamed for the frequent failure of the police to intervene when a pacifist gathering ended in a fracas. Certainly, there were gangs that made it their business to break up anti-war rallies, and they did so very efficiently, but they were privately organised. The ultra-patriotic National Union of Seamen called on the services of 'Captain' Tupper who led two hundred 'torpedoed seamen' from the East End on an assault on a socialist rally held at Finsbury Park in June 1917. These rowdies belaboured participants and hoisted some on to the park railings and suspended them by their trousers. As so often happened, servicemen on leave weighed in; in this instance Australians who tried to throw one agitator into a lake.[13]

A contingent from the National Federation of Discharged Soldiers and Sailors appeared at an open-air pacifist rally at Plumstead in August 1918 behind a banner that announced: 'All patriots, so to hell with Ramsay MacDonald and his German comrades.' By now everyone knew what to expect and both patriotic and pacifist stewards were equipped with staves. Stones were hurled once MacDonald began speaking and he was soon silenced by roars of disapproval. Appeals for free speech were ignored and when some women appeared on the platform in the hope that their presence would calm the crowd, someone shouted: 'Is it a man's place to have a woman shield him?' The pelting and barracking continued. 'Do you consider yourselves Englishmen?' pleaded one of MacDonald's supporters. His opponents did, and believed that it was an Englishman's right to silence or knock over anyone whose politics he found repugnant. The meeting dissolved into a series of scuffles.[14] There was a strong tradition of political violence in Britain which stretched back into the eighteenth century and beyond and it was still very much alive.

It showed itself in Glasgow during the city's first celebration of that socialist festival, May Day, in 1918. A procession of anarchists, pacifists and ILP members got a dusty reception; there was jeering ('Get away to work!' and 'Go and join the army!'), and a fight in which a banner was seized and destroyed.[15] These outbursts were spontaneous and some bystanders clearly suspected that the demonstrators were shirkers or cowards. This was to be expected, for the right-wing press was doing its bit to keep passions high. *Punch* portrayed pacifists as holier-than-thou humbugs and the *Saturday Review* described them as 'home-bred fools and lunatics' who were given far too much leeway in expressing their views.[16] The *Daily Express* dismissed James Scott Duckers, the ex-chairman of the Stop the War Group, as 'the chief of the Pasty-Faced peace cranks' when it gleefully reported his arrest in April 1916.[17]

II

Scott Duckers, a London solicitor, was a conscientious objector who refused to assist the war-effort in any way. His fate was that of others who defied the 1915 Military Service Act and its successors. After being fined two pounds for disregarding his call-up summons, he was bundled off to a barracks where he declined to put on a uniform. For this disobedience he was sentenced to ninety-eight days' imprisonment, and his continued obduracy secured a further three and a half years in gaol with hard labour. Conditions were stern and, in January 1919, the governor of Maidstone reported to the Home Office that in spite of Scott Duckers's 'placid temperament' and 'sense of humour' he was on the verge of a physical breakdown. Three other objectors were suffering from 'general debility' and a fourth had died in Dartmoor from diabetes.[18]

In all, there were fifteen thousand conscientious objectors, nearly all of whom were willing to come to an accommodation with the authorities and undertake non-combatant work, sometimes as medical orderlies and stretcher-bearers. For Scott Duckers and the remainder of the 1500 'absolutists' such a compromise was apostasy and they preferred to go to prison rather than dilute their principles. They believed the 1915 Military Service Act was anathema, for it assumed that the state had the right to override an individual's conscience. Religiously or ethically based objections to shedding blood were inviolate and no public emergency, however grave, could justify the government's demand that they should be suspended or jettisoned. An ancient and fundamental liberty was in jeopardy.

Even those who reluctantly accepted that conscription was a necessity were morally uncomfortable about how it was being enforced. Individual cases were raised in the Commons, including those of thirty-four 'absolutists' who had been transferred to France where they were court-martialled and sentenced to be shot. These sentences were commuted to long stretches of hard labour which were served in English prisons.

Appeals against conscription were assessed by tribunals whose members included local worthies and a military representative, usually a retired officer. Proceedings were public and reported in the provincial press. In the market town of Ludlow in the Welsh Marches, the mayor presided over a tribunal of six councillors who were shopkeepers and a solicitor, figures who were also prominent in the committees that ran food-saving drives and, augmented by farmers and retailers, oversaw food distribution and pricing. By decentralising the everyday enforcement of its wartime measures, the government to some extent dispelled anxieties about an all-powerful and distant state imposing its will from on high. If an unwilling man was sent to face death in the trenches, it was by representatives of his community. This arrangement also made practical sense, with Whitehall working in partnership with men and women already experienced in local government. Such people could be expected to make decisions in the light of peculiar local conditions.

These were raised many times before the Ludlow tribunal. In May 1917, the town's only picture-house proprietor, a married man aged forty with two children, pleaded that he alone could operate the projectors, which might prove dangerous in untrained hands. He asked for an exemption from call-up and promised to perform some agricultural work, perhaps on Sundays when his cinema was closed. Councillor Evans, a draper and Ludlow's mace-bearer, told him that the food committee would find work for him. He was instructed to keep a record and present it to the recruiting office in a month's time as evidence of his usefulness to the war-effort. The only local saddler also argued that he was vital to the community, as did Ludlow's clock and watch repairer, a man of twenty-six whom the army classified as Class A, that is robust enough for front-line soldiering. He was told that he would be exempt if he could secure 350 signatures attesting to his usefulness.[19]

'A lady pianoforte and music dealer' argued the case for Ludlow's last remaining piano tuner. 'That goes rather in our favour,' remarked one tribunal member, 'if they have sent them all into the army, then we ought to take this one.' The man was ordered to report to the recruiting office and no doubt many parlour vocalists had to make do with off-key accompaniments. A dental mechanic, a thirty-two-year-old Class A man with two children, had a dentist speak on his behalf and was represented by a solicitor, Mr Jones. 'Have you got toothache, Mr Jones,' asked Mr Hunter, the military member. 'No, but I believe I shall have, Hunter. You talk too much, you had better go home.' Hunter stayed and argued that the army needed false teeth. Another tribunal member observed: 'Let people do without them or with their old ones; perhaps then they will eat less food; which we are asked to do.' The upshot of these exchanges, with their echoes of Justices Shallow and Silence, was that the dental mechanic's exemption was extended for three months.[20]

One pacifist, a twenty-eight-year-old post office linesman, was summoned to the Ludlow tribunal in April 1918. He explained his views in a written submission in which he stated that 'militarism demands unquestioning obedience and complete subjection to external authority. It takes no account of a man's personal feelings or convictions.' The war, he believed, had been caused by the machinations of capitalists. His case was transferred to a higher appeals tribunal.[21]

III

There were no tribunals in Ireland. Irishmen were spared conscription for political reasons, the most important of which were misgivings over the capacity of the government to enforce it. Divisions within the country had widened since the home rule crisis of 1914, with the moderate, prowar Home Rule party losing substantial ground to Sinn Féin. That was a party utterly opposed to war waged solely in British interests. Its outcome was irrelevant to the problems of Ireland, which could only be solved by the creation of an independent Irish republic. To this end, and mindful of the not altogether propitious precedent of 1798, Sinn Féin made an ultimately fruitless attempt to seek German help through Sir Roger Casement. An armed coup de main in Dublin by Sinn Féin in 1916 also failed, but the condign measures used to suppress the Easter Rising increased the swing of opinion towards Sinn Féin. From the beginning of 1917 it was the main nationalist party in southern Ireland.

Since the beginning of the war, Sinn Féin had conducted an anti-recruiting campaign. One ingenious flysheet adopted the layout, typeface and style of the royal appeal for volunteers. It read: 'Lord Kitchener is confident that he can entrap, cajole, gull and force 100,000 IRISHMEN to enlist in the demoralised, decadent, crime-stained and blood-sodden BRITISH ARMY.' Anyone contemplating doing so was reminded of their country's past and present grievances, including the fear that starving Britain would confiscate Ireland's food supplies.[22] There were also songs, like this one which mocked Irishmen who had enlisted:

> We've promised to give our obedience, boys,
> To King George and his toffs
> To the Cecils and Goughs . . .[23]

General Gough's actions at the Curragh still rankled.

Despite Sinn Féin's appeals, 140,000 Irishmen joined the services, sixty-five thousand of them Catholics. In some communities there was friction between the wives of soldiers and local nationalists. On 20 March 1916, at Tullamore, County Cork, a Sinn Féin activist selling flags to raise funds for a memorial to a hero of 1798, Wolfe Tone, was accosted by a loyalist. The flag-seller drew a revolver, but no one was hurt. This incident triggered brawls between supporters of the war, including wives of men serving in the 7th Leinsters, and followers of Sinn Féin.[24] In Drogheda in July 1917 there was a demonstration by soldiers' wives shouting 'Up the Khaki!' which prompted a nationalist mob to wreck the 'small tenements occupied by soldiers' dependents'. The occupant of one, Mrs Marcella Flood, the mother of four chil-dren, afterwards testified that she heard one rioter shout: 'this is the Floods. Fire!' Thirty or so stones were then thrown at her windows.[25] On 21 March 1918, three soldiers in Omagh were confronted by a drunken nationalist, who asked them why they had joined up and expressed the hope that Germany would win. After hearing the evi-dence, the local magistrate observed that, 'Up to this time, they had, thank goodness, no row of this description in Omagh.'[26] The town had been fortunate; elsewhere disagreements about the war and Ireland's part in it added to the growing number of disturbances.

The executive in Dublin was paralysed, unable either to prevent the dissemination of sedition, or to suppress lawlessness. The police were under strength and the garrison lacked the manpower to undertake large-scale security operations. All that the government could do was to sit tight and hope that once the war was over it would be possible to contrive a political settlement. Disorder proliferated to the point when, in late 1917 and early 1918, the most turbulent districts were placed under martial law.

It was against this background of growing restlessness that the 1918 Military Service Act was introduced, making men between forty-one and fifty liable for conscription. Hitherto, and in acknowledgement of local conditions, Ireland had been exempt from the draft. Its exclusion provoked fury in the press and the Commons. Cecil Harmsworth, the MP for Luton, spoke for many when he asked: 'What am I to say to my friends in Bedfordshire when they ask why they should be conscripted up to fifty-one when there are tens of thousands of the best military age in Ireland not doing their duty?'[27] The government conceded the point and extended the new act to Ireland, and then postponed its execution there.

No one was satisfied by this arrangement. Tories and Unionists believed the Irish had been indulged, and Sinn Féin was presented with a new and potent grievance. The threat of conscription at some future date was treated by the nationalists as a direct challenge that could only be met with force. Passive resistance was pointless, argued one Sinn Féin pamphlet, for it would invite massive and brutal coercion, perhaps massacres. It was better to fight, for 'if more die for Ireland first then fewer will die later in the barrack squares and prisons and asylums of England, and on the shameful fields of France and Flanders.'[28] In the meantime, young Irishmen publicly defied the government; in October 1918 seven hundred from Fermanagh, Tyrone, Donegal and Londonderry declared that they would never be conscripted.[29] This gesture proved unnecessary, for the war ended a few weeks later. With a sigh of relief, the government dropped plans for a measure that would have exacerbated the tension in a country that was now all but ungovernable.

IV

There was far greater relief among British servicemen. The armistice of 11 November 1918 was universally interpreted as a victory, although some officers vainly pointed out that no peace had yet been formally signed. No one cared: what mattered was that the fighting had stopped and Germany had been vanquished. Three months of intermittent disorders followed in which thousands of servicemen in France, Britain and Egypt did as they pleased rather than what they were told. It was as if a contract had existed in which each individual had agreed to forfeit his rights and submit to authority so long as the war lasted. His obligation performed, the serviceman became a civilian again and retrieved his former freedoms.

Army technicians, engineers and clerks reverted to peacetime habits and demanded higher wages and shorter hours as if they were members of a trade union, which of course many had been. There were sporadic outbreaks of cussedness and sometimes insubordination in which symbols of authority were assailed. 'Officers only' signs were wrenched from station waiting rooms, and at Al Qantara in Egypt a sergeants' mess was demolished. Elsewhere, men protested against routine drills and fatigues which now seemed even more irksome for they had become pointless.

If there was a driving force behind private and mass acts of disobedience it was anger at the government's mishandling of the process of demobilisation. Arrangements were based on economic necessity, rather than equity. Priority was given to men in vital occupations such as coalmining, rather than to length of service. This denial of fair play led to noisy demonstrations in London and various towns in south-eastern England during January 1919. The worst was at Calais at the end of the month when five thousand men went on 'strike' in protest against demob blunders, poor accommodation and rations. It was the largest mutiny since 1797.

Haig panicked and ordered the disturbances 'to be quelled at all costs', even if that meant shooting down the strikers. The men gave up without a fight, which did not stop Haig from asking permission to execute the ringleaders. Churchill, the new Secretary of State for War, refused and reminded the commander-in-chief that the death penalty was now only to be used in cases of murder.[30] General Sir William

Robertson sympathised with the protesters and told Haig that conditions at Dunkirk were an 'absolute scandal' with German prisoners of war housed in huts with stoves while British troops were in tents. Haig was unconvinced. Tents were 'not really colder than Nissen huts', he assured Robertson, a judgement that could hardly have been based upon experience.[31]

What disturbed Haig was that the commotions might be the prelude to political upheaval. Accounts of them convinced him that he was facing a 'plot of considerable dimensions' in which 'professional agitators' and 'regular Bolsheviks' were sowing the seeds of revolution.[32] If such creatures existed, they failed miserably. There certainly was a leaven of former trade unionists and socialists among men from the RASC and the Royal Army Ordnance Corps during December 1918 and January 1919. Despite some concessions on rates of pay and hours, the mood in the base depots was sulky and defiant. It exploded on 13 January with a fresh wave of strikes which extended to Dunkirk, Calais and Boulogne and threatened to paralyse the BEF's lines of communication. Anger focused on the treatment of John Pantling, a private who had been involved in negotiations at Calais and who was subsequently arrested for sedition. In the argot of trade unionists he had been 'victimised' and it was everyone's duty to rescue him. Agitators fanned out to workshops and offices to bully those still working into joining the strike. One activist discovered a group of NCOs still doing clerical work. 'Don't you know there's a strike on,' he told them. They showed no interest and were then brusquely informed: 'I've no time to waste arguing with you, come on now, out of it.'[33] Like its military counterpart, trade union discipline required Pavlovian responses.

The authorities showed wisdom and forbearance and within ten days the strikes were over. Thanks to Churchill's intervention, the machinery of demobilisation improved and technical staff had their wages increased and hours cut. Troops earmarked for the occupation of the Rhineland had their pay doubled and were promised bonuses. Concessions and compromises were a sign that the newly elected Lloyd George coalition was keen to restore tranquillity, whatever the price. Minds had been concentrated by events in Russia since October 1917, the current Spartacist insurrections in Germany and the spread of Bolshevism across eastern Europe. It was revealing that Haig's first reaction to the restlessness among his troops was to imagine that it presaged a red uprising. The evidence for communist subversion of servicemen was slight and confined to a handful of minor incidents. During the summer of 1917, a tiny number of isolated and ephemeral 'soviets' had been declared by groups on the extreme left, including one that included soldiers in, of all places, Tunbridge Wells.[34]

Lenin's coup in October 1917 and Russia's withdrawal from the war the following December had had an enormous impact on the left in Britain. These events were both a resounding blow against capitalism and a signpost towards future action. Soldiers and sailors had played a decisive part in the Bolshevik seizure and consolidation of power, a fact that together with often sensational press accounts of how the rich and respectable were being abused in Russia, scared the middle and upper classes. They and the government were further discomposed by the knowledge that there were now millions of men in the country who knew how to use arms and were familiar with violence. They might form the nucleus of a 'Red Guard' on the Russian model and would be hard to beat. 'In the event of rioting,' wrote a Home Office official, 'for the first time in history, the rioters will be better trained than the troops.'[35]

The soldiers' protests during the final week of January had coincided with a spate of industrial stoppages. The largest were on Clydeside and in Belfast where transport and power supplies were seriously disrupted. There was violence in both areas and troops, supported by tanks, were deployed in Glasgow after rioting and looting on 31 January. The more jittery officers believed the authorities were taking a bit of a gamble since the Scottish garrison consisted largely of unfit men and those described by one officer as 'educated and ill-disciplined', and therefore possibly sympathetic to the strikers.[36] This may explain why English and Australian units were transferred to Glasgow.[37] In the event the soldiers carried out their orders and their appearance prevented further disturbances and hastened the collapse of the strikes, which ended within ten days. In Belfast, where there had also been looting, trade union officials sent pickets to assist policemen protecting property.[38]

Nothing but will-o'-the-wisp conspiracy theories emerged from the strikes and soldiers' disorders of 1919, although some Bolshevik rhetoric was heard, particularly on Clydeside. In all, over twenty-six million days were lost from strikes during 1919. All were the result of the failure of wages to keep pace with wartime inflation, which continued to gather momentum, rather than a general desire to overthrow the political and economic system. Nonetheless, those who listened to trade unionists and left-wing firebrands were convinced that the wartime language of patriotism had now been replaced by that of class war. National unity had been no more than a product of the war and dissolved within weeks of its end.[39]

Early in 1918, the security services had begun surveillance of anarchists, revolutionary and pacifist groups and ex-servicemen's associations. The latter came under closer scrutiny from early 1919 onwards, for fear that they might involve themselves in political activities. The National Association of Discharged Soldiers and Sailors and the National Federation of Discharged Sailors and Soldiers had unsuccessfully put up candidates during the December 1918 general election, but thereafter concerned themselves with lobbying their members' interests.[40] The electoral triumph of those Conservatives, Liberals and Unionists who backed Lloyd George and his coalition was proof that voters were still satisfied with the established parties.

Ex-servicemen's associations joined with opposition Liberal and Labour MPs and some elements in the press, including the *Daily Express*, in opposition to the government's continued military and financial support for the ragbag armies of Russian social democrats, liberals and monarchists fighting the Bolsheviks. Throughout 1919 and the first quarter of 1920, British soldiers, sailors and airmen (many of whom who had been looking forward to demobilisation) found themselves campaigning in the Baltic, the Caucasus and north Russia. It was a highly unpopular war at home, and many who had been ordered to fight it had no stomach for an enterprise whose purpose they could never fully understand. Bolshevik propaganda exploited this puzzlement and told working-class servicemen that they were undertaking the dirty work of capitalism and betraying their class. This material was directed towards men who were already disheartened and discontented. In February 1919, a marine detachment protested about being detained in north Russia where they were tormented by cold in winter and heat and mosquitoes in summer. 'We are *not* in a state of *Mutiny*,' they claimed, 'far from it, we are simply asking for our rights.' We 'have been messed about like a flock of sheep' and 'are shivering all night with five blankets and a roof over us . . . we simply won't do it.'[41] During the next few months there were further outbreaks of mass disobedience.

Attempts to persuade them that the war had a useful purpose failed. The local commander at Murmansk asked his officers to reassure their men that the Bolsheviks were not the Russian equivalent of the Labour party and to remind them that the reds proposed 'the nationalisation of women', something that, he believed, would horrify every service-man. Admirable though it was, the prospect of rescuing Russian womanhood did not persuade men that service in Russia was worthwhile or in the national interest.

In October 1919, 150 sailors from a force of destroyers ordered to return for a second spell of duty in the Baltic deserted en masse after holding protest meetings. When the flotilla commander, Commodore Tweedie, attempted to mollify those who remained, an able seaman from the most intractable ship, the *Wryneck*, asked him what they were fighting for. With remarkable candour he replied that he did not know. What he did know was that a good many of his officers and sailors were similarly bewildered and wanted no part of any further operations.[42] 'We are not at war with Russia,' observed one sailor, 'and had nothing to fight them for.' He added: 'It was generally said that the wealthy people in England would benefit by our fighting and we had had enough of that during the last five years.' Another pertinently remarked that 'we were not fighting for our country but for people we did not know anything about.'

Fifty-five of the disaffected sailors decided to lay their complaints before the prime minister. They left Rosyth, evaded police patrols and caught the train from Aberlady to King's Cross, where they were met by the police, who had been forewarned. After being told by an inspector that it was too late to go to Downing Street, the deputation agreed to be put up in a local police station. There were cheers and a ringleader announced: 'Get together, boys, no trouble, go with the inspector.' And off they went, marching in good order and good faith. This was misplaced: arrests, courts-martial and prison sentences followed, retribution for what the navy considered a dangerous mutiny.

This episode threw the intelligence services into a frenzied hunt for evidence of clandestine Bolshevik activity. Many hares were started, but none was worth pursuing in a chase that revealed more about official paranoia than Bolshevik plots. The unpalatable truth was that the sailors were thinking for themselves and had concluded that they were unwilling to die in a conflict that served no national interest. All were men who, in normal circumstances, would have performed their duties unquestioningly and well. One of the ringleaders, William Selmes of HMS *Versatile*, had a ten-year record of exemplary service and had been wounded during the Zeebrugge raid.[43] By the time he had begun his sentence of one year's hard labour, the government had started disengaging from the Russian imbroglio.

This forgotten episode, like the ruckuses earlier in the year, was an indication of a new independence of mind among servicemen which extended to regulars as well as volunteers and conscripts. In future, all would be more willing to ask the reason why and expect answers based on more than blind patriotism or the traditional quietism of the armed forces. Soldiers' and sailors' objections to the Russian campaign were a symptom of a wider spirit of defiance among the working classes in the years immediately after the war. It manifested itself in the soldier's demonstrations during the winter of 1918 to 1919 and the dramatic increase in strikes throughout the rest of the year.

It was as if a political truce had been ended. In terms of the politics of grievance and protest, the war years had witnessed a suspension of activities thanks to the co-operation of trade union leaders, censorship, propaganda, intelligence surveillance of militant groups and official and unofficial persecution of pacifists. Radical dissidence was not, however, driven underground or extinguished. With the re-establishment of normal political life in 1919, it reappeared to take advantage of the social and economic problems of the postwar world.

7

The cemetery of all that is best: Remembering and counting the cost

I

A few minutes before midnight on 14 February 1918, a flotilla of German destroyers surprised and wreaked havoc upon armed drifters on an anti-submarine patrol in the Dover Straits. The commanders of the British destroyers, whose job it was to protect them, were unclear as to what was happening and offered no opposition. It was a short and unequal fight. One shell shattered the wheelhouse and boiler of the *Violet May*, killing the skipper, and the second set the boat on fire, wounding two crewmen, one fatally. Two survivors bundled the injured into a lifeboat and wrapped them in blankets. They then clambered back on board and doused the fire with buckets of seawater. The German warships steamed away and four hours later the crippled drifter was picked up by the destroyer *Courage*. It was one of thousands of episodes on sea and land in which things went badly wrong, as of course they always do in war.[1]

Seven drifters were sunk, seventy-eight sailors killed and thirteen wounded. Their names were listed by Admiralty clerks, the addresses of their next of kin were extracted from records and telegrams duly sent out. One was received by Mrs Terris, who lived with her three young children in a cottage in St Andrews. Her husband, James, was forty, had worked for a local coal merchant and had been in the navy for over three years, serving as a second engineer. His widow publicly thanked friends for their condolences and flowers, and in due time her husband's name appeared on the city's war memorial, close to where I live.[2] Like thousands of others, it stands in a prominent place and represented the gratitude of the community.

Death was inescapable throughout the war. Every provincial newspaper carried announcements of local men killed or missing in action, sometimes under columns headed 'Roll of Honour' and accompanied by photographs and brief biographies. Close relatives of the dead wore the customary sombre clothes of mourning, with widows in black veils or, if they could not afford these trappings, a black armband. In some streets shrines were spontaneously set up, adorned with crosses, flowers and the names of local men who had died, a gesture not unlike today's habit of laying flowers on the place where a murder or fatal road accident has occurred. These impromptu memorials resembled the wayside crosses familiar to soldiers in France and Flanders, and may have been inspired by them.

It went without question that the memory of the dead and their deeds had to be preserved. In June 1916, someone suggested that designs should be invited from artists for a sort of household reliquary which would contain 'war mementoes', either for the 'Happy Warrior' when he returned, or in remembrance of the man who had given his life on some field of France of Flanders.[3] The contents would have included medals, the named black plaque with its grieving Britannia that was sent to the family of every man killed in action, photographs, regimental badges and any souvenirs that the serviceman had managed to collect and send home. Trophy-hunting was an obsessive and sometimes unpleasant front-line activity, with the German pickelhaube being highly prized. Private Conn spotted one on a German corpse: 'I lifted his helmet, half the top of his nut was in it. I'm not very squeamish, but I didn't fancy scraping that out.'[4]

The idea of each family having its own private war museum did not catch on, although there was plenty of hoarding of mementoes – I once found a red and blue French kepi in a Suffolk curio shop with an English nametape sewn in the band; presumably its owner had exchanged it for his own khaki cap. The concept of national memorials incorporating objects from the war did gain widespread support. According to its prospectus of 1917, the Scottish National War Memorial would be 'a shrine and place of pilgrimage' for 'our men who have fought all over the world to point out in days to come to their children and grandchildren the very gun they had helped capture or the actual object they remembered in foreign lands.'

Souvenirs could be brought home, but not human remains. The dead remained where they had died, for it would have required an impossible effort to transport them. Those who mourned were deprived of the normal focus for their grief: the funeral. Before the war, funeral processions had often been extravagant street spectacles with elaborate hearses drawn by black-plumed horses. These displays were an expression of respect and exhibition of status, which was why the poor had their burial clubs in which money was put aside each week to provide a decent funeral for the subscriber. Denied this rite, some families held memorial services. At the end of January 1917, the widowed mother, fiancée, relatives and friends of Private Cyril Evans gathered in Wistanstow church, below Wenlock Edge. He had died from illness in France while serving with the Shropshires, and in a service of remembrance the parson paid tribute to a young man of 'exceptional amiability' who had played a lively part in his community. 'He suffered much without complaining and the severe hardships and weather had no doubt been too much for him, he being not of strong constitution.' Nevertheless, 'when the grand victory came at the end such lives which have been so nobly sacrificed would not have been sacrificed in vain.'[5]

Although Evans's body lay in a French cemetery, he had been honourably remembered and the sorrow of those who mourned him had been partly assuaged by the knowledge that his death benefited his country. No doubt such ceremonies and the roadside shrines added to the nation's resolve to fight on, come what may. To have done otherwise would have been tantamount to sacrilege. The analogy with Christ's self-sacrifice was universal and comforted mourners, in so much as those who had died in battle had a mark of divinity for they had followed the teachings of the gospels to the letter. It was a point repeatedly made in sermons and on war memorials.

These monuments represented public grief and placed individual deaths within the context of the great absolutes of the war: God,

Patriotism, Duty and Selflessness. These were not hollow words for many who grieved, since they gave death a nobility and purpose. On hearing that her son, Edward, had been killed in action in March 1915, Mrs McCarthy of Abersychan in Monmouthshire declared: 'I love soldiers and sailors and if I had a hundred sons I should like every one to join the Army and the Navy. It is a glorious death to die for your King and Country, and I am proud of my Edward.'[6] Her sentiments were sincere and often echoed elsewhere, although they may seem strange, even unnatural, to us. Mrs McCarthy had been born in 1842 and lived through the many spasms of patriotic exultation that accompanied the Victorian wars of Empire. Her son had enlisted in 1898, fought in South Africa, been discharged, worked as a miner and volunteered in November 1914.

Private responses to death were seldom revealed in an age that disapproved of excessive displays of emotion. T. E. Lawrence warned his mother against these after the deaths in action of his younger brothers, on the grounds that women of her background had to set an example of stoicism. Some refused to believe that their loved ones had been killed, or clung to the hope that 'missing in action' meant a disappearance rather than a death. The War Office, the Red Cross and other charities did all in their power to trace those who had vanished; between four and five million servicemen were interviewed about missing personnel in France, and over a third of a million reports were compiled in response to requests from the bereaved.[7]

Hope sometimes overcame reality. The facts of Lieutenant Joseph Macnamara's death were irrefutable: in June 1917 his aircraft had been flying at six thousand feet over German lines when it was struck by anti-aircraft fire. One man was seen to leap from the machine, but the bodies of Macnamara and his observer were never found. The aeroplane's engine could be identified by its number. All these details were relayed to Mrs Macnamara, but she would not relinquish the hope that her husband had somehow survived: 'It would be a great relief if I could hear something definite,' she told the War Office in December 1918. Nothing new emerged and, after further pleas, she was told in 1920 that the matter was closed.[8]

Others probed for precise information as to how their loved one had met his death. The parents of Midshipman Archie Dickson, killed when the battlecruiser *Queen Mary* sank at Jutland, tracked down the handful of survivors and asked them what they knew of their son's last moments. One, who had served in the same gun-turret as the boy, could only remember 'an awful explosion' after which the lights went out and men began to scramble out through a hatch as the ship went down.[9] If he knew more, he did not say. There were things better left unsaid: shell blasts burned bodies to cinders, shrapnel ripped them apart and escaping steam scalded men to death. Letters of condolence from commanding officers invariably stated that death had been instantaneous and without the mutilation and suffering that the recipients knew were common on the battlefield. Decency and kindness demanded that many lies were told.

Ignorance of when and how a man had died and the whereabouts of his body drove some perturbed relatives towards spiritualism, which gained a considerable following during and after the war. The séance might uncover what the authorities could not and provide reassurance of an afterlife in which the deceased enjoyed tranquillity. This was the experience of 'W.T.P.' who published a clairvoyant's revelations of the testimony of a private who had been killed in action.[10] The book struck a chord with the public and went through four editions between August 1917 and August 1918. It is easy to understand why, for the dead man claimed: 'Physical death is nothing. There really is no cause for fear.' There followed an account of an ethereal journey to the 'Rest Halls' of what was clearly paradise where, in time, he experienced a remarkable spiritual rebirth.

The key to this book's success was its insistence that the dead moved on to an infinitely happier world. This was a consolation for those whose heartache had been intensified by the awareness that the destruction of young lives had terminated ambitions and left dreams and talents unfulfilled. In a silly attempt to comfort those with such regrets, and it must have been hard to have resisted them, a poetess asked:

> Are they not the lucky ones, those dead, plucky ones?
> Though their joys were shadows – did they miss so much?[11]

What had been snatched from them was the future, not only their own but that which they had hoped to share with someone they had loved. Memory and the thoughts of what might have been were bound to remain, points that were simply made by another poetess, Marian Allan:

> We walked along the tow-path, you and I,
> Beside the sluggish-moving, still canal;
> It seemed impossible that you should die;
> I think of you, the same and always shall.
> We thought of many things and spoke of few,
> And life lay all uncertainly before,
> And now I walk alone and think of you,
> And wonder what new kingdoms you explore.
> Over the railway line, across the grass,
> While up above the golden wings are spread,
> Flying, ever flying overhead,
> Here still I see your khaki figure pass,
> And when I leave the meadow, almost wait
> That you should open first the wooden gate.[12]

This regret was one of the most enduring sentiments of the war. One of the wooden crosses laid under the Menin Gate memorial on 11 November 1998 had a note which read: 'We never had time to get to know you, from your nieces.'[13] Even before the war was over, people spoke ruefully of a 'lost generation'.

Its grandest memorial was Sir Edward Lutyens's Cenotaph in Whitehall. A symbolic, uninscribed empty tomb was not enough. Something more immediate and personal was required, particularly for the families of the 'missing'. In 1916, David Railton, an army chaplain, had noticed a wooden cross on which was written: 'An unknown soldier of the Black Watch'. Might not, he wondered, a national memorial be contrived for 'an unknown soldier'? He passed on his idea to the dean of Westminster, who was enthusiastic and asked George V for his backing. The king wavered, fearing that such a monument could easily offend the proprieties of taste, but he succumbed. A committee was formed and proposed an elaborate ritual for procuring an anonymous corpse from the cemeteries of France and Flanders.

Six bodies were exhumed from unnamed graves and placed in coffins which were taken to a hut where one was chosen by a blindfold officer. Encased in a substantial casket, the coffin was shipped to Dover and conveyed by train to Victoria station. On Armistice Day 1920 the casket was placed on a gun-carriage, draped with a Union Jack and, followed by a cortège led by the king, his generals and admirals, the funeral procession proceeded to Westminster Abbey. The burial service was simple with the singing of 'O valiant hearts' and 'Lead, kindly Light'. Afterwards the king unveiled the Cenotaph.

The concept of the 'Unknown Warrior' caught the public imagination. A gramophone record of the service was immensely popular and within five days a million people had visited the grave, laying flowers and small offerings on the slab. One hundred thousand wreaths were placed below the Cenotaph. The funeral of the Unknown Warrior had given everyone the opportunity to bury their own dead in a dignified manner; the one nameless soldier became many and his tomb provided an object of reverence for families distraught by the knowledge that their loved ones had no known resting place.

II

Defeating the Germans was celebrated in spectacular fashion. On 21 November 1918, and in accordance with the terms of the armistice, the German fleet crossed the North Sea to a rendezvous off the Firth of Forth. There it was met by the Grand Fleet and units of the French and American navies and was shepherded into the estuary. The official surrender complete, the German warships steamed north towards Scapa Flow and internment. Schoolchildren had been invited to watch history being made, but girls from St Leonard's School were forbidden to cheer by their headmistress who reminded them that the German navy had not been beaten in battle.[14] This was true and it galled everyone in the navy from Admiral Beatty downwards. Watching the German battlefleet steam into the Forth, sailors felt 'contempt and pity' for adversaries who had denied them the chance of another Trafalgar.[15]

The public's faith in the navy had not been vindicated in the way that everyone had expected. Jutland had not been a decisive victory in terms of enemy vessels sunk or crippled and the battle soon became a 'what might have been' of history, the subject of acrimonious wrangling among experts, some of whom had been present. In so far as it confirmed the maritime status quo, Jutland was a glorious victory. The sealanes remained open for Allied shipping, men and supplies for the BEF crossed the Channel, the American money-markets were still at the disposal of the Allies and the blockade continued to cause hardship and resentment in Germany. All this made winning the war possible, although it did not constitute the Nelsonian triumph of which everyone had dreamed.

Nonetheless, there was compensation in the sight of the eleven German battleships, five battlecruisers and fifty-odd cruisers and destroyers moored in Scapa Flow. Surrounded on all sides by low-lying islands, the fleet anchorage has the appearance of a lake and its shores are littered with the detritus of war. There are derelict gun-emplacements, lookout towers and storehouses built in a durable grey-brown concrete, and a slipway for flying-boats at Houton which has decayed to the point where it is barely distinguishable from the pebbles on the beach. At Lyness, overlooking where the German destroyers were anchored, there are more substantial remains – workshops, an ironwork jetty and dry-dock – which date from the Second World War.

Life here for the 1800 German sailors left behind as skeleton crews was tedious, distressful and humiliating, with some forced to barter Iron Crosses for food. They were, however, permitted the luxury of alcohol which was a valuable unit of exchange, for Scapa had been designated a 'dry' base by the Royal Navy. On 21 June 1919, the German commanding officer ordered the scuttling of the fleet rather than have it parcelled out among the Allies. Most British warships were on exercises in the Pentland Firth so little could be done to prevent this marine mass suicide. Efforts were made to drive the Germans back on to their ships and ten were killed and sixteen wounded when naval boarding-parties opened fire. These were the last shots in the war. Hun-hatred was still prevalent among newspaper editors, and the press railed against what was seen as a further example of German duplicity and wickedness. In time, most of the sunken vessels were salvaged and sold for scrap, but three dreadnoughts and four light cruisers remain under the Flow. They quickly attracted all kinds of sea-creatures and are now heavily encrusted, but it is still possible to detect the outlines of guns, superstructures and masts, which makes the wrecks popular with scuba divers.

III

The scuttling of the High Seas Fleet was a nine-day wonder for a country that was beginning to assess the cost of the war and adjust to peace. There was little cause for euphoria and plenty for anxiety. National unity was rapidly crumbling as the now heavily unionised working class endeavoured to protect itself against inflation and retain wartime gains. Class antipathy returned in a new and more virulent form. Manufacturing industry, freed from state controls, faced an uncertain future in a world where markets had slipped into the hands of foreign competitors, most notably the United States. The coalition government of Lloyd George, elected by an overwhelming majority in the snap election of December 1918, struggled with balancing the books and decided that settling the country's wartime debts took priority over national reconstruction.

The immediate bill for the war was £10,755 million, of which £7251 million had been borrowed and £503 million had been raised by taxation.[16] These figures represented a Herculean effort, excelling that made during the French and Napoleonic Wars. These had been exalted as an example of fiscal sacrifice by Lloyd George in his emergency budgets of November 1914 and March 1915. By 1917, 70 per cent of the national income was being channelled into the war-effort. Nothing like this had happened before and would never be repeated; in 1943, when Britain's war expenditure reached its peak, it was only consuming 57 per cent of the country's income.[17]

There were hidden costs that could not yet be estimated exactly. Those whom the war had left permanently injured, disordered or deprived of a breadwinner were entitled to small pensions from the public funds. In 1922 the annual bill for war pensions was £96.4 million and a further £13.5 million was spent on treatment for the disabled. These payments would be made as long as the recipients lived, although they were eventually subject to the cuts made by interwar governments in response to dwindling revenues, themselves a consequence of successive slumps.

Cycles of booms and depressions were the result of an economy that the war had put out of joint. Inflation had not ended with the armistice, but continued to gather momentum so that in 1924 the pound was worth 11s 4d (57p) in terms of its 1914 purchasing power. In large part, the pace of inflation had been set by spiralling food prices, with staples such as eggs, bread, fish and mutton costing 80 per cent more than they had at the outbreak of war. House prices rose dramatically because building had had a low priority during the war; a villa that had cost four hundred pounds in 1912 fetched £850 in 1919.[18]

High property prices were part of a general boom in land sales during 1919. Estates to the value of £21.5 million exchanged hands at prices 25 to 50 per cent above the prewar level. Many purchasers were tenant-farmers who mistakenly imagined the seller's market for produce would survive the end of the war. It did not, and when patterns of international trade were re-established, cheap imports pushed down food prices. By 1921, agriculture was entering a recession that would last thirteen years.

Manufacturing industry and mining were similarly afflicted. The war had suspended the rules of supply and demand with the state becoming industry's principal customer. Economic distortions and dislocations followed. In March 1915, the War Office ordered Dundee's jute manufacturers to provide five million sandbags, a target that had risen to forty million by the close of the year.[19] Everywhere official contracts came first, and so, by 1918, nine-tenths of Clydeside's steel alloy output was being purchased by the government. Former buyers had to be turned away and found other suppliers; early in 1915 Clydeside's Japanese customers were turning to American steelyards.[20]

United States businessmen were quick to exploit what they had correctly identified as a massive opportunity to exploit markets temporarily abandoned by their British competitors. Between 1914 and 1918 the annual value of America's exports increased from $2364 million to $6290. At the same time, American manufacturers took advantage of their pre-eminence in modern technology and production methods; in 1927, 83 per cent of all cars sold in New South Wales were American models, and 13 per cent British-made. This otherwise obscure statistic revealed one of the greatest costs of the war: the irrecoverable loss of export outlets, even in markets such as Australia that had traditionally favoured British products.[21] An official investigation into the prospects for manufacturing, compiled in 1926, concluded that the war had struck a 'staggering, and for a time numbing blow' to industry. Moreover, wartime measures introduced to promote efficiency had failed to cure old malaises. British firms were still spending a pittance on research and development compared with their American and German counterparts.[22]

The year immediately following the end of the war witnessed a boom. Unemployment increased during the early months of 1919 and then fell to just below 1 per cent in the spring of 1920. By the end of that year, the boom had fizzled out and the numbers of jobless began to rise inexorably with the mining, shipbuilding, textile and metallurgical industries in South Wales, the north and Clydeside suffering heavily. Thousands of unemployed veterans abandoned their medals for the 1921 Armistice Day parade and marched down Whitehall carrying pawn tickets.[23] Men who had been hailed as heroes soon found themselves in the dole queue and facing the iniquities of the Means Test.

IV

The domestic political and social repercussions of the war were complex. Unlike the Second, the First World War witnessed no systematic government planning for postwar reconstruction and regeneration, and the state was relieved to extract itself from managing the economy. There was, however, considerable concern as to the war's demographic consequences, which was reflected in the extension of welfare services for children.

Nearly nine-tenths of those killed in the war were men aged between thirty and fifty. No one was agreed as to the cumulative effect of this loss on society. Writing in 1917, Harry Campbell, a distinguished neurologist, claimed that Britain was in the middle of a primitive, tribal struggle for survival. The fittest and strongest would win and emerge hardier than ever. Modern warfare simultaneously toughened the combatants and taught them 'discipline and respect for authority', qualities that had been neglected by democracies.[24] Major Leonard Darwin, son of the naturalist and president of the Eugenics Society, believed the reverse would occur and the British race would be weakened. Early in 1916, he predicted that if the present casualty rate continued, 13 per cent of the adult male population would disappear. Worse still, a disproportionately high number of the dead were public school and university men, and their loss and that of their potential offspring would prove a 'check on the intellectual and material progress of the country'. Another eugenicist calculated that five hundred thousand children had been lost because their fathers had been killed. Equally disturbing was the fact that those who had not volunteered – the shirkers and the morally and physically feeble – would predominate, with dire results for the future.[25]

Eugenics was not then tainted by association with Nazism and enjoyed a strong following among intellectuals, politicians and men of science. Ways of improving the national genetic stock had been widely discussed before the war, largely in response to disquiet over the unhealthiness of the poorer classes. High infant mortality rates and the sickliness of those who reached childhood had caused the greatest concern and much prewar welfare legislation had been aimed at remedying these problems. Action in this field gathered momentum during the war in the hope that sturdier, fitter children would replace losses on the battlefield. National Baby Week was introduced in July 1916 to promote schemes for infant welfare. Its aims were interpreted solely in terms of the war by Bishop Winnington Ingram: 'While nine soldiers died every hour in 1915, twelve babies died every hour . . . The loss of life has made every baby's life doubly precious.'[26] Government and local authority health programmes were stepped up and extended to raise the numbers of antenatal clinics; free school meals were introduced and in some factories crèches and nursery facilities were introduced for working mothers.

The infant mortality rate did continue to decline, although unevenly. In Warwickshire it fell from eighty-two per thousand in 1907 to thirty-seven in 1927, but in largely industrial Renfrew the drop was from 137 to eighty-eight. Thanks to the £1 10s (£1.50) maternity allowance introduced in 1911, more women could afford the guinea fee expected by doctors for attending a birth. And yet during the war 60 per cent of practitioners were on war service.[27] Professional assistance at childbirth was obviously valuable, but what really boosted survival rates was the overall improvement in the working-class diet which was the outcome of full employment and higher wages.

A more robust generation grew up alongside survivors who had been maimed by the war. In all, four hundred thousand servicemen had been disabled, of whom forty-one thousand had lost at least one limb. Their prospects distressed the novelist John Galsworthy, who sought to lessen their misfortunes by editing *Reveille*, a journal founded in August 1918 for and about the crippled veteran, who, he believed, would be easily overlooked once the war was over. 'We see him encumbering the ground,' Galsworthy wrote, 'hopeless and embittered, often out of work and always an eyesore to a nation which will wish to forget there ever was a war.'[28] Between 1915 and 1917 under half the disabled service-men who had registered at employment offices had found work.[29]

Wartime technical improvements in artificial limbs made it easier for crippled men to undertake normal jobs in factories and offices, and there were plenty of comforting press photographs that showed veterans who had overcome their handicaps riding, playing cricket and driving. These were misleading images; despite pressure from the government and charities the disabled did not find work easily or in large numbers. Like others dependent upon state pensions, they eventually became the victims of ministries that encouraged cheeseparing because they feared the welfare budget would get out of control. As Galsworthy had predicted, crippled and blinded servicemen were often reduced to reproachful beggary.[30]

Another group that found itself adrift in an ungrateful and unkind world were former officers. There were two hundred thousand of them and many had been 'temporary gentlemen' who returned home to find themselves in a social no-man's-land. Their predicament was represented by H. F. Maltby, an NCO who had been commissioned, who wrote the play *A Temporary Gentleman* which appeared in June 1919. Its hero, an ex-warehouseman who had been an officer, had social pretensions which made him set his cap at the daughter of Sir Herbert Hudson, a typical war-profiteer 'who packs his clerks off to the front while he stays at home amassing a fortune out of army contracts'. Odious though he is, Hudson forces the temporary gentleman to face up to the reality of his place in the civilian scheme of things. Chastened, he becomes a commercial traveller and marries a former Women's Auxiliary Army Corps girl who has become a housemaid.[31] The old social order has been preserved.

Other former officers were less lucky and had to choose between destitution and menial jobs. Captain Charles Sorrell, MC, the hero of Warwick Deeping's *Sorrell and Son* (1927), becomes a porter in a provincial hotel so that his son can be educated at a local grammar school. 'Will it be a gentleman's school?' the boy asks. 'Oh, yes we must see to that,' his father replies. The older Sorrell exists in a world where his former status and courage count for nothing: 'All that scramble after the war, the disillusionment of it, the drying up of fire and foolish enthusiasms, the women going to the rich fellows who stayed at home, the bewilderment, the sense of bitter wrong, of blood poured out to be sucked up by the lips of money-made materialism.'

No radical, Sorrell, like so many others, resented those who had done well from the war. Class tensions became more intense and bitter than ever. John Buchan had hoped that the 'brotherhood of the trenches' would somehow lay the foundations of a new social order in which 'class hatred will abate because class selfishness was gone'. He symbolised this fraternity in paternalist terms with 'the light-hearted public schoolboy' subaltern leading the 'stalwart working man' over the top.[32] Buchan was correct in that this had occurred on numberless occasions, but wrong in his belief that the bonds created by shared danger would outlive the war. When it was over, officer and private re-entered a society in which they had to protect their own interests. And yet, two of his public schoolboy subalterns, Clement Attlee and Harold Macmillan, who became MPs in the 1920s and eventually led the Labour and Conservative parties, revealed throughout their public lives a powerful urge to do all in their power to help the sort of men they had once commanded. The trenches did make a few young middle-class men aware of the humanity and foibles of those they had been taught to regard as inferiors and with whom they would otherwise have had little intimacy.

The class politics that Buchan detested had been a prewar phenomenon. What had changed during the war was the self-confidence of the working class, who seemed less willing than ever to submit to what their bosses defined as inexorable economic laws. The working man was conscious of the power that union solidarity gave him and had become less tractable. Furthermore, the success of the Bolsheviks in Russia encouraged those on the left to see socialism as a practical alternative to capitalism. A just world seemed within the working man's grasp, which was why in 1918 the Labour party committed itself to national-isation in the famous Clause Four of its manifesto. The Communist party did not flourish; in 1921 it had only three thousand members and serious revolutionary agitation was almost entirely restricted to South Wales and Clydeside, where it made little headway.

Nonetheless, Marxist theories were widely studied on the left, par-ticularly by the growing number of middle-class recruits to the Labour party. The weekly *The Communist* had a readership of fifty thousand in 1921, including Leading Seaman Walter Dyer who joined the party. His expression of opinions 'of a nature antagonistic to the existing order in society' upset one of his messmates, who reported them to his superiors. Dyer was discharged by the navy which was taking no risks when it came to lower-deck radicalism.[33] There had been two cases of subver-sion of sailors the previous year, one involving Sylvia Pankhurst, who had been sentenced to six months.

For all their passion and energy, those on the postwar extreme left did not seriously upset the country's equilibrium, beyond giving the middle classes a nasty scare. Outside Ireland, the nation's faith in con-ventional politics was as strong as ever. In 1918 the franchise had been extended to all males and women over the age of thirty, and the new electorate plumped for Lloyd George and a coalition in which Tories dominated. Candidates put forward by ex-servicemen's associations did badly, but anxieties about such bodies playing a partisan political role led to the formation of the British Legion. Its chief sponsor, Haig, saw it as an antidote to a postwar malaise. 'Subversive tendencies are still at work,' he wrote in 1922, 'short cuts to anarchy are still the fool's task of unstable intellectuals.' The British Legion provided a 'rallying ground' for 'all who have worn the King's uniform' and who 'realise the nobil-ity of service, to enrol themselves to win the peace, even as they won the war'.[34] Half a million ex-servicemen joined the Legion.

Old-fashioned Liberalism had been irreparably damaged by the war. Total war could not be waged effectively by politicians still under the spell of laissez-faire principles, and the Liberal party was split by the coup in which Lloyd George supplanted Asquith as prime minister. Individual Labour politicians and trade union leaders prospered, in that they were admitted into the corridors of power and were given responsible administrative posts. The Labour party as a whole fared less well and between 1918 and 1922 occupied the political wilderness. Associations with wartime pacifism did not help: in the 1921 Woolwich by-election, Ramsay MacDonald was taunted by the slogan 'A traitor for Parliament' and lost to Captain Robert Gee, VC, a Conservative Unionist.[35] The past was forgotten by 1924 when Labour came to power in coalition with former Liberals on a programme from which socialist measures were distinctly absent. Then and in subsequent elections, the debate was over how best to remedy the economic consequences of the war.

Women have traditionally been regarded as beneficiaries from the war; after all they got the vote in return for what everyone agreed was a vital part in the war-effort. In 1916 a convalescing soldier summed up the common view in a poetic appreciation of his nurses:

> It's a pill for Mr Kaiser,
> And sadly him it vexes
> When he fights well he knows
> That his toughest foes
> Win the war by BOTH sexes.[36]

The volunteer amateur nurses, who, like their male counterparts in uniform, were learning on the job, were upholding a tradition begun sixty years before by Florence Nightingale and were acceptable to society. The same was true of women who undertook charitable work in connection with the war. Women who stepped outside their normal roles and trespassed in areas that had hitherto been masculine preserves faced disapproval. There were misgivings about those women who, largely for patriotic reasons and out of a sense of adventure, enlisted in the QMAAC, WRAF and WRNS.[37] Working-class families in particular objected to their daughters volunteering for these corps and there were persistent but false rumours that the QMAAC girls who went to France were merely chasing men and many returned pregnant.[38] Such prejudices did not evaporate during or after the war.

Those women who ignored convention and threw themselves into the war-effort did not do so to win the vote or to secure future equality; most were inspired by the same sense of patriotism and duty as men. There was no sudden postwar emancipation of women and their gains were deceptive. In 1919 parliament admitted them to all the professions and simultaneously deprived them of access to industrial jobs through the Restoration of Pre-War Practices Act passed in the same year. This legislation, and the subsequent behaviour of employers and unions, were reminders that the mass recruitment of women during the war had been a temporary measure. Men took back their old jobs and the numbers of women workers fell dramatically; where they kept their jobs their wages were lower than men's. Admitted to full citizenship, however, women were now able to exert political pressure, particularly on issues that directly involved them, such as family welfare.

V

Britain the global and imperial power gained little of permanent value from the war save the temporary eclipse of Germany, and it is possible to argue that this was not in Britain's interests. The Versailles treaty and the subsequent settlement of the Middle East were disappointments in that they failed to secure harmony within Europe and stability within the former Ottoman Empire. The trouble was that the victorious powers, including Britain, wished both to uphold President Wilson's ideal of national self-determination and at the same time to share prizes among themselves in the manner of the statesmen of 1815. There was also an urge, far stronger in France than in Britain, to punish Germany and exact retribution for human and material losses. 'Hang the Kaiser' had been a slogan during the 1918 general election.

As a result, the Austro-Hungarian and periphery of the Russian Empires were split into a mosaic of fragile states loosely defined by ethnicity, which either succumbed to dictators (Poland and Hungary) or fell prey to stronger neighbours (Austria and Czechoslovakia). In southern Europe, Bosnians, Slovenes, Croats, Macedonians and Albanians were corralled into Yugoslavia, an artificial polity designed to compensate Serbia for its efforts in the war. The creation of what amounted to a greater Serbia has had dire results for the region and Europe as a whole. Another victor state, Italy, was dissatisfied with its share of the spoils and under Mussolini looked for recompense in the Mediterranean and Africa. Britain obtained Iraq, Tanganyika and Palestine from the postwar treaties, all held in trusteeship from the new international forum, the League of Nations.

Germany was compelled to shed territory and people to its new eastern neighbours, Poland and Czechoslovakia, and face a bill for reparations that, had it been paid, would have reduced it to destitution. As it was, the account was never fully paid, but the vindictive terms of the treaty made the Germans susceptible to Hitler's promises of national resurgence. Those in Britain who had not succumbed to the prevailing mood of vengefulness recognised where it would inevitably lead. On the last day of 1918, Admiral Lord Fisher, who had joined the navy under the sponsorship of one of Nelson's captains, inspected the aircraft-carrier *Furious*. Looking at the new torpedo bombers he remarked: 'Scrap the lot, or put them in cotton wool till the next war!' Asked when that would occur, he replied, 'Twenty years time.'[39]

Everyone was terrified by the prospect of another war. In October 1919, the *Economist* spoke for many when it described 'shell-shocked humanity' still coming to terms with the suffering of the past five years. That experience and an overwhelming desire never to see it repeated were powerful inducements to back movements for international peace and in particular the League of Nations which provided the machinery for settling disputes through arbitration. The alternative was a renewed arms race which Britain could no longer afford.[40]

The pursuit of peace through international co-operation, systematic disarmament and interlocking nonaggression pacts would both prevent war and serve as a worthy memorial to those who had died. This was the theme taken up by Edmund Blunden – significantly, a poet and former subaltern, rather than a general – whom the BBC asked to deliver a broadcast on the anniversary of the Somme in 1929. 'War had been "found out",' claimed Blunden, 'but none of his masks and smiles and gallant trumpets can any longer delude us; he leads the way through the cornfields to the cemetery of all that is best.' Those who had been killed 'will never be excelled in honour, unselfishness, and love; except by those who come after and resolve that their experience shall never again fall to the lot of human beings.' If the present negotiations succeeded and a permanent international peace followed, then the country would have paid its debt to the dead and given quittance to those like him who had suffered in the war.[41] Otherwise, the wartime slogan 'the war to end wars' would have been just another piece of hollow propaganda contrived by deceitful politicians.

VI

Blunden's talk was delivered at a time when Britain was beginning to reassess the war. Between 1919 and 1926 nearly everyone, including those who had taken part in it, had been curiously reticent about the conflict.[42] Then, roughly between 1926 and 1933, came an autopsy undertaken by a handful of literary men, mostly former officers like Blunden. They produced a sequence of factual and semi-fictional narratives of their own experiences which caught the public attention and proved highly influential in shaping attitudes towards the war in that and later generations. Together with the poetry of Graves, Sassoon and Owen, these books form the canon of First World War literature which has become a fixed part of school and university curricula. R. C. Sherriff's play *Journey's End* (1928) has been performed regularly and filmed. T. E. Lawrence's *The Seven Pillars of Wisdom* (1926), and its shortened version, *Revolt in the Desert* (1927) were the basis for a stunning and very popular film, and Vera Brittain's *Testament of Youth* (1933) has been adapted for television. Whether we like it or not, and those military historians who have taken on the Sisyphean task of rehabilitating the generals do not, the verse of Sassoon and Owen and the prose of Aldington, Blunden, Graves, Ford Madox Ford and Brittain still provide many people with their most lasting impressions of what the First World War was like.

None of these works claim to be history, although they describe recognisable historical episodes (*Journey's End* is set in the few days before the German offensive of March 1918) and contain material drawn from the authors' diaries and letters. Each saw his work primarily as literature, a creative personal response to the extraordinary, morally perplexing and terrifying circumstances in which they found themselves. The recurrent themes of noble, carefree enlistment, the horrors of the battlefield, patriotism betrayed and subsequent disillusionment run through much of the poetry and prose. Above all there is the nagging feeling that the suffering would not yield anything of value; not surprisingly, what these writers had to say about war did much to foster pacifism during the thirties.

These sentiments were not novel; they were felt, written about and published during the war. Consider the observations of Arthur West, written towards the end of the Somme and published shortly after his death in 1917: 'Most men fight, if not happily, at any rate patiently, sure of the necessity and usefulness of their work. So did I – once! Now it all looks to me so absurd and brutal that I can only force myself to continue in a kind of dream-state; I hypnotise myself to undergo it. What *good*, what *happiness* can be produced by some of the scenes I have had to witness in the last few days?' West was an aesthete and intellectual who had won a Balliol scholarship in 1910 after several wretched years at the games-crazy Blundells School. Like Blunden and Graves, he had volunteered out of a sense of duty and patriotism and found himself occupying a humble position in a rigid hierarchy dominated by men whom in peacetime he would have dismissed as dim, hearty conformists. How these men of letters tried to come to terms with the unnatural and hostile world in which they found themselves, how they analysed themselves and how they, in Owen's phrase, reacted to and explored 'the pity of War' have been exhaustively analysed.

At the same time, in what is to some extent an excellent corrective to the common view of First World War literature, Dr Martin Stephen has produced an anthology of wartime verse that contains much that is jaunty, patriotic, droll and cheerful. Much of this stuff is not great poetry and does not have the same appeal to posterity as profounder works, but it is a reminder that the experiences of the front did not always generate introspection and despair.[43] And there are masses of often unpolished reminiscences, letters and diaries that exude a simple quietism and the capacity somehow to make the best of things.

Or there were men like the father of Mavis Nicholson who had told her little about the war save that the trenches had been full of rats and animals had been better treated than soldiers. On the morning of

3 September 1939 he listened with millions of others to Neville Chamberlain's quavering voice declare: 'This country is at war with Germany.' Mr Nicholson's reaction was that 'he was bloody glad he was too old to be called up.' He would not be defrauded again: 'He pitied the poor buggers who would go off believing, as he had done, that this was the war to end all wars.'[44]

PART SIX

THE PEOPLE'S
WARS:
1919–2000

1

Britannia's Huns with their long-range guns: Civil wars in Ireland, 1919–23

I

And from the plains of Royal Meath
Strong men came hurrying through
While Britannia's Huns with their long-range guns
Sailed in through the foggy dew.[1]

Each civil war in Ireland has yielded its crop of inspirational song; this one describes the 1916 Easter Rising. Britannia's Huns were the British soldiers who converged on Dublin with their heavy artillery during the last week of April 1916. Troops summoned from the mainland imagined that they were disembarking in France.[2] It was perfectly understandable for a Tommy to mistake the sights and sounds of Dublin for those of, say, Ypres. On entering the city he would have heard artillery, machine-gun and rifle fire and seen shops, offices and public buildings in ruins or on fire. Snipers were everywhere; there were rumours that German troops had landed at Galway Bay and escaped German prisoners of war were believed to be on their way to help the Irish insurgents.[3]

Outgunned and outnumbered, the rebels surrendered on 29 April after four days of street-fighting and sieges in which they had lost sixty-four dead and had killed just over twice that number of British troops.

The roads were soon cleared and damaged buildings repaired, although there are still bullet marks on columns of the General Post Office which had been the main rebel stronghold. A few yards down O'Connell Street, one of the bronze allegorical figures beneath O'Connell's statue has a neat round hole in the centre of her breast, clearly the work of a marksman. Or, perhaps, the shot was fired some years later by a trigger-happy Auxiliary or Black and Tan, for it was the sort of vandalism they went in for.

The attempted coup de main by Sinn Féin volunteers marked the beginning of a new and still unfinished phase in an intermittent, eighty-four year struggle to decide how and by whom Ireland should be governed. The war spread into the rest of Britain, which suffered from sporadic outbreaks of terrorism during 1920 and 1921, 1938 and 1939 and the 1970s onwards. Seen from an Irish perspective, the 1916 rebellion and its protracted sequel were an extension of a contest for the control of Ireland that had started in the middle of the twelfth century. Of this the nationalists had no doubt. 'Our fathers fought before us', ran one of the lines of 'The Soldier's Song', which became the marching song of the Sinn Féin volunteers and, eventually, the national anthem of the Irish Republic. For Sinn Féin, the goals were the same as they had been in 1798: an undivided Irish republic, totally detached from the United Kingdom.

Independence of a kind had seemed within Ireland's grasp in September 1914 when parliament passed the home rule bill, dissolving the union of 1800 and promising the restoration of the old Dublin parliament, now to be elected on democratic lines. Self-government was, however, postponed for the duration of the war and Home Rule MPs urged their countrymen to be satisfied and throw themselves behind the British war-effort. This appeal was largely directed towards the 188,000 men who had joined the INV during 1914 in readiness to fight the UVF.

The war split the INV and the whole nationalist movement. Some Irishmen took the British government at its word and volunteered. Others were sceptical and refused to hazard their lives in Britain's overseas war. In mid-August 1914, two thousand Cork Volunteers pledged to defend their homeland but refused 'to be turned into militiamen to be led by General Roberts and Kitchener'.[4] Volunteers drawn towards

Sinn Féin remained at home and drilled secretly, as had their predecessors in 1798. Memories of that year and its 'martyrs' were revived by speakers during a review of volunteers at Bandon, County Cork, in mid-August 1914.[5] If they knew their nationalist lore, the listeners would have been well aware of the similarities between Ireland's present situation and that in 1798. Then the republicans had canvassed and secured French assistance for a revolt against an unpopular administration distracted by a continental war.

History now presented Sinn Féin with the opportunity to do likewise. Like republican France, imperial Germany might be persuaded to support a nationalist uprising that would force Britain to withdraw troops from the front. During the winter of 1914 to 1915, Sir Roger Casement had attempted to repeat history by travelling to Germany, where he pleaded for arms and attempted to suborn Irish prisoners of war. He secured fifty-five defectors and a shipment of arms and ammunition which were shipped in a Norwegian trawler, the *Aud*. It heaved to off Tralee Bay, but found no one waiting to unload its cargo, and was sunk by its commander on 20 April 1916, after being challenged by a British warship. On the same day, Casement was put ashore from a U-boat and almost immediately captured.

This sequence of blunders was the prelude for the coup in Dublin on Easter Monday, 23 April. As a military operation it was an utter failure; once the British authorities had recovered their balance and called in reinforcements, they had little difficulty in dislodging the two thousand or so rebels from their strongholds. As a political gesture, the Easter Rising was an unlooked-for success. This owed much to the policies of the local commander, General Sir John Maxwell, who was convinced that the insurrection had been masterminded by German intelligence. Condign measures were necessary to strike fear into the rest of Ireland and fifteen of the rebel leaders were tried for treason by courts-martial and shot. Many more, including Eamon de Valera, the future president of Sinn Féin, and Michael Collins, who directed the war against Britain between 1919 and 1921, were given long terms of imprisonment in British gaols.

These proceedings were legal and owed much to Maxwell's experience of dealing with the enemies of the Empire in the Sudan. After the fall of Khartoum in 1898, he helped organise the summary executions of prominent supporters of the Khalifa Abdullah.[6] It was axiomatic among commanders on imperial frontiers that severe measures simultaneously instilled obedience and won respect. Like dervishes, Irishmen would respond to the iron fist.

One of Maxwell's subordinates, Captain John Bowen-Colthurst of the Royal Irish Rifles, was of the same mind. During the fighting he ordered the execution of three nationalist journalists being held prisoner in the Portobello barracks. 'It is the right thing to do,' he announced, believing that the men were about to be rescued, or so he claimed afterwards. Bowen-Colthurst came from an Ulster protestant landowning background and his sixteen years in the army had included service in India and in the Tibet campaign. After the retreat from Mons, he had a breakdown and at his trial confessed to having panicked. He was judged insane and sent to Broadmoor, where he was diagnosed as a 'neurasthenic' with symptoms of insomnia and a 'morbid religious zeal'. He was released after treatment in January 1918, much to the fury of Irish nationalists, and finally settled in British Columbia from where he conducted an extended postal vendetta against one of his former commanding officers.[7] Moral callousness was not confined to one deranged British officer. The volunteers murdered several unarmed men, including an indignant Dubliner who attempted to remove his cart from a rebel barricade.[8] Another tradition of previous Irish conflicts had been resuscitated in 1916: the easy and promiscuous resort to extremes of brutality.

II

Maxwell's firing squads turned out to be Sinn Féin's recruiting-sergeants. At first, the uprising had provoked largely hostile emotions ranging from vexation to rage, but the systematic killing of its leaders aroused pity and indignation. At worst, the rebels had been foolhardy and misguided idealists. Dead and in British gaols they became martyrs, heroic figures who had proved beyond question their sincerity and courage. By fighting and dying for Ireland, they had elevated themselves and their country. Henceforward, the test of a nationalist was whether he was willing to follow their example and risk his life for his country. During the next seven years and beyond, militant nationalism would draw immense strength from acts of self-sacrifice, including those of hunger-strikers who starved themselves to death.

The true nationalist now thought of himself as a soldier, engaged in a war against his country's enemy, Britain. In March 1918, when five Dundalk Sinn Féiners were charged with illegal drilling, one told the magistrate: 'As a soldier of the Irish Republic I refuse to recognise the court.' To emphasise the point, his fellow accused defiantly kept their caps on and lit cigarettes. The five were committed to Dublin's Mountjoy gaol and were given a cheery send-off by crowds singing 'The Soldier's Song' and shouting nationalist slogans.[9]

This incident was one of many that were symptoms of the disintegration of government authority over large parts of southern Ireland and the growth of popular support for Sinn Féin. The shift of allegiance and mood was reflected in boisterous demonstrations in villages and towns. At Drimoleague, County Cork, the 1917 St Patrick's Day celebrations were described by a police inspector as a 'bear garden' with a crowd of fifty or so shouting 'Up Germany' and 'Up Sinn Féin' and singing nationalist songs. A few miles away at Dunmanway, a howling seditious mob gathered on the night of 10 May 1917, hurled imprecations at the police barracks, shouted Sinn Féin slogans and pelted the house of the local magistrate. One activist pointed to Carbery House and reminded the crowd that its owner had lent his car to the police during the Easter Rising.[10] In a war, the enemy had to be identified.

As well as working up a head of nationalist steam, Sinn Féin extremists were preparing for the possibility of a prolonged campaign against the authorities which they imagined was now unavoidable. Sinn Féin's arsenal had been severely depleted after the collapse of the Easter Rising but was topped up by privately owned revolvers and sporting guns which were stolen from farms and country houses. In January 1918, a man was killed attempting to steal the rifle from a soldier on leave and a raider was peppered by a farmer's shotgun. Between sixty and eighty men ransacked Baronscourt, the seat of the Duke of Aberdeen, but found only antique weapons.[11] Early in 1918, County Clare appeared to be sliding into anarchy with gunmen ambushing police patrols and rumours of plans for concerted assaults on barracks. The district was placed under army control, which did not prevent parties of Sinn Féiners from drilling openly and without interference.[12]

At the same time, moral pressure was put on the police and anyone who chose to supply them with intelligence. Tradesmen who supplied the police in Clare were threatened with that traditional instrument of Irish popular disapproval, the boycott.[13] Attempts were made to subvert members of the Royal Irish Constabulary (RIC), some of whom received leaflets in August 1918 that reminded them of where their loyalties ought to lie and who their enemies were: 'Your name is not Price or Maxwell or French; it is Kelly or Burke or Shea. You were reared in an Irish household and your mother sang Irish songs . . . Private Hodgkins of Yorkshire, or Berkshire, or Pigshire, is an important man here. He can carry a gun and ammunition, and his vile language into that household which you once loved . . .'[14]

'French' was Field-Marshal Lord French of Ypres, sometime commander of the BEF and, from May 1918, Lord-Lieutenant of Ireland. He had been instructed to pacify the most turbulent areas, which were placed under military control, and curtail the activities of Sinn Féin, which he accomplished by using the terms of DORA to intern some of its leaders. It was a hopeless mission: the administration's prestige had been severely, perhaps irredeemably, damaged and French had just under ten thousand troops available for security duties.[15] At best, he could keep the lid down for the time being and hope that some political settlement could be devised, based upon the Home Rule Act.

This possibility was becoming increasingly remote, given the Unionist objections to a single Irish state. The people of Ulster 'will never submit to a Dublin Parliament dominated by the Roman Catholic hierarchy', declared William Coote, MP, to his South Tyrone constituents in April 1918.[16] The rest of Ulster's protestant community heartily concurred and Lloyd George, whatever his past commitment to home rule had been, now depended upon Unionist support in his cabinet and the Commons. Furthermore, any future political decision over Ireland was complicated by the imperial dimension. In 1921, when the guerrilla campaign was at its height, Field-Marshal Sir Henry Wilson, the Chief of the Imperial General Staff, predicted that the 'loss of Ireland' would lead directly to the loss of the Empire. Revealingly, he confided to the Unionist leader, Sir James Craig, that 'I often tell these unfortunate English fellows that when they have made a hash of the Empire we Ulster boys will take over the show for them and let them see how to run a real Imperial idea!'[17]

Armistice Day 1918 revealed that the old Irish polarities were unchanged. At Omagh, soldiers and local girls danced and kissed in the streets, union flags appeared on houses and cars and there was a procession through the streets. Sinn Féiners watched with 'sullen disregard'.[18] The Blacklion Orange Lodge marched through Belcoo, County Fermanagh, by torchlight and held a meeting which closed with the singing of the national anthem. Nationalists replied with cries of 'Up Dublin' and 'Up de Valera' and Father Caulfield, a passionate and outspoken Sinn Féiner, declared: 'To hell with the Kaiser, and to hell with King George, his first cousin.'[19]

Some Belcoo nationalists carried American flags. President Wilson's expression of support for small nations seeking autonomy had been taken by Sinn Féin to mean that the United States might treat Ireland favourably, so long as it could be proved that the Irish people wanted sovereignty for themselves and Sinn Féin was their voice. For this reason, party activists were endeavouring to establish in some districts what amounted to a shadow administration, with its own courts. Thanks to the Easter Rising and its growing temerity, Sinn Féin was winning Irish hearts, strongly appealing to strains of romantic nationalism. Its future political programme was simple – an independent republic – but it possessed few solid proposals as to how this might be accomplished. Imprecision as to methods did not matter greatly since its rival, the Home Rule party, had failed in that it had been unable to prevent the British government from tacitly approving the future partition of Ireland. While Sinn Féin was prepared to fight for independence, Home Rule candidates lamely admitted that Ireland could never hope to overcome the might of the British Empire.[20]

The December 1918 general election gave Sinn Féin what it wanted: proof that it spoke for the majority of Irishmen and was the sole inheritor of the nationalist tradition. Sinn Féin candidates swept the south and, in January 1919, thirty-three assembled in Dublin's Mansion House (thirty-six were in prison) and declared themselves the parliament (Dáil Eireann) of the new Irish Republic. Triumph at the polls was a reflection of the swing in opinion towards Sinn Féin during the preceding thirty months, although the party had secured less than half the popular vote. There were 1.9 million electors in Ireland, of whom eight hundred thousand were newly enfranchised women, and of these 485,000 had voted for Sinn Féin with 557,400 for the old Home Rule party and (mainly in the north) the Unionists.[21] This was not an overwhelming mandate, but it was sufficient for the Sinn Féiners in the Dáil to regard themselves as the legitimate government of Ireland and to behave accordingly.

As a test of its executive powers, the Dáil took the odd step of banning hunting as a protest against the continued imprisonment of nationalists by the British. This infringement of liberty was not well received and local Sinn Féiners had to use force to get their way. Twenty youths attempted to halt the Ward Union stag hounds on 19 February and two shots were fired, one wounding a horse. In Kilkenny volunteers stopped the Coolagh hunt, much to the annoyance of local farmers who held a protest meeting.[22] By and large, this gesture succeeded and most hunts had acquiesced by 1 March.

There was no way of knowing what course events would take. Much, some believed everything, would depend on whether the fledgling and so far unchallenged state could secure American support and investment. To this end, de Valera set off to the United States. It was not clear how the British government would react, although the preponderance of Unionists and imperialists within Lloyd George's cabinet made it highly improbable that London would acquiesce to what was tantamount to a unilateral declaration of independence by a part of the Empire. The situation was rather like that in Massachusetts in 1775 when the authorities had had to decide how much defiance they could tolerate.

Some sort of armed confrontation could reasonably be expected and French's policy during the second half of 1918 indicated that, as in 1798, the British would employ martial law once things got out of hand. When demobbed soldiers returned to Belcoo at the end of December 1918, Father Maguire asked the Catholic community to treat them well, for 'they were good Irishmen who had been led astray, who knew how to shoot and might be useful to them.'[23] Within Sinn Féin, a powerful group not only expected a fight but welcomed it. By early 1919 its various bodies of volunteers were being called the IRA

(Irish Republican Army), the name by which they would subsequently be known.

It was a force that had evolved during 1918 and 1919 under the guidance of Cathal Brugha (who became defence minister in the Dáil), Richard Mulcahy, who was chief of staff, and Michael Collins, who served as director of intelligence and minister of finance in the Dáil. The IRA's structure followed that of the British army with a general headquarters and locally recruited brigades comprising between three and six battalions. Each of these was split into companies under elected officers. The chain of command was tenuous, with district commanders often doing more or less as they wished. Until March 1921, when the Dáil officially took responsibility for the IRA, it was theoretically free of political control. Women and schoolchildren formed support units, the Cumann na Mban and Fianna Eireann, which provided supplies, ran messages, kept safe-houses and collected intelligence and gave operational assistance, organising escape routes and taking weapons from fugitive gunmen. Throughout the war, the IRA was desperately short of explosives, arms and ammunition and the greater part of its efforts was concentrated on acquiring them by raids on industrial stores and police, army and naval depots. Success was limited; in November 1921 the IRA's GHQ calculated that it possessed three thousand firearms.[24]

III

Ireland slithered into war during 1919. The desperate nature of the IRA's quest for arms and its endeavours to intimidate the RIC made bloodshed inevitable. The lack of a tight command structure also encouraged more militant district commanders to act on their own initiative. This is what happened on 21 January 1919, when Seán Treacy and eight Tipperary volunteers ambushed a police detachment escorting gelignite to a quarry at Soloheadbeg and two constables were killed in the exchange of fire. Dan Breen, one of the attackers and later commandant of the 3rd Tipperary Brigade, hinted afterwards that the attack had not entirely been prompted by military necessity. It had been partly intended to rekindle popular enthusiasm for the armed struggle which he feared had been dulled by Sinn Féin's recent success in the polls.[25]

Throughout the next two years the IRA needed to provide constant reminders of its capacity to strike at the enemy, often in a spectacular fashion. Whatever their immediate tactical and strategic value, these coups were invaluable propaganda and they kept IRA men busy. Inactive guerrillas became stale and lost heart like soldiers in any other army. Publicity, experience and arms were simultaneously provided by another raid in March, this time against the RAF airfield at Collinstown near Dublin. It was a signal and, for the authorities, alarming example of the IRA's audacity and powers of organisation. Between thirty and forty men in cars surprised sentries, bound them, incapacitated ten military cars and drove off with seventy-five rifles and four thousand rounds of ammunition.[26]

Even if the IRA secured weapons from these and other sources, it lacked the numbers to engage British troops openly. A guerrilla war was the only option and, if it was to have any chance of success, the British intelligence-gathering system would first have to be neutralised through assassination and intimidation. The IRA's first target was the RIC, which Dan Breen rightly identified as 'the brain of England's garrison'. At the same time, and sometimes through the same methods, the IRA had to secure the co-operation or benevolent neutrality of a majority of the Irish people, whose help would prove vital once the authorities retaliated with coercive measures. Progress on this front was well advanced by the beginning of 1919. The local police reported that a council workman who had witnessed the Soloheadbeg murders 'cannot or will not identify' the gang responsible and there was a 'bitter hostility' to the RIC in the area. After the Collinstown raid, the government decided it was prudent to pay off the eight hundred local civilians employed at the airfield whose loyalty was no longer assured.[27]

Then and afterwards, the old apparatus of the eighteenth- and nineteenth-century Irish secret societies was reactivated with their sinister and frightening rituals of nocturnal threats and vengeance on suspected collaborators and informers. After a scuffle involving two constables at Holywell, County Fermanagh, in September 1919, the militant republican Father Caulfield warned that, 'Any men who was seen talking to a policeman in future, no matter who he is, is dangerous . . . Sinn Féin have their secret service and they will know about it.' As a parting shot he added: 'Lord French is a whore.'[28]

In all likelihood, some of the IRA's victims had no connection whatsoever with the security forces. One night in April 1921, Hugh Newman, a former soldier from Lisdegan, County Cavan, was taken in his nightshirt from his wife and family and shot three hundred yards from his house. According to the police, he had never been an informer, nor could have been, for 'the IRA take good care that loyal people such as this ex-soldier will be kept in the dark as to their movements.'[29] This being so, his murder was a device to coerce others who were unwilling to accept Sinn Féin's brand of nationalism. In the same month, Daniel McCarthy's bullet-ridden corpse was found by a roadside in Ballincollig, County Cork, with a notice attached to it that read: 'spies and informers beware.' It is difficult to understand what value he could ever have been to the intelligence services, for a police report described him 'a native of Bantry and half-witted'.[30] At the time, the IRA in the area were under pressure and had become very jumpy about informers.[31]

Whether random or not, terror worked. Breen thought that many RIC men recognised him and other IRA suspects as they passed through the countryside, but said nothing. A constable who did otherwise 'would not be serving his wife and family by attempting to arrest us'.[32] Like every other IRA man, Breen knew enough history to appreciate that the combination of 'English gold and Irish greed' had been a canker that had destroyed previous revolutionary movements.

Public and private animosities became entwined in the IRA's campaign of coercion. In the remote Galway village of Loughanbeg, which a police inspector described as 'a regular warren of small, poverty stricken cottages', Patrick Thornton had a reputation as a 'local bully' with a record for assault. He had served with the British army at Mons and been invalided out in November 1915. His brother, Martin, was also unloved but for different reasons, since he had 'kept aloof from Sinn Féin when drilling started in 1917 and incurred their hostility'. On the night of 2 February 1920, when the two brothers were returning from the pub, they were attacked by five men who beat them with sticks and fatally shot Patrick. After some difficulty scouring the 'wild, rocky moorland country' the police rounded up four suspects, including the three Feeney brothers, all Thornton's neighbours. The murder charge was dropped and the Feeneys each got eighteen months for assault. The police report of the case concluded that 'the people there and all along the coast are a very savage race' and, it would appear, quite happy to settle their private disputes in the way of their ancestors.[33] Whether they would have done so anyway, or were encouraged by a background of civil war, is not known.

This episode occurred during the second phase of the IRA's campaign. Towards the end of 1919 there had been an upturn in the scale of violence, and attacks on British troops and an attempt to murder Lord French revealed that the terrorists were growing bolder. The terminal decline in police recruitment, numbers and morale indicated that the IRA was getting the upper hand and getting closer to its objective of knocking down the scaffolding that shored up the Dublin administration. While the objectives of Sinn Féin and the IRA were all too clear, those of the government were not. London vacillated between prescribing placebos, in the form of amnesties for Sinn Féin detainees, and astringents, in the shape of military reinforcements and the imposition of martial law in Dublin, Meath and Wicklow between April and June 1920.

Anxieties about the depletion and ineffectiveness of the RIC forced the cabinet's hand and, in October 1919, it was decided that since Irishmen could no longer be induced to join the force, the shortfall would be made up by recruits from the mainland. This proved to be a self-defeating stratagem for it produced the 'Black and Tans', who first appeared on Ireland's streets in the spring of 1920, and the 'Auxies' or 'Cadets' (Auxiliary Division of the Royal Irish Constabulary), another scratch force which began to arrive in the summer. Collectively known as the 'Tans', this body of 12,200 men soon won a place of infamy in the nationalist demonology alongside Cromwell's Ironsides and the 'Orange' Yeomanry of 1798. The Tans, whose dark green and khaki uniform reminded some wit of a pack of Limerick foxhounds, were largely ex-soldiers who were paid ten shillings a day (50p). The Auxies were paid twice that amount and were a cut above their colleagues, having been recruited solely from former officers. For this reason, a Cork IRA man adopted 'a strong Scotch accent' and 'a gentlemanly bearing' when he posed as an Auxie in an attempt to entrap a suspected informer.[34]

The Tans and Auxies turned out to be a Frankenstein's monster which refused to do its creator's bidding and ran out of control. This was bound to happen: both units had limited training and no local roots. Finding themselves in a hostile country, they treated its people and their property with contempt and spite. For the Irish, the Tans were an overbearing army of occupation whose members rode around in their lorries, robbing, destroying property and killing at will. They did so as much out of frustration as malice, for what came to be known as reprisals were invariably random retribution for some IRA outrage. Acts of retaliation, taken by vengeful men on the spur of the moment against real or imagined Sinn Féin supporters, began in the spring of 1920 and continued to the end of the war. They were undertaken by policeman, Tans and soldiers, and often included setting fire to creameries – a crude form of economic warfare against rural communities suspected of assisting the IRA.

While deploring what was evidence that the security forces were becoming a law unto themselves, some senior police and army officers admitted that spontaneous reprisals had a value. The local commander-in-chief, General Sir Nevil Macready, was sympathetic, and General Sir Henry Wilson suggested that such actions were beneficial, having produced 'cringing submission' in hitherto truculent districts. The cabinet was ambivalent, recognising the salutary effect of reprisals, while regretting their indiscriminate nature.[35] After discussing the subject in November, it was decided to let matters take their own course while publicly instructing the military and civil authorities to restrain their men. On 10 December, a detachment of Auxies burned down several public buildings and private property in Cork. The IRA responded to this and other reprisals by burning the houses of loyalists. Thereafter, and in the wake of martial law, official retaliation was permitted.

Ministerial agonising over the value of reprisals and whether or not to sanction them coincided with an intensification of the IRA's campaign against everyone working for or loyal to the crown. On 21 November, assassins acting under Collins's orders murdered fourteen officers in Dublin who were believed to be intelligence agents. Seán Lemass, a future prime minister of the Irish Republic, was one of the hit-squad and a veterinary officer one of its victims.[36] Later that Sunday, a unit of Tans opened fire on players and spectators at a Gaelic football match at Croke Park, killing nine.

A week later, the war spread to mainland Britain. Ever since the

1916 rising Sinn Féin had been organising volunteer units among Irish immigrants in London, Liverpool, Glasgow and Tyneside, and by the end of 1920 the IRA could call upon about a thousand volunteers.[37] On 28 November, the Liverpool cell set fire to warehouses on the waterfront as the first blow in a concerted campaign against British economic targets. Cathal Brugha wanted to go further and contemplated murdering ministers and machine-gunning cinema queues.[38]

During 1920, the military response to the IRA had been faltering and unfocused. Army and police units operated under separate commands and their intelligence networks were snapping under IRA pressure. Soldiers who had learned their trade on the Western Front or pacifying tribesmen on imperial frontiers were confronted with a novel form of warfare against a highly mobile enemy who was hard to identify and chose only to fight on the most favourable terms. There was a serious lack of wireless equipment, armoured cars and lorries – pro-Sinn Féin trade unionists made moving troops by rail well-nigh impossible. Most of the soldiers were young and raw with few trained marksmen and skirmishers, both vital in ambushes. In October 1920, a proposal to employ aircraft to bomb hostile mobs was rejected as too haphazard a form of chastisement, although it had recently been used in India.[39] Constraints imposed on the punitive application of air power were a reminder that the Irish conflict could not be undertaken with the sort of vigour that was being displayed in contemporary policing actions in Egypt, Kurdistan, Iraq and the North-West Frontier.

Prestige counted in these imperial campaigns, as it did in Ireland, where the cabinet could not afford to buckle under IRA pressure. Nevertheless, ministers were nervous about extending martial law, a measure that would transfer power from Whitehall and Dublin Castle to officers in the field. Brigadier-General Rex Dyer's shooting into a crowd at Amritsar in April 1919 and brutalities inflicted elsewhere in the Punjab by other, often junior officers, were baleful reminders of what could go wrong. In the end, the escalating disorder compelled the cabinet to give way and in December 1920 martial law was declared across what had been the province of Munster. Between January and June 1921 it was extended to Clare, Kilkenny, Wexford, Waterford, Cavan, Monaghan and Louth.

At the same time as it was gaining a new dispensation of power, the

Roughing it on campaign: English and Imperial soldiers light fires and dig into their tins of bully beef. Although this is South Africa in 1900, the scene might be any camp on any campaign in the previous century. NATIONAL ARMY MUSEUM

Industrial warfare: troops, transport carts and supplies move up to the front by train, South Africa 1900. NATIONAL ARMY MUSEUM

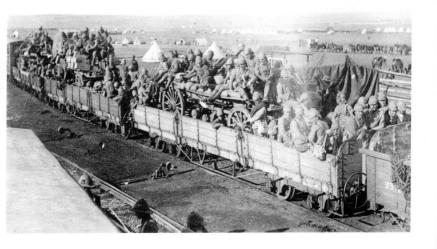

[above] Maxim machine-gun, the North-West Frontier, 1897. Just as new technology made it possible to deploy and supply larger numbers of men in battle, it provided the means to kill them in greater numbers than ever before. NATIONAL ARMY MUSEUM

[left] 'We're here, because we're here, because we're here': Infantry prepare for another futile offensive, Arras, March 1917. POPPERFOTO

[left] Remembering: Field-Marshal Earl Haig prepares to unveil the war memorial at St Andrews, Fife. Its imagery of Celtic cross and sword are traditional. COURTESY OF ST ANDREWS LIBRARY

[right] Remembering: the War Memorial at Ballywater, Co. Down. Here, as elsewhere, the image of a modern infantryman, one of the Ulster Division, looking much as he did when he advanced at the Somme in 1916. COURTESY OF ST ANDREWS LIBRARY

[*above left*] Escaping the bombs: Gravesend evacuees set off on an adventure which will bring joy for some and sorrow for others, September 1940. TOPHAM

[*above right*] Spectators: London schoolchildren take a pause from hop picking and watch Spitfires win mastery of the skies over Kent, September 1940. TOPHAM

[*below*] Safety underground: Mancunian families in a communal shelter while the Luftwaffe attacks their city, September 1940. POPPERFOTO

All clear! A turbanned housewife is given a hand out of her Anderson shelter by a neighbour. To judge by the vegetables in the garden and on the shelter roof, she has taken seriously the official exhortation: 'Dig for Victory'. TOPHAM

Getting on with the job: a wartime August Bank Holiday with munitions girls at their benches, testing Bren gun barrels. Tea cups and milk are ready for a break and the flowers evoke a happier world. TOPHAM

[*above left*] Shopping spree: a factory girl goes spending, accompanied by Hitler's accomplice, the Squander Bug; she should have put her money in National Savings. IMPERIAL WAR MUSEUM

[*above centre*] Welcome aboard: The Wrens were seen as a cut above the other women's services, but, like them, suffered their share of groundless and crude sexual innuendo. IMPERIAL WAR MUSEUM

[*above right*] Supporting the war effort: Utility clothing made the best use of scarce materials and in this case gave the warmth needed when fuel was rationed. IMPERIAL WAR MUSEUM

[*below left*] The voice of Britain: J B Priestley and Leslie Howard at the BBC.
IMPERIAL WAR MUSEUM

[*below right*] Swinging together: A Glad WRAC at a dance, *c.* 1943
IMPERIAL WAR MUSEUM

On a charge: American military policemen ['Snowdrops' from their white helmets] take a professional interest in an untidy and seedy trio in a London park, September 1945. POPPERFOTO

Icebound: the crew of the destroyer *Vansittart* chip away ice on convoy duty to North Russia; an official photo whose caption claimed that the convoys 'always get through to our heroic ally'. TOPHAM

Straggler? An officer examines a merchantman steaming astern, North Atlantic, 1941. POPPERFOTO

Doomsday deterrent: British H-Bomb successfully tested on Christmas Island, June 1957; many present, including national servicemen, would subsequently claim that exposure to radiation triggered debilitating and fatal illnesses. POPPERFOTO

Preventing civil war: British troops on the streets of Londonderry, 1971.
POPPERFOTO

An umbrella of safety: An Irish Guardsman chats to an Albanian boy in Pristina in 1999 after Nato forces intervened to halt the massacre of Albanians by Serbians. POPPERFOTO

army in Ireland was reinforced, bringing the total deployed there to just under forty thousand, and supplied with additional transport and over one hundred armoured cars. Aircraft were used for reconnaissance over remote areas, although they were not allowed to attack IRA forces on the ground. In consequence, the army was able to adopt more aggressive tactics. During the first six months of 1921, new methods were adopted by which the British copied their opponents, deploying small, self-supporting detachments in open country to launch surprise attacks on IRA units. In May and June extra manpower enabled the army to conduct large-scale cordon and search operations, not unlike those that had been undertaken during the second phase of the Boer War. The IRA command was also developing new tactics, employing mobile, flying columns of between twenty and thirty men for sudden ambushes.

Lessons learned the hard way were turned to good use. Old hands lectured officers posted to Ireland on how to raid houses and winkle out wanted men, weapons and incriminating documents.[40] First, troops secured the front and rear of a building simultaneously and then rushed to the top storey and herded all the occupants into one room. The other rooms were systematically searched and men were ordered to look out for false doors and walls and give special attention to attics, cisterns and clothes-baskets. During a raid on the house of George O'Grady in March 1920, soldiers had found rifle ammunition in his wife's knicker drawer, much to her indignation.[41] Advice was also offered on interrogation, an art in which 'bluff' was essential: a still-disorientated suspect had to be convinced the authorities already knew everything about him. High-ranking IRA men withstood torture so that 'ill-treatment, blows &c' were pointless, a conclusion that suggests that such methods had yielded nothing in the past.[42]

Officers were ordered never to reveal any surprise at what they uncovered. This must have been particularly hard for Major Tottenham, an Auxiliary, after he arrested Father D—, who had links with Collins and helped raise funds for Sinn Féin. Among this cleric's possessions were thirty envelopes, each containing a 'little snitch of pubic hair', dates of and remarks of assignations and a snapshot of a girl stripped to the waist in his garden. The find was delivered to the Bishop of Ossory.[43]

The security forces were stronger in 1921 and better prepared than they had been before. But numbers and innovations did not prove decisive. Senior officers feared that, while the odds were no longer so heavily against them, they could not avoid becoming bogged down in a mutually corrosive war of attrition. The IRA, too, was feeling the pinch. It was suffering from shortages of money and arms, and Collins, for one, feared that having fought its enemies to a standstill it could not do more without suffering irreplaceable losses. The extension of martial law was marked by a stiffening of sentences; men found guilty of 'unlawful' assembly, who had been sentenced to between two and five years in 1920, were receiving fifteen the following year. Convictions for treason (i.e. levying war against the king) and 'improper possession of arms, ammunition and prejudicial documents' were followed by death sentences and execution by firing squads during the first half of 1921.[44]

A general election at the end of May confirmed the republican majority in the south and Unionist paramountcy in Ulster, which was granted its separate parliament. The protestants had at last got what they had always wanted and had been ready to fight for in 1914. Lloyd George, now all too aware that Britain could not win the war and conscious of the growing public disquiet as to how it was being waged, put out peace feelers and an offer of dominion status for the south. Negotiations were opened with de Valera and Arthur Griffiths, vice-president of the Irish Republic (both hurriedly released from detention) and a truce was agreed which began on 11 July.

Liam Deasy of the West Cork brigade welcomed it as 'a respite from the incessant strain of the war, and particularly of the period of almost two years during which I was "on the run".' It was not, he believed, an outright victory, for the enemy had only been 'forced to a halt', but it did mean an end of the perpetual disturbances which had been a 'nightmare' for civilians. He feared that his men might lose the habits of discipline to which they had grown used and become lax and therefore unfit to continue the fight if the truce collapsed.[45] It did not, and for the next five months, representatives of the Dáil, including Collins and Griffiths, and British ministers hammered out a peace treaty.

IV

'A week has seen Dundalk become like Liège or Ghent' at the time when they had been under German occupation, commented the local newspaper in April 1920. There were soldiers guarding the local post and revenue offices and patrolling the streets. Things got worse and in September the editor remarked: 'The music of the rifle and revolver is now recognised as familiar to the people of Dundalk as the selections of the itinerant fiddler.'[46] In time, these disruptions would be known, perhaps euphemistically, as 'the Troubles'.

No one, whatever their political allegiance, could avoid being drawn into a war in which there was no front line and where the distinction between civilian and combatant was ignored by both sides. No area was immune from the IRA's terror and the government's counter-terror, and no individual could escape entanglement in a web of violence that could deprive them of their life, home and property. The chances of involuntary involvement were highest if they lived in Dublin or the south western counties. In all, 1400 were killed, two-thirds of them in the first six months of 1921 when the conflict reached its final and most intense phase. Half the casualties were soldiers and policemen.

In the six northern counties, incidents of terrorism were less than elsewhere because it was less easy for IRA men to move undetected among a predominantly protestant population, although they did establish themselves in the urban Catholic ghettos, as they would in the 1970s. Sectarian tension increased as the war in the south intensified, and was made worse by the competition for jobs and the summer round of Orange parades. On 21 July 1920, five thousand Unionist Belfast shipyard workers declared that they would no longer work alongside Sinn Féiners and began to hustle them out of the yards. Slogans and blows were exchanged, trams were stopped and Catholics hauled off, and by the evening a full-scale sectarian riot was underway. Fighting was heaviest along Cupar Street which connected the Unionist Shankill Road with the nationalist Falls Road. Twenty people were killed, including a girl of sixteen, and over two hundred were arrested for looting; a temporary breakdown of order always offered opportunities for the poor, and the Catholics were among the poorest in the city.[47]

Sectarian animosities grew. There were further disturbances in Belfast during August, when the murder of a policemen sparked off mass evictions of Catholics from their homes. Similar expulsions occurred in rural districts and many of the victims shifted south. Horrified Roscommon Catholics collected cash for the refugees and alarmist fundraisers predicted that Ulster's Catholics might face extermination.[48] Religious riots occurred sporadically for the next two years, with the worst trouble coinciding with the Orange marches; over three hundred Catholics took the ferry to Scotland and joined friends and kinsfolk in Glasgow rather than remain at home for the 12 July celebrations of the Battle of the Boyne in 1922.[49]

As in the south, the RIC was the principal target of the IRA, and in November 1920 the government authorised the raising of the A- and B-Specials, armed volunteer policemen who were predominantly protestant. They, too, matched terror with terror. 'As a reprisal' for an IRA attack on the Specials at Dromoe on 6 April 1921, three Sinn Féiners were taken from their houses and shot dead. Two B-Specials were among the suspects. After four Specials were attacked and one killed by an IRA gang on their way to church in Creggan, two Catholic homes were burned down.[50]

Violence and death overtook people suddenly and unexpectedly, usually at night. On the night of 29 October 1920, three drunken soldiers from the 2nd Argyll and Sutherland Highlanders ran amok in Ballagh, demanding more drink and smashing household goods. They fired their rifles wildly into the darkness and one bullet hit Ellen Nevil, the sixty-five-year-old wife of a peddler who was sleeping in a tent. 'I am very poor,' she told authorities, 'and live as a travelling hawker, neither my husband or I get old age pensions.' In compensation for her injured leg, she was given the fifteen shillings (75p) a week pension.[51] Three marines were carrying provisions for the Ballyvaghan coastguard station on the coast of Clare on the night of 29 April 1921 when they were fired on by three men a hundred yards away. The marines dropped their victuals, ducked behind a wall and, using what cover they could, ran back to the station where they collected their rifles. A patrol moved out to find the gunmen, leaving a lookout behind. He saw three men approaching the station and fired two rounds. One of them wounded a fourteen-year-old youth. What he was doing there is not known.[52]

Isolated coastguard stations were a favourite IRA target, for they contained stocks of weapons, ammunition and explosives and were lightly manned. Eleven rifles and four pistols were seized by a gang of over a hundred who attacked Ballycrovane station near Castleton Bearhaven just after midnight on 29 July 1920. No sentries had been posted which suggests that even by this date the threat from the IRA was not being taken too seriously. Nonetheless, the outnumbered defenders fought back, wounding four of their assailants before their ammunition ran out. Two coastguards were killed; one, Charles Brown, left a widow with two teenage children. 'My heart is nearly broken,' Mrs Brown told the authorities in an appeal for compensation and, although now destitute, she hoped she might buy a small house in Middlesbrough. Six months after her husband's death she was awarded four thousand pounds.[53]

During the first six months of 1921 the IRA burned down the houses of coastguards as part of their counter-reprisal campaign. On occasion, the terrorists' approach was almost apologetic with offers of help in carrying out the families' furniture and utensils. At Howestand, five armed men helped empty two coastguards' homes and then blindfolded the pair and took them to a derelict building, where they were held prisoner for three days. At the end, an IRA man announced: 'Gentlemen, you have been tried: I did my best for you and it has been decided to release you.' Presumably they had been tried, in absentia, for making war on the Irish Republic in the same way as IRA men were being court-martialled for the same offence against the British crown.[54] Others were denied even a kangaroo court: Corporal Ernest Williams of the marines was snatched at gunpoint from a 'jaunting car' filled with rations and shot dead on the beach at Rosses Point, Sligo, in May 1921. His murderers warned the civilian driver that he, too, would die if he continued to work for the coastguards.[55]

Off-duty soldiers were always at risk. After the Dorsets had fired on nationalist rioters in Londonderry in April 1920, the warning 'Dorsets Beware' appeared on walls. Two soldiers were beaten and chased to a servicemen's club by a mob, which then tried to storm the building. Isolated soldiers in theatre queues were also attacked.[56] Circumspect soldiers took private precautions against such violence. Travelling on the Cork–Limerick line in May 1919, Lance-Corporal Farrington was ready for trouble when an IRA gang ambushed his train at Knocklong Halt. 'I directly prepared for a scrap with civilians, and being in possession of a large knuckle duster, I put it on quietly.' It was of no value in a gunfight, but, 'in emotion I struck two civilians who tried the bully [sic]'. These may have been among the passengers who were shouting 'Up Dublin!' to encourage the IRA men. This chorus was taken up by a Scottish soldier who was later arrested. After the attack, the daughter of the postmaster at Kilmallock did what she could for two wounded policemen, for which she was ostracised by a Roman Catholic curate and several local shopkeepers.[57]

Even during its first phase, the conflict was creating a new moral universe in which a priest could feel free to abandon the compassion and charity of his vocation. The IRA would, of course, have been encouraged by this show of solidarity. Soldiers and policemen were also corrupted by a war against an all-but-invisible adversary who held the initiative and wrote the rules of engagement. Unable to get to grips with the gunmen, the security forces vented their frustration and rage against those whom they imagined to be their accomplices. After an ambush at Thomastown on 28 October 1920 in which three men from the Northamptons had been killed, their colleagues paid their last respects to them as they lay in open coffins. The mourners showed 'considerable indignation' and 'were very angry and disgusted'. In this mood, fifty of them wreaked havoc on the nearby township, smashing and stealing property to the value of five thousand pounds. No one was arrested, but henceforward medical officers were ordered not to allow men to view the corpses of comrades killed in action.[58]

Hitting back at someone was deeply satisfying. If it made the Irish more frightened of the British authorities than the IRA, so much the better. Officers from the commander-in-chief downwards believed that reprisals would have this effect. What they failed to grasp was that while many men and women wished to be left alone and unharmed, there was a strongly held belief that, whatever its faults, the IRA was fighting for a free, independent Ireland and that the security forces represented an alien power and ancient enemy.

The IRA was not only the protector of the new and fragile Irish Republic, it represented the romantic tradition of resistance in which closely knit fraternities of warriors undertook nocturnal sorties against the oppressors of the people. This was why the Irish were prepared to overlook or even forgive the IRA for its terror, but not the authorities for theirs. Perverse as it may have seemed from above, Irish men and women whose homes and lives were inconvenienced by the security forces' raids blamed the government and not the IRA. For this reason, the IRA gunman was able to shift across the countryside, passing from village to village, and find shelter, warmth, sustenance and words of encouragement. Those who offered them were rewarded by the knowledge that they were helping to liberate their country. This conviction was not seriously shaken by reprisals, unofficial or otherwise.

Retribution extended beyond arson, random murders, damaging property, abductions and theft. Allegations of torture were made by the IRA, for they had excellent propaganda value, but some were true.[59] What, one wonders, happened to J. Hinkey, known to the army as an IRA 'captain', who died on 21 December 1920 in the guard room of Tipperary barracks 'whilst suffering from DTs [delirium tremens]'.[60] 'There were no injuries to the joints' of Kevin Barry according to the doctor at Mountjoy prison, refuting the widespread accusations that the eighteen-year-old medical student had been roughly handled.

Barry had been captured during an ambush on a military lorry collecting rations from a Dublin bakery on 20 September 1920. It was a typical IRA attack and three soldiers died in the exchange of fire, one just a little older than Barry. Barry was knocked over by the lorry and found underneath it, stunned and carrying a revolver that had fired one round. Forensic evidence suggested that the missing bullet was like that found in the body of a soldier, and Barry was sentenced to hang. Before his death, he chatted with the warders about soccer and hurling and expressed some 'very strange ideas' about England which he took to be 'all one industrial area', a common misconception among his countrymen.[61] He 'considered himself unlucky to be caught', and 'Toward the end he lost all hope of a reprieve and remarked somewhat cynically that these were only known in the cinema world.' 'He went to the drop with callous composure,' the report continued, which was appropriate for a young man who would soon be celebrated in a famous ballad as a martyr-hero of Ireland.[62]

Fifty years after Barry's execution, the Irish post office issued a stamp in his honour. Had he lived by that time he would have probably been a respected but obscure doctor, perhaps on the verge of retirement. Instead, his operational misadventure and death made him a shining example of that youthful courage that was winning Ireland its freedom, and of a Christian selflessness similar to that which had recently impelled other young men to lay down their lives in France and Flanders. Barry's self-sacrifice was acknowledged by the five thousand mourners who gathered outside Mountjoy prison on the morning of the hanging; many sang hymns and women knelt and told their rosaries.

Barry saw himself as a soldier and so did every other IRA man. Taken prisoner and hustled into an armoured car during an ambush on a raiding party in Dublin, Thomas Traynor pleaded with his captors: 'For God's sake shoot me now, I am only a soldier and I have to do it.' He was forty, had ten children and had been an IRA messenger. Two of his colleagues and one Auxie had been killed in the shooting and Traynor had a pistol on him when he was seized. Like Barry, he was an accessory to murder and was hanged at the end of April 1921.[63] An RIC inspector was shot as a reprisal; his murderers remembered him as 'a kind and cultured gentleman and brave officer'.[64]

Neither side had a monopoly of bravery or patriotism during the Troubles. Dan Breen admired the constables who fought back at Soloheadbeg because they 'were Irishmen, too, and would rather die than surrender'. Before the ambush on Lord French's motorcade, one of Breen's men recited verses and sang ballads about 'the glory of dying for one's country'.[65] 'God bless the King. I would love to die for him,' were the last words of a captured British intelligence agent shot by IRA gunmen.[66] Inevitably many who were drawn into this war were veterans. The authorities hoped that former servicemen were still loyal to the crown and would be glad to serve it again. At the end of April 1921, plans were made to recruit such men and employ them in the maintenance of public services in Fermoy which was 'a particularly rabid part of Ireland'.[67] Five ex-soldiers were involved in the murder of a policeman in Londonderry, one of whom had volunteered in 1914 while under age, served at Gallipoli, been gassed on the Western Front and taken prisoner.[68]

Surprisingly, the war did not stem the flow of Irishmen into the British army: twenty thousand volunteered between 1919 and 1921.[69] Poverty rather than a desire to serve George V must have been the most compelling motive, for Ireland, like Britain, was suffering from inflation and unemployment. Other jobless men stayed at home and collected their dole while engaged in IRA activities. An official sourly remarked that the system involved 'the government paying a number of idle young men to commit outrages six days of the week and draw their wages on the seventh'.[70]

Those who took the king's shilling and served in predominantly Catholic regiments were not posted to Ireland, for obvious reasons. Two, the Connaught Rangers and the Leinsters, were stationed in India, where the latter took part in the suppression of the Mapilla uprising in March 1921, when the measures adopted exceeded in severity any then being employed in Ireland. Letters from home that described Black and Tan outrages distressed some men of the Connaught Rangers stationed at Jullundur in June 1920, who compared their role in India to that of the British army in Ireland. This self-knowledge prompted a protest against 'British atrocities' in Ireland and a collective resignation from the army. Demonstrations followed during which soldiers sang unofficial songs and shouted 'Up the Republic!' The upshot was a mutiny in which a crowd of men tried to storm an armoury and shots were fired. Jim Daly, a republican and a veteran of the First World War, assured his comrades that other Irish regiments would follow their example and someone hoisted Sinn Féin's orange, white and green tricolour over a bungalow. Seventy-five mutineers were tried and thirteen were found guilty and given long gaol terms. Daly was executed.[71]

V

It was extraordinarily hard for British administrators, policemen and soldiers to penetrate the minds of men like Daly. Seen from above and from behind a protective screen of barbed wire, the Irish appeared an irrational, temperamental and exasperating race. With some amusement, General Sir Nevil Macready recalled how a Unionist politician had complained of the even-handed way in which men from the Norfolks dealt with Catholic and protestant rioters. He assumed that they must have been Catholics since the Duke of Norfolk was the leading lay Catholic in Britain.[72] Not all Irish were beyond reason or redemption. An army memo on future approaches to propaganda in 1921 suggested that the Irish were a mixture of English, Scots, Spaniards and Huguenots, while 'the native Irish are very few and not the best'. These, it was to be hinted, were 'the lazy, dirty element' who, it went without saying, backed Sinn Féin and the IRA.[73]

This bizarre anthropological and historical analysis was part of an official propaganda offensive begun in the spring of 1921 and intended to win hearts and minds in Ireland and to answer domestic criticism of the government's policy there. Brigadier Charles Foulkes, an expert on gas warfare, took charge of this overdue propaganda offensive. He and his subordinates took a contemptuous view of their audience. The 'chief characteristics' of those farmhands and shop assistants who had hitherto been so susceptible to the IRA were 'ignorance, emotionalism, credulity and unquestioning obedience to the Roman Catholic clergy', ran a preliminary report.[74]

This being so, British propaganda emphasised the financial losses endured by Irish farmers, the futility of continued resistance and the cowardice of the IRA. The last two points were made by the girlfriend of an IRA detainee in a letter that had been intercepted by intelligence and reproduced in a leaflet: 'Things in Dublin seem to grow worse every day, and it's dreadful to see Black and Tans sometimes left dead on the roadside . . . Well you know, Paddy, while this goes on we cannot expect peace . . . Why don't they come out and fight the Black and Tans and not hiding [sic] and killing half the civilians.'[75] One suspects that 'Paddy' and those of his mind might well have been cheered by the news of Black and Tan corpses littering the pavements.

As well as dissuading Irishmen from supporting the IRA, Foulkes's intelligence officers were endeavouring to put the authorities' case to the British press. Sir Alexander Sprot, a sympathetic Unionist MP, agreed to ask questions in the Commons that were favourable to the army, and anti-IRA material was supplied to the ultra-Unionist *Morning Post*.[76] Public opinion counted more and more in the early months of 1921, when there was a growing feeling in Britain in favour of an accommodation with Sinn Féin and an end to a war that was arousing moral disquiet.

Incomprehension, indifference and its offshoot, boredom, had always been the common British reaction to Irish politics. The establishment of the Dáil in January 1919 and its possible significance for Anglo-Irish relations were hardly touched upon by a press that was dominated by news of the Versailles peace conference. During the next eighteen months, manifestations of Irish restlessness were overshadowed by events in Russia, the former Ottoman Empire, Egypt and India. Then, in September 1920, came reports of the 'sack of Balbriggan', a small town on the coast to the north of Dublin where property had been destroyed by RIC men as a reprisal for the murder of an officer. Press photographs showed refugee families with their possessions bundled into carts and perambulators against a background of ruined cottages, scenes that had appeared six years earlier when the fugitives had been Belgians and French escaping from the German army. The comparison was made by the *Manchester Guardian* which called Balbriggan 'the Irish Louvain', the city that, with its university library, had been destroyed by the Germans.[77]

Subsequent newspaper reporting of 'reprisals' was haphazard, but there were enough harrowing stories to disturb consciences. Of course, there had been provocation, but striking out wildly against whoever and whatever was close at hand offended the public's sense of justice and fair play. Given that these qualities were essential elements in the national self-image, there was a feeling that the war in Ireland was being waged by methods that were somehow 'un-British'. Opposition to the Irish campaign grew during 1920 and embraced the trade union leadership, various Labour, Liberal and Conservative MPs (including Sir Oswald Mosley), churchmen and men of letters and learning. The Peace in Ireland movement that emerged was an unusual alliance, embracing G. K. Chesterton, Bertrand Russell and Harold Laski. Lloyd George dismiss them as 'Bolshevists, Sinn Féiners and cranks of all sorts'. How far the movement reflected the mood of the country cannot be assessed accurately, not least because the audiences at its meetings contained a high proportion of Irish.[78]

At the end of 1920 the Irish war spilled over into Britain. In accordance with Collins's instructions, the IRA's mainland offensive was one of economic sabotage and the disruption of the rail network and telegraph system. The forces available were Sinn Féin followers in the large Irish communities in the north-west, London and Glasgow and the campaign was directed by Rory O'Connor. Expatriate support for

Sinn Féin had followed the Irish pattern. A 1922 police report on Paisley's large Irish population revealed passionate patriotism in 1914 with large-scale volunteering. Loyalty withered after the 1916 rising and Paisley's Irish turned towards Sinn Féin, with some young men proposing to spend their summer holidays training with the IRA.[79] Duty and pleasure were combined by some Glaswegian Sinn Féiners who spent a weekend in June 1920 at a popular beauty spot, Campsie Glen. Here, they pitched bell-tents and just after dawn were drilled in companies for one and a half hours. A police observer thought their instructors were ex-NCOs and noted that 'they were fairly well dressed, wore collars and ties of a green hue and had badges on their pockets'. On Sunday evening they returned in hired charabancs to Bishopriggs tramway terminus and made their way home.[80] Here and elsewhere, many Sinn Féiners were first-generation immigrants who had arrived during the war to take munitions jobs.

Targets for arson during the winter and early spring of 1920 to 1921 were warehouses, business property and farms around Liverpool and Manchester. Some participants convinced themselves that they were avenging their countrymen at home. 'We are doing what you are doing in Ireland,' one shouted as he brandished a revolver at the frightened staff of a Manchester café while his colleague poured paraffin over the floor.[81] At the same time, fires were started in other restaurants and hotels in the city. That night, armed detectives and police raided the Hulme Irish Club and in an exchange of shots a policeman was wounded and a terrorist killed. He was John Morgan and bullets and details of targets were found on his body. Inside the club were incendiary materials. Like its co-ordinator, several of those involved in this campaign were IRA men who had travelled from Ireland. Henry Coyle from Mayo and Charles McGinn from Belfast were identified by police in Liverpool three weeks before their arrest near Dunfermline on 4 December 1920. They had taken their Austin car into a local garage for repair and the mechanic had noticed rifles in the back. He alerted the local police and, following a car chase, its occupants were caught after having tried to hide their weapons, explosives and detonators in a field. The Austin's owner was a Glaswegian, as was its driver; as in Ireland, the IRA was depending on local sympathisers for operational mobility.[82]

There were other ways in which Sinn Féin's British operations resembled their Irish counterparts. In April 1921 the pattern of punitive and intimidatory murder was adopted by IRA units on the mainland. On the 4th a corpse was found on an Ashford (Middlesex) golf-course with a note: 'Let spies and traitors beware, IRA.'[83] A month later, about a dozen gunmen ambushed a prison van carrying Frank Carty, a Sinn Féiner who was wanted in Ireland, as it passed through the Cathedral Square in Glasgow. An inspector was killed and attempts to arrest suspects in a Catholic area led to a riot in which the police were showered with stones and bottles. After arrests had been made, there were well-founded fears that witnesses would be intimidated.[84] A few days afterwards, during the Whitsun weekend, fifteen attacks were made on the homes of ex-RIC men and their families and those who were still in the service. These incidents occurred in Liverpool and the London suburbs, where houses were set on fire, one person was killed and several wounded, including a man of seventy-seven who grappled with a gunman.[85] In each case the identities and addresses of the victims were known to their assailants. Just as in Ireland, the IRA had built up an effective intelligence-gathering service which made particular use of sympathisers among telephone operators, telegraphists and post office workers.

The police and intelligence services responded to the mainland outrages vigorously. There were mass arrests and deportations to Ireland which considerably shook the IRA's confidence.[86] Nonetheless, the wave of terrorism had demonstrated the vulnerability of a complex, industrial society to sabotage undertaken by a relatively small body of dedicated and ruthless terrorists supported by a capable intelligence network. If the Irish war had continued, it is certain that the IRA would have extended its range of targets. In June 1921 the Royal Navy's oil pipeline at Old Kirkpatrick, west of Glasgow, was sabotaged, and the local police were considering using soldiers and sailors to guard installations where explosives were stored and the RAF aerodrome at East Fortune.[87] Given the closeness of Glasgow with its large and strongly pro-Sinn Féin Irish population, the increased tempo of IRA operations, such precautions were wise.

How far the extent of the IRA's mainland war was a factor in persuading the government to pursue a peace settlement is not known.

Some Irish nationalists assumed that it was, which explains why a similar but far more ambitious and deadly campaign was undertaken by the IRA in England between 1972 and 1997. Their purpose was the same as it had been in 1921: to force concessions from the government and bully the public into supporting a total British disengagement from Ireland.

VI

The Anglo-Irish Treaty signed in December 1921 ended one civil war and started another. Sinn Féin split. One faction, led by de Valera, denounced the constraints the treaty placed on Irish self-determination. It was a betrayal of nationalist ideals because the new Irish Free State remained within the orbit of the British Empire and the separation of the north with its Catholic minority was recognised. Collins and supporters of the treaty argued that it was the best bargain they could get and infinitely preferable to reopening the war. Some freedom was better than continued bloodshed and destruction without any certain hope of total victory at the end. After a narrow vote in the Dáil, the pro-treaty faction won. In June 1922 the issue was put to the test of a civil war which lasted until the following August when anti-treaty forces surrendered to the Free State army. Fighting continued in Kerry until the end of 1923.

In many respects, the civil war over the treaty was an unequal contest. As Collins had correctly diagnosed, the Irish were suffering from war-weariness and were disinclined to support those who wished to continue fighting for principles that seemed irrelevant, given that the Union had been dissolved and British forces were withdrawing. Moreover, the fighting caused severe economic disruption and, in some areas, the breakdown of the machinery for food distribution. With a total of 55,000 men (many recruited from the unemployed), the Free State army outnumbered its opponents and had access to British weapons, including machine-guns, armoured cars and artillery. The latter was used to eject anti-treaty forces from the Four Courts in Dublin after Collins had unsuccessfully asked for aircraft.[88] As the war progressed, Free State forces made full and rigorous use of emergency powers: courts-martial were able to try and sentence to death anyone found in illicit possession of firearms. One of those shot for this offence was the English writer and passionate Sinn Féiner, Erskine Childers.

It was paradoxical perhaps that all but one of the aims of the anti-treaty faction were eventually obtained peacefully. British naval bases retained under the treaty were evacuated in 1938 and by 1949 Eire had severed all links with the Empire. Its detachment did not halt freedom of movement between the republic and Britain.

The Irish civil wars of 1919–23 radically altered the nature of the United Kingdom. The Union of 1800 disappeared and two new states were created, one independent and the other, Ulster, attached to Great Britain in the same way as Wales and Scotland, but with its own legislature. From the nationalist standpoint, this arrangement was a not entirely satisfactory outcome of an intermittent contest for the control of Ireland that had started in the twelfth century and which, from the sixteenth, became and remained a struggle for religious supremacy between Catholics and Protestants.

Whilst the Catholic Church had traditionally if not always happily supported the Irish national movement, the events of 1919 to 1922 had presented an imponderable moral problem. What line should the Church take when many of its communicants, whether they were gunmen or policemen, were daily repudiating the Commandments. Many priests followed their political instincts and openly sided with Sinn Féin and assisted the IRA. Their bishops, sympathetic to nationalist aspirations, were horrified by moral anarchy, condemned the slaughter, threatened excommunication and pleaded with both sides for peace.

Ulster's political culture was a creation of previous religious conflicts that made the province distinct from the rest of the United Kingdom. Sectarian differences were so ingrained that, in 1912, the protestants of Northern Ireland were ready to fight to uphold what they considered their peculiar identity. After 1921 they were free to do so, leaving the Catholic minority isolated in a hostile polity. Ulster's Catholics therefore looked towards the Irish Free State and, thanks to their experiences during the tumults of 1920 and 1921, regarded the IRA as their protectors. It was to the IRA that Ulster's Catholics appealed in 1969 and 1970, when again they faced systematic protestant violence. The Irish Free State, too, looked backwards as it moved forwards. Under de Valera, the government fostered what was imagined to be a distinctive Gaelic culture whose roots lay in Ireland's ancient past, and there was an intimacy between the state and the Catholic hierarchy. This was strongly felt in the evolution of the Irish Republic's social and public health policies, a point not missed by Ulster protestants.

The sheer daring and determination of the IRA between 1919 and 1921, together with the capacity for self-dramatisation of many of its members, won it a special place in Irish hearts. Sentiment drew the Irish towards brave men whose exploits made exciting stories, but from 1923 onwards the IRA's programme of a united, socialist Ireland won little support at the polls. In 1938 and 1939, the IRA mounted a campaign of bombing in England in which several people were killed. Bombings in Dublin during 1940 and fears that the IRA might act as a pro-German fifth column which might stage a coup and invade Ulster forced de Valera's hand. A thousand IRA members were interned and what was left of a severely shaken organisation went underground. A recrudescence of IRA activities against the Irish state in the mid 1950s was met with internment. Then and earlier, public support for the movement was very thin and intelligence agencies in London and Dublin co-operated against a body that threatened the stability of both countries and co-operation between them.

In spite of its operational weaknesses and lack of popular sympathy, the IRA was treated with exaggerated respect by both the British and Irish governments. Between 1919 and 1923 it had proved itself a formidable adversary, possessing what sometimes appeared to be an omniscience in gathering intelligence, collecting weaponry and explosives and using them to cause the maximum of terror and dislocation. This reputation was still strong forty years later; early in 1966, when the IRA was comparatively run-down and inactive, MI5 and the cabinet were extremely nervous about whether and how it would celebrate the fiftieth anniversary of the Easter Rising. Of one thing there was no doubt: if the IRA did stage a coup, it would be dramatic and devastating.[89] Nothing happened, nor did it in the summer of 1969 when civil rights demonstrations triggered violent clashes between Catholic nationalists and the Royal Ulster Constabulary, backed by the B-Specials and protestant mobs. In what turned out to be a reopening of Ireland's civil war, the IRA was nowhere to be seen and frightened Catholics, who had looked to the IRA for protection, scrawled on walls: 'IRA = I Ran Away.'

2

A war of peoples and causes: Duties and ideals, 1939–45

I

Pillboxes are among the most enduring mementoes of the Second World War. They are found everywhere. No one knows how many were built, or where they all are, because most were put up in a desperate hurry during the summer of 1940 when a German invasion seemed imminent. Massive, reinforced concrete pillboxes overlook the steep shingle beach at Cley-next-the-Sea in Norfolk which, like hundreds of other towns and villages along the east and south coasts, was part of Britain's first line of defence. Among the pebbles at Cley there are skeins of rusted barbed wire and steel corkscrews, all that survives of the entanglements intended to hamper the invaders as they came ashore. Inland is a small brick pillbox with an arc of fire overlooking the saltings across which the Germans would have advanced to establish their beachhead. There are thousands of other tactically sited pillboxes at road junctions, by bridges or alongside railway tracks, each testifying to the fact that in 1940 the whole country could have become a battlefield. After the war their iron doors and shutters rusted away and pillboxes became dark, dank places into which children ventured, nervously as I remember. Many were enveloped by sand dunes, nettles and bushes.

Clusters of pillboxes surround those other permanent memorials of the war, the abandoned airfields that are strewn across eastern England

and Scotland. These were home to the RAF's Bomber and Coastal Commands and the 8th USAAF (United States Army Air Force), which alone required a quarter of a million acres for its runways, hangars, workshops and fuel dumps. Most of the buildings have decayed or been demolished, although some runways survive and are now used for practice by learner drivers. But for the greater part, these airfields have reverted to what they had been before the war, farmland.

Derelict buildings still mark the site of the RNAS (later known as the Fleet Air Arm) aerodrome at Crail from which aircraft harried German coastal shipping and hunted U-boats. Later, during the Cold War, it housed bright young national servicemen studying Russian. Today, it is still easy to imagine what Crail was like in wartime. There is the stump of the old flagpost close to the main entrance, a flat-roofed, modernistic control tower, corrugated-iron hangars streaked with rust and bunkers to which men and women ran when the warning siren sounded. The brick and concrete huts, messes, canteens and offices where they worked, ate and relaxed are now in a state of unpicturesque but evocative decay. A few have been converted into makeshift pigsties and cattle byres. A frieze of barbed wire stretches across the wall of the guard-room and inside are rotting wooden shelves and doors, a sink and lavatories. Cream distemper covers some walls and the woodwork is painted in sea green: nasty colours which characterise wartime austerity and service uniformity. Iron chimneys protrude from the roofs of the living quarters, but the coke-burning iron stoves have vanished. They were the sole source of warmth for the men and women stationed at Crail. Feeling cold was one of the commonest experiences of the war, equalled only by boredom and anxiety.

So too was noise. Now Crail aerodrome is silent, but between 1939 and 1945 it was full of sounds, mostly discordant. There was the drone of machinery, the hums and growls of aeroplane engines, trucks and cars and, of course, voices shouting orders. Competing with the cacophony of war was popular dance music and songs played on gramophones and wireless sets. Hearing these catchy tunes again, Richard Passmore, a RAF wireless operator, found that they retained the power to 'glaze the eyes and tug at the heartstrings'.[1]

One was Anne Shelton's 'Comin' in on a Wing and a Pray'r', a jaunty song which had a special poignancy for aircrew. Walking around

Crail on a cold but bright October afternoon one could imagine hearing it played somewhere in the distance. Its opening line – 'One of our planes is missing . . .' – must have had a chilling resonance in the NAAFI and mess. Sixty years before, in October 1940, the crews from 218 Squadron at Crail were undertaking raids against German destroyers moored in Brest harbour. First, they had flown their obsolescent and slow Albacore biplanes to the base at St Eval in Cornwall. Then, between 9 and 16 October they flew three sorties against Brest. The flight took three-and-a-half hours and on arrival the airmen faced heavy anti-aircraft fire which brought down one machine. Its crew was captured and spent the next four-and-a-half years in a POW camp. The Albacore crews who returned could only guess at the damage they had caused; aerial photographs taken from great height and in poor weather conditions were indistinct. On 18 October the Crail airmen were stood down and given some leave in which to recover from six days of intense concentration and fear. Afterwards, they flew their aircraft back to Crail.[2]

Even if there was no clear indication as to what harm they had inflicted on the enemy, such missions satisfied the public. Britain was biting back, which mattered greatly in the autumn of 1940 when cities and towns were suffering devastating, nightly air raids. Rage and frustration generated a widespread desire for vengeance in kind, which lasted until the end of the war. Three years later, when the mass bombing offensive against Germany was gaining momentum, airmen would write messages on their bombs, dedicating them to the people of British towns and cities that had been raided.[3] Prewar professionals were dispassionate, at least to begin with. 'This, at last, was what we were here for,' thought Richard Passmore after he heard news of the declaration of war on 3 September 1939. Like many others, he also speculated about his chances of survival.[4]

II

Passmore was engaged in a war the immediate aim of which was to restore the equilibrium of Europe which had been upset by Hitler. Those who described the Second World War as 'Hitler's war' are correct; he believed that unending conflict was the natural state of humankind and was ready to use war, or the threat of it, to impose his will on Europe. In the autumn of 1938, he had opened a new phase of German expansion with demands for the detachment of the Sudetenland from Czechoslovakia. At Munich, Neville Chamberlain let him have his way. Six months later, in March 1939, Hitler occupied the rump of Czechoslovakia and Memel. The Anglo-French response was a pledge to defend his next target, Poland. Unperturbed, Hitler negotiated a non-aggression pact with Russia in which he and Stalin agreed the partition of Poland. It was invaded on 1 September and two days later, Britain and France declared war, a Quixotic gesture, for there was nothing that the Allies could do to prevent the defeat and dismemberment of Poland.

The only alternative was to stand aside and concede Hitler a free hand in Europe. Restoring the balance of power on the continent was a cause that did not generate much passion, at least among the soldiers of the British Expeditionary Force (BEF) in north-west France. In the spring of 1940 their officers were disturbed to discover that few of their men had the slightest idea what they were fighting for.[5]

No one had any doubts on this score by June 1940. After the conquest of Poland, Hitler shifted his attention westwards and, in April, launched a series of offensives that successively defeated Norway, Denmark, the Netherlands, Belgium and France. For a few days at the end of May, it appeared likely that Britain too might succumb. The BEF was in danger of being stranded in north-western France and faced with surrender or fighting an unwinnable, last-ditch battle. At first, War Office analysts estimated that a mere thirty thousand men could be evacuated and a jittery cabinet briefly discussed whether to seek terms from Hitler. The crisis quickly passed. Thanks to German operational hitches, good luck and improvisation, 334,000 British, French and Belgian troops were withdrawn from Dunkirk. Small ships, including fishing boats and pleasure craft, ferried the troops to destroyers and transports. The resolution, steadiness and courage of those who manned them were held up as shining examples of the qualities that were needed from every citizen in what was now a war for national survival.

Some welcomed Britain's predicament. After France's surrender, a sailor was overheard to say: 'Well, the last of our allies has gone under, and a good job too. Now we can do a bit of fighting on our own account, and I'm ready to start.'[6] These defiant words were passed on to Churchill, who had become prime minister on 10 May at the head of a coalition of Conservatives, Liberals and Labour. Within three weeks of the formation of this government of national unity and in the immediate aftermath of Dunkirk, there were angry recriminations against the men and policies that had brought the country to its present, perilous position. The culprits were identified as the 'Old Gang' or, in the title of a highly partial version of recent history, *Guilty Men*. Among its authors was the journalist and future Labour leader, Michael Foot, and it sold fifty thousand copies in a fortnight. The book's central contention was that Chamberlain and his advisers had encouraged Hitler through appeasement in the hope that he would eventually fall upon the Soviet Union and make the world safe for capitalism.

This crude thesis was widely accepted during and after the war, although it rested on a complete ignorance of Britain's diplomatic position and military capacity in 1938. If Chamberlain had defied Hitler at Munich he would have gambled recklessly with the nation's security. France was unwilling to fight in defence of Czech integrity, as were the dominions, which had provided invaluable manpower during the previous war. Most important of all, Britain was vulnerable to aerial attack and Air Ministry experts were predicting that once war came, the Luftwaffe would deliver a sequence of hammer blows that would raze much of London and leave tens of thousands dead and wounded. Fighter Command could not repel these attacks; only six of its twenty-nine squadrons were equipped with Spitfires and Hurricanes and half the remaining fighters were outdated. Work on the network of radar stations was unfinished, air defence systems were not yet operational and the civil defence programme was incomplete.[7] When Chamberlain met Hitler, his intelligence services insisted that Germany had 5600 aircraft, although the actual total was 3300.[8] Obstinacy over Czechoslovakia could easily have begun an aerial war that analysts feared Britain would lose.

These factors were not known in July 1940, which was why Acting Petty-Officer George James declared to his colleagues at Chatham that, 'Chamberlain was a traitor.' A Labour supporter, he told one messmate that, 'it was the capitalists of this country who had started the war and he and I, the under-dogs, who fought it.'[9] James considered himself 'a good loyal Englishman', but a court-martial reduced him to the ranks for his intemperate opinions which were judged harmful to discipline. The officers who sentenced him would have been astonished if they had known that within three years they would be officially encouraged to stimulate political discussions among ratings.

Those who castigated the Conservatives for their pusillanimous treatment of Hitler also blamed them for prewar economic stagnation and its outcome, huge pockets of unemployment and poverty in the old mining and industrial heartlands of Wales, the north and Clydeside. The victims had placed their hopes in the Labour party which, since 1931, had been in the political wilderness. Now it was an essential part of the government and the *New Statesman* confidently believed that the new dispensation of political power would prove advantageous for the Labour party and those it represented: 'Organised labour in alliance with the Liberal opposition and a small group of mutinous Tories has challenged and overthrown the men who for ten years have controlled the obsequious Conservative majority in the Commons.' For a decade it had danced to a tune played by 'the Nuffields, the Austins and the City financiers, whose guiding principle has been that the good of the country must be subordinated to the short-term interests of British business both at home and abroad'.[10] For those on the left, there could be no going back. The crisis of May 1940 marked a historical watershed: after ten, some would say twenty, years of social and economic rifts, the people were finding a new cohesion in the face of a common peril. This unity also involved a repudiation of the politicians and dogma that had got the country into its present mess and had presided over a decade of economic decay and social antagonism.

In the meantime, there was a war to be fought and an isolated Britain faced aerial bombardment and invasion. 'We are all in it,' declared a BEF medic soon after his return from Dunkirk. 'Totalitarian war', which he had just witnessed in Belgium and France, was about to overwhelm Britain. 'Nothing less than the BEF's standards of courage and endurance will be enough for the civilian population under bombing attacks from the air and the attempts to land troops.' Was, he wondered, the population as well nourished and cared for as the fighting men had been?[11]

Everyone, whether in uniform or not, was now on permanent active service, facing uncertainty and danger and submitting to irksome rules. Civilians were chivvied by ARP (Air Raid Precautions) personnel if their windows were not fully blacked out at night, if they neglected to carry their gas-masks, or if they loitered in the street after the warning siren had sounded. They walked in darkened streets where they might easily be knocked down by cars whose headlight beams had been reduced to thin pencils of light by the blackout regulations. Their children were removed to places of safety in the countryside and, if their houses were destroyed or damaged, billeting officers would send them and what remained of their possessions to lodge with kinsfolk, neighbours, friends or, if these were not forthcoming, strangers. To these inconveniences were added fretful nights huddled in personal or public shelters.

Civilians were subject to the same discipline as servicemen and women. When they failed to comply, they were prosecuted and punished. In July 1941 a nineteen-year-old Greenock fire-watcher who failed to report for duty was imprisoned for sixty days.[12] His excuse, toothache, might have got past a prewar employer, but this youth was now in the front line where such discomforts had to be endured. An eighty-year-old Middlesbrough widow's understandable plea of momentary forgetfulness was rejected by a local magistrate after she had allowed a streak of light to show through a window. She was fined two pounds and told that German airmen dropped bombs wherever they saw a light, a fact he had been told by a friend in the Home Guard who had heard it from a captured German flier.[13]

The 1.5 million civilians who had volunteered to join the Home Guard during the summer of 1940 were bound by the same constraints as professional soldiers. Public duty always came before private responsibilities. In August 1942, when the threat of invasion had been briefly revived, a Devon farmer failed to pass on a telephone message ordering his Home Guard unit to turn out immediately, so that the final muster was fourteen men short. His wife had just given birth and he was distracted by police inquiries about foot and mouth disease. The magistrate was unsympathetic; he was fined four pounds and reminded that his negligence might have been 'a matter of extreme danger to the country'.[14] The Bedford bench took the same stern line in April 1944, by when the danger of invasion had all but disappeared, and fined a factory worker four pounds (more than half his weekly wage) for missing a Home Guard parade. A plea of mitigation based upon problems created by an ailing child and night-shift work was ignored.[15]

III

What amounted to the mobilisation of the entire population in the summer of 1940 gave rise to the phrase 'People's War' which then and afterwards enjoyed widespread currency. No one was exempt from the war-effort and every personal sacrifice, however trivial, had value. Of this there was no doubt, and government advertisements constantly exhorted the public to do its bit. There were myriad ways in which the individual could help beat Hitler. The chilled man or woman would feel some satisfaction in the fact that five pounds of coal not burned in the domestic grate provided the energy that helped produce a hundred rounds of Bren-gun ammunition, according to one official advertisement. Another asked phone users to 'cut out social gossip on trunk lines' which might otherwise become overloaded and so impede vital military messages.

Posters implored women to 'Make Do and Mend', so that textiles could be saved for more important purposes. By cutting up her husband's 'civvie' suit and one of his shirts and turning them into a pinafore, blouse and turban (the factory girl's headdress was now chic), the housewife was contributing to victory. *Woman's Own* provided the pattern, and alongside the instructions was a drawing that showed her uniformed husband watching the destruction of his wardrobe with approval.[16]

Individual complemented communal abstinence and ingenuity. Across the country and throughout the war, communities held fundraising rallies in support of the war-effort. All involved self-denial. Posters and press advertisements constantly reminded people that the 'squanderbug' was Hitler's accomplice. This demon was sent packing during the 'Wings for Victory Week' in Bath early in April 1943. In common with other, similar campaigns, there were whist drives, dances and rallies in which cash was raised to pay for aircraft. At one meeting, the citizens of Bath were reminded of the air raids they had recently suffered and promised that 'greater and harder blows' were about to be struck against Germany. Survivors of the Bath blitz were encouraged to buy stamps that would be stuck on bombs destined for German targets. Individuals formed groups that set themselves cash targets and then proceeded to meet them. The 177 children of Widcombe Junior School pledged themselves to raise six hundred pounds and managed to collect eight hundred. The names of individuals, schools and streets and the amounts they had raised were published in local newspapers, just as those of subscribers to patriotic funds had been during the Napoleonic Wars. Bath raised £915,000, an impressive amount for a city that had already contributed £794,000 in an earlier 'Warship Week'.[17]

During the Bath 'Wings for Victory Week' rally an American air force chaplain had reminded listeners of what they were fighting against. Their aim was the defeat of an enemy whose purpose was the extinction of 'all things held high in our philosophy of life'. No one would have quarrelled with this interpretation of Italian fascism or German Nazism, but it was less easy to define 'our philosophy of life' or agree on what its essentials might be. Both subjects had been the cause of urgent concern during the summer of 1940 when the threat of invasion had concentrated minds on what exactly Britain was fighting for. The same phenomenon had occurred in the 1790s and early 1800s when the country had faced a similar danger and needed a unifying cause. Then, old-style Francophobia had been superseded by a patriotism that contrasted the blessings of the British system of law and government with the anarchy of Revolutionary France and, later, the tyranny of Bonaparte. Such an antithesis could not be contrived in 1914, and so a patriotic spirit was distilled from straightforward king-and-country loyalty and a perception of Britain as holding the moral high ground.

This formula would not work in 1940. There was a powerful sense that the nation had been misled in the last war. The partnership between rulers and ruled had ended in acrimony with the latter believing that four years of bloodletting and sacrifice had yielded them nothing. There were no 'homes fit for heroes' and bitter memories of Lloyd George's duplicity were still strong in 1940. Would, a young soldier asked, this conflict end like the last when the survivors returned to 'find that there is no room for them in their homeland'?[18] The Labour party suspected that 'the 1918 trick would be worked again' and the war would end with the clock being turned back, as it had been then.[19] Such political legerdemain would no longer be tolerated; the men, women and children of Bath who handed over their coppers to pay for bombs and had put up with shortages and air raids expected tangible rewards when peace came.

Following Napoleonic precedents, it was necessary to devise a fresh exposition of Britishness, an abstraction that was attractive and would bind the nation together. On a simple ideological level, this presented few difficulties. Britain represented the moral antithesis of its adversaries, Italy and Germany, especially the latter. Britain stood for democracy, personal liberty, the toleration of individual idiosyncrasies and voluntary submission to laws that had been framed according to the common will. The Third Reich was a dictatorship in which a monolithic state directed the thoughts and actions of its citizens, whose highest duty was purblind obedience to the Führer. Hitler's will was law and all former moral codes were superseded by Nazism. The German state encouraged Mercedes-Benz, BMW and other corporations to man their production lines with slaves and allowed the Gestapo and special police units to torture and kill anyone who did not subscribe to its dogma. Jews, gypsies and the congenitally disabled were excluded from Hitler's new order, stripped of their humanity and, from September 1939 onwards, systematically murdered. Among the earliest German Enigma signals to be deciphered were those of police detachments undertaking massacres in Poland. In June 1940, Dr J. M. Herth, the Chief Rabbi, told British Jews that their faith gave them no exemption from active service in a struggle 'against heathen forces that have the annihilation of the Jews as one of their main aims'.[20] Over the next two years the government accumulated often detailed evidence of the mass murders being committed across occupied Europe and Russia, which confirmed where the moral battlelines were drawn. This information, sometimes accompanied by photographs, regularly appeared in the press.

The People's War was also a 'good war' in which the Allied victory turned out to be of immeasurable benefit to humanity. Those across the world who watched the sickening newsreel footage of the survivors of the concentration camps discovered by British, American and Russian troops during the spring of 1945 could have been in no doubt that the war had been waged against evil on a historically unprecedented scale. This view prevailed then and has never been challenged, nor can it be. The world order that was restored in 1945 was far from perfect, but it was infinitely preferable to that which would have existed if the Allies had not won or had been compelled to make an accommodation with their adversaries.

The vindictiveness of Hitler and the hell he and his satraps were creating in Europe meant that Britain was not fighting just to preserve itself. In 1940 it became the last hope for the revival of freedom and decency in Europe. On 14 July, Churchill had told the country that it was now engaged in 'a war of peoples and causes' that would only end when 'the dark curse of Hitler' was 'lifted from our age'.[21] The same message was repeated over and over again. 'The destiny of civilisation and all freedom-loving nations is at stake,' the mineworkers' leader Will Lawther told an audience of striking miners in July 1941.[22] An advertisement of 1943 described the thousands of young women in the armed forces as 'Our girls – the fearless girls of freedom'. Defined in negative terms, Britain's cause was undeniably just, in that it was fighting to stem and reverse the spread of what Churchill called a new 'Dark Age'.

IV

But the war was not just an exercise in a higher altruism in which Britain single-handedly restored liberty and enlightenment to Europe. In mid 1940 this prospect seemed far distant, although Churchill's faith in ultimate victory was unshakable. Then, the country was fighting for survival, and to do so it needed to remind itself of its identity and, in particular, of those peculiar qualities of mind and conduct that bound the people together and for which they would hazard their lives.

This process of introspection produced results that were largely flattering. Much was made of the English countryside which, with official encouragement, became a symbol of all that was worth preserving at any cost. 'New values bring new visions,' ran the editorial of the July

1940 edition of *Vogue*. 'Our present danger illuminates, like lightning, the familiar English landscape making it vivid, strong and new.' Readers were asked to wander again in the 'dear, snubbed English countryside' and return 'knowing more of England – fairest isle, all other isles excelling'. On the following pages models displayed the new summer fashions against a background of the Sussex Downs, a Lakeland hillside, a beach and a riverbank.

This theme was expanded by *Country Life* in a 'British Issue' which contained articles on British birds, gardens and waterfalls and photographs of Cotswold villages, Suffolk cottages and Tudor manorhouses. The editorial declared that 1940 was 'one of the beacon years of history' which occur between 'long dull intervals of prosperity and selfishness', and the historian A. L. Rowse wrote of the 'dream of happiness and content' that 'lay at the heart of every Englishman'.[23] The countryside was the real England, a sort of 'l'Angleterre profonde', or, as the chorus of the popular song 'There'll always be an England' put it:

> There'll always be an England while there's a country lane,
> As long as there's a cottage small beside a field of grain.

This Arcadia was in dire peril. The danger was immediate and vivid; newspapers and magazines showed pictures of the familiar country landscape and village streets that had become the backdrop to scenes of soldiers marching, road blocks and the erection of anti-tank defences. Southern and eastern England were about to become a battlefield and hypothetical drawings of the fighting depicted tanks ambushed as they drove past shops, inns and churches. One area designated as a future war zone was Sussex, where, according to the rector of Buxted, the country people were bewildered by the preparations for war but nonetheless somehow remained cheerful and calm. He believed that this stoicism was an expression of their innate 'character and faith'.[24]

These qualities distinguished the British people as a whole. This theme was expanded in the official documentary *This England* of 1941 which was tactfully renamed *Our Heritage* when it was shown in Scottish cinemas. Audiences saw footage of a countryside whose inhabitants lived in a harmony that would have been recognised by Jane Austen: the squire and the parson ruled gently and benevolently over communities of farmers and craftsmen who laboured patiently and were proud of their skills. By contrast, the urban world was blighted by dirt, ugliness, materialism and social tension.[25]

This was true, particularly in areas of industrial dereliction and unemployment. While official propaganda portrayed the English landscape as the symbol of a country worth fighting for, there were nagging questions about the moral landscape of prewar Britain. The nation was engaged in a life-or-death struggle in which all distinctions between fighting men and civilians had vanished. And yet, among the men who were being drafted, forging the steel for barbed wire and constructing pillboxes were many who had spent the last ten years without jobs or the hope of ever finding them – a million men were still without work at the beginning of 1940. As people prepared for bombs that did not distinguish between slum and suburb, the disconcerting but pertinent question was raised as to whether an equality of danger and distress would merit an equality of recompense after the war. If 'our way of life' was at stake, then there were many who had gained little from it and had no reason to perpetuate it, argued the editorial in the August 1940 issue of *Horizon*.[26] The *New Statesman* was already characterising the war as a catalyst for profound social and economic change: 'This is a workers' war; if we are determined, the peace will be a workers' peace.'[27]

Britain was shifting leftwards. George Orwell, a percipient barometer of the wartime mood, recognised this and concluded that the country was hoping for far-reaching social and economic changes. War was providing both the momentum for these changes and their goal: national regeneration. At its heart, this would require what Orwell called 'a decent standard of living for everyone'. This would be achieved because the total war that Britain was fighting was accelerating historical processes already underway. Social distinctions were dissolving and people were being compelled to confront reality.[28] The voice of an intellectual found echoes in unexpected quarters. During the summer of 1941 an advertisement for Pears' Soap showed a pensive young boy alongside a globe. The copy claimed that the present impetus for victory should be maintained beyond the end of the war 'to give Britain at peace better health, a better standard of living and a happier life for all'.

Practical necessity complemented such ideals. In 1940 Britain was an ignorant nation in which 90 per cent of children left school at fourteen. Basic literacy and numeracy were inadequate qualifications for the thousands of service jobs that required scientific and technical proficiency, especially in the navy and air force. By August 1940, the RAF was compelled to accept 'reasonable standards of intelligence and mathematics' as a substitute for school-leaving certificates from those applying for aircrew training. The problem got worse and in May 1943 courses had to be devised to bring up to scratch those who had left school at fourteen and were unable to cope with the syllabus. Their 'lack of mental training' was remedied by a course designed to 'sharpen wits' and show trainees how 'to examine and elucidate a problem'. Potential pilots, navigators, bomb-aimers and wireless operators received lessons in mathematics, science, geography and modern history. Here, 'as much time as possible should be given to discussion and debate', particularly on 'postwar problems'.[29]

By this time, all the services were actively encouraging men and women to discuss how and according to what principles Britain was to be ordered after the war. All syllabuses took it for granted that national regeneration was both necessary and desirable. In 1944 soldiers heard about new approaches to the problems of urban and rural planning, public health and education schemes, all of which were intended 'to cure evils which make it hard for men and women to live a decent life'.[30] Even those whose preferred topics of conversation were beer, girls and the fortunes of their local football team found themselves caught up in the process of improvement. After the commander of the cruiser *Delhi* had introduced 'Discussion Groups' designed to get his ratings 'to think for themselves', 'a well-known scallywag' was overheard addressing his shipmates 'on postwar housing policy in the heads [latrines]'. 'Well, all I can fucking well say is I fucking well wouldn't live in one of those fucking council houses if I was fucking well paid to.'[31] Exchanges with British servicemen in 1943 prompted a GI to write home: 'They seem much more politically conscious than our soldiers and far more radical. I doubt whether even the Labour Party will be able to satisfy them after the war.'[32]

These socialist soldiers would have taken their views from several sources. The *Daily Mirror* and *Picture Post*, both of which had a large service readership, had continuously exposed the inequalities and injustices of prewar society and suggested how they might be corrected through state intervention and planning. The Ministry of Information's documentary film unit followed the same, radical line, which was not surprising since it was under the supervision of Sidney Bernstein, owner of the Granada cinema chain and a Labour supporter, and Jack Beddington, who had produced films for Shell. Below them were directors whose views ranged from pink to crimson.

The result was a series of subjective and emotional documentaries in which the past appeared wretched and the future bright. In the closing moments of *New Towns for Old* (1945), a town councillor from the fictional industrial town of 'Smokedale' delivers an appeal: 'You [the workers] are the only folk who can make true not only plans for this town but for every town – YOUR TOWN.' *Wales – Green Hill, Black Mountain* (1943) ends with a glance at the recent past:

> Remember the procession of the old young men,
> From dole queue to corner and back again . . .
> Nothing in their pockets, nothing now to eat,
> Lagging from slag heap to the pinched back street.
> Remember the procession of the old young men.
> It shall never happen again.

Then, against the sound of a Welsh choir: 'Out of the huddle of slum and valley must come the clean broad roads and the clean white houses.'[33]

A blueprint for Britain's postwar renaissance, the Beveridge Report, appeared in December 1942. It specified poverty, disease, squalor and idleness as the afflictions that had hitherto troubled the mass of the population and proposed their elimination through a free health service, child allowances and provision for full (i.e. 90 per cent or more) employment which would be funded by the state and industry. Over six hundred thousand copies of the report were sold and a synopsis was distributed among servicemen and women. The implications of Beveridge's scheme were extensively dissected in the press. Readers of *Woman's Own* were given comments on the report from various luminaries, including the actor Laurence Olivier who hoped that 'free education' would be available for everyone after the war and that the spirit of good neighbourliness would survive. The philanthropist Dame Elizabeth Cadbury hoped that slums would disappear and genuine 'communities' replace 'suburban dormitories'. Clement Attlee, the deputy prime minister and Labour leader, affirmed that his party unequivocally endorsed Beveridge's proposals.[34] He was preaching to the converted, for a contemporary opinion poll revealed that 86 per cent of the population were in favour of Beveridge's recommendations.[35]

They were debated in the Commons in February 1943. Herbert Morrison, the Labour MP for Lambeth, echoed what he believed were the feelings of his constituents. 'They have had bombs of all kinds dropped on them' and been praised as 'heroes' by journalists and statesmen. 'They say they did so because they could think of nothing else to do but to stand up to bombardment' and they did not expect to receive 'the reward of heroes'. What, above all, they desired was for the same sense of urgency, drive and energy that was being applied to the war-effort to be directed towards the solution of 'postwar problems'.[36] Morrison was speaking at a time when fears for the nation's survival had receded. During the preceding four months the British had won the battle of El Alamein and the push was underway that would conclude with the expulsion of German and Italian forces from North Africa. The surrender of the German Sixth Army at Stalingrad marked the limit of German conquests in Russia. The following April witnessed a decisive tip of the balance in the Allies' favour in the Battle of the Atlantic. The way was now open for the concentration of American men and supplies for the forthcoming campaign in Italy and the projected invasion of north-west Europe.

Henceforward, defeat was out of the question. The British people were free to speculate about and prepare for the peace. In doing so, they turned not only to the Beveridge Report but to their immediate experiences of war, which had revealed a capacity for selflessness and co-operation. The war had also demonstrated how the state could successfully plan and co-ordinate every form of human activity from grand strategy to the evacuation of hundreds of thousands of schoolchildren. The same idealism and teamwork that had manifested themselves under the pressure of war could, surely, be applied to the creation of a fairer and kinder society that truly reflected those values that lay at the core of Britishness.

V

Substantial postwar rewards were well deserved. Churchill had said as much in his broadcasts, although his main preoccupation was strategy rather than postwar reconstruction. Thanks to modern technology, a nation in arms was prepared for battle by the oratory of its leader, just as fighting men had been in the past. His themes would have been perfectly understood by commanders over the preceding thousand years. The prime minister appealed to the courage that he believed was latent in each of his countrymen and women and which had been assayed many times before. The future actress Molly Weir remembered how her mother responded to Churchill's words. 'She loved above all things, listening to Churchill – and even though she was pretty deaf his voice got through to her: "Here he comes. The British bulldog. By God he puts new life into you."' For her own part, Molly believed that Churchill 'could touch the soul and heart of the nation' and that victory would have been impossible without him.[37]

In the summer of 1941, *Picture Post* photographers had toured the country catching men and women as they paused and listened to Churchill. Workers drinking in a pub, men and women huddled in the doorway of a wireless shop, farmers and labourers in their village inn and the well-to-do dining in a fashionable restaurant all show the same concentration. Not only was Churchill speaking with 'a voice worthy of Britain', his sentiments were binding together the whole nation, rich and poor, town and country. His mood was stubborn and pugnacious and he dismissed Hitler ('a bloodthirsty guttersnipe') with a mixture of fury and disdain that was felt by everyone. Total war waged the British way had always required a bogeyman as a focus for animosity; Hitler played the same role as had been played by Bonaparte, and the Führer's appearance on newsreels prompted hisses, boos and raspberries.

Churchill did much more than vilify an odious adversary. He appealed to the nation's imagination and sense of destiny: the people were now fulfilling their historic mission under the same providence that had been so generous to them in past conflicts. 'This is indeed a grand heroic period in our history and the light of glory shines on you all,' he told listeners in April 1941.[38] Churchill believed the people could and would live up to his high expectations. Once he remarked that victory could only be secured if everyone matched the intensity of dedication and effort that had been displayed by his friend T. E. Lawrence during the last war.

The prime minister's powerful atavistic appeals were repeated by the novelist J. B. Priestley, whose thoughtful, often radical, comments on the war were broadcast immediately after the nine o'clock news during the summer and autumn of 1940. His voice was the counterpoint to Churchill's. The grandson of the 7th Duke of Marlborough spoke in the patrician tones of Britain's traditional leadership, while Priestley's Yorkshire accent was that of the working man.

In 1940 their voices were complementary, although Priestley's caustic asides about the rich raised many hackles. Here he is on 8 September, explaining how the man and woman in the street were being elevated into the makers of history:

> . . . just now we're not really obscure persons tucked away in our offices and factories, villas and back streets: we're the British people being attacked and fighting back: we're in the great battle for civilisation . . . we're bang in the middle of the world's stage with all the spotlights focused on us; we're historical personages and it is possible that distant generations will find inspiration when their time of trouble comes, in the report in their history books of our conduct; just as it is certain that our airmen have found a shining place for ever in the world's imagination, becoming one of those bands of young heroes, creating a saga that men can never forget.[39]

Priestley moved among the people and listened to what they had to say. So too did Churchill, whose sense of touch was flawless. Tom Harrisson, one of the co-founders of that imaginative exercise in amateur anthropology, Mass Observation, was certain that Churchill was the first politician for twenty years to understand precisely what the public was thinking.[40] A popular song of November 1941 (sung by the comedian Max Miller) called him Britain's 'guiding star', a national asset beyond value, distinguished by his 'bulldog grin' and 'big cigar'. Both made Churchill universally identifiable as he stepped through the rubble of bombed streets and inspected training camps, airfields and coastal defences. These images of the prime minister, familiar from newsreels, also evoked a heroic past: here was a man who was leading from the front and sharing common danger. Cinemagoers cheered whenever he appeared.

There was a paradox here. Churchill was a member of the nation's traditional ruling élite who had fought the wars of the late Victorian Empire on horseback. Now, he was a leader of a war dominated by machines which was being waged by the masses who wanted something more than the glory that had satisfied the fighting men of Churchill's youth. To achieve victory, he harnessed the energies of figures who saw the war as the means to create a more egalitarian society. As an anglophile American journalist perceptively observed in August 1940: 'The plutocratic England is today a socialist state, created with class war, created of love, and led by an aristocrat.'[41] This would have pleased Churchill, for he needed all the sympathy he could get from the United States, where Britain was commonly believed to be a class-ridden, pyramidal society dominated by the rich. Dispelling this image was vital, for Churchill was convinced that the country could only survive if America became its banker and armourer.

3

Only scratches:
Invasion fears and
blitz realities

I

Moments after Chamberlain had told the country that it was at war with Germany, the sirens sounded across London and everyone trooped into the air-raid shelters. Among them were MPs, including Lloyd George, who appeared 'very white and greatly excited'. His apprehensiveness struck Sir Samuel Hoare, the Lord Privy Seal, who wondered why 'this great and courageous war leader' was so frightened. In 1966 Harold Macmillan gave the answer: 'we thought of air warfare . . . rather as people think of nuclear warfare today.'[1]

Everyone was scared in September 1939, for they had been conditioned to expect an aerial Armageddon once war was declared. Technical developments over the previous twenty years had produced bombers that could carry high explosives for hundreds of miles. As warplanes had evolved, strategic theories were contrived for their use in battle. Relentlessly and ruthlessly applied, aerial bombardment could disrupt economies, fracture communication systems, destroy housing and terrorise populations to the point where their will to fight would evaporate. In Britain, a handful of influential senior RAF officers had talked themselves into believing that offensive air power alone might win a war. This hypothesis appealed to politicians who welcomed a potentially decisive method of securing victory without the mass slaughter of a continental land war which, it was rightly believed, the public would never again condone.

Instead of killing millions of soldiers, the new war of attrition would kill civilians on a similar scale. Potential casualties were in no doubt of their fate; in 1932 Stanley Baldwin had warned 'the man in the street' that 'the bomber will always get through.' He was repeating what his expert advisers had predicted, and they remained unshaken despite the gradual introduction of ARP programmes, the network of radar stations, anti-aircraft batteries and new, faster fighters. The two high priests of bomber orthodoxy, Air-Chief-Marshal Sir Charles Portal and the future chief of Bomber Command, Air-Vice-Marshal Sir Arthur ('Bomber') Harris, insisted that enough bombers would get through to create havoc. The outcome of an aerial conflict would depend, they argued, on the resolution of the British working man, and both believed that his nerve and willpower were superior to those of his German counterpart.[2]

They would need to be. Air Ministry statisticians calculated that the Luftwaffe could drop eighteen thousand tonnes of bombs a day on London, which would kill or maim twenty thousand in the first twenty-four hours of the attack and 150,000 within a week. Pessimism came easily, for no one knew exactly what to expect, and where facts were unavailable guesswork was substituted. In 1936 officials had simulated an air raid on the Billingham chemicals complex by throwing paper darts at a model.[3] Experience of the bombing of cities by the Nationalists in Spain and the Japanese in China was discounted on the grounds that in terms of intensity and duration these operations had been on a smaller scale than those planned by the Luftwaffe. Other pertinent evidence was also disregarded. Throughout the 1920s and 1930s the RAF had regularly bombed insurgents and their villages on various imperial frontiers, where it was found that the attacks often aroused resentment and an urge to hit back. Somali warriors fired back at bombers in 1920 and were heard singing songs to keep their spirits up.

The British public had an inkling of what was in store. In the autumn of 1938, as the Munich crisis had unfolded, Londoners hastily prepared for an air attack. They were taught how to provide their houses with 'gas-proof rooms', instructed to collect gas-masks from distribution centres in local schools and to dig protective trenches in their gardens. Commuters found Underground stations shut while fireproof doors were installed and, as they walked to their offices, they saw bulwarks of sandbags being piled against public buildings. Families made hasty arrangements to send mothers and children to rural retreats. Visions of the forthcoming calamity were clear and baleful. Alexander Korda's film of H. G. Wells's The Shape of Things to Come (1936) had vividly shown London under aerial bombardment and, more recently, newsreels had shown the real thing in Shanghai and Barcelona.

Premonitions of catastrophe turned out to be exaggerated. The Air Ministry men had got their sums wrong; between June 1940 and June 1941 the Luftwaffe dropped 36,000 tonnes of bombs on London and other cities and towns, which demolished 350,000 houses, killed forty-two thousand and wounded forty-five thousand. High-level doubts about the toughness of civilian morale also proved unfounded. Just like soldiers after a battle, air-raid survivors congratulated themselves on their good luck, cursed Hitler and the war, and somehow managed to live their lives as normally as possible. There was little else they could have done.

By just hanging on, the British people 'won' the aerial war and gave Germany its first defeat. The Luftwaffe's failure first to secure air superiority over Britain and then to coerce its government and people into a compromise showed that the Third Reich was not invincible. Plans for invasion were shelved; the German navy had never been happy about the enterprise and, by mid September, Hitler and his strategists were concentrating their minds on an offensive against Russia. Most important of all, in terms of the course of the war, Britain's resistance during the second half of 1940 convinced the United States that it was worth backing with credit and matériel.

Apprehension about an invasion remained. Hitler's attack on Russia on 22 June 1941 triggered fresh alarm, for analysts of the Joint Intelligence Sub-Committee (JIC) predicted that Soviet forces would be overwhelmed within six weeks, leaving Hitler free to invade Britain.[4] Countermeasures were immediately implemented, including large-scale and realistic exercises designed to test the country's defences. At the end of August, Scotland suffered a mock invasion: a gas attack was launched against Lanark which left thousands dead and injured, frightening rumours were disseminated to confuse civilians and local fifth columnists (ultra-right-wing subversives) unsuccessfully stormed the local defence commissioner's HQ.[5] A similar exercise was staged in February 1943 when German forces landed on the south Devon coast under cover of fog. They gained a bridgehead and penetrated northwards into Somerset where they met strong resistance from the Ilminster Home Guard. Local police, ARP personnel and the Women's Voluntary Service (WVS) were involved, and the public had been warned beforehand to behave as if they were under occupation. Many ignored these shenanigans and it was officially regretted that 'the public in Chard and other districts did not obey instructions.'[6] There was no point in doing so in the wake of the news of El Alamein and Stalingrad, and when local pubs and dance halls were full of American servicemen who were to form the armies that would eventually invade Europe.

II

The people of Chard would not have shown such insouciance in June 1940, nor would it have been tolerated. Britain was bracing itself for aerial bombardment and seaborne invasion. Defences had to be made ready, fresh troops conjured up and emergency laws made to neutralise anyone inclined to impede the war-effort or chip away at the people's confidence in themselves and their leaders. The paradox of 1914 was repeated: the preservation of freedom and cherished legal rights demanded their suspension, and the state assumed dictatorial powers which were rigorously exercised.

In May a Napoleonic precedent was revived when the secretary for war, Anthony Eden, appealed on the BBC for men to join the Local Defence Volunteers. They were the equivalent of the fencibles and militia, and within six weeks a million and a half men had volunteered for what soon became known as the Home Guard. These amateurs symbolised the nation's new cohesion and sense of purpose. The *Sphere* boasted that Home Guard drill and exercises were uprooting the 'barrier between class and class' and fostering 'the mutual understanding between man and man'. A photograph of the Maidenhead detachment showed young and middle-aged men, some in suits and others in workmen's aprons and dungarees, marching during their lunch hour.[7]

Weapons were in short supply, ingenuity was not. Newspaper articles suggested often hair-raising ways in which ordinary men and women could fight in their homes. A tank could be immobilised by a bed-spread thrown into its tracks, by a Molotov cocktail (a weighted bottle filled with petrol, with a burning rag for a fuse) hurled into its turret, or even by heaving a cart filled with burning straw into its path. Considerable interest was aroused by the Home Guard's mounted units which were preparing to hunt down nocturnal parachutists. Sportsmen practised their marksmanship on clay pigeons so that they could shoot the intruders in mid air. Churchill instinctively knew the public temper and contemplated telling the people that they could 'always take one with you'.

Parachutists made everyone tremble. They might fall from the skies either in mass or in small parties as saboteurs. Tales circulated of para-chutists who had already landed and were wandering about dressed as nuns or policemen. Lord Croft, the under secretary of state for war, was certain that the German army had a hundred thousand paratroopers ready for an invasion.[8] MI6 warned that men had been planted among German prisoners of war with orders to co-operate with parachutists who would land close to their camps.[9]

The danger from above turned minds towards that within. Unease about the possibility of covert collaborators waiting to assist the invaders became a mania during May 1940. The source of a brief spasm of national paranoia was a belief in the existence of a shadowy and therefore infinitely frightening fifth column. The phrase had first been used during the Spanish Civil War by General Mola who in 1936 had claimed that while four Nationalist columns were converging on Madrid, a fifth, consisting of secret supporters, was already inside the city and when the battle started would hinder its defenders. Fifth columnists were thought to have assisted German forces in the Netherlands and France, not least by spreading defeatism and panic among civilians. Vigilance and tough precautionary measures were vital to uncover and forestall the British fifth column.

Its existence and capacity for mischief could only be guessed at. In April the Home Office became anxious about the seventy-four thou-sand Germans and central European refugees who had flocked to Britain during the preceding five years. Among them were commu-nists who, it was suspected, might help their British co-believers in their campaign against the war.[10] It was not unreasonable to imagine that some of the fugitives from Nazism were German agents, although there was no hard evidence for this. None was required by the military authorities, who were taking no chances; during the second week of May they secured a mandate to intern all male aliens in southern and eastern England. By the end of the month the trawl was widened and there was mass internment. Many detainees, including passionate anti-Nazis, were shipped to Canada, and some were drowned when their transports were torpedoed.

An obvious source of fifth columnists was in the ranks of those ideologically opposed to the war. They were few, marginalised, often dotty and highly unpopular. There were outright fascists, members of Mosley's British Union (formerly the British Union of Fascists) and crackpots whose admiration for Hitler was equalled by their loathing for Jews. On the left there were communists who, following the Soviet-German pact, parroted the Moscow line that the war was a struggle in which the capitalists would enrich themselves at the expense of the workers. Pacifists of the Peace Pledge Union and Anti-Conscription League opposed the war on purely moral grounds.

Given the jumpy mood of the country, all opponents of the war were considered potential fifth columnists with a capacity for sabotage quite out of proportion to their numbers. This was certainly true of the British Union. It was a minute party, funded by Mussolini, and its leader, Sir Oswald Mosley, perhaps one of the most overrated British political figures of the century, and certainly the most objectionable. His adherents included anti-semites, conspiracy theory fantasists and roughnecks who relished the brawls that occurred whenever Mosley and his blackshirts held rallies. During the winter and spring of 1939 to 1940 Mosley reiterated Nazi propaganda that claimed that Jewish interests had covertly manoeuvred Britain into the war against the national interest. No one took him seriously, but what worried the Home Office and the intelligence community was the 'leadership' principle that lay at the heart of fascism and gave Mosley theoretical power over cells of dedicated followers scattered across the country.[11] This, as much as his opinions and daydreams about a coup, persuaded the cabinet to order his arrest and detention without trial under section 18B of the Emergency Powers Act at the end of May.[12]

Senior fascists were also interned, along with some of the rank and file. Among these were four army officers, a Kent squire, a Bridgwater policeman and Bertha Graham.[13] Her husband, the rector of Old Bolingbroke in Lincolnshire, had been prosecuted for ringing his church bells in defiance of a ban imposed after the government had decided that they were only to be rung as a signal that the Germans had landed. These precautions were justified, for even though leaderless a handful of fascists attempted to disrupt the war-effort. William Gutheridge was discovered cutting cords in West London telephone kiosks to hinder ARP operations and spent the rest of the war in prison. Another of Mosley's men lit a bonfire during an air raid and, when arraigned, gave the fascist salute in court.[14] Ex-fascists were suspected of spreading subversive rumours in the Bath and Bristol area in December 1940. One, Charles Hewitt, toured pubs near Bristol and stood rounds of drinks for workmen, giving some of them clothes and money. He would then inform his appreciative audience that their poverty was the fault of the government.[15]

Closely linked with the British Union were the Right Club, the Link and the Nordic League – tiny organisations that were magnets for anti-semites and anyone infatuated with Hitler. These bodies attracted a dozen Tory MPs and some social heavyweights who imagined they could still pull strings, including the Dukes of Buccleuch, Montrose, Wellington and Westminster. All wanted an immediate end to the war and an accommodation with Hitler. In what must have been an extraordinary convergence of prejudices, the anti-semitic ('in my boyhood the German Jew was a byword for all that was objectionable') Marquess of Tavistock shared a Glasgow platform with local communists on 29 March 1940. One of them denounced 'this useless bloody war' which was filling the pockets of capitalists, and the marquess insisted that Hitler sincerely desired peace.[16] It is not known whether his hosts introduced Tavistock by his title or as 'Comrade Russell'.

Soon afterwards, Tavistock succeeded his father as the 12th Duke of Bedford. In December 1940 the Home Office contemplated detaining him, but he masked his Nazi sympathies with pacifism and so avoided internment on legal grounds.[17] Captain Archibald Maule Ramsay, Tory MP for Arbroath and co-ordinator of the Germanophile anti-war lobby, was less fortunate, for he was imprisoned at the same time as Mosley.

There was widespread speculation as to whether he and Mosley might have served in a puppet Nazi administration if the invasion had succeeded. This may explain why, in July, army officers serving in southern England were surprised that Mosley had not been shot.[18]

Bizarre as it seems, there was some collusion between Mosley's supporters and pacifists. Members of the Anti-Conscription League encouraged former British Union men to evade the draft by claiming to be conscientious objectors. Officers of the Home Office's G Division detected fascist undertones in some of the articles in *Peace News*.[19] This weekly magazine was the mouthpiece of the Peace Pledge Union. It had been founded in 1935 by an East End parson, the Reverend David Sheppard, who had invited pacifists to send him declarations that they would refuse to fight in another war. By 1939, the Peace Pledge Union had 130,000 members, many of whom were tormented by a moral dilemma. How could men and women of leftist inclinations stand aloof when their beliefs were being extinguished in Spain and central Europe. Was there, pacifists wondered, a point where armed resistance was morally justified?

A few believed never. In 1938 the Bloomsbury Group artist and writer Clive Bell declared in *Peace News* that, 'I see no reason why Germany should not have colonies and hegemony too . . . we welcome the idea of a United States of Europe, even though that Europe be policed by Germans.' Blithely delivering Africans and Czechs into the hands of the SS seemed a step too far for pacifists less sympathetic to Hitler and better informed about his philosophy and methods. The author Rose Macaulay at times imagined that she had purchased the *Blackshirt* in mistake for *Peace News*.[20] Nazi victories and the imminence of the invasion prompted some hasty moral gymnastics. In the summer of 1940 Clive Bell was clamouring for 'ceaseless war against Hitler' and the Peace Pledge Union repudiated militants who had produced a poster that challenged servicemen: 'War will cease when soldiers refuse to fight. What are you going to do about it?'[21]

During the second half of the year, the Home Office recorded a sharp decline in pacifist and communist agitation.[22] Nonetheless, dissidents were kept under close surveillance and those who voiced anti-war or pro-German sentiments were prosecuted. Undeterred, the quirky continued to express their views. In July 1940, W. O. Brown, a

Scottish Nationalist, told an Aberdeen audience that, while he disliked the Nazis, they deserved credit for reducing Germany's infant mortality rate. In December, Jack Thomas, a Yorkshire miner from a communist family, astonished a cinema audience by shouting 'Sieg Heil!' and giving a Nazi salute during the playing of the national anthem.[23] After the invasion of Russia, he and his kind threw themselves into the war-effort and were soon clamouring for a second front.

Public animus towards anti-war groups was strong and justified official bans on their demonstrations on the grounds that they would provoke disorder. Between eight hundred and a thousand ex-service-men promised to break up a rally of pacifist students from Aberystwyth University in March, which provided the local chief constable with a good reason to forbid it.[24] At the same time, Caernarfon farmers refused to accept conscientious objectors who had been drafted as labourers. There was considerable anger that such men were being paid farm labourers' wages, which were below those of servicemen.[25] Hertfordshire Land Army girls were indignant that in some quarters they were regarded as 'conchies' attempting to evade conscription, and that occasionally they had to take orders from men 'whose outlook on life prevents them from serving their country at the Army rate of pay - but allows them to idle away their lives at the very minimum of £3 a week'.[26] As in the last war, there was a general feeling that conscientious objectors were shirking their duty.

The prevailing atmosphere during the summer of 1940 produced some expedient retractions from those who had hitherto opposed the war. In March the pacifist Professor Cyril Joad declared that the Chinese, Abyssinians and Poles would have been wiser not to have resisted their Japanese, Italian and German conquerors. 'You cannot,' he insisted, 'keep a virile nation, e.g. Germany, down by force of arms.' Six months later, he was urging BBC listeners to fight that virile nation to save the 'common heritage of Western Civilization'.[27] On the extreme right, the former Nazi apologist and anti-semitic journalist Arthur Bryant reinvented himself as a patriot and settled down to write stirring histories of Britain's struggle against Revolutionary and Napoleonic France.[28]

III

Nothing could be allowed to erode national morale. A trust in the capacity of ordinary people to take the strain of continuous air raids emerged in the early phases of the blitz, but there was no way of knowing whether people's endurance would prove infinite. A breaking-point might be reached, and it seemed close in mid October when the Air Ministry predicted that the 'vigorous' night attacks on London 'and to a lesser extent Liverpool' were 'likely to have a considerable moral effect in the near future'. The popular will in these cities would be stiffened if two squadrons of night-fighters were stationed close to each city. Practical objections were put forward by Air-Chief-Marshal Sir Hugh Dowding, the head of Fighter Command, who pointed out that unsolved technical problems meant that these aircraft would have 'negligible success'.[29]

Perhaps so, but what mattered above all to Londoners and Liverpudlians was the consolation of being able to hit back. People aware of their own and their homes' vulnerability needed the assurance that they were not the helpless victims of a one-sided battle. If this were so, then despair and defeatism would spread. This was the message of the city fathers of Leicester in a telegram to Churchill after a raid on the night of 19 to 20 November: 'Morale of [the] people is high and it can best be maintained by instant retaliation.'[30] For the same reason, thirty-two additional anti-aircraft guns were moved to Birmingham, another city under severe and regular attack.[31] The noise alone of the ack-ack batteries heartened those in shelters, for it meant that the enemy was not having everything his own way, which was why Glaswegians cheered when they heard the sound of 'our' guns firing during the raids of 5 to 7 May 1941.[32] Few of the bombers would have been hit. Experts estimated that anti-aircraft fire was largely ineffective with a 1 to 2 per cent chance of bringing down an aircraft. Nevertheless, and this would have been deeply satisfying to those on the ground, flying through flak scared aircrews.[33]

The explosions of the anti-aircraft shells were part of the spectacle of air raids, which provoked curiosity as well as terror. Early sorties against Rosyth and the Forth Bridge in September 1939 drew hundreds of spectators, including the nine-year-old Richard Demarco who was making sandcastles on Portobello beach with his younger brother. He got a good view of a crippled bomber just before it crashed into the sea and saw its pilot wave as it passed. The young Demarco picked up some shrapnel, which turned out to be some compensation for the walloping he got from his mother, who had been terrified by his rashness in the face of a danger he could not wholly comprehend.[34] Night raids were even more dramatic with searchlights traversing the sky, exploding shells and fires illuminating the horizon. 'Cor! Looks just like a fairy land,' exclaimed a marine sentry during a night attack on Portsmouth in 1940.[35] In March 1941 people in Selkirk were 'reluctant to take shelter', preferring to watch the bombers pass over, outlined against a full moon, on their way to Glasgow.[36]

An urge to witness history and, if one was lucky, gather keepsakes could outweigh the urge for self-preservation. During a raid on London in September 1940, George Orwell watched two young men and a girl in the hallway of his Marylebone lodgings. The trio were 'openly and unashamedly' frightened, but rushed into the street during a pause in the explosions to catch a glimpse of a bomber and pick up fragments of shrapnel.[37]

Such recklessness was discouraged. As on the Western Front, safety lay under the ground in some kind of shelter, which was where everyone was expected to go when they heard the warning sirens. There was no consensus as to the most effective type of shelter. The government favoured the Anderson shelter and had distributed 1.5 million by September 1939. This was an arch of corrugated iron which was either placed inside the house or, as the civil defence authorities recommended, over a brick-reinforced trench in the garden. These dugouts for families, and sometimes neighbours, were often lined with bricks and furnished with beds, bunks and chairs and a paraffin stove for warmth and making cocoa and tea.

The price of security in an Anderson shelter was often a fitful night's sleep in a fetid atmosphere. Uxbridge had up to four warnings each night during the second week of September and local people were soon flagging. A doctor noticed that while overall morale was good, many of his patients suffered from residual sleeplessness; in one family the parents were 'nervy' while their ten- and eleven-year-old children had 'pale, washed-out faces', poor appetites and short tempers.[38]

Conditions were just as bad in the communal shelters. Before and during the blitz, these were a bone of political contention. Sir John Anderson, the minister responsible for civil defence, opposed communal shelters on economic and psychological grounds. Their construction would waste manpower and resources required elsewhere and would transform the population into 'troglodytes'. Anderson predicted that once the bombing began, everyone would go underground and remain there so that the war-effort would grind to a halt. This strange conjecture was challenged by those on the left, who accused the minister of jeopardising the lives of the poor.

The row about the provision of shelters came to a head early in September 1940 as the night raids on London were increasing in frequency and intensity. It was settled, spontaneously and unilaterally, by the people. Individuals purchased twopenny (1p) tube tickets, took refuge in Underground stations during the afternoon and early evening, and stayed there throughout the night. Rather than risk confrontation, the London Passenger Transport Board and the government bowed to the popular will. By the end of the month, 186,000 men, women and children were sheltering in the stations. This demonstration of people power was a victory for commonsense and must have saved thousands of lives.

Stress and discomfort were the price of security in the mass shelters, as a young Cockney girl discovered when she stepped into one, a converted underground store near the docks:

> [The] first impression [is] of a dense block of people, nothing else. By 7.30 p.m. each evening every available bit of floor space is taken up. Deck-chairs, blankets, stools, seats, pillows – people lying on everything, everywhere. When you get over the shock of seeing so many sprawling people, you are overcome with the smell of humanity and dirt. Dirt abounds everywhere. The floors are never swept and are filthy. People are sleeping on piles of rubbish. The passages are loaded with dirt. There is no escaping it.

After half an hour a great coughing started which lasted for the rest of the night. There was also self-imposed segregation: Jews congregated on the right-hand side of the building, whites in the middle and Indians on the left.[39]

Indulging what a Ministry of Health doctor dismissed as the 'herd instinct' and desire for 'companionship' of the masses in times of peril presented enormous medical problems.[40] The most urgent was the containment of the contagious diseases that were bound to spread rapidly when up to two thousand people were crammed into airless stations in temperatures that rose to seventy degrees. First, tuberculosis sufferers were weeded out and either directed to hospitals or given Anderson shelters. Insecticides were sprayed to kill bed-bugs and lice, chemical lavatories and ventilator fans were installed and stations where more than five hundred people gathered were provided with medical centres. These proved to be an unlooked-for blessing, for they gave doctors and nurses the opportunity to persuade mothers to have their children inoculated against diphtheria and to advise those who had never bothered to do so to attend child welfare clinics.[41] Smoking, then the habit of an overwhelming majority, was restricted to designated areas and half a million gauze anti-germ masks were distributed as a further precaution against contagion.

Public and private organisations fed the crowds in the Underground stations. Tea, cocoa and vegetable soup were offered by the local authorities, the Salvation Army, the WVS and the armed forces and were distributed from trains. Sandwiches, sausage rolls, buns and cakes were sold cheaply from stalls. Advertisements urged shelterers to eat the 'Woolton sandwich', an officially promoted delicacy with a filling of shredded raw vegetables and chutney, but Londoners stuck to their familiar faggots, made of offal, and fish and chips delivered by chippies who had followed their customers into the shelters. Nutritionists were disappointed.[42]

The crowds packed into the shelters became one of the enduring symbols of the blitz. Two official artists, Edward Ardizzone and the sculptor Henry Moore, were sent to record the scenes and returned with images of masses huddled together, often cocooned in blankets, sleeping on platforms and escalators. They were moving images: here were ordinary people, unbeaten, persevering and making the best of things. There was plenty of backbiting. On a visit to one shelter during the second week in September, Orwell found that its elderly and predominantly working-class occupants were 'grousing bitterly about the hardness of the seats and the longness of the nights'. There was no trace of defeatism, although he noticed that the comradeship of danger and inconvenience had not eliminated selfishness. Many queued early to secure the best seats or sent others to reserve them.

That same week, Orwell fell into conversation with a mechanic of about twenty. He was 'very embittered and defeatist . . . and horrified by the destruction he had seen in South London' and peeved by the deferment of his application to join the RAF. Prompted by Orwell, he agreed that houses abandoned by their rich owners in the West End should be commandeered by the authorities and given to the homeless. Orwell had already encountered the dispossessed, 'disconsolate-looking people trudging the streets burdened with suitcases and bundles'. His own lodgings had a 'bomb-proof' room where his landlady and five other women assembled each evening. When the bombs fell there was 'screaming in unison' and the pauses between explosions were filled with 'animated conversation' about everyday, trivial matters.[43]

IV

Were Orwell's impressions of Londoners under bombardment typical? No definite answer can be given: twelve months of intermittent air raids on cities and towns across Britain affected millions of people and prompted myriad responses, some perverse and eccentric. In Bolton, Lancashire, a woman with a reputation for being a little daft announced to her neighbours that she had watched a stick of bombs fall and then seen them rise, pass over the rooftops and finally fall on the town hall.[44] As a child I remember a somewhat frightening elderly woman who wandered about with all she owned in shopping bags. I was told that she had been bombed out of her home and refused ever to sleep under a roof. She was easily startled when unkind children made banging noises.

In the autumn of 1940 air raids were still a novelty. They supplanted the weather as the chief topic of everyday exchanges. Extraordinary events and common misfortune dissolved inhibitions and provided everyone with a story to tell, which they did to anyone who would listen. The same phenomenon occurs today whenever travel systems disintegrate. Outside the capital and before the provinces had been bombed, Londoners would bore the curious and uninitiated with 'gather round boys and hear about my bomb' anecdotes.[45] Glaswegians admired the fortitude shown by Londoners and were resolved to match it when their turn came.[46]

'It's our turn next' was a common, fatalistic remark. It was exploited by the former fascist and German radio propagandist, William Joyce, whose ridiculous attempts to adopt an upper-class accent earned him the mock title 'Lord Haw Haw'. In April 1941 he taunted his listeners: 'Look out Devonport, it's your turn next.'[47] Haw Haw's revelation of exact details of raids disturbed the government since they were weakening morale. The Home Office suspected that former fascists were somehow relaying information to Germany.[48]

By now official anxieties about the fragility of public morale were receding. The worst time had been immediately after Dunkirk when there had been concern about an invasion causing the same sort of hysteria and mass evacuations as had occurred when the Germans advanced into France and Belgium. A condign measure was needed to prevent this and, on 10 July, the cabinet approved Section 119 of the Emergency Powers Act. Anyone found guilty of forcing their way through a roadblock or army and police pickets guarding property was liable to the death penalty. No one was hanged for this crime, and by the end of the month the public mood had become calmer. Official observers in Scotland reported that 'coolness and courage' had replaced 'feelings of novelty and nervousness'.[49]

According to official analyses there was no panic nor 'mass anti-social behaviour' in either Birmingham or Hull in spite of 'a degree of alarm and anxiety' during the raids of 1940 and 1941.[50] Hull, the smaller city, had suffered very badly with 3500 houses demolished and eighty thousand damaged. The qualities shown by its inhabitants were also displayed in Glasgow and Clydebank during night raids of 13 to 14 March and 4 to 5 May 1941 in which 1500 were killed and fifty thousand made homeless. Secret reports praised the population's 'general calm' and 'patience and fortitude'. In Dumbarton there was 'no sign of panic in any form and all behaved with splendid courage'.[51] Discrepancies between what people saw or heard and official accounts of the attacks aroused some bitterness, especially the withholding of the local death toll, whose publication was seen as proof that Glaswegians could 'take it' as stoically as everyone else. What were euphemistically called 'disputes about the rights of occupation' were common among early arrivals at communal shelters, and two drunks were overheard blaming the raids on the 'capitalist bosses'.[52]

The conduct of the people of York was judged 'excellent' during a surprise two-hour raid in the early hours of 29 April 1942 which destroyed five thousand houses.[53] The city had been a victim of one of the Baedeker Raids which were directed against targets with outstanding architecture in retaliation for the RAF's bombing of Rostock and Lübeck. Since York had never been considered a prime target, it had no anti-aircraft batteries and barely enough shelters.[54] Ulster was also unready. Before the war, the Stormont government convinced itself that the province was beyond the range of bombers based at airfields five hundred miles away, which was why it had pressed Whitehall for rearmament contracts for local shipyards and factories.

Conjectured immunity meant that Belfast possessed few ack-ack guns, no searchlights, limited fighter cover and no Anderson shelters. On the night of 15 to 16 April 1941, the city was attacked by 180 bombers which dropped incendiaries and parachute-mines, designed to smash the prestressed, industrial concrete used for factories and, therefore, able to flatten entire streets and tenement blocks. Over seven hundred were killed in the raid and extensive fires started, some of which were put out by volunteer firefighters from Dublin who rushed to Belfast in response to an official plea for help. After a night of pandemonium, tens of thousands fled from a city whose civil defence arrangements were defective and took their chances in adjacent towns and villages. Those who failed to find lodgings slept in fields or under hedges. A further raid early in May triggered a similar exodus. Many fugitives were slum-dwellers, whom Richard Dawson Bates, the minister of home affairs, characterised as 'sub-human' on account of their appalling 'personal habits'. Watching these people leave the city, a Presbyterian clergyman was horrified and wondered whether there would be a revolution after the war if nothing was done for them.

In Belfast and other areas under bombardment there were innumerable instances of bravery and selflessness. A doctor attached to a

London mobile first aid unit was impressed by survivors who dismissed their injuries as 'only scratches', or told their rescuers: 'Go look for someone worse hurt than me'.[55] Courage appeared unexpectedly. Felix Brown, a psychiatrist at Guy's Hospital, was struck by the 'thoroughly heroic manner' in which a young dental mechanic extricated the wounded from the rubble while bombs were still falling. Extreme peril and the chance to be useful had transformed a shy, mother-dominated and sexually disturbed 'psychoneurotic'. Brown speculated as to whether this metamorphosis would have occurred if the young man had been part of the disciplined, institutional world of the services rather than a free agent in a first aid post.

Brown's clinical duties gave him a unique opportunity to observe the emotional impact of sudden encounters with death and mutilation. Like army psychiatrists treating shellshock cases during the previous war, he noticed that some victims of breakdowns had previous histories of neuroses. A female patient stunned by the shockwaves from a bomb that struck her flat imagined she had had a stroke and collapsed. Questioned, she revealed a deep revulsion towards sex, which, Brown concluded, made her susceptible to trauma. Another woman, also a blast victim, succumbed to delusions and attacked a neighbour and an ARP warden, thinking them to be Germans. She was still resisting her rescuers when she reached Guy's and kept shouting: 'Oh, help, it's the Gestapo. Go away. I'm a gas-mask.' Brown uncovered a previous life of inhibition caused by a strict, late Victorian upbringing which had given her an aversion to sex, something that her husband had accommodated by remaining celibate throughout their sixteen-year marriage. Sedation and rest in the outpatient department restored her equanimity.

Perhaps the most intriguing of Brown's cases was that of a salesman who had served in Iraq during the First World War. A direct hit had demolished his house and sliced apart its shelter, from which he struggled free to find his wife buried with just her feet protruding from the rubble. He could not help her, for his left arm had gone numb, a condition diagnosed as 'hysterical paralysis'. As he came round from an anaesthetic, he revealed his emotions during the desperate moments after he first saw what he imagined was his wife's corpse: 'I'll get you out Dolly – I can't use my left arm. Say something. I'll pull you out.

Someone will come soon. Let me catch hold of your feet, Dolly. I want you so . . . Damn old Hitler, if only I could get the swine. Why can't I fit wings on my car? I'll teach him to bomb girls and the kids. House, car, all the damn lot's gone. Never mind we can sleep in the tent . . .'

The drug also unlocked memories of his campaign experiences twenty-five years before, which he described vividly. What is revealing is the sequence of his reactions: first concern for his wife, then vengefulness and finally a recognition that his life would somehow continue. His wife was rescued and survived. The mind's balance was also tilted by sickening sights. A seventeen-year-old girl machinist, who had been sitting in a pub when it received a direct hit, survived but soon began suffering from headaches and insomnia. Under Epivan, she released her suppressed memories of the ghastly moments after the explosion: 'There's a man's head under the piano – I can't see where the body is. It's horrible. I'm going mad.' Brown believed this induced confession had helped restore his patient's stability. From this and other cases, he concluded: 'A very severe bombing experience is needed to provoke hysterical reaction in a normal person.'[56]

Children's reactions to air raids were measured from a sample of fifteen thousand evacuees, of whom 420 showed symptoms of trauma which included hysterical vomiting, bed-wetting, sleepwalking, fits and nervous tics. The source of disturbance was sometimes traced to a feeling of guilt at having 'run away' from their parents. Miss A. T. Alcock, a play therapist who undertook the survey, noted that most victims responded quickly to conventional clinical treatment. Foster-parents occasionally resorted to their own hit-or-miss remedies. A farmer's wife took an incontinent child to the pigsty and said: 'Look at the old sow, now, she wouldn't wet 'er straw, she wouldn't and no more must you.'[57]

Before the war, the Ministry of Health had expected a flood of mental breakdowns and earmarked two London psychiatric hospitals to handle them.[58] They were not required because many who might have collapsed under the strain of air raids were able to secure a temporary respite by staying with friends in the country. These refugees often took to their beds for weeks on end, behaving as if they were chronic invalids. Whether this was the result of continuous restless nights, or, as one doctor suggested, delayed concussion, was the subject for clinical debate.[59] Hostesses were advised to indulge this urge to sleep. 'If you're

temporarily housing a friend from a much-raided area, spoil her by
sending up breakfast in bed at midday, supper in bed at night, letting
her get up when she feels like it.'[60] Those unable to escape could fall
back on Horlicks as the perfect nostrum for broken or shallow sleep. An
advertisement of January 1941 showed how it revitalised a drooping
shelter marshal who, well rested, was able to maintain his own temper
and soothe that of others.

V

After the all-clear sirens sounded there was looting. It is forgotten now,
understandably given the popular image of the blitz as a period when
individuals helped each other rather than themselves. During October
1940, 150 looters were indicted: two were professional burglars, thirty-
nine soldiers (some deserters) and twenty-seven council workers, ARP
staff and firemen.[61]

The breakdown of looters' occupations indicates a large proportion
of chancers who succumbed to the temptation presented by their war
work. The police knew this, which may explain why two plain clothes
detectives paused to watch four firemen picking among the rubble of
the Black Swan and adjacent warehouses near St Paul's churchyard on
the afternoon of 30 September. One, Reginald Ledster, a section officer
from Harrow, extracted a bundle of socks and a trilby, which he tried on
for size. He hid these spoils under a damaged cistern and, for the next
three hours, he and his colleagues made frequent trips to their tender,
parked twenty yards away. Their purpose was revealed when the detectives approached the vehicle: 'We saw one of the men climb into the
tender, heard a clink of glass against bottle and heard a voice – "That
was a good drop of Scotch".' The beano ended when a motorcyclist
summoned the crew to return to their station. Thirty-seven bottles of
whisky, a dozen of gin, fifty pairs of socks, some underwear and the hat
were later recovered and the four firemen each received five years'
penal servitude.[62]

None had any previous convictions. The same was true of seven soldiers from the Norfolks who, while clearing away rubble, discovered and
stole several bottles of whisky which had been stored in a garage.[63]

Easily consumed and easily disposable, liquor and cigarettes were common plunder. Less so were two cucumbers, stolen by a middle-aged Hull firewatcher who passed them on to a demolition contractor in May 1941; both men got three months.[64] Stiff sentences were the rule, for judges and magistrates were determined to deal severely with symptoms of a collapse in the moral order. Misinterpreting section 1B of the Emergency Powers Act, a Liverpool magistrate warned a seventeen-year-old looter that he could have been hanged, before sentencing him to three years of 'Borstal treatment'.[65] There were exceptions: a regular police officer was bound over for stealing a fur coat worth eighteen pounds which he gave to his wife. Regretting this leniency, Air-Vice-Marshal Sir Philip Game, the Metropolitan Police commissioner, remarked that it was the consequence of the accused having hired 'a clever counsel who enlarged on his misfortunes', which included being bombed out of his house and sickness.[66]

Other looters came from the margins of urban society. They had supple consciences and snatched at whatever opportunities for profit came their way, including petty crime. It was a way of life that demanded several identities and a capacity to elude authority. Percy Bishop, also known as Jack Desmond, had enrolled as an auxiliary fireman at the beginning of 1940, had fallen under suspicion of stealing from his colleagues, and had been placed on extended sick-leave in August. For him and his kind, the blitz presented the chance to make a little money, either by theft or by dealing in stolen goods. Offered some cutlery for five shillings (25p) by a man in Cambridge Road, Bethnal Green, Bishop accepted. 'He told me it was stolen and I said, "All right. I'll take my chance."' Luck deserted Bishop in September, for he was bombed out of his house and compelled to stay with his wife's aunt. There were quarrels, inevitable in overcrowded houses, and the Bishops moved on to the home of a Mrs Barnett. She had members of her own family staying and the sight of one undressing upset Mrs Bishop, so the pair returned to her aunt.

In the meantime and in spite of his illness, Bishop was doing casual work, helping shift loads of furniture and household goods for homeless neighbours. One, a man with a wooden leg, paid him two shillings (10p) for three days' graft and Bishop made up what he considered the shortfall by taking some of his possessions. When arrested, Bishop and three accomplices were found to have a store of looted goods including a cotton frock, lino and household utensils.[67]

Similar items, together with a Bravington alarm clock and five Dulwich College ties, were among the hoard recovered from another gang of looters and fences. They included A. J. S. Allan, a reserve policeman, and Jack Sandler, a former housebreaker who had been called up at the outbreak of war and deserted on 25 October 1940. Two days later, he had helped remove broken glass from a damaged house in Brixton, which included a flat occupied by a moneylender, Mr Isaacson, who had taken himself off to Dublin. Sandler entered and stole twenty-five pounds in cash and a diamond pendant which he tried to sell. A clandestine, no-questions-asked market existed for such goods, as a fence. Alfred Allen, a discharged soldier, explained to the police. He had purchased grey suit cloth in 'Wally's Café', a white fur coat at a dancehall, and a pair of lady's fur-lined boots from a prostitute in Piccadilly.[68]

VI

Deterrent sentences passed on looters were well advertised in the press. Other aspects of the blitz were deliberately withheld from the public for good psychological and strategic reasons. In July 1940 the cabinet agreed to suppress casualty figures because it was feared they would reach such high levels that their disclosure would encourage panic-stricken stampedes from cities and towns, either after or in anticipation of attack. Newspapers and the BBC were forbidden to identify targets until it was certain that German intelligence knew that they had been hit – an important consideration, given that British scientists were endeavouring to jam or deflect the wireless signals that guided German bombers at night. Thus the raid on Bristol on the night of 24 to 25 November was reported as an attack on 'a West Country town' in which, among things, water mains had been fractured and reinforcements of firemen brought in from other areas.[69]

No injunction could curb the tendency of journalists to describe the damage caused in what the Air Ministry described as 'extravagant terms', as they had done after the 14 to 15 November bombing of Coventry. Such coverage could easily lead to a 'reluctance' by the

Americans to 'let us have machine tools' and other necessities.[70] These objections were to be expected from a ministry that was notoriously secretive. In September, *The Times* had indiscreetly mentioned that the Air Ministry censors filtered its communiqués twice, a fact that German wireless propaganda exploited by claiming that the public were being deceived about the air war.[71]

'Mr Knowall' knew the whole truth and was keen to share his knowledge with everyone. He and the pessimistic 'Mr Glumpot' appeared on official posters in July 1940 with a warning that sensible people ignored whatever they said. Rumours masquerading as facts and doom-laden predictions were, paradoxically, the by-products of censorship. Speculation was the child of official secrecy and the authorities were anxious to control or stifle it at birth. During the Dunkirk crisis local figures of 'distinction' and 'integrity' were instructed to refute scaremongers in the event of the BBC or the press being put out of action.[72] On 11 June anyone spreading rumours or misinformation that could damage morale became liable to prosecution under the Emergency Powers Act. Among the first victims of this regulation was a seventy-four-year-old Home Guard volunteer who spent seven days in gaol for declaring that the swastika would soon fly over the Palace of Westminster.[73]

Very few such cases came before the courts; during June and July there were only seventy-four prosecutions for spreading 'alarm and despondency'.[74] At the end of August, attention was focused on the playground, and headmasters and headmistresses were ordered to punish children overheard repeating rumours.[75] A fortnight later the Home Office was contemplating stifling those whose views could fragment 'national unity', presumably communists who were protesting against inadequate shelters for the poor.[76]

It was impossible to smother rumours, which flourished throughout the war. Despite War Office injunctions, veterans of Dunkirk gossiped in pubs about officers running away and scenes of panic. These tales had a long life and in December 1942 led to brawls between British and American soldiers in Lochgilphead bars. Accusations of cowardice at Dunkirk were the last straw for men already incensed by the Argyll lasses' preference for GIs.[77] The public's appetite for the irrational and the plain silly led to rumours that the Lord Mayor of Manchester had pleaded for immediate peace the moment the first bomb fell on his city, that the Americans were about to invade Ireland, and that within a year of the first arrival of black servicemen in Britain one Norfolk girl had had three black babies in succession.[78]

Another of Hitler's helpmates, 'Miss Leaky Mouth', appeared on posters in July 1940. While Jeremiahs and gossips invented the truth, she knew it and was willing to chatter about it. As another poster put it, 'Careless Talk Costs Lives', for it was assumed that spies were everywhere, eavesdropping on conversations in which vital secrets were aired. Fortunately, there were no German agents in the Lyons' Corner House on the Strand on 11 July when Sub-Lieutenant G. C. Ames, a brother naval officer and two young ladies were talking over tea. Ames described experimental work on asdic and direction finders in which he was involved and which he thought were public knowledge. They were not and a court-martial reprimanded him and stripped him of three months' seniority for his indiscretion.[79] It was an uphill struggle to fetter loose tongues, even among those who ought to have known better. In December 1940, army intelligence was dismayed by the casual attitude being shown to operational security in Cairo. An officer revealed plans for intervention in Greece when he asked colleagues in a bar to recommend a good hotel in Athens. Soon afterwards, two barflies, both officers, were overheard discussing a forthcoming offensive against the Italians in Libya.[80]

Snippets of information communicated by those in the know, or who pretended they were, gained credibility because the public suspected that the government was not always candid. Everyone in 1940 knew that censorship was a fact of life. Mischievous Orcadians, whose islands were host to extensive naval and RAF installations, knew that all their letters were opened and deliberately inserted enigmatic phrases to fox the censors.[81] What angered people was that they were being kept in the dark because the government feared that they could not withstand bad news. In March 1941, when provincial cities were suffering heavy air raids, Midlothian sceptics deduced that the brevity of BBC news bulletins and the abundance of peripheral material on the wireless were evidence that bad news was being suppressed. Reporting their conclusions, the local chief constable declared that no one would flinch from the truth, however grim. 'Instead of shaking the morale of the public a report of heavy casualties is much more likely to stiffen the

resistance of the country.'[82] Similar sentiments were expressed in soldiers' letters after the fall of Singapore in February 1942. Army censors
reported that they believed that 'the country could be trusted' and
would 'stand being told the truth'.[83] In its absence, soldiers were swal-
lowing rumours that the capitulation had been the result of bungling by
highly placed 'Blimps'. This turned out to be the truth; for once, 'Mr
Knowall' had got it right.

VII

People were most impressionable during the immediate aftermath of air
raids. This was why the authorities moved swiftly to scotch rumours and
calm the stunned survivors. The morning after the attack on Glasgow
in March 1941, Ministry of Information loudspeaker vans toured devastated areas. Survivors were directed to an administrative centre in a
local theatre, advised to boil their water and keep clear of rickety gable-
ends. They were reassured that work was already in hand to restore
supplies of gas, electricity and water and told to stay in their houses if
they were undamaged. On the whole, these instructions were obeyed,
despite a residual scepticism about all statements made by 'authority'.[84]

Public confidence was best maintained by effective practical measures rather than words of comfort. The dead had to be removed,
identified and buried, rubble and broken glass cleared away, roads
reopened, telephone lines reconnected, tottering buildings demolished,
and damaged ones repaired. The homeless had to be given hot food,
provided with a change of clothing and housed. If necessary, transport
had to be commandeered to carry them to billets in outlying towns and
villages. Between thirteen and fifteen thousand people, mostly women
and children, were evacuated from Glasgow in March by train and bus.
Within two months of the raid, an army of joiners, slaters, plumbers and
glaziers undertook emergency repairs to make over three thousand
houses habitable.[85] Everywhere the task of clearing up the human and
physical detritus of the air raids was done under the direction of the
civil defence and local authorities. Private firms contributed manpower,
as did neighbouring municipal councils.

At the street level, ARP wardens took charge. They were local men, familiar with their neighbourhood, who knew how many people were in a house that had been hit. Over 1100 wardens were on duty in York during the April 1942 raid. After explosions had severed telephone lines, they and the rest of the emergency services depended on motor-cycle despatch riders or foot messengers to report damage and summon fire-engines and ambulances. Time and time again, neighbours and passers-by would lend a hand in the fraught and often painstaking task of recovering the dead and wounded from the rubble. Strangers might find themselves working as members of a rescue party, gingerly picking over the debris and forming the human chains that passed broken woodwork and bricks from hand to hand.

Press photographs and newsreel footage of such scenes were proof not only of the nation's resilience, but of what could be accomplished through selfless teamwork. This shared self-image of the nation during the blitz had a political dimension: it showed that planning and co-operation worked for the common good. At the same time, victims of the bombing and those who cleared up afterwards wanted revenge. Perthshire civil defence workers rushed to Clydeside in March 1941 returned home incensed by what they had seen and demanded that parachute-mines and incendiaries should be dropped on German cities.[86]

4

You may go for a Burton next time: Attrition in the air and at sea, 1939–45

I

Blitz survivors who clamoured for revenge in kind against Germany were well satisfied. From mid 1942 onwards, Bomber Command and 8th USAAF launched the Combined Air Offensive, the former bombing the Reich by night, the latter by day. 'We shall continue to batter Germany from the air with increasing severity and keep the seas open and ourselves alive,' Churchill promised Stalin at the beginning of September 1942.[1] There were no strategic alternatives. Britain and, after December 1941, the United States had no choice but to embroil themselves in two wars of attrition: one in the skies over Germany and occupied Europe, and the other against submarines in the Atlantic and Mediterranean.

In the meantime, the Soviet Union bore the brunt of the land war, which was going entirely Germany's way. By January 1942, 3.1 million Russian soldiers had been killed, three million captured and five thousand Soviet warplanes had been lose. A calamity on this scale appeared to rule out further resistance, let alone a resurgence, or so Anglo-American experts concluded. The outlook was forlorn for British forces on the Mediterranean and North African fronts: during 1941 and the first half of 1942 they had been evicted from Greece and Crete, their grasp on Malta was precarious and Rommel's Afrika Korps was edging towards the Suez Canal.

At each stage in the war, all fronts were interconnected. Reverses on one had repercussions on others. None alone was decisive, although both Churchill and Roosevelt rightly agreed that if the Allies lost control over the Atlantic, British and American forces would be incapable of engaging Germany on land in North Africa and western Europe. From the beginning of 1941 until the middle of 1943 the war at sea had absolute priority.[2] Hitler acknowledged the significance of the contest in the Atlantic, but, from June 1941, his overriding preoccupation was the extinction of the USSR. This would destroy forever the phantom forces of the Jewish-Bolshevik conspiracy and thereafter the new Nazi order in Europe and Russia would be unassailable. Hitler's ideology dictated German strategy, disastrously as it turned out.

Pragmatic considerations shaped Allied war plans. During 1941 and 1942, geography prevented Britain and America from giving direct assistance to Russia beyond supplies, in particular wireless equipment and transport, which were conveyed by sea at considerable risk. The other form of relief available, a formidable aerial bombing offensive against Germany, was what Churchill offered Stalin in August 1942 when they met in Moscow. He had flown there to refute Soviet insinuations that Britain and America were not pulling their weight in the war-effort and to persuade the Russians that Germany would be gravely, perhaps fatally, hurt by aerial pounding. Stalin was pleased and Anglo-American planners entertained visions of a victory gained solely by air power.

It was a tempting strategy. Superficially, Germany was highly vulnerable to the persistent and intense bombing that the Allied air staffs had in mind. Of the Reich's eighty million inhabitants, twenty-six million lived in towns and cities with a population of over one hundred thousand. Moreover, and this was welcomed in Moscow, once the aerial war gathered momentum, the German high command would be compelled to withdraw fighters and anti-aircraft guns from the east. Two-thirds of the Luftwaffe's combat aircraft were eventually deployed for home defence, which contributed immeasurably to the superiority achieved by the Soviet air force in 1944. Inside Germany, a low priority was given to civil defence which, together with endemic economic mismanagement, meant that there were never enough shelters to go round. This shortfall left 6.5 million Germans unprotected, including the citizens of Dresden who suffered forty thousand casualties when it was attacked in February 1945.[3] Hitler was indifferent to civilian deaths – he never visited a bombed area – and placed his hopes in retaliation using secret weapons (jet planes and 'V' missiles) which were fitfully developed after 1943.[4] Neither did anything to reduce the air raids.

The aerial onslaught against Germany was dictated by two theories, one psychological, the other strategic. The first hypothesis claimed that unceasing and methodical bombardment was bound to generate mass hysteria and social chaos which together would bring about the implosion of the German state. This dénouement was confidently predicted by Air-Chief-Marshal Portal's mathematicians in November 1942: 1.75 million tons of bombs would kill or injure 1.9 million Germans and leave a further twenty-five million, nearly the whole urban population, without homes.[5]

This equation could work only if the Allies could muster between four and six thousand bombers, which would require a concentration of resources and industrial capacity that was bound to deprive the army and navy of equipment. But the price was worth paying, for, if the men with slide-rules were correct, victory would be achieved by air power unaided. This was an enticing prospect since it would remove the need for an Anglo-American amphibious assault on France, an operation that worried British strategists. Unlike their American counterparts, they were haunted by memories of the Gallipoli débâcle and had more recent, perturbing experience of being expelled from France by the Wehrmacht. Severe casualties suffered during the Dieppe raid in August 1942 confirmed these misgivings.

Everyone had got their sums wrong. D-Day did not end in catastrophe and German nerve did not crack under bombing. The calculus of aerial death was checked in 1945 by USAAF investigators in occupied Germany. They discovered that the 2.76 million tons of bombs that had fallen on Germany had killed three hundred thousand civilians, injured a further 780,000 and made 7.5 million homeless. The German authorities estimated the death toll at twice the total reached by the Americans and the statistical basis for the survey has been called into question.[6] Nevertheless, the conclusions were sound. Morale had not been significantly impaired by the air raids, although they had contributed to that growing sense of helplessness and defeatism that followed the surrender of the Sixth Army at Stalingrad. Before, when victories had been abundant, optimism had been high, but by early 1944, 70 per cent of Germans were secretly convinced that the war was lost. Nearly half the pessimists based their misgivings on news of reverses in Russia, North Africa and Italy. Only 15 per cent blamed Allied air raids.[7] The American findings corroborated the results of investigations undertaken after the air raids on Hull and Birmingham in 1940 and 1941. In both cities there was no significant decline in civilian morale. It was a fact that the advocates of bombing deliberately ignored, preferring instead tentative theories about bombing producing collective despair.[8]

While there were differences of opinion over whether bombardment would gnaw away at the civilian will to fight, there was agreement that it would cripple German industry and communications. The evidence for this was incontrovertible. Aircraft production plummeted after 1943 and, unable to replace machines lost in action, the Luftwaffe slid into terminal decline.[9] For the final year of the war the Allies had aerial supremacy everywhere. The aerial offensive coincided with a last-ditch programme to establish the German economy on an efficient war-footing, and doomed it to failure. German forces were bedevilled by dire shortages of fuel, transport, equipment and ammunition.

Destroying the Reich's war industries killed civilians. Until the closing months of the war, neither the RAF nor USAAF possessed the technology accurately to bomb military and economic targets. Since most lay within or near areas of civilian housing, it was impossible to prevent what today's euphemism calls 'collateral damage'. American statisticians reckoned that during 1942 only 20 per cent of bombs hit their specified targets. The proportion had risen to 70 per cent by February 1945, thanks to improved bomb-sights and navigational instruments.[10] Bomber crews were well aware of their bombs' waywardness. One remarked to a government scientist: 'You can think it damn lucky, old boy, that we drop bombs in the right country.'[11] His superiors were unconcerned about misses; every bomb that exploded on German soil counted. Objecting to a proposal to deploy more aircraft in the campaign against U-boats, the head of Bomber Command, Air-Marshal Sir Arthur Harris, remarked that nearly every bomb dropped at sea missed. Whereas on land, a stick of bombs that fell short of a factory could still demolish the houses of those who manned its production-lines and so help weaken the German war-effort.[12]

Official versions of the bombing offensive strenuously repudiated suggestions that it was being waged to kill civilians. 'We never set out to bomb indiscriminately,' declared the *Daily Herald*'s air correspondent in July 1941, a message that was repeated throughout the war.[13] Rather, bombing operations were an integral part of Allied exertions in what the *Spectator* called 'one' war and they were securing benefits on other fronts, particularly the Russian.[14] In broadcasts regularly made during the first half of 1944, the BBC's air correspondent, Squadron-Leader John Strachey, emphasised how the raids were paralysing Germany's industry and communications. In every theatre its forces were being starved of fuel and equipment. Strachey dismissed suggestions of vindictiveness, reminding listeners that the current onslaught against Berlin was being undertaken because the city was the centre of the Reich's electronics industry.[15]

Government propaganda was challenged by George Bell, the Bishop of Chichester, during a House of Lords debate in February 1944. He detested Nazism, but had moral reservations about a bombing policy that made no distinction between Germany and the 'Hitlerite state'. Bell wondered whether the motive behind the aerial offensive was the annihilation of the German people. Even if this was not achieved, he felt sure that the legacy of devastation and death would be resentment, which would hamper the postwar political reconstruction of Germany. Bell also regretted the destruction of churches, art galleries and museums. The government's spokesman, Lord Cranborne, insisted that the RAF had never launched a 'pure terror raid' and reminded the peers how the Nazis were treating the Jews and the people of occupied Europe. War and suffering were inseparable, Cranborne concluded, and in so far as the bombing offensive would shorten the war, it was contributing to the reduction of human misery.[16]

Bell's moral unease was not widely shared. The public agreed with

Cranborne and welcomed any strategy that would accelerate the coming of peace. Nor was there much sympathy for a velvet-glove approach to Germany after the war. It was wickedly parodied by Noël Coward's 'Don't let's be beastly to the Germans' (1943) in which he suggests that their postwar renaissance might be assisted by the export of some bishops. What Coward understood and Bell did not was that there was a strong feeling that the Germans deserved to be punished. The bombing represented retaliation for the blitz and was, after all, a form of warfare that Germany had started. It was an attitude summed up by John Strachey's barber: 'Well, they wanted to play, didn't they?'[17] As Britain entered the fourth year of the war, Clement Attlee reminded BBC listeners how the Germans had first used mass aerial bombardment 'ruthlessly and so lightheartedly against defenceless cities'. Nemesis was approaching and its advent would be marked by more and heavier attacks on the Reich.[18]

A vengeful spirit pervaded parts of the American documentary *Memphis Belle*, which was released in June 1944. Filmed in colour and dramatically narrated, the film told the story of a Flying Fortress and its long-serving crew. Their targets are the industrial 'foundations' of the 'Nazi Empire', but as footage of the German coastline appears, the commentator observes that below is the nation that had started two world wars and 'flooded the world with suffering'. Press coverage of air raids left nothing to the imagination. 'Dessau Goes Up In Flames' ran the *Daily Herald* headline on 9 March 1945 over a story that described how over half a million tons of incendiaries had fallen on an important industrial and communications centre for the Eastern Front.

Revenge was not a reason for the bombing strategy, although its architects proceeded on the tacit assumption that high explosives did not distinguish between the human and the physical wherewithal to wage war. In secret, Harris and those of similar mind mistakenly imagined that high civilian casualties were a bonus because they would create problems for the German authorities. This aspect of the campaign has subsequently attracted criticism to the point where the policy has been likened to the Holocaust. This is a perverse analogy, resorted to by writers bent on exonerating Hitler's state. There can be no reasonable comparison between operations openly conducted in the justifiable belief that they were contributing substantially to an overall

Allied victory, and the furtive, meticulously planned, mass murder of civilians whose death could have no bearing whatsoever on the outcome of the war.

II

Retrospective morality, which took no account of the complex realities of wartime strategy, lay behind objections to the setting up of Harris's statue in front of St Clement Danes church in the Strand and acts of vandalism against it. He was called 'Butcher' or 'Butch' by his crews, but not because he ordered them to kill civilians. Harris earned his nickname because, like Haig, he had an inflexible mind and never let casualty rates deflect him from pursuing a strategy that he believed to be right. Again like Haig, he was popular with those he ordered to their deaths. In Harris's war of attrition, twenty-two thousand aircraft were lost, 55,573 British and dominion aircrew killed and nearly ten thousand taken prisoner.

Those who died had joined a service that had a positive, modern and romantic image. The RAF had emerged from the First World War with credit and could boast that it had replaced the navy as the nation's first line of defence. The air was the last frontier and the pioneers engaged in exploring it were lionised by the public. The thrills and spectacle of the Hendon air shows, the derring-do of Biggles and adventure films such as *Wings*, *Dawn Patrol*, and *Hell's Angels* attracted young men for whom flying was exciting and glamorous.[19] Richard Passmore was 'hopelessly in love with aircraft and flying' when he joined in 1938, after five years in a provincial grammar school and two in business. In return for five shillings (25p) a day (office boy's wages) and poor marital prospects, he trained to be a wireless operator on Blenheim bombers.[20]

Flying duties attracted many of Passmore's mould, restless young men from lower-middle-class backgrounds whose grammar school education gave them the necessary sharpness of mind and basic mathematical and scientific knowledge. Trenchard, the RAF's founding father, and the Air Ministry did not want an egalitarian service and preferred public schoolboys as officers. 'You've got to be a gentleman to fly, my lad!' a recruiting officer told Harry Jones, a brewery worker's son, when he enlisted in 1935.[21] He was put to work as a rigger, but like many other ground crew found a way to satisfy his urge to fly. When war was declared there was a gratifying deluge of applications for flying duties from public school men. An advertisement of November 1939 appealed to ex-public schoolboys who knew how to handle men and were 'addicted to sport, especially shooting', to apply for commissions as air gunners.[22] Just the sort of fellows who had been the mainstay of the air force in 1918.

Wastage in battle and from accidents compelled the RAF to cast its net widely and forget nostrums about leadership qualities residing solely among former public school prefects. Nor could it be too choosy about basic education. Over four-fifths of the candidates who applied for air-crew training courses at Locking in Somerset in September and October 1942 were accepted, a large proportion of them former ground crew. [23] Among this new intake were men like Flight-Lieutenant T. W. Fox from Renishaw in Derbyshire, who had left school at fourteen to work in the local Co-op. His protective and fearful parents had asked him not to volunteer for flying but, after three years as a fitter, he did. He was attached to 77 Squadron, based at Full Sutton in East Yorkshire, and during 1944 and 1945 flew Halifax bombers on missions in support of the D-Day landings and the parachute drop at Arnhem. His eight-man crew included a former bank teller, a Metropolitan police detective and a Glasgow constable; the youngest member was nineteen.[24]

Old snobberies lingered. Infuriated by reports of excesses at a station dance in 1944, the commanding officer at Coningsby in Lincolnshire carpeted the aircrew sergeants, whom he called 'errand boys and chimney sweeps', and accused them of lowering the tone of his flying crews. The graffito 'Errand boys make Berlin' appeared on one Lancaster and the officer apologised. At the next dance he made amends by dancing a tango with his wife and turning a blind eye to a senior warrant-officer who did an Apache war dance 'with a red-haired bit of stuff from the Orderly Room' and two squadron-leaders who played rugger with a squashed bun and ended up under a billiard table.[25]

This was just the sort of 'dash' that aircrew instructors at Birmingham considered appropriate for fighter rather than bomber pilots. Reports from this training centre during the autumn of 1941 indicated that shortages had forced selection boards to accept many who were temperamentally unsuited for flying. Many trainees were 'not interested in outdoor sport and are not mechanically minded', but they were balanced by young men who had owned motorbikes and, therefore, were adept with machinery. Former schoolmasters were judged 'rather slow or dull', musicians were 'generally good'. There was also a correlation between age and aptitude: seventeen- to nineteen-year-olds tended to be unstable, married men over twenty-six with children were 'not so hot', and trainees over thirty were disheartened by crashes.[26]

Behind these sweeping assessments of character and how it might influence the performance of flying duties were high-level anxieties about how aircrew reacted to the psychological pressures of continuous operations. The dilemma was the same as it had been in the previous war: what was the proper way to deal with the flier whose nerve had failed, or was about to do so? Was he a patient in need of therapy, or a coward who needed to be shamed and degraded? Clinical indulgence was out of the question, for faintheartedness was infectious. As one officer observed: 'You can't have any member of the crew windy – it hazards the whole crew.'

This axiom guided the small group of senior officers who assembled at the Air Ministry in April 1940 to devise a policy towards 'personnel who will not take operational risks'. The result was a code of punitive sanctions: courts-martial tried those who had shown 'flagrant cowardice' and those who had been traumatised to the point where they could no longer perform their duties were humiliated. Aircrew who had lost their commanding officer's confidence or revealed symptoms of stress were categorised as LMF (Lacking Moral Fibre) and dismissed from flying duties. Officers forfeited their commissions, NCOs lost their stripes and flying badges and were deliberately allocated menial tasks. Their papers were stamped 'W' for 'waverer'. After 1944, 'waverers' were liable to be transferred for compulsory service in the coalmines. Dangers beneath the earth were easier to live with than those above it, or so it seemed to the Air Ministry mind.[27]

Between 1941 and the end of the war the criteria for LMF were reconsidered, largely as a consequence of political pressure. A maximum of two hundred flying hours was set for the first tour of duty in March 1941, with reductions for men of 'less robust constitution'. In March

1943, when longer missions were being flown deep into Germany, a total of thirty was fixed for the first tour and twenty for the second. An Air Ministry pamphlet, distributed to station medical officers in 1943, listed the symptoms that indicated imminent nervous exhaustion. They were the same as those of shellshock victims and faltering pilots in the First World War: headaches, insomnia, nightmares, indigestion, loss of appetite, giddiness and hypochondria. The stigma implied by LMF was partially lifted in June 1943, when it was officially superseded by the clinical description 'No Ascertainable Disease: Lacking Confidence'.[28]

Cases of failure of nerve were astonishingly few given the danger and stress involved in flying sorties day after day for weeks on end. Out of a total of 288,000 British and dominion aircrew, there were just over one thousand instances of LMF or its equivalent between 1942 and 1945, a third of them in Bomber Command. Injustices occurred. A bomb-aimer was categorised LMF and removed from his station after he had fallen through a hatch while his plane was in mid air. He had been hauled back in the nick of time and after landing announced that he would never fly again, an understandable sentiment given what he had just endured.[29]

Like men from all services and throughout all wars, bomber crews found fear hardest to suppress during the hours spent waiting for action. A mood of apprehension pervaded the aircrew of 218 Squadron during 7 November 1941. They were based at Marham, on the edge of the Fens, and flew Wellingtons. Over the previous three and a half weeks the squadron had undertaken eight missions against Nuremberg, Duisburg, Bremen, Essen, Ostend and Antwerp. On four they had been unable to identify their targets, but jettisoned their bombs anyway. This happened frequently, particularly when aircraft got lost or faced heavy flak, and getting rid of the bombs lightened the plane for its return flight. No machines had been lost during these missions, but a rear-gunner had been killed in an engagement with a fighter during the Bremen raid.[30]

Those who quantified their odds of survival, as many did, would have considered this a remarkable run of luck which was bound to end. This possibility must have contributed to the tense atmosphere when the crews assembled for a briefing at six in the morning. Flight-Lieutenant John Dobson, a prewar volunteer reservist, recalled the mood, so utterly unlike that portrayed in screen versions of such occasions: 'No celluloid sallies here, no carefree chatter which film-struck spinsters associate with an operational briefing: no "wonder where it will be". We all wondered. We were all in the bluest of blue funks so that no-one dared speak for fear of voicing with his eyes or gruffness, his innermost, uppermost fear of the unknown.'

The commanding officer opened with a patriotic appeal: 'Gentlemen . . . His Majesty, the King, has seen fit to select 218 Squadron, Bomber Command, for a special mission over enemy territory.' After outlining details of the targets, which included a secret weapons establishment (two aircraft were designated to the Ruhr, the remaining eleven to Berlin), he returned to his theme: '. . . the King recognises the sterling work accomplished hitherto. Don't let him down chaps. You each have a great hope of saving your life by a parachute descent and, at worst, being taken prisoner.' This discouraging afterthought drew a sardonic 'Amen' from one of the audience. For the rest of the morning, the men sat around in a mess listening to a gramophone. There was plenty of time for morbid speculation and lunch was eaten without any relish. The king was toasted and afterwards everyone stood to attention for the national anthem. Dobson was moved: 'I could hardly help a rather patriotic lump filling my mouth and the thought that England could never be lost whilst such men as these were ready to lay down their greatest gift at her feet.'

His crew were untouched by these emotions. Just before take-off, Dobson's navigator told him that he had undertaken thirty missions and was entitled to a rest. He feared he would never have children and, speaking for his four colleagues, declared that they were 'certainly not going to chuck our lives away on this damned death but no glory stunt'. The navigator had suspected, probably correctly, that the raid had been contrived to provide a 'newspaper headline which was scarce worth the paper on which it would be printed'.[31] Dobson was allocated a fresh crew, all novices, and the sortie proceeded. For the next week, the squadron was stood down, flying its next mission against Emden and Kiel on 15 November. It is not known what happened to the five defiant crewmen; there is no mention of their misconduct in the squadron's war diary and wartime RAF court-martial transcripts are still embargoed.

III

Firm and inspiring leadership were the official antidotes to flinching, backed by the threat of punishment and degradation. At the lowest level, where it counted most, an aircrew's cohesion and fighting spirit derived from the personality of their pilot, the 'skipper' of the aircraft. There was no perfect paradigm. Guy Gibson, who led the famous 'Dambuster' raid in 1943, was described by his group commander as 'the kind of boy who would have been head prefect in any school'. On the other hand, and much to the annoyance of senior officers, the demotic familiarity of officers from the dominions could work wonders.[32] A skipper with a knack for flying who earned the confidence of his crewmen enhanced their chances of survival.

Nonetheless, there were always those whose temperament made them calculate their chances of survival. These increased with training and experience, although neither could eliminate that constant factor in warfare, mischance. Loss rates fluctuated. They were less than 0.5 per cent among Coastal Command crews laying mines and hunting U-boats during 1944, operations in which they were unlikely to encounter fighters or heavy ground fire. Casualties among bomber crews operating over occupied Europe, where targets tended to be less heavily defended, were 2.76 per cent, and over Germany, where they were well defended, nearly 5 per cent. A breakdown of these figures revealed the obvious: inexperienced crews were most at risk and the odds on survival increased after fourteen missions.[33]

Air Ministry averages were misleading, for they disregarded periods of large-scale operations during which casualty rates soared, as they had done in the trenches. Ten per cent of aircraft were lost during the mass night attacks on Berlin between November 1943 and March 1944, which Harris wrongly believed were a war-winner. Wastage was even higher during the simultaneous onslaught on other cities; of the 795 machines that attacked Nuremberg on 30 March 1944, ninety-six failed to return and a further twelve were damaged beyond repair.[34] Losses were even greater among American aircraft flying daylight raids with nearly one in four machines being lost during the attack on Schweinfurt in October 1943.

Technical innovations reduces casualties. New navigational systems guided pilots through cloud and mist, and strips of aluminium foil ('window') were dropped to confuse German radar. The Luftwaffe's initial effective detection and fighter control system was analysed and broken. German fliers seeking the whereabouts and course of bomber formations found themselves listening to Hitler's speeches, relayed on Luftwaffe wavelengths from transmitters in Britain. The decisive breakthrough was the hurried development of long-range fighters – the American Lightning and Thunderbolt and the Anglo-American Mustang – which escorted the USAAF's bombers. By mid 1944 these fighters had tipped the balance in the Allies' favour. The Luftwaffe had been beaten and was unable to make good its losses.

The turn in the tide came just too late for Flight-Sergeant George Hull, a navigator, flying in a Lancaster from 61 Squadron, which was shot down over Frankfurt in March 1944. He was an articulate, intelligent young man from Stepney who enjoyed the theatre and ballet. For the last ten months of his life, he conducted a candid and frequently introspective correspondence with Joan Kirby, a 'winsome Wren', whom he met whenever their leaves coincided. She was the sister of one of his colleagues who had been killed in a training accident. Such mishaps were common; even experienced pilots misjudged height, got lost in clouds and fog, or ran out of fuel. Of forty-five aircraft lost between September 1939 and January 1940, eight were victims of enemy action, twenty-four went down due to pilot error and thirteen developed technical faults.[35] Losses among novices were naturally higher; eight trainee Australian pilots out of a batch of thirteen were killed during training in July 1943.[36] One cause of accidents – sudden instrument failure – was identified by RAF medics as a trigger for nervous collapse among pilots.[37]

'Tense co-ordination of judgement with action' was required to fly a bomber, according to one pilot. He found the experience intoxicating: 'It is not only the excitement of plunging through the clouds and darting over the world. It is also the grace and movement. One seems to dance in the air. I like, for instance, stall turns – the tense climb, the momentary pause at stalling speed, the gentle sideways going-over, the drop; or loops – the rushing down, the slow involution . . . But how can one speak of such things in prose?' There was something essentially 'feminine' about the rhythms of an aircraft in flight.[38] George Hull concurred in his lyrical description of 'A Able', the Lancaster he navigated: '. . . she's a beautiful woman to be taken care of, treated with respect. She's strong and reliable, never grudging that extra height or speed that we need for safety, obeying the stern vigour of circumstances with grace and efficiency . . . Her manner is self-assured and sophisticated, spurning mascot, insignia and bomb-score paintings; who would mar her smooth skin with weird drawing and boastful advertisements?'[39]

The machine was a demanding mistress. Hull was 'too busy to think about anything but navigation' during his first mission. One man's inattention could imperil the entire crew; gunners kept a permanent lookout for night-fighters and, as a navigator, Hull had to keep the machine on course. A Mosquito that had strayed from its flightpath in September 1944 was attacked by fighters from 219 Squadron whose pilots took it for an intruder.[40] A safe return was greeted with a mixture of relief and elation. Hull wrote: 'How beautiful to see England spread beneath your wings in the morning sunlight after a night of doubt and tenseness.'[41]

Between missions, his mood swung between purposefulness and dejection. He and his brothers-in-arms wholeheartedly supported the strategy they were fulfilling. They were driven by an 'enthusiasm to finish the war by carrying on' simply because it was the only way to 'get things done'. Prosaic pragmatism was common among bomber crews. Explaining the aerial war to BBC listeners in March 1944, Colonel Kermit Stevens of the 8th USAAF described warfare at twenty thousand feet as 'impersonal'. 'I think that is why fliers, more than other fighting men, often speak of aerial warfare as "A job to do".'[42] Getting it done was expensive in terms of lives. Hull bitterly regretted the deaths of his comrades; in September 1943 he confessed: 'I hate the RAF, this camp in particular. I hate the job I do, not for myself, but for those who are lost in the gamble, but I do like to fly, it fascinates me.'

What disturbed him most was the precariousness of his world. After one operation he told Joan Kirby: 'Friendships are so often short-lived – you appreciate that as I do, memories are so dear but there's no-one present to remember them.' Among the dead were the crew of 'O Oboe, with its proud row of bright yellow bombs painted alongside the cleverly executed drawing of Olive Oil [Popeye's girlfriend] seated on a bomb carrying a machine-gun'. Like medieval knights, bomber crews entered battle with their own distinctive insignia. Contemplating the loss of this boldly decorated Lancaster and its crew, Hull concluded that to 'retain sanity . . . we must forget it – nobody in the squadron even remembers O Oboe this morning'. Forgetting preserved sanity, for 'we must think in terms of life – not death.'[43]

Hull persevered, but with increasing difficulty. Two months before his death he wrote to Joan: 'I want to hold on to life with both hands and get out of this war somehow to live in certainty – a dangerous idea when it is for people like you that I will fight this to the end.' Alcohol regularly but temporarily obliterated such reveries and Hull admitted that he and his comrades drank plenty of it in their mess and local public houses. A mordant humour pervaded these sprees: 'Drink up mates, you may go for a Burton tomorrow.'[44]

Beer and whisky dulled memories and blocked out tomorrow. It was also a solvent for discipline and the Air Ministry became concerned at reports of frequent binges. It frowned, too, upon station dances to which all ranks were invited and where, it appeared, anything went. It usually did, for during 1943 there was an increase in sexually transmitted diseases among Bomber Command aircrew, especially Canadian squadrons.[45] Hull was appalled by the brazenness of prostitutes accosting airmen in Lincoln pubs: 'The girls make me sick, they fling sex at you with both hands – I am no Puritan, but when I see young girls of seventeen and eighteen offering themselves for the price of a dance ticket or a glass of port – well, as I say, it makes me sick.'[46]

These may have been the sort of women whom two officers smuggled into their quarters, for which they were subsequently court-martialled. In July 1943 a court-martial heard how a Norwegian warrant-officer had intercourse with a WAAF in the mess and had tried to kiss another in a women's lavatory.[47] This debauchery was the outcome of familiarity fostered in station dances and had to be stamped on. 'Aircrew personnel must be disabused of the idea that their sole responsibility is to fly,' ran an official memo on this subject issued in 1943. In future 'their leisure hours must be freely devoted to training and hard work.'[48] It is unlikely that this astringent produced a change in habits that were already deeply ingrained. Posted to Jamaica in January 1942 for anti-submarine operations, Lieutenant-Commander E. Barringer noticed that RAF officers found naval discipline 'a little tedious' and that their 'humorous irrelevance' irritated naval officers. No doubt eyebrows, and probably hackles, were raised by the conduct of one pilot, 'Taffy' Jones, who flew his Swordfish low over Kingston on the lookout for unclothed ladies sunbathing on their patios.[49]

IV

When not playing Peeping Tom, Taffy's job was to patrol the Caribbean on the lookout for long-range U-boats which were sinking oil tankers and merchantmen carrying bauxite. His squadron was playing its part in a vast war of attrition fought at sea and in the air for the control of the Atlantic sealanes along which men and matériel were being carried from America to Britain, much of which was relayed, also by sea, to the Russian and Mediterranean fronts. It was a crucial contest that would decide when and how the war was ultimately won. Once the Allies had achieved mastery at sea, America's overwhelming industrial might and manpower could be concentrated for the amphibious assault on north-western Europe which was scheduled for 1944. If the German submarine fleet made the Atlantic impassable, then Allied strategy would collapse and forces everywhere would be starved of reinforcements, equipment and fuel. Each cargo was vital. A torpedo that sank a six-thousand-ton merchantman deprived the Allies of forty-two tanks, fifty Bren-gun carriers, over 5000 tons of ammunition and 2500 tons of stores and spare parts.[50] All were manufactured in the United States and, if destined for the British army, would have been paid for by American loans.

As in the First World War, Britain had access to America's money-markets, industry and oilfields and, early in 1941 when its credit was exhausted, the United States government extended it under a series of accommodations known as lend-lease. Two-thirds of Americans approved of Roosevelt's underwriting the British war-effort. They did so because of strong emotional ties between the two countries, shared ideals, an admiration for Britain's defiance of Hitler, and fears that a British defeat would have adverse strategic and economic repercussions for the United States.

This was a possibility during the first half of 1941 when the flow of transatlantic convoys was in danger of being staunched. The British and Canadian navies were overstretched and unable to cope with the 'wolf-pack' tactics being adopted by U-boat commanders. Rather than allow the Atlantic to become a German lake, America intervened in the naval war. The United States Navy (USN) was deployed to escort convoys, with orders to engage U-boats. Construction work began on air and naval bases in Scotland and Northern Ireland, and American forces moved into Greenland and replaced the British in Iceland.[51] One American destroyer was sunk by a U-boat, and in one of the great might-have-beens of the war, a USN squadron, including three battleships, was ordered from Iceland to intercept the *Tirpitz* after it had ventured out from its Norwegian anchorage in November.[52] It returned to base.

The USN had been drawn into a contest for which neither the British nor the German navies had been adequately prepared, although in September 1939 the commander of the German submarine fleet, Admiral Karl Dönitz had predicted that, 'The U-boat will always be the backbone of warfare against the English.' Yet at the time he had only forty-eight operational submarines available and it was a year before an expansion programme began. It yielded 430 boats by April 1943, of which 235 were operational. The Admiralty was also unready. Escort vessels were in short supply and an under-strength Coastal Command had no anti-submarine aircraft.[53] On both sides, shipyards worked all-out to replace losses and enlarge existing stocks of submarines and destroyers, frigates and corvettes. In the meantime, the strain on existing ships was enormous; at the beginning of 1941, 70 per cent of the Royal Navy's destroyers were in dock undergoing repairs and refitting.[54] This shortfall was made good by fifty obsolescent American destroyers, which were exchanged for bases in Newfoundland and the West Indies. Lend-lease further reduced the pressure, with American yards turning out escort vessels at the rate of a hundred a month, compared with the eight produced by British and Canadian yards. By 1945, thirty-three American-built escort carriers and over one hundred frigates and corvettes were in service with the Royal Navy.

Numbers mattered in a conflict in which the winner had to sink ships at such a rate that they could not be replaced. From the outbreak of war until June 1943 the reckoning was in the Germans' favour, and then it changed dramatically and, as it turned out, irreversibly:

	Merchant ships sunk by U-boats in Atlantic		U-boats sunk
1939	98		9
1940	456		22
1941	409		35
1 Jan–31 July 1942	510	1942	87
1 Aug 1942–31 May 1943	656	1 Jan–31 May 1943	95
1 June–31 Dec 1943	85	1 June–31 Dec 1943	140

The cumulative erosion of Allied shipping had been halted. More and more merchantmen ('Liberty ships') left American slipways, where the production rate had soared to a million tons a month by September 1943.[55] The Germans never retrieved their advantage nor could they adequately replenish their submarine fleet, which lost a further 392 vessels between January 1944 and May 1945.

The turning-point had come in May 1943. Looking back on a month in which forty-one U-boats had been sunk, Admiral Dönitz blamed Allied air power and radar.[56] His conclusions were correct in that both made it possible to intercept submarines where they were most vulnerable, on the surface. U-boats travelled to their hunting-grounds on the surface and, using the wolf-pack tactics developed during 1941, one vessel tracked a convoy by sight, summoning others for night attacks. The Schnorkel device, which allowed U-boats to cruise at periscope depth, came into use during 1944, too late to influence the course of a war that had already been lost.[57] Moreover, submarines had to ascend regularly to recharge their batteries and provide the crew with fresh air. A survivor of U-91, sunk in February 1944, told his captors that his shipmates had been scarcely able to breath after having spent thirty-eight hours submerged.[58]

Convoys were the most effective defensive measures against the U-boats. Only 40 per cent of Allied merchantmen sunk were sailing in convoys, the remaining 60 per cent were attacked travelling on their own or after having become detached from a convoy. The system, the value of which had been proved during the Napoleonic Wars and in 1917 to 1918, required vessels to assemble outside ports and them steam in parallel lines under the direction and protection of naval ships. Speeds varied between five and fifteen knots and dawdling was fiercely discouraged.

Convoys provided a degree of security, but to gain the upper hand the Allies had to take the offensive, detecting and striking at U-boats as they proceeded to and from their bases in western France or as they laid their ambushes. Allied offensive capacity increased rapidly during the winter of 1942 to 1943. Radar sets were distributed to all escorts, and the number of long-range bombers such as the Liberator, which flew from bases in Britain, Iceland and Newfoundland, was growing. Auxiliary aircraft-carriers, introduced at the same time, provided supplementary air cover for convoys in mid Atlantic. Patrolling aircraft deterred all but the most reckless U-boat commanders. In May 1943 two refused to risk shadowing convoys that had permanent aerial protection. During 1944, Allied aircraft alone destroyed seventy U-boats.

Some aircraft were guided to their targets by deciphered enemy signals. How they were obtained was a secret confined to a small circle of senior British and American officers and there were often delays in the assessment and dissemination of this intelligence. Its operational value was enormous; J. M. Parish, an observer serving with 269 Squadron based in Iceland in 1943, was amazed by the 'detailed dispositions' of German submarines laid out in the 'ops room'.[59] The markers and lines plotted on maps were the fruit of the hidden labours of cryptanalysts at Bletchley Park who produced Ultra, a priceless intelligence source based on signals encoded by Enigma machines. During 1941, using Enigmas and codebooks captured from German vessels, it had been possible to secure intelligence of U-boat operational orders and to reroute convoys accordingly.[60]

New and temporarily impenetrable codes deprived the navy of this information for much of 1942. For a year the signals war swung in Germany's favour with German naval intelligence breaking Admiralty ciphers. Convoy schedules and courses were disclosed in advance and it was estimated that over two-thirds of those attacked during the winter and spring of 1942 to 1943 had been pinpointed from British signals. An Enigma machine and coding instructions taken from U-559 by sailors from the destroyer *Petard* off the Egyptian coast in November 1942 helped recover Britain's advantage in the signals war.

The German codes were again broken and, from early 1943 until the end of the war, the Allies had prior intelligence about operational orders given to U-boat commanders and the routes they had been assigned.[61]

V

Superior technology and intelligence complemented the perseverance, tenacity and courage of sailors and fliers and the men and women who tracked the enemy, uncovered his secrets and co-ordinated operations. Those who oversaw the war from a distance were not detached from its human consequences. Death is 'so apparent here all the time', Wren Joan Kirby told her parents early in 1944. Once of her recent duties had been to dispatch 'a signal to tell the captain of an aircraft-carrier that one of his planes crashed near Campbelltown'. One of the crew had been killed. Like herself, he was twenty-one and she heard that he was 'our B H pilot boy'[62]

Admission to the Wrens was considered a privilege. They were part of a proud and confident service and applicants had to pass an exam in which a knowledge of naval history was required together with definitions of such words as 'starboard' and 'fo'c'sle'.[63] Drafted sailors penetrated these mysteries during their first days at sea. Cyril Dawson, who joined the newly commissioned destroyer *Paladin* in August 1941, found coming to terms with what he called his 'alien environment' was 'a very gradual and traumatic process'. 'The first thing to do was learn a new language, walls became bulkheads, floors became decks, passages were gangways . . .'[64] The body also had to adjust. W. H. Bates, an apprentice window-dresser, suffered from chronic seasickness on his first voyage in the corvette *Hibiscus*. 'I was useless,' he remembered, 'I couldn't stand.' In his enfeebled state he was barely able to remove his seaboots and oilskins. After three days of wretchedness, a sympathetic shipmate offered him kippers with the advice: 'If you can keep them down, you'll never be seasick again.' This pungent nostrum did the trick and Bates soon felt himself part of the crew or, as he and many other sailors called it, his 'family'.[65]

Familiar metaphors were commonly used to describe a 'happy ship'

and, as in Nelson's time, its general state of wellbeing and purposefulness were the key to its fighting efficiency. It was the first duty of the
captain and his officers to foster that harmony, mutual dependence
and competence, which distinguished a crew in which every man performed his duty gladly and well. Although driven by oil-fired engines,
packed with electronic gadgetry and guided by radio messages, how a
ship was handled in battle still depended on discipline and seamanship.
Commanding officers were expected to live up to Nelsonian models
and show audacity, aggression and an eye for the main chance. All
were amply displayed by Lieutenant Desmond Machin, a Canadian in
command of the submarine *Tuna*. While cruising in Arctic waters in
April 1943, the Asdic operator picked up a target on the beam and two
minutes later Machin sighted a U-boat through the periscope as it
passed across *Tuna*'s stern. Within three minutes the submarine had
turned through 240 degrees and fired five torpedoes, two of which
struck and sank U-644. For his presence of mind, Machin received the
DSO and five petty-officers and ratings were decorated for the alacrity
and precision with which they carried out their orders.[66]

Whatever its causes, professional ineptitude and discord among the
crew imperilled a ship. On the night of 1 to 2 August 1940, the submarine *Oswald* was patrolling in the Ionian Sea when the officer on watch
spotted the Italian destroyer *Ugolini Vivaldi* one and a half miles away
steaming on a parallel course. He ordered action stations, but confusion
and fumbled responses gave the destroyer time to change direction and
prepare to ram the *Oswald*. Evasive submersion or counterattack were no
longer possible and the *Oswald*'s captain, David Fraser, ordered 'Abandon
ship'. The survivors, who were picked up and transferred to an Italian
prisoner of war camp, felt they had been 'let down by officers', and that
Fraser had prematurely thrown in the towel. Able-Seaman Ernest Tooles
expressed their bitterness to his captain: 'Were it not for a foul gutted
cunt like you, we should not be here.' An inquiry into the circumstances
of the *Oswald*'s sinking was held in 1945 and a court-martial found Fraser
guilty of negligence through failure to issue exact orders to the watch and
slowness of response once it was obvious that his ship was in danger. The
outspoken Tooles continued to make trouble; he took 'every opportunity
to embarrass his captors' which frequently landed him in solitary confinement. 'I did not like Italians', was his explanation.[67]

Investigations into the sinking of the *Oswald* also resulted in the dismissal of a junior officer for cowardice. He was considered 'temperamentally unsuited' to submarines, suffered from unspecific stomach ailments and shoved men out of the way in a helter-skelter rush to get off the ship. Lectures in psychology given to seagoing medical officers emphasised the difficulties men would face overcoming their instincts for self-preservation the moment their ship came under fire. Fear could be subdued by discipline, confidence in their own and their shipmates' capacity to undertake their duties properly, a faith in their officers, and, above all, a pride in their ship which, if carefully cultivated, would become an integral part of every sailor's personal self-esteem.[68] The recipe worked; Cyril Dawson remembered how a flexible attitude, willingness to work as a team and 'constant practice' created a fierce sense of 'pride and loyalty' among the crew of the *Paladin*.

His shipmates did not find much time to think about the purpose of the war. 'Ratings and especially boys knew very little of what was going on,' remembered Bertram Hubbard, a boy on the cruiser *Sussex*. 'I suppose the less they knew the less they could worry about.'[69] Bad news during 1941 and 1942, which included the loss of the aircraft-carrier *Ark Royal* and two battleships, did not trouble the stoical 'lower deck' at Devonport, although the impudence of the dash through the English Channel by the *Scharnhorst* and *Gneisenau* enraged patriots. 'It's not their bloody Channel. It's our bloody Channel.'[70]

Letters from home were always welcomed, although some were a source of concern for officers. The arrival of a 'Dear John' letter or some other disturbing news would distress the recipients and medical officers noticed how they often reported sick with some trifling ailment. To prevent this impediment to efficiency, the Admiralty persuaded the BBC to broadcast a talk in which wives were advised not to burden their husbands with their domestic problems.[71] Doctors were instructed to be vigilant for symptoms of fatigue, in particular declining alertness, among officers who had spent long spells at sea. The warning signs – impatience with subordinates and anxieties about potential mishaps – were like those of other servicemen who had undergone prolonged and severe strain.

VI

Sailors and airmen who stalked and destroyed U-boats needed all the attentiveness of a huntsman. A brief lapse of concentration could mean an opportunity lost, and conditions on ships and aircraft were not always conducive to vigilance. At the end of November 1941, and after a Chestertonian twenty-first birthday party and three hours of sleep, C. A. Smee took off at six in the morning from Chivenor for a routine patrol over the Bay of Biscay. He found himself dozing, but it was 'too cold, draughty, and noisy' onboard a Whitley bomber for sleep. Suddenly the radar revealed a ship on the surface, eight miles away. The pilot approached and, two miles distant, shouted: 'Christ! It's a U-boat.' The Whitely dived on its target, dropping depth-charges and machine-gunning the submarine which rapidly submerged. At the limit of its fuel range, the plane returned to base, having, it was afterwards discovered, sunk U-206.[72]

Routines had to be followed methodically, for oversights led to disaster. Captain Guy D'Oyly Hughes, commanding the aircraft-carrier *Glorious*, failed to order reconnaissance flights and his ship was unready for action when it encountered two German pocket-battleships off the Norwegian coast on 8 June 1940. After an unequal fight, the *Glorious* and its escorts the *Acasta* and *Ardent*, were sunk with the loss of over 1500 men. Subsequent investigations revealed that D'Oyly Hughes, a submariner with a high reputation, knew nothing of aviation and had quarrelled with the flying officers under his command. This may explain delays in launching aircraft once the action had started.[73] The scandal was hushed up for sixty years, for the navy loathed admitting its mistakes.

Commanders and crews who had spent weeks on end fruitlessly combing the sea sometimes became intoxicated once they made contact with the enemy and the chase began. Exhilaration could distort judgement. 'In the excitement of the moment', the commander of the corvette *Asphodel* forgot to release 'foxers', devices that deflected the new Germans' acoustic torpedoes. One struck his ship as it manoeuvred to engage a U-boat and it sank in three minutes with the loss of over seventy men.[74]

Asphodel's seven survivors remembered little of the ship's final minutes. One recalled falling debris, another several explosions which were probably depth-charges detonated when the torpedo hit. When the frigate *Tweed* was torpedoed in mid Atlantic in January 1944, the chief stoker heard a 'dull thump' which 'lifted me off my feet'. 'The next minute the fire was coming towards me.' Like thousands of other sailors whose stations were below-decks, his experience of battle consisted of hearing the reverberations and sounds of the engines. For the man sealed off from the outside world by bulkhead doors which were always shut when a ship was at sea, battle was test of discipline and training. Both taught the rating that he was a vital cog in a fighting machine and that if, for any reason, he failed to function, his ship's efficiency would be diminished and his crewmates endangered. During an air attack on an escort destroyer off the Norwegian coast in 1942, a medical officer noticed that a sailor whose job it was to convey orders from the bridge to the gunnery officer was trembling with fear. His voice rose to a 'high-pitched squeak' but somehow he overcame his terror and continued to perform his duty. This was how the vast majority behaved, although the nervous did crumple, desert their posts and rush above to see what was happening. One man was brought to the doctor in a state of 'hysterical collapse' and, on being told to 'get a grip on himself', ran off and hid.[75]

When a large ship was struck, sailors could not always ascertain the whereabouts or extent of the damage. The company on the battleship *Royal Oak* was 'not much disturbed' by the explosion of the first torpedo that struck it as it lay at anchor in Scapa Flow just after midnight on the morning of 13 October 1939. Some conjectured that the noise was a nearby air raid or an internal accident. Further hits a few minutes later dispelled doubts as to what was happening; power supplies failed, the ship heeled to starboard and began to capsize. There was no panic and many acts of selfless heroism; a wireless telegraphist lit matches to guide men towards a hatchway, a marine corporal supported a hatch on his shoulders to let men through, a petty-officer 'on his own initiative' released prisoners from the ship's cells and an 'unknown' rating dived into the sea three times to rescue men. Rear-Admiral H. E. C. Blagrove remained on deck, warning sailors not to jump too close to the pro-pellers and, when a steward with a lifejacket asked him to go overboard with him, he replied: 'Don't worry about me; try to save yourself.' He was among those drowned.[76]

Inside the *Royal Oak* 'balls of orange fire' surged through the labyrinth of gangways and decks, igniting hammocks and, as the ship turned turtle, hatches slid shut, blocking escape routes. Memories of men trapped and their own desperate attempts to reach the main deck haunted the stunned survivors. After their transfer to transports, many insisted that they slept in gangways, ready for a swift flight.[77] Many of those who suffered the extremes of horror as shells and bombs punctured armour plate and fire spread below-decks also witnessed the courage and humanity of individuals who did all in their power to help others to safety. After bombs had hit the *Gracie Fields* during the Dunkirk evacuation, the decks were littered with human debris and awash with blood. In the middle of this a gunner was carrying the wounded on his shoulders 'as if they'd been children' and comforting the wounded and dying.[78]

VII

It was best not to think about such things. Like others before him, merchant seaman C. Harwood trusted to 'luck and God's will' as he crossed the Atlantic in a tanker in March 1943.[79] Faith in providence and one's own fortune must have been hard to sustain as sailors watched ships sink or encountered survivors in lifeboats, on rafts, or swimming in oily waters. One can imagine the thoughts of the seamen on the *Empire Opal* when they watched 'flames shooting hundreds of feet in the air' from another tanker, the *Empire Spencer*. Its master remained onboard to turn his burning ship to starboard so that it would not endanger vessels astern.[80]

Such incidents created a distressing moral dilemma for captains. It was imperative that convoys kept moving come what may, for a stationary vessel picking up survivors was a perfect target. Humane instincts had to be suspended in the interests of the convoy, and if he surrendered to them a commander also risked censure. When, in high seas and a strong wind, the commander of the destroyer *Matchless* endeavoured to pick up a man who had fallen overboard, one rating was appalled. 'The Captain's gone crazy, he's going to risk the lives of two hundred men to look for some silly bastard that hadn't the sense to keep off the upper deck.'[81] The man was not saved, nor was a merchant seaman who fell from his ship which was part of a convoy bound for Alexandria in September 1943. He swam away from the ships astern to avoid their propellers, but when he realised that none would stop, he pleaded, screamed and cursed. Among the vessels that passed was the repair ship, HMS *Blenheim*; one of its crew later recalled: 'the messdecks were rather quiet that night.'[82]

Destroying the enemy took priority over saving the shipwrecked. After U-91 sank the frigate *Gould* off the Azores in February 1944, it was attacked and forced to the surface by the *Gould*'s sister ship, the *Gore*. The sea was full of swimmers, survivors from the *Gould* and the submarine, and some may have been killed when one of *Gore*'s depthcharges fell among them. 'Many were drowned,' reported the *Gore*'s commander, but once the U-boat had been sunk he managed to rescue thirty-five British sailors before looking for 'Huns'.[83] Solitary survivors were sometimes miraculously rescued. In September 1941 the crew of C. A. Smee's Whitley spotted a single sailor clinging to a spar a hundred miles west of Rockall. A smoke float was dropped and a few moments later the airmen saw the 'horrible sight of a half-submerged burning vessel' surrounded by oil, planks, doors and barrels. There was also a crowded lifeboat which the fliers were able to guide to the sailor using an Aldis lamp. He was picked up and the position of his shipmates was passed on to a destroyer.[84]

A doctor who treated shipwrecked seamen calculated that those who reached a Carley float, in which they were partly immersed and which, before 1942, possessed no emergency rations or water, might expect to stay alive for three and a half days. Men lucky enough to get aboard a raft could survive for forty-eight days, and those who made it to a lifeboat, up to seventy, assuming that it had stocks of water and food. There were exceptions; a sailor stayed alive for fourteen hours in the Barents Sea at a temperature of thirty degrees Fahrenheit before being found. The examination of survivors revealed, not surprisingly, that they suffered from thirst, dehydration and ulcers which induced tension and irascibility. Many suffered hallucinations, believing themselves at home, or in a bar, or back on board their ship. Delirious men would slip overboard, assuring their shipmates that they were 'going across to the pub' or 'below to get a drink'.[85]

There were many remarkable instances of stamina and endurance. Among them were the survivors of the *Viking Star* which was sunk two hundred miles off the coast of Sierra Leone by U-30, whose crew took photographs of the survivors. One boatload made it to the shore, after sometimes violent squabbles about whose turn it was to boil the water. They then spent six days proceeding through the bush from village to village until they reached Sherbro.[86] 'Thick chocolate' and 'biscuits' kept another party alive, one of whom remembered the 'awful silence' in his lifeboat. 'Conversation was at a minimum, we just wrapped our blankets round to keep warm.'[87] Perhaps the most famous incident involving sailors cast adrift was that of the tanker *San Demetrio*, which was damaged by the pocket-battleship *Admiral Scheer* in November 1940. After two nights at sea in a lifeboat in a heavy gale, sixteen survivors sighted their ship, still on fire, and reboarded it. They dowsed the fires, restarted the engines, improvised a course and steered the *San Demetrio* to the Irish coast, from where it was escorted to the Clyde. Of its cargo of twelve thousand gallons of petrol, eleven thousand were saved.

This exploit was the subject of an official book and, in 1942, the realistic Ealing Studios film *San Demetrio, London*. On one level, the perseverance and heroism of the crew were a glowing example of what was expected from ordinary people, on another they were a tribute to the merchant service as a whole. In one scene, the chief engineer reminds the audience that 'the British merchant seaman is the most neglected beggar in the world. It's only when war comes along that he gets any thanks.' There follows a rebuke to the public who squandered the fuel carried at such risks by ships like the *San Demetrio* on driving in cars and taxis when they could walk or use public transport.[88]

Nearly twenty-three thousand seamen lost their lives at sea during the Battle of the Atlantic, a large proportion between June 1940 and May 1941.[89] They bore the brunt of the maritime war of attrition and, according to an analysis produced in August 1943, suffered a lower rate of depression and mental disorders than men in other services. One physician who remarked on this also observed that 'by and large, they were small in stature, thin, wiry, gnarled and underfed'. They were also, and this was perhaps invaluable in a contest of wills, rolling stones with an independent and rebellious temperament.[90]

5

Don't fence me in: Women, GIs, black men and evacuees

I

The Second World War was a time of temporary migrations. In September 1939, 827,000 schoolchildren, sometimes accompanied by their mothers and teachers, left their urban homes for the countryside where they would be safe from air raids. Under regulations introduced early in 1942 to remedy the shortfall in volunteers, the Ministry of Labour began drafting women into the forces, the Land Army and those industries essential for the war-effort. Two million women were mobilised and directed towards factories, engineering works, dockyards and farms where they were joined by smaller numbers of workers who had been recruited in Eire and the British West Indies. In mid 1942 the first American servicemen began to arrive in Britain; by June 1944 there were two million, of whom 130,000 were black.

Demographic shifts on this scale, even though they were temporary, had widespread social and moral repercussions. Some were anticipated; before the war and with the experience of the previous war in mind, the government believed that physical dislocation would lead to moral anarchy. Once young men and women were detached from the discipline of their family and neighbourhood, they would assert their emancipation by sexual promiscuity.[1] It was not just a matter of an absence of constraints. People whose lives were in perpetual jeopardy naturally felt that today had to be enjoyed to the full, come what may, for tomorrow might be snatched away. Or, as Richard Passmore observed: 'Our horizons were bounded by next week: only the present and the immediate future mattered.'[2] In these circumstances prewar moral conventions no longer applied.

For some they still did; a girl writing to the agony aunt of *Woman's Own* in 1943 admitted to being very much in love with a soldier who, just before embarkation overseas, 'asked me to do wrong'. She did not and afterwards he wrote to her to say that he was glad she had refused, for it set 'his mind at rest'. The columnist warmly endorsed her decision and used it to remind potential waverers that, 'No boy respects a girl after she has given way to him.'[3] For the unchaste there were admonitions. 'I gave way to my boyfriend in a foolish moment, as he said it would be safe,' one wrote. Afterwards she went out with others, became pregnant and wanted to know whether she ought to compel one of her other lovers to marry her. No, was the reply: 'You girls who always think you can slip out of the consequences of folly honestly deserve what you get.'[4]

The war placed women in an invidious position. They were expected on the one hand to do everything they could to further the war-effort, which meant undertaking men's work in the masculine worlds of the services and industry, and on the other to remain attractive but virtuous. 'This is total war . . . I am totally involved,' was a new year's resolution recommended by *Vogue* in January 1943. As the year progressed, patriotic girls were advised to shift from voluntary to part-time work and then on to full-time. At the same time, they were urged not to neglect glamour, although this involved the sort of improvisation demanded in the official poster that invited women to go through their wardrobes and 'Make Do and Mend'. Overcoming shortages and the constraints of clothes-rationing was by now a staple of women's magazines. In February 1943, *Vogue* revealed how a prewar evening-dress with its 'yards of unrationed material' could be transformed into blouses, slips, cami-knickers, jackets and shirts. At the same time, the actress Ursula Bloom was sharing her tips on how to spend less on make-up with *Woman's Own* readers. When cash or clothing-coupons ran out, there were various ingenious expedients, including simulating stockings by painting legs with gravy browning and drawing the seams with an eyebrow pencil.

Cosmetics and nylons were not welcomed on the parade-ground or production-line, where all displays of glamour were considered as immodest, provocative and potentially distracting.[5] Men's heads were easily turned and their imaginations aroused. This was the official position, and it had its roots in the collective male mentality of the period which assumed that women who joined the forces or ventured into factories were either vamps or innocents who would quickly and easily be corrupted. It was a supposition that revealed as much about men's predatory inclinations as it did about female frailty. The former were also reflected in the smutty innuendoes that branded the Woman's Land Army as 'Backs to the Land' and the Auxiliary Territorial Service (ATS) as the 'Groundsheet of the Army'. Those who found these allusions funny would also have smirked at 'Up with the lark and to bed with a Wren'.

These aspersions were taken seriously and the War Office attempted to dispel them by issuing ATS girls with a uniform designed to smother desire. It included boned corsets, khaki bloomers and stockings and lace-up shoes. Subsequent complaints that the ensemble was slatternly led to adjustments, but ATS girls were enjoined not to wear make-up. Connie Harris, a Glaswegian working in a Manchester engineering factory, found on arrival that slacks were compulsory for moral rather than practical reasons. As a foreman explained: 'there's stairs to climb and so we'd rather have ladies in trousers.'[6] Soon after joining the Wrens, Maureen Wells and her fellow trainees were given a lecture in which they heard, no doubt to their surprise, that 'sailors and naval officers do not like glamour.'[7]

Hearsay and conjectures about servicewomen's delinquent sexuality had wide currency. They particularly disturbed better-off working- and lower-middle-class parents for whom propriety was an integral part of that respectability that marked their standing in society. One working-class mother threw her daughter's ATS papers on the fire and declared: 'You're not ending up as an officer's groundsheet.' The girl became a bus-conductress and had to endure sniggers about what clippies and bus-drivers got up to at the end of each shift. Soldiers in the Middle East wrote home to urge their wives and daughters to shun the ATS because of its flighty reputation, a slur that the authorities blamed on fifth columnist rumour-mongers.[8]

These disparaging generalisations contained an element of male wishful-thinking and anxiety. The jealous husband who objected to his wife leaving home each night to work as an ARP warden believed that she would be faced with irresistible sexual temptations.[9] Untrammelled by domestic and communal constraints, women would do as they pleased and were somehow inclined towards waywardness, a weakness that men would exploit. This trepidation was not entirely groundless. Trainee Wren Maureen Wells was shocked by her cabinmates' obsession with sex. 'Over and over again they describe their "experiences", their friends' experiences, the dirty books they've read, the men they've know. And married women do it too.'[10]

Connie Harris recalled that there was some 'carrying on' in her workplace, although those caught were sacked. After clocking off, she had plenty of fun: 'We really did live it up. We were out at night, worked in the day and spent our money. If we were on nights, we used to go to the Ritz in the afternoon, we were knackered by the time we went to work . . . we worked hard, but we didn't sleep around in those days . . we liked dancing and so on.'[11] Dances vied with the cinema and the pubs as the most popular source of diversion during the war. For millions of young men and women they were exuberant occasions which punctuated the closely controlled routines of camp and factory and where inhibitions were dissolved by alcohol and the rhythms of American 'swing'. There were opportunities for flirtation, smooching and seduction. One female factory worker recalled a canteen staff dance at which the spot prize for the waltz was 'a pair of mauve satin French knickers' for the woman and sixty Capstan cigarettes for her partner.[12]

The woman's trophy might have struck some as naughty but harmless, but for those who agonised over the decay of the nation's morals it was another unwelcome token of an increasing sexual freedom. Young women seemed to be becoming more and more shameless and abandoned. How else could one interpret a letter sent to *Woman's Own* in December 1943: 'I am nearly sixteen and feel despair. I love dancing and my parents won't let me out at all since the soldiers came to our town.'[13] Given the date and her parents' prohibition, there is good reason to believe that these arrivals were Americans. In just over a year they had gained a reputation for licentiousness and a capacity to attract headstrong and flighty girls like the one whose parents barred her from dancehalls.

II

American servicemen's public behaviour attracted a great deal of attention and comment, much of it critical and envious. Yanks could not be ignored: in all, two million were stationed in Britain between 1942 and 1944, many in country towns and rural villages where their presence was bound to be obtrusive. They wore smarter, better-tailored uniforms than their British counterparts, were better paid, had access to apparently unlimited quantities of rationed or unavailable commodities and appeared to have plenty of time on their hands. There was also a tendency to brag, which was widely noticed and regretted. Friction was bound to occur despite the US authorities' efforts to instruct servicemen about the sensibilities and idiosyncrasies of their host.

Money was a permanent source of grievance. In December 1942, American servicemen were using their purchasing power to buy up whisky and beer in East Anglian pubs. Many left their change on the counter 'which has a bad effect on British soldiers in the pubs who have to count their pennies'. An army captain stationed in Taunton in August 1943 was apoplectic when he saw 'a Buck Nigger private call for and absorb two double whiskies, the cost of which equals two days' pay for one of our privates'. Over the border in Dorset, GIs were more discreet and 'don't boast and flash money about'.[14] Among Americans, there was admiration for British grit and determination, and many were moved by the evidence of the blitz. There was also bewilderment over some of their hosts' more arcane conventions. An officer attached to a British regiment for training referred to the actress Ingrid Bergman in the mess and was warned that the penalty for mentioning a lady's name was buying a round of drinks for everyone present. 'Polo, cricket, dogs and war' and the jokes from the latest *Punch* comprised the conversational repertoire of his new colleagues and he lost eleven pounds living off British army rations. 'In their way the English are all right,' he tolerantly concluded.[15]

The reactions of British servicemen to Americans were mixed. A private in the 1st Royal Tank Regiment attached to the American 5th Army in Italy early in 1944 found his new comrades 'grand fellows'. The news of an American reverse at Kasserine in Tunisia filled one British private with secret joy: 'it will do the swell-headed blighters a world of good to get a thrashing, it will take away some of that cocky air they so often have.'[16] Such sour competitiveness led to street-fights; men from the Black Watch battled with American servicemen in Chichester on New Year's Eve 1943, and one thought the pleasure of beating them worth the price of his subsequent punishment.[17] Sexual jealousy may have been one of the causes of this shindig, for an army chaplain reported in July 1943 that many soldiers deeply resented the 'poaching' of their girlfriends and wives by Americans.[18]

All these observations are drawn from official files in which British and American censors' reports were collated with material gathered from domestic agencies to provide a weekly overview of Anglo-American relations. Both governments wanted to do everything to cultivate harmony between guests and hosts, and prevent misunderstandings and sexual liaisons that would generate distrust and tension. On a local level, goodwill was fostered by 'America Weeks' and social events organised by the English Speaking Union, the WVS and the Red Cross which had set up seventy-nine clubs for American servicemen by July 1943. Moral precautions were taken when drawing up guest lists, which were vetted to exclude the 'wrong type' of girl.[19] At the same time, those who might otherwise have been considered the 'right type' were discouraged from attending American dances. Joan Kirby and several Wrens were confined to barracks for fourteen days and given three hours a day of galley chores after they went to an American squadron dance in December 1943.[20] English local authorities shared the navy's misgivings about the ambience of such revels and by mid 1943 were becoming increasingly reluctant to sponsor them on the grounds that they attracted prostitutes and were marred by drunkenness.[21]

Young, mostly unmarried men, far from home and facing an uncertain future were bound to seek sexual experience whenever the opportunity occurred. Their desperation and candour were often distressful for those they encountered. In December 1942, a 'professional man' from Cheltenham complained that whenever his wife walked to and from the shops she was propositioned five or six times by Americans seeking sex. Some offered her as much as twelve pounds.[22] A Wallasey girl described how: '. . . a jeep drew up beside me and an American soldier popped his head out and in a very loud voice said to me: "Say, honey, my name's Bob, what's yours, tell me quick before I forget." I stuck my nose in the air and very haughtily walked on, the next minute the jeep was after me, and the same voice said, "Gee, I thought all angels were in heaven".[23] Unmoved, she sent him packing. Other GIs were more persevering and less pleasant. In April 1944 a Bedford girl protested that, 'In the last fortnight I have been molested by Americans on no fewer than four occasions.' On one, just before ten o'clock, as she was returning from the cinema, a 'Yank' asked her the way to the chip shop, offered to walk her home and then forced her against a wall, pulling off her turban She threatened to call for help and he disappeared.[24] Incidents like this had prompted the local paper to observe that, 'The way of a man with a maid . . . may not be the same in the United States as it is in England.' It was imperative that Americans should recognise this and behave accordingly.[25]

But did the fault always lie with the Americans? A Bedford house-wife blamed local girls who were 'very wild' and flocked to the dances in the town's Corn Exchange in pursuit of GIs. This was denied by William and Mabel Chamberlain: 'We are often in the centre of the town during the evening and keep a sharp look out for undesirable conduct.' They were pleased to report that they had seen none.[26] This pair of busybodies, various clergymen, journalists and social workers, and members of such organisations as the National Vigilance Association and the Church of England Moral Welfare Council believed that the country was teetering on the verge of moral anarchy. Before the war, the prevailing moral climate had encouraged young women to play 'hard to get', a message that was underlined in the plots of popular romantic fiction and film scenarios.[27] Now, they appeared to be doing the opposite, prompting Americans to gibe: 'The only thing that is cheap in England is the women.'[28] Those who sought out Americans risked being considered fast, as Connie Harris remembered: 'It was more permissive during the war, with the Yanks it was wartime and you didn't know when you were going to die. But you knew what kind of reputation you would get if you went out with Americans, one we called *Yankee Betty*.'[29]

Yankee Betty and her kind were a source of annoyance to both the British and American governments. Her behaviour, particularly in public, caused muttering and blighted relations between ordinary people and American servicemen. It also blemished the self-image of the British as a composed, determined and purposeful people. There was the problem, too, of sexually transmitted diseases which placed servicemen in hospitals when they ought to have been training or in action. Prostitutes were blamed for this. In March 1943, 40 per cent of GIs infected had contracted the disease in London, which is not surprising given that it was calculated that there was one prostitute every ten yards on the streets in the centre of the city. A further 27 per cent were infected in Manchester, Liverpool, Bristol and Bedford.[30]

The legal machinery existed to forestall an epidemic. Under regulation 33B of the Emergency Powers Act, women named by men as a source of infection could be detained and compelled to undergo treatment. Prostitutes arrested for soliciting were processed by local magistrates in what was a morning ritual with each pleading guilty and receiving a two-pound fine. Inquiries made early in 1943 as to why prostitutes were not being drafted under the wartime labour legislation revealed, amazingly, that local registration officers of the Ministry of Labour were inclined to grant them exemption.[31] Among them must have been N— W— and Miss P— of Friar Lane, Leicester. On 1 July they came home with two Americans, much to the annoyance of Miss P—'s mother who called the police. They arrived but the GIs escaped across the rooftops.[32]

If these two women had been younger, they would have been brought before a magistrate as in moral danger and placed in care under the 1933 Children and Young Persons Act. It was used to restrain a sixteen-year-old labourer's daughter who was described as 'dirty and ragged' and 'beyond parental control' after she had been found with GIs.[33] In the same category was a seventeen-year-old Leicester girl who visited pubs, spent her nights in an air-raid shelter and was infatuated with two Americans. When they were transferred to another camp, she stole a bicycle to follow them.[34] Similar devotion was shown by two other local girls, aged fifteen and sixteen, who absconded from a Nottingham remand home and made their way to the American camp at Ollerton in December 1943.[35] Women found in American bases were prosecuted and either fined or placed on probation. In February 1943, Chard magistrates fined Rualine Cownden, aged twenty-one,

five pounds for trespassing after she had been found with a black GI
whom she had known for some time. A neighbour testified that she was
'a very good girl'.[36]

III

Miss Cownden's attachment to a black soldier was a small part of a
growing problem that was vexing the British government and the
American military authorities and causing disorder in many areas,
notably in the midlands and north-west. Its principal features were
bluntly outlined by the regional commissioner for south-west England
in August 1942. 'A very large number of girls, some of them outwardly
of respectable class, are now walking out with coloured troops,' he
reported to the Home Office. Sixteen- to eighteen-year-old girls were
slipping out of control and women whose husbands were on service
abroad were striking up liaisons with black soldiers. 'The darky is a
simple minded child,' the commissioner commented, who, if given too
much leeway, would press for more, 'Only yesterday I was given an
authentic account by a responsible person of two young girls coming out
of a public house, escorted by one buck nigger, all of them in drink.'
'The matter is of some urgency,' he concluded, 'in order that we may
prevent calamities which will become apparent in nine months' time.'[37]
Other calamities were already occurring; a month before, Liverpool
police had had to separate black GIs from white women after they had
been threatened by white American servicemen. One black soldier
objected: 'It is no democracy if we cannot do what we like.'[38]

Sexual jealousies and white Americans' conceit of their racial superiority were an inflammable mixture, which was why the British
government had been uneasy about an influx of black GIs into a country where they would experience the novelty of theoretical racial
equality. Blacks were banned from the American navy, and the army was
segregated with blacks relegated to helotry as labourers and pioneers.
The US military authorities hoped that this separation could be
extended. In July 1942, when white servicemen were already arriving in
Oxfordshire and black GIs were expected, the local American commander, General L. A. Hawes, proposed importing southern-style

segregation. Pubs in large towns were to be reserved for whites and those in smaller market-towns and villages for blacks. The local chief constable thought publicans might object and pointed out that there was no colour bar in Britain. Furthermore, he argued, giving the sanction of law to American racial prejudices would provoke popular outrage.[39]

Some voices were raised in favour of the sort of discrimination that then obtained across the southern states of America. It was proposed by Sir James Grigg, Secretary of State for War, in September 1942, but rejected under pressure from the Colonial and Home Offices. Britain was an imperial power, the benevolent ruler of millions of blacks in Africa and the West Indies, many of whom were playing an important part in the war-effort. Reports of racial segregation in Britain would cause discontent among the king's black subjects who were 'British citizens', according to Brendan Bracken, the minister of information, and therefore entitled to 'the same rights as Englishmen'. Broadcasting in September 1942, Harold Macmillan, the under-secretary of state for the colonies, urged his listeners to treat individual black men and women from the colonies with warmth and courtesy so that each would return home 'a convinced Ambassador of Empire'.[40]

To a large extent, ordinary people, brought up to believe in a paternalist Empire, were prepared to be tolerant, or at least to ensure that blacks were treated fairly. After black GIs had been expelled by whites from a Cambridge dancehall, a woman onlooker perceptively remarked, 'really at bottom we are more truly democratic than America'. An assault by white soldiers on a black one in a Cambridge canteen provoked a similar outburst of national pride: 'We don't usually behave in such a brutal and Nazified way.'[41] In July 1943 the local people of Cosham intervened when US military police waded into a crowd of blacks who were blocking the traffic after closing time. There were catcalls: 'that's democracy!' and 'Why don't you leave them alone? They're as good as we are.' Encouraged by this support, a black sergeant shouted at an officer: 'We ain't no slaves, this is England.' Hampshire passions were again aroused at East Tytherley the following month. Three American officers accompanied by some ATS girls emerged from a pub and ordered their black driver to give them the key of the car and walk home. The officers manhandled him and knocked him into a ditch before he was rescued by some locals.[42]

The Home and Colonial Offices got their way: there was no colour bar in Britain. In September 1942, a Home Office circular informed all police forces that if the American authorities attempted to enforce segregation, they were to be given no assistance.[43] This was a bold and decent decision that was bound to incense a large section of white American servicemen, many of whom were southerners who had been taught to believe that the black was an inferior creature, born to occupy the bottom of the social and economic pile. For blacks the world had been temporarily turned upside down, for they found themselves in a country where familiar taboos did not exist and where they were accorded a degree of equality by whites. One night in February 1944, outside a Leicester pub, an ATS girl, offended by the sight of a black GI with an English girl, bawled out: 'A white girl with a black, she ought to be ashamed of herself.' 'Why should she be ashamed?' a black soldier riposted.[44]

White GIs, not all of them from the south, would have taken the part of the ATS girl. The war had witnessed an upsurge in racial tension; in June 1943 twenty-five blacks and nine whites were killed in race-riots in Detroit, and there were further, equally violent outbreaks in Chicago and New York.[45] This antipathy was reflected in Britain where there were sporadic street-fights between white and black troops in which knives and, occasionally, firearms were used. The worst was at Preston in June 1943 when military police fired a shot during a scuffle with black soldiers as the pubs turned out. The military police brought up an armoured car, the blacks secured guns from their camp at nearby Bamber Bridge, and several were killed in an exchange of fire. A party of ten blacks hunting for military policemen shot dead the wife of a publican and a black military policeman in Kingsclere in Hampshire in October 1944.[46] There was a tendency, regretted by their British civilian counterparts, for American military police to use their sidearms unnecessarily. Revolvers were drawn and brandished when they intervened to break up a scrimmage between two white women and a group of black soldiers in Leicester in December 1943.[47]

Black men consorting with white women provided the commonest source of disorder. Early in August 1942 white soldiers were 'incensed' by white women, including ATS and WAAF girls, walking with blacks in the Belle Vue Gardens, Manchester. Less than a fortnight later, there were brawls and knife-fights in Huyton between white GIs from Woolfall Heath camp and blacks from Maghull. Superintendent A. Aberdeen of the Manchester police, for whom these disturbances were an added burden, wondered whether the fault lay with American discipline which he thought 'lax in the extreme'. Perhaps so, but the roots of the problem were explained to him by an American officer, Captain Hick. His black troops were from the southern states where 'blacks are forbidden contact with white women and such instances as do occur are dealt with in a drastic manner.' Hick warned his men that if they did approach white women 'the same punishment would be inflicted', but the 'free manner' in which Lancashire girls were behaving made it impossible for him to prevent familiarity.[48] For a black man brought up in the south between the wars, 'a drastic manner' would have meant death, for lynchings of blacks suspected of sexual assaults on white women were common. American military law punished rape with death and of the eight rapists hanged at the US military prison at Shepton Mallett between 1942 and 1945, five were black.[49]

Behind such severity were primal sexual fears. They were summed up by one American officer who spoke for many others when he observed in a letter home: 'The good Lord was extra kind to the Negro so they say.'[50] Well membered, potent and promiscuous, the black man was a source of both temptation and danger. Both were recognised by the 8th Duke of Buccleuch, who had travelled to Berlin for the celebrations of Hitler's fiftieth birthday and had been prominent in the pro-German peace movement of 1939 to 1940.[51] In August 1942 his mind was disturbed by the proximity of local lasses and foresters from British Honduras (Belize) who had been imported to the Borders to increase timber production. He expressed his apprehension in a letter to Macmillan, who humoured him by instructing the local police to investigate. They discovered that eight women 'of an undesirable type' had travelled from Edinburgh to the loggers' camp at East Linton and had been sent back. The duke was unsatisfied and reminded Macmillan that 'loose relations between black men of totally different standards, both moral and material, and our simple country girls have unpleasant features, and that improper intercourse with decent young women should be strongly discouraged.'[52]

Fears of miscegenation were uppermost in the fevered imagination of

Maurice Petherick, a Cornish Tory MP, who pestered the Foreign Office with demands that every black GI should be transferred to North Africa or Italy 'to go and fertilise the Italians who are used to it anyhow'.[53] He would have sympathised with the American GI who, incensed by the Englishwoman's apparent preference for blacks, was keen to 'shoot it out' with black GIs.[54]

'White trash' was how black soldiers stationed at Gaddesby in Leicestershire described the girls and women who appeared in droves around their camp during the spring and summer of 1943. 'Girls come for miles in buses,' reported the local police, who also noted that the black GIs did nothing to encourage them. The nuisance value of these visitors was enormous; the schoolmistress was justifiably enraged by 'certain rubber devices' which her pupils found and tried to inflate as if they were balloons. There was also, as in nearby Leicester, a spate of brawls and indecent assaults.[55] Such incidents were reported, often luridly, by local newspapers which also received a flow of bad-tempered correspondence from those who were outraged by what they had seen, or more commonly by what they had seen and subsequently imagined.

'Huddersfield Girls and Coloured Soldiers' and 'Gold Diggers who prey on American Troops' were two headlines in the local paper in September 1943. Beneath was a report that described couples embracing in parked vehicles and side-streets and how an enterprising youth was directing truckloads of black GIs towards public houses. There were plenty of accommodating teenage girls around, but they were ignored by the soldiers and there were no signs of drunkenness. At eleven the revellers parted company as the blacks went back to their lorries; one woman was heard to cry out: 'Good night, my darkie boy. I'll see you at eight tomorrow night.' There was not much here to stimulate the prurient imagination and the picture was confirmed by subsequent readers' letters. One, from a young girl, suggested that the blacks' reputation for womanising was exaggerated, that they did not wolf-whistle and many girls were 'afraid' of them.[56]

A completely different impression was conveyed by a story in the *Sunday Pictorial* in August 1945, which described shameless scenes outside an American barracks near Bristol when the news arrived that the black GIs were about to be shipped home. Several hundred women aged between seventeen and twenty-five gathered outside their barracks on a rainy night in this 'most English of English cities'. 'This was too much for the coloured men who, singing "Don't Fence Me In", began to break down the barbed wire. In a few minutes hundreds of girls and US soldiers were kissing and embracing.' There were further scenes of passionate parting at the railway station where fifty girls crowded on to the platform. One eighteen-year-old told the *Pictorial*'s reporter: 'I don't mind getting wet. I intend to give my sweetie a good send off.'[57] This astonishing display of affection was not reported in the staid *Bristol Evening Post* which, a week before, had denounced the 'scurrilous myth' then circulating that British soldiers in the army of occupation were flirting with German women and, in some instances, taking them into the woods.[58] Connie Harris, the Manchester factory worker, gave some credence to such stories. While not exonerating the female 'Yank basher', she wryly observed that 'our lads in the army were not doing too badly with the German girls.'[59]

Double standards were being exercised. While the army discouraged what was called 'fraternisation' by troops in Germany and Austria, it was severe in cases when a soldier was disturbed by news of his wife's misdoings. Administrative machinery was activated and, if the local social services discovered that the woman was playing fast and loose then she would forfeit her allowance from the Ministry of Pensions. This was £2 3s (£2.15) for a woman with two children and although barely adequate in the face of inflation it often represented a family's entire income. A soldier's wife in Leicester who was enjoying a 'good time' with an American serviceman who visited her regularly had her small child taken into care.[60] Stories like this and the predilection of local girls for blacks angered British troops who had returned from North Africa and were stationed near Leicester early in 1944.[61]

Observers, whether in ministries or on the streets, imagined that moral standards were collapsing around them. 'We must be sex mad,' declared an army chaplain in a letter to a Bath newspaper in May 1943. 'Man has always been prone to indecency from the dawn of history,' he continued, 'it is a primitive weakness.' Now, to make matters worse, servicemen were receiving lectures on sex and contraception. This protest against the official programme for the prevention of sexually transmitted diseases struck a chord. 'The youth of nowadays are indecent enough without sex teaching,' one sympathiser claimed. Another ('Old

Fashioned') announced: 'I never received a word of sex teaching from either of my parents, at either of the schools I attended. But I am none the worse today.'[62] A glance at the correspondence columns of provincial newspapers will always reveal a world in a state of chronic deterioration, but what people saw and read during the war suggested that the country was in a state of sexual revolution. But the behaviour of Bristol girls and Leicester housewives was misleading: they were responses to extraordinary and, as it turned out, temporary circumstances rather than features of a permanent shift in the nation's moral attitudes.

The birth rate increased between 1941 and 1945, as it did in Europe and the United States. It rose from 14.9 per thousand of the population in 1939 to 18.0 in 1944, and there was a corresponding upturn in the proportion of illegitimate babies from 0.6 per thousand to 1.4. This was hardly an index of permissiveness and was more than equalled by a rise in the number of marriages. 'Has there been a relaxation of discipline, a feeling of recklessness, of now or never?' asked the *Lancet*. Another explanation offered itself: 'The sheer overwhelming magnitude of the problems of war and security against which many have increased the individual's sense of isolation in the community. Marriage has been the shock absorber, and children once again the main source of interest and pleasure. In a sense, the people of Europe, frightened and unable to understand the world around them, have retreated into the home.'[63]

At the same time, there was a noticeable increase in the number of women who did not marry once they found themselves to be pregnant.[64] The numbers of rapes and sexual assaults on women, a feature of the 'permissive' last quarter of the twentieth century, rose slowly. There were ten cases of rape in London in 1939 and seventeen in 1951, while indecent assaults increased from 415 to 706. In Scotland, the number of sexual offences actually fell; in 1938 there were 363, with small increases in 1941 and 1942, then a fall in 1943 and 1944, with a rise again in 1945.[65] Amazing as it may seem, there were fifteen cases of rape in 1945, three less than in 1914. The licentiousness that appeared to be enveloping the country, and for which there was abundant anecdotal evidence, was purely a wartime phenomenon that did not survive 1945. It was twenty years before a lasting revolution in sexual values and habits got underway.

It was estimated that there were twenty thousand GI babies, and Congress insisted that the fathers had their pay docked in accordance with affiliation and maintenance orders issued by British courts.[66] How many of these babies were black is not known; those born in Somerset were immediately taken into care by the local authority, where they remained, for adoptions were rare.[67] Rejection was also the fate of Margaret Goosey who, in 1947, married her black boyfriend, but the racial purity laws of Virginia were as strict as those of the Third Reich. Her husband was sent to an 'industrial farm' and she was gaoled and then deported.[68]

For a generation brought up in the shadow of Hollywood, whose films dominated British cinemas, America was an attractive country, particularly, as George Orwell observed, to the working classes. Relaxed and free-spending, American servicemen offered the pleasures of conviviality, drink, living dangerously and shocking one's elders. The GI provided an escape from dreary routines, careers that followed unchanging patterns of courtship, marriage and children, and the constrictions of life in industrial towns or rural backwaters where the opportunities for independence and excitement were limited.

IV

If there had been an American camp in the vicinity of Malfrey, then Doris Connolly would have beaten a path towards it. 'Her figure was stocky, her bust prodigious, and her gait, derived from the cinematograph, was designed to be alluring.' She, her younger brother, a delinquent, and sister, an imbecile, were the three obnoxious evacuees whose disposal gave Basil Seal the chance to make some dishonest cash in Evelyn Waugh's *Put Out More Flags* (1943). Real-life Connollys, and there seem to have been plenty of them if the uproar that followed the September evacuation was anything to go by, were among the children removed from towns and cities and placed in the countryside in anticipation of air raids. If, as was expected, these were imminent and likely to be devastating, it was imperative to preserve as many of the next generation as possible.

There is a large and still expanding literature of the experiences of evacuees and, in acknowledgement that they were participants in total war, a contingent of them was allowed to join the Armistice Day parade in 2000. Stories about the fortunes of evacuees form a staple of modern children's fiction, and understandably so. Removal from a familiar to an unfamiliar, often mysterious and sometimes hostile, environment provided the fictional evacuee with opportunities for adventure and self-discovery. Many evacuees did not adjust to their new world and were glad to join the stream of those who returned home once it was clear that there was not going to be a mass bombing offensive. When it did arrive, in the summer and autumn of 1940, there was a second exodus, and a third in 1944 when London was attacked by flying-bombs. In each instance, once the danger was perceived to have passed, the migrants returned. They were pleased to do so: 'Once evacuated, twice shy' became a popular East End saying.

In some idealistic quarters, mass evacuation was a brave experiment in which the people of the countryside would share responsibility for the largely poor children of the cities and towns. It has been suggested that the sickly and unkempt condition of many, but not all, of these evacuees and their mothers stirred the consciences of the rural middle class and inclined them towards welfare legislation. This is largely wishful-thinking; country people of all classes were indeed horrified by the condition of their guests, but their reaction was usually to demand their reallocation. The historian R. C. K. Ensor was appalled by the irruption into his Home Counties town of 'the lowest grade of slum women – slatternly, malodorous tatterdemalions trailing children to match' who were foistered on to 'prosperous artisans with neat clean homes and habits of refinement'. Another historian, W. L. Burn, scorned the concept of evacuation as an exercise to promote cultural understanding between town and country. 'What good is served by intimate knowledge of those town children who represent the antithesis of all that the decent patient country housewife has striven to install into her own children?'[69] These outbursts appeared in the *Spectator* and provoked further grousing from readers, one of whom ('Victim') denounced the powers of the billeting officers to compel householders to take children accompanied by their mother. 'Is the Englishman's home no longer his castle?'

Evacuees prompted a wave of grumbling during the autumn of 1939 and a short-tempered debate in the Commons, where Labour MPs defended their working-class constituents against allegations of uncleanliness and immorality. Host communities complained about 'verminous' and incontinent children, 'loud' expectant mothers, unruly youngsters and boys with 'dirty' or 'filthy habits' (i.e. masturbation). The chorus was taken up again the following year; a survey conducted by members of the Women's Institute revealed a body of mothers who were unwashed, idle, unable to cook, sew, darn or control their off-spring.[70] Such creatures were a small minority in Ayrshire, where the following exchange occurred between a mother and a woman voluntary worker in May 1941:

> Mother: Hey you. Come here.
> [Voluntary Worker – passing on job, halts and looks.]
> Mother: Come on here. Wipe that bairn's arse [pointing to child].
> Voluntary Worker: But . . .
> Mother: Get on with it. You're paid for it.[71]

It is beyond question that many refugees from the slums suffered from hygienic and moral deficiencies, misbehaved and had truculent and slatternly mothers. It is also beyond question that these shortcom-ings received excessive prominence at the time in the press and wherever the outraged gathered to relate their unfortunate experiences. Distortion was bound to happen and one genuine awful child or family became ciphers for thousands of others, real and imaginary. Or, as Evelyn Waugh put it, whenever the iniquities of evacuees came under discussion, 'the chances were that the scandal originated with the Connollies. They were cited in the House of Commons; there were paragraphs about them in official reports.'

Bad news always drives out good. There were a substantial number of generous and kindhearted foster-parents and helpers who did all in their power to care for their charges. They organised parties and pan-tomimes and offered more in food and clothing than the official 8s 6d (43p) weekly allowance for an evacuee could ever provide. 'We have very nice food such as venison, pheasant, hare and other luxury [sic] which we cannot afford at home,' a fourteen-year-old girl reported from her billet in Cambridge. Not everyone welcomed a new diet; one girl missed 'fish and chip suppers and my pease pudding and saveloy suppers', while another, placed with a continental family, yearned for 'proper English food'.[72] These comments came from a detailed survey of evacuees undertaken in Cambridge which strongly suggested that a majority were impressed by the hospitality of their foster-parents, although one teenage girl in a middle-class household was upset by squabbling housemaids.[73]

These Londoners' reactions to their surroundings were quirky and unpredictable. An eight-year-old boy listed 'Cauliflowers, Sweets, Country Walks, Pets [and] Apples' as the delights of Cambridge. 'Cambridge is a dull, dismal and awful place with hardly any entertainment,' grumbled a thirteen-year-old boy. Pleasures were discovered, principally walking, and a thirteen-year-old boy declared: 'I like playing football here [better] than I do in London, the ground is softer.' Reading through these responses it soon becomes clear that there was no pattern beyond a common homesickness. There was concern for the strain caused by evacuation and a special effort was made by welfare workers to monitor and, if possible, remedy the worst cases. In some, the problems stemmed from the individual's home circumstances, and for them evacuation was a benefit. An incontinent six-year-old whose parents fought one another found contentment in 'a home run in a haphazard sort of way' where there was a large extended family and 'much spontaneous affection'.[74]

There was disagreement among those responsible for allocating children to households in Cambridge as to whether it was best to place them in families with similar incomes to their own. As some of the remarks above suggest, a few found themselves billeted in rich households. It was hoped that such arrangements would be for 'the ultimate good of the community' and social cohesion.

It would be dangerous to generalise too much on this point, given the evidence of the social tensions created by evacuation. In one town, a seventeen-year-old girl complained 'well brought up middle-class girls and boys' were placed in 'tiny, dirty houses' where the girls were treated as 'unpaid maids'. The extremes of poverty, unhealthiness and delinquency of the mothers and children from the slums confirmed common stereotypes of the urban poor and upheld the contention that their condition was the direct consequence of ineradicable fecklessness and indolence. The Victorian ethic of 'self-help' and the notion that the poor had only themselves to blame for their misfortunes still had plenty of adherents, not only among the middle classes. For their part, the have-nots asserted that when it came to the allocation of evacuees, the better-off shirked their responsibilities, often with the connivance of billeting officers. In Salisbury, the old cry of 'It's always the same, the poor helping the poor' was raised.[75] Seen from the perspective of a harassed billeting officer, a reluctant host and an evacuee from the back-streets of the East End, Britain's social divisions were as strong as ever.

6

---◆---

Tactful handling:
Command and combat

I

At the beginning of Evelyn Waugh's *Brideshead Revisited* (1945), Captain Charles Ryder was falling out of love with soldiering. His men were similarly disenchanted: 'In the company office there was a crop of minor charges and requests for compassionate leave; while it was still half light, day began with the whine of the malingerer and the glum face and fixed eye of the man with a grievance.' And there was Hooper, Ryder's subordinate officer who had failed to win his men's respect because he was professionally inept and over-familiar. Waugh the soldier was well acquainted with all this; while a company commander in Scotland early in 1942 he noted in his diary: 'Every day D Company gave evidence of low morale. The men mean-spirited, lazy, untruthful. My senior subaltern, Hand, a Lancashire solicitor, fat, garrulous. I found him one day carrying his equipment up to company lines. "Why don't you make your servant do that?" "Well you know how it is. If you get on the wrong side of them they take it out of you in other ways."'[1] Hooper's batman was likewise under-employed. Perhaps he and his master shared the view advanced in the aggressively egalitarian *Picture Post* that 'many of the most progressive officers' believed there was no place for servants in a modern, democratic army.[2]

Nor was there a place for Waugh. He had shown great courage during the Crete débâcle, but men and events had eclipsed his romantic view of the noble profession of arms. Like Ryder, Waugh became disillusioned and isolated among soldiers who had never shared a passion rooted in past glories: 'Gallipoli, Balaclava, Quebec, Lepanto, Bannockburn, Roncevalles, and Marathon – these, and the Battle in the West where Arthur fell, and a hundred such names whose trumpet-notes, even now in my sere and lawless state, called to me irresistibly across the intervening years with all the clarity and strength of boyhood, sounded in vain to Hooper.' Hooper and thousands like him were in uniform reluctantly and above all wanted to get the job done quickly so they could return to normal life in a postwar world shaped by principles that Waugh detested.

Ryder, Hooper and the sullen squaddies were part of an army that was spending long periods doing little more than train, drill and perform routine camp chores. One and a half million soldiers were stationed in Britain between 1940 and 1944, roughly 60 per cent of all the men in the army. Some manned anti-aircraft batteries, others were busy with logistical and administrative duties and, between 1940 and 1942, all were on hand to resist an invasion. Such a concentration of manpower at home was only possible because of the unprecedented recruitment and deployment overseas of troops from the dominions, India and East and West Africa, who comprised just over half of the British army's 108 divisions. In October 1941 the Eighth Army in North Africa consisted of seventy-three commonwealth, Indian and colonial divisions and twenty-seven British. Two-thirds of the British units in Italy in August 1944 were dominion, Indian and Polish. Less than a fifth of the army that reconquered Burma in 1944 to 1945 was British, the rest were Indians and Africans.[3]

Between 1940 and the invasion of Italy in 1943, imperial troops were implementing an essentially imperial strategy: the security of communications through the Mediterranean, the defence of the Suez Canal and the protection of the Iranian oilfields which supplied all British forces in the region. After 1943, Commonwealth, Indian and colonial soldiers played a vital part in Allied strategy in Europe. In Italy they helped the Allies divert Germans from the Eastern Front and from north-west Europe, and Canadians were prominent at D-Day and in the subsequent offensives through France and Germany. It was a situation that would have pleased Victorian statesmen: imperial manpower giving substance to Britain's pretensions as a global and European power.

Even in the spring of 1945, when purely British forces were most heavily committed on the continent, there were still a million soldiers stationed at home, a third of the army's manpower. Nearly all were conscripts aged between eighteen and forty-one, bound to serve for the duration of the war by the terms of the 1939 National Service Act. The military authorities were uncomfortably aware that this generation of draftees was less deferential than its predecessors in 1914 and contained a far higher proportion of men who were acutely aware of their legal and moral rights. During the interwar years, the Labour party and the trade union movement had deepened the working class's sense of its own identity and its members were readier than ever to defend their interests. This self-confidence became stronger thanks to propaganda that emphasised the struggle as a people's war and demanded equality of effort and sacrifice. At the same time, there were many working-class recruits whose attitudes towards the army were coloured by their fathers' often chilling memories of the Western Front. Folk memories of the horrors of the trenches persuaded young men in the South Nottinghamshire Hussars in September 1939 that service in the cavalry or artillery would raise their chances of survival. As one put it: 'the infantry get too close, they're real brave lads – and I thought, "Let's be in the artillery, they stand off and keep lobbing it in!"' This optimism was sadly misplaced: the Hussars, serving as gunners, suffered heavy losses in North Africa in 1942.[4]

Sir James Grigg, the secretary of state for war, blamed soldiers' attitudes on 'Pansydom' cultivated among the young over the preceding twenty years and the now common assumption that the state fulfilled the individual's needs without any reciprocal obligation.[5] Whatever the cause, servicemen in general were less willing to knuckle under and, if they thought that their real or imaginary rights had been overridden, they protested to their MPs and the left-wing press. The *Daily Herald* had 'The Forces Write' column which became a forum for venting grievances, including those of 'Yorkshire Wren', who grumbled about a lack of baths and privacy in her quarters and a ban on off-duty conversations with men.[6] Service attitudes of mind were also criticised.

A sapper private wrote to *Picture Post* after his sergeant had rejected his request to study mathematics with the observation: 'I thought we might make a soldier out of you.' How typical, the private thought, of an army that regarded education as 'an effeminate civilian game'. The blame lay with 'Blimps', as it usually did whenever the army was charged with outmoded or rigid thinking.[7] Caricature, reactionary senior officers became the scapegoats for all that was wrong with the army, particularly its instinctive conservatism and attachment to out-dated and pointless routines and rituals. Furthermore, Blimp and his fellow brass-hats carried the stigma of the now discredited high command of the previous war.

Discontented servicemen and women appealed directly to the authorities and their MPs, who raised cases with the appropriate min-istries or asked questions in the House. During the debate on the naval estimates in March 1944, S. P. Viant, the Labour MP for West Willesden, intervened to ask whether candidates for commissions in the Wrens were asked their father's occupation, the name of their banker, where they went to school and who had recommended them. A. V. Alexander, the first sea lord and a former trade unionist, denied that social background counted for anything with commission boards, who were solely concerned with 'character and ability'. He added that he had been commissioned from the ranks in the last war.[8] Viant, a sailor's son, took an interest in the misfortunes of Wren P. M. Scott. Although not one of Viant's constituents, her father wrote to him about her new posting, which involved working long hours in an air-conditioned bunker. Before, she had been 'a sweet, fresh, wholesome, physically sound and mentally balanced girl, a working class girl – not given to hysteria or illusions'. Now, she was deeply distressed, claiming that her new life was 'hell on earth' and threatening to 'run away'. Her miseries were compounded by sessions of 'Blimp' drill and the obligation to salute superiors. A naval doctor sensibly suggested that she might well have been claustrophobic.[9]

Multiplied many times, one unhappy Wren became a problem for all the services. They had somehow to balance the needs for efficiency and its vital concomitant, discipline, with the rights and sensibilities of individuals. Moreover, the discontented occasionally ignored the recog-nised procedures for venting their complaints and exercised their civilian right to strike. Between two and three hundred men gathered on a Glasgow dockside in January 1942 in protest about bad conditions on a troopship that was about to take them to the Middle East. They embarked after officers reminded them that they were on active service and were liable for court-martial and punishment.[10] There was a similar incident in Cape Town the same month when sailors, soldiers and airmen walked off the *City of Canterbury* after they had discovered that its berths were filthy and there was a shortage of usable lifebelts. Just over two hundred were court-martialled, but their sentences were suspended and they proceeded to the Far East.[11]

Officers were not immune from this refractory spirit. At New York in January 1946, fifteen (seconded from the merchant navy) refused to embark on the transport *Fifeness* after they found that they had been allocated quarters formerly occupied by lascars. Signs that read 'Native Quarters' and 'Native Latrines' aroused indignation and a feeling that full naval officers would never have been treated in this manner. The navy dealt gently with the protest, for it recognised that such officers were prickly about their status and 'it is well known that men in this position are likely to be umbrageous and so need tactful handling.'[12]

The same approach was adopted by the commanding officer at Plymouth in July 1943 after the crew of the Canadian destroyer *Iroquois* went on strike, causing the captain to suffer a heart attack. He had banned shore leave after no one owned up to the theft of a U-boat officer's badge which had been stolen as a trophy. The senior officer listened to the men's complaints, ordered no further action and the *Iroquois* proceeded to sea.[13] In the First World War such an incident would have led to prison sentences, and in the Napoleonic Wars to floggings and executions.

II

The navy was better at handling citizens in uniform than the army. This was the conclusion of a US intelligence report on British service morale prepared in March 1942. The 'spirit' of the Royal Navy and RAF was good, perhaps because both were continuously engaged in operations. By contrast, the army was bedevilled by 'problems of officer-men relationships' caused by 'a new generation of subalterns' who upheld 'the old military hierarchy'.[14] This impression of simmering class antagonism was confirmed by the army censors whose reports were collated for weekly assessments of morale. In September 1940 it was noticed that the recruit was 'quicker than before to resent what he calls "the old school tie" stand-offishness when conditions lend themselves to closer comradeship.'[15] A year before, a popular song, 'We Must All Stick Together', had urged everyone 'to forget the old tie'. Like Blimp (who doubtless possessed one) the old school tie became a familiar Aunt Sally, representing social divisions that had no place in wartime and the suspected promotion of men because of their connections rather than their talents.

The War Office was untouched by this sentiment. It stuck to the time-worn belief that ex-public schoolboys made the best officers. 'Teach a man to march and shoot. Give him the right type of officer. Leave the rest to him', was the formula for successful command according to a veteran colonel in *Put Out More Flags*. Much to his annoyance, Basil Seal remarked: 'It's an odd thing that people always expect the upper class to be good leaders of men. That was all right in the old days when most of them were brought up with tenantry to look after. But now three-quarters of your officers live in towns. *I* haven't any tenantry.'

Nonetheless, the deracinated, urban public schoolboy was still expected to have acquired the qualities needed for junior command. But, as in the previous war, such fellows were in short supply and so the army had to tap other less satisfactory sources. During the winter of 1942 to 1943 it was officially regretted that, 'Most candidates for commissions now have not a "background" which helps them adopt the right attitude towards their men.' The same defects were prevalent among ex-public schoolboys, some of whom were guilty of 'selfishness and negligence' in handling their men. A year later, another report on morale warned that 'one selfish or stand-offish officer produces more potentially disaffected soldiers than six communist agitators.'[16] To make matters worse, these shortcomings were not being corrected by commanding officers, many of them regulars, to the detriment of what the army was now calling 'man management'. Courses in this arcane skill, once believed to be inborn in the officer class, were laid on with instruction from psychiatrists. Evelyn Waugh attended one and treated his mentors and their proceedings with contempt.

A problem that had troubled Wellington was solved in part by measures that curtailed the privileges enjoyed by officers which, if the soldiers' letters were anything to go by, caused considerable envy and griping. Officers relinquished their previous monopoly of hotel bars and lounges and were no longer able freely to use military transport for private purposes. During 1942 and 1943, and in response to the findings of its morale reports, the War Office tackled other sources of discontent. Remedies for ennui and frustration included an end to stewed tea in the NAAFI, where teapots replaced urns; the dropping of dud ENSA shows; and improved and extended recreational facilities. Reductions were made in the number of parades and there was less insistence on what soldiers called 'spit and polish', cosmetic activities designed to consume time. Welfare officers were appointed to advise and assist soldiers with domestic problems and legal help was made available for men with errant wives.

The institutional confidence of the army, which had been bruised by three years of defeats in France, Germany, the Dodecanese and North Africa, was restored by the victory at El Alamein in November 1942. And not before time; a morale report from the beginning of the year included the ominous comment: 'The effect of the Russian successes and our own reverses has been to make men take an increased interest in the Russian system of discipline and Government.'[17] No one then knew that the former rested upon a ruthless recourse to the death penalty for any soldier who faltered, even momentarily. Measures to reduce discomfort, tedium and friction between officers and men, together with continued successes in North Africa, Sicily and Italy restored the army's morale, which reached its highest point on the eve of the D-Day landings.

Flaccid morale was also eliminated by more conventional methods which drew upon the army's traditional regimental and regional loyalties. These had always been strong in Scotland and were exploited to the full by Major-General Douglas ('Tartan Tam') Wimberley when he revitalised the 51st Highland Division between 1940 and 1942. Everything possible was done to emphasise the division's Scottishness, which became a source of pride, and to cultivate self-respect among its members. Unlike many of his contemporaries, Wimberley believed that 'spit and polish' and formal rituals helped bond men to each other and their unit. He ordered his senior training officers to cultivate smartness, avoid 'blood and hate' methods of battle-training, make officers change for dinner and maintain 'all those old-fashioned things that were regarded as bow and arrow by the War Office theorists'.[18] Wimberley's methods were successful; the 51st Division secured a high reputation and he won its lasting affection.

The overall recovery of the army's spirit by 1942 owed much to another enlightened officer of a different kind, General Sir Ronald Adam, the adjutant-general. 'This war is going to be won or lost on morale,' he predicted in September 1940. Since it was a subject that his fellow generals found disconcerting, he added: 'We are too apt to leave the problem alone. Morale is a psychological problem like sex, and therefore the Britisher is almost ashamed to talk about it.'[19] An Old Etonian and baronet, Adam had served as a gunner and staff-officer in the previous war and was prepared to take its human lessons seriously. 'Bravery is not the absence of fear, but the subordination of it,' he informed all senior officers in December 1943. 'In fact, a man cannot be truly courageous unless he has felt and conquered fear. Conversely, cowardice is not the presence of fear, but the succumbing to it without a struggle or excuse.'[20]

This was true of fighting men in any war. As in the past, bravery was often an inconstant quality. Sub-Lieutenant A. G. C. F—, who had begun his naval service as a rating in June 1940, endured air raids in Portsmouth and London and on board his first ship, the destroyer *Warwick*. Although categorised as unfit for active service, he was a gunnery officer on the battleship *Prince of Wales* when it was attacked and sunk by Japanese bombers on 10 December 1941. He was rescued and, six days later, placed in charge of a party of ratings who were manning river ferries conveying retreating troops and civilians in Malaya. According to one of his detachment, he was in a 'blue funk', and everyone was alarmed by the stories told by soldiers as they passed. F— confessed his nervousness and wish to get away and believed that his men felt the same. Some said that they would stick it out until the job was finished, and one later remarked that 'all officers were brought up on silver spoons.' Nine did desert, were arrested and given nine months each. Their officer was court-martialled for not preventing their flight and reprimanded. Medical evidence suggested that F— was psychologically unsuited for active service and he was transferred to less stressful duties.[21]

All the services were now listening to the advice of psychiatrists, who could not only treat men like F— who had given way to the strain of battle but were able to detect those who might do so. The value and influence of psychiatrists was described to a professional audience in December 1945 by Brigadier G. W. James, who was psychiatric consultant to the Eighth Army between 1940 and 1943 and to home forces for the rest of the war.[22] He and his colleagues had the prime duty of creating 'a relentless fighting army' which required them to reject draftees whose temperaments or previous mental histories did not fit them for soldiering. During the first phase of the North African campaign selection had been so haphazard that 'men with a mental age of seven years or under were "trained" mainly in camp cook-houses or latrines' in Britain before being shipped out to fight in the desert. There was, James believed, a period of transition from civilian to soldier in which men learned 'new standards of health and fitness' and personal responsibility for their own 'cleanliness and hygiene'. 'There are no wives and mothers to "clear up" for them, to cook, mend and make their bedding' in the front line.

When they were there, those who suffered breakdowns were no longer considered as moral delinquents but as legitimate casualties. Moreover, they responded well to clinical treatment. For those who were simply worn out, camps were established behind the lines where they could rest, sleep, enjoy simple amusements and comparatively decent rations. The body, James noted, had immense recuperative powers. Injured minds, too, could be healed; three-quarters of the men treated as 'psychiatric casualties' were returned to their units, and of these 10 per cent suffered a relapse within nine months. Interestingly, James's statistics revealed that in 1941, when the Eighth Army was enduring a string of reverses, the proportion of 'psychiatric casualties' to physically injured was 24 per cent to 38 per cent. In 1943, when the tide of battle had swung in its favour, the figures had fallen to 15 and 24 per cent.

The drop may in part have reflected the policy introduced in July

1942 by which recruits were more rigorously examined as to their suitability. Hitherto, the procedures had been hit or miss, with more of the latter than the former; half the men drafted into the Royal Armoured Corps were later discovered to be utterly unsuited.[23] Afterwards, efforts to uncover recruits' aptitudes and place them accordingly reduced the number of square pegs in round holes. At the same time, it was revealed that out of 710,000 processed during the next three years, only thirty-six thousand were graded as suitable for combat. General Sir Alan Brooke, the Chief of Imperial General Staff, noted ruefully: 'The trouble with our British lads is that they are not killers by instinct.'[24] What was absent was the kind of powerful ideological impetus that drove the German soldier. It was summed up by a pamphlet of 1944 distributed among the Wehrmacht in which Hitler proclaimed: 'He who fights with the purest will, the staunchest belief and the most fanatical determination will be victorious in the end.'[25] This injunction would have been easily understood by young men who had already absorbed Nazi ideology and believed themselves the advance guard of a new world order.

By contrast, the British soldier had undergone no programme of political indoctrination. His mood was one of unromantic fatalism; he wanted to make the best of it, get the job done and then return home where he would be left in peace. There was a prevailing but not always closely defined sense of the righteousness of the Allied cause, a loathing for Hitler and an urge to take revenge for the air raids, but democracy and British values aroused less interest than football, beer and women.[26]

There were pockets of old-style Hun-hatred. Denis Healey encountered a 'beastly captain' who announced: 'If you meet a German parachutist, don't offer him a cigarette. Kick him in the balls. Treat him as dirty as you know. Never forget he's a Hun. The Hun knows no law. Shoot as many as you can; but remember to leave a few for our intelligence boys.'[27] There was a perfectly understandable loathing of the SS, whose cruelty and tendency to murder the wounded and prisoners of war were well known and earned them rough treatment. In July 1944 the army authorities deliberately suppressed details of SS atrocities so as not to enrage troops in Normandy.[28] As in the previous war there was a reluctance to accept the surrender of units that had continued firing until the last moment and, as in all wars, soldiers took personal revenge

for the death of a close comrade. One recalled an incident at Sidi
Rezegh in November 1941 when the battle resolved itself into a private
contest: 'Poor old Smudger got his lot. I made sure of the sod that did
him. Filled his guts with the bren, close range, the bastard.'[29]

III

A few senior officers retained a faith in fear as a stimulus for 'fighting
spirit'. After what appeared to be a crimewave among the BEF in
Belgium, including 144 instances of gross insubordination and assaults
on officers, the commander-in-chief, Lord Gort, asked for the restoration of the death sentence for desertion. It was refused, as was a similar
application made by three senior officers serving in the Middle East in
April 1942. The local commander-in-chief, Lieutenant-General Sir
Claude Auchinleck, disagreed on the grounds that it would increase
social antipathies within his army. Shooting deserters and falterers was
'undemocratic' in that there would emerge 'an underlying suspicion
that distinction of rank or class may be made in its enforcement'.
Nonetheless, his chief-of-staff, Brigadier Thomas Corbett, ordered corps
and divisional commanders to set up posts for the reception of stragglers. To prevent panic, officers were allowed to 'take the strongest
measures' against any soldier' who cannot otherwise be stopped'.[30]

A willingness to engage the enemy with the bayonet was still seen as
a touchstone for the killer instinct. In December 1944, Lieutenant-
General Harold Franklyn emphasised that bayonet-drill instilled
recruits with 'dash' and a 'determination to close with the enemy'. It
was also an assay of the soldier's virility for only 'feminine squeaks'
would be repelled by such training.[31] Those engaged in proving their
manhood with the bayonet were not all convinced as to its value; one
soldier complained of 'a blood on the bayonet' officer whose attitude
seemed to belong to the era of the Boer War.[32] Another commented: 'If
I had a bloody bullet in my rifle there wouldn't be any bayonet fighting.
I'd fire the bugger before I got near enough for the bayonet.'[33]

How men behaved during battle in the Second World War is a subject that has been extensively described and dissected. Perhaps the
most all-encompassing and revealing study is John Ellis's *The Sharp End*

of War (1980), which drew heavily on memoirs and the anatomies of combat experience compiled by Allied military psychiatrists and doctors during and after the war. Detailed analyses of what commanders began to call 'battle motivation' became increasingly important after the onset of the Cold War in 1945 and with it the prospect of another world war, this time against the Soviet Union and its allies. How would the civilian-soldiers of the increasingly materialistic western democracies perform in battle against adversaries who were imagined to be as ideologically inspired and ruthless as the Nazis?

Reading through the raw material of Second World War battle experiences it is impossible not to draw comparisons with previous conflicts. Periods of static operations in Italy produced conditions akin to the trenches: 'The ground for fifty yards outside is MUD – six inches deep, glistening, sticky, holding pools of water . . . My men stand in the gun-pits stamping their feet in the wet, their heads sunk in the collars of their greatcoats. When they speak to you they roll their eyes up because it makes their necks cold to raise their heads. Everyone walks with their arms out to help keep their balance.'[34] This happened to be Italy in October 1944, but it might easily have been a section of the front during the winter of 1917 to 1918, or the siege lines outside Sebastopol in that of 1854 to 1855. 'Muddle and incompetence reigned', remembered one participant in the withdrawal to the French coast in May 1940, and another described his battalion as 'a starving, disorganised mob'.[35] Both observations were equally applicable to the retreat from Kabul just under a hundred years before. The emotional and physical stresses of war remained to a great extent constant. Eyewitness accounts of the extremes of heat and cold, flies, mosquitoes, the irregularity and inadequacy of rations, and memories of a chilling sense of vulnerability all have resonances from previous conflicts.

War still excited the whole range of emotions and the modern soldier sometimes felt the same mixture of exhilaration, detachment and anxiety that possessed the young Nikolai Rostov when he was first in action. 'I was surprised that I did not feel frightened,' John Verney recalled in his account of his first action, fought against Vichy French forces in Syria in 1941. He and the rest of his yeomanry unit were being carried by trucks in preparation for a night attack against a French fortalice. An explosion, possibly a mine, suddenly concentrated his mind. 'Any martial ardour I had worked up in myself evaporated instantly, like the smoke, and my first thought was to leap out of the truck and run for my life.' Instead he helped the wounded from the damaged truck, one a sergeant with a shattered leg. '"Oh God, sir," he gasped, when I tried to comfort him, "I've fairly dropped a bollock this time."'

In a freezing wind and by moonlight, Verney and the yeomanrymen shifted up the hillside and he suffered from 'a violent attack of diarrhoea which was decidedly awkward though really rather funny (afterwards)'. Advancing, the unit came under fire. 'Darting about among rocks dodging bullets was at the time quite good fun and quite unreal – like some Wild Western picture. I simply could not believe that it was *me* taking part and consequently felt moderately safe, as indeed I was, so long as I kept behind cover.' Unfortunately, the detachment came under fire from French forces placed on surrounding high ground and it was pinned down for six, hot, weary and thirsty hours. 'I saw men sleeping, literally sleeping with bullets spattering round them.'

Before 'heat and tiredness had worn the edge off enthusiasm', Verney had approached the French position and seen two Senegalese infantry pop their heads up over the parapet. He ordered a trooper to fire a machine-gun, which jammed. Verney cleared it and fired and the two black faces vanished. 'Thus, with the wantonness of a boy destroying some harmless bird for "sport", I contributed my share towards the never-ending story of man's inhumanity to man. But at the time I thought I had behaved rather splendidly and the trooper was impressed too.' Recalling his emotions long afterwards, Verney looked to the past. 'The irrational, not to say poetic, uplift of the spirit which sweeps over men sometimes during battle is a well-authenticated experience, from Homer's day to our own.' This was how he had felt and subsequent attempts at rationalisation left him puzzled. How could he have felt that 'joy' that Homer had described, for, 'No battle, after all, is bloodless and no one *joyfully* risks being killed and maimed'?[36]

Much was changing on the battlefield. The badly wounded sergeant survived and eventually recovered the use of his legs, something that would have been extremely unlikely even in the First World War. Improvements in surgery and new drugs increased survival rates dramatically. Penicillin, used increasingly from 1942 onwards and in great quantities, was reducing deaths from sepsis and, incidentally, provided an effective treatment for sexually transmitted diseases. In the First World War the death rate for chest wounds was 54 per cent and for amputees 70 per cent; in the Second they fell to 6 and 7 per cent respectively.[37]

Scientific and technical innovations brought new terrors and discomforts. Tanks, which appeared so formidable on the battlefields, forced men into cramped, often foul conditions, choked by the fumes from shells and machine-guns. Unable to cook their rations, tank crews lived off bread and jam for days on end. 'When a shell bursts near,' one officer recalled, 'the turret acts like a drum – that's how my gunner got concussed.' The noise, another remembered was endess and jarring. '. . . The perpetual "mush" through the headphones twenty-four hours each day, and through it the machinery noises, the engine as a background, with the whine of the turret trainer and the thud and rattle of the guns as an accompaniment.'[38] Amid this mechanical cacophony, sounds from the heroic past were heard as many tank units had been formed from former cavalry regiments. One was John Verney's yeomanry, and he heard that at El Alamein its former adjutant had blown his hunting-horn during the pursuit of German armour. 'We picked them off like pheasants,' he declared, echoing warrior-sportsmen across the ages.

7

It's all for you: Peace and perceptions of the war

I

Victory in Europe was celebrated in 8 May 1945, a day after the remnants of Germany's armed forces agreed an unconditional surrender. The mood was relieved and exuberant and there were spontaneous festivities throughout the country, just as there had been on 11 November 1918. Street-parties were held everywhere. Edward Kanter, then aged fourteen, remembered how each family in his London street placed a florin (10p) in a bag and those who could not afford it 'would be supported by others'. 'Trestle tables were hastily erected, bunting came from nowhere and the whole street was ablaze with colour and children laughing – none of them knowing why all this excitement was taking place.' The local publican had kept a barrel of beer which he produced and kicked down the road, shouting, 'there you are, it's all for you.'[1]

The novelist Mary Wesley heard the news of peace while walking along the Cornish clifftop. She wept and told her son, who was furious. 'I want my war, it's not over, I want my war.' He had been taken to London a month before and had been excited by what he had seen of the V-bombs. His mother was 'thinking of the people who had been killed'.[2] More would be: the war against Japan continued. British forces were preparing for an amphibious landing in Malaya and were earmarked for the seaborne invasion of Japan, which was scheduled for

November. Given the fierceness of recent Japanese resistance on Okinawa, heavy losses were predicted once the Allies came ashore on Kyushu. As it turned out, Japan surrendered in August after atomic bombs had been dropped on Hiroshima and Nagasaki.

By this time, normal life was returning to Britain. Beaches were now open and masses flocked to them for the August bank holiday, which gave many children their first experience of the seaside. But there was still much that was missing. A disconsolate child appeared on an advertisement with the caption: 'Please *when* can we have Chivers' Jellies?' She would have to show forbearance, for jelly, like sweets, was rationed and would remain so for some years.

The dead were not forgotten, although there were far fewer people wearing the tokens of private grief on 8 May 1945 than there had been on 11 November 1918. The total of the dead was 264,000, of whom a sixth had been killed in air raids. Losses were more evenly shared among the three services, and included four thousand women. Unlike 1918, there was no obsessive urge to commemorate the dead. Servicemen and women did not want a 'crop of monuments' to spring up across the country, concluded General Sir Andrew Thorne, the army commander in Scotland. Rather, he suggested, 'the young men and women of today preferred memorials which were more than ornament.'[3] Nonetheless, manufacturers of tablets and stained-glass windows were advertising their wares in the press as suitable for remembering the dead.[4] They did not do as much business as they had done after the previous war; in most towns and villages new names were added to existing memorials and their sacrifice was acknowledge by practical symbols such as 'victory' community halls. In 1945, Britain preferred to move forward rather than to pause and grieve.

Of course, people mourned, not only for loved ones and friends. Joan Kirby spoke for many when she wrote to her parents in July 1944: 'words can't express how I hate this war, the parting from people, the loneliness that is always with you, the losing of people you love and who love you without ever saying goodbye.' Futures were eclipsed. 'How dreadful for those parents with only one child – they have no-one to comfort them at all and will grow old with only themselves for company – no grandchildren to look forward to – absolutely nothing.[5] For the survivors, there was a proud sense of achievement; they had stuck it out and endured nearly six years of hardship, fatigue and inconvenience with a resilience that still rouses wonder and admiration. Neither is anywhere better expressed than in George Barker's 'To My Mother':

> *Most near, most dear, most loved and most far,*
> *Under the window where I often found her*
> *Sitting as huge as Asia, seismic with laughter,*
> *Gin and chicken helpless in her Irish hand,*
> *Irresistible as Rabelais, but most tender for*
> *The lame dogs and hurt birds that surround her, –*
> *She is a procession no one can follow after*
> *But like a little dog following a brass band.*
> *She will not glance up at the bomber, or condescend*
> *To drop her gin and scuttle to a cellar,*
> *But lean on the mahogany table like a mountain*
> *Whom only faith can move, and so I send*
> *O all my faith and all my love to tell you*
> *That she will move from mourning into morning.*

J. B. Priestley likened the condition of survivors to train passengers who had just completed a long night journey and were emerging into the first light of dawn. During their dark transit they had, he believed, discovered a lofty sense of community.[6] Others reached the end of their odysseys glad to be free of tiresome restrictions. Joan Kirby, who had become bored with the Wrens, was pleased to part company with 'their petty officialdom'.[7] She and millions of others would have sympathised with the girl in an Osbert Lancaster cartoon of January 1943 who remarks to a friend: 'Frankly, can you think up a single New Year resolution that the Government hasn't taken for us already?'[8] Behind the pair are posters exhorting passers-by to save more fuel, question the necessity of their journeys, shop early in the day and collect scrap metal for the war-effort.

Peace did not terminate official hectoring or blow away the sheaves of regulations. If, as J. B. Priestley had suggested, the British people were awakening to a new dawn, it was a wintry one which heralded a cold, comfortless day. There were still acute shortages; Britain was on the verge of insolvency, and an economy distorted and exhausted by the war-effort had somehow to adjust itself to peacetime production to redress the massive balance of payments deficit. Austerity remained and new sacrifices were demanded by the government, this time to win the peace through the export drive.

II

Restoring the economy, like beating Hitler, required scrimping and going without. Within three weeks of VE-Day, further ration cuts were announced by the Ministry of Food. The weekly personal allocation of milk was halved to two pints, the bacon ration fell from four to three ounces and that for cooking fat was reduced to one ounce. One-seventh of all meat available was tinned corned beef.[9] In July 1946, the government was faced with a global dearth of grain and cereals and was compelled to introduce bread rationing. It lasted for the next two years and provoked much anger. A working-class housewife, who had been used to feeding four men on sandwiches, was 'bloody fed up'. 'And 'oo dus it 'it?' she asked. 'The poor man all the time. The rich 'uns they can go inter resterants.'[10]

Then and during the war, those with extra cash could always secure extra food through the black market. Early in 1945 the going rates were 5s 6d (28p) for a pound of bacon, 7s 3d (35p) for a pound of sugar and ten shillings (50p) for a pound of tea. It was calculated that goods worth £2.5 million were being stolen from docks and marshalling yards by workers who sold them to racketeers; there were stories that dockers filched rations from ships' lifeboats.[11] There were plenty of entrepreneurs (the 'spivs' of folk mythology) on hand to satisfy the public's need for what was otherwise scarce or only available illegally. In January 1944, a GI wrote home that he never had any difficulty in procuring an egg, although one of his suppliers charged 2s 6d (13p) each, five times the regulation price.[12] No doubt this spiv shared the common view that Americans were as naïve as they were rich. Those who produced food tended to fare better; Joan Kirby was given scones, butter and cheese at a farmhouse while cycling in Argyll in February 1944.

By 1945, four-fifths of Britain's admittedly restricted diet was home-grown or reared. After two decades in the doldrums, farming was thriving again. There were 370,000 farms in England and Wales, two-thirds of them small enterprises of under twenty acres. All were prospering and, early in 1945, the demand for land was outstripping supply, encouraging many older farmers to sell up and retire.[13] The government intended to replace some of them with ex-servicemen who were offered a year's training and low-interest loans for land and stock. Many Land Army girls, who knew what to expect in terms of graft, were keen to stay in farming. Among a group of sixty who attended a conference at Worcester in February 1944, three-quarters wanted to stay on the land, including a small group who hoped to set themselves up as contractors. Here and elsewhere, there was a widespread wish to emigrate to the dominions and farm there.[14]

Present and future rural prosperity in large part depended upon agricultural subsidies which had spiralled during the war in order to forestall the inflation that had occurred between 1914 and 1919. Then the index of retail food prices had soared from 100 to 168, whereas between 1939 and 1945 the increase was from 100 to 120.[15] Holding down the price of food was expensive; between 1942 and 1944 the total of subsidies rose from £127 to £200 million, with just under one-third spent on grain and cereals. Nearly a third of the price of a four-pound loaf was made up by the Treasury.[16] Government-guaranteed prices swelled farmers' incomes: between 1939 and 1945 the wholesale price of wheat rose from 9s 9d (49p) to 18s 10d (94p) and potatoes, the unrationed national staple, from £2 2s 6d (£2.13p) a ton to £7 15s 7d (£7.78p).

Farmers now possessed the wherewithal for investment in machinery. The total number of combine harvesters more than trebled between 1942 and 1946, to 3500, and that of tractors quadrupled to over two hundred thousand in the same period. Nonetheless, the horse-drawn plough still dominated the fields; there were just over three hundred thousand of them in use in 1946.[17] By 1949, the number of plough-horses had fallen to two hundred thousand.[18] For the unsentimental the gradual extinction of these beasts was a token of how farming had adapted to meet the demands of war.

Peace brought new challenges. Like everyone else, farmers had to shoulder the burdens of reconstruction. Imports of foreign food had to be kept to a minimum to conserve Britain's currency reserves and the government hoped that low food prices would act as a brake on wage claims. For these reasons, the wartime system of subsidies was perpetuated by the 1947 Agriculture Act and, like Topsy, they grew and grew. In the next year £491 million was poured into farming, and the annual bill for the protection of farming soon equalled that for the new National Health Service. How this money was invested is still a matter of controversy. As in the war, the overall goal was high production rather than competitiveness, and so farmers were encouraged to adopt intensive methods. These included 'overkill' applications of chemical fertilisers and pesticides which have defaced the landscape and decimated wildlife.[19] At the same time, dependency on the state has made agriculture a highly vulnerable sector of the economy; few wartime expedients would have such extended and unlooked-for repercussions.

The image of horse- and tractor-drawn ploughs operating in neighbouring fields was as appropriate to postwar industry as it was to agriculture. Innovation and obsolescence co-existed as did extremes of managerial and technical proficiency and incompetence. For the previous five years, the government had directed a command economy in which it was the largest customer for manufacturing, mining and farming. All were circumscribed by rules that gave absolute primacy to war production. The Ministry of Labour controlled man and woman power and, by 1945, five million workers of both sexes were engaged in essential war work. Sluggish production levels and an upsurge in man-hours lost through strikes led the government to draft eighteen-year-old conscripts into the collieries. They were called 'Bevin Boys', after the minister of labour, Ernest Bevin. One who refused, preferring to join the merchant navy or the fighting services, was sent to prison for two months in February 1945.[20]

There was a limit to what ministers and civil servants could demand. They and the Ministry of Information could not eliminate attitudes that had their roots in the preceding hundred or so years of industrial history. Workers did not allow their patriotism to supersede attachments to restrictive practices or the trade union rulebook. Many operated antiquated plant under the supervision of managers and directors with ossified minds. These were an extension of the old enemy within, according to the Daily Herald, which labelled them the 'Blimps of the directors' parlours and Stock Exchange bars'.[21] Whether or not boardroom blimpishness was to blame, the war did very little to modernise production methods or exorcise animosities between bosses and workers, which were as bitter as they had been in the thirties. There was a considerable element of truth in J. M. Keynes's flippant observation that the best way of regenerating British industry would be for the USAAF to flatten the factories and shipyards of the north-west and north-east, having first evacuated all employees, but not their boards of directors.

Alongside the dead wood were green shoots; in the months after May 1945 the public read about hitherto secret projects which revealed an abundance of native ingenuity, among them radar, the Mosquito, jet aircraft, penicillin and Pluto, the underwater pipeline that had conveyed fuel to the armies in north-west France. The true value of inventiveness was only realised through planning; of this the war gave ample evidence. His experiences of amphibious operations convinced Major Denis Healey that the diligent planning that had made them a success ought to be applied to the economy. This approach was infinitely preferable to the capitalist free-market philosophy, which 'usually depends on the uncoordinated plans of innumerable private groups'. A few servicemen, impressed by the Red Army's victories, wondered if this was a vindication of the Soviet faith in planning.

The talismanic value of planning at every level and in just about every area of human activity was central to Labour's manifesto and helped secure the party a 146-seat majority in the general election of July 1945. The new prime minister, Clement Attlee, believed that Labour had caught the mood and imagination of the nation. 'I think the general feeling was that they wanted a new start. We were looking to the future.'[22] Its shape and direction had been defined during the last five years when people had toiled, gone without and put up with every form of discomfort, fortified by the knowledge that their perseverance would be rewarded by a better tomorrow. A sentimental optimism pervaded many wartime favourites – 'We'll Meet Again', 'It's a Lovely Day Tomorrow' and 'The White Cliffs of Dover' with its promise of 'There'll be love and laughter/and peace ever after/when the world is free.' And then there was the spectre of 1918 which Attlee invoked in an address to Hackney voters: 'The young people, and those who have been fighting for us, are asking at the present time that we who fought in the last war will not let them down.'[23]

Future aspirations required the rejection of the immediate past. The world of joblessness, poverty and despair was irrevocable, although some still feared that it might creep back. In the north-east, a social worker observed during the election that: 'When you speak of future employment, it is like touching a part of the body which has a very deep bruise, and they need much convincing that history will not repeat itself.'[24] It would not, according to Labour's pre-election broadcast in which George Tomlinson declared that those who had won the war were entitled to more than 'a chance in a lottery' – they deserved 'homes', 'security' and 'happiness'. All were within the nation's grasp so long as it adhered to principles that had proved their value during the war, when, 'All along the line we could see the value of state initiative and enterprise.'[25]

What was latent within individuals had been harnessed by the state and the result was victory. In June 1945, Labour pledged itself to maintain this union of national willpower and government wisdom to rebuild the economy, sustain full employment and create a welfare state as proposed in the Beveridge Plan. Movement in this direction was already underway. The 1944 Education Act had opened up secondary education to every child with talent and, early the next year, the coalition government had set a target of 320,000 houses to be constructed over the next two years. Labour endorsed and enlarged this ambitious programme, which would simultaneously replace the 450,000 dwellings that had been destroyed or seriously damaged by bombing and rehouse the millions whose present accommodation was unwholesome and dilapidated. The new 'prefabs' that were appearing offered many families their first experience of bathrooms and inside lavatories.

Decent housing, low rents, family allowances and free access to the 'better' (i.e. grammar) secondary schools were the postwar priorities of twenty-thousand women surveyed in January 1945.[26] Reports from the Army Bureau of Current Affairs confirmed these concerns, although there is no evidence that the votes of men serving overseas tipped the balance in Labour's favour. Nonetheless, an illicit poster appeared at Dundee that claimed that the 'Navy, Army and Air Force' urged voters to chose Labour.[27] Certainly, educational programmes had heightened political consciousness, and one junior officer believed the routines of army life had fostered radical values. 'In a world of wage-earners and wage-slaves the Army teaches a man a wage corresponds to his personal needs, not to the work he does – that work is not measurable by money. A soldier may be digging drains or typing in the office, his pay is the same.' There were also lessons in mutual dependence. 'To be efficient in the Army means to do something as well as you can, because on your work depends the convenience and happiness of others.'[28] Not every squaddie would have shared such a lofty view of humdrum fatigues, or their rewards. Nevertheless, these remarks indicate something of the spirit of the time and help explain why Attlee believed that it was in tune with Labour.

The radicalism of many young army officers astonished Indian nationalists who had hitherto only experienced the unbending imperialism of career officers.[29] Bob Rogers, a communist serving with the Fleet Air Arm in India in 1945, visited the party headquarters in Coimbatore, introduced himself to its members (including an Old Etonian) and spoke at several meetings where he noticed that a white man in uniform evinced a certain amount of anxiety among Indians. Rogers's activities upset his superiors and he found himself facing a charge of 'making a political speech in uniform', but it was pointed out that what he had said was immaterial.[30] He had a good record and the war had just ended so the matter was dropped. He was demobbed early in 1946 and became a sculptor who drew on the forms and patterns he had seen in India. For Indians, contact with such men and the knowledge that considerable support existed for Labour, the party that was pledged to independence, was encouraging.

While everyone agreed that the people had won the war, a divergence of opinion would emerge as to whether they secured the peace. For idealists on the left, a wonderful and never-to-be-repeated opportunity for a far-reaching, radical renaissance had been timidly grasped. Much was achieved, but much was left undone. The pragmatic disagreed: in the circumstances, Labour had done remarkably well and given the country a fair return for its wartime effort. Moreover, the Conservatives, who had fiercely opposed Labour's programme of nationalisation and welfare legislation, accepted both in principle when they came to power in 1951. This was not surprising since the ethos of the welfare state and the principle of state intervention to prevent unemployment fitted the concept of one-nation Toryism which dominated party thinking between 1951 and 1974. 'Fairness' and 'Compassion' were part of the political lexicon of both Harold Wilson and Edward Heath.

Hitches occurred in the implementation of Labour's policies. No one had foreseen how the cost of the National Health Service would spiral; it stood at £439 million per year by 1951, and was set to rise further as more and more patients, no longer deterred by consultation fees, visited their doctors. A 1949 CIA assessment of Britain's performance and progress was favourable: production was increasing, exports had been restored to their prewar level and 'democratic socialism' had achieved a revolution in social life. There were, however, misgivings about the country's future competitiveness once the severely crippled economies of France, Germany and Japan returned to par.[31] Popular confidence in Labour and its programme remained high; despite six years of austerity, shortages and high taxation, Labour polled fourteen million votes in the 1951 general election. By this time, an unexpected event, the Korean War, was placing fresh burdens on the nation's finances; between 1950 and 1952 the defence budget soared from £780 to £1114 million. In the next two years, as the CIA had warned, Britain had to face competition from Germany, France and Japan which, thanks to the RAF and USAAF, had build their manufacturing industries and infrastructure up from scratch and were able to modernise both in the process.

Apostles of the free-market right, who gained prominence in the Conservative party during the late 1970s, have condemned the 1945 settlement as a recipe for future catastrophe. Given Britain's economic predicament and the resources then available, Labour's policies were unrealistic and self-indulgent. This was the view advanced in Corelli Barnett's *The Audit of War* (1986) and it accorded well with the new Thatcherite economic dogma which repudiated postwar collectivism, state aid to enfeebled industries and nationalisation. Attlee's welfare state had produced 'a segregated, sub literate, unskilled, unhealthy and institutionalised proletariat hanging on the nipple of state maternalism'.[32] As for the economy, its decline was accelerated to the point when in 1973 it was unable to withstand the shock of the fourfold oil-price increase decreed by OPEC. The road taken in 1945 had led inexorably to the incurable malaise of old industries, sluggish growth, Edward Heath's candle-lit winter of 1973 to 1974, the IMF loan two years later and the messy suicide of old-style trade unionism in the winter of 1979 to 1980. Only a stringent dose of free-market policies, including privatisation of the nationalised industries, restored the nation's economic health.

Whether this medication would have been chosen by the electorate in 1945, and how a war-weary but hopeful country would have reacted to its traumatic side-effects, are matters for speculation. Any conjecture that I might offer would be coloured by personal considerations. I was a beneficiary of the 1944 Education Act, wartime and postwar provision for babies and infants (in the form of cod-liver oil and delicious free orange juice) and the National Health Service. I went to school with the children of families who were clearly glad to live in the new prefabs that sprang up close to my home and whose building sites provided me with a source of wood and nails, the raw material for forts manned by my toy soldiers. In June 1945 my father, then in Palestine, broke a lifetime's habit by voting Labour, a choice he later explained as a reflection of his own feelings and those of his fellow airmen, all of whom were looking forward to a new and better world. They were right: the people's peace was the proper outcome of the people's war.

III

The idealism abroad during and immediately after the war was a reflection of the nation's self-esteem and self-confidence. There was self-congratulation too; if total war was a test of a country's moral strength, then Britain had passed with outstanding success. British society had survived the enormous strain of war, although in the process the suppositions that had underpinned it had been revised. Democracy had proved itself stronger and more flexible than dictatorships, as wartime propaganda had always claimed it would. There was a paradox in this, in that throughout the war the state had assumed authoritarian powers and was prepared to override those liberties the country was defending. This was tolerated in what were perceived as the interests of necessity and the greater good and, for the same reason, people were willing to elect a government in 1945 that proposed to retain state control over transport, food distribution and sections of industry.

Physically damaged by the war, Britain emerged with its moral reputation enhanced as one of the three nations that had rescued Europe. It could and did feel proud of what it had accomplished. By contrast, Germany had the unpalatable task of 'overcoming the past', that is uncovering and facing up to collective and individual guilt for all manner of crimes. Naturally many Germans preferred to avoid a painful dissection of their recent history, but the curiosity of a younger generation has made inquiry impossible to avoid. The results have been unsettling, particularly those that have appeared in print within the last decade which have called into question the matter of culpability. Genocide and massacre were not solely committed by Nazi fanatics, but the ordinary Germans in uniform who were often untouched by ideology. Moreover, their actions and the policies that guided them enjoyed the tacit approval of millions of civilians.[33]

The French have been afflicted by similar although less severe traumas. As in Germany, the past was evaded or, during the Gaullist era, glossed over for political reasons. The official version of the war related how a divided and badly led France surrendered after the British had withdrawn and then, from 1940 until 1944, resisted bravely. Its ancient honour was reclaimed when de Gaulle and the Free French forces liberated Paris. Its self-esteem restored, France proceeded to fulfil its historic destiny as the leader of Europe under de Gaulle. This travesty was challenged in 1971 by a four-hour TV documentary, Le Chagrin et la Pitié, that exposed the massive scale of active collaboration. It was banned for ten years. 'Certain myths are necessary to the happiness and tranquillity of the people,' explained the head of ORTF.[34] Only in 1983 was the war admitted to the history syllabus of French schools, where children learned, among other things, that thirty thousand French men and women worked for German intelligence and French policemen helped round up nine thousand Parisian Jews who were exiled and subsequently murdered in concentration camps.

Britain was spared such an agonising self-examination. But national pride has always been prickly when it comes to allocating credit for wartime achievements. It matters to get things right, which was why recently there was a furore when a Hollywood film, U 571, claimed that an American rather than a British warship had secured a vital Enigma machine from a U-boat. Over fifty years previously, there had been an even greater uproar when another Hollywood movie, *Burma Story*, showed Alan Ladd sweeping all before him in a campaign from which Americans were conspicuously absent. *The True Glory* (1945), an Oscar-winning, Anglo-American documentary account of the campaign in north-west Europe, ran into production difficulties when it came to apportioning the honours between United States and British forces. If the latter's efforts were overstressed, an American official believed the film would so incense the average GI that he would be 'ready to start a fight with every English soldier he meets'.[35] Passions were certainly aroused by film portrayals of the war. At a Hove cinema in January 1944, newsreel footage of American soldiers was booed by an audience of dominion and British servicemen who cheered when Australians appeared.[36]

This remarkably durable concern over how the cinema treated the war was both appropriate and significant. There was almost universal coverage of the war on film, then the most popular medium of entertainment and information. If all the existing footage of the war, documentary and fictional, was played consecutively, it had been calculated that the performance would last longer than the conflict itself.[37] At least five years before the outbreak of war, the government had been examining approaches to propaganda and it was inevitable that the cinema would become its most potent and persuasive vehicle. In 1939 an average of nineteen million people visited the cinema once a week, a total that rose to thirty million (roughly 60 per cent of the population) in the next six years. They went primarily for escapist diversion, and there was plenty available, mostly from American studios whose productions had an 80 per cent share of the market.

Cinemagoers also learned about current affairs, the subject of the weekly newsreels. The five companies that produced them depended entirely on the co-operation of the government for their wartime material and were subject to censorship. Everyone was aware of this, which explains why in 1940 half the population mistrusted the newsreels and there was widespread dislike of over-optimistic propaganda, understandably given the way the war was going.[38] For some, the newsreels were an unwelcome distraction. On leaving a cinema in May 1940, an elderly, middle-class woman crossly remarked: 'with the other two pictures I forgot about the war for an hour or two, but those horrid pictures brought it all back.'

The newsreels were complemented by Ministry of Information-sponsored documentaries and semi-fictional documentaries that covered the everyday work and achievements of the services and were designed to boost morale. *Eastern Command* and *One of Our Aircraft Is Missing* were among the repertoire of the RAF Film Projection Unit which toured stations during 1941.[39] Inspiring words and images would have shown airmen and WAAFs how people like themselves were contributing to the overall war-effort and the qualities that were required from them. Like the newsreels, such material was often sceptically received. After watching a somewhat overblown puff for the Royal Navy, *Ships with Wings* (1942), one cynic remarked: 'Rotten, what's the good of the Navy when they can't stop the Japs in Malaya.' Another cinemagoer did not bother to watch: 'I dodged it. It was all flag-waving wasn't it?' Audiences were allergic to exaggerated patriotism and Hun-hatred, perhaps because the previous war had exposed both as bogus and deceitful.[40]

Audiences were captivated by dramatic films based upon real events and with characters with whom they could emotionally engage. Perhaps the most popular was Noël Coward's *In Which We Serve* (1943), which follows the fortunes of Captain Kinross, played by Coward, and various members of the crew of his destroyer and their families. All face up to the responsibilities war has imposed on them, withstand its shocks and perform their duties cheerfully. Throughout there is a low-key realism; during the final scenes Kinross helps rescue his men as their ship sinks, just as Lieutenant-Commander R. S. Miller of the frigate *Tweed* did after it had been torpedoed. He was 'paddling around, assisting others to reach some form of support, keeping their spirits up with cheering remarks and for a long period holding a stoker until the whaler arrived to relieve him of his burden'.[41] The same humour in adversity shown by the rating in *In Which We Serve* was reflected in real life. When Keith Fawcett was hauled from the water after the destroyer *Warwick* sank in February 1944, his rescuer quipped: 'That will cost you a pint.' Everyone displayed what Fawcett called a 'true British "never say die" spirit'.[42]

Too much realism upset audiences. Shots of corpses in *Next of Kin* (1942) shocked cinemagoers, as they were intended to in a film designed to alert the public to the dangers of 'careless talk'. Indiscreet words provide German intelligence with a forewarning of an amphibious landing, which is repulsed with heavy losses. There were high casualties, too, in *Went the Day Well* (1942) in which a force of Germans, disguised as British troops, occupies an English village. Its inhabitants are treated with the same brutality as their counterparts in Poland and France. Nazi terror provokes British anger, transforming the gentle, motherly postmistress into a Judith who kills an unwary German soldier. In a revealing twist, the villagers' 'natural' leader, the squire, turns out to be a fifth columnist who hampers their efforts to get help. This betrayal would not have surprised many; when the film was released there were rumours that at least five dukes secretly favoured coming to terms with Hitler.[43] In *The Foreman Went to France* (1941) a fifth columnist army officer bears a close resemblance to Mosley.

In a people's war it was necessary to dispel notions that the upper classes were natural leaders, although Noël Coward's Captain Kinross is unmistakably out of the top drawer. The young platoon commander in *The Way Ahead* (1944) is a former garage owner, although as played by David Niven, himself a former subaltern, it would be easy to imagine otherwise. The film's theme is the creation and training of a fighting unit from a group of men from widely different backgrounds, including a spiv, who, under Niven's guidance, finally meld together. To remind the bored tommy that weeks of training had a purpose, the film concludes with the platoon in action in North Africa. The fighting scenes are realistic and the soldiers have acquired the necessary blood-lust. One remarks: 'Did you see that bloke who dropped his tin hat and tried to pick it up. Blimey, did I catch him bending.'

On this screen battlefield, the enemy were Italians ('macaroni eaters') who, like the rest of Britain's opponents, were stereotyped by film-makers. The Germans were tough, ruthless and fanatical; the Italians were at best lukewarm soldiers and inclined to cravenness; and the Japanese were sadistic automata. The Ministry of Information played its part in propagating these images. In a wonderful memo issued to newsreel scriptwriters in 1940 the ministry forbade them to refer to Italians as 'ice-cream merchants', which insulted worthy tradesmen, but allowed the use of 'wops'.[44]

IV

There was no place for such gibes in the BBC's news coverage. Its tone was serious and, from July 1940, newsreaders announced their names at the beginning of each bulletin as an earnest of its authenticity. Restrained, authoritative and dispassionate, the nine o'clock news was the nation's chief source of information as to how the war was progressing, and it was widely believed. In 1939 nearly nine million wireless licences were issued, a total that had risen to 9.7 million by the end of the war, giving a distribution of one radio to six people. The BBC's mass audience made it an invaluable partner in the government's campaign to raise morale and reveal to individuals the ways in which they could help the war-effort. The corporation also had the unique capacity to convey background information about the war, and the moral and political issues it raised, through talks by experts. During February 1944, Home Service listeners heard about family life in the Soviet Union, the American invasion of the Marshall Islands and how the Dutch had coped with occupation. There was advice on keeping ducks and geese, gardening tips, and recipes that were cheap, nourishing and used easily available ingredients. Among them were orange-peel biscuits, which sounded attractive, and prune fritters, which did not. The prewar tradition of educational public service broadcasting was kept alive with programmes on theology, glass manufacture and seal-hunting in Newfoundland.

Lord Reith, the BBC's austere and high-minded first director-general, would have approved. The corporation existed to improve the nation in the widest sense and not to pander to popular tastes. For this reason, there were sometimes five-minute gaps between programmes to prevent listeners from treating the BBC as a provider of background noise. This approach to broadcasting changed radically in 1939 in response to the need for entertainment that would directly engage the masses and raise their spirits. This was provided by the Forces' Programme, six hours of popular music and variety shows which began at 6.30 in the morning. Favourites included 'Bandwagon' and the comedy series 'ITMA'. 'Music While You Work' and 'Workers' Playtime' were both aimed at factory workers, the latter coinciding with their lunch hour. The content and breezy style of presentation of these programmes was copied from that of the prewar commercial station, Radio Luxembourg, which had attracted a huge working-class audience.

Giving the people what they wanted obviously helped morale. But the BBC, like the cinema, had also to provide what was good for them, programmes that defined Britain's war-aims and helped foster national identity and cohesion. The traumas of 1940 had focused attention on 'Britishness' or 'Englishness' (the terms were interchangeable, although the latter tended to be more commonly employed) and analysis of its essential components. In October 1944, the *New Statesman*'s film critic had praised *The Way Ahead* for its 'Englishness', assuming that readers and the film's audience would know what to expect in terms of sentiments and treatment. Watching the film today, one is struck by the way in which social barriers dissolve and how the men learn to depend on each other, although this comradeship evolved in abnormal conditions. Yet the fact that this band of conscripts behave as they do can be attributed to latent values, most notably decency and tolerance, which contemporary commentators considered important features of Britishness.

Perhaps the most famous attempt to distil Britishness was George Orwell's *The Lion and the Unicorn* (1942). The British emerge from this essay as a humane, good-natured, humorous and quirky people who set great store by commonsense. They are mad about sport, animals and gardens and, while instinctively tolerant, are quickly aroused by bullying and injustice. Authority is regarded with an inbuilt suspicion which turns to indignation whenever it throws its weight about.

All these qualities are manifest in the 1944 film *The Tawny Pipit* which, true to its theme of Englishness, is set in the idyllic countryside of the Downs, which until recently had been the nation's front line. The story revolves around the appearance of a rare bird, a migrant from Europe, whose survival is threatened by the army, which wants its nesting site for tank exercises, the Ministry of Agriculture, which seeks to plough it up, and egg-collectors, who are portrayed as pseudo-fifth columnists. Threatened by high-handed authority, expediency and selfishness, the pipit is defended by the fair and independent-minded locals, including the squire and parson. Various representative figures are drawn into the contest to save this bird, including a nurse and an RAF pilot who is convalescing locally. Asked by some young boys what it felt like to fight in the Battle of Britain, he answers by comparing himself to a batsman stepping out to the wicket in a test match in which the odds are stacked against England. Another player from another war, Lieutenant Bokolova, a Russian woman sniper, appears, throws herself into the struggle on behalf of the pipit and gives a stirring rendition of the 'Internationale' to the villagers. They and their quintessentially English values prevail and the bird is saved, as will be the continent from which it escaped.

National virtues cultivated during the war are also exemplified in a postwar film, *Passport to Pimlico* (1949), in which a district of London finds itself legally detached from the rest of the country as an enclave of the defunct medieval state of Burgundy. The local people assert their new independence by destroying their identity cards and ration books and dealing brusquely with overbearing civil servants. An official blockade is thwarted by Londoners who bombard the 'Burgundians' with food which is served to the community as a whole, re-creating the wartime spirit of 'togetherness' and sharing.

National ideals were inseparable from the culture in which they had their roots, the history that shaped them and the environment in which they evolved. The public exposition of Britishness therefore involved an examination of the country's art and literature and an exploration of its past and landscape. Much of what was being presented had hitherto been taken for granted. In a BBC talk on 'The English and their Architecture', the artist John Piper observed that, 'A cynic might say that it has taken a world war with heavy bombing to make the British conscious of their architecture.'[45] His address was largely concerned with the National Buildings Record, a project begun in 1941 the aim of which was a complete photographic record of the country's architecture. Piper was one of the artists who contributed to a similar enterprise, the 'Recording Britain' exhibitions. These were sponsored by the new Council for the Encouragement of Music and the Arts (the forerunner of today's Arts Council) and consisted of images of rural and urban scenes. The countryside predominated, as it did in Edward Seago's *Peace in War* (1943), a collection of essays and pictures of East Anglia, the New Forest and Sussex. All might have been painted a century before and so suggest the timelessness and continuity of English rural life. Explaining his choices of subject, Seago observed that his pictures evoked 'the placid days of a country at peace and the simple delights of a life now unobtainable'.

Pictures of churches, windmills and shire-horses plodding along country lanes represented a common national inheritance which was now endangered and which everyone had to do their utmost to protect. The nature of this common inheritance was revealed in photographs, paintings, words and print. Today, few secondhand bookshops do not have copies of Collins's 'Britain in Pictures' series or the equally well-illustrated King Penguins, both of which appeared during and after the war. The wartime titles of the King Penguins included *Some British Moths*, *Elizabethan Miniatures* and *British Ballet*. The last ends with a tribute to dancers who performed several times a day in London during the blitz, drawing large audiences who queued for hours. People also waited patiently for Myra Hess's free lunchtime concerts in the National Gallery, which were highly popular with servicemen and women. For John Masefield, the poet laureate, these occasions symbolised what the nation was fighting for:

> And the great pianist is here, the crowd
> *Has longed for this a week, a month, a year*
> *The freedom they enlist for is here,*
> *The larger life to which lives are vowed.*[46]

These concerts were also a striking reminder that embattled Britain represented that civilisation that had been so thoroughly extinguished in Europe.

The accompanying drawings of the servicemen in the audience gave no indication of their social background, although all are rankers or NCOs. Possibly they were from the lower middle and working classes, groups that normally preferred 'Bandbox' to classical piano pieces. If so, their presence at this concert would have pleased those government agencies that were then endeavouring to stimulate a greater interest in the creative arts and to broaden their audience. Servicemen, detached from the culture of their respective backgrounds, were thought to be susceptible to learning and understanding subjects that were new to them or would be considered as the preserve of their social superiors. This was why Allen Lane of Penguin began the Penguin Forces Club which followed his prewar policy of offering 'Good Books Cheap'. His pocket-sized books by serious writers offered an alternative to the coarse, tough, bloodthirsty 'pulp' and largely American fiction of the *No Orchids for Miss Blandish* genre that was favoured by the lower ranks.[47]

This process of mass enlightenment became government policy. Under the terms of the 1944 Education Act, local authorities were enjoined to expand facilities for adult education. These would complement and extend the cultural missionary work already being undertaken by the services and, in the words of the statute, would offer everyone the chance to enjoy 'a full and satisfying life' as part of a 'civilised community'. In the new Britain the working man and his wife would no longer be strangers in the art gallery or concert hall.

V

Putting the higher forms of culture in the way of the masses was a contribution towards the erosion of class barriers, which were seen, particularly on the left, as an obstacle to national unity and efficiency. In 1939 there were still 'Two Nations' in Britain and their mutual incomprehension seemed as great as it had been when Disraeli had coined the phrase nearly a hundred years before. The dispensation of favour and fortune was vividly described by a working-class soldier in North Africa:

> Have you ever heard of Class Distinction, sir? I'll tell you what it means, it means Vickers-Armstrong booking a profit to look like a loss, and Churchill lighting a new cigar, and the 'Times' explaining Liberty and Democracy, and me sitting on my arse in Libya splashing a fainting man with water out of a steel helmet. It's a very fine thing if you're in the right class – that's highly important sir, because one class gets the sugar and the other class gets the shit.[48]

This image of a polarised nation was common among the working classes for whom the world was split between 'Us' and 'Them'. 'Them' included the upper and middle classes who were viewed with distrust because they always managed to take care of their own interests.

Class distinction was not just about inequalities of income and possessions, although these mattered; it was about expectations. Reporting on the comforts and meals provided for Land Army girls at West Barsham Hall in Norfolk in January 1940, the owner observed that, 'They are all educated girls and therefore it has been necessary to provide greater comfort than would have been expected for working girls.'[49]

Education, or the lack of it, marked a person's place in society: there were those who left school at fourteen, and those who remained there until sixteen or eighteen. Of the latter, a proportion attended public schools, whose old boys' ties became associated with exclusiveness and arrogance of the ruling élite. In the August 1940 edition of *Horizon*, an anonymous young literary radical denounced those 'concentrations of snobbery, envy and caution' which, he hoped, would soon be 'bombed out of existence'. Five months later, readers of the magazine were reminded of how those at the top had let down the country in the previous war when, 'The thick-necked cavalry generals remained at the top, but the lower-middle classes and all the colonies came to the rescue.'[50] J. B. Priestley added to this assault on the nation's traditional leaders in his broadcast with references to 'Fat General Staffers' and 'Commanders in the Carlton Club' whose collective myopia and inertia could lose the war.[51]

Social animosity was a powerful political weapon. A *Daily Herald* cartoonist revealingly represented 'Unrestricted Private Enterprise' as a hunstman in the saddle brandishing his riding crop.[52] During the 1945 general election, the *Sunday Pictorial* reminded its predominantly working-class readership that one in five Tory candidates were Old Etonians, one in sixteen had been to grammar school and one in a hundred to elementary school.[53] A vote for the Conservatives would preserve inequalities and, it went without saying, ensure the return to power of the same vested interests that had dominated the country before the war.

Class prejudices and allegiances did not disappear during the war, however much they were deplored or blamed for restricting the war-effort. Togetherness might be accepted as an ideal, but people remained attached to what was familiar and reassuring. After meeting a 'very well educated' young artilleryman at a Harrogate dance, Sylvia Watts told her mother that she was bound to like him because 'he is "our" class of person.'[54] Old attitudes prevailed in many quarters. An ex-public school sailor on board the cruiser Penelope, who deserted his post when the ship was bombed, was sentenced by the captain to thirty days' imprisonment and given an admonition. 'The whole ship's company know your background, and they are intently watching this case. The very fact that you come from a public school, as I do, makes it impossible for me to show you leniency or to suspend your sentence.' A stoker charged with the same offence was let off with a caution in which he was reminded that his wife and children would suffer a loss in income if he was imprisoned.[55] Was the disparity of punishment an indication of the captain's wish to appear even-handed, or did he feel that the public school man had forfeited his honour by behaving in a way that was not expected from those of his background? One suspects the latter.

In the film Millions Like Us (1944) social barriers appear to be crumbling on the factory floor when the upper-class Anne Crawford falls in love with the foreman (Eric Portman). Marriage is out of the question for the moment, for the foreman suspects that the easing of social relations will prove temporary and peace will restore old barriers. Old habits of mind did return in 1945 and old hierarchies survived the war undamaged. There had been an increase in incomes for the working and middle classes, particularly when wives were working, but high taxation rates, shortages and rationing prevented any equivalent increase in consumption. It was changes in spending, together with rising incomes and the greater availability of goods, that turned out to be the great leveller. From the mid 1950s onwards, those who had lived through the war were invited to forget self-sacrifice and austerity and to indulge themselves in a wide range of enticing goods. 'You've never had it so good' materialism was the catalyst that dissolved social divisions – but not entirely, hence the continued pleas by politicians for the creation of a classless society.

One who voiced his dreams of a future without class was John Major, a former grammar school boy and product of the 1944 Education Act. Equally emphatic in his denunciation of class was Tony Blair, an alumnus of a public school. What each has said on this subject echoes wartime dogma, and, incidentally, repeats its questionable assumption that membership of a particular class is inseparable from endorsement of all its prejudices about both itself and other social groups. As reactions to evacuees indicated, the war did not eliminate class stereotypes.

Nor did the war eliminate discrimination against women. In all, seven million had jobs, just under half of all those aged between fifteen and forty-four, and their rates of pay were below those of men. A survey undertaken in 1943 showed that a quarter of working women were happy to give up their posts after the war, and 39 per cent believed that when peace came men deserved automatic precedence in the job market. Of those who wanted to remain in employment, 44 per cent had worked before the war.[56] This was far short of a revolution in terms of equality of opportunity, changing expectations or numbers of working women. Of course, the status of women had been enhanced and as in 1918 no one would deny the value of their contribution to the war-effort. As a curious acknowledgement of their endeavours, in May 1945 the RAF flew parties of WAAFs over German towns and cities where they could see the indirect results of their labours.[57]

And yet those who had predicted in 1940 that the war would produce far-reaching social changes were not entirely mistaken. Most imagined that the tempo of change would be faster than it in fact was and that new expectations would be swiftly fulfilled. What could not be predicted was the acceleration of changes in material comforts, outlook and ambitions which gathered momentum after 1945. In large part, this occurred not from measures designed to promote equality, although these were significant, but from increases in disposable income and the abundance of goods on which to spend it. The signs were already there just after the war; in 1945 just under eight thousand private cars were licensed, a total that rose to nearly 120,000 during 1946.

VI

The Second World War has become embedded in the national psyche and its position is now unassailable. Unlike the First, its contemplation does not provoke agonising over why it was fought and why such a colossal sacrifice was so sparsely rewarded. The commanders were not subsequently caricatured as mindless Blimps, and later generations have continued to admire Churchill. Those who fought the war received tangible compensation and the postwar years were marked by growing prosperity rather than chronic recession Above all, the British people can feel a justifiable pride in their defiance of Hitler in 1940 and their part in his final obliteration.

Because the war was fought for such positive and praiseworthy reasons, its history could be quarried without guilt by writers and film-makers in search of thrilling, intriguing or uplifting scenarios. Whether or not they were based upon actual incidents, and a great many were, wartime books and films commanded an immense and highly appreciative audience. Paul Brickhill's *The Dam Busters*, which described the destruction in May 1943 of the Mohne and Eder dams, has been in print for over fifty years and sold a million copies. It was filmed in 1955 with a stirring score by Eric Coates and the spectacular footage of the bouncing-bombs has become a familiar image. It was employed, together with the film's music, in the 1990s for an advertisement that showed how drinkers of Carlsberg lager could frustrate German holidaymakers' attempts to colonise swimming pools.

The Dam Busters was one of over a hundred films with wartime subjects made by British studios between 1945 and 1960, many of which were box-office success. Whether fictional or not, the genre presented the war in a heroic manner; brave men and women performed brave deeds, frequently against the odds and in a manner that often bordered on nonchalance. Favourite subjects were escapes from prisoner of war camps – *The Wooden Horse* (1953) – espionage and covert, behind-the-lines operations – *Odette* (1950) and *Carve Her Name with Pride* (1958) – and straightforward, dramatic accounts of operations – *The Battle of the River Plate* (1956) and *Sink the Bismarck* (1960).

Realism was avoided by directors. The charred corpses and skeletons in lifejackets that were described in Nicholas Monsarrat's *The Cruel Sea* were not reproduced in the screen version, but the film does show shipwreck survivors being hit by depth-charges. This incident emphasises the loneliness of a commander and the cruel choices he has to face, but elsewhere plots concentrate on the sort of individual resourcefulness and courage that G. A. Henty would have applauded. It was exemplified by such actors as Kenneth More, John Mills, Dirk Bogarde and Jack Hawkins whose clipped accents and mannerisms were very much those of the traditional officer class. Richard Todd, who starred in *The Dam Busters*, explained that its cast of former officers gave verisimilitude to the 'breezy, friendly atmosphere' of an RAF officers' mess.[58]

The other ranks, like Pistol, Bardolph and Nym in *Henry V*, tend to be roguish or comical stereotypes, leaving the stiff-upper-lipped officers to fill the centre stage. Their attitudes invited parody. In the early 1960s, a *Beyond the Fringe* skit had an officer calling for a 'futile gesture' to be made in the interest of national morale – just the sort of request to which Richard Todd would have responded. Not everyone was amused. One incensed theatregoer, who appeared to be a former officer, shouted out: 'What do you young bounders know about it?' Not much, would probably have been the answer, but the impudent satirists would have undergone national service and, like many others, poked fun at the many absurdities of army life. As it was, like their predecessors, the post-1945 war films and the impression of the conflict they conveyed were destined for a long, probably indefinite life. Since the 1960s they have been and still are regularly shown on television, providing new generations with a version of the war that conveys more of its spirit than of the reality of the battlefield.

The spirit of 1940 is matchlessly conveyed in *Dad's Army*, an affectionate television comedy series which traces the misadventures of a Home Guard platoon based in a south-coast town. Script and characters ring true to time and place: the amateurs of Warmington-on-Sea are easily flummoxed by the demands of military efficiency, refuse to relinquish their civilian rights, suffer the taunts of the rest of the community and fall victim to blunders of their own making. But we know that when put to the test, they and their pompous, prickly and often bewildered commander, Captain Mainwaring, will sell their lives dearly, for their sense of purpose is indomitable.

Television has also enabled the story of the war to be retold through documentaries, and specific episodes to be scrutinised, sometimes microscopically. Contemporary footage is superabundant, revelations are still to be made (particularly concerning wartime intelligence-gathering), and plenty of participants are glad to relate their experiences, often with remarkable candour. During the last decade of the twentieth century, there was a huge upsurge in popular interest in the war. Anniversaries of the war's outbreak, conclusion, the evacuation of Dunkirk, the Battle of Britain and the D-Day landings were publicly and emotionally celebrated. Veterans congregate, revisit old battle-fields and exchange stories with each other and attendant news reporters. Each occasion produces a crop of documentaries and the rerunning of old films on television, and schoolchildren have been encouraged to ransack their grandparents' memories to discover what it was really like and to rummage in attics for abandoned gas-masks, ration books and medals. The war has become central to school syllabuses already heavily weighted towards the twentieth century; and, in recent years, the Holocaust has tended to crowd out other subjects so that schoolchildren may end up knowing more about the Final Solution than, say, why and how the Allies won.

Accuracy is still a sensitive issue. Twice in the last ten years there have been lengthy lawsuits in which wartime events have been minutely picked over to discover the truth. In the first, a jury awarded Lord Aldington an astonishing one million pounds after he had been libelled by Nikolai Tolstoy, who had accused him of being a war criminal. The allegation concerned events in the early summer of 1945 when Aldington had been involved in the repatriation of Soviet and Yugoslav renegades and deserters who had fought alongside the Nazis. Their surrender had been agreed among the Allies at the Yalta Conference, some of the deportees had committed atrocities and nearly all were subsequently executed for treason, although a small number were genuine refugees. During 1999, the writer David Irvine defended himself in another protracted libel trial in which he failed to refute the charge that he had 'denied' the Holocaust. What is interesting about the two cases is that at heart each concerned an ethical issue: if Tolstoy had been correct, then British troops had been accomplices to a crime; and, if Irvine was to be believed, the Nazi leadership's culpability in the murder of Europe's Jews was minimal. Had either been vindicated, then the moral battlelines of the war would have had to have been redrawn.

The immense media interest in both cases provided further evidence of how the war continues to command the public's attention. Hollywood has responded, resuscitated the large-scale war epic and made significant changes to provide the authenticity audiences can now take without flinching. Television pictures transmitted directly from the front line in Vietnam during the late 1960s and early 1970s gave everyone the opportunity to see exactly what a battlefield looked like, and documentaries have also accustomed the public to the realities of war. *Saving Private Ryan* (1998) opened with horrific scenes of the D-Day landing on Omaha Beach in which soldiers were mangled and shattered. More of the same, in terms of scale and realism, are offered in *Enemy at the Gate* (set against the battle for Stalingrad) and *Pearl Harbor*, both released in 2001.

The political and psychological context of this recent resurgence of interest in the war is important. At the end of 1988 the Cold War finished and the prospect of a third global war between the great powers vanished. For the first time since 1945, people no longer had to contemplate the possibility of a new conflict which, given the immense nuclear and conventional arsenals of the adversaries, was bound to be infinitely more destructive than the Second World War. With Europe, America and Russia on the threshold of an era of peace and stability, it became possible to consider the last war without wondering what it might teach us about the next. Other, more fundamental questions remain, and help explain the hold that the Second World War, and, for that matter, its predecessor, have over our imaginations. Individuals from generations that have experienced peace ask themselves what they would have done if they had been drawn into a war. Would they have overcome fear, been willing to sacrifice their lives, endured the loss of familiar comforts and found the inner will to see it through come what may? The corpus of war literature and films of all kinds does not provide the answers, but it does give inquirers an idea of how people like themselves coped.

Wartime behaviour is now considered a model for how people ought to react in a national crisis. When one occurs, the press inevitably summons up the spirit of the blitz, that peculiarly British distillation which enables the nation to improvise and carry on calmly with an often mordant humour. Invocations of the spirit of 1940 were common during the autumn of 2000 when Britain successively faced temporary fuel shortages and the sudden disintegration of the railway network. A few months afterwards, younger inhabitants of Ambridge spoke admiringly of the older Mrs Archer's 'old wartime spirit' when, like the rest of the farming community, she was faced with the possibility of foot and mouth disease.[59] Listeners would have understood exactly what was meant, although it is absurd to compare having to live through six years of intermittent bombardment, uncertainty and deprivation with having to cycle to work for a few days or confronting a temporarily empty supermarket shelf.

How the country faced up to wartime adversities is now an integral part of Britishness. The war years have become an extension of that happier but sadly lost age known as 'the good old days'. In the popular imagination, it was a time when the country counted for something, was united and determined, and its lean, fit inhabitants supported each other in a generous, neighbourly manner. Romanticised or not, our simple perceptions of this period have become a source of regret and moral unease at a time when egoism and greed appear to be out of control.

8

A normal hazard: Cold War and hot war, 1945–98

I

Labour's election victory was good news for airmen in India who imagined that it would expedite their demobilisation. They were wrong, and during the winter and spring of 1945 to 1946 their impatience turned to anger. The result was a spate of strikes and demonstrations which the authorities called mutinies. Subsequent investigations by the RAF security police revealed that fifteen of the thirty-one ringleaders were communists and uncovered a network of communist 'cells' spread across units in India and Aden. The director of MI5, Sir Percy Sillitoe, wondered whether the incidents were part of a sinister conspiracy; the mutinies had harmed British prestige in India, always a source of concern for the authorities there, and had coincided with Russian political intrigues in central Asia.[1] Within a year of the war's ending, Britain's former ally had become a bogeyman, bent on expansion and with a limitless capacity for mischief-making.

The Cold War had started. Its origins could be traced to the winter of 1944 to 1945 when senior British and American diplomats, strategists and politicians began to express disquiet about Russian contrariness in dealing with its allies and its future ambitions in eastern and south-eastern Europe. It ended in December 1988, when Mikhail Gorbachev announced the withdrawal of Soviet forces from Poland, East Germany,

Czechoslovakia and Hungary, and the dissolution of the Warsaw Pact which had bound them to Russia for the preceding thirty-eight years. Any chance of the Cold War resuming disappeared in 1991 to 1992 with the dismantling of the Soviet Union.

Throughout its existence, the Cold War was about perceptions of danger and assumptions of motive. It resolved itself into a contest in which the antagonists tested each other's willpower and endeavoured to secure political and strategic advantage through propaganda, espionage and intimidation. The course of the Cold War was unpredictable and, particularly between 1958 and 1962, there were some nerve-racking crises, first over Berlin and then Cuba. These highlighted the inherent risk of a real war breaking out. If it did, there was every reason to believe that both sides would resort to nuclear weapons and Europe would experience a third world war in which the devastation would be far greater than in the previous two, and the chances of national and individual survival far less. Preparations for this conflict were intensive, for it became axiomatic that if one contestant showed signs of lagging behind in the arms race, the other would exploit its advantage.

There was plenty of conventional fighting, since the western and eastern blocs were willing to wage war by proxy in Asia, Africa, the Middle East and Central America in order to defend or extend their spheres of political influence. The by-products of nuclear confrontation in Europe were wars in Korea, Malaya, Vietnam, Angola, Afghanistan and Nicaragua and between America's unofficial ally Israel and its Arab neighbours. Wherever possible the two superpowers preferred to let their local clients do the fighting, providing them with cash, arms and technical guidance. This arrangement broke down in Korea in 1950 to 1951, when America and its allies had to rescue the South Koreans, and China the communist North Koreans. Similarly, the United States was compelled to commit large forces to support its faltering dependants in South Vietnam in the late 1960s, and the Soviet Union was driven to invade and occupy Afghanistan in 1979. Neither intervention proved decisive, and when it became clear that both wars were unwinnable there were widespread domestic protests, particularly from conscripts and their families.

Britain was deeply involved in the Cold War. In terms of resources, it was a second-rank participant in a contest between the postwar superpowers, Russia and the United States. Nonetheless, successive governments, both Labour and Conservative, were convinced that Britain remained a 'great power' with international prestige and responsibilities, although these diminished as the Empire was dissolved. As late as 1966, substantial British forces, including eighty warships, were still stationed in the Far East. They had gone within two years, a sign that it was becoming harder and harder for the country to pay the price of global status.

Waging the Cold War turned out to be an expensive business. In 1951, 10 per cent of Britain's gross national product was being spent on defence, although subsequent governments struggled to keep the proportion down to 7 per cent. This figure was the source of agonising by Macmillan's cabinet in February 1964, when it debated whether to spend sixty million pounds on a fifth Polaris-carrying nuclear submarine. If, the service chiefs warned, a coincidence of routine refitting and accidents put the other four out of action, then Britain's nuclear deterrent would be useless. For over a decade, atomic and nuclear weapons had been considered a good return on investment. In 1952 the price of a twenty kiloton bomb was one million pounds, which prompted one Admiralty analyst to remark that it represented 'a reasonable exchange' for an aircraft-carrier which had cost fourteen million pounds. This was confirmed by experts who calculated that an atom bomb of a quarter of that size could sink any warship within a thousand yards of its point of detonation.[2]

Cheapness was only comparative when it came to defence estimates. Soon after the outbreak of the Korean War in 1950, the cabinet allocated £4.7 billion to a hurried, three-year rearmament programme. By 1975 the annual defence budget had risen to £5.3 billion and at the conclusion of the Cold War in 1988 to 1989, after a period of inflation, it had reached nineteen billion pounds. To begin with at least, these charges were a heavy imposition on a nation whose economy was beginning to flourish and which was faced with an unexpectedly high bill for new welfare services. The impact of the spiralling defence costs was soon felt; medical prescription charges had to be introduced and a balance of payments surplus of £307 million in 1950 became a £369 million deficit the following year. Ironically, given the problems of competitiveness that would bedevil Britain in the second half of the twentieth century, its future rivals, Japan and Germany, were then on the threshold of their economic 'miracles'. How far Britain's growth was retarded as a consequence of inflated defence expenditure during the Cold War remains one of the great 'what ifs' of recent history.

And yet a period of unparalleled peacetime military spending was also one in which standards of living rose as never before. The Cold War coincided with an era of prosperity in which people earned more and had more to spend it on; Britons had never been richer. Some became wealthy as a direct consequence of the Cold War. Government contracts and subsidies for research and development created a flourishing arms industry whose sophisticated products were eagerly sought abroad. In 1975 exports of weaponry were worth £447 million, and in 1995 five billion pounds, one-fifth of the world's arms trade. By that date, the armaments industry was employing ninety thousand, a consideration that carried some weight in countering moral criticism of a business whose customers included some of the world's most brutal tyrannies.

There were other domestic repercussions from the Cold War. The postwar decision to retain forces in West Germany for its defence in the event of a Russian invasion, together with the maintenance of the imperial garrison, forced the Labour government to take a step that would have been unthinkable in the past: the introduction of peacetime conscription. The 1947 National Service Act drafted all eighteen-year-olds for eighteen months in the services, a term that was extended to two years during the Korean War. After discharge, national servicemen spent four years in the reserves, ready for immediate recall in an emergency.

Over the next ten years nearly 1.3 million young men were conscripted. They formed the backbone of another innovation, the British Army of the Rhine (BAOR), a force permanently deployed on the continent. National servicemen also replaced sepoys in Middle and Far Eastern garrisons after Indian and Pakistani independence in 1947 deprived Britain of that invaluable reservoir of manpower, the Indian army. In Palestine, Kenya and Cyprus, national servicemen were engaged in operations against nationalist guerrillas. National servicemen were also involved in Cold War conflicts; they fought against communist partisans in French Indochina in 1945 to 1946, against regular

Chinese and North Korean forces in Korea, and between 1948 and 1954 helped defeat communist insurgents in Malaya.

Even with the influx of draftees, Britain's armed forces were stretched to breaking-point by imperial and Cold War commitments. In 1950 the Admiralty was hard pressed to find men and ships to cope with the unlooked-for crisis that followed Iran's nationalisation of the Abadan oilfields and refineries.[3] In the meantime, the War and Colonial Offices were examining plans to recruit an army of four hundred thousand men from Britain's African colonies, and pleas were sent to Commonwealth states for men and aircraft for operations in Malaya and the Middle East garrisons.[4] The manpower problem was solved by gradual withdrawal from the Middle East and the decision taken in 1957 to concentrate resources on an independent nuclear arsenal. National Service was abolished (Macmillan feared that its perpetuation might become an awkward political issue) and henceforward Britain's armed services would be manned by professionals.

Britain had become a nuclear power as a direct consequence of the Cold War. And yet, even if relations with the Soviet Union had stabilised in the immediate postwar period, it is highly likely that Britain would have seriously considered developing nuclear weapons. They were, as successive politicians insisted, an advertisement that Britain was still a 'great power'. Like the dreadnought before 1914, the atomic bomb was a prestigious status symbol. This was certainly how it appeared to Ernest Bevin, the foreign secretary, who in February 1947 persuaded a small cabinet committee that it was imperative for Britain to develop its own nuclear weapons. If, as was extremely likely, Russia obtained them, then Stalin could extort whatever he wanted. It would be 'Munich all over again', Bevin predicted, and Greece, Turkey and Iran would be seized by the Soviets.[5]

Bevin assumed that no reliance could be placed upon America. In August 1946 its government had repudiated the 1943 Quebec agreement by which the two powers shared atomic research. There was no guarantee that the United States would defend Europe if the Russians attacked, and the British chiefs of staff believed that when they did, they would advance to the Rhine and possibly beyond. In this event Britain might expect an aerial attack by conventional, biological, chemical and, once Russia had produced them, atomic weapons.[6] For

Britain not to adopt a nuclear programme was a reckless gamble with its own and western Europe's security. It did so in the knowledge that it might have to use the threat of employing atomic bombs to forestall any Soviet aggression in Europe and possibly the Middle East.

Within two years the international situation had changed dramatically. Through the Truman doctrine, the Marshall Plan and NATO (North Atlantic Treaty Organisation), the United States had provided unequivocal proof that it would do all in its power to checkmate Russia in Europe and elsewhere. Henceforward, Britain became again what she had been between 1941 and 1945, America's junior partner and helpmate. It performed these tasks at the same time as claiming to be a 'great power', a status that was enhanced by what British politicians still call the 'special relationship' with the United States. This comforting commonplace obscured hard economic, military and political facts of life. Britain was the subordinate partner in the alliance and, whenever interests diverged, as they did in the Middle East in the 1950s, America's prevailed.

Nor, as has sometimes been assumed, did this special relationship give British prime ministers the intimate confidence of American presidents at moments of crisis, or the power to restrain them. When, after the Chinese intervention in the Korean War in November 1950, President Truman publicly hinted that he might use the atom bomb, Attlee flew to Washington to dissuade him. The prime minister was informed that the weapon would only be dropped in response to a 'major military disaster' and he went home satisfied. In private, the president insisted that he would never tolerate 'Limeys' interfering in strategic decisions. Several atomic bombs were sent to Guam the following April in readiness for use against the Russians, who were mobilising in Manchuria for what the Americans feared might be an attack on Japan.[7] The mistaken belief that Attlee had moderated American policy prompted the Labour leader Hugh Gaitskell to urge Macmillan to do the same and fly to Washington at the onset of the Cuban missile crisis in October 1962.[8]

Britain's geographical position made it an ideal Cold War ally for America. If the Soviet Union flexed its muscles provocatively or made encroachments on the territory of any NATO member, Britain was designated as the staging-post for American reinforcements and the base for an aerial offensive. Britain's future role was demonstrated in June 1948 after the Russians had imposed a land blockade on the British, American and French zones in Berlin. In answer, the United States sent sixty B-29 bombers to its airfields in Britain. Although none had yet been adapted to carry atomic bombs, the implication of the gesture was clear. America's 'Trojan' war plan of 1949 included nuclear bombardment of Russian cities by aircraft based in Britain. It was estimated that between three and five million would be killed and twenty-eight million made homeless.[9]

II

On the outer fringes of the Conservative and Labour parties there was a degree of resentment about a strategy that seemed to relegate Britain to the status of an American aircraft-carrier, permanently anchored off the coast of Europe. Or, put in another, less emotive way, Britain was now playing the same role that Malta and a string of similarly well-sited imperial garrisons had during the heyday of Empire.

Subordination to America was bound to affect the psyche of a nation that had helped win the last war and was still proud of its international and imperial status. At the onset of the 1956 Suez crisis, many politicians, newspaper editors and Conservative and Labour supporters welcomed the chance to demonstrate to the world that Britain was still a power that made things happen, rather than one to which things happened. The jingoes were disappointed; the subsequent, brief war against Egypt confirmed the existing dispensation of power. Under American pressure, Anglo-French forces retired, and during the next few years the United States replaced Britain in the Middle East.

There were other, equally galling indications of inequality. Imported American films, popular music, comics, slang, television programmes and, in time, fast food became evidence of what was known as 'cultural imperialism'. A sense of endangered identity, together with jealousy, snobbery and awareness of relative impotence, became the ingredients of both visceral and intellectual anti-Americanism. Paradoxically, it was an unintended product of the Cold War and, to many Americans, seemed like ingratitude. Anti-Americanism has survived the Cold War and has intruded into the current debate about Britain's relations with another consequence of the Cold War, the European Union. The institutions and agencies that now form the European Union had their origins in efforts to strengthen western Europe through economic and political integration which were prompted by the Cold War. America encouraged closer European harmony and co-operation, believing that they would provided the stability needed to resist communism. The decade after the collapse of communism has witnessed intermittent bickering between America and the European Union, mostly over trade and security. Discord between the United States and Europe has been reflected in Britain by a debate about whether the country should disengage from the latter and attach itself more closely to the former.

During the Cold War, British hostility towards America was strongest on the left, where there was a residual sympathy towards communism, and on the far right, which had never come to terms with the loss of the Empire. The Vietnam War briefly transformed anti-Americanism into a political force which expressed itself in several mass demonstrations outside the United States embassy in London. Students were prominent among the protesters, as they were in the ranks of the Campaign for Nuclear Disarmament (CND) which had been founded in 1957.

CND's purpose was to persuade the government to make a grand moral gesture by renouncing nuclear weapons and destroying those it possessed. It was assumed that Britain still enjoyed the same moral authority that it had in the last century, when it had successively outlawed the slave trade and then slavery itself. The rest of the world followed, admittedly gradually and sometimes reluctantly, and CND supporters believed that it would do the same if Britain abandoned its atomic and nuclear arsenal. Idealism would prove contagious. Furthermore, by jettisoning its atomic weapons, Britain would detach itself from the bipolar politics of the Cold War and free itself from American influence. 'We could become a great third force in this world with our traditions and knowledge and all our experience,' predicted R. Willis, a trade union delegate to Labour's October 1961 conference.[10] Greatness beckoned again.

Making converts among Labour and trade union activists was part of CND's strategy. Publicity was provided by the movement's annual

Easter march from the nuclear research establishment at Aldermaston to Trafalgar Square. CND grew rapidly and the 1961 march attracted a hundred thousand demonstrators. Its popularity was understandable, given that the Cold War was in the middle of a fraught and bad-tempered phase. In November 1958 the Soviet leader Nikita Khrushchev, had demanded the evacuation of West Berlin to stem the growing exodus of often talented East Germans. At one stage up to three thousand fugitives were crossing the border each day, attracted by the freedom and opportunities of the west. During the summer of 1961, there was the prospect of a second land blockade and with it the possibility of a collision between Warsaw Pact forces and a NATO relief convoy. For a time, President Kennedy contemplated a possible nuclear response.[11] 'Berlin was not worth a war,' declared one delegate at the 1961 Labour conference, while, in Berlin, American and Soviet tanks faced each over Checkpoint Charlie with their guns loaded.

Nuclear war appeared both unavoidable and imminent. In 1961 the scientific guru C. P. Snow predicted one within the next ten years, adding portentously: 'I am saying this as responsibly as I can; *that* is a certainty.'[12] Relying on the unprovable and untestable assumption that the Soviet Union would not drop atomic bombs on a neutral, disarmed Britain, CND offered a means to evade Armageddon. The hope of survival attracted many followers. There were British communists and those on the outskirts of the Labour party and trade union movement who claimed that Soviet belligerence had been exaggerated and the communist system provided justice, prosperity and happiness for those who lived under it. This was the line that had been unswervingly followed by the eighty-seven-year-old Melita Norwood, who was exposed as a Russian spy in September 1999. A communist and CND supporter, she had been recruited into Soviet intelligence in 1937 by Andrew Rothstein, the leader of the British communist party, and had delivered secret atomic data to her employer. By doing so, she had hoped to 'prevent the defeat of a new system which had at great cost given ordinary people food and fares they could afford, a good education and health service'.[13] This was a remarkable testament to purblind faith. Communism had delivered these benefits, but sparingly and unevenly, and, as the implosion of Russia and the Warsaw Pact nations had shown, the price had been economic mismanagement, shortages, pollution and distant governments that ruled by a mixture of secret police surveillance and coercion.

Ideologues like Norwood were outnumbered by Christian and secular pacifists; the Anglican canon Lewis Collins and the philosopher Bertrand Russell, a veteran of the First World War anti-conscription campaign, were among its leaders. There were also those who were genuinely frightened by the human and physical consequences of a nuclear war and its aftermath of desolation and contamination. This anxiety was felt most strongly by the young. They recognised that such a conflict would rob them of their futures and were impatient with their elders, who seemed either unable or unwilling to halt what appeared to be an irreversible slide towards catastrophe. On 24 October 1962, as the Cuban missile crisis began to unfold, forty sixth-formers from Midhurst Grammar School in Sussex refused to attend lessons. Instead, they wrote a letter to Macmillan in which they deplored the way in which the world had been allowed to reach a situation 'in which war is imminent'. Their headmaster was sympathetic.[14] Students were plentiful among the crowds that protested in various cities and towns on 17 to 20 October. Many adopted Gandhi's methods of passive resistance and sat or lay down in public places, waiting for the police to carry them off and charge them with obstruction. When found guilty, some chose brief imprisonment rather than pay a fine and so secured a form of martyrdom.

Not all students took to the streets to demonstrate that week. Mischievous Sheffield students used the missile crisis for a hoax in which they set up newspaper vendors' placards inscribed 'War Declared, Official'. The culprits were suspended by the university.[15] A student of my acquaintance blew all that remained of his grant on a binge, believing it might be his last, and spent the rest of the term living off the charity of friends.

During the 1960s, CND converted many young men and women, particularly the radically inclined and better educated. These were more numerous than ever, for the government's expansion of universities (in part a reaction to alarms over the superiority of Soviet education) had increased the numbers of students from 113,00 in 1961 to over two hundred thousand in 1969. Funded by the state, as the right-wing press constantly reminded its readers, students filled the ranks of CND and the closely allied protest movements against apartheid in South Africa and the war in Vietnam.

Early in 1965, CND attempted to proselytise servicemen with a leaflet that suggested that as accomplices to nuclear war they were no different from the Nazis who had herded people into gas-chambers. There was a tiny trickle of pacifist converts, including some national servicemen. Much to their displeasure, they discovered that while conscientious objection was a valid reason for exemption from national service, there were no legal provisions to release those who subsequently changed their minds. Some who did found themselves in detention for disobedience.[16]

In spite of repeated efforts by CND activists in the trade unions and constituency parties, the Labour party rejected unilateralism. The postwar party consensus on nuclear weapons remained unshaken and disarmament never became a vote-winner. Pacifist and anti-nuclear candidates stood at Bromley in the two 1964 general elections, and got under five hundred votes each time, and at Twickenham where one secured 1073 votes. In 1966, CND-backed candidates fared even worse, with under two hundred votes in Fulham and less than three hundred in Hull North. Although New Labour's cabinet contains former CND supporters, it is determined to retain Britain's nuclear arsenal and has allocated large funds for the purchase of the latest American missile, Trident.

Britain's largest pacifist movement failed. Marches, sit-downs and protracted vigils by groups of women camped outside American bases at Greenham Common and Molesworth in the 1980s had no appreciable effect on Britain's nuclear policy. This is surprising, given that opinion polls revealed an underlying apprehension about a nuclear war among a large section of the population. In 1982, 70 per cent of the country admitted to being worried about a nuclear war, and 38 per cent felt certain that one would occur. The young were particularly fearful; in 1984, 52 per cent of teenagers believed that a nuclear war might break out during their lifetime, and 70 per cent were convinced it was unavoidable.[17] CND never benefited from this fatalism, perhaps because it was unable to convince people that renunciation of nuclear weapons would automatically guarantee immunity from nuclear attack. Furthermore, perceptions of national weakness during the Munich crisis remained strong.

Nevertheless, CND's persistence and methods of persuasion have served as models for subsequent single-issue groups such as Amnesty International and Greenpeace. The latter campaigns against anything that increases global warming, which, from the 1970s onwards, has largely replaced nuclear war as a source of mass anxiety. Imagining a future catastrophe of unprecedented proportions has become a peculiarly twentieth-century phenomenon: the prewar generation trembled in contemplation of aerial bombardment and gas; the postwar generation dreaded nuclear war; and the present generation is disturbed by the consequences of global warming.

Even if CND had convinced a government to abandon nuclear weapons, there is no indication that other nations would have followed suit. Atomic and nuclear armouries were symbols of prestige, independence and international clout, as they had been for Britain in 1947. 'Hoorah for France,' exclaimed General de Gaulle on hearing the news of his country's first atomic bomb test in 1960. 'Since this morning she is stronger and prouder.' Likewise, India and Pakistan tested nuclear weapons and intermediate range missiles in 1998 as proof that they were nascent global powers that would have to be heeded in the future. The new Russian Federation, like Britain in the 1940s and 1950s, is strapped for cash and, therefore, has concentrated its resources on nuclear rather than conventional forces, again conscious of the equation between nuclear muscle and global status.[18]

NATO still retains its stock of nuclear warheads and delivery systems despite the conclusion of the Cold War. Ever since 1954, the alliance had accepted the possibility that it would open an exchange of nuclear weapons in the event of numerically superior Warsaw Pact forces gaining the upper hand in a conventional battle. The knowledge that, if necessary, NATO would launch a 'first strike' fitted with theories of deterrence in so far as the Warsaw Pact was thereby restrained from exploiting its advantages in manpower, tanks and aircraft. Of course, the bluff might be called and the stakes raised to the point where strategic weapons would be launched and cities eliminated. The rapid accumulation of warheads and missiles by both sides during the 1960s created a doomsday scenario which American strategists called mutually assured destruction (MAD). Such traditional concepts as victory and defeat were no longer valid.

III

Preparing for a war that never was concentrated the intelligence and energies of legions of scientists and planners. They evaluated weaponry, assessed its battleworthiness and constructed and analysed conjectural situations to create models for forms of crisis management that could be applied to stop a helter-skelter slide into war. Beyond these academic investigations, there was all manner of popular speculation as to how a nuclear war might start and what might be its consequences for ordinary people. A world apparently living on the edge of an abyss was morbidly fascinated by what it might contain.

The unthinkable has become the impenetrable. A decade or so after the end of the Cold War, the British government is still chary about releasing precise details of plans for a nuclear offensive and what measures would be introduced if Britain suffered such an attack. To start with at least, a degree of resilience was confidently expected. An Admiralty analysis of 1956 imagined that if the Suez Canal was destroyed by a Soviet atomic bomb, 'a rotation of men' using earth-moving machinery would be able to reopen the waterway within four months. In the same time, Port Said would be restored to operational efficiency, a conclusion based on another, still secret, report that had examined the effects of an atomic attack on Liverpool.[19] The problems of residual contamination or persistent radioactive particles in the atmosphere seem to have been overlooked.

Everyone concerned with preparing for a nuclear battle had some inkling of what to expect after an atomic or thermonuclear device had exploded. There was extensive material gathered by the Americans from Hiroshima and Nagasaki; British observers had watched the American bomb tests on the Bikini Atoll in 1946; and, from 1952 onwards, Britain conducted its own tests on the Monte Bello Islands, fifty miles off the coast of Western Australia, and at Woomera. Between April and September 1957, a series of thermonuclear tests were held at Christmas Island in the south-west Pacific. All were massive operations, involving aircraft, warships, scientists, senior officers and forces personnel, including national servicemen. Precise data were gathered, recording the effects of the explosive flash, blast waves, radiation and the behaviour of minute radioactive debris or fallout. Measurements were made of subsequent levels of contamination in the area around the test site. In so much as it reveals in what condition and for how long human beings might survive nuclear explosions, this corpus of knowledge has been confined to those whose job it is to prepare fighting men and civilians for atomic and thermonuclear war. Publicly available material on this subject is still sparse, but enough has filtered through to provide glimpses of the official version of how Britain might have fared under nuclear bombardment.

Radiation was obviously a primary concern. Relying on information collected earlier, officials responsible for the 1956 Monte Bello test expected contaminated particles to drift at least forty miles downwind. 'The dust hazard could exist indefinitely,' in spite of 'washing away or other dispersal'. Radiation measurements indicated that aircraft flying two hundred miles from the point of detonation absorbed twelve Roentgens, and those closer just over twice that amount. Neither dosage would have caused sickness, but these readings were sufficient to warrant a ten-hour ban on flights within a four-hundred-mile radius of the next tests.[20] Human reactions to gamma rays were also monitored. It was correctly acknowledged that there would be biological variations in how individuals would respond to exposure, with a 'fraction of one per cent' of the population having a 'low threshold'. For the rest, 'unfissioned material' would be naturally eliminated from the body during its lifetime, but, 'it is advisable not to increase the body burden beyond that recommended, as the effect cannot be predicted.'[21]

Contact with radiation levels of one hundred Roentgens and over would make half the victims seriously ill. 'Those not obviously ill would equally have been harmed and it is thought that a number of them would break down under mental and physical stress more readily than before,' concluded a 1952 Admiralty assessment of a nuclear attack on warships. This was an overestimate, although the blood-cell counts of those exposed to this level of radiation (two hundred Roentgens would be fatal) would have been reduced. Survivors were expected to be 'less reliable' but could be kept on operational duties.[22] It was, therefore, imperative that sailors should become accustomed to considering atomic weapons as 'a normal hazard of war that is understood and countered in a rational manner'.[23] In the event of seamen facing nuclear attack, it was to be remembered that half the radiation would be absorbed in the first second after detonation and that 'dosimeters' would be available to diagnose cases. Drill would be invaluable. It would have to be; an assessment of a nuclear attack on a warship suggested that its crew would successively face three seconds of intense heat, and ninety seconds of blast waves and radiation.

Afterwards they would be exposed to a 'radioactive mist' (i.e. fallout) which would emit radiation and could last for hours or 'possibly days and even weeks'.[24] This would prove the greatest and most enduring hazard of nuclear war because the radioactive particles would be driven by the wind and easily absorbed.

Sealing a ship against radiation was one countermeasure. It was used on board the destroyer *Diana*, which had been earmarked to enter the fallout zone and collect samples during the May 1956 test. Protective clothing was available for men whose duties forced them to leave the 'citadel', but none of it was suitable. The plastic 'Windscale Alpha Suit', used at the ill-fated atomic power station that was renamed 'Sellafield', was too fragile, and a fabric suit had no hood and was too uncomfortable and heavy.[25] Eye damage was another hazard faced by the crew of the *Diana* and others participating in these tests. A 1957 Air Ministry memo on nuclear warfare reassured medical officers that 'actual experience' had shown that the eye seeing an atomic flash twenty-five miles distant and twenty-five degrees from the line of sight recovered from blindness within five minutes.[26] Whether this 'actual experience' was that of men who had been told to turn their backs and cover their eyes is not known. Those who took these precautions recalled that for a moment they could see the bones of their fingers against the light.[27]

In time, British units serving with NATO were issued with protective overgarments, gloves, boots and respirators so that they could maintain fighting efficiency after a nuclear or chemical bombardment. This gear offered a barrier against thermal blast but not residual radiation.[28] New dosimeters appeared in 1982 but, like their predecessors, they could sap morale; once the fighting man discovered that he was suffering from radiation, his natural impulse was to give up and get away.[29]

What emerges from the fragmentary information available from British nuclear tests is that there was a vast blank area: the long-term consequences of exposure to radiation. Nor could anyone tell for how long the land around the test sites would remain contaminated. Time has provided some answers. It was not just certain people who were more vulnerable than others to radiation, but certain organs. As the dissemination of airborne radioactive particles after the 1986 Chernobyl disaster revealed, these caused cancer in the thyroid, a gland close to the skin's surface. Exposure to radiation could also trigger leukaemia by accelerating the proliferation of white blood cells in the bone marrow. Depleted uranium, employed for conventional explosive warheads during the 1999 Kosovo campaign, may also be carcinogenic. Just how far contact with gamma rays as opposed to radioactive debris can be directly linked to subsequent cancers remains a contentious issue, and it should be remembered that currently one in four of the population is likely to contract some form of cancer.

What would be the experience of civilians in a nuclear war? This question has perturbed successive governments because addressing it calls into question the theory of mutual deterrence. Providing civil defence measures was an admission that things might go terribly wrong, a point often made by CND which took a great interest in this potentially embarrassing subject. It also exercised the imagination of science-fiction writers. In a plot that closely parallels the physical results of a nuclear war, John Christopher's *Death of Grass* imagines a plague that destroys grass, and the nation slides into anarchy. A well-armed group of survivors establishes a defended sanctuary in a remote Cumberland valley, where they are beset by starving marauders from devastated cities. A primeval world replaces a civilised one, just as it had done in Britain during and after the twilight of Roman rule. Alan Watkins's semi-documentary *The War Game* (1965) realistically chronicles events after a nuclear attack in which there is panic and mayhem. Public order dissolves and there are scenes in which looters are executed by police firing squads and a policeman shoots dying, mutilated victims of the blast. The film was banned by the BBC on the grounds that it would scare the elderly, children and those 'of a nervous disposition'. It certainly would have generated despondency and dispelled any notion that the British would behave in the next war as they had in the last.

Before 1960, civil defence plans were largely based on wartime experience and the knowledge that the Soviet Union possessed limited stocks of nuclear weapons. As these increased in number, it became obvious that the scale of devastation would be vast. Prime targets were military and industrial complexes, including the plutonium-manufacturing power station at Sellafield. Many were close to cities and towns and civilian casualties were expected. Estimates of these varied depending on wind direction, but figures of between six and eight million were forecast. Many would be suffering from radiation burns and the effects of blast, and the medical authorities would face the predicament of whether or not to treat those whose chances of survival were minimal. There were also the long-term problems of homelessness, disrupted communications and power supplies and, most serious of all, climatic aberrations. The so-called 'nuclear winter' might last two years, paralyse agriculture and produce a protracted famine.

Keeping up to fourteen days' supply of food was among the suggestions made by the government to households in leaflets on civil defence. Advice was also offered on how to improvise a radiation-proof room. Early in the 1980s, when there was a revival of official interest in the civil defence programme, various firms offered to construct private shelters which cost between six and eight thousand pounds.[30] Underground bunkers were already available for ministers, service chiefs and civil servants who had to be preserved in order to co-ordinate relief work and govern what was left of the country. The location of these 'regional centres of government' was kept secret, but CND uncovered some and held demonstrations near them. Two, near Anstruther in Fife and at Kelvedon Hatch in Essex, have been sold and made into tourist attractions. The latter was built in 1962 and contained desks, telephones, a generator, a television studio, a decontamination unit, food supplies (oatmeal blocks and canned soup) and living accommodation. The bunker was occasionally attacked by Territorial Army units, presumably acting as Soviet saboteurs and fifth columnists, and was once occupied by two hundred or so administrators as part of another simulation exercise. When this occurred, local people detected a smell 'like rotten cabbage', which suggests that the air-conditioning worked.[31]

The men and women who gathered underground were no doubt taking part in one of those periodic civil defence exercises designed to test responses to various nuclear scenarios. The records of one, code named Hard Rock, undertaken in September 1982, shed some light on what the government imagined might happen in the event of a sudden deterioration of relations with the Warsaw pact and a conventional war in which overwhelmed NATO forces were compelled to use tactical nuclear weapons against enemy concentrations. There was sabotage by Soviet agents, conventional air attacks, runs on banks, panic purchases of food and fuel with consequent shortages.[32] Other hypothetical projections, which involved actual nuclear attacks, included panic-stricken mass evacuations, epidemics, localised famines, looting, scavenging and the imposition of what amounted to martial law with police and soldiers firing on mobs.

Whether or not these were chilling flights of fancy can never be known. Only once during the Cold War was Britain on the brink of nuclear war, a situation that was hidden from the public. On 24 October 1962, when the Cuban missile crisis took a turn for the worse, American nuclear forces in Britain passed from Defcon (Defence Condition) 3, in operational readiness for a surprise attack, to Defcon 2 in which they were posed for immediate offensive action. Three days later, the RAF's V-bombers were placed on fifteen-minute standby and sixty Thor missiles were primed for action, according to Air-Vice-Marshal Sir Stewart Menaul, then a senior air staff-officer at Bomber Command.[33] It is not known whether the prime minister or the relevant cabinet ministers knew of these precautions; if they did, they said nothing subsequently.

In the end, deterrence worked. The Cold War between the superpowers ended, leaving one, the United States, supreme, and the other economically debilitated. The threat of a war involving nuclear, chemical or biological weapons has not disappeared. Up to the close of the Cold War, American scientists were contriving microbes designed to devour metal, plastic, rubber and concrete.[34] From 1947 until 1998, the Soviet Union and Russian Federation also developed biological weapons, including anthrax spores, some of which were released into the atmosphere after an accident at a factory at Sverdlovsk in 1979. Casualties were believed to be high. Since their abandonment, scientists who worked on these projects have been dispersed, adding to fears that their expertise might be purchased by countries anxious to obtain weapons of mass destruction on the cheap. Another, equally chilling possibility is that Cold War nuclear weaponry could find its way into the hands of terrorists.

IV

Terrorist bombings and assassinations have been the British people's only direct experience of war since 1945. The explosions and murders began in British cities and towns in 1973 and were an extension of the three-hundred-year-old civil war between Irish protestants and Catholics. The fighting began in the summer of 1969 and continued with intermittent and short truces until a peace agreement between the IRA and the Unionists was signed on Good Friday 1998. This accord was rejected by diehard nationalists in the Real IRA, who have continued the struggle to compel Britain to dissolve the Union. In August 1998, the Real IRA planted a bomb that killed twenty-nine people in Omagh (the highest death toll in any single incident), and a further two exploded in London during the summer of 2000.

Throughout the hostilities, Unionists and nationalists appealed to and were comforted by their distinctive versions of history. At the onset of the troubles, the hardline Unionist, Ian Paisley, declared that the Roman Catholic church had been meddling in Ulster's affairs since 1641 and denounced its hierarchy as the 'enemies of this province'. He also evoked ancestral memories when he described the Irish Republic as a 'bog country inhabited by a bog people'. A seven-year-old stone-thrower from a nationalist family told a British army officer: 'You bastards have been exploiting us for three hundred years and we are not putting up with it any more.'

What quickly evolved into a war waged by the IRA to overturn the 1921 settlement and create a united Ireland began as a domestic conflict within Northern Ireland over jobs, electoral chicanery and the distribution of public resources. From 1967, the Northern Ireland Civil Rights Association (NICRA) had campaigned for fairer housing and educational policies and an end to gerrymandering. The movement was modelled on and inspired by the recent civil rights agitation in America; during a visit to New York in August 1969 one of NICRA's prominent figures, Bernadette Devlin, likened the injustices suffered by the Ulster Catholic minority to the discrimination suffered by blacks in the American south. Sympathetic American newspapers hailed her as a new Joan of Arc.[35]

Ulster Unionists saw the civil rights movement as a nationalist

Trojan horse and were prepared to silence it by force. During the first fortnight of August 1969 there was an outbreak of sectarian rioting, shootings and arson in Belfast and Londonderry. As was the custom in Ireland, these incidents were recorded in song:

> On the 15th of August we took a little trip,
> Up along Bombay Street and burned out all the shit,
> We took a little petrol and we took a little gun,
> And we fought the bloody Fenians till we had them on the run.

Even with reinforcements of B-Special auxiliaries, the Royal Ulster Constabulary (RUC) was unable to suppress the disorder, not least because it was widely distrusted by Catholics who did all in their power to keep its men out of their districts. The RUC's chief inspector, Sir Anthony Peacock, appealed to Whitehall for troops. They appeared on the streets, to the relief of embattled Catholics. One told a journalist: 'If the British army had not come in we would all have been massacred. 'We knew the "Prods" had guns, some of the Bs [B-Specials] who had more than one had given their pistols to relatives.'[36]

A large-scale civil war had been averted, but only temporarily, as British officials subsequently concluded. Oliver Wright, sent by the cabinet to survey the situation, reported bleakly: 'The Catholic barricades are manned by people who genuinely fear for their lives and property. The Protestant barricades are manned by people who hate Catholics.' An immediate return to civil order was imperative before legislation could be introduced that would allow equitable treatment for the Catholics. The process, he predicted, would be bloody: 'In the last resort it must suit the Catholics to get clobbered by us if it is the only way we can get justice for them.'[37]

Not only new laws would be required, the entire Ulster system of government would have to be reconstructed. Stormont had manifestly lost the 'general consent' of the people, concluded a memo sent to the new Conservative prime minister, Edward Heath, in August 1970. It would have to be superseded by direct rule, even if this evoked sour memories of Dublin Castle, before a new and more equitable constitution could be devised.[38] By this time, the IRA had intervened in its traditional role as guardian of Ulster's Catholics and was considering

how it might exploit their grievances and harness them to the nationalist cause. As early as July 1970, intelligence sources warned the
government that the IRA would use violence during the approaching
'marching season'. Disengagement was impossible, the cabinet was told,
because it would lead to a civil war into which the Irish Republic would
be drawn. At this stage, the situation would acquire a Cold War dimension, for 'it is not beyond the bounds of possibility that in those
circumstances other people might try to fish in those troubled waters.'[39]

These disturbed waters became a whirlpool, the eddies of which
bewildered and exasperated successive British governments. In 1969
there were 1.5 million people in Northern Ireland who were divided by
religion, history, patterns of behaviour and habits of mind. Rifts were
widened by twenty-nine years of guerrilla war, terror and counter-terror,
and voluntary segregation has now become the rule. According to the
1991 census, 90 per cent of the Northern Irish chose to live surrounded
by their coreligionists, which offered a degree of safety. Tribal loyalties
dominated protestant and Catholic ghettos and, within these enclaves,
paramilitary units usurped responsibility for enforcing the law. Car
thieves, drug peddlers and sexual deviants faced at best expulsion from
their communities and at worst tarring, beatings, 'knee-capping' and
murder. Informants were killed as they had been in the 1919 to 1922
war. Gunmen, whether IRA or loyalist, became idolised; the war offered
many young men the opportunity to secure a respect and status they
could never have hoped to acquire otherwise. Both would diminish if
the fighting permanently ceased.

Folk art perpetuated the memories of the new heroes and the old.
Walls and gable-ends in working-class districts are decorated with naïf
but forceful images of gunmen and women, wearing khaki drill and
berets and carrying automatic weapons. Many of these warriors are
'martyrs' and, like their religious counterparts, these icons are memorials to steadfastness and self-sacrifice. Their message is plain: stay strong
in the cause. In protestant districts, 'King Billy' rides his horse as he did
at the Boyne, and the battle is annually remembered by Orangemen
marching to fife and drum. His victory will not be abandoned or bargained away.

The sequence of events during the war was in part dictated by British
governments which, from 1969 onwards, stuck to bipartisan policy. Its

ultimate objective was to construct a new, democratic constitution that would allow power to be distributed and exercised even-handedly. On the assumption that prosperity would dilute militancy and remove one of its causes, there has been considerable investment in the province. The sum of £315 million was allocated to the province as part of the 1998 Good Friday agreement. This inducement made long-term financial sense in that the annual bill for maintaining troops in Ulster was five hundred million pounds. At the same time, it was accepted that no settlement would be agreed without the consent of the protestant majority, of whom four-fifths wanted to maintain the Union with Britain. Their suspicions have been repeatedly aroused by another strand of British policy: the involvement of the Irish Republic in negotiations about Northern Ireland's future.

Northern Ireland's detachment from Britain and inclusion in an all-Irish, socialist republic was the aim of Sinn Féin and the IRA. This, they imagined, could be achieved by a war of attrition, first fought in Ulster and then through bombings on the mainland, which would persuade the British people to withdraw the army from the province. Simultaneously, IRA/Sinn Féin would defend the Catholic communities and secure their active support for the terrorist campaign.

This has passed through various stages of intensity. To begin with, the RUC was the IRA's target, but in February 1971 British forces were attacked. Republican logic argued that since Ulster was a 'colony', and that Britain had just evacuated Aden after losing twenty-six men, it would withdraw from Ulster once it had lost that number of servicemen. Within a year, 102 had been killed and there was no sign of a 'Bring the Boys Home' backlash in Britain. Direct attrition was then applied when, following the precedent of 1920 to 1921, the IRA began a pitiless mainland campaign of bombing and assassination. Targets included politicians, servicemen on and off duty and public buildings, and every outrage produced the intended headlines and television news footage in Britain and across the world. Anniversaries had a potent symbolism for the IRA, which was why on 21 November 1974, seventy-four years after the mass assassination of intelligence officers and the retaliatory shooting of spectators at Croke Park, two bombs were placed in crowded Birmingham pubs. Seventeen were killed and 120 injured, and an eyewitness compared the scene outside one pub to 'a First World

War casualty clearing station'. A doctor treating flash burns compared the injuries to those suffered by victims of napalm, many of whom had recently been seen on television in reports from Vietnam.[40]

More bombings followed and there was further distressing television footage of shattered or burning buildings and bloodied survivors. There was and still is inconvenience as a result of the precautionary measures adopted; wastepaper bins disappeared from some public places, including railway stations. The public was enraged, but never to the point of demanding disengagement, rather the contrary. The government's policy remained unchanged. In August 1971 internment was introduced in Ulster, and in May 1972 the Stormont government was superseded by direct rule. This was a preliminary to the creation of a new power-sharing executive. Its brief existence was terminated in May 1974 by a general strike of the predominantly protestant labour force which brought the province to a standstill and demonstrated beyond question that the majority could, if they so wished, make it ungovernable.

The strike that revealed the limits of London's power was organised by the militant protestant groups that had emerged during the previous three years in response to fears that the British government lacked the will to retain the province and might eventually abandon it. The largest was the UDA (Ulster Defence Association) which soon had twenty-five thousand members, some of whom were willing to answer the IRA's terror with their own. Often random killings, known as 'sectarian murders', became an everyday feature of the wider war between the IRA and the security forces.

For the British army, trained either to fight the Warsaw Pact armies or to contain colonial insurgency, the war in Northern Ireland was a novel experience. For the most part, it involved constant patrols, checking vehicles and pedestrians and overall surveillance of those areas that gave sanctuary to IRA men. Since the major overall strategic objective was containment, it was vital to deprive the gunmen of arms and explosives. Between 1971 and 1986, the RUC and army undertook 271,000 searches which uncovered just under ten thousand firearms and 189,000 pounds of explosives.[41]

Serving governments that were convinced that the province's problems would be solved politically rather than militarily, the soldier found himself faced with constraints designed to show that the army was even-handed. The stern measures of 1919 to 1921 were never revived for fear they might alienate domestic opinion, as they had done then. In an urban battlefield of streets and alleyways from which gunmen suddenly emerged and then disappeared, or where snipers waited, the soldier was instructed to overcome his instinct to save himself by swift retaliation. A yellow card issued in 1970 circumscribed when and against whom he could open fire. He could not shoot an assailant after he had stopped firing, although this was permissible if someone had already been killed or seriously wounded, or when a gunman was spotted close to an area where there had been shooting.

These restrictions were revised during the war, and some soldiers who opened fire after snap decisions found themselves tried for murder in the civilian court. Their predicament aroused considerable sympathy in the British press which suspected that the trials were a sop to republicans. At one stage a Mancunian policeman was sent to the province to discover whether a 'shoot-to-kill policy' existed in the police and army, which suggests that in the middle of an ambush crossfire men should pause and take aim only to disable their assailants. Soldiers were also sorely tried by the open hostility they faced in Catholic districts, and by being in the invidious position of recognising known terrorists whom they could not arrest for lack of evidence. There was no resort to martial law, as there had been during the last 'Troubles', although judicial tribunals replaced juries.

The IRA never accepted any restraints, beyond giving often inadequate warnings as to the whereabouts of bombs. As in 1919 to 1922, it indulged in a policy of reprisals, particularly against the Parachute Regiment, whose members had opened fire on rioters in Londonderry in January 1972 in the belief that the crowd contained snipers. Thirteen were killed, and afterwards the graffiti 'Paras 13 Derry 0' appeared on local walls. What actually happened is still a matter of contention and is currently being reinvestigated. Early in the 1980s, the IRA revived the hunger-strike, a feature of the earlier war, to rally support among Catholics and to bring domestic and overseas moral pressure to bear on the British government.

The 'dirty protests', in which IRA prisoners daubed their excrement on their cell walls, and the hunger-strikes were reminders that this was a war of attrition and a test of willpower. How long, the IRA wondered, would the British government tolerate the expense and bloodletting before seeking an accommodation that would involve political and military withdrawal? It imagined and worked towards a hypothetical point when the British government and people would say 'enough'. It was never reached, despite soaring casualties during the 1970s. Between 1969 and 1982, 287 RUC policemen and auxiliaries, 438 soldiers, 199 members of the UDA and 2104 civilians were killed. Thereafter, the death rate slowly dropped; between 1990 and 1992, thirty-seven soldiers and policemen were killed. In the meantime, the loyalist paramilitary groups were becoming more aggressive, having secured supplies of arms from South Africa in 1988. Their targets were often Sinn Féin activists.

By this stage, the people of Ulster were managing to live with violence and disruption. Surprisingly, nearly thirty years of war did not have the expected psychological effect on those for whom it had become a routine hazard of everyday life. Although there were areas of relative calm, one-fifth of 522 ten and eleven-year-olds surveyed in 1985 had been close to an explosion and one-eighth were anxious about their safety. Mass traumatisation did not occur as had been expected, although this was a period in which the young were becoming accustomed to witnessing more and more violence on television and videos.[42] Other investigations revealed that the young inherited the attitudes of their parents and acted accordingly, which was why so many appeared on the streets throwing stones and shouting slogans.

War-weariness did become apparent. In 1994 an opinion poll revealed that 70 per cent of people in Britain were prepared to countenance Ulster's detachment from the rest of the country.[43] As so often with such surveys, there was no indication as to whether those who wanted disengagement would have accepted the Irish civil war that might easily have followed. Chilling television footage of civil war and massacre in Bosnia in 1992 and 1993 had been instrumental in swinging public opinion towards intervention on humanitarian grounds. Given that Ulster had witnessed a spasm of limited 'ethnic cleansing' in August 1969, there was a distinct possibility that it might have recurred once British forces had gone home. As it was, public tiredness and exasperation with an unruly and seemingly implacable province coincided with the period of political initiatives that allowed the Irish government a say in discussions about Ulster's future (1985) and the admission of Sinn Féin representatives to negotiations on what form this might take (1993).

What had been a protracted test of nerve and willpower ended with the 1998 Good Friday agreement, which was successively endorsed by an overwhelming majority of Unionist politicians and by Ulster as a whole. Accommodations were made in which the hitherto unthinkable was accepted: Unionists admitted Sinn Féin ministers into a new government, and Sinn Féin conceded that its ancient goal of a united Ireland was unobtainable without Unionist consent. There were dissenting voices. One nationalist complained of betrayal. 'We as Republicans elevated the physical force tradition to a sacred level. For years we argued that it was justified to fight and kill to get rid of the British. Now Sinn Féin tries to say it is no longer justified, yet the British are still there.'[44] There were echoes here of the anger that followed the 1921 treaty. On the Unionist side, the sceptics constantly complain that one of the terms of the agreement is not being honoured: the decommissioning of the IRA's arsenal. But then, only a defeated army hands over its weapons, and neither the IRA nor the protestant paramilitaries would admit that they had lost. It remains to be seen whether the Good Friday agreement represents a peace or another armistice in a civil war that has yet to run its course.

Envoi: What next?

I

The twenty-first century will not be free of conflicts. Its first year has witnessed wars in the Balkans, Chechnya, the Middle East and various parts of Africa and Asia. All are being waged for traditional reasons: the pursuit of national survival, security, political and economic power (often masks for personal ambition) and the protection of what are seen as vital interests. Two protagonists, the Russian Federation and Israel, possess nuclear weapons, and events of the past ten years have convinced other states of their value. If either Saddam Hussein or Slobodan Milošević had had a nuclear arsenal, their treatment by the United States and its allies might have been very different.

Both Iraq and, until recently, Serbia existed outside and in defiance of what President George Bush (senior) called the 'new world order' which emerged after the end of the Cold War and in which America was the only global superpower. Britain has given wholehearted support to this new dispensation, and committed forces to uphold it in the Gulf War of 1991, the subsequent aerial surveillance operations over Iraq, and in the Balkans. It has done so for a mixture of practical, selfish and ideological reasons; like America and the nations of the European Union, Britain wishes to create a world filled with 'safe' (i.e. unwarlike) democracies that adhere to free-market, capitalist philosophies and respect the human rights of their subjects. The result would be stability and everyone would get richer.

Iraqi expansion into a region that contains about half of the world's oil reserves, and Serbia's ferocious efforts to preserve its dominance over what had been Yugoslavia, were affronts to the new world order. Both were checked in a salutary manner which demonstrated not only the will of America and its supporters but also their overwhelming technical superiority. The wonders of the electronic battlefield with its laser-guided bombs and missiles were seen on television across the world in 1991. The Gulf War was an unequal contest: 240 Allied personnel were lost, while the Iraqis counted their dead in thousands.

This condign lesson was not, however, understood by the Bosnian Serbs, who went ahead with massacring their Muslim neighbours. The new world order had to assert itself again and did so, again in spectacular fashion, by an aerial attack on Serbia in 1999 after it had refused to stop killing Albanians in Kosovo. The upshot was a war won by air power alone, which proved that Slobodan Milošević could no longer protect his own people and so hastened his overthrow. Like the Gulf War, this conflict was reminiscent of those nineteenth-century colonial wars won by superior technology at little cost to the victor.

Victorian statesmen would have recognised the practical value of the new world order and applauded its ethical justification, although contemporaries would have described its enforcement as 'gunboat diplomacy'. The phrase is avoided today, because it has connotations of the bullying of the weak by the strong, and because armed intervention has the theoretic sanction of the United Nations. British servicemen who fought in the Gulf, or who joined units from other nations in the peacekeeping contingents in the Balkans, did so with the approval of the United Nations which, in turn, expressed the view of the rest of the world. They may expect to do so again and also as part of a permanent European Rapid Reaction Force which is being constructed for unspecified overseas duties in the future.

Britain's participation in this force has provoked the wrath of those opposed to the European Union, who fear a further dilution of national sovereignty. Yet the idea is not new; in the past the European powers improvised armies and armadas to cope with sudden overseas crises. This occurred during the Greek War of Independence, when British,

French and Russian warships destroyed the Turkish fleet at Navarino in 1827, and in 1900 when a multinational army saved the Peking legations and restored order in northern China. Leaving aside the tricky question of relations between the new force and NATO, its creation suggests further wars of intervention and pacification in the interests of stability as defined by the western European industrial powers. Two, Britain and France, have already shown themselves disposed to play the admittedly humanitarian policeman in their former colonies. Anarchy in Sierra Leone and the incapacity of nearby African powers to restore order has led to the despatch of British warships and troops.

Such ventures by democracies demand public support. Henceforward, it will depend on how the conflict is presented on television. Satellite transmission beams the battlefield into the living-room, provoking instant emotional reactions. Images of destruction, famine, refugees from war and genocide and, often discreetly filmed, corpses have become familiar and give distant crises an unprecedented immediacy. Such footage, including shots of a Bosnian Serb concentration camp, together with the testimony of the victims of rape, torture and coercion arouse popular anger which expresses itself through demands that something should be done. Elected governments cannot ignore such pressure, especially when humanitarian issues appear to be at stake, as they obviously were in the Balkans. What has been called the 'CNN effect' can cool as well as inflame war-fever. In October 1993 eighteen American soldiers and several hundred Somalis were killed in a fight in the streets of Mogadishu. Film of the American corpses being abused and taunted by Somalis provoked outrage and demands for the immediate evacuation of all forces from a country where the United States had few if any interests. Likewise, and this occurred in 1986 when the Americans bombed Libya and during the Gulf War, satellite television enables people to view the human and physical consequences of wars being waged in their name.

Handling the media has become as vital a part of making war as supplying men with rations. At the start of the war in Northern Ireland, the RUC had two press officers and by 1971 it had forty. News presentation mattered, as was discovered during the 1982 Falklands campaign in which, against all apparent odds, a British task-force retook the islands after they had been seized by forces of the Argentinian military junta. It was the last of the old wars in so far as the public relied on the voices and despatches of war correspondents and cohorts of armchair strategists. There were also official communiqués flatly delivered by the defence secretary, John Nott, and a ministry official, and more spiritedly by Mrs Thatcher who famously invited journalists to 'Rejoice' at the news that South Georgia had been recaptured.

Her gung-ho mood matched the temper of the country during a war that was widely seen as a reversal of thirty years of international impotence. The liberation of the Falklands was a sign that Britain was no longer a country to which things happened, but that could make them happen. During this war and that in the Gulf, the tabloid press reverted to a strident jingoism that had scarcely been heard since 1914. Not without some justice, Saddam Hussein was demonised in the old way; he was 'The Butcher of Baghdad' in the *Daily Star* and a 'New Hitler' in *Today*. The *Daily Mirror* exploited the fact that this was a desert campaign and evoked memories of another during the Second World War by calling the British forces the new 'Desert Rats'. 'Rats Get Stuck In' ran one triumphant *Mirror* headline as the land battle began. Both the Falklands and Gulf Wars produced a crop of 'instant' books and souvenirs. *Daily Star* readers were offered a T-shirt with the British and American flags and the words 'These Colours Don't Run'. Its 1914 equivalent would have been a mug decorated with the flags of the Allies.

The pugnacity recently shown by the popular press has for some been an uncomfortable reminder that the British are still a belligerent people. Further evidence of this is the often random aggression shown by football fans at home and abroad. There has been much editorial and political breast-beating about this phenomenon, which is variously interpreted as a modern malaise and evidence of a wider lack of discipline within society. Perhaps so; but it must be remembered that 'hooligan' is a late Victorian word coined to describe a creature who was as familiar then as he is today, and that Dr Johnson observed that what was seen as 'insolence' by the masses in peace became courage in war. It is of passing interest that some of the most violent football supporters wear a form of uniform and organise their affrays in a military manner, using mobile phones to convey orders and situation reports. When 'in action' abroad they prominently display the union flag.

The armed forces that recovered the Falklands, helped defeat Iraq and presently keep civil order in parts of the Balkans and Sierra Leone are entirely professional and admired for their discipline, integrity, devotion and ability to do a job well. Britain is still proud of its servicemen, whose reputation is far higher than that of other public servants, most notably the police, teachers and judiciary, all of whom are losing public confidence. The armed services enhance Britain's status in the world and remain a focus of national unity at a time when regional separatism is gaining political ground.

As in the past, the forces reflect the composition and values of the society they defend and cannot avoid entanglements in its preoccupations. At present there are intermittent rows about whether the forces reflect a multicultural society, whether women should be permitted to serve in the front line, and whether military law should be amended to permit homosexual servicemen and women openly to display their inclinations. A further, extremely contentious issue is that of compensation for illness and mental disorders contracted on active service. The last decade has witnessed a pandemic of lawsuits for such redress, and policemen have secured huge sums for witnessing horrific incidents that their predecessors during the blitz would have accepted as part of their normal duties. The imposition of what may turn out to be transient civilian values has aroused resentment in the service, which claim that they will curtail their efficiency and undermine morale.

Current economic dogma has also intruded into service life. Ancillary and support systems, including the ordnance, warship refitting and the management of non-military stores have been handed over to private companies. This has reversed the course of history, since these activities have been undertaken by the state since the eighteenth century on the grounds that private entrepreneurs might sell short or defraud the army and navy. Many did, but now competition is imagined to have a talismanic effect on the efficiency, so the services will somehow get good value for money and provide a profit for the contractors as well. This policy has been followed by successive Conservative and New Labour administrations. The latter has faced considerable disquiet about defects in the latest army rifle, a product of the new system.

II

The public remains mesmerised by war, past, present and future. The last quarter of the twentieth century has seen the immense popularity of three very different warrior heroes: George MacDonald Fraser's roguish and craven Flashman, who fights for Queen and Empire; Bernard Cornwell's gritty promoted ranker, Sharp, who takes on the French in the Peninsula and Waterloo; and Patrick O'Brian's wayward patrician, Jack Aubrey, who fights them at sea. The First World War provided the backgrounds for successful novels by Sebastian Faulks and Pat Barker, and the cinema continues to quarry the Second World War for often epic plots.

The most recent global conflict, the Cold War, has generated its own peculiar genre of espionage fiction and films. As the MI5 agent Peter Wright revealing observed, he and his fellows were the Cold War's 'storm troopers' who were serving in the 'front line'. What they did there was disclosed in his memoirs, *Spycatcher* (1987), which caused a scandal. And yet his audience was probably not astonished by what they read, for much of it was the staple of the spy fiction that had been in fashion for over thirty years. Len Deighton and John Le Carré offered a fascinating and plausible insight into a clandestine world of intrigue and deception. Their characters and serpentine plots gained credibility when the identity and activities of real spies were uncovered. Guy Burgess, Donald Maclean, Kim Philby and Anthony Blunt gave an element of authenticity to spy stories. Glamour was provided by Ian Fleming's creation, James Bond, a sophisticated, indestructible and sexually irresistible secret agent who waged war against communism and criminal masterminds while enjoying the high-life in exotic locations. He was assisted by an arsenal of gadgets, all British-made, which was reassuring at a time when Russia and America seemed to share a monopoly of inventiveness.

Equally comforting as evidence of enduring British courage and stamina were the action-filled memoirs of former members of the SAS (Special Air Service) which disclosed details of covert operations against the IRA and behind enemy lines in Iraq. It was thrilling stuff, *The Seven Pillars of Wisdom* augmented by arcane information about the SAS's techniques, weaponry and endurance training. That Britain should still produce such resourceful, brave and ruthless warriors is a source of pride and explains the current obsession with the SAS. It has become the modern counterpart of the 'Few' of the Battle of Britain or Henry V's 'band of brothers', helping to prove that numbers do not matter in war, which is consoling for a nation that has never been able to field mass armies on the continental or American scale. Agincourt, Rorke's Drift and the defence of the Imjin River in Korea all testified to a peculiar British capacity not to be deterred by overwhelming odds.

Gruelling SAS survival training programmes are among the many commercial courses that promise adventure and danger to those who seek them on land or water, or wish to prove themselves capable of overcoming the outdoor discomforts and some of the perils of war. Paradoxically, the enervating experiences of a sailor in Nelson's navy or a soldier in the Peninsula are now regarded as a form of therapy that will foster self-discovery, self-reliance and self-respect. Just as the eighteenth-century rogue was forced into the army or navy and sent across the world, his modern counterpart is sent for 'adventure training' in the hope that it might be the key to his redemption.

Fighting mock skirmishes with paint guns helps prepare businessmen and women for battles in the boardroom or on the trading-floor and, since groups are organised as platoons, encourages teamwork. For the past forty years, others have discovered some of the experience of war by dressing up appropriately and refighting engagements of the English and American Civil Wars or practising the drill of Napoleonic or Victorian soldiers. Others adopt the armour of Vikings, Normans and medieval knights and give realistic displays of hand-to-hand fighting.

It is a curious phenomenon. Generations that have escaped real wars fight make-believe ones, or choose to endure the conditions under which they were once fought in distant places. Huge numbers are absorbed by books about war and watch war films and videos, safe in the knowledge that they are extremely unlikely ever to have to fight. Here, perhaps, lies a clue to this unending fascination with war. Experiencing it at second hand or stripped of its lethal risks provides a chance for the individual to contemplate the question of how he or she would behave in the face of death. That eternal prerequisite of war, the capacity to suppress primordial fear, remains highly prized even in peacetime.

Notes

Abbreviations

AJ *Archaeological Journal*
ANS *Anglo-Norman Studies*
BAR British Archaeological Reports
BL British Library
BMJ *British Medical Journal*
BRO Buckinghamshire Record Office
CDRS *Calendars of Documents Relating to Scotland*
CP Cumberland Papers
CSPD *Calendars of State Papers, Domestic*
CSPI *Calendars of State Papers, Ireland*
CPSAWI *Calendars of State Papers, American and the West Indies*
DAR *Documents of the American Revolution*
EcHR *Economic History Review*
EHR *English Historical Review*
HJ *Historical Journal*
HMC Historic Manuscripts Commission
HPJP *Historical Papers relating to the Jacobite Period*
IHR *International History Review*
IHS *Irish Historical Studies*
ILN *Illustrated London News*
IWM Imperial War Museum
IWMR *Imperial War Museum Review*
JCH *Journal of Contemporary History*
JMH *Journal of Modern History*
JSAHR *Journal of the Society for Army Historical Research*

LASPFS Lists and Analyses of State Papers, Foreign Series
LHC Liddell Hart Centre
MM Mariner's Mirror
NAM National Army Museum
NLS National Library of Scotland
NMS Nottingham Mediaeval Studies
PP Past and Present
PRO Public Record Office
RCHMW Royal Commission for Historic Monuments, Wales
REBP Register of Edward the Black Prince
RPCS Register of the Privy Council of Scotland
SAUL St Andrews University Library
SRO Scottish Record Office
TCBH Twentieth Century British History
TT Thomason Tracts
WMQ William and Mary Quarterly
WS War and Society

Sources: unpublished

British Library, London

Additional Mss 36,613; 38,102; 42,615; 70,829
Hurlulun Mss 504, 7747
Keyes Papers
Thomason Tracts
Luttrell Collection of Broadsides &c.

Buckinghamshire Record Office, Aylesbury

D/X 1059 Hilda Gosling
D/X Pt. P. J. Darbyshire
TA 3/517 E. F. Lawson, Royal Buckinghamshire Hussars
TA 3/8; 3/20; 3.120 Buckinghamshire Imperial Yeomanry
TA 8/7 Buckinghamshire Home Guard

Imperial War Museum, Lambeth, London

Edith Airey (81/9/1)
Lieutenant-Commander E. E. Bainbridge, RN (91/17)
Captain H. G. Boys-Smith, RN (99/5/1)
Alfred Bradburn (95/16/1)
A. W. Conn, Devonshire Regt (81/41/1)
Flight Sergeant J. P. Dobson, RAF (92/2/1)
W. H. Firth (88/29/1 and 2)
Flight-Lieutenant J. W. Fox, RAF (98/8/1)
Flight Sergeant G. Hull

Joan Kirby, WRNS
Major A. C. D. Lees (91/22/1)
Flight-Lieutenant R. Passmore, RAF (83/1/1)
Lieutenant C. H. Perkins (87/18/2)
Major B. A. Pond (78/21/3)
Sergeant A. V. Reeve, RAF (90/21/1)
Hiram Sturdy
Olive Turner (83/17/1)
Sylvia Watts, WAAF
Captain G. R. Waymouth, RN (87/16/1)
Gabrielle West (77/156/1)
Misc 2645

Liddell Hart Centre, King's College, London

Papers of:
Lord Burnham
Lieutenant-General Laurence Carr
Captain Ralph Covernton
Lady Gertrude Denman
Brigadier-General Sir James Edmonds
Major-General Charles Foulkes
Lieutenant-General Sir Launcelot Kiggell
Field Marshall Sir William Robertson
Wing-Commander Maurice Wells
Edward Wickens, Middlesex Regiment

National Army Museum, Chelsea

Letters, diaries and papers of:
Anon. (Private 38th Regt) (7912–2)
Anon. (Loyal North Lancashire Regiment) (8404–124)
Ralph Clerk, Lincolnshire Regiment (7606–45)
Sergeant F. G. C. Cross, Royal Irish Rifles (8207–91–2)
Lieutenant William Fleming, 45th Regiment (7202–36–5)
H. Pope Hennessy (7402–7–3)
Lieutenant R. Jelf, Rifle Brigade (6903–46)
Colonel H. Jourdain, Connaught Rangers (5603–10,11,12)
Colonel Lloyd (7709–43–37)
Lieutenant-Colonel W. I. Maxwell (7402–28)
Quartermaster-Sergeant F. Nunn, Royal Berkshire Regiment (8012–74)
Private Andrew Philip, Royal Artillery (8009–9)
Colonel George Preston (6510–11)
Colonel Henry Ross (8004–40)
Private W. Sykes, West Yorkshire Regiment (7607–48)

National Library of Scotland, Edinburgh

Ancram Papers (Acc 5750)
Sir George Browne Papers (Ms 1859)
Cochrane Papers (MS 2313, 2335)
Diary of Colonel Sir John Crabbe (Acc 11460)
Letters of Midshipman Archie Dickinson (MS 13,589)
Dundas of Ocherlyne Papers (Acc 16719/4)
Fettercairn Papers (Acc 4796)
Papers of Major Granville-Egerton, Seaforth Highlanders (Acc 166926)
Diary of Field Marshal Earl Haig (Acc 3155)
Diary and papers of General Sir Aylmer Haldane (Ms 20247–2054)
Letters of Lieutenant H. Munro, Argyll and Sutherland Highlanders (Ms 26,930)
Letters of Major Alexander Robertson, Bengal Artillery (Ms 1855)

Public Record Office, Kew, London

Admiralty: Adm 1; Adm 97; Adm 101; Adm 103; Adm 137; Adm 156; Adm 167; Adm 178; Adm 199; Adm 265; Adm 296
Air Ministry: Air 1; Air 2; Air 14; Air 29; Air 35; Air 37; Air 40
Avia 65
Cabinet: Cab 45
Exchequer: E 34; E 404
Colonial Office: CA / 71 \ A7 137; CO 876, CO 201
Criminal Prosecutions: Crim 1
Foreign Office: FO 371
Home Office: HO 45; HO 50; HO 139: HO 144
King's Bench: KB 27
Metropolitan Police: Mepo 2
Prime Minister's Office: Prem 4; Prem 11; Prem 15
War Office: WO 1; WO 3; WO 32; WO 35; WO 79; WO 92; WO 95; WO 108; WO 135; WO 138; WO 141; WO 154; WO 158; WO 164; WO 165; WO 169; WO 179; WO 231; WO 352

St Andrews University Library

Cumberland Papers [CP] microfilm of originals in Windsor Castle

Scottish Record Office, Edinburgh

GD 1 (Various); GD 13; GD 24 (Abercairney); GD 26 (Leven and Melville); GD 45; GD 46 (Seaforth); GD 51 (Dundas); HO 50; HH 52; HH 57

Part One: Conquests AD 43–1100

1 A warlike province: Britain, AD 43–410

1. Shirley, 124–7.
2. Holder, 25–8, 107.
3. Henig, *Religion*, 13; the original is in the Lincolnshire Museum at Lincoln.
4. Wheeler, 351, 353.
5. Richmond, II, 32–3.
6. Stewart, 'Inventing Roman Britain', 3.
7. Braund, 107.
8. *Ibid.*, 3, 12–13, 15, 22.
9. *Ibid.*, 103.
10. Henig, 'The Veneration', 249–51.
11. Webster, *Rome against Caractacus*, plate 10.
12. Henig, *Religion*, 90.
13. *Ibid.*, 89; Davies, 'The Training Camps', 73.
14. Henig, *Religion*, 97–8; MacMullen, 107, 124.
15. Davies, 'The Training Camps', 77.
16. Webster, 'The Military Situation', 181.
17. Webster, *Rome against Caractacus*, 29.
18. Webster, *Boudica*, 126–6; the head is in the British Museum.
19. Jones, *The End &c.*, 13–17.
20. Kendal, 'Transport Logistics', 132.
21. Breeze and Dobson, 'The Development', 113–14.
22. Hind, 'Who Betrayed Britain', 2.
23. Jones, *The End*, 206–8, 215–16.
24. Bowman and Thomas, 90, 95.
25. Birley, 127.
26. Jones, *The End*, 188, 192–3, 198, 216.
27. Cunliffe, 1, 419–31.
28. Hind, 'Who Betrayed Britain', *passim*.
29. Elton, 41.
30. Breeze, *Roman Scotland*, 112–14.
31. Johnson, *Late Roman Britain*, 59.
32. Hornsby and Laverick, 'The Roman Signal Station', 210, 217; Hornsby and Stanton, 'The Roman Fortress', *passim*.
33. *Maritime Celts*, 111–12.
34. E. and I. Gifford, 'The Sailing', 149–50.
35. Jones, *The End*, 84–5, 91–3.
36. Holder, 120.
37. Jones, *The End*, 90.

2 Stern in contest: Arthur and after, 410–800

1. The Gododdin, 112.

2. Halsall, 'Anthropology', 162.
3. Elton, 137–8.
4. Wormald, 'Bede', 34.
5. Woolf, 'The Ideal of Men', 64, 66.
6. Page, 5–6.
7. Jones, *The End*, 39.
8. Brooke, 'The Northumbrian Settlements', 121, 316; Cunliffe, II, 301.
9. Welch, 'Late Romans', 232.
10. Keefer, 'Hwaer', 115–16.
11. Jones. *The End*, 64.
12. Clarke, 'The North Sea', 41.
13. Alcock, 214–15.
14. *Ibid.*, 230–32.
15. Halsall, 'Anthropology', 166.
16. Jones, 'The Early Evolution', 20.
17. Report in *Journal of Roman Studies*, 21, 232–3.
18. Charles-Edwards, 'Irish Warfare', 45.
19. *Annals of Ulster*, 113.
20. Davison, 'The Training of Warriors', 17.
21. *Annals of Ulster*, 127.
22. Alexander, 175.
23. Jones, *The End*, 67.
24. Hawke, 'Warrior Queen', 36.
25. Introduction, ed. Hawkes, 4.
26. *The Gododdin*, 100.
27. Poole, 'Skaldic Verse', 277.
28. *Early Irish Myths and Sagas*, 155.
29. *The Gododdin*, 103, 11.
30. Davison, 'The Training of Warriors', 18.
31. Russom, 'A Germanic Concept', 6.
32. *Early Irish Myths and Sagas*, 136.
33. *The Gododdin*, 103, 11.
34. Davison, 'The Training of Warriors', 12.
35. *Ibid.*
36. *The Frenzy of Suibhne*, 15.
37. Henry of Huntingdon, 130.
38. Tatlock, 'The Dragons', 223.
39. Henry of Huntingdon, 130.
40. Poole, *Viking Poems*, 37.
41. Wenham, 'Anatomical', *passim*.
42. Cunliffe, II, 241–2.
43. Bone, 'The Development', 69–70; Lane and Ager, 'Swords', 101, 110.
44. Examples of such hilts can be seen in the British Museum (from Sutton Hoo); the City Museum, Sheffield; and the Yorkshire Museum, York.

45. *The Gododdin*, 135.
46. The Sutton Hoo helmet is in the British Museum; the Benty Grange in the City Museum, Sheffield; and the Coppergate in the Castle Museum, York.
47. Owen, 13–14.
48. *Ibid.*, 14–15; Arent, 'The Heroic', 133–4.
49. *The Gododdin*, 107.
50. Abels, 12.
51. Byrne, *High Kings*, 190.
52. Abels, 13.
53. *Ibid.*
54. *Anglo-Saxon Chronicle*, 50–51.
55. Pelteret, 'Slavery', 120, 122.
56. Abels, 20.
57. Charles-Edwards, 'Early Mediaeval Kingship', 31.
58. McCone, 'Werewolves', 4.
59. Christison, 'Report', 306.
60. Bannerman, 147.
61. *Ibid.*, 119.
62. Illustrated in Chalmers.
63. *The Frenzy of Suibhne, passim*.
64. Smythe, 66, 74, 78.

3 A people accustomed to be conquered: 800–1100

1. *Orkneyinger's Saga*, 59.
2. *Ibid.*, 15–16.
3. *Annals of Ulster*, 179; Page, 3–5.
4. *Annals of Ulster*, 43.
5. Poole, 'Skaldic', 281.
6. *Orkneyinger's Saga*, 13
7. *Ibid*, 36–7.
8. Abels, 'English Tactics', 144.
9. Moberg, 'The Battle of Helgeå', 4.
10. Brooks, 'Arms, Status', 97.
11. Florence of Worcester, 143.
12. *Orkneyinger's Saga*, 403.
13. Brooks, 'Arms, Status, 83.
14. Ordericus Vitalis, VI, 349.
15. *Anglo-Saxon Chronicle*, 105.
16. *The Gododdin*, 118, 137.
17. Ordericus, VI, 342–3.
18. *Ibid.*, 236–8.
19. Keefer, 'Hwaer', 122, 128.
20. Strickland, 'Military Technology', 360–66.
21. Green, 35.

22. Beauroy, 'Le Conquête', 36.

23. Bachrach, 'Some Observations', 12.

24. *Ibid.*, 9.

25. Allen Brown, 'The Battle of Hastings', 7.

26. *Orkneyinger's Saga*, 411.

27. Strickland, 'Military Technology', 369.

28. Ordericus, VI, 348–51.

29. *Orkneyinger's Saga*, 76.

30. Thordeman, I, 185–7.

31. Ordericus Vitalis, II, 173; ed. Morillo, 47.

32. Briese, 'The Courage', 9.

33. Ordericus, VI, 239–40.

34. Brown, 'The Bayeux Tapestry', 27–8.

35. Ed. Morillo, 49.

36. Ordericus, II, 177.

37. Petre-Turville, 94–5.

38. Ordericus, II, 203.

39. Petre-Turville, 96.

40. Powell, 'The Three Orders', 115–16.

41. *The Annals of Roger Hoveden*, I, 142.

42. *Domesday Book: Yorkshire I*, 311 a, c, d.

43. Ordericus, IV, 161–2.

44. *Ibid.*, VI, 19.

45. *Ibid.*, II, 260–61; III, 137–42, 145.

46. RCHMW, *Glamorgan*, III, 1c, 59–60.

47. Beresford, 99.

48. Ordericus, II, 260–61; III, 137–42, 145.

49. *Ibid.*, VI, 241.

50. Beresford, *passim*.

51. Colvin, I, 24.

Part Two: Disputed lands: 1100–1603

1 Just quarrels: Britain at war, 1100–1063, an overview

1. Henry of Huntingdon, 323–4.

2. Owst, 72–3.

3. *Calendar of Inquisitions Miscellaneous, 1219–1307*, 637–8.

4. Madden, 209–10.

5. Brieze, 'The Courage, 7–4.

6. *The Chronicle of Lanercost*, 341.

7. Fraoli, 'The Literary Image', 823–4.

8. *Calendar of Memoranda Rolls (Exchequer) 1326–27*, 97–8.

9. Edwards, 'The Cult', 118.

10. Brieze, 'The Courage', *passim*.

11. Knighton, 73.
12. Ibid., 423.
13. The Actes and Deides, VI, 491.
14. The Bruce, Bk XII, ll. 235–9.
15. Salacronica, 146.
16. The Chronicle of Lanercost, 240.
17. The Actes and Deidies, II. 7–8.
18. Robbins, 263.
19. Hodgson Part III, Vol. 2, 217, 225, 244.
20. Calendar of Border Papers, II, 333.
21. Suppe, 21.
22. Nitze, 'The Exhumation', passim.
23. Vale, Edward III, 18–20.
24. Spenser, 43.
25. CSPI, March to October, 1600, 295.
26. Acts of the Lords of Council, I, 345, 348.
27. Wormald, Lords and Men, 4–5.
28. Brown, Bloodfeud in Scotland, 161.
29. Owst, 72–3.
30. Bernard, 32–4.
31. PRO, E 34 1b, 139, 167–8, 193.
32. HMC, Fifth Report, 492, 521.
33. Further English Voyages, 28, 35.
34. Documents Concerning English Voyages, 120–21.

2 So haughty a spirit: Chivalry and command

1. The Siege of Caerlaverock, 62–3.
2. Langtoft, II, 381.
3. Brut, I, 69.
4. Burnley, 30–31.
5. The Bruce, Bk XI, l. 525.
6. Anglo, The Great Tournament, 25n.; The Bruce, Bk XI, l. 321.
7. The Penguin Book of French Verse, 214–15.
8. Le Clerc, 8.
9. Sir Perceval of Galles, 18.
10. Lloyd, 'William of Longespee', 83.
11. Hume's History of the House of Douglas, I, 125.
12. Greene and Whittingham, 'Excavations', 285–7.
13. De Pisan, 35; Knyghthode and Bataile, 10.
14. Anglo, 'How to Win', 248–9.
15. Ibid., 256.
16. Mann, II, 241–2.
17. The Bruce, Bk III, ll. 115, 138.
18. The Death of Arthur, 67, 121.

19. Thordeman, I, 163.
20. *Calendar of Inquisitions Miscellaneous 1219–1307*, 593.
21. *L.P. Henry VIII*, I, ii, 1021.
22. Mann, I, 1–5, 92–3.
23. *The Bruce*, Bk XIX, l. 396.
24. Mann, I, 13.
25. Mann, 'A Further Account', 319–21.
26. *Hamilton Papers*, II, 616.
27. Barwick, 10d; Smythe, 3.
28. *CDRS*, II, 258–9, 304–6; V, 208; *REBP*, IV, 289, 326, 361.
29. PRO, E 101/509/11.
30. *REBP*, IV, 502, 532.
31. *CDRS*, II, 304–5, 404, 406.
32. *REBP*, II, 127–8.
33. Gillmor, 'Practical Chivalry', 116.
34. *Testamenta Eboracensia*, I, 42–3.
35. Anglo, *The Great Tournament*, 10.
36. *REBP*, IV, 67.
37. Crouch, 75–6.
38. Anglo, 'How to win', 260–61.
39. Anglo, *The Great Tournament*, 38–40.
40. Knighton, 95.
41. Gillingham, 'War and Chivalry', 17.
42. Maddicott, *Thomas of Lancaster*, 41–2.
43. HMC, *Various Mss*, II, 304.
44. PRO, E 101/71/4, 18.
45. *Calendar of Patent Rolls 1452–1461*, 321.
46. HMC, *Twelfth Report*, App 4, 2–4.
47. *The Buke of the Laws of Armys*, 159.
48. Macfarlane, 154.
50. *L. P. Henry VIII*, I, ii, 1294–5.
51. Virgoe, 'Some Ancient Indictments', 241–2.
52. PRO, KB 9/369, 22.
53. Ordericus, VI, 241.
54. *Testamenta Eboracensia*, I, 20.
55. Contamine, 257–8.
56. Macfarlane, 151–2.
57. *Ibid.*, 186.
58. Williams, *A Brief discourse*, 6.
59. HMC, *Twelfth Report*, App 4, 35.
60. *Ibid.*, 202.
61. HMC, *Salisbury*, IV, 18–19.
62. Styward, 34–5.
63. *Ibid.*, 137.

64. Barwick, 6.
65. Styward, 138–9.
66. *The Chronicle of Lanercost*, 270–71.
67. HMC, *Twelfth Report*, App 4, 33, 35.
68. *LASPFS*, I, 171.
69. HMC, *Salisbury*, VII, 286; *CSPI, March–October 1600*, 284.
70. HMC, *Salisbury*, VII, 570–71; *CSPI March–October, 1600*, 278–9.
71. Williams, *A Brief discourse*, preface, n.p.

3 The small folk: Infantrymen and technology

1. *The Bruce*, Bk 1, l. 399.
2. *The Chronicle of Lanercost*, 266–7.
3. *LASPFS IV*, 175.
4. *British Naval Documents*, 46.
5. HMC, *Twelfth Report*, 47–8.
6. *The Chronicle of Lanercost*, 270–71.
7. *Calendar of Patent Rolls, 1452–1461*, 406–10.
8. Prestwich, 93.
9. Cruikshank, *Elizabeth's Army*, 25.
10. *Further English Voyages*, 146.
11. Cruikshank, *Elizabeth's Army*, 290.
12. *CSPI, March–October 1600*, 217.
13. HMC, *Twelfth Report*, 381.
14. *Stonor Letters*, II, 96–7.
15. Wormald, *Land of Men*, 44.
16. *LASPFS IV*, 242.
17. HMC, *Salisbury*, IV, 4.
18. *The 1341 Inquisition*, 66, 67, 96.
19. *Calendar of Inquisitions Miscellaneous*, II, 630–31.
20. CDRS, II, 282, 288; *Calendar of Close Rolls 1296–1302*, 379; *Calendar of Patent Rolls, 1292–1301*, 529–30.
21. *Coventry Leet Book*, 363–4.
22. HMC, *Sixteenth Report*, 163–4.
23. Carr, 'Welshmen', 43.
24. *Naval Songs and Ballads*, 25.
25. *Plumpton Correspondence*, liv–lv.
26. Simms, 'Gaelic Warfare'.
27. *Hamilton Papers*, II, 390, 406.
28. *CSPI, March–October 1600*, 172.
29. *London Trialbaston Trials*, 30.
30. Ayton, 'Military Service', *passim*.
31. *A Plea Roll*, 51, 59.
32. Owst, 338.
33. Wright, 'Pillagers and Brigands', 15–17.

34. Contamine, 257–8.
35. *The Spanish War, 1585–1587*, 179.
36. *CSPI, March–October 1600*, 338.
37. *CSPD, 1595–1597*, 441.
38. *CDRS*, II, 276.
39. *The Spanish War, 1585–1587*, 171–2.
40. HMC, *Twelfth Report*, 40, 43.
41. *The Spanish War, 1585–1587*, 103.
42. *LASPFS*, IV, 108.
43. *CSPI, March–October 1600*, 272.
44. *Hamilton Papers*, II, 603.
45. Styward, 142.
46. Virgoe, 'William Tailboys', 35, *passim*.
47. *L. P. Henry VIII*, XIII, 194: *Ibid.*, XIV, i, 450–51.
48. *CSPD, 1598–1601*, 441.
49. *Plumpton Correspondence*, liv.
50. Williams, 'The Welsh Border', 25.
51. *The Spanish War, 1585–1587*, 254.
52. McGurk, 'Rochester', 64.
53. Smyth, *Certaine Discourses*, 3, 20–22.
54. Le Clerc, 27.
55. *The Bruce*, Bk XIX, ll. 399–400.
56. Nicholson, 'The Siege of Berwick', 27.
57. PRO, E 404/71, 160.
58. *Hamilton Papers*, II, 390.
59. HMC, *Twelfth Report*, App. 4, 6.
60. Rodger, *A Naval History*, 168–9.
61. Parker, 'The *Dreadnought* Revolution', 289.
62. *CSPD, 1595–1597*, 131.
63. *Naval Songs*, 18.
64. *Ibid.*, 20.
65. Robinson, 'A Seventeenth Century Sailor', 313.
66. BL, Harleian Mss 540, 73.
67. *CSPI, 1601–1603*, 379.
68. BL, Harleian Mss 292, 154.
69. PRO, E 404/71, 4, 47.
70. BL. Add. Mss 41. 615, 1.
71. 'A Contemporary Account', 143, 147, 150; *L.P. Henry VIII*, 1, 2 (1513), 1021.
72. BL, Harleian Mss 540, 73.
73. *Hamilton Papers*, I, 310.
74. *CSPI, 1601–1603*, 624–8.
75. HMC, *Salisbury*, IX, 35.
76. Robinson, 'A Seventeenth Century Sailor', 313–14.

77. *The Taking of Madre de Dios*, 111.
78. Breight, 264–5.
79. Ohlmeyer, 'Civilising', 132.
80. PRO, E 404, 79, 63.
81. *L.P. Henry VIII*, XIX, ii, 172, 284.
82. CDRS, III, 160–61, 163.
83. Summerson, 'Response', 157–8.
84. CDRS, III, 157.
85. *British Naval Documents*, 36–7.
86. *The 1341 Royal Inquest*, 8, 90–91.
87. Maddicott, *The English Peasant*, 9, 17.
88. *CSPD, 1598–1601*, 22, 130, 428.
89. Barwick, 4–5.
90. *English Privateering Voyages*, 330–37; Andrews, 87–8.

Part Three: Civil wars, 1637–1800

1 Sharp sickness: The Wars of the Three Kingdoms, 1637–60

1. *The Last News from the King's Majesties Army*, 1–2 (TT E 127, 44); *An Extract and True Relation of the Battle*, 5 (TT E 127, 8).
2. *CSPD 1641–1643*, 373, 387; RPSC, IV, 134–5; Spalding, I, 222, 224, 228.
3. Suckling, 111.
4. Underdown, 85.
5. Hainsworth, 7.
6. Ridpath, 359.
7. Firth, 'Ballads', 263.
8. HMC, *Fifth Report*, 351.
9. *An Encouragement to Warre*, 2 (TT E 122, 2).
10. *The Christians Incourgement*, 1 (TT E 157, 3).
11. Firth, 'Ballads', 260.
12. *CSPD, 1640*, 494, 496.
13. Ibid., *1641–1643*, 371.
14. *A Blazing Starre*, passim (TT E 127, 17); *A Barbarous and Inhuman Speech*, passim (TT E 83, 17); *A Wonderful and Strange Miracle*, 2–3 (TT E 122, 36).
15. *Mercurius Britannicus*, 15–22 Sept 1645; BL, Sloane, 1519, 20.
16. *Laws and Ordnance of War*, passim (TT E 127, 31); Adair, 'The Court Martial Records', 221.
17. HMC, *Marr and Kellie*, I, 211.
18. *Dundee Court Martial Records*, 12–13.
19. BL Add. Mss 70,829, 29, 31.
20. *Tracts Relating to the Proceedings in Lancashire*, 71, 150.
21. HMC, *Fourteenth Report*, App. 2, 190–91.
22. *Generall Cromwell's Letters*, 7 (TT E 301, 18).
23. Gentles, 118–19, 131.

24. *Ibid.*, 131.
25. Andriette, 176–7.
26. *Diary of Sir John Hope*, 146–7, 148–9.
27. Luke, I, 1.
28. Martindale, 31–2; *Calendar of Proceedings*, II, 1029.
29. Luke, III, 249.
30. Martindale, 34–5.
31. *Ibid.*, 36–41.
32. HMC, *Fourteenth Report*, App. 2, 156.
33. Gentles, 149.
34. HMC, *Fourteenth Report*. App. 2. 157.
35. *CSPI, 1660–1663*, 457–8.
36. Stevenson, 142, 245.
37. Carlton, 123.
38. HMC, *Kellie and Mar*, I, 56.
39. *A Contemporary History of Affairs &c.*, III, ii, 191–6.
40. *Ibid.*, 271–2.
41. *Ibid.*, I, ii, 684–5.
42. *Ibid.*, III, ii, 188–9.
43. *Ibid.*, I, ii, 526–7.
44. Ohlmeyer, 'The War of Religion', 123.
45. Murtagh, 'Irish Soldiers Abroad', 29.
46. *A Contemporary History of Affairs*, III, ii, 298
47. *Ibid.*, III, ii, 226, 239.
48. *CSPI, 1660–1663*, 420.
49. Connolly, 'The Defence of Protestant Ireland', 232.
50. *Ibid.*, 231–2.
51. Carlton, 212–14, 386.
52. Dills, 'Epidemics', 45, 46–47, 50.
53. Ohlmeyer, 'The War of Religion', 184–5.
54. Carlton, 211.
55. Stoyle, 'Whole Streets', 71–2, 79.
56. Porter, 'The Fire Raid', 31–3.
57. Luke, I, 71.
58. *Ibid.*, III, 109–201.
59. *Dundee Court Martial Records*, 42–3, 60–63.
60. Brodie, 73–4.
61. Spalding, II, 317–18.
62. *CSPD, 1641–1643*, 354, 373, 379–81.
63. Adair, 'Court Martial Papers', 218.
64. *Dundee Court Martial Records*, 15–16.
65. Quaife, 49–50, 123.
66. Luke, I, 69.
67. *Cavalier Songs*, 9.

68. Carlton, 295.
69. Durston, 45.
70. Bennett, 'My Plundered Towns', 37–8, 42, 44–5.

2 The Highland bagpipes mak' a din: Rebellions 1660–1746

1. *RPCS, 1690*, 311.
2. *CSPAWI 1702–1703*, 225.
3. *HPJP*, I, 274, 277.
4. Albemarle, I, 29.
5. HMC, *Lothian*, 159.
6. Colley, *Britons*, 74.
7. *HPJP*, II, 375.
8. Clifton, 'Lessons', 115.
9. *RPCS, 1690*, 82–3.
10. *Ibid.*, 1686, 1.
11. PRO, Adm 1/5270 nn.
12. *CSPAWI, 1714–1715*, 234–5.
13. *RPSC, 1689*, 497–8.
14. HMC, *Lothian*, 145.
15. SAUL, CP, Box 11, 224.
16. PRO Adm 1/5253, 98.
17. Albemarle, I, 18–19.
18. *CSPAWI, 1738*, 224, 240, 272.
19. PRO WO 71/38, 30–31, 37–41, 41–3.
20. *HPJP*, I, 147.
21. *RPCS, 1665–1669*, 205.
22. *Ibid.*, 1686, 3.
23. *HPJP*, II, 501.
24. SAUL, CP, BOX 11, 202.
25. SAUL, CP, Box 12, 439.
26. SAUL, CP, Box 12, 172.
27. SAUL, CP, Box 12, 101.
28. *HPJP*, I, 271.
29. *Ibid.*, II, 391, 395.
30. *Ibid.*, II, 384–5.
31. *Ibid.*, II, 417.
32. SAUL, CP, Box 11, 229.
33. *HPJP*, II, 427–8.
34. *Ibid.*, II, 415.
35. SAUL, CP, Box 12, 83.
36. BL, Add. Mss. 35, 451, 32d.
37. Ed. Jackson, I, 369–71.
38. *HPJP*, II, 474–5.
39. *Correspondence of Duke of Richmond*, 197; HMC, *Lothian*, 156.

40. SAUL, CP, Box 11, 238; Box 12, 228.
41. WO 71/8, 150, 168, 308.
42. Charteris, *William Augustus*, 227.
43. *Ibid.*, 236; Lenman, 262.
44. *Correspondence of the Duke of Richmond*, 209.
44. SAUL, CP, Box 11, 239.
45. Albemarle, I, 2.
46. SAUL, CP, Box 12, 140–41; Box 13, 3.
47. SAUL, CP, Box 12, 101.
49. SAUL, CP, Box 12, 101, 105; Box 13, 25.
50. Charteris, *William Augustus*, 273.
51. Albemarle, I, 365.
52. SAUL, CP, Box 12, 83; BL, Add. Mss 35, 451, 41–41d.
53. Charteris, 273; BL, Add. Mss 36, 257, 60d.
54. SAUL, CP, Box 13, 74.
55. Albemarle, I, 179.
56. R. Forbes, *The Lyon in Mourning*, ed. H. Paton, 3 vols (Scottish History Society, 1895); J. Prebble, *Culloden* (1960). The latter is a highly emotive account of a subject which continues to generate much passion.

3 A parent's hand: North America, 1775–83

1. Fischer, 215, 406–7.
2. Brown, 'The Death of Lexington', 505.
3. Evelyn, 39–40.
4. Graymont, 1.
5. Selig, 'A German Soldier', 581.
6. Tiedemann, 'Patriots by Default', 49.
7. *Orderly Book*, 102, 217.
8. Sandwich, I, 63.
9. PRO, CO 5/88, 184–5, 180, 190.
10. *Ibid.*, 197–8; Hoerden, 208.
11. *Ibid.*, 223.
12. *Ibid.*, 225.
13. PRO CO 5/88, 217.
14. Bellesiles, 'The Origins of Gun Culture', 427, 428–9, 433, 444.
15. HMC, *Hastings*, III, 180.
16. Mackenzie, *A British Fusilier*, 27, 29.
17. *DAR*, 14, 47.
18. Tiedemann, 'Patriots', 36–7.
19. Conway, 'To Subdue', 381, 384, 385.
20. *Orderly Book*, 880.
21. SRO, GD 24/1/58, 3, 7; Conway, 'To Subdue,' 392.
22. Tiedemann, 'Patriots', 47.
23. PRO, WO 71/84, 262–70.

24. PRO, WO 71/85, 154–5.

25. Ibid., 159–61.

26. Peebles, 71.

27. NLS, Fernyhough, Box 75, F2, F3.

28. Conway, 'The Great Mischief', 386–7.

29. DAR, 17, 55.

30. Orderly Book, 38–9, 56, 273, 455, 476.

31. NLS, Fernyhough, Box 75, F2.

32. Orderly Book, 476, 880.

33. Graymont, 146–7.

34. Atwood, 130.

35. Shy, A People Numerous, 168–70.

36. Einstein, 115–17.

37. Shy, A People Numerous, 171–3.

38. PRO WO 71/85, 142–4.

39. Orderly Book, 50.

40. Adm 1/484, 307–7d for Dyer's confession. He later claimed he had been kidnapped aboard a British warship and hailed as a patriot hero (Stiles, I, 462–3).

41. PRO WO 71/85, 142–4.

42. Ibid., 128–30.

43. Orderly Book, 273, 275.

44. DAR, XVII, 53–4.

45. Peebles, 108.

46. NLS, Fettercairn, Box 75, F2.

47. Smith, Loyalists, 77.

48. DAR, 21, 277–8.

49. Smith, Loyalists, 35, 63.

50. NLS, Fettercairn, Box 75, F3.

51. Smith, Loyalists, 92.

52. DAR, 17, 53–4.

53. Conway, 'To Subdue', 393.

54. Graymont, 166.

55. Ibid., 55.

4 By Jesus, we have dirks and arms a-plenty: Ireland, 1798–1800

1. SRO, GD 26/9/527, I, 5, 12, 13, 46.

2. Ibid., 44, 74.

3. Curtin, 'The Transformation', 490.

4. Musgrave, I, 184, 189.

5. Curtin, 'The Transformation', 476–7; Bartlett, 'Defenders', 377.

6. Ibid., 378–9.

7. NLS, Ancram, 125.

8. SRO, GD 26/9/527, I, 141.

9. BL, Add. Mss 38, 102, 4–6.
10. Bartlett, 'Counter-Insurgency', 247.
11. SRO, GD 26/9/527, I, 27, 58.
12. PRO, WO 79/44, 103, 162–3.
13. *Ibid.*, 188–9, 193.
14. Curtin, 'The Transformation', 479, 481.
15. NLS, Ancram, 133d–34.
16. Blackstock, 'A Dangerous', 393.
17. NLS, Ancram, 119.
18. *Ibid.*, 120d.
19. Bartlett, 'Counter-insurgency', 270.
20. Moore, I, 273, 275.
21. Byrne, I, 35.
22. BL, Add. Mss 38, 102, 11–12, 17.
23. SRO, GD 26/9/527, I, 19.
24. Musgrave, I, 303–4.
25. Byrne, I, 52.
26. Musgrave, I, 270.
27. Byrne, I, 72, 92, 94, 98, 125.
28. NLS, Ac 5750, 38d.
29. Byrne, I, 169.
30. Bartlett, 'Counter-insurgency', 263.
31. BL, Add. Mss 38, 102, 37, 43.
32. BL, Add. Mss 40, 166N, 70d.
33. SRO, GD 26/527/9, II, 36.
34. BL, Add. Mss 40, 166N, 72d–73, 74.
35. *Two Diaries*, 67, 69.
36. James, *Mutiny*, 185–95.
37. PRO, Adm 1/5351; Adm 1/5370.
38. PRO, WO 1/18, 182–182d.
39. *Ibid.*, 189–201.
40. Cookson, *The British*, 155.
41. Costello, 7.
42. PRO, HO 50/461, 6.
43. PRO, WO 141/4, Memo, 31 March 1914, 21.
44. *Times*, 7 July 1798.

Part Four: Overseas wars, 1660–1870

1 You fight for a good cause: Patriotism and the pursuit of power

1. Bowen, 25.
2. Webb, 'The Frigate', 23, 39.
3. Bowen, 24.
4. Coad, 227–8, 230–32.

5. *Ibid.*, 237–8.
6. *CSPAWI, 1738*, 102–3.
7. PRO, CO 137/61, 27, 29, 40, 46.
8. NLS, Ms 2313 [Cochrane], 138–9.
9. BL, Luttrell Collection, 2, I, nn.
10. *Naval songs and Ballads*, 234–5.
11. *Naval Chronicle*, 2, 67.
12. BL, Lutterell Collection, 2, I, 84.
13. Winstock, 'Hot Stuff', 3.
14. Naphine and Speck, 'Clergymen', 249.
15. *The Anti-Jacobin*, I, 308.
16. *Hansard*, 3rd Series, 85, 449, 451.
17. Beckett, 'Responses', 72.
18. Woodforde, V, 149.
19. *Scottish Songs*, 179.
20. *Aberdeen Journal*, 26 Oct 1803.
21. Frothingham, 137.
22. NLS, Acc 10719/4/7.
23. PRO WO 71/38, 46–78.
24. Knox, I, 109.
25. SRO, GD 51/1, 899, 921.
26. PRO, WO 1/1099, 57–8.
27. *Naval Chronicle*, 3, 136.
28. *Anti-Jacobin*, I, 35.
29. Whiting, 'Frampton Volunteers', 25–6.
30. *Anti-Jacobin*, I, 311.
31. Hudson, 'Volunteer Soldiers', 171.
32. Buckley, 85–7.
33. Cookson, *The British*, 27.
34. Bingham, 26, 27–31.
35. *Illustrated Crimean War Song Book*, 11.
36. Gowing, 3.
37. *Aberdeen Journal*, 8 Nov 1854.
38. PRO, Adm 1/5125.
39. Elmsley, 'The Military', 102.
40. Bell, 'Letters', 77.
41. Paget, 73.
42. *Five Naval Journals*, 162.
43. Blakeney, 54.
44. Donaldson, *Recollections*, 198–9; *A Continuation*, 19.
45. Dillon, I, 128.
46. NAM, Anon 38th Regt. 20d.
47. Costello, 144.
48. ed. Jackson, *Lives*, I, 169.

49. Blakeney, 74.
50. Laurie, 9, 23, 28.
51. HMC, *Hastings*, III, 179; *Naval Chronicle*, 31, 123.
52. Baldwin, 61.
53. Donaldson, *Continuation*, 97–8.
54. PRO, Adm 1/5370.
55. Dillon, I, 150.
56. Baldwin, 46.

2 *A wild rattling man: Recruitment and discipline*

1. Anglesey, I, 115.
2. PRO, Adm 1/5123/25, 131–2.
3. PRO, Adm 101/80/40.
4. Hutton, 75.
5. PRO, WO 12/8823.
6. Cookson, *The British*, 128–9.
7. ed. Jackson, I, 280.
8. *Ibid.*, III, 178.
9. PRO, Adm 1/3991, 36 (Enclosure).
10. Donaldson, *Recollections*, 66.
11. Costello, 2.
12. Baldwin, 21.
13. Pindar, 6
14. Neuburg, 'British Army', 44.
15. Anglesey, I, 123.
16. Ryder, 3.
17. PRO, Adm 1/5468.
18. Anglesey, I, 117–19.
19. Bell, *Songs &c*, 3, 4–5.
20. *The Health of Seamen*, 134.
21. PRO, Adm 1/579.
22. PRO, Adm 1/5114/3/
23. PRO, Adm 1/5116/10, 130.
24. Codrington, I, 207–8.
25. PRO, Adm 1/579.
26. PRO, Adm 1/580.
27. PRO, Adm 1/579.
28. PRO, WO 3/13, 159–60.
29. PRO, Adm 1/5127.
30. *Naval Chronicle*, 31, 31; Scott, I, 35–7; III, 131.
31. PRO, Adm 1/5116, 10, 191.
32. PRO, Adm 1/579.
33. PRO, Adm 1/5361.
34. *CSPAWI, 1711–1712*, 57.

35. *Ibid.*, 228, 351.
36. Scott, III, 120.
37. Buckley, 87, 194.
38. PRO, WO 11246.
39. *Ibid.*; PRO, CO 137/127, 149.
40. Richardson, 67.
41. Harris, 10.
42. Wetherell, 28.
43. Donaldson, *Recollections*, 85.
44. Quinney, 10–11.
45. Donaldson, *Recollections*, 89.
46. PRO, Adm 1/5125.
47. PRO, Adm 51/1214, Pt 6.
48. Dillon, I, 23.
49. *Five Naval Journals*, 129.
50. Clowes, VI, 217.
51. BL, Add. Mss 36, 257.
52. *Five Naval Journals*, 357.
53. PRO, Adm 1/5385.
54. PRO, WO 154/333, 8.9.14.
55. Richardson, 105.
56. PRO, Adm 1/5468.
57. Scott, I, 208.
58. PRO, WO 90/2, 2, 18, 118, 120, 133.
59. Anglesey, I, 135.
60. PRO, Adm 1/5370.
61. PRO, Adm 1/5385.
62. *Five Naval Journals*, 153, 159, 173.
63. *CSPAWI, 1702–1704*, 273–4.
64. Qunney, 171.
65. NAM 8009–9, 3.
66. PRO, WO 71/181.
67. PRO, Adm 1/5444.
68. *CSPAWI, 1711–1712*, 57, 103.
69. PRO, WO 25/2907, 90, 92, 379–80, 975–6; WO 92/1, 36, 38.
70. NLS, Ms 2335 [Cochrane], 18.
71. Gleig, 186.
72. PRO, Adm 1/5444.
73. Spinney, 'Hermione', 183.
74. PRO, WO 71/180.
75. PRO, WO 71/63.
76. PRO, WO 3225, York to Bathurst, 20 Oct 1813.
77. PRO, WO 25/2906, 73.
78. SRO, GD 26/9/527, I, 31.

79. PRO, WO 71/54, 50.
80. PRO, Adm 1/3991.
81. PRO, WO 25/2906, 58; WO 25/2907, 675.
82. PRO, Adm 1/5346.
83. PRO, Adm 1/5345.
84. Wetherell, 39–40.
85. PRO, Adm 1/5375.
86. Dugan, 375, 377.

3 Honourable danger: Command, courage and rewards

1. *Times*, 23 April 1803; *NC*, 9, 317–25.
2. Sterling, *Letters*, 187.
3. *DAR*, 20, 33, 91.
4. Anglesey, I, 279–83.
5. Dundas, 24.
6. Wood, *Subaltern Officer*, 15, 52.
7. Donaldson, *A Continuation*, 170.
8. BL, Egerton, 2135, 31.
9. Anon, 'The Fights', 658.
10. Watkin, 'Captain Hugh Crow', 181, 184.
11. NLS., Browne, 66–7d.
12. Vanson, 53.
13. Dowling, 18.
14. Kinglake, III, 97.
15. Paget, 179.
16. *Health of Seamen*, 146–7.
17. PRO, Adm 101/104/6.
18. Gleig, 93.
19. Dillon, I, 130.
20. Sandford, 106.
21. Knox, II, 57.
22. *Waterloo*, II, 44.
23. Blacker, 20.
24. Strachan, *From Waterloo*, 43.
25. Sterling, *Letters*, 354.
26. *Five Naval Journals*, 105.
27. Southey, 224.
28. Markham, 18.
29. Eastwood, 'Patriotism', 145.
30. Fernyhough, 66.
31. *Naval Chronicle*, 13, 259.
32. *Ibid.*, 267; Guttridge, 'Aspects', 51.
33. BL, Add. Mss 36, 613, 51, 52.
34. *Naval Chronicle*, 31, 31.

35. Clowes, IV, 526.
36. Dillon, I, 101, 160.
37. *Five Naval Journals*, 24–5.
38. *Naval Chronicle*, 9, 153–4; Guttridge, 'Aspects', 151.
39. *Naval Chronicle*, 31, 31.
40. PRO, WO 164/418.
41. PRO, WO 164/172.
42. PRO, Adm 97/128/1.
43. BL, Harleian 7025, 81–2.
44. Baldwin, *Indian Gup*, 50.
45. Swinhoe, 216, 244, 309, 312.
46. Notes, *JSAHR*, LVII, 186.
47. Stanley, 'Highly Inflammatory', 239–40.
48. *Hansard*, 3rd Series, 136, 2136.
49. *Ibid.*, 2159.
50. Maclean, *The Raising*, 17.
51. Sunter, 'Raising the 97th', 95, 102.
52. Glover, 'Purchase', 223–4, 232–3.
53. Razzell, 'Social Origins', 253.
54. Bittner, 'Jane Austen', 78.
55. Wood, *Subaltern Officer*, 10.
56. Thackeray, 42.
57. Surtees, 213.
58. Borrow, 331.
59. Wolesley, 119.
60. Stanley, 'Highly Inflammatory', 238–9.
61. Sterling, *Letters*, 118.
62. *Hansard*, 3rd Series, 137, 1535.

4 Duty must be done: Killing, dying and surviving

1. Codrington, I, 317.
2. Anon., 'The War', 11.
3. McGuffie, 'Kelly of Waterloo', 97, 104.
4. Swinhoe, 137–8.
5. Harris, *Recollections*, 18–19.
6. Frothington, 74.
7. Gleig, 106.
8. *Lancet*, 14 July 1855.
9. *Fifeshire Journal*, 28 Sept 1854.
10. Anon, 'The Indian Rebellion', 57.
11. *Edinburgh Medical Journal*, 1 (1855–56), 605.
12. Glissop, *Passim*.
13. Teichman, 'The Yeomanry', 132–3.
14. Baldwin, 31–2, 37.

15. Pearman, 138, 165.

16. Elers Napier, II, 265–6, 333.

17. Anon, 'The War', 15.

18. Ryder, 23.

19. Donaldson, *Recollections*, 147–8.

20. Hall, *Diary*, 57.

21. Robinson, *Diary*, 201.

22. *Aberdeen Chronicle*, 18 Oct 1854.

23. Paget, 181; Astley, I, 212.

24. Egan, I, v.

25. Gleig, 106.

26. Costello, 18–19.

27. Baldwin, 6.

28. Anon, *Letters from Crimea*, 57–8.

29. Astley, I, 213, 227.

30. NAM, Anon. 38th Regt., 21d.

31. Pinar, 28.

32. *Five Naval Journals*, 9–10.

33. PRO Adm 1/5361.

34. ed. Jackson, I, 164–5.

35. *Ibid.*, II, 165, 174.

36. Hall, *Diary*, 62.

37. Harrington, 94.

38. Einstein, 361.

39. Uhry Abrams, 206.

40. *Naval Chronicle*, 31, 176.

41. BL, Add. Mss 73, 526, nn.

42. *Naval Chronicle*, 14, 52.

43. Glanville Evelyn, 90.

44. Gleig, 78–9, 160.

45. *Ibid.*, 161–2.

46. Bingham, 46.

47. Moore Smith, 47.

48. PRO, Adm 101/11/1.

49. *Health of Seamen*, 173.

50. Shepherd, I, 114–15.

51. Solly, *Lancet*, 17 Feb 1855.

52. Macleod, 'Surgery', 1087.

53. Nicholls, 'A Surgeon', 219–21.

54. *Lancet*, 6 Jan 1855.

55. Solly, *Lancet*, 17 Feb 1855.

56. Maclean, 'Surgery', 1093.

57. *Lancet*, 14 June 1856.

58. *Health of Seamen*, 134.

59. Scott, III, 240; PRO Adm. 1/5125.
60. James, III, 129–30, VI, 241.
61. NLS, MS 2312, 149d.
62. Rothenburg, 247–53.
63. Buckley, 60, 102–3.
64. Browne, *Journal*, 93.
65. Buckley, 273.
66. Pinckard, II, 9–11.
67. Robinson, *Diary*, 258.
68. Rothenburg, 237–8; Keep, 339.
69. PRO Adm 101/116/1.
70. Robinson, *Diary*, 71.
71. PRO, Adm 101/99/7.
72. Shepherd, I, 324–5.
73. PRO, Adm, 101/93/3.
74. PRO, Adm 101/80/4.
75. PRO, Adm 101/93/3.
76. PRO, Adm 101/104/6.
77. PRO, Adm 101/116/1.
78. *Lancet*, 14 June 1856.
79. PRO, Adm 1/3533.
80. *Health of Seamen*, 248–9.
81. Pinckard, I, 14–15.
82. PRO Adm 101/93/3.
83. *Health of Seamen*, 229.
84. *Lancet*, 27 June and 26 Sept 1846.
85. Knox, I, 3–4.
86. ed. Jackson, 77.
87. Browne, *Journals*, 174.
88. PRO, WO 71/239.
89. Pinckard, I, 115.
90. Buckley, 165.
91. PRO, WO 71/94.
92. Buckley, 160–61, 163.
93. *Five Naval Journals*, 131–2.
94. Ramsbotham, 'Soldiers', 46.
95. PRO, Adm 1/5361.
96. PRO, Adm 1/5385.
97. *Ibid.*
98. PRO, Adm 101/110/4.
99. *CSPAWI, 1702–3*, 75.
100. *Ibid.*, 212.
101. *Annals of Medicine for the Year 1798*, 347.
102. PRO, Adm 1/110/4.

103. *British Parliamentary Papers, Medical*, 8, 215, 232.
104. *Ibid.*, 577–9, 609–10, 733.
105. Kinglake, III, 20, 312–13.

5 *Each honoured name: Memories and attitudes*

 1. Porter, 'Bureau and Barrack', 27, 408–10.
 2. King, 'George Godwin', 102.
 3. *Diary of John Bright*, 192.
 4. *Naval Chronicle*, 19, 31.
 5. *Times*, 30 Oct and 6 Nov 1843.
 6. Colley, *Britons*, 159–60.
 7. Pearce, *The Duke of Wellington's Funeral Ode*, 5.
 8. Samuel, 'Workshop', 19.
 9. Lloyd, 'The Rating', 115.
10. *Hansard*, 3rd Series, 94, 123.
11. Sterling, *Letters*, 363.
12. *ILN*, 30 Jan 1855.
13. Introduction, i–ii.
14. BL, Add. Mss 45, 524, 28.
15. Hudson, 'Volunteer Soldiers', 172–3, 177.
16. Bower, 125; Cookson, 'Patriotism', 161.
17. *The Poor Man's Guardian*, 12 July 1831.
18. Beckett, 'The Amateur', 7, 14
19. Western, 'The Formation', 416.
20. SRO, GD 1/49/166 nn.
21. Emsley, 'The Military', 109–10.
22. *Ibid.*, 108.
23. PRO HO 50/4, 313–14.
24. Emsley, 'The Formation', 106.
25. Western, 'The Volunteer Movement', 617.
26. SRO, GD 51/942/1.
27. Whiting, 'Frampton Volunteers', 17.
28. Hudson, 'Volunteer Soldiers', 176.
29. Cookson, 'Patriotism', 167, 175–6.
30. Beckett, 'The Amateur', 8.
31. Porter, 'Bureau and Barrack', 423.
32. Sweetman, 13.
33. Speirs, 92.
34. Anglesey, I, 87.
35. Crossman, 'The Army', 373, 376.
36. Bartlett, *British Naval Policy*, 270.
37. PRO, Adm 1/5124/1, 313.
38. *Hansard*, 3rd Series, 111, 283.
39. Colley, 'Whose Nation?', 101.

40. *Annual Register, 1802* (Principal Occurrences), 65.
41. *ILN*, 3 March 1849.
42. *Ibid.*, 10 March 1849.
43. *Ibid.*, 27 January 1849.
44. *Fifeshire Journal*, 7 Dec 1854.
45. NLS, Ms 1855, 85–85d.
46. Sterling, *Letters*, viii–ix.
47. Vanson, 93.
48. Astley, I, 238.
49. *ILN*, 20 Jan 1855.
50. Harrington, 137–8.
51. Isichei, 150–51.
52. *A Solemn Review*, 9n.
53. *War Inconsistent*, 5–6.
54. *Sketch of the Horrors*, 3.
55. *A Solemn Review*, 4.
56. Royle, *Crimea*, 117–18.
57. *Diaries of John Bright*, 163.
58. Speirs, 50–51.
59. *Aberdeen Chronicle*, 1 Nov 1854.
60. Browne, *Napoleonic War Journal*, 73.
61. Graves, *Goodbye To All That*, 75.
62. Thomson, *Eighty Years*, I, 63–4.
63. *Quarterly Review*, 84, 345.
64. Scott, *Letters*, III, 76–7.
65. Bartlett, *Great Britain*, 315.
66. Mawson, 'Not a Very Nice Regiment', *passim*.
67. *Illustrated Crimean War Songbook*, 10.

Part Five: Total War, 1914–19

1 For civilisation: The nature of total war, 1914–18

1. Moriarty, 'Christian Iconography', *passim*.
2. Aldington, 227.
3. Gallagher, 57.
4. French, 'The Meaning', 387–8.
5. NAM, Maxwell, 31.
6. NAM, Anon, Loyal North Lancashire Regt, 4–5.
7. LHC, Burnham 8 June 1900.
8. Neilson, 'That Dangerous', 25.
9. Beckett, 'The Amateur', 8.
10. Wyatt, 'Air Raids', 38.
11. *Documents Relating to the Naval Air Service*, I, 173, 188–91.
12. Wilkinson, 16.

13. Dockville and French, 69–70.
14. Foyle, III, 444.
15. Marder, V, 108.
16. PRO WO 161/97, 227.
17. Fayle, III, 61.
18. *Economist*, 10 April 1917.
19. PRO WO 154/73, 16 Sept 1916.
20. LHC, Foulkes, 6/7, nn.
21. PRO, HO 139/5/9.
22. PRO, HO 139/7/25.
23. PRO, HO 139/7/27, II.
24. Ferguson, figure 14.
25. *Evening Standard*, 13 July 1916.
26. Smither, 'A Wonderful Idea', 4.
27. Reeves, 'Film Propaganda', 469.
28. Wilkinson, 20.
29. IWM, Pond, 1.
30. Griffith, 43.
31. *Daily Sketch*, 17 June 1917.
32. *Evening Standard*, 13 July 1917.
33. Wells, *Anticipations*, 181–2, 185–6.
34. Wells, *Correspondence*, 2, 423.
35. Hartcup 13 13, 29.
36. Charteris, *At GHQ*, 77–8.
37. Griffith, 36.
38. Harris, 'Haig and the Tank', 146–7.
39. *Aeronautical Journal*, Feb 1919; Snowden Gamble, 210.
40. Prior and Wilson, 294.
41. Hartcup, 146–7.
42. LHC, Foulkes, 6/4, 34.
43. Griffith, 163.
44. Snowden Gamble, 216 ff.
45. Prior and Wilson, 294.
46. LHC, Wickens, 1.
47. PRO, Air 1/2288/11/84, 5.
48. Hartcup, 154.
49. Jones, VI 464–5.
50. Hartcup, 178.
51. Jones, VI, 482–8; Hartcup, 154.
52. Jones, VI, 476.
53. Griffith, 12 ff.
54. Sassoon, 323–4.
55. *Statistics of Military Effort*, 183, 878.
56. *Ibid.*, 500, 505.

2 Their officers' example: Preparations for command and civil war postponed, 1870–1914

1. NLS, Ms 20, 247, 88.
2. Haldane, 402–3.
3. Woodhead, 117.
4. *Daily Express*, 6 Nov 1998; private information.
5. *Lancet*, 23 April 1923.
6. PRO, WO 141/37, 152–3.
7. PRO, Adm 156/28.
8. Razzell, 'Social Origins', 253.
9. *Saturday Review*, 20 Oct 1917.
10. Anon. [Martello Tower], 7–8, 33.
11. NAM, Ross, 12–14.
12. *Spectator*, 20 April 1918.
13. Lyttleton, 'The Loom of Youth', 659.
14. *Hansard*, 5th Series, 70, 1434, 1598–9.
15. NAM, Ross, 18.
16. Temple-Patterson, 'A Midshipman', 351–3.
17. PRO Adm 156/21.
18. Barrow, 107.
19. NAM, Maxwell, 74.
20. NAM, Jelf, 3.
21. LHC, Burnham, 22 July 1900.
22. NLS, MS 11460, I, 8.
23. Travers, 50.
24. NAM, Preston, 26 June 1904.
25. Ballard, 'Letters', 77–8, 80.
26. NLS, Ac 1669, 26, 1 and 28 March and 28 August 1898.
27. Temple Patterson, 'A Midshipman', 356.
28. Bennett, *Cowan's War*, 56–7, 59.
29. Barrow, 62–3.
30. Travers, 39, 41.
32. Ballard, 'Letters', 70.
33. NLS, Ms 20,248, 25.
34. Ponsonby, 'The Army Crisis', 611.
35. PRO, WO 141/4, Memo 31 March 1914, 20–21; Intelligence Summary 21/31; 31/3; 35/3, 68/3.
36. *Saturday Review*, 21 March 1914; *Spectator*, 28 March 1914.
37. Beckett and Jeffery, 'The Royal Navy', 62, 65.
38. Beckett, 'Some Further Correspondence', 104.
39. Beckett, *The Army*, 337.
40. *Hansard*, 5th Series, 60, 431.
41. Beckett, *The Army*, 385–6.
42. *Droghedea Argus*, 9 April 1918.

43. Beckett and Jeffery, 'The Royal Navy', 65.

44. Beckett, 'Some Further Correspondence', 104.

45. *Hansard*, 5th Series, 60, 435.

46. Beckett, *The Army*, 370.

47. Adm 156/157 nn.

48. Beckett, *The Army*, 124.

49. LHC, Edmonds VII/5, IA, 7.

50. BL, Keyes 2/2.

51. Dangerfield, *The Strange Death of Liberal England* (1935).

52. Hamilton, 1, 62.

3 The stern business of war: Command and discipline

1. Travers, 39; Echevarria, 'On the Brink', 82.

2. *Lancet*, 16 June 1917.

3. PRO, WO 154/8, List of absentees up to 30 June 1917.

4. Childs, 139.

5. NLS, Ms 20,249, 211.

6. PRO Air 1/2288.11, 87, 2.

7. *Spectator*, 30 March 1918.

8. Travers, 251.

9. Manning, 181.

10. Crozier, *The Men*, 33.

11. IWM, Conn, 21.

12. PRO, WO 158/17, 286–7.

13. NLS, Ms 20,248, 152, 277.

14. PRO, WO 95/1415, 12 March 1915.

15. PRO, Cab 45/166, nn.

16. PRO, Cab 45/133, 279.

17. PRO, Cab 45/136, 160.

18. PRO, Cab 45/133, 283–4.

19. Graves, 200.

20. IWM, Perkins, 2.

21. PRO Cab 45/138, 47–9.

22. NLS, Ms 20,249, 88.

23. Travers, 182.

24. PRO, Cab 45/135, 362–3.

25. PRO, Cab 45/30, Lt-Colonel W. E. Beazley, 21 Oct 1937.

26. PRO, Cab 45/133, 357–8.

27. NLS, Ms 20,248, 99.

28. NLS, Ms 20,249, 29.

29. Prior and Wilson, 91.

30. De Groot, *Haig*, 407.

31. *Ibid.*, 241.

32. NLS, Acc 3155/118, 38–9.

33. PRO, WO 161/100, 4044.
34. PRO, WO 154/151, 19 April 1917.
35. BRO, T-A 3/517, 10 August 1915.
36. *Times*, 22 Jan 1918.
37. Woodward, 335.
38. *John Bull*, 26 Jan 1918.
39. *Ibid.*, 2 and 16 March and 25 May 1918.
40. Crozier, *Impressions*, 196.
41. Crozier, *The Men*, 54.
42. *Ibid.*, 71–2.
43. PRO, Cab 45/137, 201.
44. PRO, Air 1/2288/228/11/87, 2.
45. BRO, T-A 3/20 nn.
46. LHC, Burnham, 5, 9 and 24 April and 2 May 1900.
47. NAM, Lloyd, 221.
48. PRO, WO 108/372, 8; NAM 5603-10-2, 29 Jan 1900.
49. PRO, WO 108/372, 104, 106, 116.
50. NLS, Ms, 20,048, 82.
51. *Ibid.*, 41–2, 56–7; PRO, WO 154/33, 25–6 and 28 August 1914.
52. LHC, Edmonds VI, 4, 26 August 1914.
53. PRO, WO 33/713, 136, 186–7.
54. PRO, WO 141/37, 3, 4, 35, 77–8, 163–5.
55. NLS, Ms 20,2048, 85.
56. PRO, WO 71/387; WO 153/33; Babington, 6–7.
57. Peaty, 'Haig and Military Discipline', 99–100.
58. Hurst, 'Administration', 324–5.
59. NLS, Ms 20,249, 197.
60. PRO, WO 71/397; Putowski and Sykes, 30–31.
61. PRO, WO 71/388.
62. NLS, Ms 20, 248, 150; 20, 249, 107.
63. PRO, Cab 45/116, nn.
64. LHC, Edmonds, III/ 12, 16–17.
65. PRO, WO 154/73, 18 August 1916 and 5 January 1917.
66. *John Bull*, 16 March 1918; *Hansard*, 5th Series, 106, 847–51.
67. *Ibid.*, 107, 529; 108, 719–20.
68. *Drogheda Argus*, 17 August and 28 Sept 1918.
69. PRO, Adm 156/19, 14.
70. PRO, Adm 156/89, Minutes of Enquiry, I, 42.
71. Dallas and Gill, *Unknown Army*, 74.
72. Dallas and Gill, 'Mutiny', 92n.
73. PRO, WO 154/101, 2 August 1917.
74. *Ibid.*
75. Dallas and Gill, *Unknown Army*, 76, 81–2.
76. PRO, WO 106/401.

77. Ferguson, 348.
78. Gurney, 95, 139.
79. Brophy and Partridge, 45.
80. IWM 87/37/1, nn.
81. Brophy and Partridge, 67.
82. Gurney, 136.
83. PRO, WO 161/95, 285.
84. Sheffield, 'The Effect', 89, 98.
85. Ferguson, 348.
86. Bion, 41.
87. PRO, Cab 45/31, Sir Morgan Crofton, 26 Dec 1937.
88. Owen, Letters, 393.
89. Fuller, Troop Morale, 51.

4 The intensity of the moment: Survivors and casualties

 1. NAM, Clark, 62.
 2. IWM, West, nn.
 3. PRO, Cab 45/207.
 4. Dewey, 'Military Recruiting', 204–5.
 5. Saturday Review, 12 Sept 1914.
 6. I am indebted to Father Aidan Berenger for this point and showing me the memorial.
 7. IWM, Turner, nn.
 8. South Wales Argus, 25 April 1915.
 9. Cork Eagle, 15 April 1916.
10. IWM, Sturdy, 19–20.
11. NLS, Ms 26,930, 26, 44–5, 81–2.
12. South Wales Argus, 19 April 1915.
13. Cork Eagle, 17 Oct 1914.
14. South Wales Argus, 19 April 1915.
15. IWM, Firth, 29 June 1916.
16. PRO, Air 1/2288/11/83, 4.
17. LHC, Carr, 14.
18. James, Imperial Warrior, 123.
19. IWM, West, nn.
20. Veitch, 'Play Up', 370–72.
21. Brophy and Partridge, 230.
22. PRO, Cab 45/30, Sir Morgan Crofton, 20 Dec 1937.
23. PRO, Cab 45/212, nn.
24. PRO, Cab 45/212, W. Dalziel to Col. Chapman, 22 May 1930.
25. Times, 8 Jan 1918.
26. South Wales Argus, 6 March 1915.
27. IWM, Reeve, nn.
28. IWM, Conn, 38.

29. Sassoon, 94.
30. Lewis, *Sagittarius Rising*, 45.
31. PRO, WO 161/96, 549.
32. PRO, Air 1/1219/204/2634, ii, 54–5.
33. Jones, II, 202.
34. PRO, Air 1/2288/11/80.
35. PRO, Air 1/1219/5/2634/27.
36. PRO, Air 1/1219/5/2634, 203.
37. PRO, Air 1/1219/204/2634, 12, 20.
38. PRO, Air 1/1219/204/2634, 31.
39. PRO, WO 161/95, 172.
40. English, 'A Predisposition', 16.
41. Birley, 'The Principles'.
42. PRO, Air 1/2288/228/81, 1, 4.
43. Jones, VI, 441.
44. PRO, Air 1/2288/228/11/71, 4.
45. 'Medical Aspects of Aviation'.
46. Anon, 'Physiological Aspects of Flying'.
47. Anon, Stamm, 'Medical Aspects', 11–12.
48. Birley, 'The Principles'.
49. *Lancet*, 23 Jan 1915.
50. Talbot, 'Soldiers, Psychiatrists', 437.
51. *Medical Services: Diseases of the War*, II, 7, 8, 57; *Lancet*, 20 Dec 1930.
52. *Medical Services: Diseases of the War*, II, 5.
53. *Ibid.*, 34–9; May, 'Lord Moran', *passim*; Summerfield, 'Shell-shock'.
54. *History of the Great War: Medical Services: Diseases of the War*, II, 10.
55. Bogacz, 'War Neuroses', 227.
56. Savage, 'Mental War Cripples', 4.
57. Burton Fanning, 'Neurasthenia'.
58. Bogacz, 'War Neuroses', 255–6.
59. Mott, 'War Pyscho-Neurosis'.
60. Rivers, 'Repression'.
61. *Hansard*, 5th Series, House of Lords, 39, 1102–3.
62. PRO, Adm 156/93, Deposition of Major W. Williams.
63. BL, Add. Mss 71,558, Letters of Frances Emily Scott, 103–4.
64. Bogacz, 'War Neuroses', 259.
65. May, 'Lord Moran', 98.
66. Leese, 'Problems', 1058–63.
67. Anon. 'The Adventures of an Ensign', 609.
68. Ferguson, 377.
69. *Medical Services: Surgery of the War*, I, 481.
70. IWM, 78/21/1, nn.
71. IWM, 87/18/1, 8–9.
72. Ferguson, 376–9.

73. Bourke, *An Intimate*, 189.
74. Horne and Kramer, 'Atrocities', 11–12.
75. E.g. PRO, WO 161/97. 228; WO 161/98, 115; WO 161/99, 1601, 1839; WO 161/100, 2422, 2782, 2891, 2893, 3224, and for a case in East Africa, PRO, Cab 45/31, J. J. Drought, 17 Nov 1938.
76. PRO, WO 161/95, 74.
77. PRO, WO 161/95, 2; WO 161/100, 3110.
78. PRO, WO 161/99, 1583, 1597, 1615.
79. PRO, WO 161/99, 1612.
80. PRO, WO 161/100, 2403–7.
81. Ferguson, 3690.
82. PRO, WO 161/98, 160, 186, 199, 243, 285, 687.
83. PRO, WO 161/95, 72.
84. PRO, WO 161/96, 105.
85. PRO, WO 161/96, 175.
86. PRO, WO 161/99, 1586.
87. PRO, WO 161/100, 2735–6.
88. PRO, Cab 45/211.
89. Schneider, 'The Cross', 44–5.
90. *Life and Work*, May 1915.
91. *The Layman's Book of the General Assembly of 1915*, 63; *Life and Work*, Nov 1917.
92. Wilkinson, 180, 81.
93. *Ibid.*, 135–8, 141, 182.

5 *Same as the lads: Women, work and wages*

1. Hinsley, 21.
2. Account from Oliver Turner's narrative (IWM, 83/17/1).
3. *Saturday Review*, 23 March 1918.
4. IWM, Airey, 3.
5. PRO, HO 45/10783/283152, i, 7.
6. PRO, HO 45/10783/238152, ii, 26.
7. PRO, HO 45/10783/238152, ii, 3.
8. Jones, VI, 143, 152.
9. PRO, Air 1/2288/228/11/86.
10. *Lancet*, 3 Sept 1919.
11. Creighton, 'Women Police', 166.
12. *Saturday Review*, 19 May 1918.
13. Levine, 'Walking the Streets', 44.
14. PRO, WO 154/8, January (Appendix V); July (Appendix V).
15. PRO, WO 154/104, *passim*.
16. PRO, HO 45/10802, 307990, 64.
17. PRO, HO 45/10802/307990, 63.
18. PRO, Mepo 2/1720.

19. Fuller, *Troop Morale*, 75–6; *Hansard*, 5th Series, 107, 335.
20. Account from Miss West's diary (IWM 77/156/1).
21. Culleton, 'Working-class Women', 6–7.
22. Waites, 163–6.
23. *Economist*, 16 Nov 1918.
24. Lewchuk, 114.
25. *Documents Relating to the RNAS*, 19, 102.
26. LCH, Foulkes 6/4.1.
27. Lewchuk, 154.
28. Whiteside, 'Welfare Legislation', 382.
29. *Times*, 22 July 1918.
30. Ward, 123–4.
31. Waites, 189–90.
32. MacLean, *The Legend*, 13.
33. *Ibid.*, 109.
34. Scott and Cunnison, 94, 108–9.
35. Maclean, *The Legend*, 31.
36. *Ibid.*, 35, 61.
37. *Times*, 10 July 1918.
38. Rubin, 33–4.
39. *Ibid.*, 246.
40. MacLean, *The Legend*, 79–83.
41. *Times*, 23 July 1918.
42. PRO, Mepo 2/1719.
43. Waites, 135.
44. Coles, 'The Moral Economy', 174–6.
45. *Economist*, 31 August 1918.
46. Dewey, 'British Farming', 382.
47. *Times*, 12 and 16 Sept 1918.
48. *Scotsman*, 7 Sept 1918; *Times* 9 Sept 1918.
49. *Cork Eagle*, 19 May 1917.
50. *Scotsman*, 3 Sept 1918.
51. *Times*, 10 Sept 1918.
52. *Cork Eagle*, 16 June 1917.
53. *Tyrone Constitution*, 22 Feb 1918.
54. Dewey, 'British Farming', 374–5.
55. Bowley, 151.
56. *Economist*, 24 Sept 1918.
57. Balderston, 'War Finance', 235.
58. Scott and Cunnison, 173.
59. Waites, 101.
60. Sassoon, *Diaries*, 43–4.
61. IWM, Bradburn, 13 Nov 1915; 16 Jan 1916.
62. PRO, Adm 167/55, 405.

6 *Ramsay MacDonald and his German comrades: Objection to war,*
1914–19

1. PRO, HO 45/10814/312987, 9.
2. Ward, *Red Flag*, 166.
3. Wilkinson, 28.
4. MacLean, *The Legend*, 45, 106–7, 244.
5. Ferguson, 221.
6. PRO, HO 45/10814/312987.
7. PRO, HO 139/26/96.
8. Ferguson, 221.
9. PRO, HO 139/23.
10. PRO, HO 45/10814/312987, 1.
11. PRO, HO 45/10814/312937.
12. PRO, HO 45/10814/312987, 9.
13. Weller, 56–7.
14. *Times*, 1 Sept 1918.
15. *Scotsman*, 2 May 1918.
16. *Punch*, 22 March and 5 July 1916; *Saturday Review*, 29 Jan 1916.
17. *Daily Express*, 19 April 1916.
18. PRO, HO 45/10808/311118, 7.
19. *Bishops Castle Advertiser*, 4 May 1917.
20. *Ibid.*, 11 May 1917.
21. *Ibid.*, 2 April 1918.
22. PRO, CO 904/61, 916.
23. PRO, CO 904/61, 978.
24. *Cork Eagle*, 22 Jan 1916.
25. *Drogheda Argus*, 2 July 1917.
26. *Tyrone Constitution*, 19 April 1918.
27. *Hansard*, 5th Series, 107, 993.
28. PRO, CO 904/161/1154.
29. *Tyrone Constitution*, 4 and 11 Oct 1918.
30. NLS, Acc 3155, 135, 29–31 Jan 1919.
31. LHC, Robertson, 5/3/3, 4.
32. NLS, Acc 3155, 29 Jan 1919.
33. Dallas and Gill, *Secret Army*, 97–8.
34. Englander and Osborne, 'Jack, Tommy', 604–5.
35. Ward, 'Intelligence', 179, 187.
36. Dennis, 'Territorial Army', 707.
37. Evans, 'Some Forces', 80.
38. PRO, CO 904/108, 58.
39. Ward, *Red Flag*, 148.
40. Ward, 'Intelligence', 183–4, 187.
41. PRO, Adm 156/179, 482.
42. PRO, Adm 156/94.

43. PRO, Adm 156/49.

7 The cemetery of all that is best: Remembering and counting the cost

 1. PRO, Adm 137/3833, 12.
 2. *St Andrews Citizen*, 22 Feb, 2 March 1918.
 3. *Spectator*, 27 June 1916.
 4. IWM, Conn, 29.
 5. *Bishop's Castle Advertiser*, 2 Feb 1917.
 6. *South Wales Argus*, 13 March 1915.
 7. Bourke, 'Heroes', 43.
 8. PRO, WO 374/45209.
 9. NLS, Ms 13, 589, 254–5.
10. [WTP], *Thomas Dowding* (1918 ed.), *passim*.
11. *Spectator*, 29 April 1918.
12. *Scars upon my Heart*, 1–2.
13. *Daily Telegraph*, 12 Nov 1998.
14. Private information.
15. Marder, V, 192.
16. *Economist*, 31 Jan 1920.
17. Horn, 'The Concept' 6.
18. *Economist*, 17 Jan 1920.
19. Lloyd, *Experiment*, 36.
20. Scott and Cunnison, 61.
21. Tweedale, 'Business', 59.
22. *Factors*, I, 66, 518–20.
23. Wilkinson, 305.
24. *Lancet*, 15 and 19 Sept 1917.
25. Darwin, 'On the Statistical'; Crook, 'War', 49.
26. Winter, 'The Impact', 498.
27. Winter, 'Aspects', 724.
28. Koven,' Remembering', 1168–9.
29. Hammond, 228.
30. De Groot, *Blighty*, 258–61.
31. Petter, 'Temporary Gentlemen', 132–3.
32. Grieves, 'Nelson's History', 538–9.
33. PRO, Adm 153/43.
34. De Groot, *Blighty*, 268.
35. Ward, *Red Flag*, 169.
36. Watson, 'Khaki Girls', 34.
37. Robert, 'Gender', 60–61.
38. Watson, 'Khaki Girls', 43.
39. Marder, V, 345.
40. *Economist*, 10 October 1919.
41. *Listener*, 10 July 1929.

42. Hynes, 68.
43. M. Stephen, *Never Such Innocence* (1988).
44. Nicholson, *What Did You Do*, 1.

Part Six: The people's wars, 1919–2000

1 Britannia's Huns with their long-range guns: Civil wars in Ireland, 1919–23

1. I am indebted to Mark Hunter for a copy of this song.
2. I am indebted for this point to Dr Tony Macgilligot.
3. PRO, HO 144/21349. These rumours were cited in defence of Captain Bowen-Colthurst [see p.566].
4. *Cork Eagle*, 22 August 1914.
5. *Cork Eagle*, 29 August 1914.
6. James, *Rise and Fall*, 283.
7. PRO, HO 144/21349.
8. Kee, 566–7.
9. *Drogheda Argus*, 16 March 1918.
10. *Cork Eagle*, 19 May and 23 June 1917.
11. *Tyrone Constitution*, 11 Jan, 1 Feb, 24 May and 12 July 1918.
12. PRO, CO 904/228.
13. PRO, CO 904/228.
14. PRO, CO 904/161, 916
15. Townshend, 14.
16. *Tyrone Constitution*, 3 May 1918.
17. Wilson, *Letters*, 267, 273.
18. *Tyrone Constitution*, 15 Nov 1918.
19. PRO, CO 904/161, 319–321d.
20. *Drogheda Argus*, 14 Dec 1918.
21. Kee, 626–7.
22. PRO, CO 904/108, 249; *Kilkenny People*, 1 Feb, 22 Feb, 1 March 1919.
23. PRO, CO 904/161, 313.
24. Fitzpatrick, 'Militarism', 406.
25. Breen, 74.
26. PRO, CO 904/108, 496.
27. PRO, CO 905/108, 9, 496.
28. PRO, CO 904/161, 251d.
29. PRO, CO 904/115, 687–8.
30. PRO, CO 904/115, 346.
31. Breasy, 200–201.
32. Breen, 109–110.
36. Coogan, 159; Kee, 693.
37. Hart, 'Operations', 73.
38. Coogan, 179.

39. PRO, WO 141/44.
40. LHC, Foulkes, 7, 29–32.
41. PRO, WO 35/170, 40/636.
42. LHC, Foulkes, 7, 32.
43. LHC, Foulkes, 7, 23.
44. PRO, WO 35/91.
45. Breasy, 314–15.
46. *Dundalk Examiner*, 24 April and 15 Sept 1920.
47. *Times*, 22 July and 13 August 1920; PRO, CO 904/115, 685.
48. *Roscommon Journal*, 11, 19 and 26 September 1920.
49. SRO, HH 55/68, 300033/22.
50. PRO, CO 904/115, 8, 26.
51. PRO, WO 35/170, 7/98.
52. PRO, WO 35/170, 52/789/1.
53. PRO, Adm 178/106, 3153 R 15.
54. PRO, Adm 178/108, R 109.
55. PRO, WO 35/170, 52/781/1.
56. *Belfast Telegraph*, 19 April 1920.
57. PRO, CO 904/41.
58. PRO, WO 35/170, 2/3089.
59. Coogan, 146.
60. PRO, WO 35/89.
61. PRO, CO 904/42; Figgis, 176.
62. PRO, CO 904/42.
63. PRO, CO 904/43, 38887.
64. Breen, 233.
65. Breen, 39, 135–6.
66. Coogan, 130–31.
67. LHC, Foulkes, 7, 9.
68. *Belfast Telegraph*, 15 May 1920.
69. Fitzpatrick, 399–401.
70. CO 904/115, 331.
71. James, *Mutiny*, 204 ff.
72. Macready, II, 609–10.
73. LHC, Foulkes, 7, 14.
74. LHC, Foulkes, 7, 11.
75. LHC, Foulkes, 7, 25.
76. LHC, Foulkes, 7, 15.
77. Boyce, 52–4.
78. *Ibid.*, 79–81.
79. SRO, HH 55/68, 30033/22.
80. SRO, HH 55/62, 300033/2.
81. *Times*, 4 April 1921.
82. SRO, HH 55/63, 300033/13.

83. *Times*, 4 April 1921.
84. SRO, HH 55/63, 300033/13.
85. *Times*, 16 May 1921.
86. Hart, 'Operations Abroad', 81.
87. SRO, HH 55/63, 300033/14.
88. PRO, Air 8/40.
89. Private information.

2 A war of peoples and causes: Duties and ideals, 1939–45

1. IWM, Passmore, 1, 20.
2. PRO, Adm 199/838, 419–20.
3. IWM, Hall, 178d.
4. IWM, Passmore, I, 89.
5. French, 'You Cannot', 3.
6. PRO, Prem 4/37/5A, 387.
7. Wark, 'The Air Defence Gap', 522–3.
8. Cox, 'The Sources', 562.
9. PRO, Adm 152/214.
10. *New Statesman*, 1 June 1940.
11. *Lancet*, 15 June 1940.
12. *Daily Herald*, 5 July 1941.
13. *Times*, 28 Jan 1941.
14. *Cleveland Engineer News*, 13 March 1943.
15. *Bedfordshire Times and Standard*, 21 April 1944.
16. *Woman's Own*, 22 Jan 1943.
17. *Bath and Wiltshire Chronicle*, 3, 7 and 13 April 1943.
18. *Spectator*, 15 Jan 1943.
19. *Labour and the Wartime Coalition*, 110.
20. *Times*, 7 June 1940.
21. Gilbert, *Finest Hour*, 665.
22. *Daily Herald*, 15 July 1941.
23. *Country Life*, 24 August 1940.
24. *Times*, 20 July 1940.
25. Richards, 'National Identity', 43–4.
26. *Horizon* 2 (August 1940).
27. *New Statesman*, 1 June 1940.
28. Morgan and Evans, 48.
29. PRO Air 29/603.
30. Morgan and Evans, 48.
31. IWM, Waymouth, II, 100–101.
32. PRO FO 371/34126, 165.
33. Pronay, 'The Land of Promise', 76–7.
34. *Woman's Own*, 15 and 22 Jan 1943.
35. Hennessy, 76.

36. *Hansard*, 5th Series, 386, 1687.
37. Nicholson, *What did You Do*, 143.
38. *Listener*, 1 May 1943.
39. Priestley, 69.
40. Harrison, 'The Popular Press', 167.
41. *Listener*, 1 August 1940.

3 Only scratches: Invasion fears and blitz realities

1. Bialer, 158.
2. Murray, 'The Influence', 244–5.
3. Smith, 'The Air Threat', 621–2.
4. Hinsley, I, 481–2.
5. *Daily Herald*, 1 Sept 1941.
6. *Chard and Ilminster News*, 20 Feb 1943.
7. *Sphere*, 15 and 22 June 1940.
8. Mackenzie, 'The British Home Guard', 52.
9. PRO, WO 165/38, 11 June 1940.
10. PRO, HO 45/26025, memo of 25 April 1940.
11. PRO, HO 45/26018, nn.
12. Thurlow, 'The "Mosley" Papers', 180.
13. PRO, HO 45/25747, 863001, 2A.
14. *Times*, 20 July 1940; Hinsley and Simkins, 53.
15. PRO, HO 45/26027, 24, 5; 25, 4.
16. SRO, HH 55/7 PWD 1/1/3/1.
17. PRO, HO 45/26027, 24, 3; HO 45/25747, 863001/20, 7.
18. *New Statesman*, 30 July 1940.
19. PRO, HO 45/26018, nn.; HO 45/25747, 836001/20, 7.
20. Lukowitz, 'British Pacifists', 121, 123.
21. *New Statesman*, 27 July 1940; *Times*, 7 June 1940.
22. PRO, HO 45/25747, 86300/20, 7.
23. SRO, HH 55/23, PWD 1/1/2, 22; PRO HO 45/26027, 26, 5.
24. PRO, HO 45/26024.
25. *Country Life*, 11 May 1940; SRO HH 55/23, PWD 1/1/22, 22.
26. LHC, Denman, nn.
27. *Peace News*, 8 March 1940; *Listener*, 12 Sept 1940.
28. Roberts, Ch. 6.
29. PRO Air 2/8420, 1A, 4A.
30. Prem 4/3/24, 1979.
31. Prem 4/3/24, 1961.
32. SRO, HH 55/28, PWD 1/1/2, 42.
33. PRO, Air 2/8654.
34. I am indebted to Richard Demarco for this reminiscence.
35. IWM, Waymouth, 75.
36. SRO, HH 57/27, PWD 1/1/2, 12.

37. Orwell, 12, 262–3.
38. *BMJ*, 21 Sept 1940.
39. *New Statesman*, 29 Sept 1940.
40. *BMJ*, 4 Jan 1941.
41. *BMJ*, 12 April 1941.
42. *BMJ*, 11 Feb 1941.
43. Orwell, 12, 255–65, 262–3.
44. I am indebted to Percy Wood for this story.
45. *New Statesman*, 2 Nov 1940.
46. SRO, HH 55/23, PWD 1/2/23.
47. Webb and Duncan, 145.
48. PRO, HO 45/26067, 26, 5.
49. SRO, HH 55/23, PWD 1/2/23.
50. Crook, 'Science and War', 88, 99–100.
51. SRO, HH 55/27, PWD 1/1/2, 39, 42; HO 50/2 [16], 2–3.
52. SRO, HO 50/2 [16], 1.
53. Price, 'Politics', 302.
54. Fisk, 51–2, 412–15.
55. *BMJ*, 10 June 1941.
56. *Lancet*, 31 May 1941.
57. *Lancet*, 25 Jan 1941.
58. Calder, 129–30.
59. *BMJ*, 12 April, 10 May 1941.
60. *Vogue*, November 1940.
61. PRO, HO 45/25557, 824286, 12.
62. PRO, HO 45/25557, 824286, 22.
63. *Daily Herald*, 29 Oct 1940.
64. PRO, HO 45/25557, 824286, 20.
65. Manchester *Guardian*, 6 May 1941.
66. PRO, HO 45/25557, 834286, 12.
67. PRO, Crim 1/1252.
68. PRO, Crim 1/1251.
69. *Evening Standard*, 25 Nov 1940.
70. PRO, Air 2/7725, 18.
71. PRO, Air 2/6163, 9A.
72. *Times*, 30 May 1940.
73. *Times*, 19 July 1940; *Spectator*, 19 July 1940.
74. *Economist*, 3 August 1940.
75. *Sunday Graphic*, 1 Sept 1940.
76. PRO, HO 45/25747, 863001/20, 11.
77. PRO, FO 371/34123, 9.
78. PRO, FO 371/34126, 78; I am indebted to A. N. Wilson for the Manchester tale, which he heard from his father.
79. PRO, Adm 156/98.

80. PRO, WO 169/11: Intelligence summary 209, 6; Intelligence summary 22, 7.
81. SRO, HH 55/27, PWD 1/2/38, 22.
82. SRO, HH 55/27, PWD 1/2/2.
83. PRO, WO 32/15772, 16A.
84. SRO, HO 50/12 [16], 1–3.
85. SRO, HO 50/1, *passim*.
86. SRO, HH 55/27, PWD 1/1/2, 39.

4 You may go for a Burton next time: Attrition in the air and at sea, 1939–45

1. Gilbert, *Finest Hour*, 1182–3.
2. Overy, 18, 26, 45.
3. Groehler, 'The Strategic', 287.
4. Kershaw, 598, 620–21.
5. Terraine, 'Theory', 489; Hastings, 489.
6. *U.S. Strategic Bombing Survey*, I, 1.
7. *Ibid.*, IV, 1, 7, 17, 44–9.
8. Crook, 'Science', *passim*.
9. Morrow, 'German Aircraft', 46–7; Groehler, 'The Strategic', 294. ·
10. *U.S. Strategic Bombing Survey*, I, 4–5.
11. Crook, 'Science', 84.
12. Murray, 'The Influence', 245.
13. *Daily Herald*, 4 July 1941.
14. *Spectator*, 31 March, 14 April and 2 June 1944.
15. *Listener*, 2 March, 1 June 1944.
16. *Hansard*, House of Lords, 5th Series, 130, 747–51.
17. *Listener*, 2 March 1944.
18. *Listener*, 6 January 1944.
19. Paris, 'The Rise', 123–4.
20. IWM, Passmore, I, 20, 73.
21. Hastings, 15.
22. McCarthy, 'Aircrew', 87–8.
23. PRO Air 29/603.
24. IWM, Fox, 3–4.
25. IWM, Hull, 179, 195.
26. PRO, Air 29/603.
27. PRO, Air 2/4935; McCarthy, 'Aircrew', *passim*.
28. PRO, Air 2/4935.
29. Hastings, 215–16.
30. PRO, Air 27/1349.
31. IWM, Dobson, 4–7.
32. Hastings, 215–17.
33. PRO, Air 14/3230, 1B, 2B.
34. Hastings, 125–6; 267.

35. PRO, Air 35/160, 6A.
36. McCarthy, 'Aircrew', 91–2.
37. PRO Air 2/4935, Notes for the Guidance of Medical Officers [Air Ministry Pamphlet 100A].
38. *Spectator*, 9 June 1944.
39. IWM, Hull, 138–9.
40. PRO, Air 37/643, 1A, 1B.
42. *Listener*, 13 April 1944.
43. IWM, Hull, 137.
44. IWM, Hull, 65d, 75–75d, 110, 179–179d.
45. Hastings, 215.
46. IWM, Hull, 89.
47. PRO, Air 44/15, 410, 468.
48. Hastings, 215.
49. IWM, Barringer, 15, 40.
50. Morison, I, 127–8.
51. Morison, I, 53.
52. Morison, I, 82.
53. *Defeat of the Enemy*, 17–19, 21.
54. Morison, I, 26.
55. *Defeat of the Enemy*, 40.
56. *Defeat of the Enemy*, 93.
57. *Defeat of the Enemy*, 178–9.
58. *Defeat of the Enemy*, 216.
59. PRO, Adm 199/958.
60. *Battle of the Atlantic*, xxvii.
61. *Battle of the Atlantic*, xiv–v, xvi–xvii, xxvii.
62. IWM, Kirby, 277–8.
63. PRO, Adm 1/15304.
64. Letter to author.
65. IWM, Misc 2645, nn.
66. PRO, Adm 1/14346.
67. PRO, Adm 156/280.
68. Coulter, I, 94–5.
69. IWM, Misc 2645, 19.
70. MM, 82 (Letter from S. A. Williamson).
71. Coulter, I, 95.
72. IWM, Misc 2645, nn.
73. Levy, 'The Inglorious', 303, 305.
74. PRO, Adm 199/958.
75. PRO, Adm 199/958; Coulter, I, 20.
76. PRO, Adm 199/158, Pt 1, 75, 77–9, 183, 188.
77. PRO, Adm 199/158, Pt 1, 141.
78. IWM, Boys-Smith, 32.

79. IWM, Misc 2645, 238.
80. IWM, Misc 2645, nn.
81. *The War at Sea*, 149.
82. IWM, Misc 2645, nn.
83. PRO, Adm 199/158
84. IWM, Misc 2645, nn.
85. Critchley, 4, 7, 26, 73, 78, 81.
86. IWM, Misc 2645, nn.
87. IWM, Misc 2645, 64.
88. Coultass, 'Film', 84–5.
89. *The Defeat of the Enemy*, 45.
90. *Lancet*, 14 August 1943.

5 Don't fence me in: Women, GIs, black men and evacuees

1. Summerfield and Crocket, 'You weren't', 436.
2. IWM, Passmore, I, 45.
3. *Woman's Own*, 16 April 1943.
4. *Woman's Own*, 9 April 1943.
5. Goodman, 'Patriotic Femininity', 282.
6. Summerfield and Crocket, 'You weren't', 438.
7. Wells, *Letters*, 62.
8. Summerfield and Crocket, 'You weren't', 437–9, 442–3.
9. *Woman's Own*, 10 August 1940.
10. Well, *Letters*, 69.
11. Goodman, 'Patriotic Femininity', 286.
12. Goodman, 'Patriotic Femininity', 286–7.
13. *Woman's Own*, 23 December 1943.
14. PRO, FO 371/34124, 4, 8; FO 371/34126, 77.
15. PRO, FO 371/34126, 161–2.
16. PRO, FO 371/38263, 78, 83; FO 371/34124, 43.
17. PRO, FO 371/38263, 77.
18. PRO, FO 371/34126, 73.
19. Rose, 'Girls and GIs', 150–51.
20. IWM, Kirby, 130.
21. PRO, FO 371/34126, 19.
22. PRO, FO 371/34123, 4–5.
23. PRO, FO 371/34126, 131.
24. *Bedfordshire Times and Standard*, 14 April 1944.
25. *Bedfordshire Times and Standard*, 18 February 1944.
26. *Bedfordshire Times and Standard*, 17 and 31 March, 21 April 1944.
27. Rose, 'Girls and GIs', 148–9.
28. PRO, FO 371/24123, 4, 9.
29. Goodman, 'Patriotic Femininity', 288.
30. PRO, FO 371/34124, 26.

31. PRO, FO 371/34124, 15–16.

32. PRO, FO 371/14124, 32.

33. Rose, 'Girls and GIs', 150.

34. Rose, 'Sex', 1151–2.

35. PRO, FO 371/38263, 91.

36. *Chard and Ilminster News*, 13 Feb 1943.

37. PRO, HO 45/25604, nn.

38. PRO, HO 45/25604, nn.

39. PRO, HO 45/25604, nn.

40. Buggins, 'West Indians', 96–6.

41. PRO, FO 371/34124, 56, 66.

42. PRO, FO 371/34126, 235.

43. PRO, HO 45/25604, 871266.

44. PRO, FO 371/38623, 189.

45. Thorne, 142–3, 283–4.

46. Shaw, 148–9.

47. PRO, FO 371/38623, 91.

48. PRO, HO 45/25604, nn.

49. The US Prison at Shepton Mallet, *After the Battle*, 59 (1986), 36.

50. PRO, FO 371/34126, 177.

51. Griffiths, *Patriotism*, 207.

52. PRO, CO 876/41, 120, 123, 127, 148.

53. Shaw, 100

54. PRO, FO 371/38623, 226.

55. PRO, FO 371/34124, 24, 67, 120, 168, 196d, 243.

56. *Huddersfield Daily Examiner*, 20 and 29 Sept, 1 Oct 1943.

57. *Sunday Pictorial*, 26 August 1945; Rose, 'Sex', 1175.

58. *Bristol Evening Post*, 18 August 1945.

59. Goodman, 'Patriotic Femininity', 288–9.

60. Rose, 'Sex', 1165.

61. PRO, FO 371/38623, 189.

62. *Bath and Wiltshire Chronicle*, 21 and 27 May, 1 June 1943.

63. *Lancet*, 7 July, 18 August 1945.

64. Summerfield and Crockett, 'You weren't', 440.

65. *Report of the Commissioner of Police for the Metropolis for the Year 1949*, 39; *Criminal Statistics Scotland: Summary of Statistics . . . for the years 1939–1945*, 6.

66. Smith, *When Jim Crow*, 205: PRO, Mepo 2/7005.

67. Smith, *When Jim Crow*, 208, 212–13.

68. Smith, *When Jim Crow*, 206.

69. *Spectator*, 15, 22, 29 Sept 1939.

70. Crosby, 4–5, 31–5, 52; *Cambridge Evacuation Survey*, 117.

71. SRO, HH 55/28, PWD 1/1/2/43, 37.

72. *Cambridge Evacuation Survey*, 79–80.

73. *Cambridge Evacuation Survey*, 81–2, 87.
74. *Cambridge Evacuation Survey*, 115.
75. Crosby, 4–5, 46, 50–51; Calder, 62.

6 *Tactful handling: Command and combat*

1. Waugh, *Diaries*, 518.
2. *Picture Post*, 4 Oct 1941.
3. French, *The British Way*, 198, 205–6.
4. Sheffield, 'The Shadow', 32.
5. Crang, 'The British Soldier', 61.
6. *Daily Herald*, 14 April 1944.
7. *Picture Post*, 3 May 1941.
8. *Hansard*, 5th Series, 397.
9. PRO, Adm 1/17100.
10. SRO, HH 55/7, PWD 1/2/1C.
11. PRO, Air 2/9204.
12. PRO, Adm 156/285.
13. PRO, Adm 178/305.
14. Throne, 153.
15. Crang, 'The British Soldier', 65.
16. Crang, 'The British Soldier', 56–67.
17. Crang, 'The British Soldier', 73.
18. French, 'The Fashioning', 282.
19. Crang, 'The British Soldier', 61.
20. French, 'Discipline', 356.
21. PRO, Adm 156/224.
22. *Lancet*, 22 Dec 1945.
23. Crang, 'Square Pegs', 295.
24. French, 'You Cannot', 1–2.
25. Forster, 'Motivations', 271.
26. French, 'You Cannot', 6.
27. Healey, 48.
28. French, 'You Cannot', 17.
29. French, 'You Cannot', 12.
30. French, 'Discipline', 538–9.
31. Bourke, *An Intimate*, 92–3.
32. PRO, WOI 32/15772, 51A.
33. French, 'You Cannot', 11.
34. Ellis, 25.
35. Bond, 'The British', 45.
36. Verney, 94–100.
37. Ellis, 189–91, 225.
38. Ellis, 168–9.

7 It's all for you: Peace and perceptions of the war

1. Gilbert, *The Day the War Ended*, 263.
2. *What Did You do in the War, Mummy*, 253.
3. *Daily Herald*, 24 Jan 1945.
4. e.g. *Country Life*, 23 Feb 1945.
5. IWM, Kirby, 277–8.
6. *Listener*, 17 May 1945.
7. IWM, Kirby, 409.
8. Lancaster, 18.
9. *Economist*, 26 May 1945.
10. Zewinger-Bargielowski, 'Bread Rationing', 79.
11. *Daily Herald*, 7 Feb 1945.
12. PRO, FO 371/38623, 135.
13. *Country Life*, 16 Feb 1945.
14. LHC, Denman, nn.
15. *Economist*, 7 April 1945.
16. *Studies in War Economics*, 215.
17. *Annual Abstract of Statistics*, 84 (1935–1946), 171.
18. *Country Life*, 2 Sept 1949.
19. Bowen, 'British Agricultural Policy', 75–6.
20. *Daily Herald*, 30 Jan 1945.
21. *Daily Herald*, 31 July 1945.
22. Hennessy, *Never Again*, 57.
23. *Times*, 26 June 1945.
24. *Times*, 26 June 1945.
25. *Listener*, 5 July 1945.
26. *Daily Herald*, 30 Jan 1945.
27. *Times*, 26 June 1945.
28. *Convoy*, 3, 17.
29. I am indebted to Trevor Royle for this point.
30. I am indebted to Bob Rogers for this point.
31. Hennessy, 'Never Again', 3–5.
32. Barnett, 304.
33. E.g. D. G. Goldhagen, *Hitler's Willing Executioners: Ordinary Germans and the Holocaust* (New York, 1996) and E. Johnson, *The Nazi Terror: Gestapo, Jews and Ordinary Germans* (1999).
34. Nettlebeck, 'Getting the Story Right', 91.
35. Krome, 'The True Glory', 23.
36. PRO, FO 371/38623, 85.
37. Ramsden, 'Refocussing', 35.
38. Richards and Sheridan, 381, 401.
39. PRO, Air 2/6354.
40. Richards and Sheridan, 228, 318–19, 322.
41. PRO, Adm 199/958.

42. IWM, Misc 2645, nn.

43. Richards, 'National Identity', 49.

44. *New Statesman*, 28 Sept 1940.

45. *Listener*, 8 June 1944.

46. Masefield and Seago, 54.

47. Chibnall, 'Pulp', 140–42.

48. Ellis, 321.

49. LHC, Denman, nn.

50. *Horizon*, 2 (August 1940), 10–11; *Horizon*, 2 (December 1940), np.

51. Nicholas, 'Sly Demagogues', 259.

52. *Daily Herald*, 23 March 1945.

53. *Sunday Pictorial*, 24 June 1941.

54. IWM, Watts, 27 Jan 1941.

55. *The War at Sea* ,189.

56. Smith, 'The Effect', 217–18.

57. IWM, Watts, nn.

58. Ramsden, 'Refocussing', 43n.

59. BBC Radio 4, 'The Archers', 16 March 2001.

8 A normal hazard: Cold War and hot wars, 1945–98

1. PRO Air 20/11516, 1A, 8.

2. PRO Prem 11/5104, 26; Adm 1/26922.

3. PRO Adm 1/27285.

4. James, *Rise and Fall*, 531–2.

5. Hennessy, *Never Again*, 267–70.

6. Cornish, 16.

7. Dingman, 'Atomic Diplomacy', 66–70, 90–91.

8. *Times*, 24 Oct 1962.

9. Herken, 283, 287.

10. *Times*, 5 Oct 1961.

11. Gearson, 'British Policy', 113.

12. Harknett, Wirtz and Paul, 86.

13. *Times*, 11 September 1999.

14. *Times*, 24 Oct 1962.

15. *Times*, 30 Oct 1962.

16. PRO, Air 20/11264, E 1, E 61, E 159, E 166.

17. *London Under Attack*, 177.

18. Harknett, Wirtz and Paul, 81; Kamp, 'The Relevance', 295.

19. PRO, Adm 1/26927.

20. PRO, Adm 296/1.

21. *Ibid.*

22. PRO, Adm 1/26922, 3.

23. *Ibid.*, 137.

24. PRO, Adm 265/88.

25. PRO, Adm 296/41; Adm 296/26.
26. PRO, Air 20/10950, 37.
27. I am indebted to Susie Dowdall for this, which she heard from her father.
28. *JRUSI*, Dec 1981, 12.
29. Private information.
30. Campbell, *War Plan*, 373–5.
31. *Times*, 4 Sept 1999.
32. Campbell, *War Plan UK*, 387–402.
33. Scott, 'Close to the Brink', 509–14.
34. Kier and Herser, 'Military Intervention', 100–101.
35. *Times*, 28 August 1969.
36. *Times*, 26 August 1969.
37. *Sunday Telegraph*, 2 July 2000; this document has since been withdrawn from public scrutiny.
38. PRO, Prem 15/102.
39. PRO, Prem 15/100.
40. Hogan and Walker, 63.
41. Cairns and Cairns, 97, 101–2.
42. Sheeney, 'Interest', 311.
43. *Scotland on Sunday*, 11 March 2001.
44. *Ibid.*

Bibliography

Except where otherwise stated, all books are published in London

R. Abels, *English Tactics, Strategy and Military Organisation in the Late Tenth Century*, in D. G. Scragg (ed.), *The Battle of Maldon* (Oxford, 1991)

The Actes and Deidis of the Illustrere and Vail and Campion Schir William Wallace Knicht of Ellersie by Henry the Minstrel commonly known as Blind Harry, ed. J. Moire (Scottish Text Society, 1889)

A Book of the State of the Frontiers and Marches betwixt England and Scotland written by Sir Robert Bowes &c at the request of the Lord Dorset, Warden-General, in J. Hodgson, *A History of Northumberland*, Part III, ii (1827)

'A Contemporary Account of the Battle of Flodden, 9 September 1513', *Proceedings of the Society of Antiquaries of Scotland*, VII (1863–67)

A Contemporary History of the Affairs in Ireland from 1641 to 1652, 3 vols, (Dublin, 1879–1880)

J. Adair, 'The Court Martial Papers of Sir William Waller's Army, 1644', *JSAHR*, 44 (1966)

P. Addison and A. Calder, eds, *A Time to Die: The Soldier's Experience of War in the West 1939–1945* (1997)

Adoman of Iona, *Life of St Columba*, trans. R. Sharpe (Penguin, 1995)

The Albermarle Papers: Being the Correspondence of William Anne, Second Earl of Albermarle, Commander-in-Chief in Scotland, 1746–47, ed. C. S. Terry, 2 vols (Spalding Club, Aberdeen, 1902)

L. Alcock, *Economy, Society and Warfare among Britons and Saxons* (Cardiff, 1987)

R. Aldington, *Death of a Hero* (1927)

M. Alexander, *Old English Literature*, (New York, 1983)

R. Allen Brown, H. M. Colvin, and A. J. Taylor, *History of the King's Works*, I (1963)

R. Allen Brown, The Battle of Hastings, *ANS*, 3 (1980)

K. A. Andrews, *Elizabethan Privateering* (Cambridge, 1964)

E. A. Andriette, *Devon and Exeter in the Civil War* (Newton Abbot, 1971)

The Marquess of Anglesey, *A History of the British Cavalry*, I, 1816–1850 (1988 ed.); II, 1851–1971 (1975)

S. Anglo, *The Great Tournament Roll of Westminster*, 2 vols (Oxford 1968)

S. Anglo, 'How to Win at Tournaments: The Technique of Chivalric Combat', in *The Anglo-Saxon Chronicle*, Everyman Edition (1938) *Antiquaries Journal*, 68, (1988)

Annals of Medicine for the Year 1798 (1799)

The Annals of Roger Howden, trans. H. T. Riley, 2 vols (1843)

The Annals of Ulster, ed. S. M. MacAirt and G. MacNiocaill (Dublin 1983)

Annual Abstract of Statistics, No 84: 1935–1946 (1948)

Anon., 'The War', *The Journal of Psychological and Mental Pathology*, 9, (1856)

Anon., 'The Indian Rebellion in its Moral and Psychological Aspects', *The Journal of Psychological and Mental Pathology*, 11 (1858)

Anon., 'The Fight at Peiho', *Blackwoods*, 86, (1859)

Anon., *'Letters from the Crimea during the Years 1854 and 1855* (1863)

Anon. ['Martello Tower'], *At School and at Sea: or, Life and Character at Harrow, in the Royal Navy and in the Trenches before Sebastopol* (1899)

Anon. [W. T. Pole], *Private Dowding* (1919)

Anon., 'Some Medical Aspects of Aviation', *BMJ*, 27 April 1918

Anon., 'Physiological Aspects of Flying', *BMJ*, 11 May 1918

A. M. Arent, 'The Heroic Pattern: Old Germanic Helmets, *Beowulf* and the Gettis Saga', in E. C. Polomé (ed.), *Old Norse Literature and Mythology* (Austin, 1969)

J. D. Astley, *Fifty Years of My Life*, 2 vols (1904)

R. Attwood, *The Hessians: Mercenaries from Hessen Kassel in the American Revolution* (Cambridge, 1980)

A. Ayton, 'Military Service and the Development of the Robin Hood Legend in the Fourteenth Century', *NMS*, 36 (1993)

S. Bachrach, 'Some Observations on the Military Administration of the Norman Conquest', *ANS*, 8 (1986)

T. Balderston, 'War, Finance and Inflation in Britain and Germany', *EcHR*, 42 (1989)

J. R. Baldwin, *Indian Gup: Untold Stories of the Mutiny* (1897)

J. W. Baldwin, *A Narrative of Four Months Campaign in India* (Norwich, c. 1853)

C. R. Ballard, 'Letters from South Africa', ed. H. C. B. Cooke, *JSAHR*, 79 (1991)

J. Bannerman, *Studies in the History of Dalriada* (Edinburgh, 1974)

C. Barnett, *The Audit of War* (1986)

G. de S. Barrow, *The Fire of Life* (1942)

C. J. Bartlett, *Great Britain and Sea Power, 1815–1853* (Oxford, 1963)

T. Bartlett, 'Defenders and Defenderism', *Irish Historical Review*, 24 (1985)

T. Bartlett, 'Defence, Counter Insurgency and Rebellion in Ireland, 1793–1803', in T. Bartlett and K. Jeffrey (eds), *A Military History of Ireland* (Cambridge, 1996)

H. Barwick, *A Breefe Discourse Concerning the force and effect of all manuall weapons of fire and the Desirability of the Long Bow* (1594)

The Battle of the Atlantic and Signals Intelligence: U-Boat Situations and Trends, ed. D. Syrett (Navy Records Society, 1998)

J. Baylis, 'The Development of Britain's Thermonuclear Capacity 1954–61', *Contemporary Record*, 8, (1994)

Beaumont and Fletcher, *Dramatic Works*, ed. F. Bowers, IV (Cambridge, 1974)

Bede's Ecclesiastical History of the English Nation, trans. D. Knowles (1958)

J. Beauroy, 'La Conquête clericale de l'Angleterre', *Cahiers de civilisation médiéval*, 27 (1984)

I. F. W. Beckett, 'The Amateur Military Tradition in Britain', *WS*, 4 (1986)

I. F. W. Beckett (ed.), *The Army and the Curragh Incident, 1914* (Army Records Society, 1986)

I. F. W. Beckett, 'Some Further Correspondence Relating to the Curragh Incident of March 1914', *JSAHR*, 79 (1991)

I. F. W. Beckett and K. Jeffery, 'The Royal Navy and the Curragh Incident', *Bulletin of the Institute of Historical Research*, 63 (1989)

J. Beckett, 'Responses to War: Nottingham in the French and Napoleonic Wars, 1793–1815', *Midland History*, 12 (1997)

Songs from the Manuscript Collection of John Bell, ed. D. I. Harker and F. Rutherford (Surtees Society, 196, 1984)

'The Letters of William Bell, 89th Foot', ed. B. W. Webb-Carter, *JSAHR*, 33 (1970)

J. G. Bellamy, 'The Coterel Gang: An Anatomy of a Band of Fourteenth-Century Criminals', *EHR*, 79 (1964)

M. M. Bellesîles, 'The Origins of Gun Culture in the United States, 1760–1865', *Journal of American History*, 83 (1996)

G. Bennett, *Cowan's War: The Story of the British Naval Operations in the Baltic, 1918–1920* (1964)

M. Bennett, '"My Plundered Townes, My Houses Devastation": The Civil War and North Midland's Life, 1642–1646', *Midland History*, 22 (1997)

G. Beresford, *Goltho: The Development of an Early-Mediaeval Manor, c. 850–1150* (1987)

G. W. Bernard, *The Power of the Early-Tudor Nobility: A Study of the Fourth and Fifth Earls of Shrewsbury* (Brighton, 1985)

B. J. Bernstein, 'Eclipsed by Hiroshima and Nagasaki', *International Security*, 15 (1990–91)

P. Berton, *The Invasion of Canada, 1812–1813* (Toronto, 1980)

U. Bialer, *The Shadow of the Bomber: The Fear of Air Attack and British Politics* (1990)

W. R. Bingham, *The Field of Feroshah, a Poem in Two Cantos* (Agra, 1846)

W. R. Bion, *War Memories 1917–19*, ed. F. Bion (1997)

J. L. Birley, 'The Principles of Medical Science Applied to Military Aviation', *Lancet*, 29 May and 5 June 1920

J. L. Birley, 'A Lecture on the Psychology of Courage', *Lancet*, 21 April 1923

R. Birley, *Vindolanda: A Roman Frontier Outpost on Hadrian's Wall* (1977)

'The Bisshop Papers During the War of 1812', ed. R. S. Allen, *JSAHR*, 61 (1983)

D. F. Bittner, 'Jane Austen and Her Officers', *JSHAR*, 82 (1994)

V. Blacker, *Memoir of the British Army in India during the Mahratta War of 1817, 1818 and 1819* (1821)

A. F. Blackstock, '"A dangerous specie of ally": Orangism and the Irish Yeomanry', *IHS*, 30 (1997)

R. Blakeney, *A Boy in the Peninsular War* (1899)

R. Blakiston, *Twelve Years of Military Adventure*, 2 vols (1829)

T. Bogacz, 'War Neuroses and Cultural Change in England, 1914–22: The Work of the War Office Committee of Enquiry into "Shell Shock"', *JCH*, 24 (1989)

R. Bogin, '"The Battle of Lexington": A Patriotic Ballad by Lemuel Haynes', *WMQ*, 3rd Series, 42 (1985)

B. Bond, 'The British Field Force in France and Belgium, 1939–40', in P. Addison and A. Calder (eds), *A Time to Die* (1997)

B. Bond and N. Cave (eds), *Haig: A Reappraisal 70 Years On* (1999)

P. Bone, 'The Development of Anglo-Saxon Swords from the Fifth to the Eleventh Century', in S. C. Hawkes (ed.)

H. Boog, (ed.), *The Conduct of the Air War in the Second World War: An International Comparison* (New York, 1992)

The Book of the Law of Armys or Boke of Battles, ed. J. H. Stevenson (Scottish Text Society, 1901)

G. Borrow, *Romany Rye* (1907 ed.)

J. Bourke, 'Heroes and Hoaxes: The Unknown Warrior, Kitchener and "Missing Men"', *WS*, 13 (1995)

J. Bourke, *An Intimate History of Killing* (1999)

H. V. Bower, *War and British Society, 1688–1815* (Cambridge, 1993)

J. K. Bowers, 'British Agricultural Policy since the Second World War', *Agricultural History Review*, 33 (1985)

A. K. Bowman and J. D. Thomas, *Vindolanda: The Latin Tablets* (Britannia Monograph Series, No. 4, 1983)

D. G. Boyce, *Englishmen and Irish Troubles: British Public Opinion and the Making of Irish Policy 1918–1922* (1972)

D. Braund, *Ruling Roman Britain* (1996)

D. Breen, *My War for Irish Freedom* (Dublin, 1924)

D. J. Breeze, *Roman Scotland* (1996)

D. J. Breeze and D. Dobson, 'The Development of the Mural Frontier in Britain from Hadrian to Caracalla', *Proceedings of the Society of Antiquaries of Scotland*, 102 (1969–70)

D. J. Breeze and D. Dobson, 'Hadrian's Wall: Some Problems', *Britannia*, 3 (1972)

C. C. Breight, *Surveillance, Militarism and Drama in the Elizabethan Era* (1985)

J. R. E. Brieze, 'The Courage of the Normans' *NMS*, 35 (1991)

British Naval Documents, 1204–1960, ed. J. B. Hattendorf, R. J. B. Knight, A. W. H. Pearsall, N. A. M. Rodger and G. Till (Naval Records Society, 1993)

British Parliamentary Papers: Medical Relief and Public Health General (Shannon, 1970)

The Diaries of John Bright, ed. P. Bright (1930)

B. Brivati and H. Jones, *What Difference Did the War Make?* (1993)

The Diary of Alexander Brodie of Brodie MDCLII–MDCLXXXV (Spalding Club, Aberdeen 1863)

D. Brooke, 'The Northumberland Settlement in Galloway and Carrick: An Historical Assessment', *Proceedings of the Society of Antiquaries of Scotland*, 121 (1990)

M. Brooks, 'Women in Munitions, 1914–1918: The Oral Record', *IWMR*, 5 (1990)

N. P. Brooks, 'Arms, Status and Warfare in late Anglo-Saxon England', in D. Hill (ed.) *Ethelred the Unready* (BAR British Series, 59, 1978)

J. Brophy and E. Partridge, *The Long Trail: What the British Soldiers Sung and Said in the Great War of 1914–18* (1965)

K. Brown, *Bloodfeud in Scotland, 1573–1625* (Edinburgh, 1986)

S. A. Browne, 'The Bayeux Tapestry: Why Eustace, Odo and William?', *ANS* 12 (1990)

The Napoleonic War Journal of Captain Thomas Browne, 1807–1816, ed. R. N. Buckley (Army Records Society, 1987)

The Bruce, John Barbour, ed. W. W. Skeet, 2 vols (Scottish Text Society, 1894)

The Brut, or, Chronicles of England, ed. F. W. D. Brie, 2 vols (Early English Text Society, 1906)

J. Buckley, 'Air Power and the Battle of the Atlantic', *JCH*, 28 (1993)

R. N. Buckley, *The British Army in the West Indies: Society and the Military in the Revolutionary Age* (Gainseville, FL, 1998)

J. Buggins, 'West Indians in Britain during the Second World War: A Short History Drawing on Colonial Office Papers', *IWMR*, 5 (1990)

J. Buggins, 'The End of the British Mandate in Palestine: Reflections from the Papers of John Watson of the Forces Broadcasting Service', *IWMR*, 8 (1993)

D. Burnley, *Courtliness and Literature in Mediaeval England* (1998)

F. W. Burton-Fanning, 'Neurasthenia in Soldiers of the Home Forces', *Lancet*, 16 June 1917

F. T. Byrne, *Irish Kings and High Kings* (1973)

Memoirs of Miles Byrne, 2 vols (1906)

E. and T. Cairns, 'Children and Conflict: A Psychological Perspective', in S. Dunn (ed.) *Facets of the Conflict in Northern Ireland* (1995)

A. Calder, *The Myth of the Blitz* (1991)

Calendars of Border Papers, 2 vols (1894–1896)

Calendars of Close Rolls, 1296–1302 (1906)

Calendars of Documents Relating to Scotland, II (1273–1307), III (1307–1357) and Supplementary (1884–1986)

Calendar of Inquisitions Miscellaneous, 8 vols (1916–1966)

Calendar of London Trailbaston Trials under the Commissions of 1305 and 1306, ed. R. B. Pugh (1975)

Calendar of Memoranda Rolls, 1326–27 (1968)

Calendar of Patent Rolls, 1292–1302 (1895); *1452–1461* (1910)

A Calendar of the Proceedings of the Committees for the Advance of Money, 1642–1656, 3 vols (1888)

Calendars of State Papers, America and the West Indies, 1574–1738, 44 volumes (1860–1969)

Calendars of State Papers, Domestic, of the Reign of Elizabeth 1566–1601 (1869–1871)

Calendar of State Papers, Domestic, 1640–41 (1882), *1641–43* (1887)

Calendars of State Papers, Foreign Series, of the Reign of Edward VI 1547–1553 (1861)

Calendars of State Papers, Foreign Series, of the Reign of Queen Mary, 1553–1558, (1861)

Calendars of State Papers, Foreign Series, of the Reign of Elizabeth, 1558–1589 (1865–1936)

Calendar of State Papers, Relating to Ireland, 1509–1647, 19 vols (1860–1901)

The Cambridge Evacuation Survey, ed. S. Isaacs (1941)

D. Campbell, *War Plan UK* (1983 ed.)

H. Campbell, 'The Biological Aspects of Warfare', *Lancet*, 15 and 29 September 1917

The Cavalier Songs and Ballads of England from 1642 to 1684, ed. C. Murray (1862)

C . Carlton, *Going to the Wars: The Experience of the British Civil Wars, 1638–1651* (1995 ed.)

A. D. Carr, 'Welshmen in the Hundred Years War', *Welsh History Review*, 4 (1968)

P. Chalmers, *The Ancient Stone Monuments of the County of Angus* (1848)

T. M. Charles Edwards, 'Early Mediaeval Kingship in the British Isles', in S. Basset (ed.), *The Origins of the Anglo-Saxon Kingdoms* (Leicester, 1989)

T. M. Charles Edwards, 'Irish Warfare before 1100', in T. Bartlett and K. Jeffery (eds), *A Military History of Ireland* (1996)

816 • Bibliography •

E. Charteris, *William Augustus, Duke of Cumberland: His Early Life and Times* (1913)

J. Charteris, *At GHQ* (1931)

S. Chibnall, 'Pulp versus Penguins: Paperbacks Go To War', in D. Kirkham and D. Thomas (eds), *War and Culture* (1995)

W. Childs, *Episodes and Recollections* (1930)

H. Clarke, 'The North Sea: A Highway of Invasions, Immigration and Trade in the Fifth to Ninth Centuries AD', in A. Bang-Andersen, B. Greenhill and E. H. Grade (eds), *The North Sea* (Oslo, 1985)

The Chronicle of Lanercost 1272–1346, trans. H. Maxwell (1913)

D. Christison, 'Report on the Society's Excavations in the Portalloch Estes, Argyll, 1904–05', *Proceedings of the Society of Antiquaries of Scotland*, 34 (1904–5)

I. F. Clarke, *Voices Prophesying War, 1763–1964* (1970 ed.)

P. Clayton, *Enemies and Passing Friends: Settler Ideologies in Twentieth Century Ulster* (1996)

R. Clifton, 'Lessons and Consequences of the Rebellion of 1685', in P. E. Tokespaugh and C. Brobek (eds), *Religion, Resistance and Civil War* (Washington, DC, 1990)

W. L. Clowes, *The Royal Navy from Ancient Times*, 7 vols (1897–1903)

J. Coad, *The Royal Dockyards 1690–1850* (1989)

Memoir of the Life of Admiral Sir Edward Codrington, ed. Lady Codrington, 2 vols (1873)

C. Coker, *British Defence Policy in 1990s: A Guide to the Defence Debate* (1987)

A. J. Coles, 'The Moral Economy of the Crowd: Some Twentieth Century Food Riots', *Journal of British Studies*, 18 (1978)

L. Colley, 'Whose Nation? Class and National Consciousness in Britain', *PP*, No. 113 (1986).

L. Colley, *Britons: Forging the Nation 1707–1837* (1990 ed.)

P. Contamine, *Le France en XIVe et XVe Siècles: Hommes, Mentalités, Guerre et Paix* (1981)

A Contemporary History of Affairs in Ireland from 1641 to 1642 (Dublin, 1879)

S. Conway, 'To Subdue America: British Army Officers and the Conduct of the Revolutionary War', *WMQ*, 3rd Series, 43 (1986)

S. Conway, '"The Great Mischief Complain'd of": Reflections of the Misconduct of British Soldiers in the Revolutionary War', *WMQ*, 3rd Series, 47 (1990)

T. P. Coogan, *Michael Collins* (1991 ed.)

J. E. Cookson, 'Patriotism and Social Structure: The Ely Volunteers, 1798–1805', *JSAHR*, 71 (1993)

J. E. Cookson, *The British Nation Armed* (1997)

P. Cornish, *British Military Planning for the Defence of Germany 1945–50* (1996)

E. Costello, *The Adventures of a Soldier* (1841)

J. L. S. Coulter, *The Royal Naval Medical Services*, II: Operations (1956)

The Coventry Leet Book, ed. M. D. Harris (Early English Text Society, 1907–13)

S. Cox, 'The Sources and Organisation of RAF Intelligence and its Infl
Operations', in H. Boog (ed.), *The Conduct of the Air War in th...
World War: An International Comparison* (1992)

J. A. Crang, 'The British Soldier on the Home Front: Army Morale Reports,
1940–45', in P. Addison and A. Calder (eds), *A Time To Die: The Soldier's
Experience of War in the West 1939–1945* (1997)

J. A. Crang, 'Square Pegs in Round Holes: Other Rank Selection in the British
Army', *JSAHR*, 77 (1999)

Mrs M. Creighton, 'The Women Police', *Fortnightly Review*, 114 (1920)

M. Critchley, *Shipwreck Survivors: A Medical Study* (1943)

P. Crook, 'War as a Great Disaster? The First World War Debate over the
Eugenics of Warfare', *WS*, 8 (1990)

P. Crook, 'Science at War: Radical Scientists in the Tizard-Cherwell Area
Bombing Debate', *WS* 12 (1994)

T. L. Crosby, *The Impact of Civilian Evacuation in the Second World War* (1986)

V. Crossman, 'The Army and Public Order in the Nineteenth Century', in ed.
T. Bartlett and K. Jeffrey (eds), *A Military History of Ireland* (1996)

D. Crouch, *William the Marshall: Court, Career and Chivalry in the Angevin
Empire, 1147–1219* (1990)

R. P. Crowhurst, 'Profitability and French Pirvateering, 1793–1815', *Business
History*, 24 (1982)

F. P Crozier, *Impressions and Recollections* (1930)

F. P. Crozier, *The Men I Killed* (1937)

C. G. Cruikshank, *Elizabeth's Army* (Oxford, 1966 ed.)

S. M. Cullen, 'Political Violence: The Case of the British Union of Fascists',
JCH, 28 (1993)

C. A. Culleton, 'Working-class Women's Services Newspapers and the First
World War', *IWMR*, 10 (1995)

B. Cunliffe, *Excavations at Porchester Castle*, I (Roman), II (Saxon) (1975–76)

N. R. Curtin, 'The Transformation of the Society of United Irishmen into a
Mass-based Revolutionary Organisation, 1794–96', *IHS*, 4 (1985)

G. Dallas and D. Gill, 'Mutiny at the Etaples Base in 1917', *PP*, No. 69 (1975)

G. Dallas and D. Gill, *The Unknown Army: Mutinies in the British Army in World
War I* (1975)

L. Darwin, 'On the Statistical Enquiries Needed after the War in Connection
with Eugenics', *Journal of the Royal Statistical Society*, 79 (1916)

R. W. Davies, 'The Training Grounds of the Roman Cavalry', *AJ*, 125 (1968)

R. H. C. Davis, *The Mediaeval War Horse: Origin, Development and Redevelopment*
(1989)

H. Davison, 'The Training of Warriors', in S. Hawkes (ed.), *Weapons and
Warfare in Anglo-Saxon England* (Oxford University Committee for
Archaeology, No. 21, 1989)

E. T. Dean, 'War and Psychiatry: Examining the Diffusion Theory in the Light of the Insanity Defence in Post-World War I Britain', *History of Psychiatry*, 4 (1993)

N. B. Dearle, *An Economic Chronicle of the Great War for Great Britain and Ireland, 1914–1918* (Oxford, 1929)

L. Deasy, *Towards Ireland Free: The West Cork Brigade in the War of Independence 1917–1921* (Cork, 1973)

The Death of Arthur, ed. E. Brock (Early English Text Society, 1871)

The Defeat of the Enemy Attack on Shipping, 1939–1945, ed. E. J. Grove (Navy Records Society, 1997)

P. Dennis, 'The Territorial Army in the Aid of the Civil Power in Britain, 1919–1926', *JCH*, 16 (1981)

K. DeVries, *Mediaeval Military Technology* (Peterborough, Ontario, 1992)

P. E. Dewey, 'Agricultural Labour Supply in England and Wales during the First World War', *EcHR*, 28 (1975)

P. E. Dewey, 'British Farming Profits and Government Policy during the First World War', *EcHR*, 33 (1984)

Diaries of the French Expedition, 1798, ed. N. Costello (Irish Manuscript Commission, Dublin, 1941)

W. H. Dillon, *Dillon's Narrative*, ed. M. A. Lewis, 2 vols (Naval Records Society, 1953, 1956)

J. N. Dills, 'Epidemics, Mortality and the Civil War in Berkshire, 1642–46', *Southern History*, 11 (1989)

R. Dingman, 'Atomic Diplomacy During the Korean War', *International Security*, 13 (1988–89)

B. Dobson and J. V. Mann, 'The Roman in Britain and Britons in the Roman Army', *Britannia*, 4 (1973)

B. Dobson, 'The Church of Durham and the Scottish Borders', in A. Goodman and A. Tuck (eds), *War and Border Societies in the Middle Ages* (1992)

Documents of the American Revolution 1770–1783, 21 vols (Shannon, 1972–81)

Documents Concerning English Voyages to the Spanish Main, ed. I. A. Wright (Hakluyat Society, 2nd Series, 71, 1932)

Documents Relating to the Naval Air Service, I, ed. S. W. Roskill (Naval Records Society, 1969)

C. Doherty, 'The War Art of C. R. W. Nevinson', *IWMR*, 8 (1993)

Domesday Book, Yorkshire, I, ed. J. Morris (Chichester, 1986)

J. Donaldson, *Recollections of an Eventful Life chiefly Passed in the Army* (Glasgow, 1825)

J. Donaldson, *A Continuation of the Recollections of the Eventful Life of a Soldier* (Glasgow, 1825)

M. Dockrill and D. French (eds, *Strategy and Intelligence: British Policy during the First World War* (1996)

J. Dugan, *The Great Mutiny* (1966)

J. Duncan and A. McIver (eds), *Military Workers: Labour and Class Conflict on the Clyde 1900–1950* (Edinburgh, 1992)

D. Dundas, *Principles of Military Movement chiefly Applied to Infantry* (1788)

Dundee Court Martial Records, ed. G. Davies, *Scottish History Society Miscellany*, 2nd Series, 19 (1919)

C. Durston, *The Family in the English Revolution* (Oxford, 1989)

Early Irish Myths and Sagas, ed. and trans J. Gantz (Penguin, 1981)

D. Eastwood, 'Patriotism Personified: Robert Southey's *Life of Nelson* reconsidered', MM, 77 (1991)

A. J. Echevarria II, 'On the Brink of the Abyss: The Warrior Identity and German Military Thought before the Great War', *WS*, 13 (1995)

J. Edwards, 'The Cult of Thomas of Lancaster and its Iconography', *Yorkshire Archaeological Journal*, 64 (1992)

J. Edwards, 'The Cult of Thomas Lancaster and its Iconography: A Supplementary Note', *Yorkshire Archaeological Journal*, 67 (1995)

P. Egan, *Boxiana, Sketches of Antient and Modern Pugilism*, 2 vols (1818)

B. Einarsson, 'On the Status of Free Men in Society and Saga', *Mediaeval Scandinavia*, 7 (1974)

L. Einstein, *Divided Loyalties: Americans in England during the War of Independence* (1933)

E. Elers Napier, *Excursions in Southern Africa*, 2 vols (1851)

M. Elliot, *Partners in Revolution: The United Irishmen and France* (1982)

G. Elliot Smith and T. H. Pear, *Shell Shock and its Lessons* (1917)

J. Ellis, *The Sharp End of War* (1982 ed.)

H. Elton, *Warfare in the Roman Empire, AD 350–425* (Oxford, 1996)

C. Emsley, 'Political Disaffection and the British Army in 1792', *Bulletin of the Institute of Historical Research*, 48 (1975)

C. Elmsley, 'The Military and Popular Disturbance in England, 1780–1801', *JSAHR*, 61 (1984–85)

D. Englander and S. Osborne, 'Jack, Tommy and Henry Dubb: The Armed Forces and the Working Classes', *HJ* 21 (1978)

English Privateering Voyages to the West Indies, ed. K. A. Andrews (Hakluyt Society, 2nd Series, III, 1959)

A. D. English, 'A Predisposition to Cowardice? Aviation Psychology and the Genesis of "Lack of Moral Fibre"', *WS*, 13 (1995)

R. Evans, '"Some Furious Outbursts of Riot": Returned Soldiers and Queensland's "Red Flag" Disturbances, 1918–1919', *WS*, 3 (1985)

Memoir and Letters of Captain W. Glanville Evelyn, ed. G. D. Scull (Oxford, 1879)

Factors in Industrial and Commercial Efficiency, I (Stationery Office, 1927)

R. T. Farrell (ed.) *Bede and Anglo-Saxon England*, BAR, 46, 1998)

N. Ferguson, *The Pity of War* (1997)

T. Fernyhough, *Military Memoirs of Five Brothers (Natives of Staffordshire) Engaged on the Service of their Country* (1829)

D. Figgis, *Recollections of the Irish War* (1927)

C. H. Firth, 'Ballads of the Bishops' War, 1638–40', *Scottish History Review*, 3 (1905–6)

D. H. Fischer, *Paul Revere's Ride* (1994)

R. Risk, *In Time of War: Ireland, Ulster and the Price of Neutrality, 1939–45* (1983)

W. H. Fitchett, *Wellington's Men: Some Soldiers' Autobiographies* (1900)

Five Castle Excavations (Royal Archaeological Institute, 1978)

Five Naval Journals, 1789–1817, ed. H. G. Thursfield (Naval Records Society, 1951)

D. Fitzpatrick, 'Militarism in Ireland 1900–1922', in ed. T. Bartlett and K. J. Jeffrey (eds), *A Military History of Ireland* (1996)

F. C. Forster, 'The Management of Neurasthenia', *The Practitioner*, 100 (1918)

C. E. Foyle, *The War and the Shipping Industry* (Oxford, 1927)

D. Fraioli, 'The Literary Image of Joan of Arc: Prior Influence', *Speculum*, 56 (1981)

D. French, 'The Meaning of Attrition', *ER*, 103 (1988)

D. French, 'Discipline and the Death Penalty in the British Army in the War against Germany during the Second World War', *JCH*, 33 (1998)

D. French, *The British Way in Warfare 1688–2000* (1996)

D. French, 'The Fashioning of *Esprit de Corps* in the 51st Highland Division from St Valéry to El Alamein', *JSAHR*, 77 (1999)

D. French, '"You Cannot Hate the Bastard who is Trying to Kill You . . .": Combat Ideology in the British Army in the War against Germany', 1939–45, *TCBH*, 11 (2000)

French Mediaeval Verse (Penguin, 1967)

The Frenzy of Suibhne being the Adventures of Suibhne Geilt, ed. and trans, J. G. O'Keefe (Irish Texts Society, 1913)

R. Frothingham, *History of the Siege of Boston and the Battles of Lexington, Concord and Bunker Hill* (New York, 1849)

J. G. Fuller, *Troop Morale and Popular Culture in British and Dominion Armies 1914–1918* (Oxford, 1990)

Further English Voyages to Spanish America, 1583–1594, trans. and ed. I. A. Wright (Hakluyt Society, 2nd Series, 94, 1951)

G. W. Gallacher, *The Confederate War* (Harvard, 1997)

G. N. Garmonsway, *Canute and His Empire* (1963)

J. P. S. Gearson, 'British Policy and the Berlin Wall Crisis 1958–61', *Contemporary Record*, 6 (1992)

M. Gelling, 'Why Aren't We Speaking Welsh?', *Anglo-Saxon Studies in Archaeology and History*, 6 (1993)

I. Gentles, *The New Model Army in England, Wales and Scotland* (1992)

E. and G. Gifford, 'The Sailing Performance of Anglo-Saxon Ships', *MM*, 82 (1996)

M. Gilbert, *Finest Hour: Winston S. Churchill 1939–1941* (1983)

M. Gilbert, *The Day the War Ended* (1995)

J. Gillingham, 'The Context and Purposes of Geoffrey of Monmouth's *History of the Kings of Britain*', ANS, 13 (1980)

J. Gillingham, 'War and Chivalry in the History of William the Marshall', ANS, 3 (1970)

C. Gillmor, 'Practical Chivalry: The Training of Horses for Tournament and Warfare', *Studies in Mediaeval and Renaissance History*, 13 (1992)

G. Gleig, *The Campaigns of the British Army at Washington, and New Orleans in the Years 1814–1815* (1847 ed.)

The Recollection of Miles Glissop, ed. D. Clammer, JSAHR, 58 (1980)

M. Gover, 'The Purchase of Commissions: A Reappraisal', JSAHR, 58 (1980)

The Gododdin, ed. and trans. K. H., Jackson (Edinburgh, 1969)

A. Goodman and A. Tuck (eds), *War and Border Societies in the Middle Ages* (1992)

P. Goodman, '"Patriotic Femininity": Women's Morals and Men's Morale During the Second World War', *Gender and History*, 10 (1998)

T. Gowing, *A Voice from the Ranks*, ed. K. Fenwick (1954)

G. S. Graham, 'The Transition from Paddle-Wheel to Screw Propeller', MM, 44 (1958)

A. Gransaen, 'The Growth of Glastonbury Traditions and Legends in the Twelfth Century', *Journals of Ecclesiastical History*, 27 (1976)

A. Grant, 'The Otterburn War from the Scottish Point of View', in A. Goodman and A. Tuck (eds), *War and Border Societies in the Middle Ages* (1992)

R. Graves, *Goodbye to All That* (Penguin ed., 1973)

B. Graymont, *The Iroquois and the American Revolution* (Syracuse, NY, 1992)

D. Greasley and L. Oxley, 'Discontinuities and Competitiveness: The Impact of the First World War', *EcHR*, 49 (1996)

C. Green and A. B. Whittingham, 'Excavations at Walsingham Priory, Norfolk', AJ, 125 (1968)

J. A. Green, *The Aristocracy of Norman England* (Cambridge, 1997)

S. J. Greenberg, 'Seizing the Fleet in 1642: Parliament, the Navy and the Printing Press', MM, 77 (1991)

K. Grieves, '*Nelson's History of the War*; John Buchan as a Contemporary Military Historian', *JCH*, 20 (1993)

K. Grieves, 'Improving the British War Effort: Eric Geddes and Lloyd George 1915–1918', WS, 7 (1989)

P. Griffith, *Battle Tactics of the Western Front: The British Army and the Art of Attack, 1916–18* (1994)

R. Griffiths, *Patriotism Perverted: Captain Ramsay, the Right and British Anti-Semitism, 1939–1940* (1998)

O. Groehler, 'The Strategic War and its Impact on the German Civilian Population', in H. Boog, (ed.), *The Conduct of the Air War in the Second World War: An International Comparison* (1992)

G. de Groot, *Douglas Haig 1861–1928* (1988)

G. de Groot, *Blighty* (1996)

Ivor Gurney War Letters, ed. R. K. R. Thornton (Manchester, 1983)

T. Gutridge, 'Aspects of the Naval Prize Agency, 1793–1815', MM, 80 (1994)

R. Hainsworth, *Swordsmen in Power: War and Politics under the English Republic 1649–1660* (1997)

Hall's Chronicle of England containing the History of England (1809)

W. Hall, *The Diary of William Hall of Penzeance, Cornwall, late of Her Majesty's Forty-First Regiment* (Penhryn, 1848)

G. Halsall, 'Anthropology and the Study of Pre-Conquest Warfare and Society: The Ritual of War in Anglo-Saxon England', in S. C. Hawkes (ed.)

Hamilton Papers, 2 vols (1890–92)

N. Hamilton, *Monty: The Making of a General 1887–1942* (1989 ed.)

M. M. Hammond, *British Labour Conditions and Legislation during the War* (Oxford, 1919)

T. Hancock, *The Principles of Peace Exemplified in the Society of Friends in Ireland During the Year 1798* (1839)

H. J. Hanham, 'Religion and Nationality in the Mid-Victorian Army', in M. R. D. Foot (ed.), *War and Society: Historical Essays in Honour of J. R. Western* (1973)

H. Harke, '"Warrior Graves"? The Background of the Anglo-Saxon Burial Rite', *PP*, No. 126 (1990)

R. J. Harknett, J. J. Wurtz and T. V. Paul, *The Absolute Revisited: Nuclear Arms and the International Order* (Ann Arbor, MI, 1998)

P. Harrington, *British Artists and War: The Face of Battle in Paintings and Prints, 1700–1914* (1993)

B. Harris, *The Recollections of Rifleman Harris*, ed. C. Hibbert (1970)

J. P. Harris, 'Haig and the Tank', in B. Bond and H. Cave (eds), *Haig: A Reappraisal 70 Years On* (1990)

T. Harrison, 'the Popular Press', *Horizon*, 2 (1940)

P. Hart, 'Michael Collins and the Assassination of Sir Henry Wilson', *Irish Historical Review*, 28 (1992)

P. Hart, '"Operations Abroad": The IRA in Britain, 1919–23', *EHR*, 115 (2000)

G. Hartcup, *The War of Invention: Scientific Developments 1914–1918* (1988)

M. Hastings, *Bomber Command* (1979)

F. Haverfield, 'Notes on the Roman Coast Defences, especially in Yorkshire', *Journal of Roman Studies*, 2 (1912)

S. C. Hawkes (ed.) *Weapons and Warfare in Anglo-Saxon England* (1989)

The Health of Seamen: Selected from the Works of Dr James Lind, Sir Gilbert Blane and Dr Thomas Trotter, ed. C. Lloyd (Naval Records Society, 1965)

D. Healey, *The Time of My Life* (1989)

The Poems of Felicity Hemans (1854)

M. Henig, 'The Veneration of Heroes in the Roman Army: The Evidence of Engraved Gemstones', *Britannia*, 1 (1970)

M. Henig, *Religion in Roman Britain* (1984)

Henry of Huntingdon's Chronicle, ed. and trans. T. Forester (1853)

P. Hennessy, *Never Again: Britain 1945–1951* (1933 ed.)

P. Hennessy, 'Never Again' in B. Brivati and H. Jones (eds), *What Difference Did the War Make?* (1993)

G. Herken, *The Winning Weapon* (Princeton, 1981)

N. J. Higham, *The English Conquest: Gildas and Britain in the Fifth Century* (Manchester, 1994)

C. Hills, 'The Archaeology of Anglo-Saxon England in the Pagan Period: A Review', *Anglo-Saxon England*, 8 (1979)

J. G. F. Hind, 'Who Betrayed Roman Britain to the Barbarians in AD 367?' *Northern History*, 19 (1983)

F. H. Hinsley, E. E. Thomas, C. F. G. Ransom and R. C. Knight, *British Intelligence in the Second World War*, I (1979)

F. H. Hinsley and C. A. G. Simkins, *British Intelligence in the Second World War*, IV: *Security and Counter-Intelligence* (1990)

Historical Papers Relating to the Jacobite Period, 1699–1750, 2 vols (New Spalding Club, Aberdeen, 1895–96)

HMC, *Fifth Report* (1876)

HMC, *Twelfth Report* (1900)

HMC, *Fourteenth Report* (1902)

HMC, *Sixteenth Report* (1904)

HMC, *Lothian* (1905)

HMC, *Hastings*, III (1934)

HMC, *Mar and Kellie*, 2 vols (1930)

HMC, *Sackville*, 2 vols (1910)

HMC, *Salisbury*, 24 vols (1883–1976)

HMC, *Various*, II (1904)

D. Hoerdon, *Crowd Action in Revolutionary Massachusetts, 1765–1780* (1977)

P. A. Holder, *The Roman Army in Britain* (1982)

N. Hooper, 'The Anglo-Saxons at War', in S. C. Hawkes (ed.), *Weapons and Warfare in Anglo-Saxon England* (Oxford, 1989)

The Diary of Sir John Hope, 1646, ed. P. Marshall (Miscellany of the Scottish Historical Society, 9, 1958)

M. Horn, 'The Concept of Total War: National Effort and Taxation in Britain and France during the First World War', *WS*, 18 (2000)

J. Horne and A. Kramer, 'German "Atrocities" and Franco-German Opinion: The Evidence of German Soldiers' Diaries', *Journal of Modern History*, 66 (1994)

W. Hornsby and J. D. Lowerick, 'The Roman Signal Station at Goldsborough, near Whitby', *AJ*, 84 (1932)

M. Howard, *War and the Liberal Conscience* (Oxford, 1981)

M. Howard, *The Invention of Peace: Reflections on War and the International Order* (2000)

The Annals of Roger of Hoveden, ed. and trans. H. T. Riley, 2 vols (1843)

P. Howlett, 'New Light through Old Windows: A New Perspective on the British Economy in the Second World War', *JCH*, 28 (1993)

W. Hornsby and P. Stanton, 'The Roman Fortress at Huntcliff, near Saltburn', *Journal of Roman Studies*, 2 (1912)

A. Hudson, 'Volunteer Soldiers in Sussex during the Revolutionary and Napoleonic Wars', *Sussex Archaeological Collections*, 122 (1984)

David Hume of Godscroft's History of the House of Douglas, ed. D. Reid (Scottish Text Society, Edinburgh, 1996)

A. Hurd, *The Merchant Navy*, 3 vols (History of the Great War based upon Official Documents, 1921)

G. B. Hurst, 'The Administration of Military Law', *Contemporary Review*, 110 (1919)

The Life of William Hutton, ed. L. Jewitt, (c. 1872)

S. Hynes, *A War Imagined: The First World War and English Culture* (1990)

The Illustrated Book of Scottish Songs (1854)

The Illustrated Crimean War Song Book (1856)

E. Isichei, *Victorian Quakers* (Oxford, 1970)

T. Jackson (ed.), *The Lives of the Early Methodist Preachers*, 3 vols (1837–38)

C. James, *A Naval History of Great Britain*, 6 vols (1902)

L. James, *Mutiny* (1985)

L. James, *Imperial Rearguard* (1988)

L. James, *Imperial Warrior: The Life and Times of Field-Marshal Viscount Allenby, 1861–1936* (1993)

L. James, *The Rise and Fall of the British Empire* (1994)

B. Jennings (ed.), *Wild Geese in Spanish Flanders* (Dublin, 1964)

S. Johnson, *The Roman Forts of the Saxon Shore* (1976)

S. Johnson, *Later Roman Britain* (1980)

D. E. Johnston (ed.), *The Saxon Shore* (Council for British Archaeology Reports, No. 18, 1977)

H. A. Jones, *The War in the Air*, Vols 2–6 (1928–37)

M. E. Jones, *The End of Roman Britain* (Ithaca, NY, 1996)

T. Jones, 'The Early Evolution of the Legend of Arthur', *NMS*, 8 (1964)

H-L. Kamp. 'The Relevance of Nuclear Weapons to NATO', *Defense Analysis*, 15 (1999)

H. Kearney, *The British Isles: A History of Four Nations* (Cambridge, 1989)

R. Kee, *The Green Flag* (1972)

J. Keegan, *The Face of Battle* (1978 ed.)

J. Keegan, *The Mask of Command* (1987)

S. L. Keefer, 'Hwaer Cwom Mearh? The Horse in Anglo-Saxon England', *Journal of Mediaeval History*, 22 (1996)

J. L. H. Keep, *Soldiers of the Tsar: Army and Society in Russia, 1462–1874* (Oxford, 1985)

R. Kendal, 'Transport and Logistics Associated with the Building of Hadrian's Wall', *Britannia*, 13 (1982)

I. Kershaw, *Hitler: Nemesis* (2000)

L. Kespie, 'The Antonine Wall 1960–1980', *Britannia*, 13 (1982)

S. Keynes, 'The Historical Context of the Battle of Maldon', in D. G. Scragg, (ed.), *The Battle of Maldon* (Oxford, 1991)

J. Kier and J. Merser, 'Military Intervention and Weapons of Mass Destruction', *International Security*, 20 (1996)

V. G. Kiernan, *The Duel in European History: Honour and the Reign of the Aristocracy* (Oxford, 1988)

A. King, 'George Goodwin and the Art Union', *Victorian Studies*, 8 (1964–5)

A. Kinglake, *The Invasion of the Crimea*, 8 vols (1863–87)

Knighthood in Battle, ed. R. Dyboski and Z. M. Arend (Early English Text Society, 1935)

Knighton's Chronicle, ed. and trans. G. H. Martin (Oxford, 1995)

J. Knox, *A Historical Journal of the Campaigns in North America for the Years 1757, 1758, 1759 and 1760*, 2 vols (1764)

L. K. Kooritz, *The Virginia Frontier, 1754–1763* (Baltimore, MD, 1925)

S. Koven, 'Remembering and Dismemberment: Crippled Children, Wounded Soldiers and the Great War in Britain', *American Historical Review*, 99 (1994)

F. Krome, '*The True Glory* and the Failure of Anglo-American Film Propaganda in the Second World War', *JCH*, 33 (1998)

Labour and the Wartime Coalition: From the Diary of James Chuter Ede, ed. K. Jeffrey (1987)

Lancashire Memorials of the Rebellions, MCCXV (Cheetham Society, 1846)

O. Lancaster, *More Pocket Cartoons* (1943)

The Chronicles of Lanercost, 1272–1846, trans. H. Maxwell (1913)

J. Lang and B. Ager, 'Swords of the Anglo-Saxon and Viking Periods in the British Museum: A Radiographic Survey', in S.C. Hawkes (ed.)

The Chronicles of Pierre de Langtoft, ed. T. Wright (Rolls Series, 1868)

P. G. Laurie, *My Recollections of the Crimea and the Siege of Sebastopol, 1854–1856* (1900)

The Layman's Book of the General Assembly of 1915 (Edinburgh, 1915)

Guillaume le Clerk, *Fergus of Galloway*, ed. and trans. D. D. R. Owen (1991)

P. Leese, 'Problems Returning Home: The British Psychological Casualties of the Great War', *Historical Journal*, 40 (1997)

B. Lenman, *The Jacobite Risings in Britain* (1995 ed.)

Letters and Papers, Foreign and Domestic of the Reign of Henry VIII.

P. Levine, '"Walking the Streets in a Way no Decent Woman Should": Women Police in World War I', *Journal of Modern History*, 66 (1994)

J. Levy, 'The Inglorious End of the *Glorious*: The Release of the Findings of the Board of Enquiry into the loss of HMS *Glorious*', MM, 86 (2000)

C. Lewis, *Sagittarius Rising* (1977 ed.)

T. Lewit, *Agricultural Production in the Roman Economy* (Bar International Series, 568, Oxford, 1991)

W. Lewchuk, *American Technology in the British Vehicle Industry* (Cambridge, 1987)

M. Lincoln, 'Naval Ship Launches as Public Spectacle', MM, 83 (1997)

A Lincolnshire Assize Roll for 1298, ed. W. S. Thomson (Lincoln Record Society, 36, 1944)

Lists and Analyses of State Papers, Foreign Series, Elizabeth I, 6 vols (1956–1993)

A List of Persons Concerned in the Rebellion, ed. W. Macleod (Publication of the Scottish History Society, VIII, 1890)

C. Lloyd, 'The Rating and Distribution of British Warships in the Nineteenth Century', MM, 34 (1948)

E. M. H. Lloyd, *Experiments in State Control at the War Office and Ministry of Food* (Oxford, 1924)

S. Lloyd, 'William Longespee: The Making of an English Crusading Hero', NMS, 35 (1991) and 36 (1992)

London Under Attack: The Report of the London Area War Risk Study Commission (1986)

R. S. Loomis, 'Edward I, Arthurian Enthusiast', *Speculum*, 28 (1953)

S. Lucas and A. Morey, 'The Hidden "Alliance": The CIA and MI6 before and after Suez', *Intelligence and National Security*, 15 (2000)

D. C. Lukowitz, 'British Pacifists and Appeasement: The Peace Pledge Union', *JCH*, 9 (1974)

J. D. Lunt, 'Another Angle on Recruiting', *JRUSI*, 106 (1961)

E. Lyttelton, 'The Loom of Youth', *Contemporary Review*, 112 (1917)

K. B. Macfarlane, *England in the Fifteenth Century* (Oxford, 1981)

A British Fusilier in Revolutionary Boston, Being the Diary of Lieutenant Frederick Mackenzie, ed. A. French (Boston, MA, 1936)

S. P. Mackenzie, 'The Treatment of Prisoners of War in World War I', *Journal of Modern History*, 66 (1994)

S. P. Mackenzie, 'The Real *Dad's Army*: The British Home Guard 1940–44', in P. Addison and A. Calder (eds), *A Time to Kill* (1997)

J. D. MacKie (ed.), *The English Army at Flodden* (Miscellany of the Scottish History Society, 3rd Series, VIII, 1951)

L. Maclean, *The Raising of the 79th Highlanders* (Inverness, 1980)

G. H. B. Macleod, 'Surgery in the Crimea', *Edinburgh Medical Journal*, 1 (1855–6)

R. Macmullen, *Paganism in the Roman Empire* (New Haven, CT, 1981)

N. Macready, *Annals of an Active Life*, 2 vols (1927)

P. C. Madden, *Violence and Social Order: East Anglia 1422–1442* (Oxford, 1992)

J. R. Maddicott, *The English Peasantry and the Demands of the Crown 1294–1341* (*Past and Present Supplement*, 1975)

J. R. Maddicott, *Thomas of Lancaster* (Oxford, 1975)

J. K. Mahon, *The War of 1812* (New York, 1991 ed.)

J. Mann, 'A Further Account of the Armour preserved in the Sanctuary of the Madonna delle Gracies, near Mantua', *Archaeologia*, 86 (1938)

J. Mann, *Wallace Collection Catalogues: European Arms and Armour*, 2 vols (1962)

R. Manning, *The Story of England*, ed. F. J. Furnivall, 2 vols (Rolls Series, 1887)

A. J. Marder, *From Dreadnought to Scapa Flow*, V: *Victory and Aftermath* (Oxford, 1970)

A. H. Markham, *The Life of Sir Clements R. Markham* (1917)

The Life of Adam Martindale written by himself, ed. R. Patterson (Chetham Society, 1845)

C. F. G. Masterman, 'The Temper of the People', *Contemporary Review*, 108 (1915)

M. H. Mawson, '"Not a Very Nice Regiment": Her Majesty's 63rd (The West Suffolk Regiment)', *JSAHR*, 76 (1998)

G. Maxwell, 'The Roman Experience: Parallel Lines of Predestination', in N. Macdougal (ed.), *Scotland at War AD 79–1918* (Edinburgh, 1991)

C. May, 'Lord Moran's Memoir: Shell Shock and Psychology of Fear', *Journal of the Royal Society of Medicine*, 91 (1998)

J. McCarthy, 'Aircrew and the lack of Moral Fibre in the Second World War', *WS*, 2 (1984)

K. R. McCone, 'Werewolves, Cyclopes, Diberga and Fianne: Juvenile Delinquency in Early Ireland', *Cambridge Mediaevel Celtic Studies*, 12 (1986)

S. McGrail (ed.), *Maritime Celts, Frisians and Saxons* (Council for British Archaeology Paper No. 71, 1990)

T. H. McGuffie, 'Kelly of Waterloo', *JSAHR*, 33 (1955)

J. J. N. McGurk, 'Rochester and the Irish Levy of October 1601', *MM*, 74 (1988)

C. McNamee, *The Wars of the Bruce: Scotland, England and Ireland, 1306–1328* (East Linton, Lothian, 1997)

B. McSweeney, 'Interests and Identity in the Construction of the Belfast Agreements', *Security Dialogue*, 29 (1998)

Medical Services of the War, I: *Surgery of the War*, II (History of the Great War Based on Official Documents, 1922–23)

M. Melko, 'Long-Term Factors Underlying Peace in Contemporary Western Civilisation', *Journal of Peace Research*, 29 (1992)

C. H. Mismer, *Souvenir d'un Dragon de l'armeé de Crimé* (Paris, 1887)

O. Moberg, 'The Battle of Helgeå', *Scandinavian Journal of History*, 14 (1989)

W. E. Montague, *Campaigning in South Africa: Reminiscences of an Officer in 1879* (1880)

The Diary of Sir John Moore, ed. J. F. Maurice, 2 vols (1904)

G. C. Moore Smith, *The Life of John Colborne, Field-Marshal Lord Seaton* (1903)

D. Morgan and M. Evans, 'The Road to *Nineteen Eighty Four*', in B. Brivati and H. Jones (eds), *What Difference Did the War Make?* (1993)

C. Moriarty, 'Christian Iconography and First World War Memorials', *IWMR*, 6 (n.d.)

S. Morillo, *Warfare under the Anglo-Norman Kings, 1106–1154* (Woodbridge, Suffolk, 1994)

S. Morillo (ed.), *The Battle of Hastings* (Woodbridge, Suffolk, 1996)

S. E. Morison, *The Battle of the Atlantic, September 1939–May 1943* (History of the United States Naval Operations in World War II, I, Boston, MA, 1948)

J. Morris, *Arthurian Sources*, 6 vols (Chichester, 1995)

J. H. Morrow, 'The German Aircraft Industry in the First and Second World Wars: A Comparison', in H. Boog (ed.) *The Conduct of the Air War in the Second World War: An International Comparison* (1992)

F. W. Mott, 'War Pyscho-Neuroses', *Lancet*, 26 Jan, 2 Feb 1918.

W. Murray, 'The Influence of Pre-War Anglo-American Doctrines on the Air Campaigns of the Second World War', in H. Boog (ed.), *The Conduct of the Air War in the Second World War: An International Comparison* (1992)

D. Naphine and W. A. Speck, 'Clergymen and Conflict, 1660–1763', in W. J. Sheils (ed.) *The Church and War* (Ecclesiastical History Society, 1983)

Naval Songs and Ballads, ed. C. H. Firth (Naval Records Society, 1897)

M. S. Navias, *Nuclear Weapons and British Strategic Planning, 1955–1958* (Oxford, 1991)

K. Neilson, 'That Dangerous and Difficult Enterprise: British Military Thinking and the Russo-Japanese War', *WS*, 9 (1991)

C. Nettlebeck, 'Getting the Story Right: Narratives of World War II in Post-1960 France', *Journal of European Studies*, 15 (1985)

V. E. Neuberg, 'The British Army in the Eighteenth Century,' *JSAHR*, 61 (1983–4)

S. Nicholas, '"Sly Demagogues", J. B. Priestley, the BBC and Wartime Radio', *TCBH*, 6 (1995)

M. Nicholls, 'A Surgeon in the Second Sikh War: Ludovick Stewarts's Account of the Battle of Chillianwala', *JSAHR*, 71 (1993)

M. Nicholson, *What Did You Do in the War Mummy?* (1996 ed.)

R. Nicholson, 'The Siege of Berwick, 1333', *Scottish Historical Review*, 40 (1961)

W. A. Nitze, 'The Exhumation of King Arthur at Glastonbury', *Speculum*, 9 (1934)

J. H. Ohlmeyer, 'The Wars of Religion', in T. Bartlett and K. Jeffrey (eds), *A Military History of Ireland* (1996)

J. H. Ohlmeyer, '"Civilizinge of those rude partes": Colonization within Britain and Ireland, 1580s–1640s', in N. Canny (ed.), *The Origins of Empire* (Oxford History of the British Empire, I, 1998)

The Ecclesiastical History of Ordericus Vitalis, ed. and trans. M. Chibnall, 6 vols (Oxford, 1969–1978)

The Orderly Books of the Fourth New York Regiment, 1778–1780 and the Second New York Regiment, 1780–1783 (Albany, NY, 1932)

The Orkneyinger's Saga, trans. G. W. Dasent (Rolls Series, 1894)

The Complete Works of George Orwell, 12, *A Patriot After All*, ed. P. Davison (1998)

G. R. Owen, *Rites and Religions of the Anglo-Saxons* (1989)

G. Owst, *Literature and the Pulpit in Mediaevel England* (1933)

T. O'Sullivan, 'Listening Through: The Wireless and World War Two', in P. Kirkham and D. Thomas (eds), *War Culture* (1995)

R. Overy, *Why the Allies Won* (1995)

R. I. Page, '*A Most Vile People*': *Early English Historians and the Vikings* (1986)

G. Paget, *The Light Brigade in the Crimea* (1881)

S. H. Palmer, *Police and Protest in England and Ireland 1780–1850* (Cambridge, 1989)

G. Parker, 'The *Dreadnought* Revolution and Tudor England', MM, 82 (1996)

M. Paris, 'The Rise of the Airmen: The Origins of Air Force Elistism, *c.* 1890–1914, JCH, 28 (1993)

I. D. Patterson, 'The Activities of the Irish Republican Physical Force Organisation in Scotland, 1919–21', *Scottish Historical Review*, 72 (1993)

J. Pearman, *The Radical Soldier's Tale: John Pearman, 1819–1908*, ed. C. Steadman (1988)

P. H. Pearce, *The Duke of Wellington's Funeral Poem* (1854)

J. Peaty, 'Haig and Military Discipline', in B. Bond and N. Cave (eds), *Haig: A Reappraisal 70 Years On* (1999)

John Peebles's American War, 1776–1782, ed. I. D. Gruber (Army Records Society, 1998)

D. A. E. Pelteret, 'Slavery in Anglo-Saxon England', in J. D. Woods and D. A. E. Pelteret (eds), *The Anglo-Saxons: Synthesis and Achievement* (Waterloo, Ontario, 1985)

Sir Perceval of Galles, ed. J. Campion and F. Holthausen (Heidelberg, 1913)

M. Petter, '"Temporary Gentlemen" in the Aftermath of the Great War: Rank, Status and the Ex-Officer Problem', HJ, 37 (1994)

The Penguin Book of Medieval French Verse (1970)

G. Pinckard, *Notes on the West Indies including Observations relative to the Creoles and Slaves of Western Colonies . . . interpersed with Remarks on the Seasoning for Yellow Fever of Hot Climates*, 2 vols (1816)

J. Pindar, *Autobiography of the Soldier* (Cupar, Fife, 1877)

Christine de Pisan, *The Book of Fayttes of Armes and of Chyvalrye*, trans. William Caxton, ed. A. T. P. Biles (Early English Text Society, 1932)

A Plea Roll of Edward I's Army in Scotland, 1296, ed. C. J. Neville (Scottish Historical Society, 5th Series, Miscellany XI, 1990)

The Plumpton Correspondence, ed. T. Stapleton (Camden Society, 1839)

A. Ponsonby, 'The Army Crisis and Home Rule', *Contemporary Review*, 55 (1914)

R. Poole, 'Skaldic Verse and Anglo-Saxon History: Some Aspects of the Period 1009–1016', *Speculum*, 62 (1987)

R. Poole, *Viking Poems and War and Peace: A Study iin Skaldic Narrative* (Toronto 1987)

B. Porter, '"Bureau and Barrack": Early Victorian Attitudes towards the Continent', *Victorian Studies*, 27 (1983–4)

S. Porter, 'The Fire-raid in the English Civil War', *WS*, 2 (1984)

T. Powell, 'The Three Orders of Society in Anglo-Saxon England', *Anglo-Saxon England*, 23 (1994)

M. Powicke, 'The General Obligation to Cavalry Service under Edward I', *Speculum*, 28 (1953)

M. Powicke, 'Edward II and Military Obligations', *Speculum*, 31 (1956)

D. C. Press, 'Lessons on Ground combat from the Gulf War', *International Security*, 22 (1997)

M. Prestwich, *War Politics and Finance under Edward I* (1991 ed.)

C. Price, 'The Political Genesis of Air Raid Precautions and the York Air Raid of 1942', *Northern History*, 36 (2000)

J. B. Priestley, *Postscripts* (1940)

R. Prior and T. Wilson, *Command on the Western Front: The Military Career of Sir Henry Rawlinson, 1914–1918* (1992)

Private Indentures for Life Service in Peace and War, 1278–1476, ed. M. Jones and S. Walker (Camden Miscellany, 32, 5th Series, 1994)

H. A. Probert, 'The Determination of RAF Policy during the Second World War', in H. Boog (ed.), *The Conduct of the Air War in the Second World War: An International Comparison* (1992)

N. Pronay, '"The Land of Promise": The Projection of Peace Aims in Britain', in K. R. M. Short (ed.), *Film and Radio Propaganda in World War II* (1983)

J. Putkowski and J. Sykes, *Shot at Dawn* (1989)

G. R. Quaife, *Wanton Wenches and Wayward Wives: Peasants and Illicit Sex in Early Seventeenth Century England* (1979)

T. Quinnney, *Sketches of a Soldier's Life in India* (1853)

J. Ramsden, 'Refocussing "The People's War": British War Films of the 1950s', *JCH*, 33 (1998)

P. E. Razzell, 'Social Origins of Officers in the Indian and British Home Army', *British Journal of Sociology*, 14 (1963)

E. Rees, *Sketches of the Horror of War chiefly Selected from Labaume's Narrative of the War Campaign in Russia in 1812* (1839)

N. Reeves, 'Film Propaganda and its Audience: The Example of British Films during the First World War', *JCH*, 18 (1993)

D. F. Renn, *Norman Castles in Britain* (1968)

Register of Edward Edward the Black Prince, IV (1933)

Register of the Privy Council of Scotland, 2nd Series, 8 vols (1899–1908)

Register of the Privy Council of Scotland, 3rd Series, 16 vols (1908–1970)

J. Reid, 'The Ballad and the Source: Some Literary Reflections of the *Battle of Otterburn*', in A. Goodman and A. Tuck (eds), *War and Border Societies in the Middle Ages* (1992)

J. Richards, 'National Identity in British Wartime Films', in P. M. Taylor (ed.), *Britain and the Cinema in the Second World War* (1988)

J. Richards and D. Sheridan, *Mass Observations at the Movies* (1987)

A Mariner of England: An Account of the Career of William Richardson, ed. S. Childs (Greenwich, 1970)

I. Richmond and others, *Hod Hill*, II (Excavations carried out between 1951 and 1958 for the Trustees of the British Museum) (1968)

The Correspondence of the Dukes of Richmond and Newcastle, 1724–1750, ed. T. C. McCann (Sussex Record Society, 1984)

Correspondence between George Ridpath and the Reverend Robert Wodson (Abbotsford Club, Miscellany, 1, 1837)

W. H. R. Rivers, 'The Repression of War Experience', *Lancet*, 2 Feb 1918

R. H. Robbins (ed.), *Historical Poems of the XIVth and IVth Centuries* (New York, 1959)

K. Robert, 'Gender and Class and Patriotism: Women's Paramilitary Units in the First World War in Britain', *International History Review*, 19, (1997)

A. Roberts, *Eminent Churchillians* (1994)

Daniel George Robinson's Letters from India, ed. R. N. W. Thomas (Military Miscellany, 1, Army Records Society, 1996)

C. N. Robinson, 'A Seventeenth Century Sailor', *MM*, 1 (1911)

F. Robinson, *Diary of the Crimean War* (1856)

N. A. M. Rodger, *The Wooden World: An Anatomy of the Georgian Navy* (1986)

N. A. M. Rodger, 'The Development of Broadside Gunnery', *MM*, 82 (1996)

N. A. M. Rodger, *The Safeguard of the Sea: A Naval History of Britain*, I (660–1640) (1997)

S. O. Rose, 'Girls and GIs: Race, Sex and Diplomacy in Second World War Britain', *International History Review*, 19 (1997)

S. O. Rose, 'Sex, Citizenship and Nationality in World War II', *Journal of American History*, 103 (1998)

G. E. Rothenberg, *The Art of Warfare in the Age of Napoleon* (1977)

G. Roussy and J. Lhermitte *The Pyscho Neurosis of War* (1918)

C. Routh, *Occupations of the People of Great Britain* (Oxford, 1987)

W. B. Rowbotham, 'Soldiers' and Seamens' Wives and Children in HM Ships', *MM*, 47 (1961)

Royal Commission of Historic Monuments, *Inventory of the Monuments of Glamorgan*, II, *The Early Castles* (1991)

T. Royle, *Crimea* (2000)

T. Royle, *The Best Years of their Lives: The National Service Experience 1945–63* (1988 ed.)

G. P. Rubin, *War, the Munitions Acts and Labour* (Oxford, 1987)

H. Russell, 'The Soldier's Life', in *New Songs* (1854)

G. R. Russom, 'A Germanic Concept of Nobility in *The Gifts of Man* and *Beowulf*', *Speculum*, 53 (1978)

D. Ryan, *Sean Treacy and the Third Tipperary Brigade* (1945)

M. Ryder, *Four Years Service in India* (Leicester, 1853)

R. Ryder and J. Birch, 'Hellifield Peel: A North Yorkshire Tower House', *Yorkshire Archaeological Journal*, 55 (1983)

R. Ryder, 'Mediaeval and Sub-Mediaeval Buildings in the North East of England', in B. E Vyner (ed.), *Mediaeval Rural Settlement in North East England* (Durham, 1990)

R. Samuel, 'The Workshop of the World: Steam Power and Hand Technology in Mid-Victorian Britain', *History Workshop*, 3 (1977)

D. Sandford, *Leaves from the Journal of a Subaltern, 1848–49* (1849)

The Private Papers of John, Earl of Sandwich, ed. G. R. Barnes and J. H. Owen, 4 vols (Naval Records Society, 1932–38)

G. H. Savage, 'Mental War Cripples', *The Practitioner*, 100 (1918)

Siegfried Sassoon Diaries, 1915–1918, ed. R. Hart Davies (1983)

Scalacronica, trans. H. Maxwell (1907)

Scars upon my Heart: Women's Poetry and Verse of the First World War, selected by C. Reilly (1992 ed.)

R. Schweitzer, 'The Cross and the Trenches: Religious Faith and Doubt among some British Soldiers on the Western Front', *WS*, 16 (1998)

J. Scott, *Recollections of a Naval Life*, 3 vols (1834)

J. Scott, *War Inconsistent with the Doctrine of Jesus Christ* (1839)

L. Scott, 'Close to the Brink? Britain and the Cuban Missile Crisis', *Contemporary Record*, 5 (1991)

The Letters of Sir Walter Scott, 1811–1818 (1932)

W. R. Scott and J. Cunnison, *The Industries of the Clyde Valley during the War* (Oxford, 1924)

R. A. Selig, 'A German Soldier in Colonial America, 1780–1783', *WMQ*, 50 (1993)

G. D. Sheffield, 'The Effect of the Great War on Class Relations in Britain: The Career of Christopher Stone, DSO, MC', *WS*, 7 (1989)

G. D. Sheffield, 'The Shadow of the Somme', in P. Addison and A. Calder (eds), *A Time to Kill* (1997)

B. Shepherd, '"Pitiless Pyschology": The Role of Prevention in British Military Psychology in the Second World War', *History of Psychiatry*, 40 (1999)

J. Shepherd, *The Crimean Doctors: A History of the British Medical Services in the Crimean War*, 2 vols (Liverpool, 1991)

E. A. M. Shirley, 'The Building of the Legionary Fortress at Inchtuthil', *Britannia*, 27 (1996)

J. W. Shy, 'A New Look at the Colonial Militia', *WMQ*, 20 (1963)

J. W. Shy, *A People Numerous and Armed* (Oxford, 1976)

M. Sidgwick, 'The Portland Rising and the Battle of Rullion Green', *Scottish Historical Review*, 3rd series, 3 (1905–6)

The Siege of Caerlaverock, ed. N. H. Nicolas (1828)

G. M. Smith, *When Jim Crow met John Bull* (1987)

H. L. Smith, 'The Effect on the Status of Women', in H. L. Smith (ed.) *War and Social Change* (1986)

M. Smith, 'The Air Threat and British Foreign Policy', in ed. H. Boog, *The Conduct of the Air War in the Second World War: An International Comparison* (1992)

P. H. Smith, *Loyalists and Redcoats* (Williamsburg, 1984)

R. D. Smith, '"The Unsung Heroes of the Air": Logistics and the Air War over Europe', in H. Boog (ed.), *The Conduct of the Air War in the Second World War: An International Comparison* (1992)

R. Smither, '"A Wonderful Idea of Fighting": The Question of Fakes in the *Battle of the Somme*', IWAMR, 3 (1988)

A. P. Smyth, *Warlords and Holy Men: Scotland AD 80–1000* (Edinburgh, 1995 ed.)

Certaine Discourses, written by Sir John Smyth, Knight . . . concerning divers sorts of Weapons (1590)

C. E. Snowden Gamble, *The Story of a North Sea Air Station* (Oxford, 1928)

A Solemn Review of the Custom of War showing what War is, its effects on Popular Delusion, and proposing a Remedy (1829)

S. Solly, 'A Few Observations on the Wounded in the Crimea', *Lancet*, 17 Feb 1855.

R. Southey, *Life of Nelson* (Everyman edition, 1962)

The Spanish War, 1585–1587, ed. J. S. Corbett (Navy Records Society, 1897)

J. Spalding, *The History of the Troubles and Memorable Transactions in Scotland and England from MDCXXIV to MDCXLV*, 2 vols (1828)

Spencer's Press, Worden ed. R. Gottfried (Baltimore, 1949)

E. M. Spiers, *The Army and Society, 1815–1914* (1980)

D. J. Spinney, 'The *Hermione* Mutiny', MM, 41 (1955)

L. E. Stamm, 'Medical Aspects of Aviation', *Aeronautical Journal*, 23 (1919)

P. Stanley, '"Highly Inflammatory Writings": Soldiers' Graffiti in the Indian Rebellion', *JSAHR*, 84 (1996)

Statistics of the Military Effort of the British Empire during the Great War, 1914–1920 (1922)

[Sir Anthony Sterling], *Letters from the Crimea* (c. 1871)

Sir Anthony Sterling, *The Story of the Highland Brigade in the Crimea* (1895)

P. C. N. Stewart, 'Inventing Britain: The Roman Creation and Adaptation of an Image', *Britannia*, 25 (1995)

D. Stevenson, *King or Covenant? Voices from the Civil War* (East Linton, 1996)

The Literary Diary of Ezra Stiles, 3 vols (New York, 1901)

L. Stone, 'Interpersonal Violence in English Society, 1300–1980', *PP*, No. 101 (1983)

The Stonor Letters and Papers, 1290–1482, ed. C. L. Kingsford, 2 vols (Camden Society, 1919)

M. J. Stoyle, '"Whole Streets Covered in Ashes": Property Destruction in Exeter during the English Civil War', *Southern History*, 16 (1994)

H. Strachan, *From Waterloo to Balaklava: Tactics, Technology and the British Army, 1815–1854* (Cambridge, 1986)

G. S. Street, 'War and Science', *National Review*, 120 (1917–18)

M. Strickland, 'Securing the North: Invasion and the Strategy of Defence in Twelfth-Century Anglo-Saxon Warfare', *ANS*, 12 (1990)

M. Strickland, 'Military Technology and the Conquest: The Anomaly of Anglo-Saxon England', *ANS*, 19 (1997)

Studies in War Economics (Oxford, 1947)

T. Styward, *The Pathwaie to Martiall Discipline, devided into two Bookes, verie necessarie for young Souldiers, or such as loveth the profession of Armes* (1590)

The Works of Sir John Suckling: The Plays, ed. L. A. Beaureline (Oxford, 1971)

D. Summerfield, 'Shell-shock Patients: From Cowards to Victims', *BMJ*, 14 Nov 1998

P. Summerfield, 'The Levelling of Class', in H. L. Smith (ed.), *War and Social Change* (1986)

P. Summerfield and N. Crocket, '"You weren't taught that with welding": Lessons in Sexuality in the Second World War', *Women's History Review*, 1 (1992)

H. Summerson, 'Responses to War: Carlisle and the West Marches in the Later Fourteenth Century,' A. Goodman and A. Tuck (eds), *War and Border Societies in the Middle Ages* (1992)

R. M. Sunter, 'Raising the 97th (Inverness-shire) Highland Regiment of Foot', *JSAHR*, 76 (1998)

R. S. Surtees, *Handley Cross* (1854)

C. A. Swany, 'Some Physical and Psychological Effects of Altitude', *Aeronautical Journal*, 24 (1920)

J. Sweetman, *War and Administration and the Significance of the Crimean War for the British Army* (Edinburgh, 1984)

R. Swinhow, *Narrative of the China Campaign of 1860* (1861)

Tacitus, *Daologues Agricola et Germanica*, trans. and ed. W. Hamilton Fyfe (Oxford, 1908)

Tactitus, *The Annals of Imperial Rome*, trans. M. Grant (Penguin, 1989 ed.)

The Taking of Madre de Dios, Anno 1592, ed. C. L. Kingsford (Navy Records Society, Naval Miscellany, 2, 1912)

J. E. Talbot, 'Soldiers, Psychiatrists and Combat Trauma', *Journal of Interdisciplinary History*, 27 (1997)

J. S. P. Tatlock, 'The Dragons of Wessex and Wales', *Speculum*, 8 (1933)

J. Taylor, 'The Body Vanishes: Photojournalism in the Gulf War', *Contemporary Record*, 8 (1994)

P. M. Taylor, 'If War Come: Preparing the Fifth Arm for Total War, 1935–1939', *TCBH*, 6 (1995)

R. Taylor, 'Manning the Royal Navy: The Reform of Recruiting 1852–1862', *MM*, 44 (1958) and 45 (1959)

O. Teichman, 'The Yeomanry as an Arm of the Civil Power, 1795–1867', *JSAHR*, 19 (1940)

A. Temple Patterson, 'A Midshipman in the Boxer Rebellion', MM, 68 (1977)

J. Terraine, 'Theory and Practice of the Air War: The Royal Air Force', in H. Boog (ed.), The Conduct of the Air War in the Second World War: An International Comparison (1992)

Testamenta Eborensia, I (Surtees Society, 1836)

W. M. Thackeray, The Book of Snobs (1969 ed.)

The 1341 Royal Inquest in Lincolnshire, ed. B. L. Mclane (Lincolnshire Record Society, 78, 1986)

D. Thom, Nice Girls and Rude Girls (1998)

C. Thorne, Allies of a Kind (Oxford, 1978 ed.)

A. Thomson, Eighty Years Reminiscences, 2 vols (1904)

B. Thordeman, Armour from the Battle of Wisby, 2 vols (Stockholm, 1939)

R. Thurlow, 'The "Mosley Papers" and the Secret History of British Fascism', in T. Kushner and K. Lunn (eds), Traditions of Intolerance: Historical Perspectives of Fascism and Race Relation in Britain (Manchester, 1989)

J. S. Tiedemann, 'Patriots by Default: Queen's County, New York, and the British Army, 1776–1783', WMQ, 43 (1986)

J. Tomlinson, 'Welfare and the Economy: The Economic Impact of the Welfare State, 1945–49', TCBH, 6 (1995)

C. Townshend, The British Campaign in Ireland, 1914–1921 (Oxford, 1975)

Tracts Relating to the Military Proceedings in Lancashire during the Civil War, ed. G. Ormerod (Chetham Society, 1844)

T. Travers, The Killing Ground: The British Army and the Western Front and the Emergence of Modern War (1993 ed.)

E. Turner, 'American Prisoners of War in Great Britain, 1777–1783', MM, 45 (1954)

T. Turville-Petrie, England the Nation: Language, Literature and National Identity, 1290–1340 (Oxford, 1996)

G. Tweedale, 'Business, Industrial Strategies in the Inter-war British Steel Industry: A Case Study: Hadfields Limited, Bean Cars', Journal of Business History, 29 (1957)

A. Uhry Williams, The Valiant Hero: Benhamin West and the Grand Style in History Painting (Washington, 1985)

The United States Strategic Bombing Survey, I (New York, 1976); II (New York, 1976)

M. Vale, Edward III's Chivalry: Chivalric Society in its Context, 1270–1350 (Woodbridge, Suffolk, 1982)

General Vanson, Crimée, Italie, Mexique: Lettres de Campagnes 1854–1867 (Paris, 1905)

C. Veitch, 'Play up! Play up! and Win the War: Football and the Nation in the First World War', JCH, 20 (1985)

D. Verney, *The Standard Bearer* (1963)

J. Verney, *Going to the Wars* (1957 ed.)

R. Virgoe, *Some Ancient Indictments in the King's Bench referring to Kent, 1450–1452*, in *Documents Illustrative of Mediaeval Kentish Society* (Kent Archaeological Society, Kent Records, 18, 1964)

R. Virgoe, 'William Tailboys and Lord Cromwell', *Bulletin of the John Rylands Library*, 35 (1972–3)

B. Waites, *A Class Society at War: England 1914–1918* (Leamington Spa, 1987)

The War at Sea: The Royal Navy in the Second World War, ed. J. Thompson (1996)

P. Ward, *Red Flag and Union Jack: Englishness, Patriotism and the British Left* (1998)

S. R. Ward, 'Intelligence Surveillance and British Ex-Servicemen, 1919–1920', *HJ*, 16 (1972)

W. K. Wark, 'The Air Defence Gap: British Air Doctrine and Intelligence Warnings in the 1930s', in H. Boog (ed.), *The Conduct of the Air War in the Second World War: An International Comparison* (1992)

R. Watkin, 'Captain Hugh Crow: A Liverpool Guineaman', MM, 63 (1977)

J. S. K. Watson, 'Khaki Girls, VADs and Tommy's Sisters: Gender and Class in First World War Britain', *IHR*, 19 (1997)

E. Waugh, *Diaries* (1982)

The Battle of Waterloo [By an Observer], 2 vols (1817)

I. Webb, 'The Frigate Situation in the Royal Navy, 1793–1815', MM, 82 (1996)

E. Webb and J. Duncan, *Blitz over Britain* (Tunbridge Wells, 1990)

G. Webster, 'The Military Situations in Britain between AD 43 and 71', *Britannia*, 2 (1971)

G. Webster, *Boudica: The British Revolt against Rome AD 60* (1978)

G. Webster, *Rome against Caractacus: The Roman Campaigns in Britain AD 48–58* (1993 ed.)

L. Webster and J. Backhouse (eds), *The Making of England: Anglo-Saxon Art and Culture* (1991)

M. G. Welch, 'Late Romans and Saxons in Sussex', *Britannia*, 2 (1971)

K. Weller, *Don't be a Soldier* (1985)

H. G. Wells, *Anticipations* (1902)

The Correspondence of H. G. Wells, 2 (1904–1918) ed. D. C. Smith (1998)

M. Wells, *Letters from the Home Front* (1988)

S. J. Wenham, 'Anatomical Interpretations of Anglo-Saxon Weapon Injuries', in S. C. Hawkes (ed.)

J. R. Western, 'The Formation of the Scottish Militia', *Scottish History Review*, 34 (1955)

J. R. Western, 'The Volunteer Movement as an Anti-Revolutionary Force', *EHR*, 71 (1956)

J. R. Western, *The English Militia in the Eighteenth Century* (1965)

The Adventures of John Wetherell, ed. C. S. Forester (1954)

R. E. M. Wheeler, *Maiden Castle* (Oxford, 1943)

J. R. S. Whiting, 'The Frampton Volunteers, *JSAHR*, 58 (1970)

A. Wilkinson, *The Church of England and the First World War* (1978)

G. Wilkinson, '"There is no More Stirring": The Press Depiction and Images of War during the Tibet Expedition, 1902–1904', *WS*, 9 (1991)

P. Williams, 'The Welsh Borderland under Queen Elizabeth', *Welsh History Review*, 1 (1960)

The Military Correspondence of Sir Henry Wilson, 1918–1922, ed. K. Jeffrey (Army Records Society, 1985)

Sir Roger Williams, *A Brief Discourse on Warre* (1590)

L. S. Winstock, 'Hot Stuff', *JSAHR*, 33 (1955)

J. M. Winter, 'Some Aspects of the Demographic Consequences of the First World War in Britain', *Population Studies*, 30 (1976)

J. M. Winter, 'The Impact of the First World War on Civilian Health in Britain', *EcHR*, 2nd Series, 30 (1977)

J. M. Winter, 'Aspects of the Impact of the First World War on Infant Mortality in Britain', *Journal of Economic History*, 11 (1982)

J. M. Winter, *The Great War and the British People* (1985)

J. M. Winter and J. L. Roberts (eds), *Capital Cities and the War: Paris, London and Berlin, 1914–1919* (Cambridge, 1997)

M. J. Witner, *Reconstructing the Criminal: Culture, Law and Policy in England, 1830–1914* (Cambridge, 1990)

O. J. Wolseley, *Narrative of the War in China in 1860* (1862)

F. Wood, 'The Increase in the Cost of Food for Different Classes in Society since the Outbreak of the War', *Journal of the Royal Statistical Society*, 74 (1916)

G. Wood, *The Subaltern Officer* (1825)

J. Woodford, *The Diary of the Country Parson, V (1797–1802)*, ed. J. Beresford (1931)

R. Woolf, 'The Idea of Men Dying with their Lord in *Germania* and *The Battle of Maldon*', *Anglo-Saxon England*, 5 (1976)

J. Wormald, *Lords and Men in Scotland: Bonds of Manrent, 1442–1603* (Edinburgh, 1985)

N. A. R. Wright, '"Pillagers" and "Brigands" in the Hundred Years' War', *Journal of Mediaeval History*, 9 (1983)

H. F. Wyatt, 'Air Raids and the New War', *Contemporary Review*, 82 (1917)

J. D. Young, *Socialism and the English Working Class* (1989)

A. J. Youngson, *The Scientific Revolution in Victorian Medicine* (1979)

Ywain and Gawain, ed. A. B. Friedman and N. T. Harrington (Early English Text Society, 1964)

I. Zwingor-Bargielowski, 'Bread Rationing in Britain, July 1946–July 1948', *TCBH*, 4 (1993)

Index